Cultural Anthropology

UNDERSTANDING
OURSELVES &
OTHERS 3rd Edition

Cultural Anthropology

UNDERSTANDING

OURSELVES &

OTHERS 3rd Edition

Richley H. Crapo

Utah State University

THE DUSHKIN PUBLISHING GROUP, INC.

Printed in the United States of America
Library of Congress Catalog Card
Number: 92-076096

International Standard Book Number
(ISBN) 1-56134-222-X

First Printing

The Dushkin Publishing Group, Inc.
Sluice Dock, Guilford,
Connecticut   06437

This book is printed
on recycled paper

PREFACE

Anthropology, like its study, humankind, is a tremendously diverse subject that provides a richness of information and an excitement in learning for students. The challenge is to present to students a coherent and meaningful introduction. While no text is likely to fulfill the hopes and needs of all teachers, I believe *Cultural Anthropology: Understanding Ourselves and Others,* 3rd Edition, will provide the basic insights into the field which a thoughtful student ought to have as part of a liberal education. These include not only facts and theories but, most importantly, the anthropological attitude of a commitment to understanding and appreciating cultural diversity.

Content and Organization. In *Cultural Anthropology: Understanding Ourselves and Others,* 3rd Edition, I have tried to avoid fragmentation by building systematically from one concept to the next. In the process, I cover a wide range of topics that comprise the field of anthropology.

To accommodate the needs of the majority of instructors in introductory cultural anthropology courses, the chapters of this third edition focus exclusively on the various aspects of culture. We examine the role of culture as a symbolic system that guides and gives meaning to human life and as a mechanism for human adaptation to the natural and social environments. New chapters have been added that provide expanded coverage of gender and aesthetics. Other chapters have also been substantially rewritten and expanded to accommodate the thoughtful suggestions of reviewers and those who used the second edition in the classroom. This third edition has been thoroughly revised to include information on the current status of those societies that are used as ethnographic examples of the general principles discussed throughout the text. Feminist and postmodernist viewpoints have been integrated into the text to complement the more traditional approaches.

Part I, The Science of Culture. The book begins with a succinct discussion of the often confusing subject of anthropology itself: the breadth of its content, its history and contemporary forms, its methods, and its ethics. Chapter 2 introduces the concept of culture, including discussions of both ideology and technology, as well as issues of how different cultures respond to and influence each other.

Part II, Survival and Adaptation. Building on these basics, the next three chapters focus on aspects of human survival, adaptation to the physical and social environments, and the infrastructural components of human social life. Chapter 3 discusses the physical environments in which human societies are found, the concept of adaptation, and how human societies organize their subsistence customs in various environments. Chapter 4 builds upon the concept of subsistence systems and discusses the economic customs of the world's societies. Chapter 5 considers how humans adapt to the practical problems of social life with the various mechanisms that form the political system of each society and outlines the basic types of political systems that have existed in the world's societies.

Part III, Society and Social Life. The chapters in this section discuss the ways in which meaningful systems of social life develop beyond the basic needs of mere coping and survival. Chapter 6 outlines the concept of social organization with a special focus on how the statuses of individuals change as they pass through life. Chapter 7 discusses the human notion of descent and how it is elaborated into various kinship systems. Chapter 8 discusses the customs and varieties of marriage that play a role in every descent and kinship system and surveys the family forms that arise from these marriage customs. Chapter 9 examines the roles of gender in social life and the relationships between gender and social institutions such as economics, politics, and religion.

Part IV, Ideology and Symbolism. The fourth section of the text moves to the superstructure of culture, the realm of symbolism, communication, religion, the role of culture in human personality, and aesthetics. Chapter 10 begins with a consideration of the human capacity for endowing things with meaning and then examines the unique role of language as a system of meaningful symbols with which humans communicate and create their cultural order. Chapter 11 takes an in-depth look at religion, the abstract and creatively varied use of the human ability to symbolize. This chapter not only demonstrates the varieties of human religious ideology, but also points out the role religious thought plays in social organization. Chapter 12 focuses on the individual's relationship to culture and discusses the cultural shaping of personality, altered states of consciousness, and culture-specific psychological disorders. Chapter 13 examines the nature of expressive culture such as play, recreation, and art with consideration given both to the universal human capacity for aesthetic experience and to the cultural variables in aesthetic evaluations.

Part V, Cultural Change and Diversity. The final two chapters examine the process of cultural change and the diversity of contemporary ways of life. Chapter 14 presents the general principles of cultural change, discusses the demise of the world's technologically simple societies, and analyzes the plight of the peasant cultures of the developing world and of the contemporary world's indigenous peoples. The book ends with a special chapter about the United States, interpreting its technological, economic, social, political, and ideological characteristics from the unique point of view of cultural anthropology.

I have attempted to write clearly and logically, and the vocabulary and the level of writing that I have adopted are appropriate for the serious student. I have found that when one addresses one's students with respect and dignifies them with the assumption that they possess more than a modicum of intelligence, it pays off. Students, like anyone else, live up to or down to one's expectations of them. I have written from the assumption that the classroom is a place of education and the purpose of teachers and students and their texts should be the perpetuation of wisdom and intellectual skills. I have attempted, therefore, to characterize the anthropological view of humankind in a way that may benefit and enlighten the inquiring student whether or not he or she elects to pursue a professional career in anthropology.

Learning Aids. A variety of learning aids has been systematically incorporated into the text. A list of chapter objectives informs students of the skills they will acquire from their study of each chapter. This is followed by an outline to aid students in recognizing the main concepts that are covered in the chapter and in understanding how they will be organized. To facilitate students' learning of the basic concepts of each chapter, all *terms* are defined in context and *boldfaced* for easy recognition. A formal definition of each term is also provided on the page where it occurs. These technical terms are also defined in an alphabetized *glossary* at the end of the book. Since learning the subject matter of a new field also involves acquiring a new vocabulary, students should

be encouraged to use these glossaries as a valuable learning review. By testing their knowledge of the meaning of each term, they can readily determine which parts of each chapter need further study in preparation for tests. Each chapter ends with a summary to help students review the basic concepts that have been introduced. Each chapter also contains an annotated list of readings to guide students in further readings concerning individual topics that have been covered.

Major concepts are often illustrated by *extended narrative examples* integrated with the text. These provide concrete, down-to-earth examples of the material under discussion. For instance, chapter 2 introduces students to Ruth Benedict's *Patterns of Culture* in a discussion of cultural differences in the expression of feelings, and several extended narratives about the Kwakiutl, Zuñi, and Dobuans are used to illustrate these concepts and at the same time update the current life-styles of these groups. Through the use of narrative examples drawn from the ethnographic record, students can gain a greater respect for cultural diversity as well as an insight into the underlying unity of humanity within that diversity. In so doing, they will also learn that we can better understand ourselves through an understanding of others. These narrative examples are clearly marked in the table of contents and are identified within the text by horizontal rules at the beginning and at the end.

Unfamiliar cultures to which students are introduced in the extended narratives are located geographically on maps in the narrative. All references cited within the body of the text have been compiled into a single bibliography placed immediately before the index.

Ancillaries. This edition of *Cultural Anthropology* is accompanied by a greatly expanded instructor's resource guide, *Teaching and Testing With Cultural Anthropology: Understanding Ourselves & Others,* prepared by myself and Reka F. Mosteller. Professor Mosteller's efforts have resulted in a much expanded set of teaching aids. Each chapter of the instructor's resource guide contains a chapter outline, chapter objectives, glossary, chapter overview, a lecture outline, discussion questions, a set of activities for use in-class or as outside assignments, and an annotated list of suggested readings and films.

As with previous editions, I have prepared all

of the questions in the test bank. This edition of *Teaching and Testing With Cultural Anthropology: Understanding Ourselves & Others* contains an average of 100 test items per chapter or 1500 items in all. In addition to multiple-choice, true/false, and essay questions, this edition of the test bank also includes short answer questions. The entire test bank is available for users of IBM, Apple II, and Macintosh computers on EZ-TEST, The Dushkin Publishing Group's computerized test generator.

Acknowledgments. I deeply appreciate the insightful suggestions made by Deborah Rubin, University of the Pacific, Stockton, California. Her detailed critiques have helped me to better integrate gender into the third edition. The author and publisher wish to thank the reviewers of *Cultural Anthropology: Understanding Ourselves and Others,* 3rd Edition, for their constructive criticism and expert advice.

Arthur L. Alt, College of Great Falls
Elvio Angeloni, Pasadena City College
Jeffery A. Behm, University of Wisconsin
Anne Belisari, Wright State University
Jim Bell, Linn-Benton Community College
Purnima M. Bhatt, Hood College
Anne Briton, University of Miami
William B. Brunton, North Dakota State University
James Conrad, Essex Community College
Matthew Cooper, McMaster University
John Cottier, Auburn University
Douglas Dalton, Longwood College
Mary S. de Grys, Winthrop College
James Eder, Arizona State University
Mark S. Fleisher, Washington State University
Bonita Freeman-Witthoft, West Chester University
Robert R. Gradie, University of Connecticut
Daniel A. Grossman, Cayahoga Community College
Robert C. Harman, California State University, Long Beach

Mary T. Healey, SUNY Brockport
Vernon Jantzi, Eastern Mennonite College
Donna Jones, Drury College
Ruth M. Krulfeld, George Washington University
Christine Loveland, Shippensburg University
Toby Morantz, McGill University
Reka Ferencz Mosteller, SUNY Albany
Marjorie Tallant Nam, Tallahassee Community College
Donald K. Pollack, SUNY Buffalo
Ted Presley, Abilene Christian University
Harald E. L. Prins, Kansas State University
Robert A. Randall, University of Houston
Eugene E. Ruyle, California State University, Long Beach
Daniel Schwartz, Pima Community College
James M. Sebring, University of New Mexico
Wesley Shumar, Shippensburg University
Jay Sokolovsky, University of Maryland, Baltimore
Dorice M. Tentchoff, Oregon State University
Alaka Wali, University of Maryland
Linda M. Whiteford, University of South Florida
Guy H. Wolf II, Towson State University
Newell Wright, Valdosta State College

Special thanks are also due to John Holland, managing editor of The Dushkin Publishing Group, for his careful attention to detail and for the high level of competence that he expected of those who worked on this text, to M. Marcuss Oslander who skillfully edited the second and third editions and diplomatically guided me in those difficult decisions about what to revise, to Pamela Carley for finding the right pictures, and to Bill Ferneau for bringing the publisher and me together. I wish also to thank Sharon Cannon-Crapo for her patient support of my writing efforts and for her useful criticisms of the manuscript as it evolved.

Richley H. Crapo

CONTENTS IN BRIEF

TABLE OF CONTENTS

PART V

Cultural Change and Diversity

CHAPTER 14 Cultural Evolution and the Contemporary World   325

CHAPTER 15 Contemporary American Culture   353

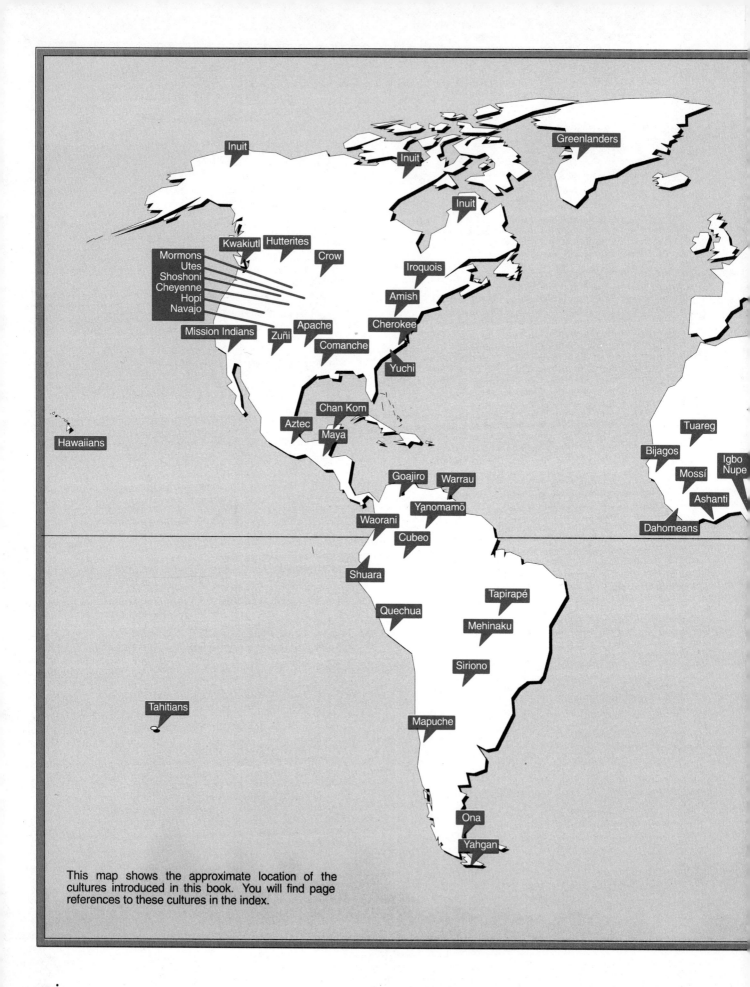

Inuit

Greenlanders

Inuit

Inuit

Kwakiutl   Hutterites

Crow

Mormons
Utes
Shoshoni
Cheyenne
Hopi
Navajo

Iroquois

Amish

Cherokee

Mission Indians   Zuñi   Apache

Comanche

Yuchi

Chan Kom

Aztec

Maya

Tuareg

Bijagos

Igbo
Nupe

Mossí

Ashanti

Goajiro   Warrau

Dahomeans

Hawaiians

Yanomamö

Waorani

Cubeo

Shuara

Tapirapé

Quechua

Mehinaku

Siriono

Tahitians

Mapuche

Ona

Yahgan

This map shows the approximate location of the
cultures introduced in this book. You will find page
references to these cultures in the index.

PART

I

The
Science
of
Culture

CHAPTER 1

**Anthropology:
A Definition**

Fieldwork and participant observation are unique methods of studying cultures employed by anthropologists. As with any discipline, the field of anthropology has evolved. The prescientific view saw all non-Western cultures as degenerated forms of an earlier divine creation. This gave way to cultural evolutionism, empiricism, and eventually to the current period of specialization in which many subfields of anthropology exist, studying many different aspects of both ancient and modern societies.

CHAPTER 2

Culture

The tendency of humans to share their ideas and emotions about their own natures and to develop survival strategies that they pass on to future generations as customs is the basis of culture. Various subsistence technologies derive from a society's pattern of culture and its adjustment to the environment in which it survives. Cultural relativism is the method of trying to understand another culture within its own context, while both the humanistic and scientific approaches provide information about a culture from two different perspectives.

Anthropology is a discipline through which we seek to understand human nature and the broad implications of social interaction. It is at once personal yet scientific. Anthropologists study societies at first hand with a humanistic interest in their cultures and customs, but use a scientific approach to gather information that they hope will ultimately lead to a greater appreciation and acceptance of the diversity in human societies. Chapter 1 defines anthropology by detailing the historical methods that have been used and describes current ideologies. Chapter 2 defines in a multidimensional way the basic concept of culture as an institutionalized system of ideas, emotions, and survival strategies passed on from one generation to another.

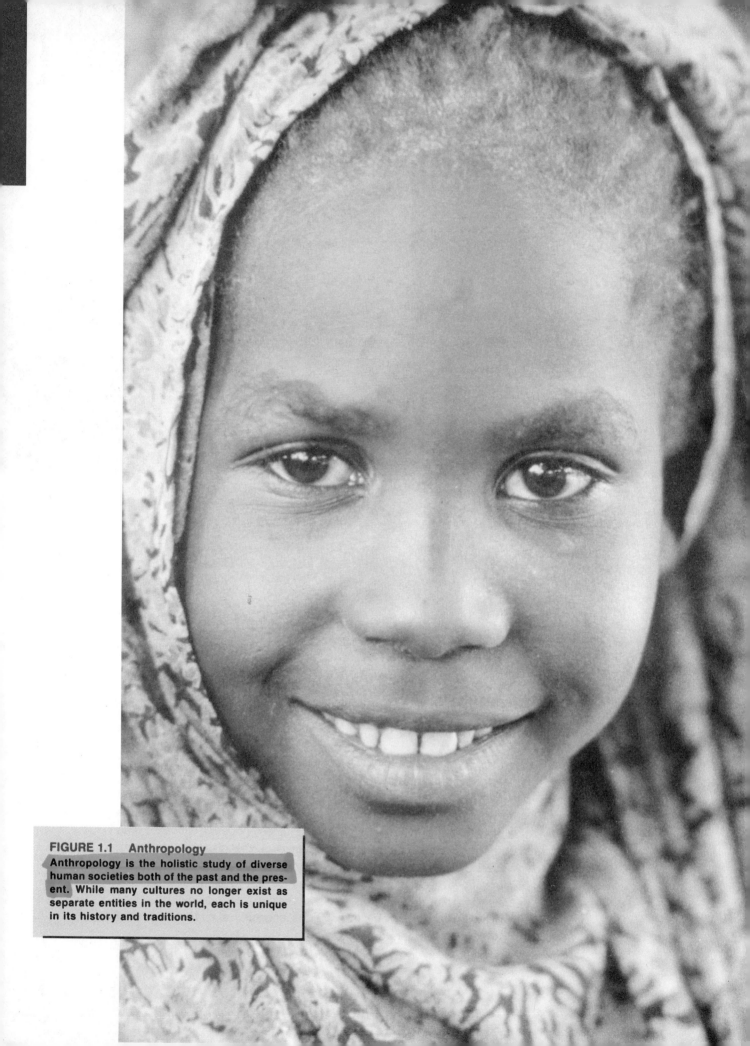

FIGURE 1.1   Anthropology
Anthropology is the holistic study of diverse human societies both of the past and the present. While many cultures no longer exist as separate entities in the world, each is unique in its history and traditions.

Many of the sciences and the humanities study humankind, but anthropology is a special way of understanding our species. In a sense, it incorporates all other ways of studying human societies. This chapter explains what anthropology is, how it has evolved as a discipline, how it gathers information about human behavior, and how it tries to keep its work on an ethical basis with respect for all its subjects.

Anthropology: A Definition

C H A P T E R   O B J E C T I V E S

After reading this chapter, you should be able to:

Define anthropology as a discipline.

Describe the diversity and interrelatedness of anthropological topics.

Enumerate the subdivisions of anthropology.

Discuss the methods of anthropological research.

Analyze fieldwork in the context of the subdivisions of anthropology.

Discuss the benefits and limitations of participant observation.

Explain the basic ethics of anthropological research.

Identify the uses of cross-cultural comparison.

Outline the history of anthropology.

Explain the basic concept of cultural evolutionism.

Describe the basic concepts of functionalism.

The Breadth of Anthropology
The Holistic Perspective
Breadth in Time and Space

Kinds of Anthropology

Methods of Anthropological Research
Fieldwork
Participant Observation
Ethics in Anthropological Research
Cross-Cultural Comparison

History of Anthropology
The Prescientific Period
The Evolutionary Period
The Empiricist Period
The Functionalist Period
The Period of Specialization

Pothunters. Fossils. Computers in the jungle. Note-takers on garbage dumps. *Ny tykka-nu. Nyet.* Analysis. Statistics. Songs. Anthropologists seek to gather information about many different ways of life, using whatever resources are available to them at any given time.

The Breadth of Anthropology

Anthropology is enlightening and exciting because of the breadth of its approaches to understanding the human condition. Classified by subject matter, it is one of the humanities, so anthropologists share some of the interests of philosophers, literary and art critics, translators, and historians. Classified by aspiration, anthropology is a science and shares a great deal with sociology, psychology, political science, economics, linguistics, geography, paleontology, and biology. Eric Wolf (1964) claims that anthropology uniquely bridges the gulf between the sciences and the humanities.

The history of anthropology has been characterized by a dynamic tension between the two poles of science and humanism. There is a fascinating paradox about the attempt to create a science of the human condition. To understand the essence of human reality is, on the one hand, to become immersed in a network of subjective meanings, and on the other hand, to attempt to analyze a human way of life with some degree of objective accuracy. The lines between objectivity and subjectivity blur in a strange way. To analyze a society or its customs with the impersonal charts and tables of a detached observer is one way to ensure that bias is avoided, yet it misses the essential meanings that every way of life has for its people.

How anthropologists have balanced the competing humanistic and scientific thrusts of their discipline is the essence of the history of anthropology. It has its roots among the social philosophers of the eighteenth century Enlightenment, who perceived cultural differences to be the result of conscious human choices rather than as the end product of natural social processes. Then Victorian scholars of the nineteenth century guided anthropology into a passion for "objective" positivist science, but followed a model of cultural evolution that seems to us today to have been strongly motivated by a desire to portray European civilization as the inevitable goal of natural evolutionary processes. Then, in an effort to purge itself of such naive biases, it developed a passion for fieldwork and for fact-collecting that gave birth both to a literary portrayal of non-Western cultures as exotic "others" and to a simultaneous call for a nonjudgmental cultural relativism. Today, anthropologists have returned to both the model of the natural sciences and to an application of the critical tools of literature and art to the study of human meanings. The former searches for causal relationships between environmental and cultural variables such as natural resources, technology, economics, and human population. The latter, an approach more like translating or novel-writing, stresses the problems of how the anthropologist, as an outsider, comes to grips with the ideological and symbolic codes that make each culture meaningfully distinct.

Today, then, anthropology is an exciting mix of diverse approaches. Cultural ecologists explore the adaptation of cultures to different habitats. Feminist anthropologists survey the influence of gender on social power, among other things. Postmodernists reinvigorate our awareness of the interpersonal processes by which anthropological insights are honed. The breadth of subject matter brings together specialists from many fields both in science and the humanities. Consider this diversity: In the past decade, the major English language anthropological journals have included articles on the origin and global spread of AIDS, the roles of gender in prehistoric societies, the rights of indigenous peoples throughout the world, agricultural and economic development in Third World countries, the rise and political influence of Islamic fundamentalism, and the origins and diversity of languages. Anthropology unites these and other diverse topics into a single field by taking as its goal the most complete understanding of the human condition possible. The goal of this book is to introduce you to the unity that defines the current field of cultural anthropology.

The Holistic Perspective

Anthropology is broader in its scope than other fields in which human beings are the topic of study. Its purpose is to paint a **holistic** picture of the human condition, that is, one that shows how different aspects of being human relate to and influence one another. For instance, an anthropologist who is especially interested in human economic life is likely to study how the economic customs of a society, a group of people who have a common identity, influence and are influenced by that society's physical environment, political system, religious customs, family patterns, or even its artistic endeavors. An anthropologist who is concerned with human biology might attempt to demonstrate that different frequencies of fractured vertebrae may result from different hunting practices. An anthropologist studying the language of a Native American society may attempt to determine the location of its ancestral homeland by comparing its words for plants and animals with those of other related languages and by considering the geographical distributions of those specific plants and animals for which the related languages share words.

Breadth in Time and Space

In addition to being more holistic than other fields, anthropology tends to be broad in scope because anthropologists develop their ideas about what is typical of human beings by comparing a wide range of different human groups before drawing their conclusions. For instance, most of the ideas set forth in a contemporary textbook on abnormal psychology are based on research that has been carried out in Europe or North America in societies whose people differ relatively little in upbringing and life experiences. By contrast, a typical anthropological textbook describing the character of mental illness will include comparisons between peoples as diverse as Ituri Forest pygmies, Canadian Inuit, traditional Chinese villagers, and Swedish city dwellers. Anthropologists want their ideas about human nature to be based on as wide a spectrum of human ways of life as possible. For this reason, anthropologists study people in all parts of the world in both simple and complex societies. Their perspective, in other words, is based on **cross-cultural research**—research that draws data from many diverse ways of life rather than just one.

Anthropology's scope extends through time as well as space. Anthropologists try to uncover as much as possible about societies of the distant past as well as about life in contemporary societies. The artifacts and fossil remains of ancient peoples are studied for clues to how people lived in the past in the hope that they will help us understand how we became what we are today.

Kinds of Anthropology

There are four main types of anthropologists: cultural anthropologists, archæologists, anthropological linguists, and physical anthropologists. Generally speaking, **cultural anthropologists** are interested in understanding the rules that govern ways of life, or **cultures**. They study the customs of human societies to discover what leads to their similarities and differences. As a part of their training, cultural anthropologists are usually expected to spend a prolonged period of time—often a year or more—living in a society that practices customs usually very different from those of their own, participating in that way of life, and recording the customs of that society as accurately as possible.

Cultural anthropologists who specialize in recording the customs of human societies are called **ethnographers**. Their descriptions of human ways of life are called **ethnographies**. Other cultural anthropologists known as **ethnologists** attempt to unravel the general laws that guide the development of human ways of life. They have their own specialties, such as people's

---

holistic emphasizing the full range of relations among parts of a system and the ways the operation of those parts helps to perpetuate the whole system

cross-cultural research research that bases its conclusions on data drawn from many diverse ways of life rather than just one

cultural anthropologists anthropologists who specialize in the study of culture in general, or of specific cultures

culture a learned system of beliefs, feelings, and rules for living around which a group of people organize their lives; a way of life of a particular society

ethnographers cultural anthropologists who spend prolonged periods living with and describing the cultures of specific peoples

ethnographies descriptions of customs, beliefs, and values of individual societies

ethnologists cultural anthropologists who formulate general laws of culture based on the study of the ethnographies of many diverse societies

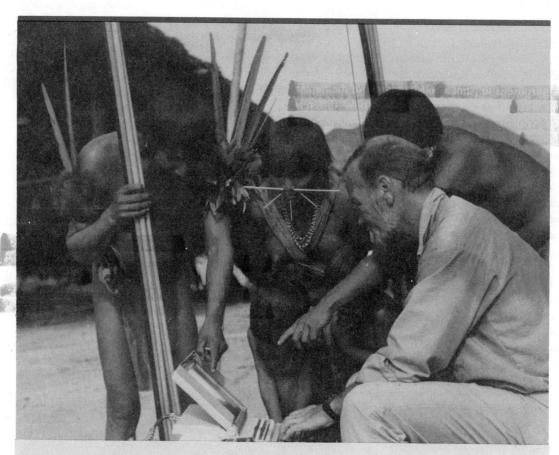

FIGURE 1.2   Ethnographer
One way an anthropologist gathers information about the culture he or she is studying is to live with and participate in the daily activities of that culture. An important part of the research is the accurate gathering and reporting of the observations made, as Napoleon Chagnon is doing on his solar-powered computer.

economic life, political systems, marriages, family and childrearing practices, art, religious practices and beliefs, or psychological traits. The specializations within this branch of anthropology tend to overlap with the interests of professionals in the other behavioral and social sciences within a university. Yet, cultural anthropology has a distinctive contribution to make: to show how each part of human life, be it language, politics, economics, family life or religion, fits into a way of life as a whole. In a sense, other social and behavioral scientists study the various parts in isolation from one another, while the cultural anthropologist is interested in how these relate to the broader context of human life.

Archaeologists, like cultural anthropologists, are interested in understanding ways of life but specialize in cultures that have ceased to exist. Ar-

chaeologists reconstruct the history and the culture of a society from the objects or artifacts its people left behind. The fieldwork of the archaeologist involves the careful, painstaking excavation of places where people have lived. The skills required for the work of excavating a site include surveying, map making, photography, and others necessary for the preservation of information about each object unearthed, including exactly where it was located compared to every other object discovered.

archaeologists cultural anthropologists who study the material remains of earlier societies in order to reconstruct their cultures

To analyze the materials obtained in an excavation, the archaeologist may use skills similar to those of botanists, zoologists, geologists, physicists, and other laboratory scientists, since the original environment of the site must be reconstructed. The archaeologist at this stage may seek to answer such questions as what plants and animals were being eaten and whether these foods were domestic or wild, what the native plants and animals suggest about the climate of the site, or how the materials left behind may provide clues about the age of the site. After such questions have been answered, the work of the archaeologist becomes much like that of the historian and the cultural anthropologist. The goal at this point becomes the description of a way of life and its history.

Archaeology: The Controlled Destruction of a Site

An archaeological site is an important historical record of how people lived in the past. Unfortunately, there are many ways in which this information can be lost. Natural processes can take their toll: Wind, rain, ice, lightning-induced fires, or flash floods can destroy an archaeological site, but human influences damage the record of our past at an even greater rate. Archaeological sites may be bulldozed into nonexistence during the construction of a road or building. They may be covered by the lake created by a new dam. The Olmec site of La Venta in western Tabasco, Mexico, one of the oldest centers of civilization in the Western Hemisphere, is now an oil refinery.

More dramatic is the impact of deliberate vandalism. Archaeological sites of tremendous public interest have been destroyed with increasing frequency in the United States in recent years. For instance, one of the most impressive prehistoric Native American rock art murals in the United States, a mural created at least 600 years ago in Butler Wash, Utah, has been severely damaged on two occasions by vandals using spray paint to cover the original paintings. In the United States, such vandalism and pothunting by collectors has doubled during the last decade, and as many as 90 percent of surveyed archaeological sites have been damaged, spurred by a now illegal multimillion-dollar artifact industry. As *Newsweek* reported in mid-1989:

"It's a hot lazy June afternoon, but things are jumping at Morton Goldberg's New Orleans auction house. 'You won't see a collection like this auctioned off again!' David Goldberg exclaims as his father hustles bids with a singsong chatter. Scattered on long tables, tacked to the walls, spilling out of cardboard boxes are the remnants of an earlier America. There are rugs, baskets, beads, necklaces, bows and arrows, pots of all sizes—even silver crosses from the graves of Indians whose souls were saved by white missionaries. When Goldberg announces that a set of shells and beads from an infant's grave has been withdrawn, the crowd moans in disappointment. Milo Flat Beaver, a Muscogee healer who came to the auction thinking it was an art sale, looks ashen. 'It's a horrible thing,' he mutters.[1]

In many tribes it is believed that disturbing the graves of ancestors will result in spiritual sickness for the living. As Maria Pearson, the Yankton-Sioux activist from Ames, Iowa, said, "When an archaeologist digs and he shakes the very roots of a living soul, it is wrong." Despite the efforts of many governments, a brisk illegal trade in prehistoric artifacts flourishes. The Archaeological Resources Protection Act (ARPA) was passed by Congress in 1979, yet it protects Indian burial sites only on federal property, not on private property. Outside the United States, just as one example, remains of ancient Mayan artifacts not yet examined by professional archaeologists have been hacked apart by looters for sale on an international underground market.

Even the excavation of a prehistoric site by professional archaeologists destroys that site. However, there is an immense difference between the trained archaeological excavator and the "pothunter" who removes artifacts from their original location without regard to the information that is lost in doing so. Archaeologists proceed carefully and systematically to record the precise location of every artifact uncovered, noting its relationship to other things around it, both natural and artificial. The archaeologist is as interested in a stain in the soil indicating the remains of an ancient fire pit or posthole as in the artifacts themselves. Grains of pollen in the soil, fragmentary bones of animals, or the charred remains of a fire may reveal much about the foods eaten, the uses of the artifacts, or the age of the material being excavated. An archaeological excavation is preceded by a careful survey of the site and methodical selection of the areas to be excavated so as to gain the greatest amount of information with the least amount of disturbance. Detailed records are kept of everything done while the work is carried out. Even so, the archaeologist of to-day is likely to leave significant parts of a site untouched, knowing that techniques developed a decade or so in the future may be used to learn even more about it.

1. From "The Plunder of the Past," by Cowley, G., et al., June 26, 1989, *Newsweek*, pp. 58-60.

Anthropological linguists are interested in the role of language in human life. They may be concerned with the origins of language, the biological characteristics of human beings that make it possible for them to use language, the ways in which languages change, or how they are used in daily life. Unlike linguists in other fields, anthropological linguists are chiefly concerned not with language for its own sake, but with the relationships between language and the human condition. Like cultural anthropologists or archaeologists, anthropological linguists may devote their efforts to fieldwork. In the field, the anthropological linguist may record the little-known languages of the world, the oral traditions, the music, the poetry, the styles of speaking, or the social and geographical dialects that are characteristic of a people. Other anthropological linguists with more theoretical interests may study the data from many related languages, much as the ethnologist compares descriptions of the customs of different societies.

Physical anthropologists are also sometimes called biological anthropologists. The purpose of their research is to answer a variety of questions concerning the origins of the human species, its evolutionary history, and the current biological variation among the peoples of the world. Some physical anthropologists study the fossilized skeletal remains of our early human ancestors and their close relatives, with the goal of developing an accurate picture of the evolution of our species. Others have a more specialized interest, such as learning about the diseases from which ancient peoples suffered. Some physical anthropologists specialize in studying how the biological characteristics of contemporary peoples differ from one another and how these differences may have come about. There are even physical anthropologists who devote themselves to the study of the biology and behavior of our close nonhuman relatives, such as the chimpanzees, gorillas, and monkeys, to learn more about the similarities and differences between us.

As diverse as the specialized interests of different anthropologists may be, what unifies them is their

FIGURE 1.3 Archaeologist
Archaeologists reconstruct the history and culture of a society that no longer exists from materials that are left behind.

anthropological linguists cultural anthropologists who specialize in the study of communication, human languages, and their role in human social life
physical (biological) anthropologists anthropologists who specialize in the study of the evolutionary origins of the human species, the relationships between the human species and other living primates, the physical variations within the human species today, and the relationships between human biology and our species' cultural capacities
biological anthropologist physical anthropologist

common desire to better understand the nature of humans and to relate their research to the broader picture of the human condition. It is this integrating tendency and holistic viewpoint that is characteristic of the anthropological enterprise and differentiates it from other disciplines that study humans.

Methods of Anthropological Research

As a science, anthropology has its own distinctive research methods. These involve fieldwork and the comparative method. In cultural anthropology, these take the form of participant observation and cross-cultural comparison.

Fieldwork

The essential method of anthropological research that is shared by anthropologists regardless of their specialization is **fieldwork**—study carried out in the field for firsthand observation. Biological anthropologists may spend time in search of fossil remains of human ancestors or observing primates such as chimpanzees or baboons in the wild to learn about the behavior of species closely related to our own. Archaeologists spend time in the field examining and excavating sites once occupied by human beings or cataloging trash in a city garbage dump. Anthropological linguists work with native speakers of diverse languages to gather data firsthand about these languages and how they are used in real-life situations. Ethnographers spend prolonged periods of time living in isolated non-Western societies, in developing countries, or in a variety of settings such as rural villages, religious communes, prisons, central city slums, or even middle-class communities in Western societies to gather data about the life and customs of those they observe.

Direct observation in natural settings is the common factor in data collection by all kinds of anthropologists. This feature contrasts with the work of other social and behavioral scientists, who have traditionally collected their data in laboratory settings, in structured interviews, or indirectly with printed questionnaires. Consider, for example, the differences in approach of a psychological anthropologist and a psychologist or sociologist interested in human aggression. A psychologist might advertise for volunteer subjects and then have these volunteers administer what they are told are electric shocks to confederates of the researcher, ostensibly to study the effects of punishment on learning but actually to study human willingness to follow aggressive role models and authority figures. Or volunteers who were exposed to a staged argument on their way to the laboratory might be compared with those volunteers who were not. Despite the insights thus gained, there are significant limitations on the usefulness of such studies. Subjects are limited to people who volunteer to come to the laboratory to participate in the research. Whether people who volunteer for such activities are typical members of society is always questionable in such research. Furthermore, it is not always clear what a subject's willingness to follow the directions of a psychologist in a laboratory setting reveals about the same person's likelihood of participating in a riot during a blackout, getting into a bar fight, volunteering for military service during a national crisis, or committing homicide.

An anthropologist interested in human aggression would be more likely to carry out research in the social environments in which violence occurs. The research would most probably be carried out over a period of months, while the anthropologist lives among the people being studied, interacting with them in their normal, day-to-day settings and recording examples of real aggression as they occur. Based on repeated observations over long periods of time, the ethnographer might then suggest some general conclusions about the situations or patterns of interaction that are most likely to trigger aggressive behavior in the particular society being studied.

Participant Observation

Most ethnographic research is also carried out using what is called **participant observation**. The anthropologist goes to the subjects in the field and

---

fieldwork the basic tool of anthropological research in which information is gathered from the context in which it naturally occurs

participant observation the technique of cultural anthropology in which the researcher spends a prolonged period participating with and observing subjects in their natural setting, as opposed to studying them in a laboratory setting remains living among them for a long enough period to earn the trust that people require to behave in the ways they usually do when strangers, tourists, or "outsiders" are not present. Ideally, the ethnographer would like to become skilled enough at following local customs to be accepted as a functioning member of the group, while maintaining sufficient objectivity about the way of life to be able to describe and analyze it fairly and impartially. In practice, complete acceptance as a member of the community being studied is rare. After all, anthropologists are usually born and reared according to customs and values different from those of the peoples they study. Nevertheless, respecting the local community's standards and customs gives the anthropologist the greatest possible chance of inspiring enough trust in the community members that they will behave spontaneously even when the anthropologist is present.

Anthropologists expect to learn the native language of the people they study, since it is a kind of record and model of a people's understandings of themselves and their environment. It also facilitates the direct questioning of a people about their customs and the meanings of those customs. Direct questioning is an important part of participant observation as opposed to simple observation. Anthropologists carry out their questioning in ways that are systematic enough to uncover implicit but not normally discussed aspects of ways of life that might otherwise remain unknown. Systematic questioning requires asking the same questions of many different informants. This is done partly to verify the accuracy of what the researcher is told—after all, anthropologists are outsiders, and they may be considered fair game to informants who may resent their presence or simply enjoy the humor of deceiving them. Asking the same questions of many informants also ensures that the information obtained is typical of the ideas expressed in the community at large.

Participant observation has limitations as well as strengths. One problem is that the time and energy it requires make it impossible for anthropologists to sample more than a fraction of the many lifestyles that exist at any time, and each anthropologist is only able to spend time in a limited number of communities within any one society. Choices such as which society to study, which communities within that society, and which members of the community to spend time with are influenced by many factors that cannot be called objectively scientific. For instance, financial limitations may determine the choice of where to do the research; national politics in the society may

influence which communities are visited; and the chance meeting of a community member who belongs to a particular political, religious, or economic faction may determine who will shun or be willing to work with the anthropologist.

Another problem in the fieldwork approach is the fact that the anthropologist's very presence can alter in important ways a way of life she or he is studying. For instance, Jean Briggs noted that "the hosts must also rearrange their lives, at some cost to themselves, to include the anthropologist and to solve the problems created by the latter's presence. The disruption may be more or less severe, depending on the nature of the role that the anthropologist adopts (or is assigned) in the society" (1986, p. 20).

Gender and fieldwork. In the past, most anthropologists were men. Since 1984, new doctoral degrees in anthropology have been earned by an equal number of women and men (*Survey of Anthropology Phds,* 1990, p. 8). This shift toward gender balance has greatly improved ethnographic data, since the gender of fieldworkers influences the information to which they have access. For instance, lives of women may be inaccessible to a male anthropologist, and the gossip in male-only settings may be unavailable to a female anthropologist.

Because both male and female anthropologists frequently assume the gender roles of the people in the society they study, the kind of topics they choose (or are constrained) to investigate is limited, as is the kind of data that they collect. For instance, Ann Fischer's first field project was the study of Trukese mothers. Since she was pregnant at the time, the Trukese spontaneously offered her many of their views on the physiological experience of pregnancy, greatly facilitating her research. She also found that she and her husband were given rather different kinds of information. She reported that "if our field notes are compared, my husband's record the more formal aspects of culture in exactitude, while mine tend to be a running account of what was happening in the village or in the homes in which I observed. This difference held in most of the cultures in which we did fieldwork together, although in New England I was in a better position to obtain formal interviews than was my husband. . . . Our access to data was different in every culture we studied" (1986, p. 282). Since the lives, customs, and opinions of men and women differ in important ways in every culture, male and female anthropologists gain different insights in the field.

The Fieldwork Experience: A Case Study

After three years of graduate training, I prepared for my first experience in anthropological fieldwork, the study of the Shoshoni language and its probability of becoming extinct. I remember one piece of advice my mentor gave me as we drove for the first time to the reservation which he had selected for my work: Don't ask directly about how many people or families lived on the reservation because such questions would raise the suspicion that I was really gathering information for the government for some nefarious purpose. I followed this advice even though it slowed considerably my building of a clear picture of the makeup of the reservation.

At first it seemed that I could not have been more fortunate in a fieldwork location. The Tribal Council had graciously offered me a rent-free ranch house that seemed luxurious. It was supplied with propane lighting, a stove, running cold water, and a propane refrigerator. It was furnished with a couch, desk, and bed. Most important of all, it actually had an indoor toilet!

My first crisis was the discovery that although the house had a mechanically perfect toilet, it was unusable. It seems a child had flushed a rubber ball down the drain. Ordinarily this might have been fixed, but the drainpipe narrowed, somewhere in the front yard, to a size smaller than the ball. Thus, my prized possession was as unfunctional as a fur-lined teacup.

The biggest initial adjustment to life in the field was loneliness. Residents of the reservation had their own work to do and lives to live. Most people were cattle ranchers, and their work kept them busy. They did not just drop everything because a young anthropologist had arrived. At first, I was at a loss to know how to go about meeting people. Residences were dispersed over the reservation. There were no stores to form a place of congregation. However, there was a third class post office, where mail arrived and departed only weekly, a small two-room frame structure where I figured people would drop by occasionally. The reservation had no telephones, there was no television reception in the valley, and only a few houses had self-generated electricity to power even a radio, so I assumed that the mail would be an important source of information about the outside world. I stopped by the post office the next time I found it open. Mail was brought out to the reservation once a week by an automobile referred to as "the stagecoach." People did come by to mail a letter or pick up their own deliveries, but few ever stayed long enough for me to get to know them. The one exception, of course, was the postmaster, Billy Mike, who became my first acquaintance. He expressed friendly interest in why I had come to the reservation, and spent many hours helping me learn the Shoshoni dialect that was spoken locally. Eventually he introduced me to other, older members of the community.

My main task was to develop an accurate description of the roles of Shoshoni and English on the reservation. I wanted to discover the rules that governed which language was likely to be spoken by which persons under various circumstances. Thus, I was interested in whether speakers' choice of language in a given conversation could be predicted by combinations of such things as the age or sex of each speaker, the topic being discussed, or the specific vocabulary items that were necessary for that topic. In essence, I was trying to characterize the degree to which English was displacing Shoshoni as the language of choice in conversations as well as the ways in which the displacement was happening.

The single most difficult barrier that I was forced to grapple with was my own lack of fluency in the Shoshoni language. I had been fortunate in having been able to study the language for two years before starting my fieldwork, but what I had learned was only "book Shoshoni," and once I was on my own on the reservation it quickly became clear to me that I lacked the conversational abilities that would be needed to follow the important but subtle nuances of day-to-day speech among native Shoshoni speakers. Shoshoni is a fascinating language whose verbs are particularly problematic for a native English speaker who is accustomed to the need for remembering only a few variations on the past, present, and future tenses. Shoshoni, by contrast, has some sixteen basic tenses that differ not only according to *when* in time the process is placed but also in the style or quality of the action. For instance, there are two simple past tenses that differ only in whether the activity was completed gradually or suddenly. Thus, the English sentence, "She died," requires in Shoshoni a choice of tense that would depend on whether the cause of death were a lingering illness or a broken neck. A third past tense in Shoshoni is used for activities that were completed only in a location different from where the speaker currently is. It is true, of course, that these distinctions can be made by adding the right words and phrases to the basic English sentence, but unfortunately for the native English speaker, these differences in meaning are grammatically obligatory in Shoshoni and —even worse—they are accomplished with suffixes that are appended to the basic verb. Consider the three Shoshoni sentences, *Ny* tykka-nu ("I ate [a leisurely meal]"), *Ny tykka-hkwa* ("I ate [quickly]") and *Ny tykka-hkooni* ("I ate [while I was over there]"). Present tenses are equally elaborate. There is one suffix for an activity that has just recently begun, another for a process that has been going on for a specific period of time, and a third for one that is happening now but has no definite time of onset. For some time, I despaired of being able to follow the sense of even the simplest conversations. I had discovered that distinctions that a student could readily notice in a neatly typed text did not linger nearly long enough in the air when spoken. For a long time, I contented myself with collecting single words, preferably nouns.

Still, some facts about language use became apparent quite soon after my arrival. For instance, although almost everyone on the reservation whom I met spoke both Shoshoni and English, there was tremendous variation in proficiency in both languages from one speaker to another. This was especially noticeable when persons of different age were compared. The oldest resident was a woman who was said to have reached her hundredth birthday and who claimed to speak no English at all. Others who ranged in age from about 60 to 80 were fluent Shoshoni speakers who typically spoke English as well but with a clear Shoshoni accent and an occasional difficulty with English vocabulary. Middle-aged speakers usually had nearly equal proficiency in both languages, while many of those under 40 appeared to be more at home with English than Shoshoni.

Even before I could follow what was being said, I noticed that conversations in Shoshoni were interspersed with English loan words regardless of the age of the speakers. When the topic dealt with technological issues, such as the repair of a water pump, English words such as *pliers*, *hammer*, or *wire* were common. Many words for recently adopted foods such as coffee, grapes, and oranges were also borrowed from English. Shoshoni has no native obscenities, so when the Shoshoni adopted the use of obscenities along with many other aspects of American culture, English words and phrases were simply borrowed and used within Shoshoni sentences. Here the pattern was noticeably age-related.

Situations and topics controlled language choice as well. Several families on the reservation were members of the Mormon religion which is a major Christian denomination throughout much of the Great Basin states. Each week a non-Indian representative of this church came to the reservation to hold worship services. In this setting, the English language predominated even in conversations before and after the meeting between Shoshonis who attended.

During my work with the Indians, I would typically tape record the examples of speech that I intended to analyze later. Simultaneously, I made handwritten notes in an abbreviated style about what was happening. They contained comments on such things as the context of conversations, persons involved, and the topics being discussed as well as any spontaneous insights into linguistic or cultural aspects of the conversations that I felt might help my later analysis. At other times, for instance when I was systematically eliciting ways of saying various things, these notes became careful transcriptions of the complete responses. Each evening at home, I would type my notes to produce a separate, neater collection of fieldnotes.

The story lines of the material I had recorded raised cultural as well as linguistic questions that also had to be answered. Why, for instance, was the weasel the animal of choice for preparing both gambling and love magic? Or when the "medicines" prepared for these purposes were "spoken to" did it imply a hearing spirit within the supernatural materials or was the speaking merely a way of manipulating the materials by invoking inanimate and unthinking supernatural forces? I made notes on such questions so that I could follow up on them the following day.

As my work progressed, I began recording conversations and folktales that were part of the oral tradition. At the same time, I was able to cross-check the accuracy of what I had learned. Such practice enabled me eventually to follow the sense of conversations that occurred spontaneously in my presence. So I began to examine the interplay of Shoshoni and English in the natural speech that was happening around me. I started recording not just when and where one of the languages seemed to be preferred over the other and how the words of one language were adopted into the other, but also how speakers might switch from one language to another as topics of their discussion changed. At the same time, as I developed an increasing facility with the native language I started to learn things about reservation life that had not been clear through English alone. For instance, I began to learn that adults, who previously had been careful to avoid suggesting that they accepted the traditional Shoshoni religious beliefs, openly discussed such matters as native curing ceremonies and native mythology when speaking Shoshoni in my presence. I began to learn something of the contemporary Shoshoni ideology, a worldview that incorporates both traditional Shoshoni ideas and those of the American mainstream.

The reservation on which I lived was one of the few places throughout the Great Basin homeland of the Shoshoni that was fortunate to have a practicing Indian doctor, a religious curer called a pohakante. Willie Blackeye was highly respected and held traditional curing ceremonies about once a month for patients who came to him from throughout Nevada. He claimed that he did not speak English, but I am still not sure whether this was so or if his fostering of this belief was a means of maintaining a certain distance from what those on the reservation called "Anglo culture." But whether it was intended or not, the contrast between the predominant use of English in the setting of Mormon worship services and the dominant role of Shoshoni in Willie Blackeye's curing ceremonies clearly marked the contrast between traditional and nontraditional aspects of Shoshoni religious ideology. Thus, as the Indians shared with me the traditional religious lore of Coyote and the other supernatural animals that populate Shoshoni mythology, words borrowed from English occurred only rarely. Stories about more recent history contained many examples of borrowed words. Finally, English was most common in gossip and tales of recent events.

My exploration of language choice among contemporary Shoshoni exemplifies the holistic and integrative nature of cultural anthropology. Although the central concern of my research was a linguistic topic, I was not primarily interested in the Shoshoni language as a closed system. Instead I sought to uncover the cultural rules that governed when and where one language would more likely be used than another. This forced me to examine how the Shoshoni discussed their environment, their artifacts, and their economic activities. I also had to examine the social facts of Shoshoni life, since their patterns of language use differed so dramatically by age. Ideology also could not be ignored, because English had not been uniformly adopted for communicating about all the various aspects of Shoshoni symbolic life.

Although my personal goal was an academic one—completing the requirements for a degree in anthropology—participant observation research is not a process of detached data gathering and analysis. I could only obtain information about the use of language in real life by living with my subjects and interacting with them in their own settings. As a matter of fact, many of the important insights into the dynamics of a society come as a result of the interplay between the fieldworker and the native participants as the researcher struggles to understand the culture. It is the give and take of participant research that is particularly central to the anthropologist's ability to translate another culture into the idiom and metaphor of his or her own way of life. I too found that I was drawn into the life of the reservation in ways that fulfilled my own goals and, at the same time, served the values of the people I had come to study. In fact, I am fortunate to be able to still maintain some contact with those people who touched my life in meaningful ways and broadened my understanding of both the range of diversity within the human condition and of the underlying similarities that make us all one human family.

Ethics in Anthropological Research

Since the subjects of anthropological research are human beings, there are important ethical considerations in doing fieldwork. It is generally agreed that the first loyalties of an anthropological fieldworker must lie with the people being studied. Our work must be carried out and reported in ways that cannot be used to harm the peoples whose lives we are investigating. When an anthropologist lives for extended periods of time with a people to thoroughly absorb the details of their lives and customs, it is almost inevitable that the researcher will become privy to information that might be harmful to the welfare and dignity of the host people were it to become public knowledge. Such knowledge is expected to be held in confidence, and anthropological research is reported only in ways that ensure the anonymity of individual informants and the welfare of the communities studied.

Because anthropological research carried out among living peoples is a matter of skilled observation and inquiry, anthropologists generally have no qualms about informing their subjects about the purposes of their research. There are, of course, situations in which the gathering of specific information about people's behavior would be made more difficult by an explicit admission of what the anthropologist is seeking, either because the informants' knowledge would make them self-conscious—thereby causing them to alter their normal behavior—or because informants may sometimes say what they think the investigator would like to hear. For instance, it would probably be self-defeating to announce one's intention to count how often people violate their own rules of public etiquette, since this would warn them to be on their best behavior whenever they see you coming! Thus, anthropologists may be open about their general topic of interest without compromising their ability to observe the specific behaviors that are relevant to learning about that topic. The real issue here is that anthropologists endeavor not to deceive their subjects or carry out research that serves interests that differ from the community's own. Clandestine or secret research is frowned on by most anthropologists. One way of avoiding conflicts of interest over allegiance to the people studied and to others with differing political aims is to avoid accepting research assignments that the funding agency requires be carried out in secrecy.

The anthropologist's second allegiance is to the expansion of a scientifically respectable body of knowledge about the human condition. Thus, anthropologists seek to do everything in their power to collect accurate information and to make it openly available to others in a form that does not violate their informants' rights or compromise their dignity. It is common practice for anthropologists to see to it that copies of their research reports and publications are made available to the communities they were studying. This ensures integrity in the research process and loyalty to the values of the subjects, and it also makes it possible for the fruits of anthropological research to be used by the subjects for their own benefit.

Cross-Cultural Comparison

The third component of anthropological research is cross-cultural comparison—examination of the varied ways a certain aspect of human life is treated in many different cultures. For instance, an ethnologist who is interested in examining the general rules that relate to aggression in any society, might compare the ethnographic data from a broad range of human societies to determine what social factors are consistent predictors of specific forms of aggression.

Anthropological fieldworkers are especially skilled at providing insights into the relationship of a custom to its broader social context. Their in-depth exposure to a particular way of life allows them to notice in detail how one part of a culture influences another. Yet, to develop truly useful generalizations about the ways in which culture functions, it is necessary to demonstrate that relationships that appear to be valid in one culture will hold true for others under like circumstances. Cross-cultural research is the typical strategy that anthropologists use for this purpose. By comparing a sufficient number of historically unrelated cultures from different parts of the world, it is possible to determine, for instance, whether warfare is more likely in societies in which there are large differences in wealth between families than in societies in which all families have about the same level of wealth. Anthropologists can also determine whether sexual inequality is more likely in societies where warfare occurs between neighboring peoples who belong to the same culture than in societies where warfare occurs between members of very different cultures.

Currently, the most sophisticated collection of data on many different societies is one which was begun in 1937 by George Peter Murdock and several colleagues (1961). This collection of cross-cultural data is known today as the **Human Relations Area Files (HRAF)**. It now contains over three quarters of a million pages of information on 335 major societal groups, each of which has been coded for the pres-

---

cross-cultural comparison basing general conclusions about the nature of culture and its influence on society on the comparison of a diverse sample of cultures from many parts of the world, so that those conclusions will be generally valid for the human condition as a whole

Human Relations Area Files (HRAF) a research data pool containing information on over 335 major societal groups, each coded for the presence or absence of about 700 cultural and environmental traits

TABLE 1.1 Correlations between Sexual Restrictiveness and Marriage Celebrations

		Sexual Restrictiveness		
		Low	Medium or High	Total
Marriage Celebration	Small	11	7	18
	Moderate or Elaborate	4	28	32
	Total	15	35	

In a sample of 50 societies from the Human Relations Area Files (HRAF), researchers have verified a relationship between few premarital sexual restrictions on women and simple weddings, and extensive premarital sexual restrictions on women followed by elaborate weddings.

Note: Association of Elaboration of Marriage Celebration with the Index of Sexual Restrictiveness for Women (from Frayzer, 1985, p. 328)

ence or absence of characteristics on a standard list of over 700 cultural and environmental traits. Use of data from the HRAF has made it possible for researchers to determine what cultural traits or environmental factors are the best predictors of the presence or absence of various customs, thereby testing their ideas about the effects of one part of a cultural system on another.

Here is a brief example of how the HRAF might be used. Suppose an anthropologist suspected that in societies in which it is important for a man to be identified as the father of his wife's children, it would be likely that those societies would have both elaborate marriage rituals (to publicly proclaim the relationship between the husband and wife) and strong rules that limit a woman's sexual behavior outside marriage. Simple weddings with few sexual restrictions on the woman might likely be found in other societies where males and females are considered equals. There should, however, be few societies in which one is prominent and the other absent. If we examined a sample of societies from the HRAF files to check how likely it is for these two traits to occur together, we would find that, although there are exceptions, elaborate weddings and restrictions on women's sexual behavior do tend to go together, as do simple weddings and few sexual restrictions (see Table 1.1).

History of Anthropology

Although anthropology is a relatively young discipline, it has its roots in earlier attempts to learn about unfamiliar cultures. Even after anthropology became systematized as a study, it evolved through many forms.

The Prescientific Period

Anthropology owes its birth to European expansionism of the fifteenth and sixteenth centuries. Exploration and colonization brought Europeans into contact with many diverse ways of life. Government officials who wished to exert political control over native peoples, and missionaries who desired to convert them to Christianity were active in recording and studying the languages of native peoples.

The Evolutionary Period

Out of the contrast Europeans saw between simple and complex societies grew the idea that cultures had evolved from simple beginnings to more

FIGURE 1.4   Charles Darwin
Darwin was the first scientist to propose the controversial theory of natural selection or the evolution of a species through change.

FIGURE 1.5   Edward Burnett Tylor
Tylor postulated, in the 19th century, that culture evolved uniformly and progressively, thus making possible the idea of progress for all societies.

complex civilizations. The idea that cultures had evolved from savagery to civilization, **cultural evolutionism**, became the dominant view among scholars.

In 1735 Carolus Linnaeus had published the *Systema Naturae*, which classified plants and animals into a hierarchical system based on their degree of similarity to one another. Although Linnaeus's purpose had been simply to demonstrate the divine order of God's creation, his systematic categorization of humans and other living things made it easy to suggest that living forms had achieved their current differences through evolution. The discovery of fossils of extinct animals also contributed to this idea. Toward the end of the eighteenth century, scholars began to consider the idea that biological species might also be evolving.

In 1859 Charles Darwin published *On the Origin of Species*, in which he set forth the first successful theory of the mechanisms by which evolutionary change occurs. About the same time, the discovery of the first known fossil remains of ancient humans added dramatic support to the applicability of Darwin's ideas to the human species.

In the nineteenth century, archaeology was also providing support for the idea that ways of life evolved. Excavation of the remains of prehistoric human groups showed that earlier human societies were simpler than later ones that developed from them. In 1871 Sir Edward Burnett Tylor published

---

cultural evolutionism the nineteenth-century emphasis on analyzing cultures in terms of their development through a series of stages from savagery to civilization
Systema Naturae the book in which Carolus Linnaeus classified plants and animals into a hierarchical system based on their degree of similarity to one another

Primitive Culture, in which he developed a theory of the evolution of religion and discussed the concept of **survivals**, remnants of earlier social customs and ideas that could be used as evidence for reconstructing the evolutionary past of societies. In 1877 a contemporary of Tylor, Lewis Henry Morgan, published another strong argument for the evolution of culture, *Ancient Society*, a book that has remained influential to this day. In 1883 Tylor became the first anthropologist to hold a position at a university and gain respect as a professional scientist, and anthropology as a professional field of study was born.

The Empiricist Period

American anthropology developed its own distinctive flavor about the beginning of the twentieth century under the leadership of Franz Boas. Originally trained in physics, Boas brought to the field of anthropology a scientific emphasis on **empiricism** that greatly influenced its history in America. He taught his students that the careful collection of accurate information about other ways of life was as important as the building of theory. He also vigorously condemned armchair theorizing—the building of grandiose theories based on speculation rather than on research. Boas was, in other words, an empiricist who viewed science as a discipline dedicated to the recording of fact. During his career, Boas published over 700 articles dealing with topics as diverse as changes in the bodily form of descendants of American immigrants, Native American mythology, geography, and the relationships between language and thought. Boas stressed the importance of fieldwork by anthropologists. Since his day it has become the rule for students to spend a period of time studying a way of life by participating in and observing it firsthand.

It was Boas and his students who established anthropology as a field of study in major universities throughout the United States. Boas set the tone of the distinctive form that American anthropology cultivated for half a century. Beyond stressing the importance of fieldwork data collection, Boas and his students strongly rejected the idea that cultures were determined by race or that races differed from one another in their ability to learn any way of life. Similarly, Boas avoided comparing cultures in ways that carried any implication of ranking them. Instead, he stressed the importance of **cultural relativism**, the idea that it is invalid to try to evaluate other cultures

FIGURE 1.6   Franz Boas
The first-hand observation of other cultures and careful collection of data about them was Franz Boas's greatest contribution to modern anthropology.

in terms of Western standards, and that each way of life is best understood by its own standards of meaning and value. This idea remains a fundamental concept in anthropology to this day.

During the first half of the twentieth century, dominated by Boas, anthropologists commonly adopted the concept of **diffusion**—the spread of customs, artifacts, and ideas from one society to another—to

survivals remnants of earlier social customs and ideas that can be used to reconstruct the evolutionary past of societies
empiricism the viewpoint that conclusions should be based on careful observation and description, rather than on abstract theorizing
cultural relativism principle that cultural traits are best understood in the context of the cultural system of which they are a part; the attempt to avoid the narrow bias of judging a custom or entire culture on the basis of one's own cultural values; the view that meanings of behaviors are best understood when interpreted in terms of the culture of the actors

18

organize their ideas about how ways of life influence each other. In the United States, the concept of diffusion led to the idea of culture areas, relatively small geographical regions in which different societies had come to share many similar traits through diffusion. A culture area can be exemplified by the Plains region of the United States. The Plains were occupied by dozens of different tribes whose people spoke many different languages. Yet these diverse societies had come to share many customs, dress, worldview, and values through diffusion.

During the first half of the twentieth century diffusionism, the approach to cultures that took the study of the diffusion of cultural traits as its major interest, was the dominant view in America. During this period European anthropologists were also abandoning their interest in cultural evolution and turning to their own brand of diffusionism as a means for reconstructing social history. European diffusionists felt that earlier anthropologists had placed too much emphasis on the independent invention of social traits and underrated the role of the diffusion of ideas. They traced the spread of social traits and ideas around the entire world from a small number of centers in which they believed those traits had been originally invented. These early diffusionists are now generally regarded to have greatly oversimplified much of the world's cultural history in their enthusiasm for their diffusionist theory. Nevertheless, although their grand schemes of all cultures having derived from a small number of great cultural centers in the world has been abandoned, the idea of diffusion itself—the borrowing of cultural traits from society to society—as an important process in cultural change is still accepted as a valid concept.

The Functionalist Period

In England the diffusionist viewpoint took on its most simplistic form. The British diffusionists contended that all important inventions had occurred but once, in ancient Egypt, and spread from there to other parts of the world. By the 1930s this overly simple view of human history had been replaced by an approach known as functionalism. Functionalists were not concerned as much with history or the origins of customs as they were with the mechanics of a society, the way in which it functioned. In their view, a society was able to continue to exist because its customs were adaptive and made it possible for people to cope with their environment and with one

another. Therefore, a society's customs can be analyzed by their functions, their contribution to maintaining the unity and survival of the society. The main proponents of this view were Bronislaw Malinowski and Alfred Reginald Radcliffe-Brown. Both Malinowski and Radcliffe-Brown stressed the importance of fieldwork and rejected evolutionism and diffusionism. Malinowski emphasized that societies survive by making it possible for their members to meet seven biological and psychological needs: nutrition, reproduction, bodily comforts, safety, relaxation, movement, and growth. He analyzed the functions of a society's customs by how they helped the individual to meet these needs. Radcliffe-Brown, on the other hand, was concerned with the functional mechanisms that operate within society to maintain an orderly social life among its members.

The early members of the functionalist school of thought were criticized by later anthropologists for having too often assumed that every custom must have some *positive* social or cultural function, a bias that led them to ignore the possibility that there are *dysfunctional* customs. The early functionalists, in their enthusiasm for discovering how customs functioned to perpetuate a culture and its society, tended to treat only the positive benefits that customs might have for some members of society, while ignoring the fact that these benefits might also prove harmful to other members of the system. For instance, Malinowski himself, when addressing the issue of cultural change in Africa, never questioned the idea that the Europeans who had invaded and conquered various African lands had a right to rule. His analysis of the colonization of Africa simply assumed that to be

---

diffusion the passage of such cultural traits as customs, artifacts, and ideas from one society to another

culture areas geographical areas in which different societies share a complex of cultural traits due to similar adaptations to their environmental zone and to the effects of diffusion of cultural traits through those societies

diffusionism the early twentieth-century approach to analyzing cultures that emphasized the historical reconstruction of the influences of one culture on another in contrast to the more general evolutionary perspective of earlier anthropologists

functionalism the approach to analyzing cultures by examining the mechanics of society while it is in equilibrium, as opposed to the more historical emphasis of diffusionism or the developmental emphasis of evolutionism

function the contribution that any one cultural trait makes to perpetuating the unity, equilibrium, and adaptation of a way of life within its environment

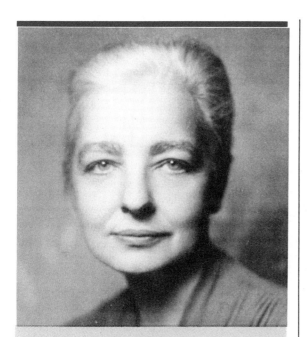

FIGURE 1.7 Ruth Benedict
Benedict was instrumental in establishing the importance of studying cultures and their behavior in comparison to other cultures.

FIGURE 1.8 Margaret Mead
Mead is best known for her study of culture and personality. The book *Coming of Age in Samoa* is her influential study of adolescent development and behavior.

the case, and argued that "what are being given to the Africans are new conditions of existence, better adapted to their needs but always in harmony with European requirements" (1945, p. 160), a viewpoint that certainly would have been disputed by the subordinated African populations.

The early functionalists also have been criticized for having ignored the fact that there are forms of change other than functional adaptations that lead to equilibrium and stability. This blind spot in the outlook of the early functionalists often expressed itself as an uncritical acceptance of the status quo, a bias that is also exemplified by Malinowski's willingness to emphasize the benefits that Africans supposedly obtained by living under British colonial domination.

Although earlier uses of functionalism have been widely criticized, the idea that customs have an effect on other parts of a culture and its society is taken for granted today by all anthropologists. Analyzing the functions of customs is probably the most common single technique used in anthropological discussions of human life, regardless of the specific school of thought.

While functionalism was on the rise in Eng-

land, one branch of American anthropology was becoming more interested in the role of psychology in ways of life. Many of the anthropologists of this tradition were students of Boas who were influenced by his interest in human psychology and worldview. The best known of these anthropologists were Ruth Benedict and Margaret Mead. In 1934, Benedict published *Patterns of Culture*, which is still among the most widely read of American anthropological works. In this book, she argued—as did the functionalists—that ways of life are integrated wholes. Unlike the functionalists, however, she found this integration in the unity of a people's mentality and values. Margaret Mead stressed the importance of childrearing practices on personality development. During the 1930s, students of **culture and personality**, or psychological anthropology, as this new subfield of anthropology came to be known, were greatly influenced by Freudian views of developmental psychology. Following World War II, their influence declined. The early practitioners of culture and per-

—

culture and personality the field of anthropology that studies the variety of psychological traits and personality characteristics among cultures

20

sonality studies have been faulted for their tendency to overgeneralize about cultural patterns, based on impressionistic stereotypes that largely ignored many variations in the behaviors of the peoples they studied.

The Period of Specialization

After World War II, the two major earlier interests—the symbolic aspects of culture and the material and social conditions to which human life must adjust—continued to be the major divisions within cultural anthropology, but many specialized subfields have developed within both of these approaches to culture. For instance, the major professional organization for anthropologists in the United States is the American Anthropological Association. Its membership has grown so much that a single, general organization is no longer adequate to meet the professional needs of its members, whose areas of specialized interest have become quite diverse. To accommodate these needs in a way that still fosters the historic goal of maintaining a holistic and integrated perspective for the field as a whole, the association was reorganized in 1984 so that it is now composed of over a dozen smaller subunits that help anthropologists coordinate their research and share their findings. Most of these affiliated societies publish their own journals, and their members meet together in smaller groups during the annual convention of the parent association. One example is the Society for Psychological Anthropology, whose members have tried to overcome the weaknesses of earlier culture and personality studies by emphasizing the use of statistical comparisons of data from many different societies. The Society for Feminist Anthropology has been formed by those who are interested in gender issues. Cultural anthropologists who are interested in cross-cultural comparative research belong to the American Ethnological Society. Anthropologists who have extended the viewpoint of their discipline to include the study of contemporary North American, Latin American, European, and Oriental cultures along with the non-Western cultures that were the historic focus of the field, find a home in the Society for Cultural Anthropology. The Society for Humanistic Anthropology houses members who advocate the use of the same techniques that are used for analyzing written literature and folklore. They interpret other aspects of culture as a system of meaningful symbols. Anthropologists who have extended the work of ethnography to include modern film and videotaping

technologies as means for recording ways of life, work together within the Society for Visual Anthropology. The National Association for Practicing Anthropologists has been formed to bring together anthropologists who use their skills for solving cultural problems and who are often employed today in settings such as industry, private consulting firms, and government.

Despite its increasing diversity, anthropology still manages to maintain an overall identity as a unified field through the activities of the parent association. For instance, the major journal of the profession, the *American Anthropologist*, regularly publishes articles, book reviews, and correspondence of general professional interest by members of all of its affiliated organizations. The *American Anthropological Association* also organizes the yearly meetings that bring together members of all of its more specialized affiliates and publishes a monthly newsletter that includes listings of employment opportunities for anthropologists and information about current trends in the profession.

Employment in anthropology. In the past, as many as 85 percent of anthropologists were employed in university settings. Today, this is changing rapidly. New anthropologists increasingly are finding employment in other settings. According to Fillmore, "nonacademic employment is expanding as anthropology Ph.D.'s fill career niches once exclusively filled by sociologists, economists, and other social scientists. These latter jobs consist of managing research programs in private firms, government agencies, and nonprofit associations, societies and institutes" (1989, p. 32). During the past decade about half of all new Ph.D.'s in anthropology have found their employment outside the traditional university and college teaching setting. Anthropologists now do consulting for the World Bank and work for companies that do independent consulting in Third World development projects. They work as business consultants for GM, Xerox, Nissan, and other corporations. In the United States, they are employed by the Centers for Disease Control, state health departments, the Bureau of Land Management, the Bureau of Indian Affairs, and the U.S. Park Service. They also find employment in private companies that do cultural and human resource management studies throughout the United States.

▬

American Anthropological Association major professional organization for anthropologists in the United States

CHAPTER SUMMARY

1. Anthropology is the broadest of the disciplines studying the human condition, for it draws on fields as diverse as philosophy, art, economics, linguistics, and biology for its conclusions.

2. The major fields of anthropology itself are cultural anthropology, archaeology, anthropological linguistics, and physical anthropology.

3. They all utilize the same basic anthropological methods of fieldwork and comparative studies.

4. In cultural anthropology, these take the form of participant observation and cross-cultural comparison.

5. As a science, anthropology has developed historically through attempts to show that cultural complexity has evolved, to gathering data on varying cultures in the field, and to demonstrating that customs and ideas have survival value to a society.

6. The two main models—culture as a symbolic system and culture as an adaptation to the environment—are represented by a number of new specialized subfields in anthropology, including feminist anthropology, psychological anthropology, visual anthropology, humanistic anthropology, and applied anthropology.

7. While most anthropologists continue their work through universities, applied and practicing anthropologists are bringing their skills to nonacademic settings.

8. Even when working for governmental or commercial employers, anthropologists try to maintain an ethical approach that safeguards the interests of the people they are hired to study.

ANNOTATED READINGS

Agar, M. H. (1980). *The professional stranger: An informal introduction to ethnography*. New York: Academic Press. A good general overview of field research.

Angeloni, E. (Ed.). (1992). *Annual editions: Anthropology*. Guilford, CT: Dushkin Publishing Group. An annually revised collection of significant articles on contemporary issues in cultural anthropology.

Bohannan, P., & Glazer, M. (Eds.). (1973). *High points in anthropology*. New York: Alfred A. Knopf. A thoughtfully selected collection of the classic writings by the major names in the history of anthropology.

Casagrande, J. B. (Ed.). (1960). *In the company of man: Twenty portraits by anthropologists*. New York: Harper & Row. Discussions of fieldwork experiences by ethnographers.

Chagnon, N. A. (1974). *Studying the Yqnomamö*. New York: Holt, Rinehart and Winston. An in-depth report of the fieldwork experience by one of the top contemporary American ethnographers.

Ginsburg, F. (1989). *Contested lives: The abortion debate in an American community*. Berkeley, CA: University of California Press. An ethnography of abortion activists in Fargo, North Dakota.

Harris, M. (1968). *The rise of anthropological theory: A history of theories of culture*. New York: Thomas Y. Crowell. An authoritative and comprehensive history of cultural anthropology by a leading figure in contemporary anthropology. Must reading for students who have decided to major in anthropology.

Lawless, R., Sutlive, V. H., Jr., & Zamora, M. D. (1983). *Fieldwork: The human experience*. New York: Gordon and Breach, Science Publishers. Aspects of fieldwork explored by 12 anthropologists.

Lowie, R. H. (1937). *The history of ethnological theory*. New York: Holt, Rinehart and Winston. The traditional view of the history of cultural anthropology in a readable style.

Moffatt, M. (1989). *Coming of age in New Jersey: College and American culture*. New Brunswick, NJ: Rutgers University Press. An ethnography of the students who attended Rutgers University in the 1980s.

Pelto, P. J., & Pelto, G. H. (1978). *Anthropological research: The structure of inquiry* (2nd ed.). New York: Cambridge University Press. A discussion of techniques of anthropological research. Especially important for the anthropology major.

Spindler, G. D. (Ed.). (1970). *Being an anthropologist: Fieldwork in eleven cultures*. New York: Holt, Rinehart and Winston. Thirteen anthropologists discuss how they and their families adjusted to life in a variety of cultures. Especially useful to the anthropology major.

Spradley, J. F. (1980). *Participant observation*. New York: Holt, Rinehart, and Winston. A step-by-step overview of how ethnographic research is conducted.

FIGURE 2.1 Intercultural Influences
Despite the now quite common influence of
one culture upon another around the world,
most social groups still make an effort to retain some of their traditions. These American
Indians watch some traditional dances of the
Mohawk, Hopi, Apache, and 22 other tribes at
the Thunderbird American Midsummer Pow-
wow at the Queens County Farm Museum in
Floral Park, New York.

Unlike other animals, we humans have a persistent tendency to try to make sense of our existence and to share those understandings with others of our group. We also feel a necessity to alter the environment so that we can survive more comfortably and predictably. These ideas and survival strategies are institutionalized and perpetuated as culture, the subject of this chapter. After analyzing the systematic patterning of beliefs, feelings, and ways of surviving, we must note that these patterns differ from one society to the next, commonly resulting in misunderstandings and mistrust between human groups.

Culture

CHAPTER OBJECTIVES

After reading this chapter, you should be able to:

Explain the nature of culture.

Define ideology.

Discuss ideological communication.

Explain the relationship between beliefs and feelings.

Enumerate the differences between real and ideal culture.

Discuss the ways cultures may influence each other.

Outline the various emotional reactions people have to other societies and cultures.

Analyze the values of cultural relativism.

Explain the difference between emic and etic interpretations of culture.

Explain the difference between humanistic and scientific approaches to culture.

Characterize the basic approaches to explaining culture.

Cockfights. Dogfights. Boxing matches. Blanket giveaways. Pig slaughters. Sacred cows. Basket moon. Harvest moon. Man in the moon. Grass skirts. Banana leaf skirts. Silk skirts. One man's diamond is another man's coal. Humans identify their world and their place in it according to what they learn from their environment, their ancestors, their families, and their schools. And despite the explosion of communications technology, one woman's diamond is still, for the most part, another woman's coal.

Culture

All human groups develop complex systems of ideas, feelings, and survival strategies and pass them from one generation to the next. Anthropologists call the system of ideas, feelings, and survival strategies of a particular human group the **culture** of that group. Great diversity exists among anthropologists' definitions of culture. Alfred Kroeber and Clyde Kluckhohn (1952) surveyed 158 definitions of culture by other social and behavioral scientists. They found that the concept of culture always centered on the idea that there is a system to the beliefs and feelings that unify a human group and give it an identity as a society. Those who share this way of life may be aware of some parts of the system, whereas their awareness of other parts of the system may be implicit in their customary behavior without their being conscious of it.

Behaviors that are guided by culture are learned, rather than acquired through biological inheritance. Thus, instincts, innate reflexes, and other biologically predetermined responses are not a part of culture. Some parts of a culture are taught explicitly; others are learned by direct and indirect observation of the behaviors of others.

In learning the customs of their culture, people are taught that they share some "common understandings" with one another and that others expect them to follow those customs. Our North American culture gives particular meanings to behaviors such as shaking hands and applauding a performance. Our common understanding about the use of these behaviors lets us know when we should perform them. A definite awkwardness or embarrassment is felt by everyone involved if someone does either behavior at the wrong time or place. In this sense, much of a way of life is like a set of rules about how one ought to live. These parts of culture, like the rules of a game, give structure and continuity to the social life of each human group. The predictability that culture lends to a people's behavior gives them security since it allows them to anticipate the behavior of others, including those they are meeting for the first time. Therefore, the parts of culture that are explicitly taught are often thought of as the *proper* ways of behaving.

Participating in a shared and traditional system of customs also gives life a sense of meaningfulness. Thus, attending the World Series, the Super Bowl, prom night, rock concerts, and sunbathing on a crowded beach are activities that help the people of the United States conceive of themselves as a society with its own distinctive culture. Customs, objects, and events acquire meanings for the participants and may be thought of as symbols of the culture. Clothing, for example, is chosen not only to protect our bodies from the elements, but also to convey symbolic messages that may be interpreted by others according to the shared meanings of our culture.

Earlier anthropologists tended to use the concept of culture as if there were no diversity within the "common understandings" of a people. This was an easy oversimplification in an era in which most fieldwork was done in small-scale societies of 50 to 300, where it is easier to stress the commonalities of thought and values that are expressed. But anthropologists who did their research in societies with larger populations could hardly ignore the fact that their descriptions of a society's culture had to take into account the fact that a culture is not fixed and

culture a learned system of beliefs, feelings, and rules for living around which a group of people organize their lives; a way of life of a particular society

symbol an object or event that represents another object or event only because of the agreement among people that it will

FIGURE 2.2   Cultural Diversity
Feminist and postmodernist anthropologists have emphasized the diversity that exists within a culture and the interactional influences that researchers and the people they're studying can have on one another.

changeless with a universally accepted pattern of customs, ideas, and feelings even within the same society. Awareness of this diversity within a culture led to the concept of subcultures, variations within a culture that are shared by different groups within a society.

The recognition that each culture may be made up of subcultures, much as languages may have various dialects, emphasizes the fact that cultures are not static. Some recent anthropologists, especially feminist anthropologists, postmodernist anthropologists, and others have emphasized the processes by which diverse viewpoints, values, and ways of behaving are negotiated by members of a society. In these approaches, the concept of culture is viewed as consisting of a polyphony of voices rather than as a solo melody.

Many anthropologists in the first half of this century emphasized the integrated quality of the values and beliefs that were characteristic of each culture, and described each as a self-consistent sys-

tem of meanings. Today, we are more likely to acknowledge that even when there are important regularities within the symbolic patterns that make up a culture, those patterns are neither rigidly present nor necessarily consistently adhered to in the behavior of people. Thus, despite some degree of internal consistency, any culture may include contradictory beliefs and competing values.

. . . .

Ideology

Within any culture, there are regularities in how people act, think, feel, and communicate, but people are not conscious of all of them. They may

subculture variations of a culture shared by different groups within a society never explicitly state an underlying rule to which they seem to be conforming, yet the regularity in their behavior may be obvious to an outsider. Suppose we observed that members of a certain society always took care to lock the doors and windows of their homes and automobiles when leaving them, that they never left their bicycles unlocked when they entered a store, that they never left valuable items unattended or in open view even at home. We might conclude that these people believe that some of their members are likely to steal, even if they never say so directly. If we were further reporting on our observations, we would include in our description of their culture the implicit rule of maintaining the security of one's own possessions, even if these people do not explicitly refer to such a rule when speaking among themselves.

A culture, then, includes all the rules and regulations that govern a way of life, both conscious, formally stated beliefs and feelings—called an **ideology** —and unconscious, informal, or implicit beliefs and feelings.

Ideological Communication

As people communicate about themselves and their environment, they build a consensus about the nature of humankind and the universe in which it exists. Much communication among members of the same society is done to reinforce this consensus. Such **ideological communication** is an important way in which people identify themselves as members of a group, declare their allegiance to it, and define their rules for behaving in the group. It frequently takes the form of highly ritualized acts, such as a pledge of allegiance to a flag or some other symbol of the group, recitation of articles of faith, or singing of hymns that glorify the doctrines of the group. Ritual affirmations of one's social solidarity with others may, of course, be less formally structured, as in so-called "small talk," the content of which is nonetheless highly predictable. For instance, North Americans recognize that the greeting "How are you?" is not a request for information but simply the opening gambit of a ritual communication of friendship and willingness to interact. The more or less predictable response—"I'm fine, thank you"—is not a measure of one's actual state of health, but an affirmation of the same willingness to interact and a declaration that one shares the same cultural code of symbolic behavior. Such ritual reaffirmations of mutuality may be

interspersed throughout an entire conversation in stereotyped communications, as in a discussion of the weather. Although ideological communication conveys little information, it reinforces the existing conventions about reality and our place in it. So it is through the efforts we devote to ideological communication that we construct and reconstruct the meaningfulness of the world. As Clifford Geertz, an anthropologist who stresses the need to understand the symbols around which people organize their lives, poetically described it, we humans are "suspended in webs of significance" (1973, p. 5) that we ourselves spin.

Beliefs

An ideology has two main interacting components: a subsystem of beliefs and a subsystem of feelings. **Beliefs** are the means by which people make sense of their experiences; they are the ideas that they hold to be true, factual, or real. By contrast, **feelings** are a people's inner reactions, emotions, or desires concerning experiences. Although beliefs are judgments about facts, they are not always the result of rational analysis of experience. Emotions, attitudes, and values—aspects of the feeling system—may determine what people believe. Within limits set by the necessities of survival, persons may choose to believe what is pleasing to believe, what they want to believe, and what they think they ought to believe. On the other hand, once people are convinced of the truth of a new set of beliefs, they may change some of their previous feelings to make it easier to maintain those new beliefs. Recognizing these interactions, we will nonetheless examine beliefs and feelings separately, beginning with beliefs.

Conformity to a belief system. People in each society have their own distinctive patterns of thought about the nature of reality. These beliefs

---

ideology the consciously shared beliefs and feelings that members of a society consider characteristic of themselves

ideological communication communication that reaffirms people's allegiance to their groups and creates a sense of community by asserting its ideology

beliefs ideas people hold about what is factual or real

feelings subjective reactions to experiences as pleasant or unpleasant, good or bad. Feelings include emotions, attitudes, and values reflect what those who share a culture regard as true: "God exists"; "The sky is blue"; "Geese fly south for the winter"; "Spilling salt causes bad luck."

The knowledge of a society is taught to its children either implicitly or explicitly, as *the proper way* of understanding the world. Thus, as children, we learn that the other members of our society share a system of thought and a pattern of thinking about the nature of the world. For example, North Americans grow up under a formal educational system in which mechanical models sometimes are used to demonstrate the plausibility of the idea that the moon is a sphere, the apparent shape of which depends on the relative positions of the sun, the moon, and the earth. By contrast, the Shoshoni Indians of the western United States Great Basin area traditionally founded their explanations of the phases of the moon on the idea that the moon was shaped like a bowl or basket rather than a sphere. The phase of the moon was thought to be simply a matter of which side of the moon was facing the observer: A crescent moon was a side view, and a full moon was the outside convex bottom.

We obtain full acceptance as members of our group by conforming to the ways in which others think. Cultural ideas are imposed on us through rewards for conformity and punishments for deviance. Individuals who violate their culture's rules for proper thinking are likely to experience punishment ranging from a mild reproof or laughter to severe sanctions such as banishment, imprisonment, or death. In the contemporary United States, normal people do not "hear voices." Those who do may find themselves placed in mental hospitals "for their own good" or "for the safety of others." In other times and places, those who heard voices have been honored as spiritual teachers. North American school children are rewarded for believing that the moon is a sphere and punished for believing otherwise. During my fieldwork on an isolated Shoshoni reservation in the late 1960s, I discovered that my attempt to describe the moon as a sphere evoked either argument or skeptical looks, and my desire for acceptance soon silenced my expression of deviant views.

Widespread acceptance of a system of beliefs gives people a sense of identity as a group. A people's knowledge that they share a set of beliefs gives them a feeling of security and a sense of belonging. When people become conscious of their shared beliefs, especially if they assign a name to their system of beliefs, this part of their ideology may begin to function as an active, driving force in their lives.

Such conscious systems are particularly common in complex societies. They are most dramatically illustrated by the named religions and political factions that can command the loyalties of great masses of people.

Types of belief systems. Each society tends to develop two different kinds of belief systems: scientific and nonscientific. The former occurs because a certain degree of practical insight into the nature of the world and its workings is necessary for any society to survive. Beliefs about such matters as how to obtain food and shelter or how to set broken bones must be based on pragmatic rather than emotional judgments if they are to be useful. The beliefs that are based on the desire to solve the practical day-to-day problems of living may be referred to as the scientific beliefs of a society.

The second basic type of belief found in every culture grows out of a people's feelings about their existence. These nonscientific beliefs are often formally organized within the framework of religious and artistic philosophies that portray the universe and express (sometimes in the guise of descriptions of reality) deeply valued feelings about the world in which people find themselves. Strong emotional commitments may also exist in political or recreational institutions. These, too, are often guided by beliefs that express the members' deeply held feelings.

Feelings

Feelings and beliefs tend to strengthen each other. Our feelings may be the motivation for believing things for which no objective support exists. Beliefs may, in turn, validate our feelings. When we believe that our feelings are the same ones that other people experience in the same situations, we are more confident that they are valid. Recognizing that our feelings are shared by others also supports our sense of belonging to a definable group.

Three major kinds of feelings find their idealized expression within an ideology: emotions, attitudes, and values.

---

scientific beliefs beliefs that are based on the desire to solve the practical day-to-day problems of living
nonscientific beliefs beliefs that grow out of people's feelings

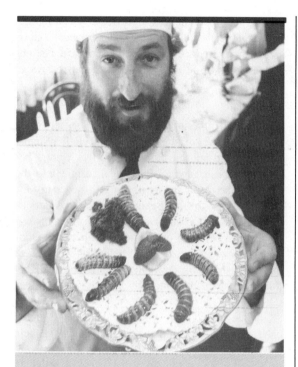

**FIGURE 2.3   Cultural Influences
on Food**

The physiological reaction to food choice is based on an emotional experience learned as a part of one's culture. Thus, it is culture that determines that cow meat is acceptable food in the United States, that dog meat is acceptable food in the Orient, and that the grubs pictured here are acceptable food in Australia.

Emotions.   An **emotion** is a reaction to experience as pleasant or unpleasant, to varying degrees. As we mature, we learn many subtle variations on the two basic emotional themes of pleasantness and unpleasantness, such as delight, elation, affection, love, mirth, happiness, surprise, or exultation, and contempt, anger, distress, terror, or grief. Which emotions we learn to experience in various circumstances depends on the culture in which we are raised.

Each society trains its members to associate certain emotions with certain situations and to experience each emotion at differing intensities in different settings. For instance, Marston Bates, a zoologist, illustrated how some foods, which are considered delicacies to people in some cultures, can be disgusting to people of other cultures:

> Even though repugnance to a particular food has a cultural rather than a physiological basis, the aver-

sion can still cause a strong physiological reaction. The big lizards called iguanas are a highly prized food item in almost all parts of tropical America where they are found; the meat has a delicate, chicken-like flavor. But for some reason lizards are not eaten in Europe or the United States, perhaps because we do not have any suitable species: our lizards are for the most part too small to be of much use as food. But whatever the reason, we clearly regard lizards as unsuitable for eating. We once served iguana at a dinner party in South America. The subject had been thoroughly discussed, and we thought everyone understood what he was eating. Certainly all the guests ate with gusto. But as the conversation continued during the meal, a French lady who was present suddenly realized that the iguana she had been eating *était un lézard* and became violently nauseated, although a few minutes before she had considered the meat delicious.

> I remember once, in the llanos of Colombia, sharing a dish of toasted ants at a remote farmhouse. This was my first voluntary experience with ants—I have eaten lots of them involuntarily, raw, when they just taste sour—and I found the toasted ants have a pleasant, nutty flavor. My host and I fell into conversation about the general question of what people eat or do not eat and I remarked that in my country people ate the legs of frogs. The very thought of this filled my ant-eating friends with horror; it was as though I had mentioned some repulsive sex habit. (1967, pp. 21–22)

Cultures also differ in how strongly or mildly feelings should be expressed and in which emotional experiences are most commonly emphasized. According to the French anthropologist Claude Lévi-Strauss, "The thresholds of excitement, the limits of resistance are different in each culture. The 'impossible' effort, the 'unbearable' pain, the 'unbounded' pleasure are less individual functions than criteria sanctioned by collective approval, and disapproval" (1950 p. xii). Cultural differences in emotional intensity were illustrated by Ruth Benedict, author of one of the most widely read anthropological books ever printed, *Patterns of Culture* (1934). For instance, she cited the late nineteenth-century Kwakiutl culture of Vancouver Island as one in which the expression of strong emotion—especially feelings of extreme self-worth bordering on megalomania—was encouraged.

---

emotion a pleasant or unpleasant subjective reaction to an experience, characterized by varying degrees of muscle tension and changes in respiration and heart rate

She described their religious ceremonies in the following words:

> In their religious ceremonies the final thing they strove for was ecstasy. The chief dancer, at least at the high point of his performance, should lose normal control of himself and be rapt into another state of existence. He should froth at the mouth, tremble violently and abnormally, do deeds which would be terrible in a normal state. Some dancers were tethered by four ropes held by attendants, so that they might not do irreparable damage in their frenzy. (pp. 175–176)

Benedict contrasted the Kwakiutl with the Zuñi of the early 1900s. The Zuñi, who lived in the southwestern part of the United States, had a culture that encouraged moderation in the expression of all feelings. Zuñi rituals were monotonous in contrast with those of the Kwakiutl. They consisted of long, memorized recitations that had to be performed with word-perfect precision. The Zuñi had no individualized prayers; personal prayers were also memorized and recited word for word. As an illustration of how Zuñi culture required moderation in emotion, Benedict cited the case of a woman whose husband had been involved in a long extramarital affair. She and her family ignored the situation, but after she was exhorted by a white trader to take some action, the wife did so by not washing her husband's clothes. In her words, "Then he knew that I knew that everybody knew, and he stopped going with the girl" (p. 108). No argument, no yelling and crying. Just a mild indication that her wifely status was in question. For a Zuñi husband, this message was strong enough.

For the Dobuans, a people of Melanesia whose culture was studied in the early 1900s by Reo Fortune (1932), the dominant feelings were animosity and a mistrust that bordered on paranoia. These feelings permeated their customs. For instance, even husband and wife would not share food for fear that they might poison each other. All deaths were regarded as murders. In deaths that other people might ascribe to natural causes, black magic was the assumed weapon, with the surviving spouse the most likely suspect as the murderer. Dobuans assumed that their spouses were unfaithful whenever the opportunity existed, so they bribed their children to spy on each other. Benedict (1934) described Dobuan paranoia:

> The formula that corresponds to our thank-you upon receiving a gift is, "If you now poison me, how should I repay you?" (p. 166)

The Kwakiutl, Zuñi, and Dobuans Today

In 1992, the Kwakiutl work at commercial fishing, in logging, in a variety of service industries, and as employees of government. The original Kwakiutl population count is not known, but it was heavily reduced by disease before 1835, when it had dropped to 8,575. After continued declines that reduced the Kwakiutl to fewer than 1,000 people in 1929, the population has risen to about 4,000, a figure that is still significantly below its original levels.

The famous Kwakiutl potlatches (discussed on p. 33), with their lavish, competitive giveaways, were outlawed by the Canadian government in the 1920s. Arrests and confiscation of ceremonial paraphernalia led to an end to Kwakiutl ceremonial life until its revival in recent times. These efforts by both the Canadian government and church leaders to undermine traditional Kwakiutl culture and economic life played an important role in incorporating the Kwakiutl, who had survived the earlier, socially disruptive population declines, into Canadian society. The acculturation of the Kwakiutl included the replacement of their traditional religious beliefs by those of Christianity under the influence of strong missionary efforts. Today, most Kwakiutl are Anglican Christians. Some belong to evangelical Protestant churches. Nevertheless, original Kwakiutl religious symbolism survives among contemporary Kwakiutl artists whose artwork is sold in many stores on Vancouver Island and elsewhere.

Today, the Zuñi, who actually call themselves the Ashiwi, live on the Zuñi Reservation in west-central New Mexico. They number over 8,000 people, many of whom occupy a pueblo, or village, that they call Itiwana, "the Middle Place." The pueblo, also called Zuñi, has lost most of its traditional outward form. It now has paved streets, sidewalks, and streetlights. Other Zuñi live outside the pueblo on various parts of the 655-square-mile reservation, which was established in 1877 and represents only about 3 percent of the land the Zuñi originally considered their territory. An unknown number live outside the reservation.

The Zuñi's traditional horticultural economy of maize, beans, squash, and other crops was supplemented by various European domesticates introduced by the Spanish, who also introduced the Zuñi to cattle and sheep.

Since their introduction, these animals have become an important source of income to the Zuñi. Many households supplement their incomes through the production of jewelry and other home crafts that are sold both on and off the reservation. Employment off the reservation has also attracted many of the Zuñi to neighboring cities.

Zuñi women continue to have high status in their society, but Americanization has shifted Zuñi inheritance patterns, which once followed maternal lines, to the common U.S. pattern of inheritance through either male or female lines. Homes and farmlands are now privately owned rather than by clans. However, the maternal clans continue to exist and play prominent roles, for instance in ceremonial activities.

Since 1970, the Zuñi have been governed by an elected Tribal Council, headed by a governor and advised by an Indian agent appointed by the U.S. Secretary of the Interior. Traditional Zuñi religious life is still very much alive, and its religious leaders, who were the traditional heads of the Zuñi theocratic government, still have great influence in the politics of the reservation. Zuñi Catholics, though a minority, make up another important political faction within the pueblo.

Dobu Island currently has a population of about 900 inhabitants, far fewer than the estimated 2,000 Dobuans of 1891. Their population decline began as early as 1884, when "blackbirders" or slavers took a number of Dobuans into slavery and killed others. By the early 1890s, copra traders had entered Dobu along with Christian missionaries, and European diseases had begun to kill many of the Dobuans.

Now, Dobuans are all followers of Christianity, although traditional practices of magic, witchcraft, and sorcery have not been lost. Dobuans still speak of yams as persons, who will leave their owners' gardens if they are not treated with the proper magical rituals and respect. They work as clerks, medical doctors, lawyers, and Christian ministers, run their own businesses, or are employed by the local Dobuan government or by the provincial government of Papua-New Guinea as public servants. Several Dobuans have stood for national parliament.

(see reference maps, pp. 32, 34, 36)

Attitudes. Our attitudes are statements of our preferences, our likes and dislikes. More generalized than our specific emotional reactions to situations, our attitudes are our general tendencies to seek or avoid types of experiences. Skydiving, for instance, may create conflicting emotions: fear and exhilaration. A general attitude toward high adventure—liking or disliking it—determines which way the scales will tip. Attitudes need not correspond to the pleasantness or unpleasantness of the emotions associated with an activity. Probably in every society individuals are taught to dislike or feel neutral about some situations that lead to pleasant emotions and to like other situations in which they experience unpleasant emotions. Athletes may learn to crave the exercise that their goals demand, even though they dread the pain that attends each workout; soldiers may be taught to seek the very situations of battle that arouse their deepest fears; and the pious may steadfastly insist that they now dislike the bodily pleasures in which they once indulged.

Values. The third part of the feeling subsystem of an ideology is values: feelings about what should or should not be considered good and bad.

Values include the moral imperatives in dealing with other humans: "Thou shalt not steal!" "Love thy neighbor as thyself!" They also include feelings about right and wrong that do not directly affect interpersonal relations but may affect one's relationship with nature or the supernatural. For instance, Jewish dietary laws, Mormon rules against drinking alcohol or coffee, and the Blue Laws outlawing liquor sales on Sundays fall into this category.

The values of different cultures can be amazingly diverse, to the extent that what is held to be supremely desirable by the members of one society may be despised by another. That which one people hold dear as a religious or moral obligation of the most sacred kind may be viewed as sacrilegious or immoral by another. When the Samoans were first met by Europeans, women did not cover their breasts

attitude a subjective reaction to an experience expressed in positive or negative terms

value a subjective reaction to experiences expressed in terms of good or bad, moral or immoral; the ideals that people long for but do not necessarily pursue. Values are often opposites of drives in public. Indeed, to do so would have been considered highly improper and immodest by the traditional Samoans. In contemporary European culture, an opposing set of evaluations prevails concerning public exposure of the breast; yet, the European woman is quite unconcerned about exposing the back of her neck in public, an act that would have resulted in strong disapproval in traditional Chinese society.

When they were first described by anthropologists, the Toda of India had no word for adultery in their language. They considered it highly immoral for a man to begrudge another man his wife's sexual favors. On the other hand, they had strong rules against being seen eating in public. Among the Dobuan islanders in the first part of the twentieth century, being happy was not a valued emotional state. In contrast, the American Founding Fathers declared the pursuit of happiness to be one of the three fundamental values of society. In the United States today, competitiveness seems fundamental to much of day-to-day life, while the early nineteenth-century Hopi of the southwestern United States carefully taught their children that it was wrong to shame others by outdoing them in competitive situations. The child who finished a race first was expected to take care not to do so the next time around.

Ideal vs. real culture. It is important to note that culture is a system of *ideals* for behavior, but that people do not always follow the guidelines of their culture. Sometimes, for example, individuals violate cultural ideals about proper communication behavior, as North Americans do when they behave rudely to show their anger. Sometimes people violate their culture's ideals for personal gain at the expense of others, but most of the time their failure to conform to cultural ideals is not consciously intended. For instance, very few United States drivers make technically legal stops at stop signs, but most do not think of themselves as breaking the law as they make their near-stops and proceed. People also tend to say that dinner is eaten about six o'clock in the evening, unaware that the most common dinner time, or the cultural ideal, in the United States is closer to seven o'clock.

In studying culture, one must recognize that there is a difference between what is called **ideal culture and real culture**. The former refers to the ways in which people describe their way of life; the latter refers to the actual behaviors they engage in as a people. The disparity between the Zuñis' ideal and real behaviors provides a good example of this

distinction. If people's actual behavior did not vary from the ideals embodied in their culture, if all members of a society conformed exactly to one another's expectations, then cultures could never change.

---

ideal culture the ways people perceive their own customs and behaviors, often more a reflection of their feelings and ideals about what it should be rather than an accurate assessment of what it is

real culture culture portrayed in terms of the actually observable behaviors of a people

---

Ideal and Real Culture Among the Traditional Zuñi

Descriptions of the ideals embodied in a culture's rules for living are not always the same as descriptions of the people's actual behavior. Ruth Benedict's portrayal of the Zuñi of the United States Southwest, and presumably their portrayal of themselves to her, was one of a culture in which emotional excess and individualism were held to a minimum. The Zuñi avoided selecting as leaders people they believed sought the office. They carefully taught their children to avoid competition and conflict. Their ritual life idealized emotional restraint. Benedict claimed of the Zuñi that "Drunkenness is repulsive to them" (1934, p. 82), that violence was so rare that only a single case of homicide could be remembered in village history, and that "Suicide is too violent an act, even in its most casual forms, for most Puéblos to contemplate. They have no idea what it could be" (p. 117).

These cultural ideals, however, do not give an accurate picture of the realities of Zuñi life. Varieties of behavior occurred among the Zuñi as they occur in all other societies. According to Ruth Bunzel (1952), the Zuñi were often split into factions that disagreed about whether anthropologists should be accepted in the village. There was rivalry along religious lines as well. Li An-Che claimed that "A strife of immense magnitude took place between the Catholic and Protestant elements" (1937, p. 69). Zuñi initiation of children into adult life, like initiations at other pueblos, involved severe whippings (Roth, 1963). Village ceremonies were often marred by drunkenness (Barnouw, 1963). Violence was not nonexistent

Zuñi

The Zuñi occupy a small territory in the United States Southwest. They describe their ideal culture as one that encourages cooperation, friendliness, and peacefulness. In reality, however, their culture has been influenced by the alcohol and violence that surrounds them.

in Zuñi life, and although their culture might foster a reticence to discuss it, even suicides did occur (Hoebel, 1949).

Culture provides guidelines that mold people's behavior, but there are conditions under which deviance from the guidelines may be more common than conformity to them. One of these conditions is the effect of contact with other societies and their customs. Was Zuñi life more emotionally constrained before its political and economic subordination within the United States nation-state? This may well have been the case, since contact with more powerful societies can be especially disruptive to the internal harmony of a way of life. Certainly the alcoholism must be understood, at least in part, as a result of disruptive outside influence on Zuñi life. Probably we will never know how much pre-contact Zuñi behavior deviated from Benedict's portrayal, but we should remember that ideal culture and behavior are never identical.

Culture as Flux

The various terms and categories used to define culture may give the false impression that a culture can be completely and accurately described by a simple listing of its characteristics as if they were homogeneous, fixed, and unchanging. Unfortunately, it's just not that simple. For culture is a dynamic system, and <u>every culture is in a constant state of flux</u>. Indeed, although we may speak glibly about a consensus or about "typical" beliefs or feelings, such descriptions are as inaccurate a portrayal of a culture as a snapshot is of a waterfall or a whirlwind. For in the real world of human life, individuals differ from one another in many ways. So it is more accurate to think of culture as a system of symbols, customs, ideas, and feelings that is constantly being negotiated and redefined by members of a society as they interact and communicate with one another. It is this dynamism also that allows—indeed, impels—each culture to change with the passing of time.

As useful as a description of a culture may be, no culture is, or ever was, fixed in stone. At best, any description of a culture merely evokes images of a way of life as it was perceived by the one who has described it at some point in time. Even that image will have lost some of its dynamism, some of its variety, in the telling. Just as an automobile repair manual fails to capture the dynamism of an idling engine, a description of a way of life may suggest homogeneity and stasis where diversity and change really exist.

Anthropologists believe, like historians, that we can learn a great deal from the past. Knowing the characteristics of a culture fifty years ago can provide as valid a source of understanding about the human condition as those characteristics found in cultures today. Thus, the illustrations of various anthropological concepts discussed in this text will be drawn from a wide range of different cultures and from different periods in history. Some societies, past or present, may seem exotic because they differ from what we are accustomed to, currently, in our own society. But even they can help us understand what it means to be human and to learn to respect the diversity that still exists among the various societies of the world today.

Cultural Differences

Cultures differ greatly in their ideologies and practical responses to their varying environments. What happens when very different peoples come in contact with each other? In some cases, contact between groups changes one of them, usually the one with less political and economic power. Even when both maintain their integrity, members of differing groups may find it difficult to understand and appreciate each other's ways. In this section, we will look at intercultural influences, intercultural prejudices, ethnocentrism (the attitude that one's own culture is the only proper way of life), and cultural relativity (understanding and appreciating other cultures in relationship to one's own).

FIGURE 2.4   Potlatch
The Kwakiutl of the Pacific Northwest coast of the United States stage periodic potlatches as a means of enhancing the status of the host chief. The more he gives away, the greater his status. The hamat'sa dance, shown at this W. T. Cranmer potlatch, Alert Bay, B.C., in 1983, is an inherited right of the dancer and is considered one of the most important events at a potlatch.

Intercultural Influences

Contact between two cultures can bring tremendous change to both societies, or especially to one of them when they differ greatly in economic and political power. Sometimes the extinction of native populations is carried out by systematic acts of war, and sometimes it is a less extreme process of assimilation. Nevertheless, the transition from the original way of life to a socially dependent status is never without turmoil. Cultural subordination of one way of life by another, even when it occurs peaceably, can be a shattering experience.

Time and time again, anthropologists have described the tragic effects on the world's agricultural peoples of contact with the industrialized nations of the world. Diseases introduced from the more densely populated societies sometimes decimate the local population. The awareness that other peoples are more powerful and have more luxuries than they do is a blow to the cultural pride that unifies a society. Often, contact with another society is followed by a rise in the rate of internal conflict, alcoholism, and suicide. For the Kwakiutl, contact with Europeans may have led to exaggerated—and destructive—attempts to display wealth and power.

The Kwakiutl Potlatch: A Reaction to European Contact?

The Kwakiutl, the indigenous population of Vancouver Island and the British Columbia coast, were described by Franz Boas (Codere, 1967), who visited them first in 1886, and by Ruth Benedict, one of Boas's students. When Boas observed them, the Kwakiutl, who now call themselves Kwakwaka'wakw, were a people whose culture encouraged emotional extremes, channeled into fierce competition for status between individuals and groups. According to Benedict, "The object of all Kwakiutl enterprises was to show oneself superior to one's rivals. This will to superiority they exhibited in the most uninhibited fashion. It found expression in uncensored self-glorification and ridicule of all comers" (1934, p. 190).

The expansiveness in the Kwakiutl personality was seen at the great give-away *potlatches*, ceremonial feasts at which gifts were lavishly given to guests as part of a public announcement of an important event in the life of the host, such as his claim to having

Kwakiutl

Indigenous to Vancouver Island and the coast of British Columbia, the Kwakiutl have been acculturated both by Canadian customs and Christianity. Their original religious symbolism, however, survives among Kwakiutl artists.

achieved a higher social status. The most dramatic of the potlatches were those at which the Kwakiutl sought to shame their rivals with demonstrations of the unmatchable superiority of their wealth by lavishly giving away food, blankets, and other valuable property. To show the host's disdain for surplus wealth, gallons of fish oil were poured by "slaves" through the smoke-holes of their longhouses onto the fires to make them blaze higher. Blankets were ripped to shreds, and holes were chopped in the bottoms of boats. Sometimes entire villages were burned by a chief and the slaves put to death in the extremes of conspicuous consumption. At potlatch feasts, a chief's retainers sang hymns of praise such as the following one reported by Benedict (p. 190):

I am the great chief who makes people ashamed.
I am the great chief who makes people ashamed.
Our chief brings shame to the faces.
Our chief brings jealousy to the faces.
Our chief makes people cover their faces by
what he is continually doing in this world,
Giving again and again oil feasts to all the tribes.

What are we to make of such extremes? To Benedict, the Kwakiutl behavior simply illustrated the diversity of culture, but later anthropologists placed this behavior in better perspective. The Kwakiutl described by Boas and Benedict had long been in contact with the Europeans. Intensive trade for almost forty years before Boas's first visit had greatly affected their culture, and many of the extremes he observed were exaggerations of their earlier customs—exaggerations that arose as attempts to adjust to the effects of European contact. Helen Codere (1950) points to the core of the problem: Smallpox and other diseases introduced by contact with Europeans decimated the Kwakiutl population, which had fallen to less than a tenth of its original size by the time Boas first met them. Marvin Harris (1974) believes that this population shrinkage and the loss of many working-age people to employment away from the Kwakiutl villages greatly intensified the competition for labor; at the same time, European wages brought unexpected wealth into the Kwakiutl economy, which was also being flooded with blankets and other trade goods in return for native furs. The native practice, common in many small-scale societies, of holding communal feasts at which food is redistributed by the chiefs to the poor, was modified into celebrations of material wealth by which the chiefs tried unsuccessfully to attract people back to the villages.

Intercultural Prejudices

When cultures meet, people may have little understanding or appreciation of groups whose ideologies and adaptive strategies differ from their own. People grow up under the nurturance of their group and learn to fulfill their needs by living according to their group's culture. As people learn their way of life, they generally identify themselves as members of the group that has cared for their early needs and has taught them the rules for living. Simultaneously, they generally develop positive feelings toward this reference group and its behaviors. Often, the training of children in the ways of the group is communicated expressly by contrasting them with the supposed behaviors of outsiders: "Other parents may let their children come to the table like that, but in our family we wash our hands before eating!" Such expressions teach children the patterns of behavior expected of group members, but they also communicate a disapproval of outsiders.

In complex societies with large populations and many competing groups, prejudices between groups within the society may become a common element of daily experience, varying from good-natured rivalry to direct antipathies. In the United States, we may think of our own state as "God's own country," our politics as the only rational way of doing things, or our religion as the only road to salvation. Even such group symbols as hair length and style of clothing have served as grounds for suspension from school, unified those in public demonstrations, and caused interpersonal violence.

The attitude that one's own culture is the naturally superior one, the standard by which all other cultures should be judged, and that cultures different from one's own are inferior is such a common way of reacting to others' customs that it is given a special name by anthropologists. Ethnocentrism, centered in one's ethnos, the Greek word for a people or a nation, is found in every culture. People allow their judgments about human nature and about the relative merits of different ways of life to be guided by ideas and values that are centered narrowly on the way of life of their own society.

Ethnocentrism serves a society by creating greater feelings of group unity. When individuals speak ethnocentrically, they affirm their loyalty to the ideals of their society and elicit in other persons of the group shared feelings of superiority about their social body. This enhances their sense of identity as members of the same society and as bearers of a common culture. A shared sense of group superiority—especially during its overt communication between group members—can help them overlook internal differences and prevent conflicts that could otherwise decrease the ability of the group to undertake effectively coordinated action.

For most of human history, societies have been smaller than the nations of today, and most people have interacted only with members of their own society. Under such circumstances, the role of ethnocentrism in helping a society to survive by motivating its members to support one another in their common goals has probably outweighed its negative aspects. However, ethnocentrism definitely has a darker side. It is a direct barrier to understanding among peoples of diverse customs and values. It enhances enmity between societies and can be a motivation for conflict among peoples whose lives are guided by different cultures.

Ethnocentrism stands in fundamental conflict with the goals of anthropology: the recognition of the common humanity of all human beings and the understanding of the causes of cultural differences. To many students, much of the appeal of the field of anthropology has been its intriguing discussions of the unending variety of customs grown out of what, from the viewpoint of the uninitiated, may seem like strange and exotic, unexpected, and even startlingly different values. A people's values generally make perfectly good sense when seen and explained in the context of their cultural system as a whole. Yet, it is often difficult to make sense out of another cultural tradition because its symbolic meanings may be so different from one's own. While negative reactions to the customs of another society may, therefore, be expected, they should be guarded against by the student of anthropology.

Culture Shock

Anthropologists who engage in fieldwork in a culture that differs from the one in which they grew up often experience a period of disorientation or even depression known as culture shock before they become acclimatized to their new environment. Even tourists who travel for only a short time outside their own nations may experience culture shock, and unless they are prepared for its impact, they may simply transform their own distress into a motive for prejudice against their host society.

---

ethnocentrism the attitude that one's own culture is the only good one and that other cultures are more inferior to one's own the more they differ from it

culture shock the loneliness and depression that are often experienced when one is in a foreign cultural setting

Doing Fieldwork Among the Yąnomamö

Napoleon Chagnon, an anthropologist who conducted his research among the Yąnomamö Indians of Venezuela, has described his initial reaction to that people when he first met them in 1966. The Yąnomamö were an extremely

Yąnomamö

Xingu National Park is an area that borders Venezuela and Brazil, where the Yąnomamö and several other tribes hope to preserve a way of life that won't be affected by pollution caused by miners, disease caused by intruders, and cultural assimilation.

fierce and warlike people who valued and cultivated extremes of aggressive behavior unequaled in many parts of the world. Their use of hallucinogenic drugs in their religious rituals added to their distinctive cultural configuration. Although it is certainly not typical of an anthropologist's first day in the field, Dr. Chagnon's uncommonly frank revelation of his feelings on first exposure to a non-Western culture gives some sense of the psychological effects of radical changes in one's symbolic environment and the ease with which ethnocentric prejudices might arise and preclude even the first steps towards the objective study of other ways of life.

We arrived at the village, Bisaasi-teri, about 2:00 p.m. and docked the boat along the muddy bank at the terminus of the path used by the Indians to fetch their drinking water. It was hot and muggy, and my clothing was soaked with perspiration. It clung uncomfortably to my body, as it did thereafter for the remainder of the work. The small, biting gnats were out in astronomical numbers, for it was the beginning of the dry season. My face and hands were swollen from the venom of their numerous stings. In just a few moments I was to meet my first Yąnomamö, my first primitive man. What would it be like? . . .

My heart began to pound as we approached the village and heard the buzz of activity within the circular compound. Mr. Barker commented that he was anxious to see if any changes had taken place while he was away and wondered how many of them had died during his absence. I felt into my back pocket to make sure that my notebook was still there and felt personally more secure when I touched it. Otherwise, I would not have known what to do with my hands.

The entrance to the village was covered over with brush and dry palm leaves. We pushed them aside to expose the low opening to the village. The excitement of meeting my first Indians was almost unbearable as I duck-waddled through the low passage into the village clearing.

I looked up and gasped when I saw a dozen burly, naked, filthy, hideous men staring at us down the shafts of their drawn arrows! Immense wads of green tobacco were stuck between their lower teeth and lips making them look even more hideous, and strands of dark-green slime dripped or hung from their noses. We arrived at the village while the men were blowing a hallucinogenic drug up their noses. One of the side effects of the drug is a runny nose. The mucus is always saturated with the green powder and the Indians usually let it run freely from their nostrils. My next discovery was that there were a dozen or so vicious, underfed dogs snapping at my legs, circling me as if I were going to be their next meal. I just stood there holding my notebook, helpless and pathetic. Then the stench of the decaying vegetation and filth struck me and I almost got sick. I was horrified. What sort of a welcome was this for the person who came here to live with you and learn your way of life, to become friends with you? They put their weapons down when they recognized Barker and returned to their chanting, keeping a nervous eye on the village entrances.

We had arrived just after a serious fight. Seven women had been abducted the day before by a neighboring group, and the local men and their guests had just that morning recovered five of them in a brutal club fight that nearly ended in a shooting war. The abductors, angry because they lost five of the seven captives, vowed to raid the Bisaasi-teri. When we arrived and entered the village unexpectedly, the Indians feared that we were the raiders. On several occasions during the next two hours the men in the village jumped to their feet, armed themselves, and waited nervously for the noise outside the village to be identified. My enthusiasm for collecting ethnographic curiosities diminished in proportion to the number of times such an alarm was raised. In fact, I was relieved when Mr. Barker suggested that we sleep across the river for the evening. It would be safer over there.

As we walked down the path to the boat, I pondered the wisdom of having decided to spend a year and a half with this tribe before I had even seen what they were like. I am not ashamed to admit, either, that had there been a diplomatic way out, I would have ended my fieldwork then and there. I did not look forward to the next day when I would be left alone with the Indians; I did not speak a word of their language, and they are decidedly different from what I had imagined them to be. The whole situation was depressing, and I wondered why I ever decided to switch from civil engineering to anthropology in the first place. I had not eaten all day, I was soaking wet from perspiration, the gnats were biting me, and I was covered with red pigment, the result of a dozen or so complete examinations I had been given by as many burly Indians. These examinations capped an otherwise grim day. The Indians would blow their noses into their hands, flick as much of

the mucus off that would separate in a snap of the wrist, wipe the residue into their hair, and then carefully examine my face, arms, legs, hair, and the contents of my pockets. I asked Mr. Barker how to say "Your hands are dirty"; my comments were met by the Indians in the following way: They would "clean" their hands by spitting a quantity of slimy tobacco juice into them, rub them together, and then proceed with the examination.

Mr. Barker and I crossed the river and slung our hammocks. When he pulled his hammock out of a rubber bag, a heavy, disagreeable odor of mildewed cotton came with it. "Even the missionaries are filthy," I thought to myself. Within two weeks, everything I owned smelled the same way, and I lived with that odor for the remainder of the fieldwork. My own habits of personal cleanliness reached such levels that I didn't even mind being examined by the Indians, as I was not much cleaner than they were after I had adjusted to the circumstances.[1]

Today, the Yąnomamö no longer live the kind of life Napoleon Chagnon witnessed. Miners, loggers, and many others have encroached on their land, destroying the forest and spreading disease (see Chapter 14, p. 338).

1. From *Yąnomamö: The Fierce People* 3rd ed. (pp. 9–10, 10–12) by Napoleon A. Chagnon, 1983, New York: Holt, Rinehart and Winston, Inc. Copyright 1983 by CBS College Publishing. Reprinted by permission.

Today, the world is much more homogeneous and interdependent than it was in the early days of anthropological fieldwork. It has been largely nationalized by states and governments that assert their sovereignty over all peoples within their boundaries. Thus, there are fewer truly simple, isolated societies that anthropologists once preferred to study. Nearly all of these independent, small-scale societies are now extinct or have changed tremendously to cope with the influences of the industrializing world around them.

Missionaries and traders have brought about many of these changes even in relatively remote areas. The search for new sources of income and for resources valued by the industries of the cities have brought many kinds of immigrants into the frontier territories that were once occupied by societies that had no direct experience with external governments.

Most ethnographic fieldwork, therefore, is carried out today among the rural and urban descendents of peoples like the Dobuans studied by Reo Fortune, the Zuñi of Ruth Benedict's time, or the Kwakiutl described by Franz Boas. Culture shock is still an experience that ethnographers must cope with, but in some ways it has become a more subtle phenomenon. The economic and political interconnectedness of most of the world's people has made us all more alike in many superficial ways. The Yąnomamö wear tee shirts and running shorts. The Navajo wear jeans and drive automobiles. Zuñi pottery and jewelry can be found in department stores. In many cases, the peoples whose lives and customs ethnographers study today speak the national language of the countries in which they live. It has become easier for anthropologists to approach their fieldwork with naivete, expecting fewer differences and misunderstandings than they actually discover because superficial similarities can mask important deeper cultural differences that may not have been lost. Culture shock can sneak up on fieldworkers in unexpected ways and catch them by surprise.

An excellent example of misunderstanding and culture shock in contemporary fieldwork is the experience of Paul Rabinow. He went to Morocco in 1968 to study the rural religion and politics of a Moslem community. He gained entry into the Islamic life of Morocco by hiring an Arabic teacher, a man he identifies as Ibrahim (1977, p. 22). Ibrahim was a merchant, hardworking and moderately prosperous. He spoke French fluently, as did Rabinow, and had worked as a middleman between other Moroccans and the French colonial administrators. Fully committed to his Islamic culture, Ibrahim considered the French and other outsiders valuable economic resources, not friends. After a frustrating month of studying Arabic with little progress, Rabinow decided to visit Marrakech for several days with two American friends who had come to visit. Ibrahim asked if he could go along to visit his cousins and to act as a guide to the Americans. Then a complication arose:

> On the second morning, Ibrahim announced not only that he had no relatives in Marrakech but that he had unfortunately forgotten to bring along enough money to pay for his room. This was one of my first direct experiences of Otherness. Ibrahim was simply testing the limits of the situation. Within Moroccan culture this is a standardized and normal thing to do, as I was to find out. He was pushing to see if I would pay for his trip. When, after much confusion and uncertainty on my part, I refused (mainly because I lacked the money at the time) Ibrahim backed down and produced his wallet. He was maximizing his resources, exploiting the situation economically, proceeding as he had in the past. We had been working together for over a month and he now felt that he could push our contractual limits more in his favor. The point is not that Ibrahim was greedy or calculating. . . .

What was upsetting was the realization that I had been engaged with this man every day for well over a month, we had spent many hours talking French together in addition to the Arabic lessons, and I had proceeded to "typify" him. But my typifications were fundamentally incorrect and ethnocentric. Basically I had been conceiving of him as a friend because of the seeming personal relationship we had established. But Ibrahim, a lot less confusedly, had basically conceptualized me as a resource. He was not unjustly situating me with the other Europeans with whom he had dealings. I had gone into anthropology in search of Otherness. Meeting it on an experiential level was a shock which caused me to begin fundamental reconceptualization about social and cultural categories. Presumably this was the sort of thing I had come to Morocco to find, yet every time these breaks occurred they were upsetting. (Rabinow, 1977, pp. 28-29)

Cultural Relativism

The alternative to ethnocentrism encouraged in anthropology students is **cultural relativism, the idea that the significance of an act is best understood by the standards of the actor's own cultural milieu.** When we try to understand the meanings of other customs in a culturally relativistic way, we search for the meanings that those customs have in the actor's own culture instead of in our own. Relativism is not an idea unique to anthropology. In every culture, people interpret the meaning of a thing depending on the context in which it occurs. In the United States, for instance, most people would not be alarmed by a masked stranger who appeared at their door at night if it were October 31st and that person were holding a Halloween trick-or-treat bag. The symbolic basis of all cultural systems invariably leads to variations in the meanings of things from situation to situation. People who share the same culture learn to take the context of one another's acts into account when they are trying to communicate. Of course, intergroup prejudices sometimes interfere with people's efforts

---

cultural relativism principle that cultural traits are best understood in the context of the cultural system of which they are a part; the attempt to avoid the narrow bias of judging the value of a custom or entire culture on the basis of the values of one's own culture; the view that meanings of behaviors are best understood when interpreted in terms of the culture of the actors

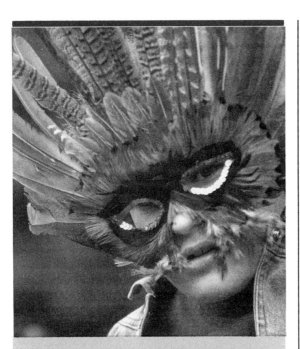

FIGURE 2.5 Cultural Relativism
A culture's symbolic systems of communication, customs, and habits are unique and can best be understood by others in relationship to the situation in which they occur. People from other cultures visiting the United States would probably find it difficult to understand the significance of masked figures going from door to door late in October with a request for treats. Only when they viewed it as a cultural custom of celebrating All Hallow's Eve would they be able to place it in the proper perspective.

to understand one another, even within the same culture.

Anthropologists have come to value cultural relativism as a first step toward understanding other cultures. A relativistic view of other cultures holds all ways of life to be equally valid sources of information about human nature. Relativism, as a research tool, reminds us that even customs that seem inhumane or irrational by our own values must be described and analyzed as objectively as possible if we wish to develop scientifically valid understandings of human behavior. Relativism reminds us that all cultures have customs that seem bizarre or repugnant to outsiders. For instance, both electroconvulsive treatment for depression and the use of machines for measuring heartbeat, blood pressure, and respiration to determine whether a person is lying might well seem inhumane or irrational to people whose cultures do not include these practices.

Cultural relativism is easy to reconcile with the anthropological goal of understanding the human condition in a way that is valid for all humankind. In support of this goal, anthropologists historically have elected to conduct most of their research among less complex non-Western societies. Such societies have cultures that differ greatly from those with which Western anthropologists would have been most familiar. In devoting their efforts to the study of diverse ways of life, anthropologists have hoped to maximize their data about the limits of diversity within and among human cultures and to preserve for future generations knowledge about ways of life that were rapidly becoming extinct as complex industrialized societies expanded their influence throughout the world.

As a result of working among peoples with ways of life very different from their own, anthropological fieldworkers commonly find that the preconceived notions they bring with them do not help them understand what is going on in the culture they are studying. Cut off from their own people and their accustomed way of life, it is they who must learn to understand the meanings of the symbols of the people they are living with, rather than the other way around. The anthropological imperative is "Respect or fail!" Learning to understand the language and the customs as they are understood by the insiders of the group is often a clear and basic necessity for survival in a foreign culture. It can also be prerequisite to the work of gathering accurate information about a culture or of developing insights about how it might have come to be the way it is and why it functions the way it does. The necessity of interpreting the meaning or value of an act within the culture in which it is found, that is, from a cultural relativistic viewpoint, has been long recognized within anthropology as a fundamental first step in learning to understand a culture as a coherent system of meaningful symbols.

Cultural relativism is a reminder to judge the meanings of any part of a culture by the role it plays with respect to the entire culture.

Elizabeth Hahn illustrates the difficulties that culture shock and ethnocentrism can impose on puzzling out the meanings of cultural behavior. Her fieldwork took her to the island of Tongatapu in Tonga. After a frustrating period of isolation in which she was unable to establish a relationship with anyone, Hahn decided to visit a government official:

> He greeted me in standard office dress—a white long-sleeved shirt and necktie, a dark brown *tupenu* (a Tongan skirt), and a *ta'ovala* (a Tongan

mat) secured around his waist by a braided cord of coconut fiber. The walls of his office were lined from floor to ceiling with papers, and reports of the Central Planning Department. I wondered how to make my vague and observation-oriented project seem like something worthwhile. Here were Tongans themselves engaged in the process of writing about and planning change in their culture and I, a foreigner, was going to have something interesting to say about their social processes, someone who half the time couldn't seem to find her way around the tiny capital of Nuku'alofa? But he was very cordial and soon put me at ease. He seemed to be willing to talk to me for longer than the polite five-minute chat. Here at last was someone to whom I could explain what I was trying to accomplish in Tonga. Indeed, he listened and he asked thoughtful questions. I fought the urge to lean over and hug him. I was having my first "anthropological" discussion—one professional to another. And then it happened—in the middle of one of my explanations, he started raising and wiggling his eyebrows at me. I was taken completely off guard and stammered to a stop. He stopped. No sooner had I resumed talking than he started giving me the eye again. We started and stopped several times. I began to get very angry. There he was, looking so innocent with a quizzical expression on his face, as if *I* were the one doing something odd. How dare he come on to me? How dare he feign interest in my project just so he could flirt with me? I decided to ignore him, but I also made a mental check of other people in the building who might be within earshot of the open office door. I did not want to be alone with him. He acted as if everything was just fine and made no reference to his pass at me. Both of us ignored the glitch even though we undoubtedly thought the other was a bit strange. As our conversation ended, I thanked him for his time, shook his hand, and departed with my head spinning. (1990, p. 73)

End of incident? No. Some time later, while Hahn was talking to a Tongan woman, the woman began to wiggle her eyebrows in the same way, and Hahn began to reinterpret the possible meanings of the gesture:

Was she making a joke or some sort of nonverbal comment? Was she teasing me? Her laughing eyes seemed to draw me in. Had a joke been made that I was too naive to catch? I acted as though I understood, smiled, and after a few minutes, in mindless imitation, I moved my eyebrows up and down as smoothly as possible. It worked well and we had

this very lively and civil conversation. I wondered how she could keep it up for so long—it felt sort of like wiggling your ears. Back in my room, I repeated the gesture in the mirror—yep, that's it all right. I felt silly. I felt like an impostor, I was certainly becoming entangled but I had no idea what I was doing. But it was also exhilarating—like flying blindly through the clouds and emerging unscathed. (p. 74)

As she interacted with other people, Hahn eventually decided the gesture did not seem to fit her idea that it might express a joke that she had missed and eventually came to realize that it was "a simple, elegant expression of affirmation—a gesture that draws the participants to each other's eyes, giving an intensity and intimacy to a friendly exchange," a conclusion that she later confirmed by a direct inquiry to a friend (p. 74).

It is not always an easy task to describe customs in terms that people who follow a different way of life can comprehend. This is especially true when we try to explain things that we ourselves have always taken for granted. Our experiences are so common in our own culture that we rarely need to talk about them or explain them—even to ourselves. This can pose problems when people of quite different cultural backgrounds attempt to communicate. Barre Toelken described an experience during his fieldwork among the Navajo that illustrates such a difficulty:

"I had lived with the Navajo family of old Little Wagon for several months before he politely asked me early one morning what kind of noise I was making on my wrist every day. I tried to explain to him that my watch was a means of measuring time, but of course since the Navajos have no word for time as we know it, and because I was still learning the Navajo language, I had no way to explain it to him. My first impulse was to believe that I could simply describe what time was like and why it was important to know it and where I was in relationship to it, but I was brought up abruptly by my realizing that nothing I could say to the old man made any sense to him at all. I pointed out to him how the hands went around a dial that was marked off in equal sections. I then told him that by watching where the hands were I could determine what kinds of things I should be doing. 'Like what?' he asked in Navajo. 'Well, eating. It tells me when to eat.' 'Don't your people eat when they are hungry? We eat when we are hungry if there is food.' 'Well, yes, we eat when we are hungry; that is, no, we eat three times a day, and we are not supposed to eat between times.' 'Why not?' 'Well, it's not healthy.' 'Why is that?' And so on. I tried another tack. I said that this machine told me when I needed to do those things that were necessary in order to make my living (there is no Navajo word for *work* that sets it apart from other useful and normal things a person might do). The old man asked, 'Aren't those things that you do anyway? What is it that this tells you to do that you wouldn't do anyway?' 'Well, it tells me when to go out and look for rocks [there was no Navajo word for uranium at the time], and then my company will know how much to pay me.' 'Do you mean if you lost that machine, you would stop looking for rocks?' 'Well, no, I guess I wouldn't.' Finally, in exasperation, I said that the watch actually was my reference point to some larger ongoing process outdoors, and this seemed to satisfy the old man. But later, when we were outside that afternoon, he stopped me and held me by the elbow and asked, 'Where is it? That which is happening out here?' Beginning to be even more frustrated, I said, 'Well, the sun comes up and goes down, doesn't it?' 'Yes,' he agreed expectantly. 'Well, I guess I can't explain it to you. It's nothing, after all. It's all inside the watch. All it does is just go around and make noise.' 'I thought so,' he said." (1979, pp. 277–278)

Anthropological Approaches to Explaining Culture

In the previous chapter, we noted that anthropology has characteristics of both the humanities and the sciences. The humanistic aspect of anthropology stems from our desire not only to know other cultures, but to understand them as well. Anthropologists with a humanistic orientation approach the study of cultures as translators who try to make the symbols of one culture understandable in terms of those of another. They attempt to portray and interpret the customs, values, worldview, or art of one culture so that they can be appreciated by readers accustomed to a different language and way of viewing life. The scientific approach searches for more mechanistic, cause-and-effect explanations of how particular cultures have developed their distinctive characteristics,

as well as what causes some cultural facts to be universal. The focus is on the role culture plays in human adaptation to the environment and survival.

This dual quality of anthropology, the humanistic desire to understand and appreciate other cultures as systems of meanings and the scientific attempt to explain cultures as mechanistic systems, manifests itself in various ways. For instance, ethnographers distinguish between emic and etic descriptions of cultures, a distinction first made by Kenneth Pike (1954, p. 8). An **emic analysis** of a culture, though written for outsiders, is one that portrays a culture and its meaningfulness as the insider understands it. As Charles Frake has pointed out, such a model may incorrectly predict the actual behavior of the people whose culture it describes, and still be valid—so long as the native member of that culture is equally surprised by the error (1964, p. 112). Ward Goodenough has suggested that the adequacy of an emic model of culture can be tested in two ways: It must not do violence to the native's own feel for the structure of what is described, and it must provide an outsider with whatever knowledge is necessary to talk about the culture or behave in the same way as a native (1956, p. 261). An **etic analysis** creates a model of a culture by using cross-culturally valid categories, that is, categories that anthropologists have found to be generally useful for describing all cultures. Such models invariably describe each culture in ways that seem alien to its own participants, but that facilitate comparisons between cultures and the discovery of universal principles in the structure and functioning of cultures. According to Harris, "Etic statements are verified when independent observers using similar operations agree that a given event has occurred," and etic models are valid insofar as they accurately predict the behavior of the native participants of a culture (1968, p. 575).

Anthropology as Humanistic Interpretation

Anthropology is a humanistic discipline in its goal of broadening our understanding of culture as a meaningful system. As Geertz put it, "The aim of anthropology is the enlargement of the universe of

---

emic analysis description of a culture as it would have meaning for an insider
etic analysis description of a culture in categories based on universal principles

human discourse" (1973, p. 14). In seeking to understand what other ways of life mean to those who live them, anthropologists have much in common with translators of foreign languages. The Talmudic scholar Jacob Neusner described the anthropologist's role as that of a translator who makes the insider's point of view meaningful to the outsider: "Anthropologists study the character of humanity in all its richness and diversity. What impresses me in their work is their ability to undertake the work of interpretation of what is thrice alien—strange people, speaking a strange language, about things we-know-not-what—and to translate into knowledge accessible to us the character and the conscience of an alien world-view" (1979, p. 17). The humanistic problem of how to understand other cultures has also been likened to translation by Jean-Paul Dumont: "Interpretation . . . can refer to three rather different matters: an oral recitation, a reasonable explanation, and a translation from another language. . . . In all three cases, something foreign, strange, separated in time, space or experience is made familiar, present, comprehensible: something requiring representation, explanation or translation is somehow 'brought to understanding'—is interpreted" (1978, p. 14).

The skill at interpreting cultures and demonstrating the significance of seemingly strange customs is probably the central feature of anthropology in the public mind—a skill analogous to that of a translator. On a deeper level, the interpretation of cultures can include the study of patterns within the symbolism, language, and ideology of a culture using analytical styles analogous to those of literary interpretation or art criticism. Anthropologists who specialize in the study of religion, art, folklore, and the influence of culture on human personality are often drawn toward the humanistic or interpretive end of the anthropological spectrum. The major traditions within cultural anthropology that stress the interpretation of culture include structuralism, interpretive anthropology, hermeneutic anthropology, and ethnoscience.

Structuralism. One of the most well known interpretive approaches is structuralism, a branch of anthropological analysis founded by the French anthropologist Claude Lévi-Strauss. The viewpoint of **structuralism** is that beneath all of the superficial diversity of cultures is an underlying unity that reflects the tendency of the human mind first to think in terms of contrasts and opposites such as black versus white, good versus bad, or female versus male

FIGURE 2.6   Claude Lévi-Strauss
The founder of structuralism, Lévi-Strauss, proposed that the human mind perceives and classifies the world around it in a dualistic fashion. In books such as *The Savage Mind* he suggested that this cognitive process is a universal constant and manifests itself in humans in every society in the world.

and, second, to resolve the dilemmas that some opposing ideas create. According to Lévi-Strauss, it is the nature of the human mind to construct these logical contrasting categories, because of the inherent dual structure of the human mind. Lévi-Strauss finds evidence of symbolic dualities in all aspects of human culture, from mythology to kinship systems. For instance, he has asserted the existence of a regularity of kinship relationships wherein two of the kinship pairs uncle/nephew, brother/sister, father/son and husband/wife will always be emotionally positive, while the other two will be emotionally negative. The combinations vary from society to society, but the duality of two positive and two negative relations among these four kinship pairs is always

structuralism Lévi-Strauss's concept of underlying unity of all cultures to think in dualities maintained. In other words, if the father/son relationship is warm and close, then the husband/wife relationship in the same society will be typically cold and distant.

For a common example of how opposites permeate human thought, consider the duality inherent in the symbols and themes of the Cinderella story. A poor young girl works in the house of a rich old woman. The girl is beautiful but unkempt; her stepsisters are ugly but well cared for. Her stepmother is mean and evil; her fairy godmother is the epitome of goodness. In the story, symbols of nature are transformed into symbols of culture. Several tiny mice become the large and beautiful domestic horses that pull the coach which is a transformed pumpkin. Two rats are transformed into elegantly dressed coachmen. Cinderella herself is transformed into a princess on the night of the ball, temporarily surpassing the superior status of her stepsisters. Her temporary triumph is made permanent after the original midnight time limit through the intervention of a paradoxical object, a slipper made of fragile glass—the only magical item that is strong enough to transcend time and survive past the midnight barrier. Another duality brings the story to a close when the slipper fits only the tiny foot of Cinderella, not the huge feet of her stepsisters.

Like Lévi-Strauss, Mary Douglas has tried to clarify the order that underlies human cultural symbolism. She argues that concepts of something unclean—either hygienically or spiritually—are intimately related to a culture's concepts of orderliness. When people categorize the world of their experience, they impose a symbolic order on it. No system of human thought perfectly mirrors the complex world in which people find themselves, so there are always things that do not seem to fit a particular classification system. Because they do not fit the normal system, they are thought of as opposite or as abnormal, disgusting, unclean, or spiritually polluting.

Douglas (1966) has illustrated her approach to symbolism by examining the food taboos of Leviticus. The ancient Hebrews classified the world of living creatures into the three basic types that corresponded to the three realms described in Genesis, the heavens, the earth, and the waters. Birds flew in the heavens and had feathers. Animals had feet and walked, hopped, or jumped. Fish swam in the waters and had scales and fins. Living things that did not fit properly into any of the categories that were believed to have been pronounced good by God in the Genesis story were spiritually unclean. Thus, locusts that flew instead of hopping, or sea animals such as the octopus or shellfish that had no scales or fins were "abominations." By mixing the characteristics thought to be appropriate to each category, these creatures seemed to cross the boundaries of creation and to oppose the order that Hebrew culture attributed to God's act of things in their proper forms. Therefore they were classified as taboo foods.

Interpretive anthropology. The anthropological approach that most parallels that of translation is known as **interpretive anthropology**, which attempts to explain how each element of a culture relates meaningfully to its original context. Interpretive anthropologists do not search for general principles that govern human cultures. Instead, they view each culture as a distinct configuration of meanings that must be understood on its own terms. An important proponent of this approach is Clifford Geertz, who has characterized the approach of interpretive anthropology as an attempt to understand "the native's point of view . . . to figure out what the devil they think they are up to" (1973, p. 58). His analysis of the cockfight as a cultural obsession in Bali is an example of interpretive anthropology at its best. Cockfights are an important occasion for gambling by the owners of the cocks, their relatives, and other spectators. The matches become statements about the honor, dignity, prestige, and respect of the owners themselves because of the high stakes in the wagers between the owners of the cocks (1972).

Geertz shows how, in its imagery, the fighting cock is both a powerful symbol of Balinese concepts of masculinity and, simultaneously, of animals, the antithesis of all that is human. Metaphors about cocks abound in Balinese discourse about men, and the word for cock, *sabung*, is used with meanings such as "hero," "warrior," "man of parts," "lady killer," or "tough guy." The owner of each cock identifies with his animal and the masculinity it represents, but this identification also implies that there is a darker, nonhuman side to men's nature—a fact that is also evident in the ritual symbolism of the cockfight. A match between two cocks, each armed with a razor-sharp steel spur, is "a wing-beating, head-thrusting, leg-kicking explosion of animal fury" (p. 8) that may last as long as five minutes and ends with the death of

interpretive anthropology explains how each element of a culture relates meaningfully to its original context one animal. Each fight is prefaced with rituals and chants, because the deaths that end each fight are regarded as sacrifices to demons that control the natural evils of Balinese life such as illness, crop failure, or volcanic eruptions. Thus, cockfights bring their participants into the realm of "The Powers of Darkness" with which humans must contend for success in life.

Hermeneutic anthropology. One of the most recent developments in anthropological thought is the emphasis on making explicit the process by which the anthropologist comes to understand an alien culture. This approach, called **hermeneutic anthropology** (from the Greek word for "interpretation"), examines the interaction of the fieldworker and the native informant, the interplay between observer and the observed. Achieving insight into how members of another culture think and feel about what the fieldworker does and says modifies the anthropologist's own understanding of the culture.

Hermeneutic anthropology is an outgrowth of the ideas of the French philosopher Paul Ricoeur, who emphasized the role of understanding others as a means for self-understanding. Ricoeur's ideas have been incorporated into the anthropological process by Paul Rabinow, who has referred to the mutual attempts of the fieldworker and informant to understand one another as "the dialectic of fieldwork" (1977 p. 39). The anthropologist is very much in the forefront of the narrative, never an "objective" analyst behind the scenes. The biases of the fieldworker are themselves usually brought to light as he or she grapples with the experience in the attempt to make sense of it. Readers are similarly exposed to the emotional and intellectual dilemmas experienced by the native informants as they too are sometimes forced to come to grips with new ways of perceiving themselves and their own culture because of their work with anthropologists.

Postmodernist anthropology. As the cultures of the world have come to influence each other, anthropologists have recently refocused their sights from the isolated "exotic" cultures of traditional anthropology, which hardly exist anymore, to *contemporary* non-Western Third World traditions. Anthropologists have begun to borrow many of the tools and much of the jargon that other disciplines such as philosophy, gender and minority studies, and literature have developed to communicate about cultural diversity from an increasingly internationalized perspective.

This not yet unified but increasingly popular approach to ethnographic writing has come to be known most widely as **postmodernist anthropology**, a viewpoint that insists that each culture must be portrayed as "an open-ended, creative dialogue of subcultures, of insiders and outsiders, of diverse factions" (Clifford, 1983, p. 137). By rejecting the notion that culture is a homogeneous system, postmodernism also denies the authority of any one mode of anthropological interpretation. Instead, postmodernists explore the diversity of meanings in human life and emphasize the exploration of cultural meanings as a cooperative quest that involves the anthropologist and native members of a society in a dialogue that evokes a variety of meanings and viewpoints and that recognizes that "there are always alternative interpretations" (Marcus, 1986, p. 191).

A number of European philosophers and intellectuals such as Jacques Lacan (1967), Michel Foucault (1977), Jacques Derrida (1976), and Pierre Bourdieu (1977) have had a major influence on postmodernist anthropology. They have expanded the anthropological concept of cultural relativism into a logical attack on the privileged status of western scientific thought. This redefinition of western science as merely one ideology among a multitude of equally valid western and non-Western ways of conceiving of the human condition implied that anthropology itself had no claim on any superior validity as a purely "objective" commentary on other societies.

The most influential postmodernist anthropologists today are James Clifford, George Marcus, and Michael Fischer. These and other postmodernists have reinvigorated ethnographic writing in two ways. Their major thrust has been the critique of traditional ethnographies that proposed they could achieve true scientific objectivity. Instead of claiming to give the reader a complete description or total explanation of a culture, postmodernist ethnographies portray a culture "as open-ended, ambiguous, and in flux" (Marcus and Cushman, 1982, p. 45).

---

hermeneutic anthropology examines the interaction between fieldworker and native informant

postmodernist anthropology a humanistic approach to anthropology that rejects the notion of ethnography as a detached, scientifically objective process and proposes the view that culture is composed of a constantly changing, open-ended, and ambiguous system of meanings that are negotiated and renegotiated by members of society as they interact with one another

Postmodernists also emphasize the participant half of participant-observation. Their work is characterized by the portrayal of the dialectic interplay of themselves and the people with whom they participate. For instance, the word "I" is much more common in postmodernist ethnographies than it ever was before. In part, this stems from the fact that postmodernist ethnographers are now living among literate peoples, who not only have developed their own traditions but who also can communicate about them. Postmodernist ethnographers must therefore collaborate with the people they live with rather than simply "describe" them.

The typical postmodernist ethnography is based on a **dialogic model**, a form of writing that, like a dialogue, brings the interaction of the anthropologist and the native members of a society into the forefront of the document. Postmodernists also emphasize the importance of diversity within, as well as among, cultures. For instance, Clifford (1983) uses the concept of **polyphony** to describe the diversity of voices and viewpoints within every human group that embodies the dynamic nature of every culture.

Ethnoscience. The methodological rigor of linguistic analysis as a tool for analyzing the symbolic patterns within ways of life is one approach to cultural interpretation, called ethnoscience. In **ethnoscience**, or **cognitive anthropology**, as it is sometimes called, the goal is to systematically describe a culture as it is perceived by its own people by uncovering the linguistic categories that informants use to discuss their culture. This is accomplished by skillfully formulating and asking appropriate questions that encourage informants to define the boundaries of each concept and its relationship to other concepts. In so doing, the ethnoscientist makes explicit the hierarchy of categories into which a society subdivides the world of its experience. In effect, ethnoscientists construct a dictionary of the native language and culture.

The systematic approach of ethnoscience results in extremely detailed and accurate descriptions of how people classify those things they talk about. One result of the rigor of this approach is that it tends to focus on rather specific and limited parts of an entire culture. Although, in theory, it might be possible to eventually outline the knowledge of an entire culture by such methods, ethnoscientists have been unable to describe more than a fraction of any single culture. For instance, Goodenough (1956) has suggested methods for systematically describing the

kinship system of a society. Conklin (1956) has examined the color categories of the Hanunóo of the Philippines. Frake (1961) has outlined how the Subanun of Mindanao diagnose the various types of diseases recognized in their culture, and (1964) has described the native categories of Subanun "religious behavior."

Anthropology as Scientific Explanation

While much of culture exists in the symbolic realm of ideas—the beliefs and feelings of an ideology—there is also a practical aspect of culture that makes it possible for a people to survive physically. Each culture, as a system of common understandings, serves as a form of social bonding and also as the action plan by which a human society interacts with its natural environment to fulfill its survival needs. Anthropologists whose interests lean toward the scientific goal of explaining and predicting human behavior emphasize the practical influences of social life, human biological and psychological needs, technology, and the environment in their descriptions of how the symbolic or ideological elements of culture arise. Their concern is for isolating the factors that give rise to the diverse cultures of the world and for developing models that show how these factors determine the form that a culture develops. The major traditions among these anthropologists include British structural-functionalism, American functionalism, Marxist anthropology, neofunctionalism, cultural ecology, sociobiology, and cultural materialism.

British structural-functionalism. British anthropologists have long emphasized the importance of **social structure**, the network of social relations among members of a society, in creating the basic customs of each culture. Their approach, called **social anthropology**, was founded by Alfred Reginald

---

dialogic model an approach to ethnographic narrative that engages the anthropologist and natives of a culture in a give-and-take exploration of cultural meanings
polyphony diversity of viewpoints within a single culture
ethnoscience (cognitive anthropology) systematically describes a culture by analyzing the linguistic categories used by informants to discuss their society
social structure the part of social organization made up of groups and their relationships with each other
social anthropology Radcliffe-Brown's idea that social interactions are important in determining customs of a culture

Radcliffe-Brown (1949). In the small-scale societies that were most often studied by anthropologists, kinship ties were determinants of how people were expected to treat one another. Because of the concern of Radcliffe-Brown and his colleagues for how a society's customs functioned to maintain its social structure, the analytical method of social anthropology has been given the name **structural-functionalism**.

American functionalism. American anthropology was more influenced by the views of Bronislaw Malinowski (1939), who asserted that cultural customs function primarily to support seven basic human **biological and psychological needs** that must be dealt with by every society: nutrition, reproduction, bodily comforts, safety, relaxation, movement, and growth. Malinowski's list is probably an incomplete summary of human survival needs, but it can be used to illustrate that cultural variation is constrained by the practical necessities of human survival. A culture can only survive if it responds effectively to its members' survival needs.

As cultural creatures, we human beings do not meet our biological and psychological needs directly. Instead, we fulfill our needs as the culture of our social group prescribes. In no society do people eat every edible plant or animal available to them. People eat only those things their culture defines as "foods," and they exclude from their diets other items of equal nutritional value. For instance, in parts of the Orient dog meat is considered a delicacy, while the Western custom of eating cheese and yogurt is considered disgusting.

Similarly, in no society is the need for reproduction fulfilled by allowing all people to mate indiscriminately. In every society, sexual acts are controlled by cultural rules, such as those determining appropriate partners, when and where sexual acts may occur, and how those acts should actually be performed. For instance, among the Navajo of the southwestern United States, sexual intercourse is forbidden between any persons of known familial relationship, no matter how distant. The pre-Conquest Quechua Indians of the Andes, on the other hand, expected their emperor, the Inca, to mate with his full sister.

The need for bodily comforts is dealt with in each society by prescribing certain forms of housing and clothing as acceptable. These cultural patterns also provide each individual in the society with a plan for making minor improvements in his or her immediate environment.

Each culture also includes plans of action for ensuring safety in dangerous situations. These include guidelines for conduct when walking down a dark street alone, when lost, or when attacked by an animal or by a human enemy. Human skills in coping with danger vary from culture to culture.

The needs for relaxation, movement, and growth are met in culturally patterned rhythms of work and sleep, exercise and rest, recreation and practical activities. Each society trains its young in the way of life of its people and teaches its members the skills they must acquire at each stage of their lives.

Neoevolutionism: Interest in the evolution of cultures was reintroduced by Leslie White, who suggested that cultural evolution could be measured by the per capita energy that a technology allows people to draw from their environment (1943, pp. 168–169). White's approach to cultural evolution has been called **neoevolutionism**, a view that describes culture as "a mechanism for harnessing energy and of putting it to work" (White, 1943, p. 390). The technological system determines the way in which a society must be organized, even those parts of culture that are not directly related to survival. Thus, White's view of cultural evolution incorporates the concept of culture into a system in which technology, the human relationships that make up a society, and nontechnological beliefs and feelings each influence one another, but in which technology is the guiding force of cultural change.

In White's concept of neoevolutionism, **technology** is described as the tools to extract resources from the environment and the knowledge and skills for making and using them. Every culture must include valid ways of coping with the natural environment, the source of energies and raw materials used to fulfill group and individual needs. In every society,

---

structural-functionalism determining customs of a culture by the analytical method of social anthropology

biological and psychological needs the needs for nutrition, reproduction, bodily comforts, safety, relaxation, movement, and growth

neoevolutionism a view of cultural evolution that describes culture as "a mechanism for harnessing energy and of putting it to work" and that measures cultural evolution by the amount of energy that a society's technology harnesses per capita per year

technology tools and techniques through which human beings harness the energy available in their environment

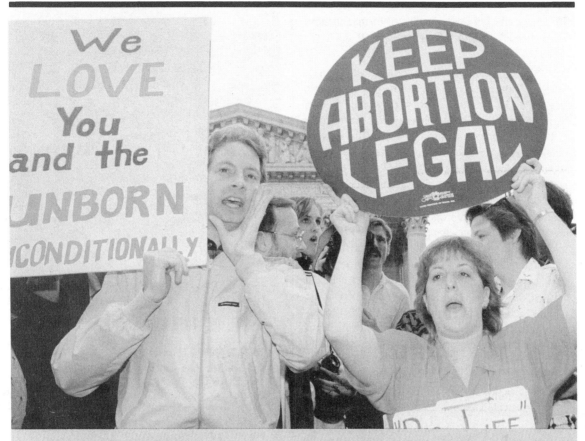

FIGURE 2.7   Neofunctionalism
Neofunctionalism states that conflict and its resolution are necessary to maintain stability in a society. The two-party system in U.S. politics usually results in spirited campaigning and ideological conflicts, but usually has elected candidates with fairly moderate views. The Supreme Court decision on abortion in 1992 provided some intense conflicts between candidates in subsequent elections.

objects are manufactured and used in undertakings ranging from recreation and worship to basic survival. Technology provides ways in which the forces of nature, whether physical or biological, are captured, transformed, and utilized to preserve human life and provide comfort. In fact, a human society might well be described as the organized patterns of human interaction through which the energies of nature are channeled from person to person.

According to White (1971), those activities that are most related to survival—the provision of food, shelter, and defense—have the biggest influence on how the rest of a cultural system is organized. Regardless of how simple or how complex a society is, its tool kit and technological know-how include the means for solving these problems and most directly influence the nature of a culture.

Multilinear evolutionism: Julian Steward, another twentieth-century cultural evolutionist, placed greater emphasis than did White on tracing the courses of evolutionary change followed by individual cultures, an approach he referred to as **multilinear evolution**. Like White, he emphasized the ways in which people adapted to their environments as determining the characteristics of the rest of their culture. Unlike White, he had little interest in broad generalizations about cultural evolution. Instead, he advocated a more empirical approach to tracing the specific course of evolution followed by each culture,

---

multilinear evolution an approach to cultural evolution that emphasizes the divergent paths that each culture follows as it adapts to its local environment an approach that he believed would discover both differences and "limited parallels of form, function, and sequence" among them (1955, p. 19).

Marxist anthropology. Marx and Engels were the first students of history to attempt to develop a deterministic theory of social change. Their viewpoint was that all history was the outcome of the conflicting economic interests of the various social classes. **Marxist anthropology** takes up on this theme and focuses on the role of social conflict, especially economic and political conflict, in determining the conditions under which people live. For instance, a Marxist anthropologist, in explaining the slow pace of economic change in a nonindustrialized nation, would suggest that one important factor is that the lands worked by many rural farmers are owned by nonresident members of the upper class. In such a situation, social policies that might benefit the landless food producers would conflict with the economic interests of the landowners who are likely to have greater influence over governmental policy decisions than are the farm workers. Thus, the Marxist anthropologist would point to the conflicting interests of the producers and owners as a barrier to economic development.

Neofunctionalism. An application of Marx's emphasis on the existence of conflict in social life and its relationship to stability in cultural systems is the hallmark of **neofunctionalism**. The neofunctionalist might point to the conflicting party ideologies in U.S. politics as a part of the system by which stability is maintained in the United States. In a two-party political system, each party strives to obtain the votes of more than half of the electorate in order to have its candidate elected. The conflict between the two parties and the positions of any two competing candidates are expressed in language that portrays them as being at opposite ends of the political spectrum, yet both parties must actually be somewhere near the center of the political spectrum represented by American voters. Thus, a campaign process that emphasizes conflicting values and political commitments is the means by which the central majority of voters are wooed by politicians who, once elected, are likely to be neither extremely liberal nor extremely conservative in practice.

Feminist anthropology. The specialization known as **feminist anthropology** is a recent model in anthropology that shares Marxist anthropology and

FIGURE 2.8   Annette Weiner
Dr. Weiner has conducted considerable research in the Trobriand Islands, Papua New Guinea, and some in Western Samoa. She is particularly interested in the study of gender, sexuality, and the part that women play in societies around the world.

neofunctionalism's common concern for how conflict and inequities of power can play themselves out in human life. The defining characteristic of feminist anthropology is its specific interest in how gender-related differences in access to various forms of social power influence social life. Although gender is always a central variable in feminist analysis of social life, these theorists also appreciate the ways in which access to social power is unequally distributed based on a variety of other social categories such as class, ethnic, and racial distinctions. Therefore, feminist anthropologists are among those, such as the symbolic and postmodernist anthropologists, who are most likely to stress the importance of diversity and

Marxist anthropology the study of the effects of class conflict on social and cultural change
neofunctionalism contemporary approach to studying functional processes of cultural systems, with emphasis on the ways in which conflict may be one of the mechanisms by which cultural stability is maintained
feminist anthropology the study of the ways in which social power interacts with gender

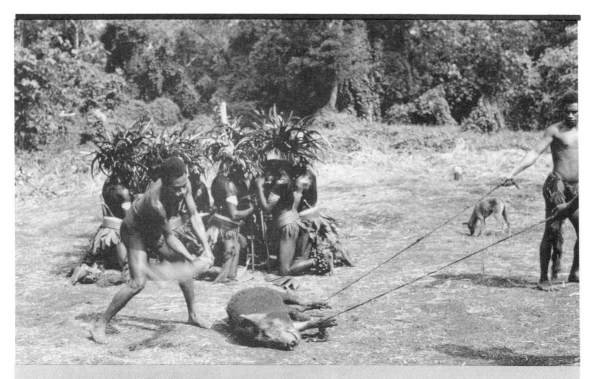

FIGURE 2.9 Tsembaga Maring Pig Ceremony
The Tsembaga pig ceremony illustrates the concept of culture as part of ecological approach. When the herd of pigs becomes too large to manage, the Tsembaga engage in a ritual slaughter intended to reduce the herds and stabilize the ecological balance among pigs, humans, and their environment.

dialogue and meaning in any culture. They are unique in their ability to bridge the gulf between humanist and scientist that more clearly separates practitioners of the other approaches to anthropology.

Cultural ecology. In the approach known as **cultural ecology**, the study of the adjustment of ways of life to different habitats, it is assumed that culture is an adaptive mechanism, and that those customs that improve a society's ability to adapt to its environment are the ones that are most likely to survive. This viewpoint is similar to that which biologists apply to evolution, so it is not surprising that cultural ecologists such as Andrew Vayda and Roy Rappaport (1968) have included the interaction of both culture and biology in their description of single adaptive systems. Thus, cultural ecologists view culture as part of a larger system that includes the natural environment and its interaction with human and animal populations, and human customs.

Rappaport's (1967, 1968) analysis of the Tsembaga Maring people of New Guinea has become a

classic illustration of the cultural ecological approach. The Tsembaga were tropical forest horticulturalists who grew taro, yams, sweet potatoes, manioc, and raised pigs. The root crops were a daily staple for the Tsembaga diet, but pigs were eaten only in ceremonial events that formed part of a longer cycle of warfare and peace between neighboring villages. When the size of the herds was small, pigs were easy to care for. They foraged for themselves during the day, and their rooting in the gardens actually aided in the cultivation of the soil.

As the herds grew, however, increasing proportions of garden crops were expended on feeding pigs. Finally, after a period of about eleven years, the costs of maintaining the herds became so great that the adult pigs began to be slaughtered in ceremonies that marked the beginning of a period of warfare between neighboring villages. The fighting continued for a

---

cultural ecology the study of the ways in which cultures adapt to their specific habitats period of weeks until one of the villages was routed. Its survivors abandoned their homes and sought refuge with their kin in other villages. Meanwhile, the victors slaughtered the loser's herds and destroyed their gardens and houses.

At the end of each war, the major ceremonial slaughter of pigs occurred, as the winners gave thanks to their ancestors for their victory and rewarded with gifts of meat the allies who had helped. The size of the herds returned to manageable numbers, and a truce remained in effect between the victors and the vanquished until the herds had once again grown large enough that they had to be culled.

Rappaport believed that the Tsembaga pig ceremonies supported the long-term balance between the human population and the food supply. Alliances were more easily formed by villages that could demonstrate their ability to support herds large enough to attract supporters who then would be rewarded during the pig slaughter ceremonies. So, the Tsembaga were motivated not to cull their herds as a source of protein throughout the year. Since the ceremonial slaughter was an integral part of the warfare process, conflicts between villages happened only periodically in a cycle that prevented human population growth from overtaxing the available land resources and geographically redistributed those who survived while their garden plots returned to nature and regenerated themselves.

Sociobiology. Like cultural ecologists, sociobiologists assume that adaptive behavior is more likely to survive than nonadaptive behavior, but unlike cultural ecologists, the concept of culture is given a less central role in the interpretation of the adaptive process. The emphasis in **sociobiology** is on the evolution of human genetic predispositions for adaptive ways of behaving that will maximize the reproductive success of human groups. In sociobiological thinking, culture is basically a system of reproductive strategies and cultural traits that are common in our species because they have been favored by biological evolution.

As one example, sociobiologists such as Pierre Van den Berghe and David Barash (1977) note that many cultures permit or even encourage men to have more than one wife, while very few societies encourage the opposite practice of a woman having several husbands. This, they argue, is because the reproductive success of men and women is normally enhanced by the former marriage pattern. For males, reproductive success is improved by having many mates.

But for females, each pregnancy represents a great expenditure of energy, so their reproductive success is enhanced by a lasting union with a single male whose characteristics will improve her children's chances of surviving. Thus, the common custom of plural marriage for men is based on the biologically evolved behavioral tendencies of both men and women. The sociobiological emphasis has not always been accepted by the traditional cultural anthropologists whose interests have centered on culture, but sociobiology is becoming increasingly accepted as one more tool for better understanding the total human condition and for possibly shedding further light on the relationships between biology and the cultural capacities of the human species.

Cultural materialism. The approach known as **cultural materialism** also shares cultural ecology's interest in the human relationship with the environment, but adds a hierarchy of technological and social variables to explain the ideology of a particular culture. Marvin Harris (1979), the anthropologist who gave cultural materialism its impetus, has summarized the major behavioral categories within which culture is manifest. He also proposed that all are ultimately linked to practical responses to the world. The first of these behavioral categories is the **mode of production**, the technology and practices by which people expand or limit their basic subsistence production in their specific habitat. A culture's mode of production includes its subsistence technology, technological relationships to ecosystems, and work patterns. The second category is the **mode of reproduction**, the technology and practices by which a people expand, limit, and maintain their population. Discussions of mode of reproduction would touch on matters of demography; mating patterns; fertility, natality, and mortality; nurturance of infants; medical control of demographic patterns; and contraception, abortion, and infanticide.

---

sociobiology emphasis on role of natural selection on genetic predispositions for specific behaviors

cultural materialism analyzes technological and social variables in explaining ideological facts of culture

mode of production the work practices by which people apply their subsistence technology within a particular environment

mode of reproduction the technology and practices operating within a particular social environment that influence the size of the society's population

Domestic economy—the organization of reproduction and basic production, exchange, and consumption within the family or household—comes next in Harris's model. This is the realm of family structure, domestic division of labor, domestic socialization, age and sex roles within the family, and domestic discipline. Next comes the category of **political economy**—the organization of reproduction, production, exchange, and consumption outside the domestic setting. Here one finds the political organization of society, its factions, clubs, associations, and corporations. Here also is nondomestic division of labor, taxation, and tribute, as well as public education, class, caste, urban and rural organization, and the mechanisms of social control and warfare. The final category, according to Harris, is the **behavioral superstructure**, the realm of art, music, dance, literature, advertising, rituals, sports, games, hobbies, and science.

Each of these behavioral categories has a corresponding component within the system of culture. The last, the behavioral superstructure, is most intimately centered within ideology, the symbolic core of culture,

and the furthest removed from the mundane influences of practical living. A link exists, nonetheless. Harris contends that the modes of production and reproduction have a major influence on the characteristics of the domestic and political economy, which in turn influence the behavioral superstructure of a culture. In brief, the means by which a people survive and maintain their population within an environment influence their social customs and even the more purely symbolic parts of human life.

---

domestic economy the reproductive, economic, and social behaviors that characterize life within the family or household

political economy the reproductive, economic, and social behaviors that are typical of life outside the family or household

behavioral superstructure those behaviors most closely linked to a culture's ideology, including art, ritual, recreation, philosophy, science

---

Practical Reasons for Dobuan Paranoia

According to Reo Fortune (1932), the Dobuans had a fierce mistrust of one another, a mistrust that bordered on paranoia. Their life was filled with sorcery. Food never grew without magic and neighbors engaged in magical theft of one another's crops; the winds did not blow except by magic; sex occurred only when one was bewitched; and all death was believed to have been caused by sorcery, with the surviving spouse the probable sorcerer. It would have been a mistake, though, to interpret Dobuan ideology as rampant mental illness. When the Dobuan outlook on life, nature, and their fellow Dobuans was seen as a cultural adaptation to their unhappy circumstances, it made a great deal of sense.

The Dobuans lived on rocky, volcanic islands that had only sparse pockets of soil that were much less productive than those of their Melanesian neighbors. Their extremely small villages never numbered more than about 25 people and they made their living from gardens they cut from the jungle. Their staple food was the yam, but the meagerness of their environment made hunger a constant threat, even though they lived in small and scattered groups. There was

never enough food and everyone went hungry for several months before each planting time to make sure there would be enough seed yams. Eating one's seed yams was the ultimate mistake, for not even a person's own family would provide new ones to someone who had proven to be such a failure. Dobuan economic life was characterized by fierce and secretive competitiveness, even within families. Husbands and wives maintained separate gardens and, although they worked together and pooled their food, they did not share seed yams.

The death of a Dobuan created severe economic obligations for the in-laws. During the period of mourning, a surviving husband had to work the gardens of his deceased wife, her parents, and her brothers and sisters, while his own brothers and sisters had the added work of caring for his. After the burial, the kin of the survivor had to make a large payment of food and yams to the relatives of the deceased. At the death of a man, his wife's children were required to cook a mash of bananas and taro, a starchy root plant, and deliver it to the relatives of their father. After the mourning period was over, the children were never again permitted to enter the village of their father or to eat food from his garden.

Dobuans

The Dobuans lived on the rocky volcanic islands of Melanesia. They made their living from gardens they cut from the jungle, but their harsh environment made hunger a constant threat. Their numbers began to decline as early as 1884 when many were taken into slavery. Currently, about 900 Dobuans work as professionals or in government service.

Is it any wonder that with conditions of economic hardship such as these, the Dobuans were not a trusting people? They lived in a world of limited resources, and their concept that one could prosper only at the expense of another was not unrealistic. This unhappy outlook on life was exaggerated when they tried to gain a symbolic modicum of security in an insecure life. Like peoples the world around, the Dobuans sought security in religion. To the Dobuans, nature was not the kind provider; it was magic alone that assured the growth of crops. Yams, the Dobuans believed, would only grow with the aid of incantations inherited from one's mother's family. When hunger still occurred each year, the Dobuans salvaged the emotional security that religion brings at an awful cost—by attributing their poor harvest to the sorcery of their neighbors. They thus affirmed that their magic did work, and in fact was so powerful that it could be used to steal the yams of others. In simplest terms, the Dobuans traded the fear of possible starvation for a mistrust of their fellow humans.

CHAPTER SUMMARY

1. Culture consists of the learned ideas and survival strategies that unify members of a particular human group. Group members are conscious that some of their beliefs and feelings are shaped by the ideology of their culture.

2. An obvious manifestation of our culture is our subsistence technology, with foraging, horticulture, pastoralism, traditional agriculture, and industrialized agriculture being the major patterns in existence today.

3. Our subsistence technology tends to shape all other aspects of our culture, including its rules about reproduction, its economic organization, and the ideological patterning of nonsubsistence behaviors.

4. Facing different environments with differing ideas about how one should live, cultures have evolved along different lines. Variations are often so extreme that people from different cultures have a hard time understanding each other's ways.

5. Cultural relativism, in which we try to make sense of the values and behaviors of other cultures within their own contexts, has long been used by anthropologists to encourage better understanding among all peoples.

6. Various orientations have developed within anthropology, each with its own approach to making sense of culture. In general, these can be grouped into two broad camps: the humanistic and the scientific approaches.

7. Humanistic anthropologists interpret the symbols of culture so that their meanings can be understood and appreciated by people of other cultural backgrounds.

8. Scientific anthropologists try to explain how cultures originate and change by considering various aspects of human life that may influence the content of a culture.

ANNOTATED READINGS

Clifford, J., & Marcus, G. (Eds.). (1983). *Writing culture: The process and politics of ethnography.* Berkeley: University of California Press. A collection of explorative writings by postmodernist anthropologists.

DeVita, P. R. (Ed.) (1990). *The humbled anthropologist: Tales from the Pacific.* Belmont, CA: Wadsworth. Accounts by twenty anthropologists of errors they made and misunderstandings they had during their fieldwork.

Geertz, C. (Ed.). (1971). *Myth, symbol, and culture.* New York: W. W. Norton. An important collection of essays on culture as a symbolic system.

Harris, M. (1974). *Cows, pigs, wars and witches: The riddles of culture.* New York: Random House. An exciting popular illustration of the cultural materialist approach to explaining human customs.

Kaplan, D., & Manners, R. A. (1972). *Culture theory.* Englewood Cliffs, NJ: Prentice Hall. A simple and straightforward discussion of the major theoretical orientations of cultural anthropology.

Lévi-Strauss, C. (1950). *Structural anthropology.* New York: Basic Books. Seventeen articles by the founder of structural anthropology, the application of linguistic techniques to the study of culture.

Rabinow, P. (1977). *Reflections on fieldwork in Morocco.* Berkeley: University of California Press. A description of how an anthropologist's encounters with Moroccans shaped his understanding of Moroccan culture.

Rappaport, R. A. (1968). *Pigs for the ancestors: Ritual in the ecology of a New Guinea people.* New Haven: Yale University Press. An excellent illustration of the approach of cultural ecology applied to the analysis of warfare among the Tsembaga Maring of New Guinea.

Ruby J. (Ed.). (1982). *A crack in the mirror: Reflexive perspectives in anthropology.* Philadelphia: University of Pennsylvania Press. A collection of studies by ethnographers who forthrightly discuss the anthropologist's role in reflexive anthropological research.

Sahlins, M. (1976). *Culture and practical reason.* Chicago, IL: University of Chicago Press. A critique of the materialist view of culture as the product of practical activity, in which the author argues for an understanding of culture as a system of meaningful symbols, the structure of which determines people's perceptions of what is and is not practical action.

Wilson, E. O. (1975). *Sociobiology: The new synthesis.* Cambridge, MA: Harvard University Press. A complex and controversial look at social systems from a biological perspective.

Wilson, E. O. (1978). *Human nature.* Cambridge, MA: Harvard University Press. A sociobiological interpretation of the human condition. Controversial but worth reading.

PART

II Survival and Adaptation

CHAPTER 3

Environment, Adaptation, and Subsistence

Humans have learned to live in such diverse environments as icy polar lands and rainy tropical forests. Foraging and food domestication are the two ways societies acquire food, a basic survival need for any society. Each has its implications for how people organize the rest of their lives. Industrialization of agriculture is a modern adaptation of the food-gathering process that has had a profound effect on the cultural and social developments of the societies that use it.

CHAPTER 4

Economics

Commodities acquire different values in different societies. Economic systems provide rules that determine how these commodities are produced, distributed, and consumed. The concepts of use rights, ownership, and division of labor are involved in production. Distribution is accomplished by some combination of reciprocal exchange, redistribution, and various types of markets. Patterns of consumption depend, in part, on need but also on status and prestige.

CHAPTER 5

Politics

Political power, the means of establishing and controlling public order, is organized and channeled in different ways in bands, tribes, chiefdoms, and states and may be vested in families, communities, associations, or specialized functionaries. The type of territorial political organization is dependent on the size and complexity of the community in which it is found. Where societies come to disagree with the established authority, conflict may arise and ultimately be resolved either peacefully or violently.

54

We humans must learn to adapt first to our physical environment and then to the cultural environment we have constructed if we are to survive as individuals and as societies. Chapter 3 illustrates the diversity of physical environments around the world and the subsistence technologies that have been developed to aid in adaptation. Chapter 4 examines how the values of commodities differ from culture to culture and discusses the development of economic systems. It includes a new section on the research of Annette Weiner. Incorporating a new section on gender and politics, chapter 5 examines the use of power to maintain an ordered society and to restore order when conflicts arise or rules are broken.

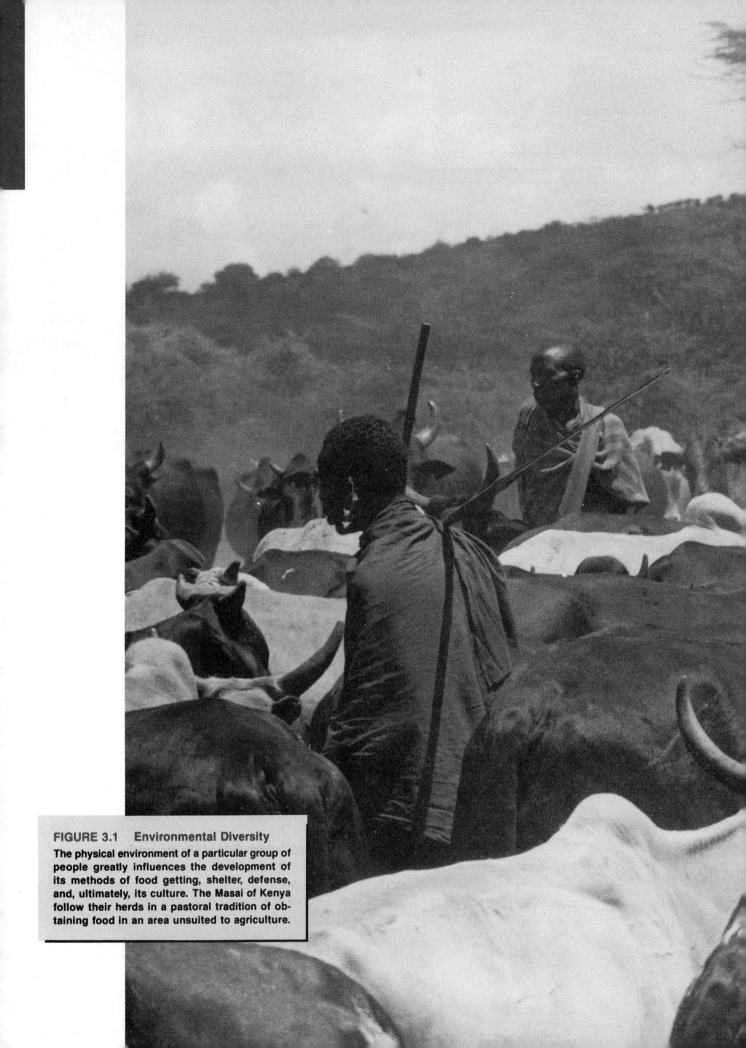

FIGURE 3.1   Environmental Diversity
The physical environment of a particular group of people greatly influences the development of its methods of food getting, shelter, defense, and, ultimately, its culture. The Masai of Kenya follow their herds in a pastoral tradition of obtaining food in an area unsuited to agriculture.

Human societies occupy territories, and their customs must enable them to cope with their environments if they are to survive. In this chapter we will examine the different kinds of environments that are found around the world, and discuss the ways in which societies have adjusted to different conditions by using the resources that their environments make available.

Environment, Adaptation, and Subsistence

CHAPTER OBJECTIVES

After reading this chapter, you should be able to:

Discuss the relationship between cultural areas and natural environments.

Characterize the world's major natural environments.

Explain the concept of carrying capacity.

Discuss the concept of adaptation in the context of biology and culture.

Define subsistence adaptation.

Discuss foraging as a subsistence adaptation.

Explain optimal foraging theory.

Discuss the major theories of the origin of food production.

Describe the kinds of food production.

Relate the different kinds of food production to the natural environments in which they are usually found.

Environmental Diversity
Cultural and Natural Areas
Natural Environments
Carrying Capacity

Biological and Cultural Adaptation

Subsistence Adaptations and the Environment
Foraging
Optimal Foraging Theory
Food Production
The Trend Toward Food Domestication

O ats, peas, beans, and barley grow. And potatoes. And tomatoes. Except in times of drought, or too much rain, or Japanese beetles. How long could you survive if you had to grow all your vegetables in your backyard and hunt for your meat in your neighborhood? If you lived in Alaska. Or Arizona. Consider the source of your lunch or dinner if you had no supermarket or McDonald's to supply it. Imagine your life without hamburgers and french fries. Imagine eating mostly rice every day. Or sushi. Or snake meat. You would probably love it. Humans have learned to adapt to many diverse types of foods.

Environmental Diversity

Human beings are unusual among the many species of animals in having successfully occupied so many different environments. Approximately 5 billion human beings are found in habitats as diverse as arctic regions, deserts, and tropical rain forests. Throughout the world, people have managed to survive challenging physical circumstances, and they have learned to exploit an amazing variety of food resources. To understand the success of the human animal in adapting to a complex natural world, it helps to be aware of the different specific environments in which people are found today.

Cultural and Natural Areas

Alfred Kroeber, an American anthropologist, noted (1939) that the culture areas of native North Americans tended to have boundaries that corresponded with important differences in their natural environments. The correspondence between cultural and natural areas can be understood in several ways. For instance, the diffusion of cultural traits from one society to another is influenced by the environment, and by natural boundaries that inhibit communication, trade, and other forms of interaction between peoples. This is not simply because such boundaries are necessarily physical barriers that are difficult to cross—although they sometimes can be—but more importantly because all aspects of a culture are in varying degrees adaptive responses to the environments in which they are found. This is particularly true of culturally governed customs that pertain to food getting, shelter, and defense technologies. Societies occupying the same or similar natural environments may readily borrow cultural traditions from one another that are relevant to successful adaptation. On the other hand, such adaptive cultural traits are less likely to be of interest to neighboring peoples who occupy different habitats.

Natural Environments

Preston James (1959) has classified the world into eight major types of natural environments that are characterized by important differences in climate, vegetation, and animal life. These differences are based, in part, on their latitude and proximity to oceans and mountain ranges, each of which plays a role in determining both the resources that are available and the kinds of problems people encounter in feeding themselves.

Mixed forests. In temperate climates there are **mixed forests**, such as those of eastern North America, that are made up of conifers and broadleaf trees. They are often accompanied by rolling plains and open areas in which the fertile soil provides an ideal situation for contemporary agricultural societies. So even though they represent only 7 percent of the Earth's land surface, they are occupied today by about 43 percent of the human population. Prior to the development of iron tools, when it was more difficult to cut down the trees, these lands may not have held such a large proportion of the human species.

---

mixed forests temperate climate with conifers and broadleaf trees

Scrub forests.   Regions between coasts and mountains that have mild, wet winters and hot, dry summers are **scrub forests** that attract a disproportionate share of human population. These areas, such as much of coastal California, represent only 1 percent of the land, but are home to 5 percent of the Earth's human occupants.

Tropical forests.   Regions such as the Amazon basin of Brazil that have warm climates, abundant rainfall, plant and animal life are **tropical forests**. Although they cover only 10 percent of the Earth's surface, 28 percent of the human species live in tropical forests.

Since heavy rainfall leaches away important soil nutrients and since tropical forest soils are typically high in acidity, they are not particularly productive as agricultural lands. Gardening techniques that rely on periodic changes in garden sites are common. Domesticated pigs have been used as food by some societies that occupy tropical forests, most particularly in Southeast Asia and the Melanesian, Micronesian, and Polynesian islands of the Pacific.

Mountain lands.   Highly complex landforms of **mountain lands** such as the Rocky Mountains or Appalachians of North America include a variety of environments, often within short distances of one another. The major environmental differences relate to (1) climate differences that are influenced by elevation and (2) local differences in rainfall and sunlight within a mountain area. For instance, slopes on the eastern sides of mountains near oceans receive greater rainfall than do the western sides, and northern and southern slopes typically receive different amounts of sunlight. These differences result in numerous different plant and animal communities that occupy specific environments within the entire mountain region. Mountain lands seem to have provided few resources to peoples who lacked domesticated foods, except at elevations below 6,000 feet above sea level, but have proven most useful to pastoralists and agricultural peoples; they represent 12 percent of the globe's land area and are occupied by 7 percent of the world's people.

Grasslands.   Twenty-six percent of the Earth's surface is covered by **grasslands**, a greater area than any other type of environment. Yet only 10 percent of the human species inhabit grassland areas. There are three basic types of grasslands that differ in climate

and in the predominant type of grass: steppes, prairies, and savannas. **Steppes**, such as the vast treeless stretches of southeastern Europe and Asia, have dry climates and extreme temperature changes during the year. Their grasses are short, hardy varieties that can tolerate their dry environment. **Prairies**, such as the North American Great Plains, have wetter climates and, consequently, support taller varieties of grass. **Savannas**, similar to some treeless plains of Florida, are found in tropical areas and are characterized by tall grasses and drought-resistant undergrowth.

Grasslands can be exploited usefully by hunters because of the large game animals, especially foraging herd animals, that occupy them. Pastoralists find them productive, since they are equally good environments for domesticated grazing animals such as cattle and sheep. Gardening in these environments is difficult without a plow or machine technology, since the grass-dominated soils are difficult to prepare for planting.

Arid lands.   The low annual rainfall in desert **arid lands**, such as parts of the southwestern United States and Great Basin, results in much of the land being sparsely covered by various plants such as grasses and low-growing desert shrubs that are capable of surviving on limited amounts of water. Isolated fertile pockets with year-round water may occur within arid lands, the only spots in which rainfall gardening is possible. Plant cultivation outside these areas requires irrigation, and pastoralism is possible but not as productive as it is in grasslands. So arid lands have typically supported dispersed bands of foragers, whose collecting of wild plants and hunting of animals permits them to live in very small no-

---

scrub forests regions between coasts and mountains with mild, wet winters and hot, dry summers
tropical forests regions with warm climates and abundant rainfall, plants, and animal life
mountain lands a variety of environments, often within short distances of one another
grasslands areas that cover 26 percent of the Earth's surface, with grasses of different types
steppes areas that cover stretches of southeastern Europe and Asia, with a short, hardy variety of grass
prairies areas with tall varieties of grass that tolerate wetter climates
savannas tropical areas of tall grasses and drought-resistant undergrowth
arid lands areas of low annual rainfall and sparse cover with low-growing desert shrubs

madic groups that exploit large territories. Thus, deserts comprise 18 percent of the world's land mass but only 6 percent of its people. Yet they are still not the most sparsely settled of the Earth's environments.

Boreal forests. Boreas, the Greek god of the north wind, gives his name to heavily wooded regions, mostly dominated by coniferous trees, the **boreal forests**. Because the climatic conditions are colder and less favorable for plant domestication than are those of other forested regions, the boreal forests such as the logging and mining areas of northern Ontario have attracted few human inhabitants. They represent 10 percent of the land surface of the world, but only 1 percent of the human species occupies these forests.

Polar lands. Regions of cold climates near the north and south poles, **polar lands** are made up of **ice-zones** of permanent snow and ice; **tundras**, level or undulating treeless plains in the arctic and subarctic regions of North America, Asia and Scandinavia; and **taigas**, swampy, coniferous forests of the northern lands south of the tundras. These are the least densely occupied environments of the world, representing 16 percent of its land area, but containing less than 1 percent of the people of the Earth. The weather of the polar lands may be continually below freezing, and even those areas furthest from the poles have short growing seasons and, therefore, few plants. As a result, polar lands do not easily support any of the basic subsistence technologies. Until recently, they have been successfully occupied only by foraging peoples who have emphasized the hunting of both land and sea mammals and fishing.

Carrying Capacity

The different natural environments of the world are not equally accessible to living creatures, including human beings. One measure of the ability of species to survive on the resources available to them in a particular environment is the **carrying capacity**, that is, the upper limit on population determined by the characteristics of that environment. Population can be limited by such things as the food resources naturally available in an environment, the potential fertility of the soil for food production, climate, and the available water resources. The most crucial factor in determining the upper limit to which population can grow is the vital resource that is least

available, since a population cannot be sustained at a level that makes its needs for any single resource greater than is consistently available, no matter how abundant the other resources may be.

Generally speaking, populations tend to stabilize at levels somewhat below the theoretical carrying capacity of their environments. The reason for this is that as populations grow toward the limit set by the available resources, competition between individuals for the resources will increase, so the effort and costs that must be expended to sustain each member of a population grow as well. The increased costs can offset the growth, making it increasingly difficult for the population as a whole to meet its needs. If this happens, the rate of population growth tends to stabilize gradually somewhere below the level that could be sustained in theory. This common pattern of regulating growth does have exceptions. When the growth rate is rapid enough, for instance, it's possible for a population to exceed the carrying capacity of its environment and thus experience massive decimation due to starvation.

....

Biological and Cultural Adaptation

The adjustment of an organism to a particular environment, **adaptation** is a two-way process, since it involves both changes in the organism in response to the demands of the environment and changes in the environment brought about by the organism. Adaptations in the organism can include biological and cultural changes that both facilitate and improve its adjustment to a particular environment.

---

boreal forests heavily wooded regions dominated by coniferous trees
polar lands regions of cold climates near North and South poles
ice-zone regions of permanent snow and ice
tundra level treeless plains in the arctic and subarctic regions of North America, Asia, and Scandinavia
taiga swampy coniferous forests of the northern lands south of the tundras
carrying capacity a particular environment's ability to support a species on the available resources
adaptation adjustment of an organism to a particular environment

LEGEND

- ■ hunting, gathering, fishing
- ⊙ horticulture, pastoralism
- □ agriculture

FIGURE 3.2 Subsistence Technologies of A.D. 1600
This map shows the worldwide range of subsistence technologies in A.D. 1600.

Biological evolution is one of the means by which living species, including human beings, are able to adjust to an environment. Over a period of time, <u>natural conditions select, or determine, which biological traits are most likely to be weeded out of a species and which are likely to remain</u>. This process was called **natural selection** by Charles Darwin (1859), who first systematically described parallels between the natural adaptation of a species and the "artificial" adaptation of breeding stock produced over many generations.

Biological anthropologists would be quick to cite examples of ways in which human beings have adapted to different environments around the world. For instance, the human trunk, head, arms, and legs tend to be longer and thinner in hot dry environments, while rounder and more compact body parts are associated with cold environments. The former traits create greater surface areas from which excess heat can be radiated efficiently from the body through evaporation of sweat. In cold environments where heat loss can endanger life, such traits would be less adaptive than the more compact shapes that make heat retention easier. Adaptive benefits have been suggested for other human differences, such as variations in average lung capacities at different elevations and skin color at different latitudes. For instance, the darkest skin tones consistently occur within about 15 degrees north or south of the equator in all parts of the world. Lighter skin shades are found as one moves further north or south. Natural selection seems to have adjusted skin tone to variations in the amount of sunlight that reach the surface of the Earth. The interaction of sunlight with the skin produces vitamin D, which is found naturally in very few foods. The right amount of this vitamin is important to the human body, since both too much and too little can be fatal. Pigmentation filters out sunlight that passes through the skin, and thus the adaptation of skin color is darkest near the equator, where it prevents overproduction of vitamin D. Away from the equator, where sunlight must pass through a greater layer of the atmosphere before it reaches the human skin, progressively lighter skin tones aid in the absorption of sunlight and thus avoid the problem of too little vitamin D production.

More interesting to cultural anthropologists are the ways in which human beings are able to adjust to

natural selection the process whereby those members of a species that are better adapted to their environment contribute more offspring to succeeding generations than do other members their diverse environments by changing their habits, customs, and cultures. Culturally governed changes in behavior make it possible for humans to adjust successfully to new environments quite quickly. Biological evolution is a much slower process. For instance, fashioning animal skins and furs into warm clothing, using dog-sledge transportation, and constructing igloos from the icy environment probably do more to explain the ability of Inuit peoples to survive so successfully in the arctic north than does Inuit body stature.

Subsistence Adaptations and the Environment

The study of subsistence is the study of how people obtain the necessities of life, particularly food, from their environment. It is in the study of food getting that we see most clearly how the forces of nature set limits and provide possibilities for human social and cultural life and how human subsistence technologies, the tools and techniques for obtaining food, help people adapt to their environments around the world.

Foraging

The oldest, simplest, and least specialized of human subsistence technologies is foraging, a food-collecting system based on fishing, hunting wild animals, and gathering wild plant foods. Depending on their environments, foragers place different relative emphases on plant gathering, hunting, and fishing.

The principal subsistence tools in those few remaining cultures that still live by foraging are digging sticks, clubs, spears, bows and arrows, fishing devices, traps, fire, and containers for storing, cooling, and transporting food. Tools are general-purpose and few in number, since they must be made on the spot when needed or transported as the people move from place to place in the quest for food. According to Alan Lomax and Conrad Arensberg (1977), who surveyed the subsistence systems of 1,308 societies, "The emphasis is on hand skills

rather than tools" (p. 668). Since individual skill is critical to success in the quest for food, foragers generally socialize their children to be independent and assertive and to rely on their own initiative rather than to be compliant to the demands of others.

Since hunting and gathering technologies rely on naturally occurring wild foods, foragers are unable to live year-round in groups as large as those supported by food domestication. Therefore, social mechanisms more complex than the family are not necessary for organizing the political and economic lives of foragers. They lack governments and warfare and tend to be highly mobile, especially when hunting provides a major portion of their food supply.

Considering the small size of their social groups, it is hardly surprising that foragers generally have been less politically powerful than food domesticators, and when in competition with them, foragers have usually been at a disadvantage. As a result, they continued to exist until recently primarily in those areas of the Earth of marginal interest to the plant and animal domesticators: the arctic wastes, the tundras, deserts, and tropical environments.

Today, there are few peoples left who rely primarily or entirely on foraging. Some of the Inuit of the Canadian arctic have returned to a tradition of self-sufficient hunting after a period of acculturation. Despite the European intrusion, many of the !Kung San people of the southwestern African desert maintained a foraging life-style until the 1970s outside South Africa, where they are no longer found. But especially since the mid-1970s, the San have undergone severe acculturation as governmental policies have aided the expansion of cattle herding into their traditional lands. Most San have been forced to find new ways to survive, such as working as herders for neighboring cattle owners. There are about 62,000 San in the desert of Botswana, Namibia, and Angola. Of these, only between 2,000 and 5,000 might still be called foragers. About 4,000 aboriginal Australians have managed to maintain a semi-nomadic foraging way of life within nationally established reserves. Some tropical forest foragers, such as the Agta of northeastern Luzon, can still be found in the Philippines. Several tropical forest peoples of South Amer-

---

subsistence how people obtain the necessities of life, particularly food, from the environment
subsistence technology the tools and techniques by which people obtain food
foraging a subsistence technology based on gathering wild plant foods, hunting, and fishing

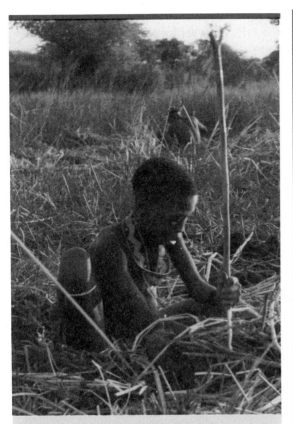

FIGURE 3.3   Foraging
Hunter-gatherers, or foragers, rely on the fish, game, or plants readily available in their environment for food. The oldest form of subsistence, foraging is being replaced in many areas of the world by some form of agriculture more suited to feeding large numbers of people. These Kalahari San are digging for bulbs after the rainy season.

ica, such as the Aché of eastern Paraguay still forage periodically despite efforts of the government to introduce them to agriculture. The Mbuti and other pygmies of Africa's Ituri forest are among the most numerous foragers today, numbering about 40,000 persons. Their ability to retreat into the forest has kept their traditional life-style viable, but it, too, is threatened as logging makes inroads into their territory.

Band cultures.   Foraging forms the subsistence base of a societal type known as the **band**. Bands are typically small groups based on kinship, with labor divided only by age and sex, sharing of resources, temporary leadership roles, material pos-

sessions limited by nomadism, and ideals reflecting these features. Wild foods are a sparse resource for people with no other means of survival. The poor environments occupied by foragers in recent times are unable to support more than about one person per five square miles, and in some places as few as one person per 500 square miles.

Nomadism and material culture.   Without a domestication technology, people must follow their food supply. This semi-nomadic pattern has an influence on the nature of a band society's material technology. Band-level peoples cannot afford to have as many different kinds of specialized tools as are commonly found among more sedentary peoples. Each tool must be able to serve many different functions and be easily carried to a new hunting ground. For instance, the Australian boomerang served not only as a throwing weapon used in the hunt but also as a flat working surface when making other tools, a digging tool, a club, a scraping tool, and a percussion musical instrument.

Group structure.   According to Julian Steward (1955) and Elman R. Service (1962), the hunting and gathering technology places certain functional demands on the social organization of the band-level culture. Permanent social groups cannot be very large. The local group that works and lives together averages about 50 people in contemporary band societies and rarely exceeds 100 people. The local groups of band cultures may have been somewhat larger in earlier times, when bands occupied areas with more abundant resources than are now found in the marginal areas to which they have been restricted by the expansion of more powerful societies. Nevertheless, wild food resources cannot maintain large local groups except in very lush environments, since the larger the group is, the farther individuals must travel from their base of operations in their quest for food.

As a general rule, in the small, local groups of band cultures, most individuals will be related, either by descent, which is commonly traced through both men and women, or by marriage. This community is the basic institution in a band society for organizing the education of children, social etiquette, and economic, political, military, and judicial practices.

band a seminomadic, kinship-based society with no full-time government, economically based on a foraging subsistence technology

64

Division of labor.

The only specialization of labor in a band culture is that based on differences of gender and age. In a band society supported by the sparse resources of wild foods, the most economical division of subsistence labor usually assigns the work of hunting to the men, while the gathering of wild plants near the camp is done by the women and older children. This specialization of labor is an adaptation to pregnancy in the female and the need for prolonged nursing of infants. Although these two biological facts might hinder her as a hunter, the woman still can be an important provider of plant foods gathered locally during periods of pregnancy and lactation. Elman R. Service (1962), R. B. Lee and Ivan DeVore (1968), and J. Tanaka (1977) have estimated that women sometimes provide as much as 80 percent of the calories in the diets of people who survive by hunting and gathering. However, in circumstances where a rigid differentiation is not important for the survival of the group, men, women, and children may play overlapping roles. In hunting and gathering societies in areas with plentiful wild foods, men may often gather wild plants as well as hunt; and men, women, and children may frequently work together in cooperative hunting activities.

Ernestine Friedl (1975) has suggested that the division of labor by gender in foraging societies takes one of four major forms, depending on the subsistence adaptation of the foraging groups to their specific environments: individual foraging, communal foraging, plant-focused foraging, and animal-focused foraging.

Individual foraging.

Subsistence based on individual foraging is common in environments in which meat is a relatively unimportant resource. In **individual foraging**, both men and women are expected to gather their own plant foods, but men provide primarily for themselves while women forage for themselves and their children. Only a small amount of time is devoted to hunting in this subsistence pattern. Men and women are typically equal in social power and prestige in these foraging societies.

Communal foraging.

In environments where the major meat resource is fish or small game, and plant foods are most easily collected by cooperative labor, **communal foraging** is common. Hunting is usually accomplished by driving animals toward nets where they are killed by the men of the group. In communal foraging, the game is normally divided at the site among all the families who participated, so

no particular prestige is gained by men from their role in hunting. The joint participation of women and men in the subsistence activities of communal foraging societies usually results in a relative equality between them.

▬

individual foraging men and women gather their own plant foods; women provide for the children
communal foraging cooperative food gathering where fish and small game are meat resources and plants are easily collected

---

Pygmy Net and Archery Hunting in the Ituri Forest

The Ituri Forest Pygmy of Zaire are a foraging people with an emphasis on hunting. Their adaptation to a tropical forest environment, described by Colin Turnbull, illustrates the interplay of technology and environment by which a society adjusts to its surroundings while meeting its subsistence needs. The Pygmy are divided into two major groups that differ in their primary food-getting technology and that have resulting differences in their social organization. One part of the Pygmy population, the Efe, emphasizes archery; the other, called Mbuti, are net hunters.

For about ten months of each year, the net hunters live deeper in the forest than do the archers, in communities of up to 30 families. Their hunt is a communal affair. According to Turnbull, "The net-hunting technique calls for each family to set up its net and fasten it to the net on each side (every elementary family owns one net, up to three hundred feet in length). As the men and youths are silently forming this semicircle, the women and girls form an opposite one, and at a given signal from the men, close in, beating the undergrowth with branches and making a distinctive whooping cry.

"Any animal falling into the nets is immediately killed with a spear, and the owner of the net into which it fell will give it to his wife to put in her basket. If the animal is too large for this, it is cut up and divided on the spot; otherwise the division takes place back in camp. The ultimate sharing follows no clear-cut kinship lines, though the owner of the net and the owner of the spear that killed the animal have first priority. Momentary individual needs seem to be given much more consideration, and portions will be given to those who were unable to come on the hunt or whose nets trapped no game" (1961, pp. 296–297).

The remaining two months of the year are a time of plenty in the forest. Game is so abundant during this period, called the honey season, that smaller groups of related families can readily provide for their own needs without participating in communal hunts. During this period, the community tends to break up into smaller groups that go their own way until food becomes scarce enough to warrant cooperating in larger groups again.

The bow and arrow hunting Pygmies follow an opposite yearly cycle of dispersal and congregation. They occupy lands near the edges of the forest that are less productive than the interior areas, partly because these areas have been changed by the presence of commercial plantations, mining activities, tourism, missions, and roads. Through most of the year the archery Pygmies wander in groups of three or four brothers and their families. Hunting is done only by men, who climb trees near game trails and wait for the opportunity to shoot animals that pass by or are flushed by the hunters' dogs. The food is carried back to the camp, where it is divided. Women in these groups do not participate in the hunt, but collect vegetable foods near the camp and take care of domestic chores. The archery hunters also supplement their food gathering by engaging in trade with nearby farming villagers outside the forest, a resource that is less used by the net hunters.

Once a year, during the honey season, game becomes abundant enough even in the territories of the archers to make communal hunts more productive than archery. During this short season, the bow and arrow hunters coalesce into a larger community that cooperates in a hunt very like that of the net hunters, although no actual nets are used. According to Turnbull, the communal hunt of the honey season "not only reaffirms the unity of the archery band as a whole, it also provides an opportunity for discussion of matters of general interest, such as betrothals, or the election of a new headman. . . . It is a time for general socializing, for song and dance (much of which is of ritual significance), and ultimately for the realignment of the smaller sections whose composition is never the same year after year. Petty hostilities and jealousies

Forest Pygmy

The Pygmy in Zaire, in Central Africa, remain one of the largest foraging populations in the world. They are divided into two types of foragers: The Efe emphasize archery and the Mbuti, net hunting. But because deforestation has greatly reduced their food resources, some Pygmies have turned to agriculture or employment on nearby farms and plantations to sustain themselves.

are removed during this festive season, which lasts about two months; old friendships are renewed and new friendships formed" (1961, p. 301).

The contrasting yearly cycle of the two groups of Pygmies is an interesting illustration of how environmental differences can influence the customs of a culture. Although historical documentation does not recount the actual development of these two patterns of Pygmy life, it is conceivable that they arose in response to a decline in game in the forest fringes due to road-building and other exploitation of forest resources by the non-Pygmy newcomers.

Today, the Ituri Forest Pygmy remain one of the largest foraging populations in the world, since the forest provides some isolation from encroaching food domesticators. The Mbuti number about 40,000 who live in bands of between 10 and 70 people. Deforestation has reduced the food resources of the Mbuti, and many have taken up agriculture or accepted employment on neighboring Bantu farms and coffee plantations.

Plant-focused foraging. Societies in environments where plant resources can readily supply the majority of the food from areas nearby engage primarily in **plant-focused foraging**. These groups that emphasize plant collecting are usually the least rigid about separating the roles of men and women. While men are occupied with hunting larger animals that may have to be pursued for long distances over a period of days, women gather plant foods near the camp, an activity that typically provides between 60 and 70 percent of the group's food. Nevertheless, men's social prestige and power are often high when compared with women, because whenever they bring more meat to camp than their own families can use, they share the surplus with the hunters of other families and are given high status by their neighbors as a result. In contrast, the plant foods that women provide their own families are the basic staple of life. They are readily available to all, so there is no need for women to share the fruits of their labor outside their own families. Thus, women lack access to a means for raising their status in the way men do. In this unbalanced system, when men share food with nonrelatives, their status rises in a way that emphasizes the dependence of women on men for the important resource that men provide.

Animal-focused foraging. Environments that offer little in the way of plant foods may be occupied by foragers when fish and animal life are abundant enough. In **animal-focused foraging**, fish and large game hunted by men are the basic food. In this subsistence system, women do not contribute directly to the food supply, but bear domestic responsibilities including the processing of the meat and skins brought in by the men. Often in those societies, men make the tools that women use. Especially where the meat resources are large game animals, the pursuit of which can encourage high levels of competitiveness and aggression in hunters, the economic dependence of women on men can result in low social status for women.

Optimal Foraging Theory

Nowhere do people use every possible available resource in their environment. Insects, for instance, are a source of protein that is ignored by a great many cultures. Dogs and cats are quite common in North American and European societies, but are culturally defined as pets rather than as foods. Some

FIGURE 3.4   Inuit Seal Hunt
After a period of acculturation, some of the Inuit, or Eskimos, of the Canadian arctic have returned to self-sufficient hunting and fishing. This hunter uses modern technological methods to bring home his seal from Bathurst Inlet.

species of dogs were raised for their food value by the Aztecs, and both dogs and cats are marketed in various parts of the Orient where milk products traditionally have not been favored as foods. This selectivity in the cultural definition of potential food resources exists even in societies that rely on the simplest of food-getting technologies that permit only foraging for wild foods.

Optimal foraging theory is a way of trying to explain why some foods are emphasized more than

plant-focused foraging plant resources are readily available, allowing hunting expeditions far from campsite
animal-focused foraging fish and animal life provide basic food supply where plants are scarce
optimal foraging theory asserts that foragers use food resources in direct proportion to the caloric effort required to obtain them

others, and why some are regularly ignored by collectors of wild foods. Basically, optimal foraging theory asserts that the likelihood of foragers using a potential food resource is directly proportional to the calories it offers as food per unit of effort required to obtain and prepare it for eating. The greater the caloric cost of obtaining and preparing a given food, the less likely it will be sought. When all potential foods in a given environment are ranked from the one with the highest rate of return on effort expended to the one with the least payoff, it will be found that those foods at the top of the list will be the ones that are most commonly used in the diet. Items lower on the list will be less and less often used. When the full dietary requirements of a foraging group are considered, there is some point on the entire list below which it is unlikely that foods will ever be sought except under unusual circumstances.

Optimal foraging theory is useful for answering a number of questions about food-collecting activities. For instance, it would be ethnocentric to suggest that insects are not used as foods by most societies because insects are unaesthetic as foods. The idea that their nutritional value is lower than that of other animals is simply incorrect. However, the tendency of many societies to ignore the nutritional value of many insects that exist in their environment does make sense on the purely practical level suggested by optimal foraging theory: The high amount of effort that an individual would usually have to expend to gather enough of them to prepare a meal simply makes most insects too costly to be worth the effort in most environments most of the time. Of course there are exceptions. The aboriginal Shoshoni of the Great Basin desert of the United States were regularly plagued by infestations of grasshoppers in sufficient numbers so that it was quite cost-effective to simply dig a trench, cover its bottom with hot coals, and then just wait until it filled itself with roasted grasshoppers. In such a situation, the usual predictions of optimal foraging theory would not be violated if grasshoppers became a temporary important addition to the normal yearly diet, as it did regularly for the Shoshoni.

Of course, a plant or animal may be collected for reasons other than its value as food. The tribes of the United States Plains hunted the bison as an important food resource, but they also used its hide for leather, its tendons for making bows, and its horns and bones for making various tools. Similarly, an animal or plant low on the list as a food resource might be sought and eaten anyway when its other uses added to its food value make the effort worthwhile. However,

the basic principle of optimal foraging theory is not really violated by such considerations. The return on invested effort is still the best predictor of a resource's being utilized, whether the return is calculated in terms of food calories or in terms of any other units of value that contribute toward survival of a social group.

Food Production

Although the shift to food domestication had been viewed traditionally as progress, the current anthropological thinking is that foraging had its advantages, too. Judging from the few groups that still practice hunting and gathering, ways of life based on foraging are usually quite satisfactory in their ability to meet the needs of people. Population density is generally low, and the communities of cooperating individuals are never very large. Under these circumstances, it is simple for the local group to move quickly from place to place. As a result, food shortages are rare among hunters and gatherers, Nomadic or seminomadic hunters and gatherers do not live amidst their own refuse, one contributor to many of the diseases with which more sedentary peoples must contend. This factor, plus the low population densities that are characteristic of foragers, means that the epidemics that often plague peoples who live under crowded conditions are also rare. Furthermore, Marvin Harris (1977) has pointed out that foragers have a much shorter work week than do food domesticators. For instance, the southern African !Kung foragers need to work only about three hours a day to obtain a nutritious diet, even though their desert environment is not nearly so lush as most of the areas occupied by hunting and gathering peoples before the rise of farming.

The Trend Toward Food Domestication

Between 10,000 and 18,000 years ago, the lifestyle of the foragers of southwest Asia began to change. Along the hilly flanks of the mountains of the Near East, there was sufficient rainfall for abundant wild grains to grow without cultivation. Foragers in these zones were able to gather a variety of wild foods in different seasons and preserve them in storage pits for off-season use. Food storage made a more sedentary life possible even while exploiting wild cereal crops that were native to the area. These wild cereals could be harvested easily by lightly beating the stems so that the seeds would break loose and fall into a basket. After grinding with stone tools, the tough seeds could be prepared for eating in a variety of ways. The use of these wild grains resulted in a more sedentary life and population growth, and laid the foundation for the eventual domestication of plants and animals.

The rise of population that may have led to food domestication can be accounted for by the interplay between human fertility and **sedentarism** (a settled rather than nomadic life-style). Rose Frisch and Janet McArthur (1974) and Rose Frisch (1975) have demonstrated that following the birth of a child, a woman will not again begin ovulation so long as less than 20 to 25 percent of her body weight consists of fat. This figure represents the approximate amount of calories that a fetus needs to develop to full term. That is, before a fertile woman will be able to conceive, her body must store enough calories of energy to nourish a developing fetus for a nine-month pregnancy. In active nomadic populations this threshold of body fat is more difficult to achieve than in sedentary populations, since the foragers burn more food energy themselves and their diets are likely to be lower in carbohydrates and higher in protein. Because nursing one child takes about 1,000 calories a day, it is unlikely that a woman will become pregnant as long as she is nursing if she lives in a semi-nomadic hunting and gathering society. Since nursing is likely to continue for at least three years in most societies, the level of fertility is, on the average, much lower in hunting and gathering societies than in sedentary societies using domesticated foods. The span of childbearing years is also shorter, for the onset of menstruation occurs later in hunting and gathering societies because a hunting and gathering diet is rich in protein. In demonstration of these theories, Richard B. Lee (1972) and Gina B. Kolata (1974) have reported growth in fertility and population among those !Kung hunter-gatherers who abandoned their native seminomadic way of life for a more sedentary food production economy.

Esther Boserup (1965) argued, on the other hand, that population growth may have been a cause for the food domestication. It would have created pressure for more effective control over the food supply than was possible with the simple gathering of wild plants. Robert Sussman (1972) pointed out that population growth eventually made it necessary for people to move into less productive areas around the margins of the zones where wild grains grew in natural abundance, and Lewis Binford (1968) and

Kent Flannery (1971) believe that it was in these marginal zones that people found it necessary to seek more direct human control over their food supply. People began to keep near to the home base a few animals such as sheep, goats, dogs, and cattle, which had previously been hunted. This practice ensured a steady supply of meat as well as other useful products such as hides, milk, and milk products. By experimenting in how to plant seeds, people acquired grains as dietary supplements in areas where they had not been common previously.

The process that led to the domestication of plants and animals began as early as 13,000 years ago. It is not possible to place a precise date on its origins, since the shift to food domestication was a gradual process. There is even some debate about where the earliest center of food domestication was. Some archaeological evidence has suggested that it may have occurred in Southeast Asia. Nevertheless, the process is best documented for the Near East. Because the distinction in the remains between wild and domesticated plants and animals is subtle, what is considered earlier materials simply may represent plants and animals in the process of being domesticated. It is safe to say, however, that by 9000 B.C. goats and sheep had been domesticated in the Near East, and barley and wheat were domesticated by 7000 B.C. in the same area. Cattle and pigs also were under human control by 7000 B.C. The domesticated grains differed from their wild relatives in that the crop domesticators favored larger seeds. As the seeds evolved to a larger size under human influence, the grain was more firmly attached to the stems and could no longer be harvested easily by shaking the stems over a basket. Thus, the domestication of grains required the simultaneous evolution of a new technology for use in the harvest, including knife blades and sickles for cutting bunches of stems. Such tool kits were in use in the ancient Near East by 7000 B.C.

Tribes. When the hunting and gathering subsistence technology gave way to sedentarism and the domestication of plants and animals, a more complex societal type arose called the tribe. In tribal societies population may approach 100 people per square mile. Local groups must maintain more or less permanent residence near the planted gardens

---

sedentarism living in permanent or semipermanent settlements

tribe a semisedentary society economically based on simple food domestication from which they draw their food. These groups can grow to be quite large in comparison with the local groups of hunting and gathering peoples. According to Marshall D. Sahlins (1960), the communities of contemporary horticultural societies have up to 200 to 250 residents. While the local groups in bands may be composed of anywhere from one to a dozen families that are loosely interrelated by ties of marriage, a tribal community may consist of as many as 20 residential families. Often, these families may be grouped into a number of larger kin groups that are united to one another by ties of common ancestry.

Horticulture. In most tribal societies, the basic means for acquiring food is h̲o̲r̲t̲i̲c̲u̲l̲t̲u̲r̲e̲, a simple form of plant and animal domestication. Horticulture involves only the planting, weeding, harvesting, and storage of foodstuffs. Techniques for irrigating the gardens may or may not be present, but there is no use of the plow, draft animals, fertilization of the soil, or crop rotation, all of which are characteristic of more complex agricultural technologies. The most common hand tools used in labor-intensive horticultural tribes are the digging stick and the hoe. Most horticulturalists have some domestic animals with which they supplement their diets, but animals are never the source of the bulk of their diet.

A horticultural technology provides a more reliable subsistence and produces more food per acre than does a hunting and gathering technology, so peoples with horticultural technologies live in larger communities than do foragers. Their denser populations give them correspondingly greater political power than foragers have, so horticultural societies are much more widespread. Four hundred years ago, they were found primarily in the tropical forest areas of South America, in many parts of North America, in most areas of Africa, throughout the islands of the Pacific, and in some of the Asian mainland. Nevertheless, the simple tools of horticulturalists give them relatively little control over the productivity of the land they cultivate, so there are natural limits on their distribution throughout the world. They were typically found in areas with warm or temperate climates favorable to the domestication of plants.

There are two common forms of horticulture: slash-and-burn and dry-land gardening. **Slash-and-burn** horticulture is also known as **swidden horticulture**, or **shifting cultivation**. This form of food cultivation is common in tropical forest environments or in savannas, where clearing the land requires heavy labor. The trees and vegetation that are cut away are

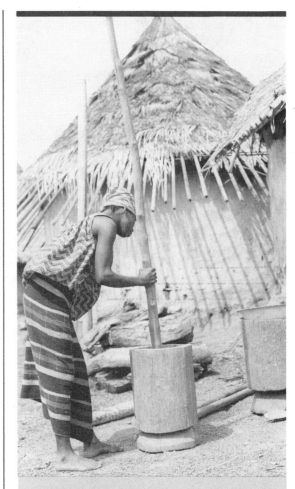

FIGURE 3.5 Horticulture
The subsistence technology of horticulture provides people with food in a simple uncomplicated way. This African woman in a village on the Ivory Coast is pounding grain into flour.

left to dry and then burned before a crop can be planted. Garden plots are cultivated for several years during which they may become less and less productive as their nutrients are depleted. Then the fields are allowed to lie fallow for a period of up to nine or

horticulture cultivation of crops using simple hand tools such as the hoe and digging stick and without fertilization of the soil, crop rotation, and often without irrigation
slash-and-burn cultivation a form of farming in which the land is prepared by cutting and burning the natural growth and in which several plots, in various stages of soil depletion, are worked in a cycle
swidden horticulture slash-and-burn horticulture
shifting cultivation slash-and-burn horticulture

FIGURE 3.6 Slash-and-Burn Horticulture
Horticulturalists use simple tools such as hoes and digging sticks to plant their crops. In order to clear a plot of land for planting, they cut down or slash the trees and brush and then burn them. The ashes that remain act as fertilizer for the soil. This type of food production is also known as shifting cultivation since a new plot of ground may be started every planting season.

ten years before they are cleared and worked again. Typically, gardeners who use the slash-and-burn technique have several gardens, each of which has been cultivated for a different length of time, so that each year the oldest may be abandoned to nature while another, abandoned previously, is again prepared for use. Ultimately, after several cycles of use and abandonment of plots, the soil will have become so depleted that the forest does not grow back, and entirely new gardens must be prepared. Eventually, gardens may be so far from the original village that an entire settlement of several hundred people may be relocated to a more convenient area.

<u>Dry-land gardening</u> is carried out in arid environments. The major problem in dry-land gardening is getting sufficient water to the crops. Some small canals may be used to channel available water resources such as the seasonal runoff of rainwater from higher land. However, in the absence of major, reliable water sources such as rivers, large irrigation

projects that require heavy cooperative labor are not a part of this system. In drier periods water may have to be hand-carried to individual plants in gardens.

In nonforested regions where cereal crops predominate, the settlements of horticulturalists may be more permanent than those of tropical forest farmers. Particularly in drier climates, horticulturalists may engage in some hand-watering of plants or limited irrigation of fields, but irrigation is not so common or complex as in agriculturally based societies.

Control over the food supply allows horticulturalists to live in larger local groups than foragers. Several hundred people may live together in villages throughout the year. Housing is more permanent and house construction more elaborate than are the temporary shelters of foragers. Village life neces-

dry-land gardening planting in arid environments using several forms of irrigation sitates greater accommodation to the presence of others, so childrearing necessarily emphasizes compliance and responsibility over independence and assertiveness in children. Family organization tends to be more elaborate among horticulturalists than among foragers, since a large number of family members may reside in the same location over many generations.

The authority of the family organization in the lives of its individual members is great, since the family is the basic governing institution in horticultural villages. Each family may be a politically autonomous component of the village except in matters that affect the common welfare. Such matters tend to be dealt with by a council of family leaders from the entire village, who seek to achieve a consensus on how to handle the problem.

The greater numbers and more complex social organization of horticulturalists and the need for control of the land as a source of income makes warfare a common element of life in horticulturally based societies. Nevertheless, just as horticulturalists have tended to be more politically powerful than foragers, they have tended to be politically less powerful than agriculturalists. For this reason, they tend now to be restricted to arable areas of the world that are less desirable to the agricultural societies.

The Shuara of Ecuador and Peru

The Shuara are a horticultural people, popularly known as the Jívaro, who have been described by Michael Harner (1973). They live within the higher reaches of the Amazonian tropical forest of eastern Ecuador and Peru. Their basic subsistence food is a starchy root crop called manioc, but they also grow maize, sweet potatoes, squash, beans, peanuts, bananas, plantains, and papayas. These foods are supplemented by fish and game such as monkeys, birds, and peccaries.

Gardens are prepared near the living site by a group of men who belong to the same family. Undergrowth is cleared from a garden area, and the small trees are ringed by removing a strip of bark from the entire circumference of each one to weaken them. When the larger trees are felled, originally with stone axes and in more recent times with steel axes, they take with them the smaller weakened trees in their vicinity, since their canopies are interwoven with vines and other jungle growth. Several months later, after the brush and trees

Shuara (Jivaro)

Living in the tropical rain forests of Ecuador and Peru, the Shuara, also known as Jivaro, subsist primarily on carbohydrate crops such as manioc, sweet potatoes, and corn. They use slash-and-burn agriculture to grow their crops and supplement their diet by hunting small game and spearing fish after they first poison them in dammed-up pools of water.

have dried, the garden area is burned. Then the gardens are planted and an elliptical, palm-thatched house is erected. The gardening itself is done by the women of the group.

Men hunt to supplement their families' diets with meat. Small game such as monkeys and birds are shot with blowgun darts that are coated with curare, a poison that suppresses the breathing reflex of the animal. Since a monkey is likely to try to pull out the dart, it is notched so that it will break off easily and leave the poisoned tip inside the animal. Within a few minutes, animals shot with the poisoned darts drop from the trees. Since the blowgun is such a silent weapon, it is often possible for a skilled hunter to pick off several monkeys from a troop before the others become alarmed. Larger game may be killed with spears, or in recent times, with shotguns or rifles. Fish are taken with traps, nets, or spears. The Jívaro (Shuara) have an unusual technique of poisoning the water and the fish in it. They build a dam to contain the fish and, using natural plants such as barbasco shrub and masu, pour the sap into the water. The poison stuns the fish so they can be speared. Little ecological damage is done by this method.

FIGURE 3.7   Pastoralism
Pastoralists focus on animal husbandry as their primary source of food. Depending on the environment, some pastoralists migrate with their herds of cattle, yak, llamas, or camels to favorable foraging areas. Camels are found primarily in northern Africa and the Arabian peninsula.

Pastoralism.   A more specialized form of domestication technology is **pastoralism**, which focuses on animal husbandry as the major source of food. It is practiced in tribal societies found in areas unsuited to agricultural pursuits: the arctic, subarctic, deserts, mountains, and grasslands, so pastoralism is probably of more recent origin than horticulture. Indeed, it is commonly argued that pastoralism in most parts of the world developed as farming peoples expanded into environmentally less productive zones and adjusted by relying more heavily on domestic animals as their basic source of income. Most pastoralists do supplement their diets with food grown in simple gardens, but plant growing is always subordinated to the demands of their animal husbandry. Thus pastoralism typically requires large areas of land and a somewhat migratory way of life, called **transhumance**, the pastoralist practice of moving their animals between at least two different primary foraging areas at different elevations in different seasons.

Pastoralism is the predominant means of subsistence in environments such as deserts, grasslands, savannas, and mountains that are unable reliably to sustain horticultural or nonindustrialized agricultural production.

There are several types of pastoralism that occupy somewhat different environments, depending on the animal that is the primary subsistence resource. Cattle herding was most common throughout sub-Saharan Africa, particularly throughout equatorial and East Africa, southern Africa, and parts of Madagascar. Cattle herding was also found in limited areas in the northern part of South America among

pastoralism a subsistence technology based on animal husbandry
transhumance a form of pastoralism in which only a part of the group moves with the herd; some stay in villages and grow crops year-round

the Goajiro, a people of mixed Native American and African origins. Many of the cattle-herding peoples combined pastoralism with some plant cultivation. Camels were the basis for pastoralism throughout northern Africa and the Arabian Peninsula. Reindeer herding was particularly important among various peoples of the far north, including the Lapps of the northern Scandinavian subarctic and various peoples in Siberia. Yak herding was limited to the high mountain regions of the Himalayan area. A similar, geographically limited form of pastoralism was found in the Andes of South America, where llama herding in combination with agricultural production was important for societies such as the Inca who dominated the area at the time of European contact. Mixed pastoralism, the predominant type throughout western Asia north of India, combined a variety of animals such as sheep, goats, horses, and cattle.

Since they occupy territory that is often marginal and unproductive, pastoralists are generally unable to produce everything they need. Therefore, they must obtain some goods from neighboring horticultural or agricultural peoples. This is often accomplished by trade, but sometimes it is more profitable to raid their more sedentary neighbors. Especially when the animals they keep, such as horses or camels, give them great mobility, these peoples can carry out their raids rapidly with little warning and leave quickly afterwards.

Since the herds of pastoralists are vulnerable to theft, pastoralists must be constantly with their herds and live in perpetual readiness for conflict. Warfare is a prominent fact of life in pastoral societies. Thus, childrearing emphasizes obedience, deference to authority figures, and a competitive and socially dominant role for male warriors.

The Northern Tungus Reindeer Herders of Siberia

The northern Tungus, many of whom identify themselves as the Evenki, occupy much of eastern Siberia. Their environment is in the treeless tundra and forested taiga zones of the northern polar region, where plant cultivation is impractical. Their source of livelihood is reindeer herding and hunting.

The Tungus keep a domesticated variety of reindeer that they milk and use for riding and as pack animals, much as horses are used

Tungus

A herding tribe in the territory of eastern Siberia, the Tungus depend on their reindeer and the land on which they graze to support themselves. During the Soviet Union's control of their territory, alcohol was introduced with disastrous effects on the health of the tribe, and the building of radar sites, airstrips, and missile facilities in northern Siberia has greatly reduced the amount of grazing land available to the tribe.

among their southern neighbors. Natural dangers such as wolves make it difficult to increase the herd, and as many as half the herd may be lost each winter. Normally, herd reindeer are only eaten at a few ceremonial events or when a weak animal is culled from the herd to prevent it from breeding; they are not a regular source of meat. The primary sources of meat in the Tungus' diet are wild reindeer, deer, elk, bear, wolves, and boars that are obtained by hunting and trapping.

The Tungus must travel with their herds as they migrate between their summer and winter pasturages. The northern tundra is the preferred feeding ground during the short summer because lichens and other foods are more plentiful than in the forest lands to the south. During the four months of summer, the herds are plagued by mosquitoes and gadflies, so the reindeer feed at night and congregate in the daytime around smoky fires built by the Tungus to repel the pests. For the rest of the year, the herds move south and pasture during the day, so that they can be protected at night from wolves.

The summer home of the Tungusic family is a birch bark lodge. In the winter, when the herds must travel constantly to forage for food beneath the snow, the home is a small skin tent occupied by a nuclear family. The husband is responsible for trapping and hunting and heavy labor around the camp, while the wife milks and cares for the herds and takes charge of the routine domestic chores. The husband's hunting and trapping activities are important, since they provide food, skins for clothing and tents, and furs that are used to trade for useful items such as rifles and metal utensils. This leaves the wife with a great deal of responsibility for the herds in the absence of her husband, including moving it to new grazing areas when this is necessary.

The northern Tungus' way of life became difficult to document during the Soviet Union's control of their territory, but it is clear that the northern Tungus' culture has changed dramatically. Frances Svenson (1980) reported that the introduction of alcohol into the society had disastrous effects, including many deaths among the Evenki. Efforts by the Soviet Union to collectivize the Siberian herds met with great resistance and led to the loss of about two-thirds of the animals. The building of early-warning radar sites, airstrips, and missile facilities in northern Siberia is believed to have resulted in the loss of lands by many of the Siberian herders, including the Tungus.

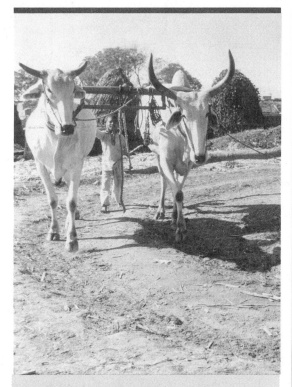

FIGURE 3.8 Nonindustrialized Agriculture

Agriculture makes use of more complicated technology than horticulture to produce food. The use of plows pulled by draft animals and simple organic fertilizers characterize the complexity of nonindustrialized agriculture. Farmers in this village of Bhadola, India, use draft animals to increase their production.

Agriculture (intensive cultivation). More intensive than horticulture in the use of land for food production, **agriculture** or **intensive cultivation** relies less heavily on human energy than on animal and technological power. The greater productivity of agriculture is made possible by the use of tools and techniques like the plow, irrigation, soil fertilization, and animal traction. Domestic animals such as the horse, cow, and ox are harnessed to pull the plow and to transport produce, and their excrement may be used to increase the fertility of the soil. Agriculture is much more recent than horticulture, being a scant 6,000 years old, but it has proven to be a very successful form of subsistence. An agricultural way of life creates large food surpluses which permit a much larger population to develop, and makes it possible for many specialists to devote their full-time labor to nonagricultural pursuits. These features, in turn, greatly increase the political power of agricultural societies relative to those with a simpler technological foundation. Agriculturalists have become the largest, most widespread, most dominant peoples in the world and occupy the most productive parts of the world's surface.

The simplest form of intensive cultivation is **nonindustrialized (or traditional) agriculture**. In this form, the major tools are hand implements such as

agriculture the intensive working of land for food production through the use of tools and techniques such as the plow, irrigation, soil fertilization, and animal traction
nonindustrialized (or traditional) agriculture intensive crop cultivation using simple tools such as hoes, shovels, and animal-drawn plows

the hoe, shovel, and animal-drawn plow. <u>Crops are grown for local consumption,</u> but the use of the plow, animal-derived fertilizers, and irrigation results in greater productivity than is usual in extensive cultivation, <u>so that market crops may also be produced.</u> Use of the plow and animal or human fertilizer to enhance the productivity of the soil makes agriculture more land-intensive than labor-intensive. While horticulturalists can expand their populations only by opening new land to cultivation, land-intensive agriculture can allow farmers to support population growth by increasing the output of their fields. The populations of towns occupied by agricultural peoples commonly number in the thousands or tens of thousands. Such large groups require a high degree of specialization and the presence of a system of government that is not based solely on the authority of the family organization. Because of the large urban populations that agriculture can support, agricultural societies frequently have class distinctions with inherited differences in political power and wealth within the local communities.

Classic Mayan Raised-Field Farming

During the golden age of Mayan civilization, the so-called classic period from A.D. 200 to 900, the ancient Maya occupied the Yucatan Peninsula, including what is now Honduras, Guatemala, Belize, and the Mexican states of Campeche, Chiapas, Tabasco, and Yucatan. Their land was dominated by tropical forests, savannas, and swamps. Their seasonal round consisted of a hot, dry season from February through May and a wet winter season that brought as much as 160 inches of rain.

In this tropical environment, the Maya built a civilization based on slash-and-burn gardening and an innovative system of raised-field intensive farming that combined plant cultivation with aquaculture. Raised-field agriculture was practiced in swampy areas and along slow-moving rivers. These fields were built by digging a series of canals around the growing areas and piling the soil thus obtained on the fields to raise them above the water level. The chest-deep canals between the fields were home to water lilies, food for fish that could be harvested. Periodically the canals were dredged, and the water plants and muck from their bottoms were added to the fields to enrich the soil.

The major crops grown by the Maya were maize, squash, beans, chili peppers, amaranth, manioc, and cacao. These were supplemented by fish from the canals and a variety of forest foods, including avocados, deer, turkeys, peccaries, tapirs, and rabbits. This combination of wild foods and domestic

Maya

The ancient Mayans (A.D. 200–900) lived in the area of the Yucatan Peninsula, a tropical land dominated by forests, savannas, and swamps. They utilized this environment to create a system of raised-field, intensive farming that allowed them to grow such things as corn, squash, beans, and cacao and that allowed fish to thrive in the canals from which the field dirt was dug.

produce supported a population of perhaps two million, divided into a number of petty states, each ruled by its own *mah k'ina* or "Great Sun Lord," who was served by an administrative class of nobles, called *cahals*. These in turn governed in the smaller cities of each state and paid tribute to their lord.

FIGURE 3.9 Industrialized Agriculture

An extremely efficient method of food production in terms of high yield with little human labor is an agriculture that utilizes the mechanization of industry such as these twin rotor combines. It is, however, inefficient in terms of the ratio of total energy used to total calories yielded.

Industrialized agriculture. The form of food production that relies most heavily on technological means for harnessing energy, such as fossil fuels and hydroelectric power rather than human or animal labor, is **industrialized agriculture**. Currently, its tool kit includes motorized equipment such as tillers, tractors, and harvesters. Chemical fertilizers are used to enhance the productivity of the soil, herbicides are used to minimize unwanted plants that compete with crops for water and soil nutrients, and pesticides play an important role in minimizing crop destruction by insects. Industrialized agriculturalists not only irrigate their fields, but also may employ various techniques for modifying the effects of adverse weather conditions—for instance, by shading crops or artificially maintaining higher temperatures around their plants during periods of cold weather.

Industrialized agricultural techniques create high yields with relatively little investment of human labor. On the other hand, they are techniques that are very inefficient in terms of the ratio of energy used to produce food to the number of calories yielded. By comparison, in horticulture, human labor is intense, but represents almost the entire investment of energy for producing food. In preindustrialized agriculture, human labor is supplemented by the work of draft animals such as oxen whose upkeep and the costs of manufacturing tools such as the plow results in a much greater investment in producing each year's crop. Industrialized agriculture carries this to an extreme. In addition to human labor on the farm, it requires the work of specialists who manufacture and maintain farm equipment, petroleum products such as gasoline and oil to fuel the equipment, and chemical fertilizers, herbicides, and pesticides to increase yields. There are also costs in transporting produce to factories, in packaging the food, in delivering the packaged goods to markets, and in marketing them. Susan Brown and J. Clair Batty (1976) estimated that the energy to produce, process, package, transport, market, purchase, prepare, and eat a single can of corn that contained 269 calories of digestible food energy could easily require the expenditure of 5384 calories of energy by the time the dishwasher finished running. Thus, industrialized agriculture is tremendously productive in that a small number of people are able to provide enough food to support a large population, but extremely inefficient in requiring much more energy to produce per calorie than do production systems that rely on human and animal labor. Industrialized agriculture also has other costs in its long-term impact on the environment. For instance, pesticides can migrate from the fields to

industrialized agriculture the use of an industrialized technology and other techniques such as chemical soil fertilization to obtain high levels of food production per acre which they are applied into the ground water and neighboring streams, where they can adversely affect humans and other animals. Industrialized farm equipment can also cause faster loss of topsoil than pre-industrialized farming.

High-yield production techniques, coupled with an industrialized system of transportation to carry the produce over great distances, have made possible the rise of farms of tremendous acreage. An industrialized agriculture nevertheless operates at great costs, when one measures the amount of energy required to produce food. But it is so productive that in the United States less than 3 percent of the population is involved in food production.

Societies whose subsistence technology is industrialized agriculture invariably support sufficiently large populations that they must be organized by full-time governments that monopolize political power. The populations commonly number in the millions or hundreds of millions. Indeed, individual cities in industrialized societies may number in the tens of millions.

CHAPTER SUMMARY

1. Natural environments place limits on the characteristics of the cultures that societies have developed in different parts of the world.

2. Each environment contains the particular resources that a society may use to meet its people's survival needs.

3. The use of some resources provides opportunities for the development of large social groups and tremendous social complexity, while the use of others may severely restrict the size and complexity of a society.

4. One traditional way of categorizing the world's natural environments divides the world into nine basic habitats: mixed forests, scrub forests, tropical forests, mountain lands, grasslands, arid lands, boreal forests, and polar lands.

5. Each of these environments has a unique set of resources that provide opportunities and set limits on cultural development.

6. In adapting to the world's various environments, human societies have developed a variety of subsistence technologies, including foraging, horticulture, pastoralism, traditional agriculture, and industrialized agriculture.

ANNOTATED READINGS

Cohen, Y. (Ed.). (1974). *Man in adaptation: The cultural present.* Chicago: Aldine. A collection of articles about the environmental adaptations of pastoral and farming societies.

Douglas, M., & Isherwood, B. (1979). *The world of goods: Toward an anthropology of consumption.* New York: W. W. Norton. Discusses economic theories of consumption and how anthropologists might study consumption.

Harris, M. (1986). *Good to eat.* New York: Harper & Row. A collection of essays on the reasons for cultural differences in what is eaten, by the founder of the cultural materialistic approach to studying culture.

James, P. E. (with collaboration by Hibberd V. B. Kline, Jr.). (1959). *A geography of man.* Boston: Ginn. One of the major and influential attempts to classify the world's major natural environments.

Kroeber, A. (1939). *Cultural and natural areas of native North America.* University of California Publications in American Archaeology and Ethnology, vol. 38. The first systematic anthropological demonstration of the relationships between cultural areas and natural environments.

Lustig-Arecco, V. (1975). *Technology: Strategies for survival.* New York: Holt, Rinehart & Winston. An examination of the role of technology in the adaptation of hunters, pastoralists, and farmers.

Rappaport, R. (1967). *Pigs for the ancestors: Ritual in the ecology of a Papua New Guinea people.* New Haven, CT: Yale University Press. A cultural ecological analysis of the Tsembaga Maring that emphasizes the role of pig herding as a regulatory mechanism in Tsembaga warfare.

Vayda, A. (Ed.). (1969). *Environment and cultural behavior: Ecological studies in cultural anthropology.* New York: Natural History Press. A classic collection of writings that illustrates the cultural ecological approach to understanding human customs in the social, demographic, and environmental contexts in which they are found.

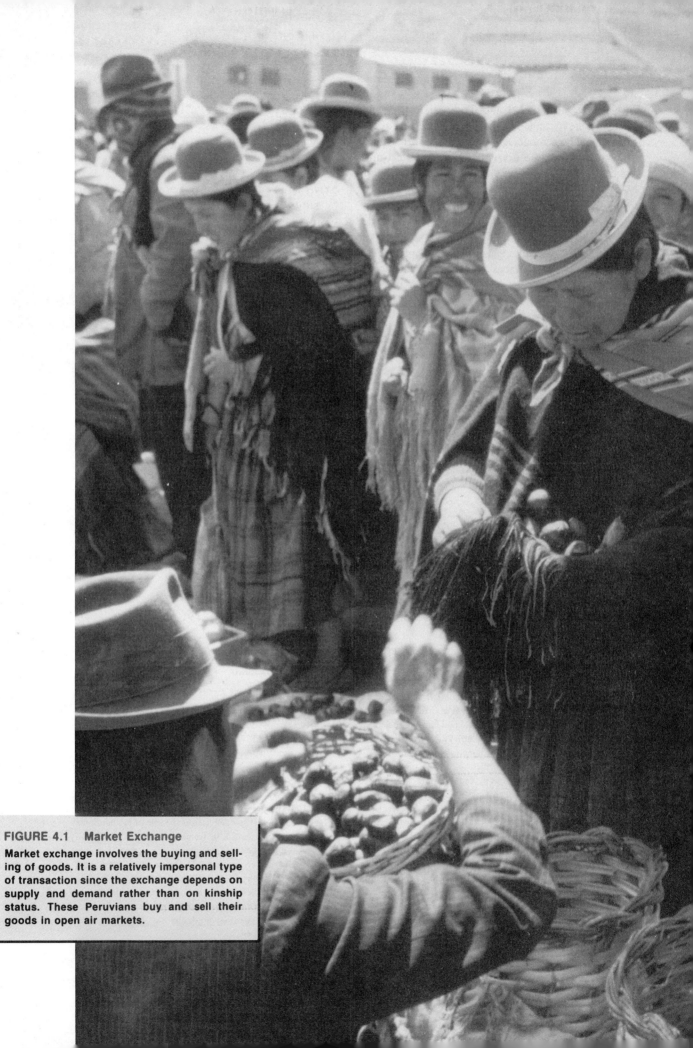

FIGURE 4.1   Market Exchange

Market exchange involves the buying and selling of goods. It is a relatively impersonal type of transaction since the exchange depends on supply and demand rather than on kinship status. These Peruvians buy and sell their goods in open air markets.

CHAPTER 4

Economics

In this chapter we will discuss how economic systems work in different societies. We will first examine how cultures define what they value as a potential economic commodity. We will consider how the relative values of commodities may vary from culture to culture, how cultural values as well as survival needs may influence the level of demand that may exist for a given commodity, and how cultures differ in the motives that are defined as normal reasons for economic exchanges. Economic systems will then be examined in terms of cultural differences in the control and use of resources, the production of valued goods and services, and in the distribution and consumption of goods and services.

CHAPTER OBJECTIVES

After reading this chapter, you should be able to:

Define elements of an economic system.

Explain the role of culture in the definition of commodities and in the determination of their economic value.

Explain the roles of use rights and the ownership of resources in the process of economic production.

Discuss the concept of division of labor in the context of economic production.

Define the three forms of economic distribution—reciprocity, redistribution, and markets.

Relate the forms of economic distribution to the four societal types—bands, tribes, chiefdoms, and states.

Compare and contrast subsistence economies and consumer economies.

Define status income and explain its economic functions.

Discuss the four systems of economic control—community, kin, association, and social class.

Relate the four systems of economic control to the four societal types.

Yen. Pieces of eight. Bull market. Penny candy. How long do you think you or your family could survive if you had to grow all the fruit and vegetables you needed? Or how many cows do you think you could raise on a tiny balcony on a high-rise apartment on the East Side of New York City? What kind of house do you think you'd live in if you had to build your own from the resources available in your immediate area? If your neighbor had more trees than you did and you had more chickens, what system would you devise to exchange the items you both need?

Definition of Economic Systems

The system by which people obtain or produce, distribute, and consume valued material goods and services is called economics. An economic system includes the subsistence customs that are most especially concerned with the production of needed goods that we discussed in the previous chapter, as well as the rules that govern what is done with those goods and how they are used. In this chapter, we will examine in more detail how people organize themselves socially to facilitate the production, exchange, and use of goods and services.

The Cultural Definition of Commodity

Cultures differ in what they define as useful or valuable, that is, as commodities. People work to produce food, provide themselves with shelter, and defend and reproduce themselves in all cultures.

However, as was pointed out in the discussion of culture, the specific goods and services that constitute food, shelter, or means of defense differ from society to society. For instance, milk and dairy products were unacceptable foods in traditional Oriental cultures, while North Americans reject the use of dog or snake meat, both of which are eaten in various parts of the Orient. These differences may be accounted for in part by an extension of the principle that underlies the concept of optimal foraging theory discussed in the previous chapter. Essentially, this is the idea that people work in order to obtain the greatest return from their efforts. Although few would argue with such a principle in general, it alone is not sufficient to account for the diversity of things that people endow with economic value throughout the world. For instance, nowhere do people rely on one food alone, as an overzealous application of this rule would imply. We also seek variety in our diets and even expend extra effort on special occasions to obtain and prepare an unusual delicacy.

Cultural differences are even greater when we consider the range of variation that exists in pleasurable activities that are not mandated by survival needs. Consider, for instance, art, recreation, and religion. Although each category is a cultural universal, and even though the psychological principles that guide people's behavior in each category may also be universal, the specific behaviors and objects people find beautiful, sacred, or fun are not readily predictable.

---

economics system by which people obtain or produce, distribute, and consume material goods and services
commodities goods, services, and intangible items that are determined to be useful or valuable in a particular culture

---

Coca Tea in Bolivia

What is an economic resource in one society can be seen as a public danger in another. Nathaniel Nash (1992), a *New York Times* correspondent, recently illustrated this in a story about coca leaf production in Bolivia, a cash-poor country that desperately needs to generate new exports as sources of income. Bolivian President Jaime Paz Zamora hopes to create an international market for coca tea and other

Aymara

In El Alto, Bolivia, the Aymara Indians are trying to market products made from coca leaves. They claim that such items as tea, toothpaste, creams, and tonics, all made from coca leaves, are beneficial to health. In their cash-starved economy, the Aymara could make more profit from the practical uses of coca leaves than from their illegal use in the drug trade.

Bolivia as a solution to the cocaine problem in other countries such as the United States. But growing coca leaves can produce more income for Bolivian farmers than other crops, so efforts to eliminate them have failed. In fact, it is ironic that the sale of coca products might actually undermine cocaine trade by encouraging coca production for its more lucrative legitimate uses. According to Bolivian experts, in an international market for coca tea, coca leaves would command about seven and a half times the price that Bolivian farmers can obtain by using them to produce cocaine for drug traffickers. Thus, acceptance of coca tea as a legitimate commodity for export could price the drug trade out of the market.

products manufactured from coca leaves. Coca leaves produce a soothing and aromatic tea that is a mild stimulant with none of the addictive or intoxicating effects of cocaine. Bolivians use it as a remedy for headaches, nausea, and weakness. Entrepreneurs have been trying to market other coca products, including toothpaste, creams, and tonics.

Because most of the world is more familiar with cocaine than with coca's other products, foreign governments have not been very receptive to the idea of marketing coca leaves internationally. At Expo '92 in Seville, for example, the Spanish government confiscated 20 pounds of coca leaves that the Bolivians hoped would demonstrate the many uses of coca. Still, a month later, the Bolivian president asked the World Health Organization in Geneva to study the possible medical and nutritional uses of coca. His hope is to have coca removed from a list of products that must be tightly controlled by governments, so that it can be exported and sold more readily.

In the past, there have been efforts to eliminate the production of coca leaves in

FIGURE 4.2 Cultural Commodities
What one culture considers valuable, another may not. The Aymara Indians of Bolivia are attempting to market products made from coca leaves, the raw ingredient of cocaine, to boost their economy. Two *yatiri*, or fortune tellers, Valentin Quispe, right, and Gregorio Quinteros, toss coca leaves to predict their future. It is bad luck if the leaves fall on the white side, good luck if they fall on the green side.

Intangible property. Cultural variation in the definition of commodities to be produced, exchanged, and consumed is not limited to tangible things. Intangibles, too, may be defined as commodities. Navajos, for example, consider the sacred chants used in their curing ceremonies to be personal property, and an individual must pay an appropriate price to be taught a chant known to another. Northwest Coast Indians of North America considered titles of nobility to be a form of property, the ownership of which had to be validated by gift giving. North Americans also assert ownership over the expression of ideas and songs in their copyright laws.

The Cultural Definition of Value

Cultures also differ in how much value they place on any commodity. The same things are not of equal worth everywhere. The sacred zebu cow of Hindu India would not command a high price at a North American cattle auction, and the dogs that so many North Americans esteem as household pets are seen as too dirty to be pets by Iranians I have known.

Supply and demand as a cultural construct. A good illustration of how culture determines the value of commodities is the law of supply and demand so widely discussed in American marketing as if it were a law of nature that operates uninfluenced by culture. Such a view of supply and demand overlooks the fact that the value of a commodity is, in many cases, culturally defined. Sahlins (1976), for instance, has pointed out that cut for cut, meat in American culture is priced higher the less closely the animal from which it comes is symbolically associated with human beings. Thus, dogs are named and live within the house like one of the family, so the eating of their meat, though perfectly nutritious, is tabooed. Horses, too, are named, but they live outside the house and work for people like servants instead of living with them as kin. Americans somewhat grudgingly admit that horses are edible, but are not commonly eaten in the United States. Pigs and cattle are clearly defined as foods, but the pig, which lives closer to the human domain as a barnyard animal and scavenger of human food scraps, usually commands a lower market price than the cow. It must be remembered that Sahlins's theory cannot be applied directly to other cultures, nor to all cultures of the United States in the early 1990s, a time when the price of pork is higher than that of beef in at least

FIGURE 4.3   Chinese Market
Cultures place different values on the type of goods they use and the food they eat. North Americans enjoy their hamburger and fries whereas Indians protect their cows as sacred and let them roam freely through the streets. Dogs and cats are popular pets in North America, yet are hung as food to be sold in this Chinese market.

some parts of the country and at certain times of the year. But the underlying idea that the desirability of an animal as food is inversely related to its symbolic closeness to humans still applies, at least *generally*, to most American food tastes.

The profit motive as a cultural construct. In the United States, people often speak of the profit motive as a basic economic incentive. Indeed, one theme of this text has been that material benefits are important predictors of customs. However, the profit motive concept is often used in an overly narrow sense, one that implies that *material* benefit is the sole motivator in economic transactions. This extreme view, common in American society, overlooks the important role of culture in defining value. Efforts to obtain valued commodities are not limited to the acquisition of material things. People also work to obtain intangible goods. For instance, people may willingly accept material loss for spiritual merit or for increased social honor such as prestige, respect, admiration, personal honor, mana, luck, or a reward after death. Thus, when the profit motive is understood as nothing more than the claim that people will always try to maximize their immediate material gain in any exchange of goods, it is understood much too narrowly.

Kwakiutl Bartering: Bidding Up the Price

A narrow, materialistic view of the profit motive can make customs in which people seek to enhance their social rank and reputation at material cost seem irrational. Consider for example the case of the Kwakiutl, whose potlatch giveaway competitions were described in chapter 2. For the Kwakiutl, prestige was a major factor to be considered in important economic transactions. After all, paying too low a price could mark one as poor, and selling high could merit the reputation of stinginess. The hallmark of Kwakiutl bartering was for the buyers to insist on paying a price high enough so that their honor was enhanced. One such transaction was the exchange of blankets for a *copper*, an engraved flat piece of metal which was a major symbol of wealth among the Kwakiutl. Benedict (1934) describes a purchase in which the buyers began with an offer that represented only a fraction of the copper's worth. Then the seller, praising himself, demanded more and more, reminding the would-be buyers that the price must reflect the current owner's greatness. Each demand was accepted by the buyers, until finally the seller was satisfied with a presentation of blankets, beautiful boxes to put them in, and three canoes, the entire offer valued at four thousand blankets:

> The owner answered, "I take the price." But it was not done. The purchaser now addressed the owner of the copper, saying: "Why, have you taken the price, chief? You take the price too soon. You must think poorly of me, chief. I am a

> Kwakiutl, I am one of those from whom all your tribes all over the world took their names. You must always stand beneath us." He sent his messengers to call his sister, his princess, and gave to his rivals two hundred blankets more, [a final payment known as] "the clothes of his princess." (p. 197)

By paying more than the seller had been willing to accept, the buyer's honor was enhanced by his demonstration of wealth. From examples such as this we can see that the old British advice, "Buy cheap, sell dear," would not be a useful guide to the practice of trade in every culture.

(see reference map p. 34)

Production: The Control and Use of Resources

Just because a resource is available to people does not mean that they have the right to use it. In every culture, the right to exploit resources is divided up among the members of a society based on concepts such as use rights and ownership.

Use Rights

The right to use a resource may belong to individuals or groups. For instance, according to Allan Holmberg (1950), the Sirionó, who (before they adopted a sedentary lifestyle based on agriculture) were a nomadic hunting people of eastern Bolivia, marked wild fruit trees with a notch as a sign that their finders had claimed the right to harvest the fruit for at least the current season. The Waorani, who are horticultural villagers in Ecuador, have more complex customs concerning the ownership of wild trees. They value the fruit of the wild chonta palm, but the trunk is impossible to climb because it is ringed with spiky thorns. When a wild chonta palm is discovered, its finder claims it by planting a cecropia tree next to it. Years later, when the cecropia is large enough, the owner harvests the chonta fruit by climbing the cecropia. The fruit is shared with other members of the village, but the chonta is considered to be owned by its finder, and is even inherited by the families of its original discoverer.

The right to use a resource may also be based on such social status characteristics as rank, age, or sex. Use right may be allocated by rules such as "first come, first served." This is common, for instance, among seminomadic foragers where it is more efficient for each group to simply begin its foraging in a location that is not already being used than to compete with others who began their work first. Another example of use rights is the treatment of beaches on the east coast of the United States, where only those who own or rent a cottage on or near the shore have the right to use the adjacent beach.

Ownership

The right to use and the right to deny use rights to others temporarily is called **ownership**, a right that is held even when it is not being exercised. Thus, people are expected to obtain permission to use property owned by others. Ownership itself can be given, bought, or sold.

ownership   the right to use property and the right to deny use rights to others as long as one owns the property

---

Shoshoni vs. Pioneer Concepts of Land in the Great Basin

The aboriginal Shoshoni of the United States Great Basin were a foraging people who occupied a desert environment. Their territory was a sparse land with food resources that supported only about one person per 50 square miles. So their society was fragmented into small groups. Throughout most of the year, the Shoshoni wandered in search of food in family groups of only four or five people. When families happened upon one another in their nomadic quest for food, they might visit and even cooperate in communal net hunts if one of the families had a net, and if they were lucky enough to have come together when large enough numbers of jackrabbits were also in

Shoshoni

The aboriginal Shoshoni were a foraging people who occupied a desert environment in the Great Basin of the United States. They valued the land as something that should be used and shared by all people, not owned by any individual group.

the area. Luck of that kind, however, was the exception rather than the rule. Most of the time it was more economical to remain distant enough from other families so as not to compete for the same limited resources. Naturally, the Shoshoni conception of their relationship to the land was not one of ownership. Instead, they thought of themselves as merely users of the resources within their native lands, and the right to use a resource could not be permanently owned by a migratory people who, throughout most of the year, had to be continually on the move in order to survive. The Shoshoni culture's rule governing the control of natural resources might be translated as "first come, first served."

In the 1840s, Mormon pioneers entered the Great Basin as settlers, bringing with them an agricultural technology. Their way of life was a sedentary one that exploited the ability of the soil to raise planted crops in enough abundance to support large, permanent populations. These farmers have a different relationship to the land than migratory foragers. Farmers who live in permanent houses near the fields they plan to work for years have a special attachment to the land. They expect to own the food they produce, and the idea of ownership of land rather than temporary use rights is a likely part of their culture's ideology.

In many parts of frontier America, there was a natural conflict between these two different concepts of the human relationship to nature. In the Great Basin, the conflict took a special twist. Mormon pioneers sought to avoid the direct hostility that had occurred elsewhere when arriving settlers had simply taken possession of land by force. Under a motto of "Better to feed the Indians than to fight them," many of the immigrants offered to "buy" agricultural land from the Shoshoni. The Shoshoni took the goods offered them willingly and went on their way. The Mormon farmers were bemused when the Shoshoni returned a year or so later and tried to "sell" them the same land again.

As might be expected, the Shoshoni view of the matter was quite different. To them the land was not something to be owned, bought, or sold. They had merely given up their temporary use rights to the foreigners in return for the goods given to them. Imagine their surprise when they again passed through their traditional hunting lands and found that the foreigners had not merely passed through but had settled down, fencing the land, and even hoarding the food they got from it. The Shoshoni regarded this as a most improper way of acting, for they valued the act of sharing and looked upon generosity as a defining quality of human beings.

Division of Labor

Production is never accomplished by requiring everyone to perform the same work. In all societies that anthropologists have visited, the labor of production is divided up by age and gender. In horticultural and pastoral societies, one also finds the beginnings of occupational specialization by age, gender, and group. Specialization becomes increasingly important the larger and denser the local groups become; it is particularly important in large industrialized societies throughout the world today.

Age and gender. Where specialization is limited to age and gender differences, the various productive forms of work are thought of as simply roles that males and females of various ages play as members of their families and local groups. Work as an activity is not divorced from one's family or community relationships and is not thought of as a specialized activity to be done for hire. Children are socialized to help the adults in their productive activities and are gradually given greater responsibilities in these tasks until they achieve adult proficiency. In most societies, the contributions of children add to the total productive resources of the family. The most productive years tend to be from puberty until the beginning of old age, when intensive work efforts are often replaced by more organizational and managerial roles.

It is common in societies throughout the world for gender differences in the division of labor to be based on the expectation that routine and domestic labor will be done by women and the heavier and nondomestic labor will be done by men. For example, men are more often expected to hunt the larger game animals, fish in offshore waters, herd large animals, clear the land in preparation for planting, do the heavier work of house construction, and manufacture stone and metal implements as well as tradegoods. Women frequently cooperate in communal hunts of smaller game, gather aquatic foods near the shores, herd smaller animals, weed and harvest gardens, take primary charge of domestic chores such as cooking and childrearing, weave textiles and make pottery. However, these common ways of dividing up the work of men and women are certainly not the only conceivable ones, and they are not necessarily rigidly enforced where they are the usual ones. There are many societies that assign individual activities to women and men differently than most do. For instance, among the Toda of southern India, men prepare the meals; among the Dani of New Guinea, men are the weavers of household textiles; and among the Great Basin Shoshoni where men were nominally called the hunters, women actually did most of the work during the communal rabbit hunts. So, although common physiological differences often may play a part in defining the roles of men and women, it is clear that biology does not control economic gender roles in any fixed or necessary way.

Occupational specialization. In societies without domesticated food resources, work tends to be unspecialized except by age and gender. Limited specialization exists only to the degree that certain individuals may devote more of their time than others do to specialized tasks such as basket making or weaving. The products of their labor are then exchanged for other things that they need.

Specialization by group. In food-producing societies, entire groups may also specialize in producing crops indigenous to their environment, which they then exchange for other foods they need. Thus, in the Andean empire of the ancient Inca civilization, villagers who lived between sea level and 11,000 feet grew maize and potatoes. Between 11,000 and 14,000 feet, potatoes were the primary crop. Above 14,000 feet, villagers specialized in raising llamas, alpacas, and quinoa, a grain that was capable of growing at high altitudes. The specialized crops of different altitudes could be easily transported from one part of the empire to another with the aid of llamas as pack animals.

Social groups such as families or age mates may also work together in some specialized productive activity. So for example, among the pig-herding Tsembaga Maring who were discussed in chapter 3, children and young adults specialized in tending the pigs, while adults worked the fields to produce root crops such as sweet potatoes.

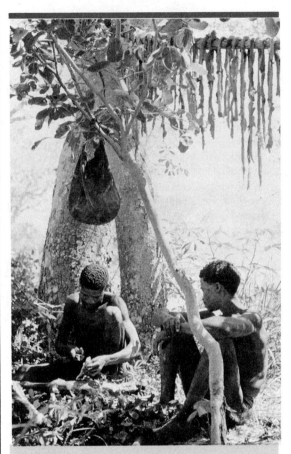

FIGURE 4.4 Reciprocity
Social interdependence in most hunter-gatherer societies is the basis for reciprocity, the giving and taking of goods without the exchange of money. These San hunters are drying strips of meat before distributing them to others.

Distribution

The movement of resources or goods from where they are found or produced to where they will be used is referred to as **distribution**. There are three major economic systems by which distribution is controlled: reciprocity, redistribution, and market.

Reciprocity

The system of exchange in which goods or services are passed from one individual or group to another as gifts without the need for explicit contracting for specific payment is called **reciprocity**. Unlike buying and selling, reciprocity does not involve bargaining over what is to be given in return. There is merely the understanding that the sharing is mutual and will be eventually evenhanded.

Reciprocity is the sole form of economic distribution in bands and tribes, where the small number of people in each local community makes gift giving a sufficient procedure to meet everyone's economic needs. The mutual sharing of surpluses in the form of reciprocal gift giving within the local community equalizes wealth and eliminates lean times for individual members. The trait of generosity, so characteristic of band peoples, is actually a very effective economic device for ensuring the survival of the entire group. When a hunter shares excess food after

---

distribution movement of resources or goods from where they are found or produced to where they will ultimately be used

reciprocity sharing of surpluses with the understanding that the party receiving the gift will respond in kind in the future a successful hunt, for example, it is a kind of insurance against future times of need. Every hunter is bound to experience some periods of poor luck in the chase. Those with whom a hunter has shared food or other useful goods in the past will make return gifts of their own later surpluses to ensure the continuation of his good will in the future. In the long run, the economic system of reciprocity maintains a balance in the distribution of goods. No one prospers at the expense of others, but neither does anyone need fear the specter of starving alone during the inevitable periods of personal failure or illness when hunting is not possible.

The enforcement of reciprocity is based primarily on the desire of the participants not to be excluded, rather than on formal sanctions. So long as everyone involved participates to everyone else's satisfaction, the rules of the exchange do not even need to be discussed. However, a group or individual that fails to engage in a fair share of gift giving may be censured or excluded by the others. In economically more complex societies, reciprocity is found within families and between acquaintances, and it typically involves symbolic goods and services such as holiday greeting cards or parties; in very simple societies, the gifts that are shared may be life-sustaining ones, such as food. In such cases, participation is likely to be self-enforcing even if it is not mandatory, since exclusion from the system may be life-threatening. As noted by Sahlins (1972), reciprocity takes three basic forms: generalized reciprocity, balanced reciprocity, and negative reciprocity.

Generalized reciprocity.   Gifts given with no expectation of immediate exchange are part of **generalized reciprocity**. The persons involved are most likely to be motivated by a sense of obligation toward the welfare of the others. For instance, in families, goods and services are provided for children by their parents even though the children may not reciprocate in kind even later in life. Generalized reciprocity may also be exemplified by the care that is given to elderly or incapacitated people who are unable to respond with a return of goods or services of equal value.

The feeling of obligation that minimizes an expectation of an immediate return of favors can be based on a sense of community as well as on the bonds of kinship. In foraging societies, generalized reciprocity is the basic economic mechanism for ensuring that everyone within the local community, nonrelatives included, is provided for. Where gener-

alized reciprocity is practiced, generosity is likely to be an expected characteristic of normal behavior. Thus, for example, in the language of the foraging Shoshoni of the intermountain region of the United States, the word *dzaande* meant both *good* and *generous*. The good human was a generous person, and since generosity in sharing was understood to be a natural attribute of the normal person rather than an unexpected or surprising behavior, no word or phrase existed that was equivalent to the English "Thank you!" Similarly, although Apache and Navajo, spoken in the southwestern desert of the United States, did have a word, *eehe'he*, with which to express thanks, it was used only for extremely valuable goods or services such as a gift of a horse or to thank someone for having saved your life. To say thanks in response to other forms of sharing, such as food or the offer of overnight hospitality to strangers caught in a storm, would have implied that the gift was unexpected—a possibly deadly insult among a people who considered generosity to be practiced by any normal human.

Balanced reciprocity.   Between persons who lack a sense of kinship or obligation to help one another with no expectation of return, but who each have something that the other would like to have, **balanced reciprocity** is likely to occur, in which a return gift is expected within a relatively short time. Although the bond between the two parties is not so great as is present where generalized reciprocity is practiced, the desire to maintain good relations is great enough that haggling over the exchange is not necessary, since both parties try to respond with something of equal value. Balanced reciprocity is commonly practiced by members of neighboring communities that each specialize in the production of different goods or that control different resources. Even without direct bargaining, balanced reciprocity may be maintained to the benefit of both groups. At appropriate opportunities each group gives what it has in surplus to recipients known to desire such a commodity. Although no immediate return is demanded, the gratefulness of the recipients and their continued interest in the commodity will ensure that

generalized reciprocity   gift given with no expectation of immediate exchange
balanced reciprocity   gift given with expectation of a return gift shortly

FIGURE 4.5   Balanced Reciprocity
A more immediate exchange of goods and services is expected in a system of balanced reciprocity. These Mennonite farmers spend their time and labor helping their neighbor in a traditional barn raising with the expectation that they each will also be helped when the need arises.

they will reciprocate within a reasonable time with gifts of their own.

Balanced reciprocity <u>may include the exchange of services as well as goods.</u> For instance, the Quechua-speaking peoples of the South American Andes in pre-Spanish times had a concept of reciprocal work obligations between communities known as the *mink'a*. Members of a *mink'a* group cooperated in performing difficult work such as harvesting, canal repair, or housebuilding. American *barn raisings* and *harvest bees* of frontier days were a similar form of balanced reciprocity of services.

Probably the most organized example of balanced reciprocity of both goods and services in a complex society operated within the caste system in India. In each local community, individuals were organized into a system of occupations deemed appropriate to members of the various castes. This *jati system* provided for the economic needs of all mem-

bers of the community because each person was obligated to provide goods or services to everyone else. The miller ground grain for all of the farmers, while the farmers provided some of the food they produced to all members of the community. The barber cut hair, and the weaver gave gifts of fabric to other members of the community. Each occupation benefited others without direct and immediate payment, and so long as everyone received as well as gave, the needs of all could be met.

The Kula Ring

Malinowski (1922) described the classic example of balanced reciprocity in his account of the Kula ring, a ceremonial exchange system between members of a ring of islands in

Melanesia. In Kula trade, there were only two kinds of valuables that were exchanged: long, red shell necklaces called *soulava* and white shell bracelets called *mwali*. Both were passed from island to island around the ring as the necklaces were traded for the bracelets. The necklaces moved only clockwise around the islands and the bracelets were traded only counterclockwise.

The necklaces and bracelets exchanged in the Kula ring were objects of prestige that gave evidence of their owners' participation in the Kula system. Each necklace or bracelet carried with it a personal history of its past ownership, so, like an heirloom, its value increased with age. Each owner kept a particular necklace or bracelet only for a year or so and then gave it as a gift to a trade partner. Men who participated in Kula expeditions had specific trade partners on islands in either direction. When they traveled on a Kula expedition, they were received as honored guests by their partners, and bracelets and necklaces were given ceremoniously with appropriate ritual speeches accompanying each bestowal. If, at that time, a partner had no object of equivalent prestige, it was understood that he was expected to work to acquire an appropriate gift to give in return on a later expedition.

Uberoi (1962) has discussed a number of social functions of the Kula ring. For instance, since the exchange of Kula valuables was a form of balanced reciprocity, trade partners should not profit at one another's expense from the exchange. What then motivated the islanders to participate in the long and sometimes dangerous sea voyages that the Kula ring required? Certainly there was an element of socializing and entertainment in the process. The Kula gift giving helped to maintain an amicable relationship between long-standing trade partners from different islands. Trading partnerships were inherited by another family member at the death of a partner and thus perpetuated friendly relationships over the generations among residents of potentially competing islands. Trading expeditions kept alive the traditions of the islands as the gift-givers recited the histories and legends associated with each Kula item bestowed.

Over time new participants were introduced into the Kula exchange system. Scoditti (1983) noted that younger men took part in

Kula Ring

An example of balanced reciprocity, Kula trade took place in the islands of Melanesia. Two kinds of valuables were exchanged: red shell necklaces and white shell bracelets. The Kula exchange enhanced the prestige of the traders and guaranteed that trading partners would be available in the long run.

Kula expeditions after they had been given necklaces or armbands by relatives or in return for building canoes. Of course, the necklaces and armbands received in this way were likely to be among the less prestigious ones. With frequent and long participation, the reputation of younger traders could rise as they acquired more valued armbands and necklaces. Campbell (1983) suggested that possession of valuable Kula objects also symbolized high social rank, since the most valued items were usually owned by the more experienced participants who were good navigators, respected expedition organizers, and—in earlier times—successful warriors.

Finally, Kula expeditions were occasions for practical as well as ceremonial exchanges. Foodstuffs, tools, and other items of economic importance were bartered by participants in the expedition to the benefit of all. Since the islands in the ring specialized in the production of different commodities, the Kula ring played an important economic role in the lives of its participants, even though it appeared to have only ceremonial significance.

Negative reciprocity. When at least one group or individual in a reciprocal exchange system attempts to get more than it gives, we speak of **negative reciprocity**. Negative reciprocity varies from simple miserliness or "Yankee shrewdness" on the part of one participant, through deceit in bargaining, to outright theft; the profit motive takes precedence over generosity. This form of reciprocity is most common among strangers within the same communities or members of different communities, especially those that differ in cultures. The traditional Apache raiding of their more sedentary neighbors exemplifies a pattern of negative reciprocity in which the neighboring groups were viewed not so much as enemies to be exterminated as a kind of resource to be exploited.

One of the most interesting examples of negative reciprocity that has been noted by ethnographers is a form called *silent trade*. In this kind of exchange, there need be no direct interaction between the trading partners once the relationship is established. Each simply leaves surplus goods known to be of use to the other at a place where they will be found. Each occasionally checks the cache site to see if anything has been left and, if so, leaves something near the offered goods. The original party may consummate the exchange by taking the goods left near the offered commodities, or may refuse to do so to indicate that the amount left by the second party was insufficient. In the latter case, the second party may add to the goods left behind or may simply retrieve them to call off the transaction. The Mbuti Pygmy foragers of the Ituri Forest carried out trade of this kind with horticultural villagers who lived outside the forest. In return for garden produce, iron knives, and pots the Mbuti partner would leave game and other forest foods. Similar silent trade has been noted in a variety of other cultures in different parts of the world, such as the Semang foragers and Malay farmers of the Malay Peninsula. Silent trade was a particularly useful form of barter among neighboring groups that did not speak a common language.

Redistribution

The second major economic system for the distribution of goods and services is **redistribution, where commodities are contributed by all members of the social group to a common pool from which they are then distributed to where they will be used.** While reciprocity is a two-party affair involving givers and receivers, redistribution requires an intermediary, a third party who coordinates the process and exercises control over the flow of goods and services. The mediating individual or group is likely to gain both prestige and power from the position of control over whatever is exchanged in this economic system. Examples of systems of economic redistribution in complex societies include taxation, social security, retirement funds, unemployment compensation, and insurance.

Redistribution, like reciprocity, is an economic practice within families around the world, occurring when their members save for a common goal. However, as a major societal mechanism within the economic system beyond the family, redistribution is not present in all societies. Service (1962) believes that redistribution developed in sedentary agricultural societies that occupied distinctly different ecological zones in which local residents specialized in producing certain types of food.

Harris (1974) also ties the rise in importance of redistribution to the presence of food domestication, but he thinks that yearly differences in productivity rather than local specialization is the central cause. He sees redistribution as merely part of a larger set of economic practices that encourage food growers to work hard enough to produce surpluses in most years. The extra produce is normally channeled to a production manager who redistributes the goods. The underlying payoff in such a system comes in lean years when climatic conditions or other crises lead to poorer than expected harvests. Furthermore, neighboring communities are not always affected by the same difficulties and may lend a helping hand at such times, if they have been beneficiaries of the suffering community's previous redistributive investments.

Those who manage the redistribution of goods and services are typically rewarded with prestige and sometimes with power and wealth. Anthropologists have been particularly interested in two kinds of redistribution managers found in societies of middle-range complexity: big men and chiefs.

Bigmanship. The economic entrepreneurs of horticultural societies are men and women who

---

negative reciprocity one group or individual in a reciprocal exchange system attempts to get more than it gives

redistribution commodities are contributed by all members of a group to a common pool from which they will be distributed to where they will be used

FIGURE 4.6   Redistribution
A hierarchical organization is the most efficient means of distributing surplus goods and services in large communities. The items are first brought or sent to a central area from where they are distributed. This system is depicted on a frieze at Persepolis where these Persians are bringing goods and livestock to the king.

engage in **bigmanship**, economic production and gift giving to achieve public recognition and respect. These "big men" and "big women" are not true officials who have power to demand the cooperation of others; rather they are prominent individuals within their community, charismatic leaders who encourage relatives and other members of their community to follow their lead in the production of surplus goods. Then a festive gathering of conspicuous generosity and hospitality that promotes the prestige of the host group and its entrepreneur is held for followers of other economic leaders.

bigmanship economic entrepreneurship by persons in horticulture societies who encourage economic production and gift giving in their communities to achieve public recognition and respect

Big Women in the Trobriand Islands

When Annette Weiner studied the Trobrianders, she found that women as well as men obtained prestige and social power through the production and distribution of wealth. Men carve, garden, and fish; women manufacture and control red skirts and banana-leaf bundles that are important forms of wealth.

According to Weiner, "Skirts and bundles have economic value, and their major use as payment to mourners after a death directly incorporates the wealth of men" (1988, p. 28). Men provide their sisters with yams from their gardens that economically benefit the sisters' husbands, since yams are a form of wealth used by Trobriand men to achieve status. A man's entire kin group is obligated to repay this debt to his wife's family when he dies in the form of gift giving which consists of the skirts and banana-leaf bundles that women own because they symbolize the wealth and status of the widows' relatives. Thus, the giveaways that are sponsored by women are even more important than those of men.

Weiner describes vividly the first women's bigmanship competition she observed:

As we entered the village, no one paid attention to yams or even to the men who were cooking. All the excitement was being generated by the activities coming from the central plaza, where hundreds of women sat or stood surrounded by as many baskets; I saw that the baskets were filled with something I had never read or heard about—banana-leaf bundles.

Women were completely involved in sorting out their bundles and arranging

Trobriand Women

In the region of Papua New Guinea, women of the Trobriand Islands gain social power and prestige through the manufacture and control of red skirts and banana-leaf bundles, which are important forms of wealth.

piles of red fiber skirts. One woman seemed to be in charge, and she continually took bundles into the center, threw them on the ground, and called out someone's name. Other women rushed to the center, adding their bundles to the pile. Finally, another woman gathered them all up and carried them to her own basket. The same throwing and retrieving went on for hours. Sometimes the pile was small, with only about thirty bundles; at other times several hundred were given, with ten or so skirts thrown on top. Women laughed and shouted among themselves; occasionally they argued over a particular distribution. A few women insisted that I throw down some bundles myself, and I was told, 'Our bundles are just like your money.'

. . . Although men did not participate in any of the action in the center of the village, they remained in the village throughout the day, sitting on the house verandas and casually watching the proceedings. When the distribution finally was over, however, they then entered the plaza to give yams to those women who now stood with empty baskets. (1988, pp. 29–30)

The importance of women's bigmanship activities is indicated by the fact that the wealth acquired by Trobriand men is subordinated to their obligation to help their wives amass women's wealth which has no utilitarian value. Its only function is to enhance the reputation of women's relatives. Yet, if their husbands do not satisfy their wives' kin by spending much of their wealth on the accumulation of women's goods for their wives, the brothers-in-law reduce the economic support to their sisters. When an important member of a woman's kin group dies, she may need to use all of her husband's yams to pay for the production of skirts and banana-leaf bundles that she will give away at her relative's funeral. If her husband refused to support her bigmanship participation at such an occasion, he would be insulting her relatives, and they would decrease contributions of yams to his wife. In the long run, his ability to participate in male competitions would be undermined. So women's production of the wealth by which they achieve rank takes priority over the accumulation of men's wealth by their husbands.

FIGURE 4.7   Women's Wealth
Trobriand Island women accumulate their own wealth and prestige in the form of skirts and banana-leaf bundles. While the woman's brother gives yams to her husband to increase the husband's stature, he is, in turn, expected to accumulate bundles and skirts for his wife so that she can repay this debt when a member of her family dies. The quantity and quality of bundles and skirts distributed are thus a measure of the wealth and political power of the dead person's lineage.

Chiefs. In somewhat larger horticultural or agricultural societies in which social ranking becomes important, the role of bigmanship merges with that of the local political official, the chief. The chief is a person of authority and prestige who is the major political official and the economic manager of the local community. Unlike the leaders in bigmanship activities, the chief does not generally participate in the productive work of the redistributive economy. Instead, the chief is a full-time political official whose duties include coordination of the redistributive practices.

In redistribution involving chiefs, festive occasions may still be celebrated using goods collected in the chief's warehouse. A more important role of redistribution, however, emerges in this system: the use of the centrally controlled goods to finance public works and services. A significant portion of the redistributive economy is channeled into such activities as building and maintaining irrigation projects, supporting a local police force or militia, and similar undertakings that enhance the general welfare of the community.

A redistributive economy that is controlled by full-time officials clearly lends itself to potential abuse. It is true that the ability of chiefs to siphon off redistributive goods for their own use allows the chiefs and their relatives in many such societies to form a social elite with special prerogatives and a higher standard of living than that of other members of society. But there is a surprisingly large number of cases in which prestige comes to the chiefs and their families only in proportion to how well they use the goods they control for the benefit of others. In these groups, chiefs may expend more than they take in and live in poverty but receive great respect in return.

Markets

The market economy is the third major approach to exchange, one that has become the major economic force in the industrialized societies of the world. The concept of the market is based on the idea of direct exchange, that is, buying and selling as opposed to mutual gift giving of valued items or services.

Marketing may occur spontaneously in any society, but it is most developed in sedentary societies in which the large number of people involved makes it convenient to establish traditional marketplaces to carry out the exchange. Especially in larger societies

FIGURE 4.8 Yam Production
The men of the Trobriand Islands raise yams not for themselves but to give to their sister's husband and to use as a medium of exchange. As they, in turn, receive yams from their brothers-in-law, they are expected to use them to acquire skirts and banana-leaf bundles for their wives. These yams are being stored in the yam house of the chief to whom these men are related by marriage.

where marketplaces may bring together strangers and persons who see each other infrequently, market exchange, like negative reciprocity, may place little emphasis on mutual obligation, since each party becomes responsible for his or her own welfare in the transaction. Thus, self-interest rather than generosity often becomes the guiding principle. This, of course, is moderated, particularly in small-scale societies

▬

chief presiding redistributive and political official of a chiefdom society or of a subdivision of a chiefdom, whose legal authority extends in at least some areas over members of families other than his or her own

market a system of distribution for goods and services based primarily on the use of established locations

FIGURE 4.9   Barter
The trading of specific items whose relative value is carefully calculated is often conducted between groups rather than individuals. These New Guineans are bartering fish for yams, taro (a starchy rootstock), and other agricultural products.

and even smaller communities within larger societies, by the fact that market exchange may be part of a long-term relationship between the parties.

Barter.   In smaller societies that have market systems, exchanges may be primarily the trading of one object or service for another, a form of exchange called **barter**. In barter a potter and a farmer might exchange a water vessel for a bag of grain, or an itinerant worker might chop firewood in return for a meal and night's lodging.

Money.   When the goods that people need are produced close at hand, barter can be the basic form of exchange, but when this is not the case or when goods and services must be obtained from many different specialists, the concept of money may be employed to obtain goods. Since **money** is fundamentally a *symbol* of value, in order to transform anything into money the parties involved only need a

mutual agreement that a particular item will be a designated standard of value. It is usually best for the common medium of exchange to be both rare and portable; it should not require less effort to obtain money than to produce the goods and services for which it is exchanged. Gold and jewelry have these characteristics, but even printed paper or electronic bits of data will work. The key is simply that people agree to accept the paper or electronic signals in lieu of the commodities they wish to exchange. Additionally, something of value in its own right may be used as money. For instance, in many parts of the world, salt or spices have been used as money. But their utilitarian value in such cases, their ability to make transactions possible when one person has

---

barter   form of exchange of goods by trading
money   standard medium of exchange that has a mutually agreed-upon value

nothing to barter that the other needs at the moment, is merely an enhancement of their real value.

Money may be either specialized or generalized. **Special-purpose money (Bohannan, 1963) is a medium of exchange that is restricted to the buying and selling of a single commodity** or at most a restricted number of designated commodities. Coins or tokens that can only be used for gambling, operating video games, or paying for bus rides, and stamps or coupons that are saved to exchange for premiums are examples of specialized money. Bohannan (1955) reports that among the Tiv, metal rods were used as a special-purpose money for buying cattle, slaves, or white cloth, all items of prestige within the Tiv economy. Subsistence goods, on the other hand, were exchanged by barter. Among native North Americans of the Northwest Coast, blankets were a special-purpose money for food, but were not a medium of exchange for other items. In various parts of Melanesia, shells are a medium of exchange for stone tools, pottery, and pigs, but not for other everyday commodities.

A universal medium of exchange, one that is not restricted in its use for only certain commodities but that can be used to buy and sell any item is **general-purpose money**. General-purpose money is particularly useful when local populations are so large that people obtain most of their daily needs by buying and selling. When many different kinds of items are regularly bought and sold, both barter and the need for several special-purpose monies can be inconvenient ways of doing business. In such situations, a single general-purpose money may replace the other forms of exchange for most transactions.

special-purpose money medium of exchange restricted to the buying and selling of a single commodity
general-purpose money universial medium of exchange used to buy and sell any item

Yapese Stone Money

The symbolic nature of money is well illustrated by an old anthropological story about the Yapese people of the Caroline Islands in the Pacific. On the island of Yap, large, doughnut-shaped stones were used as special-purpose money for major ritual exchanges between villages. Since the stones were large, they were not easily transported; therefore they were not used in everyday transactions. However, on important occasions that warranted the use of a large number of human laborers, a stone might be moved from one village to another.

On one occasion when one of the stone cartwheels was being rafted across a lagoon between two villages, the vessel sank with its precious cargo. Try as they might, there was just no way to recover the stone from the sea bottom where it still lies. The crisis was overcome when the Yapese recognized some often overlooked facts: The real value of money is not due to its intrinsic worth but is assigned to it for the convenience of its users; and since the value of money is symbolic rather than intrinsic, physical possession of the symbol of value is not necessary to its use. Both villages agreed that although the stone could not be

Yapese Money

On the island of Yap in the Pacific, the medium of exchange was, at one time, large doughnut-shaped stones. They were not easily transported and thus were not used for everyday transactions. Eventually they became symbols of a medium of exchange.

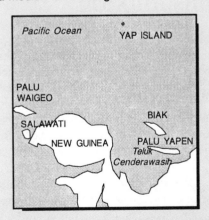

recovered, everyone knew where it was, so its ownership could still be transferred from one group to the other!

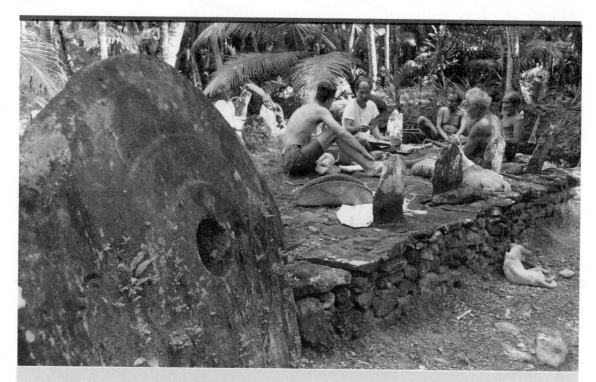

FIGURE 4.10   Special Purpose Money
When an item is designated as a specific means of exchange for a particular category of
goods, it is considered special-purpose money. These may consist of things such as shells,
brass rods, pigs, or anything a society designates. The Yapese people of Micronesia at one
time used huge stone disks, like that at the left, as special-purpose money. Today, its
presence in the village is a mark of prestige.

Consumption

In foraging bands there is little difference in the
wealth and lifestyle of individuals from one local
group to another because they all engage in the same
basic productive activities. There are few specialized
economic activities that supply goods to only some
individuals, and reciprocity tends to level out even
temporary wealth differences that may arise from
time to time due to fluctuations in productivity of a
local environment. But, with the development of food
domestication and the occupational specializations
that generally arise with it, opportunities increase for
some individuals, families, and local groups to consistently control more wealth than do others in the
same society. It is axiomatic that the more complex
and productive a society's economy is, the more
opportunities arise for differences to develop in consumption, the final use of goods and services.

Subsistence Economies

People regularly consume most of what they
produce in a subsistence economy. This is the usual
economic form in foraging societies and in simple
food-domesticating tribes, because not enough surpluses are produced for a permanent exchange of
goods to obtain what is needed. Rather, each family
produces goods for its own consumption, its own
subsistence income, and there is little need for trade.
Thus, in subsistence economies, permanent differences of wealth are unlikely to arise.

----

consumption   final use by a society of goods and services
subsistence economy   when people consume most of what
they produce
subsistence income   each family produces goods for its
own consumption

Status Income

When surplus goods are consistently available, the big men or chiefs who control the distribution process thus acquire a high social rank. The control of goods over and above subsistence needs is called status income. In the case of big men, most of such wealth is given as gifts to other groups in return for the prestige such gift giving brings. Both the redistribution of wealth to the needy within a local community and the channeling of some surpluses to host neighboring groups as a source of prestige is also a practice in many chiefdoms. However, chiefs sometimes use part of this surplus wealth to raise their own standard of living and that of their relatives above that of their subordinates. In such cases, the actual consumption of surplus goods by the elite becomes a symbol of their high standing. The use of status income as a display of social rank, a practice called **conspicuous consumption**, is found in many chiefdoms and is a characteristic of the elite in all societies in which market economies predominate. The high standard of living enjoyed by the British monarchy, the European "Upper Ten Thousand," or the American "jet set" typifies the use of income as conspicuous consumption.

Social Agents of Economic Control

Economic processes such as decision making about what to produce, what resources to use, and who will do the work is controlled by various people in various ways. In small-scale societies such as bands and tribes, control over productive work may be vested in the community as a whole, in the kin groups of society, or in special associations. In tribes and chiefdoms, the redistributive decisionmakers include individuals whose influence is based on prestige and power. In complex societies, decision-making power over production and distribution is often in the hands of members of the upper social classes, but exercised indirectly through their control of corporations or governmental bureaucracies.

Community Control of Production

In foraging bands in which the local groups are quite small and consist of members of only a few different families, decisions about the production and allocation of needed goods are sometimes a matter of discussion by the entire local group. This is especially true among foragers such as the Arctic Inuit, the Great Basin Shoshoni, and the Yahgan and Ona of Tierra del Fuego, who spend much of the year in very small local groups. It is also common among groups such as the Andamanese Islanders or Mbuti pygmy in which the local community of 20 or 30 persons functions like an extended family.

Kin Control of Production

The local kinship group is the most common institution for controlling production and allocation of goods among most foragers, horticulturalists, and pastoralists. Among foragers, this is merely a matter of the members of the nuclear family deciding about their daily needs and how best to fill them. Among pastoralists, who typically have larger local populations than do foragers, it is often the extended family that exerts ownership over the basic means of livelihood such as the fields and herds. Thus, for instance, among the horticultural Hopi of the southwestern United States, gardens were owned by kinship groups rather than by the individual woman who managed them day to day. Although she controlled the produce of her alloted plot, she could not dispose of the land without permission of her kinship group.

Association Control of Production

In other tribal societies, associations that cut through family lines and residential areas within a community may control important parts of production. For instance, the Cheyenne bison hunters of the North American Plains relied heavily on sudden kills of large numbers of migrating bison in cooperative

status income goods produced over and above subsistence needs

conspicuous consumption the acquisition and use of a surplus of goods as a way of competitively demonstrating one's success and prestige

FIGURE 4.11   Board of Directors
In complex societies where groups of producers are organized into corporations, the production and distribution of goods is directed by a group of people who are knowledgeable about its operation.

hunts. A single hunter who began to shoot too soon could frighten the herd and spoil the success of the hunt for the rest of the community. So control of the hunt was vested in the Cheyenne military association, who could police the responsibility of hunters by punishing those who did not abide by the rules that governed the bison hunt. The Tahitian islanders in Polynesia used several specialized associations or guilds for the production of expensive commodities such as chiefs' houses and boats. Chiefs' houses were built on a grand scale and could attain a length of nearly 400 feet. While a house was being erected, the carpenters of the guild were fed by the chief who was having the house built. Each guild was governed by its own chief, and the builders were respected specialists who were divided into ranks based on their training and experience. The guilds had special emblems, deities, and ceremonies that set them apart from others, and different guilds competed with one another to achieve prestige and social recognition for the quality of their work.

Social Class

Social class also plays a role in controlling the production, distribution, and consumption of goods in complex societies. Commonly, members of the higher social classes have the greatest control over the means of production and receive the greatest share of goods. Members of the social elite may sit on corporate decision-making boards. They also have greater influence than do other persons on government policymakers, to the benefit of their corporations.

Corporation and governmental decision making. Associations of employers and employees that produce goods or provide services and that are legally entitled to act as a single person with rights of ownership are **corporations**. Corporations can outlast the lifetimes of their individual members, so they can produce more than any individual and can develop tremendous economic power as their productive properties increase. Corporations may be privately or governmentally owned, but in either case those who make decisions about what corporations produce and at what prices they sell their goods and services are members of the higher social classes.

The balance of power between governmental officials and private individuals in the control of the means of production varies among complex societies. In some cases, the economic decision making of private owners of corporations is only loosely regu-

corporation   association of employers and employees that is legally entitled to act as a single person to produce goods or provide services lated. This allows the owners to play a major role in the economic life of such societies. One common outcome of this way of organizing economic decision making is a competition between corporations for sales. If the basic needs of consumers are being met by the system of production, competition in the marketplace may increase for nonessential items. In such a **consumer market**, the economic focus is on convincing consumers to purchase nonessential goods and services that enhance their standard of living rather than simply meet their basic needs. They make life easier and more comfortable. Nones-

sentials, especially those that do not improve consumers' standard of living, may still be marketed successfully because the buyers gain higher status by demonstrating their ability to purchase them. In its extreme, buyers may engage in conspicuous consumption, the use of goods merely as a display of their wealth.

consumer market where basic needs of consumers are met by the system of production, and competition for sales may focus on nonessentials

CHAPTER SUMMARY

1. Cultures differ in what they define as useful or valuable and in how much worth a given commodity may be thought to have.

2. Commodities may include intangible things such as sacred stories or titles of nobility.

3. Economic systems in all cultures are constructed out of the same rules that govern the production, distribution, and consumption of valued goods and services.

4. Production or obtaining commodities involves concepts of use rights, ownership, and a division of labor.

5. Distribution involves some combination of reciprocal exchange, centralized redistribution of goods, and markets.

6. Patterns of consumption depend on how much the producers use themselves, how commodities are used in increasing the prestige of some members of society through different levels of status income, and conspicuous consumption.

7. All societies have ways of controlling the economic system. Control may be divided between members of the community, may reside in the kinship group, or may be effected by associations such as guilds, corporations, or groups of governmental officials.

ANNOTATED READINGS

Blumberg, R. L. (Ed.). (1991). *Gender, family, and the economy: The triple overlap.* Newburg Park: Sage Publications. Examines interrelationship of gender, domestic life, and the economy.

Harris, M. (1986). *Good to eat.* New York: Harper & Row. An application of the cultural materialist perspective to the problem of cultural differences in the definitions of edible foods.

Lee, R. (1984). *The Dobe !Kung.* New York: Holt, Rinehart & Winston. A very readable description of the economic life of a foraging society in southern Africa.

Malinowski, B. (1922). *Argonauts of the western Pacific.* New York: E. P. Dutton. The first ethnographic account of the role of cultural values in the economic life of the Trobriand Islanders, with special focus on the Kula ring.

Nash, M. (1966). *Primitive and peasant economic systems.* San Francisco: Chandler. An anthropological account of economic systems that focuses on the economics of social change in nonindustrialized societies.

Neale, W. C. (1976). *Monies in societies.* San Francisco: Chandler & Sharp. A careful outline of the different kinds and different roles of money in various societies.

Plattner, S. (Ed.). (1989). *Economic anthropology.* Stanford, CA: Stanford University Press. Collection of viewpoints about economic anthropology.

Weiner, A. B. (1976). *Women of value, men of renown: New perspectives on Trobriand exchange.* Austin, TX: University of Texas Press. A reexamination of the Trobriand Islanders that emphasizes women's roles in economic exchange.

FIGURE 5.1   Political Power
Through its political system a society exercises power to maintain order internally and to negotiate with other socieites. President Corazon C. Aquino of the Philippines reviews an honor guard in Quezon City shortly before her retirement in 1992.

CHAPTER 5

Politics

Nowhere is political power, the ability to make and implement decisions about public goals, shared equally by every member of society. Whether people share power broadly throughout the entire community, divide power between their family organization and specialized associations, or place power in the hands of full-time governmental officials depends largely on the size and complexity of their societies. But whatever its form, there is always some system for maintaining social order and reestablishing order when rules have been broken. Some combination of childhood socialization, values, morality, religion, rewards for conformity, and threats of punishment is used everywhere to create an ordered society, but never with perfect success. When conflicts do arise, there are a variety of ways, both peaceful and violent, by which people seek to reestablish an orderly life.

CHAPTER OBJECTIVES

After reading this chapter, you should be able to:

Define politics.

Analyze the political structure of bands.

Analyze the political structure of tribes.

Analyze the political structure of chiefdoms.

Analyze the political structure of states.

Explain the role of gender in politics.

Define the basic mechanisms of social control: socialization, religion, rewards, gossip and community pressure, and law.

Discuss the common peaceful means for conflict resolution.

Discuss the use of power as a means of conflict resolution.

Define and explain crime.

Discuss the various means by which internal conflict is commonly addressed.

Define and explain rebellion and revolution.

102

Divine Kings. Senators. Chiefs. Taboos. Sanctions. Burning at the stake. Song duels. Electrocution. War. If someone steals your dog or cat, would you consider that a greater personal misfortune than if someone steals the radio out of your car? If a golf ball breaks your car window, is the player or the manufacturer of the golf club responsible for the damage? Who should decide on an appropriate punishment or recompense? How should the decision be enforced? Every society establishes a system by which it maintains some order.

. . . .

Types of Political Orders

According to Swartz, Turner, and Tuden (1966, p. 7), **politics** is the way in which power is achieved and used to create and implement public goals. As such, politics is involved in organizing and controlling human social behavior. It is through its political system that a society exercises power to maintain order internally and to regulate its relations with other societies. Those to whom the right to power is delegated are said to have **authority**, the legitimate right to use force or to threaten the use of force to achieve social goals. In the study of politics, it is important to consider how power is delegated, since not every use of power in society is legitimate.

Anthropologists have noted a variety of ways in which political power is channeled in different societies. Complex societies have full-time political systems with officials who monopolize the legal authority to govern others. Simpler societies make use of other mechanisms for creating and implementing common goals. For instance, governing authority may be vested in the local community, in the family

organization, in voluntary associations, or in officials whose authority is limited to those areas not governed by the family, community, or voluntary associations.

Bands: Government by Community

Societies in which people survive by foraging for wild foods in small local groups are **band** societies. They consist typically of 50 or 60 people who cooperate in economic activities. Since most political problems affect the entire local group, it is generally the seat of legal authority. When a legal problem arises, the entire community will discuss the issue in a kind of town meeting until everyone has had ample opportunity to express an opinion. The consensus that evolves out of the give and take of group discussion is the band equivalent of law.

As one example, the handling of homicide by the nineteenth century Inuit of the northern coasts of North America illustrates the legal role of the community in a band society. The Inuit occupied a harsh environment that placed heavy demands on them. In a territory that offered few plant foods, hunters were under great stress to provide for their families. Game included some rather formidable animals such as the polar bear and large sea mammals that were not easily taken. It is little wonder that successful Inuit hunters were strong-willed and aggressive men. In spite of rules of etiquette that demanded humility, politeness, and generosity, tempers sometimes did get out of hand, and violent deaths involving disputes about food and women were not rare.

Homicides were often dealt with by the families of the deceased. Revenge killings were legitimate, but might in turn lead to vengeance by the original killer's kin. So ultimate legal authority was vested in the community as a whole. It dealt with aggressive repeat offenders who were seen as threats to the common welfare. Boas (1888) described the role of community law enforcement among one group of Inuit:

---

politics manner in which power is achieved and used to create and implement public goals
authority the legitimate right, delegated to a person, to use power or force
band a seminomadic, kinship-based society with no full-time government, economically based on a foraging subsistence technology

FIGURE 5.2   U.S. Supreme Court Justices
The legal authority to govern others may be vested in the family organization, the local community, or legitimate elected or appointed officials. In the United States, the ultimate arbitrator in social and legal issues is the U.S. Supreme Court. Here, the Justices sit for their official portrait in 1991.

There was a native of Padli by the name of Padlu. He had induced the wife of a native of Cumberland Sound to desert her husband and follow him. The deserted husband, meditating revenge . . . visited his friends in Padli, but before he could accomplish his intention of killing Padlu, the latter shot him. . . . A brother of the murdered man went to Padli to avenge the death of his brother; but he also was killed by Padlu. A third native of Cumberland Sound who wished to avenge the death of his relatives was also murdered by him.

On account of all these outrages the natives wanted to get rid of Padlu, but yet they did not dare to attack him. When the *pimain* (headman) of the Akudmirmiut learned of these events he started southward and asked every man in Padli whether Padlu should be killed. All agreed; so he went with the latter deer hunting . . . and . . . shot Padlu in the back. (p. 582)

Because the entire community had acted as a judicial body and authorized the killing, it was a legal execu-

tion, and they had no need to fear any retribution by Padlu's relatives.

Leadership in bands.   As might be expected, band societies lack sufficient resources to support any full-time educational, economic, religious, military, judicial, legislative, or executive specialists. All leadership is charismatic. That is, a man or woman becomes a leader in some activity because of a personal talent in that area. Leadership also is unofficial; it is maintained only so long as a person demonstrates the qualities of excellence that draw a following. Charismatic leadership confers no authority, no power to coerce. A leader can only lend advice or take the initiative. Coming from a man or woman of respected abilities or wisdom, the advice or action is apt to be followed by others. The leader in the hunt, for example, is likely to be a man of proven ability in locating, tracking, and capturing game; a leader in political matters is respected because of his broad experience and proven wisdom. In both cases, however, as abilities decline, so does the leader's following.

The Great Basin Shoshoni: A Band Society

Steward (1938) described the native culture of the Great Basin Shoshoni. They occupied a territory that stretched all the way from near Death Valley, California, through central Nevada, northern Utah, and southern Idaho to central Wyoming. It generally is believed that the Shoshoni moved into the Great Basin from somewhere near the Death Valley area some 1,000 years ago. Throughout their territory, the Shoshoni spoke dialects of the same language, closely related to those of their Great Basin neighbors, the Northern and Southern Paiute and the Ute, who practiced a similar way of life.

The Shoshoni were a highly mobile people who hunted game and gathered wild plant foods in a sparse desert environment. Variations in rainfall made the location and amount of plant and animal foods highly variable from year to year. The Shoshoni spent much of the year in search of food, wandering in small groups of one to three nuclear families. During the spring and summer months, their food consisted of foraged seeds, berries, roots, and small game such as insects, larvae, rodents, and other small mammals.

Occasionally, several families who usually hunted separately would come upon a large congregation of rabbits. If one of the families owned a rabbit net, a collective hunt would be held. The rabbit net was about eight feet high and several hundred feet long. It was laid out in a great semicircle, and everyone would fan out to drive the rabbits toward the net. When the rabbits became entangled in the net, they would be clubbed or shot. These hunts provided both meat and furs which, cut into strips and woven into capes, provided warmth in the cold winter season. Similar communal hunts were held when antelope were available. After the hunt was completed and the meat eaten, families would again go their own ways in the search for food.

During the winter months, 20 to 30 families would camp in the same vicinity. Winter was a time for socializing. Dances and gambling were popular recreations. The most common dance was a communal one in which men and women arranged themselves in a great circle and sidestepped in one direction. This dance was believed to have some general health benefits for those who participated.

At the end of the winter, families began to disperse, some having added a new member or two by marriage. New wives left their families of birth and traveled with the families of their husbands. The Shoshoni were flexible about their marriage forms, and although most marriages were between one man and one women, both men and women occasionally had more than one spouse. When a man married several women, it was preferred that they be sisters. Marriages created kinship ties between families that were widely dispersed.

Cooperation within and between families was the basis of Shoshoni economic and politi-

FIGURE 5.3   Shoshoni Winnowing

The Shoshoni wandered in search of their food supply from season to season. This woman on the Lemhi Reservation, Idaho, in 1904 is winnowing wheat using the traditional Shoshoni method.

cal life. There was no governing authority outside the family. Property was limited to what people carried with them as they traveled, so there was little conflict over property rights. What few conflicts arose could usually be settled within the group on the basis of familial authority. Conflicts between different families were most often concerned with witchcraft accusations or wife-stealing. These might be settled by a feud, but the wandering way of life lent itself to conflict avoidance or even to settling of conflicts by each family's simply going its own way rather than pursuing the matter.

Shoshoni religion focused on the acquisition of spiritual power, called *puha*, which increased its possessor's skill, luck, and strength. *Puha* could be used to make love or gambling magic, to ensure the success of a hunt, and to cure or to kill. Religious specialists, who devoted more time than others to the acquisition and use of *puha*, were known as *puhakanten*, "power possessors." Some *puhakanten* had the particular ability to attract antelope. Their skill was especially useful dur-

ing communal antelope drives, since they could help draw the antelope into the corral. Other *puhakanten* devoted themselves to the curing of illnesses when called upon to do so. These spiritual healers were likely to have had a visionary experience in which they acquired a spirit ally known as a *puha newepea* or "power partner." During curing ceremonies, the healer would alternately chant and smoke tobacco until his spiritual ally would come and endow him with the power to cure.

Shoshoni religious beliefs included creation stories, known as Coyote stories, in which anthropomorphic animals were the central characters. Coyote, the creator of human beings, was a Trickster, a deity who enjoyed playing practical jokes. Human beings entered the world by escaping from a bundle he had opened in spite of having been told to leave it closed. He later obtained pine nuts for the hungry Shoshoni by stealing this food from wealthier tribes to the north. Coyote stories were enjoyed during the winter encampments but not at other times, since their telling could bring on a storm.

(see reference map p. 84)

Tribes: Government by Family and Associations

Societies with simple food domestication technologies that support local populations and that are small enough to need no full-time governmental authorities are known as **tribes**. Legal authority is held by the families of the local group and by voluntary associations, or **sodalities**, whose members are drawn from at least several of the families of the community. Family law typically rules in domestic matters such as the contracting or divorcing of marriage, and the punishment of family members for violation of one another's rights. Voluntary associations often play a role in the military defense of the local community and in policing the community itself, at least in matters that are not traditionally regarded as within the realm of family law.

The political role of voluntary associations is well illustrated by the tribes of the North American plains that typically had a dozen or so military societies in each community. In some tribes, young men graduated from one society into the next as they

aged; in others, they had to choose which they would join. The military associations exercised legal authority as a governing agency by preserving order in the camp during hunts, while camp was being moved, and by punishing lawbreakers. But they also performed social, recreational, and economic roles in hosting feasts and dances, holding intersociety competitions, keeping tribal traditions, and providing information about the location of buffalo herds.

Policing role. Policing authority among Plains Indians was usually held by a single military society for only a year, so that this responsibility was rotated among the associations of a community, and no one monopolized the right to police power. Enforcement

---

tribe a semisedentary kinship-based society without a full-time government. Most tribal societies are economically based on a simple food domestication subsistence technology, either horticulture or pastoralism

sodality volunteer associations whose members are drawn from several tribal families of tribal laws by military societies was also limited to crimes that harmed the community welfare. Thus, on communal buffalo hunts, someone who began to shoot too soon and frightened the herd away before others were prepared was likely to be punished. The emphasis was on making the culprit an example to discourage similar behavior by others. Punishments that were made public included the destruction of a wrongdoer's property, banishment from the camp, and death.

The Plains Indians relied heavily on the migratory buffalo that passed through their territories each year, and competition for this valuable resource brought the highly mobile, horseback-hunting tribes into recurrent conflict. The military associations protected their communities against other plundering tribes. The greatest defenders of the tribe in each military society were rewarded with honor and the plunder of war. In ceremonial meetings, these warriors recounted their exploits in battle, and it was from these men that the more formal political leaders were selected for the tribe.

Social roles. Plains military societies also played an important role in public recreation. They performed dances as public exhibitions and generally interacted with the audience in their celebrations. Among themselves, members of the military associations provided fraternal camaraderie and a place in which deep friendships could evolve.

As in bands, tribal leadership is charismatic. It is achieved by an individual's personal ability to convince others that it is in their own self-interest to follow his or her lead. Thus, leadership is a matter of skill rather than the power of an inherited status. By and large, tribal society is egalitarian like the band society, in that every individual has more or less equal opportunity to obtain the necessities of life and the esteem of others in leadership activities.

The Toda: A Tribal Society

Rivers (1906) described the Toda, a pastoral tribe of India. The Toda lived on a high plateau in southern India. They made their living by herding buffalo. Since they practiced no agriculture, the Toda supplied neighboring tribes with dairy products from their herds in return for farm products, pottery,

ironware, and other goods and services. As might be expected, buffalo were extremely important to the Toda. Cows were individually named, and their pedigrees were carefully remembered. Some herds were regarded as sacred and were tended by special dairymen at sacred dairy temples. The ancestors of these sacred herds played an important role in the creation myths of the Toda, who believed that when the first 1,600 sacred buffalo were created by one of the gods, the first human appeared holding onto the tail of the last buffalo—an apt symbol of the Toda's economic dependence on their herds.

Although families and clans were the main decision-making bodies among the Toda, their pastoral way of life had created a population density that was too great for all problems to be settled without some mechanism that superseded clan membership. This mechanism was an incipient government organization, a tribal council known as the *naim*. Its five members always came from certain families of specific clans. Lacking the authority of the true governments of more complex societies, the *naim* had no voice in criminal matters. Its primary functions were to regulate ceremonies and to settle disputes between individuals, families, and clans.

Population growth was limited by the Toda's location. Their land was bounded on all sides. In the southern directions, cliffs dropped from 3,000 to 5,000 feet. To the north were agriculturalists. With no room for expansion, the Toda had sought to solve the problem of population growth by limiting the number of women and therefore the number of children born in each generation. This was accomplished by the practice of infanticide, in which unwanted infants, especially girls, were suffocated shortly after birth. This led to a surplus of men in each generation. To rectify this imbalance the Toda practiced polyandry, a form of marriage in which one woman has more than one husband.

Marriages were arranged, and they occurred between children as young as two or three years of age. The girl was considered to be the wife of the boy with whom the marriage ceremony was performed and of all his brothers, including those born thereafter. Until she was 15 or 16, the bride lived with her own parents. Shortly before puberty, she had to be initiated into sex by a man selected from the group to which her family did not belong, that is, to a man whom she would not be permitted to marry. If this ceremonial loss of virginity did not occur before puberty, the bride was stigmatized for life, and her marriage would be canceled.

Since a woman could have many husbands, fatherhood had to be designated on some basis other than the idea of biological paternity. Thus, among the Toda, a man became a father by performing an important ritual. A man and a pregnant woman went into the forest where the man carved a niche in a tree, placed an oil lamp into it, promised the woman a calf, and ceremonially presented her with an imitation bow and arrow. She held the bow and arrow to her forehead and watched the lamp until it burned out. Afterwards, he prepared a meal, and the two spent the night together. From this time forward, he would be the father of all children to whom she would give birth, until some other man performed the same ceremony with her to supersede him as father of her children. Although it was usual for one of a woman's husbands to hold the status of father of her children, it was possible for a man who was not one of her husbands to perform the bow-giving ceremony with her.

Toda

A tribal society in southern India, the Toda made their living herding buffalo. The main decision-making government bodies were families and clans. As population grew, a tribal council was formed that regulated ceremonies and settled disputes when asked to do so. The decision of this *naim* superseded all others.

Chiefdoms: Government by Officials

A society that unites a number of villages under the legal control of a government that recognizes the right of families to exercise some autonomous legal authority is a **chiefdom**. A chiefdom's governmental official, called a chief, can legitimately use force in matters that concern the common welfare. However, kinship groups such as the family exercise a great deal of legal autonomy. For instance, laws that govern marriage and divorce are typically matters of family law, just as they are in bands and tribes. Similarly, the enforcement of laws concerning petty theft is often a responsibility of kinship groups in chiefdoms as well as in bands and tribes. However, major crimes that concern the entire community, such as grand theft, homicide, or insults to the dignity of a chief, are typically punishable by the government officials who have authority over nonrelatives in legal matters. Thus, chiefdoms have a true professional government, but one whose officials do not monopolize all legal authority to govern society. Their authority is balanced by that of each community's kinship groups, who govern themselves in those areas that most directly affect them.

Each community in a chiefdom is likely to have a chief who acts as its political head, and groups of villages usually will be unified under a district chief of higher rank than the local village ones. In some legal matters, the chiefs or their delegated representatives may be expected to play the role of mediator between the conflicting parties, with the goal of reestablishing peaceful relations between the members of the community. In other cases, the chief may have the authority to determine guilt or innocence and exact punishment for an offense without consulting the members of the offender's family. The position of chief is therefore a true office, and its holder has authority to legitimately wield power over others with whom the chief has no known kinship ties.

---

chiefdom a society, often of many villages, that has a government capable of coordinating social action within and between villages but in which governmental authority is balanced by the legal autonomy of families in many areas

FIGURE 5.4   Zulu Chief
Most societies that are organized into chiefdoms consist of several communities each headed by a chief or council. In attempting to restructure the political order in South Africa, the Zulus of the Inkatha Freedom Party are led by chief Mangosuthu Gatsha Buthelezi in negotiations with Nelson Mandela of the African National Congress and President F. W. de Klerk.

The office of chief is most often hereditary, although which relative of a deceased chief will inherit the office may be decided by the surviving family members. In some cases, the community as a whole may have some say in the selection of the new chief from the group of possible heirs.

In chiefdoms, the everyday functions of government, such as the military defense of society, the policing of local communities, the conduct of judicial activities, or the drafting of labor for various public works projects, are possible because governmental authority includes the right to tax and to redistribute produce, which all families are required to contribute. Probably the most important function of chiefs is

the economic one of serving as redistributors of goods and providers of services. In a chiefdom, all families in a community are expected to contribute a portion of their annual produce to the warehouse. The chief then sees to it that these goods are redistributed, generally at community feasts or festivals, to those most in need. It is often the case that a chief's power and prestige is maintained in direct proportion to his generosity. Indeed, the level of gift giving expected of a chief may exceed that which comes in from other families, so that the wealth of the chief's family is gradually drained, to the benefit of other less prestigious families.

Chiefdoms lack true social classes in the sense of being cross-cut by social strata whose rank depends on the importance of the occupations people hold, but they are not egalitarian either, since their kinship groups are ranked in a social hierarchy in which some families have greater social power and prestige than others. For this reason, chiefdoms are sometimes called **rank societies** (Fried, 1967; Service, 1963, 1978). Political offices are usually inherited so that they remain within certain families, and the highest ranking families normally have control over the most important political offices.

Chiefdoms are typically theocratic societies in which the chiefs are endowed with both religious and secular authority. Indeed, some of the higher ranking political officials may be considered so filled with religious aura that their very persons are sacred.

rank societies kinship groups in a chiefdom that are ranked in a social rather than occupational hierarchy

The Rwala Bedouins: A Pastoral Chiefdom

According to Musil (1928), the Rwala had the largest and most powerful tent-dwelling Bedouin chiefdom of the northern Arabian peninsula. Although much of their life was organized around the concept of kinship, the Rwala also had officials whose authority was felt beyond the boundaries of their own kin. These chiefs or *sheikhs* were officers whose positions were inherited within particular patrilineal lineages. In addition to local *sheikhs* whose authority was felt throughout an entire camp, there also were regional chiefs whose authority derived from a lineage of greater prominence than those of the local chiefs. There also was a paramount chief or *sheikh*, often called a "prince," over all the Rwala. His main duties were to conduct relations with the national government and with chiefs of other Bedouin peoples, but he had little power over the internal politics of the Rwala themselves.

Life in the camps was largely governed by kinship. Each man saw himself as the center of a group of relatives, or kindred, known as the *ahl*. A man's *ahl* consisted of all his sons and their sons, his father and grandfather, and their brothers. This group of relatives had strong obligations to him and could bear the guilt for his misdeeds. People also were organized into larger kinship groups called *feriz*, that included relatives who traced their ancestry through their fathers back to a common male ancestor. Marriages were preferably within one's *feriz*. In particular, a man was encouraged to marry his father's brother's daughter or his father's father's brother's son's daughter. This woman could marry no other without his waiving his prior claim. The marriage preference system counteracted the fragmenting effects of the Bedouin pastoral adaptation to a desert environment, kept inheritable property from being dispersed, and increased their solidarity (Barth, 1954; Murphy & Kasdan, 1959).

The Rwala made their living by herding camels, which could provide transportation, milk for food, and hides and hair for manufacturing items. Camels were traded to merchants in return for cash, weapons, clothing, and other necessities. Trade was important, for the desert environment did not permit the Bedouins to be completely self-sufficient.

Warfare was a central fact of Rwala life, and it tinged many other aspects of their culture. Stolen animals were the main reason for warfare, which consisted most often of surprise night raids on the enemy camp. Weaker groups of Bedouins and villagers paid protection tribute (*khuwa*) to more powerful ones such as the Rwala. The receiver of this protection "tax" was bound to protect those who paid it and to restore any property that was stolen from them by raiders. War was enjoyed because it was an opportunity not only for booty but also for displaying one's skill and courage. Old age was rare for males, since over 80 percent of Rwala men died as a result of warfare.

Blood feuds also were common among the Rwala. Kin were obligated to avenge the mur-

Rwala Bedouins

Living in the northern Arabian peninsula, the Rwala Bedouins organized their government around a hierarchy of local and regional chiefs with a paramount chief who had authority to negotiate with the national government and with chiefs of other Bedouin tribes. He had, however, little power over the internal politics of the Rwala.

der of a relative, and the murderer's kin shared the guilt to the third generation. The avengers therefore could take the life of a relative of the actual culprit, should they happen on one before finding the murderer. Vengeance of this kind was legitimate, a matter of family law. Guilty parties were not permitted to defend themselves against avengers, but instead had to seek the protection of a powerful *sheikh* who aided them in reaching a traditional place of refuge, where they stayed until the avengers agreed to accept a blood price of horses, camels, and weapons to compensate them for the death.

Today, the Bedouin, who number about five million, live a more settled life. Camels for the most part have been replaced by Toyota trucks for transportation, and tents have given way to cinder block houses. Sheep and goat herds remain an important source of livelihood for many Bedouin, but other occupations and sources of income have also been adopted. Some engage in dry farming. Others derive income from the tourist market. Members of the older generation sometimes complain that younger people know too little about herding and are only skilled at repairing trucks and televisions.

States: The Official Monopoly of Law

Because chiefdoms vary in their degree of social complexity and the power of their governments, the social differences between a complex chiefdom and a small state society may be slight. They are essentially differences of political ideology: a **state** is a political unit in which centralized governments monopolize the right to exercise legal force and control the affairs of local communities. It has power to levy taxes, pass laws, and draft people into work or war.

Technology. The major technological difference between the chiefdom and the state is that the agriculture of the state society is more intensive than that of the chiefdom. The plow and draft animals are almost always present, and agricultural technology is generally much more complex. Irrigation systems, for example, play such a major role in the agriculture of most states that one scholar, Karl Wittfogel (1957), has suggested that the necessity of controlling and regulating water resources led to the rise of the world's first states. This view has not been accepted widely, because it places too much emphasis on the single factor of irrigation at the expense of others, such as population growth, trade, diplomacy, and warfare. But it reminds us that irrigation was an important technological development in increasing the productivity of the state's subsistence activities.

Robert Carneiro (1970) has suggested that states arose in circumscribed environmental zones—areas surrounded by mountains, deserts, or other natural barriers to easy emigration—when population growth caused increased social competition for natural resources. This competition led to social stratification and the domination of some groups by others. Centralized political power created elites who were able to exact tribute and taxes from the dominated groups. Circumscribed habitats made it difficult for those who were losing in the competition to withdraw to other areas.

According to Carneiro (1979), once states developed they tended to expand at the expense of neighboring chiefdoms, tribes, and bands whose smaller populations made them less powerful. Due to the effects of truly intensive agriculture, members of a state society may number in the millions. They live in densely packed towns and cities in which little or no agriculture may be practiced. They also live in more rural communities of smaller size that specialize in the production of particular kinds of food, which can then be exchanged for the nonagricultural products of the larger communities.

The principle that a state monopolizes the legitimate use of force is well illustrated by Ashanti law. The Ashanti, described by Rattray (1923, 1929), were a west African state in what is now the state of Ghana. The Ashanti state was ruled by a divine king who, like Louis XIV of France, represented the very source of the state's authority. So sacred was the king's personage that cursing him was punishable by a heavy fine. Indeed, to curse the king was such a terrible thing that it could only be spoken of by the euphemism, "to bless the king."

Only the divine king or his duly authorized representatives had the authority to use any force. Since any crime involves the use of force, it was, in a sense, theft of the king's authority and an insult to the sacred ancestors he represented. All crimes were punishable by death.

The view that crimes were punishable primarily because they undermined the authority of the state and only secondarily because they victimized others led to another interesting aspect of Ashanti law. Suicide, like murder, involved taking the life of an Ashanti. Like murder, it was a contemptible affront to the king and the ancestors. So the body of a suicide was tried and, if found guilty, decapitated. By so doing, Ashanti law symbolically demonstrated the sanctity of the state's authority. Odd as this legal custom may seem to Americans, it is not very different in principle from U.S. and Canadian customs in which persons who attempt suicide may be confined in mental hospitals by judicial order for violating the law by having tried to kill themselves. Although North Americans speak of such confinement as "hospitalization" for "treatment for a mental disorder," the nonsymbolic aspects of the customs are similar. Both the Ashanti and North Americans punish suicide offenders through a judicial process.

....

Gender and Politics

In societies throughout the world, political offices are held predominantly by men. Yet, in some societies the political organization is characterized by

---

state a society with a centralized government that monopolizes the legal authority to use force a joint male-female system of authority and in some the greatest solidarity at the local village level is among women. Even in societies in which men predominate in positions of political power, women have a degree of political power and influence.

Matrifocal Societies

Women have had the greatest political power in those societies in which they are the economic producers and control economic resources. Nancy Tanner (1974), a specialist in the anthropology of legal processes, investigated **matrifocal societies**, where the primary solidarity relations involve women, and found that, in addition to their preeminent economic role, women in these societies were decisionmakers who were at least as assertive as men, and female relatives were in frequent contact with each other through mutual-aid groups that were a source of power and support that was not dependent on men. In these societies, most women generally occupied central kinship positions. For instance, the role of a mother in the family was typically more important than that of a wife.

In contemporary nation-states, women have also achieved high political positions, but not to the degree that is typical of matrifocal societies. For instance, Golda Meir of Israel, Corazon Aquino of the Philippines, Indira Ghandi of India, and Margaret Thatcher of Great Britain have all held positions as heads of state in their respective countries. Yet, worldwide statistics indicate that women continue to be numerically underrepresented in governmental offices. According to geographers Joni Seager and Ann Olson (1986, p. 115), even in the Scandinavian countries, in Ghana, and in Panama, where women have the highest rates of representation in their national government, women hold only about one in four elected positions.

The Iroquois. The Iroquois of the North American Great Lakes region often have been cited as a society whose culture defined women and men as equals. According to the nineteenth-century anthropologist Lewis Henry Morgan (1851), Iroquois children belonged to their mothers' families. Husbands were in-laws within their wives' households and had no authority over their wives or her children. Houses and gardens were owned by women and inherited by daughters, so women were not economically dependent on men. The highest governmental officials

were a council of fifty chiefs, or *sachems*. These offices were hereditary within the maternal families; they most often went from a man to his younger brother or to a sister's son, but the actual choice was made by a vote within the family. Since only women were permitted to select the candidates for other family members to accept or reject, Iroquois women exercised the authority of political office in this way. Although only males were chosen to fill these offices, it was usually possible for a family to select an infant as a sachem. Functionally, such a choice amounted to electing the infant's mother to the office, since she fulfilled all the regular duties of a sachem on behalf of her son until he became mature enough to exercise the authority of his office.

The Dahomeans. According to historian Karl Polanyi (1966), women in the West African kingdom of Dahomey, which is now the republic of Benin, played even more prominent roles in political office than did Iroquois women. In the Dahomey government, every office held by a male had a corresponding position that was held by a female who was responsible for overseeing the work of the male official. Men held their offices in various places throughout the kingdom, while the women resided at the royal palace where they could report to the king. Men who served the king could only see the king accompanied by the women who maintained oversight on their work. Even the king had such a counterpart, the Queen Mother, whose status was higher than that of the king. The Dahomean army had a similar organization. In the 1800s, the Dahomean army consisted of nearly equal numbers of male and female warriors and officers. The elite military corps that guarded the palace was comprised of about 2,500 celibate women warriors. The Dahomean joint male-female system for organizing the government and the military functioned very effectively to perpetuate the authority of the king by insulating him from male competitors.

The Lobedu. According to Eileen J. Krige and J. D. Krige (1943), the Lobedu of what is now Mozambique and some of their neighbors vested supreme authority in queens. The Lobedu queens had no military to enforce their authority. Instead, they held their office because of their religious power to

---

matrifocal societies societies in which the primary solidarity relations involve women bring rain to their people and to withhold it from their enemies. Thus, the Lobedu queen was the source of her subjects' welfare and general prosperity and they regarded her as sacred. Her life was filled primarily with religious responsibilities and ritual prohibitions designed to perpetuate the well-being of her nation, and at the end of a reign of approximately 40 years she was expected to commit ritual suicide—a custom that was done away with in the 1950s. A judicial system consisted of women who were appointed by the queen to represent the various districts of the nation.

The Lobedu queen was not permitted to marry, although she might bear children whose "father" would be selected from among her relatives. She was expected to maintain a "harem" of women who were bestowed upon her as "wives" by local chiefs and nobles of her society and sometimes by foreign leaders. This custom created a network of political alliances that ensured loyalty and good relations between other important officials and the Lobedu queen, who became a "son-in-law" to the wife-givers. The queen sometimes created similar advantageous political ties with Lobedu men by arranging marriages between them and women of the harem. In implementing these customs, the Lobedu queen played roles very similar to those that were elsewhere played by kings who entered marriages primarily for political reasons.

The Igbo.   Kamene Okonjo (1976) has described a similar female-male political organization among the Igbo of Nigeria, who had two monarchs, a queen and a king. Each exercized authority in their own areas of responsibility. The king's responsibilities dealt primarily with the lives and activities of men, while the queen was consulted on matters that affected women. Men and women had separate political organizations that paralleled each other in form and function. For instance, women settled disputes primarily among women, but made decisions that affected both women and men. Margery Perham (1937) documented how in 1929 Igbo women exercised their political power by rioting against the British colonial government to express their dissatisfaction with policies that they deemed harmful to women's interests in Nigeria. Called the "the women's war" by the Igbo, this political action influenced about 2 million people over an area of 6,000 square miles.

Social Control: The Imposition of Order

All societies have a variety of mechanisms by which the social behavior of people is controlled to maintain order or to reestablish order once rules have been broken. Social efforts to create orderly behavior begin at birth and continue through life. Some mechanisms for bringing about and maintaining conformity with acceptable behavior include early teaching of accepted customs and instilling values that motivate people to conform. Other mechanisms are punishments for rule violations and rewards for conformity. Malinowski (1926) pointed out that rules may be obeyed for a number of reasons: They may be self-enforcing due to their practical utility. They may also be followed because violating them brings public ridicule, because playing by the rules brings more rewarding interaction with others, because they are sacred and supernatural punishment will result from breaking them, or because they are matters of law that are enforced by the machinery of society.

Socialization

The basic way we learn to fit into a social order is in our childhood **socialization** or **enculturation**. We learn about our culture, and we come to see the common expectations that others have about our behavior. Those habits that are learned early in life set the pattern for later relationships outside our home and community. Effective socialization can head off problems by establishing patterns of behavior that others find acceptable.

Values.   Part of socialization is learning to feel that some ways of behaving are better than others. **Values** may be defined as our attitudes or feelings about right and wrong behavior. This broad category may then be divided into various types such

---

socialization the process of learning a culture and the role-playing skills necessary for social life

value a subjective reaction to experiences expressed in terms of good or bad, moral or immoral; the ideals that people long for but do not necessarily pursue. Values are often opposites of drives

FIGURE 5.5   Witch Trial, Seventeenth Century
Witchcraft and sorcery, uses of supernatural power to work evil, are thought to have existed in many cultures throughout the world. Witches were accused of causing sickness, death, crop failure, and all sorts of other ills. The witch trial portrayed in this lithograph took place in Salem, Massachusetts, in 1692.

as moral, spiritual, or environmental values. **Moral values** are the rules that govern our relationships with our fellow human beings. **Piety** or **spiritual values** define our relationship to the supernatural and may be circumscribed by specific religious rules of behavior such as the Jewish kosher laws, rules against blasphemy, or rules about working on a sacred day. **Environmental values** deal with our relationship to our physical environment, so that concerns here would include pollution and the protection of endangered species. Although morality and environmental values may be understood in purely practical terms such as the need for an orderly social life, or an awareness that needed resources are limited, people may accept them simply because they are tradition or because they are supported by religious teaching. Note, for instance, that the Judeo-Christian Ten Commandments begin with rules of piety such as "Thou shalt have no other gods before me" but also include moral rules such as "Thou shalt not steal."

Religion and Social Control

Another major force for the maintenance of social order is religion. The rites of passage that symbolize stages in the life of the individual as a member of society are typically religious rituals. Myths and legends also contribute an aura of sanctity to a way of life and increase people's respect for the social order. Taboos and ceremonial obligations fur-

---

moral values attitudes or feelings that govern our relationships with our fellow human beings
piety attitudes that define our relationship to the supernatural and that may manifest themselves in certain behaviors
spiritual values attitudes that define our relationship to the supernatural and that may manifest themselves in certain behaviors
environmental values attitudes that define our relationship to the environment

ther structure life in ways that demand predictable conformity from members of a community. Finally, in some societies, religious ideology directly mandates a moral life with the promise of supernatural rewards for proper social conduct and punishments for wrong living.

The role of religion in maintaining social order is illustrated by the Hopi Indians of the southwestern United States. As embodiments of evil among the Hopi, witches were called *Two Hearts*. They loved darkness, death, and other things that humans despise. Witches were put to death if they did not confess their evil deeds. So the accusation of witchcraft was a powerful force in bringing people into line with acceptable behavior.

The Hopi were a communally oriented society in which support of common values was prized over individual prowess. The person who excelled too much or too often might be suspected of being a witch. Thus, a child who won more races than others would be advised to run more slowly in other races so that others would not feel envy. In a society in which generosity and sharing were valued, the accumulation of too much personal wealth might also lead to suspicion of witchcraft. In this case, a suspect might sponsor a communal festival in which he or she distributed goods to others, an act that eliminated the surplus wealth and curried the favor of others simultaneously. Essentially any deviance was an invitation for suspicious gossip, and this suspicion helped pressure people into conforming behavior, much as the legal system in state societies is intended to do.

Rewards

Societies do not rely on punishments alone to maintain social order. Rewarding acceptable behavior also encourages conformity. The praise and esteem of other members of the community is one such reward. Promotions and salary increases provide incentives to support corporate goals. Similarly, various forms of public recognition reward contributions to the social group. In addition to money, honor, and respect, people may be rewarded with greater power within the military, police, or judicial system.

Gossip and Community Pressure

The esteem of others is valued by most people, so gossip and community pressure can be a powerful force in keeping people in line. The key to the effectiveness of gossip is that word eventually gets back to the person being criticized. The nonconformist then has the opportunity to try to regain the respect of others by changing the behavior that others have found unacceptable. Direct confrontation is another form of community pressure that is sometimes resorted to when gossip has failed.

Law

Order is also maintained through **law**, the cultural rules that regulate behavior through the threat of punishment (Hoebel, 1954). Legal rules may be formally defined and codified into a recognized body of laws, but they may also be said to exist informally, defined by custom rather than code. Pospisil (1972) has demonstrated that law in all societies has four characteristics: legal authority, universal application, legal rights and duties, and sanction. **Legal authority** is the legitimate right to compel others to obey the law, either by the use of force, by the threat of force, or punishment. All societies vest legal authority in one or more individuals who are charged with the responsibility to maintain order. They may be political specialists, heads of voluntary associations, designated members of a community, or a family. **Universal application** is the principle that the legal authority should apply the same laws uniformly in similar situations. It is this expectation of consistency that invests legal systems with tradition. Of course, legal authorities may violate this principle, but the inconsistent application of law, or favoritism, is regarded as an abuse of power in all societies. **Legal rights and duties** are the rules that define relationships between persons by specifying what recompense an injured person is entitled to receive and that legal authorities are expected to follow in enforcing contracts between persons when one or both believe their rights have been violated. Finally, **sanction** is the action taken by

law cultural rules that regulate human behavior and maintain order

legal authority legitimate right to compel others to obey the law and to punish those who violate it

universal application principle that legal authority should apply uniformly in similar situations

legal rights and duties rules that define relationships between people by specifying the type of recompense an injured person should receive

sanction action taken by legal authorities responding to violations of law

FIGURE 5.6 Law Enforcement
Most societies maintain order by investing the authority to make rules and regulate behavior in the family, an individual, or a community council. This Cherokee Indians' tribal council meets to discuss issues that affect their nation.

legal authorities when the law has been violated. A sanction may be either a punishment or the loss of a privilege or benefit to which a person was entitled before breaking a law, and may include such things as ridicule, ostracism, corporal punishment, or fines.

The Resolution of External Conflict

In all societies conflicts occur, and in all societies there are customary ways of trying to resolve them. Peaceful conflict resolution may rely heavily on the good will of those involved, whereas violent resolution may be based on the socially accepted use of force by legal authorities.

Peaceful Conflict Resolution

Antagonistic parties may sometimes resolve their conflict if both decide that it is no longer in their best interest to continue or that their losses have been restored. Even when an injury cannot itself be made right, compensation may be accepted because the payment symbolizes an admission of responsibility by the wrongdoer and allows the injured party to withdraw from the conflict honorably. For instance, the concept of compensation has been applied in many societies, even for major acts such as murder. It was called wer-gild, or "man-payment," in Anglo-Saxon England before the Norman invasion of 1066. According to Evans-Pritchard (1940), the same idea was practiced by the Nuer of the Sudan in recent times. Among the Nuer the payment took the form of cattle given by the family of the murderer to the surviving relatives.

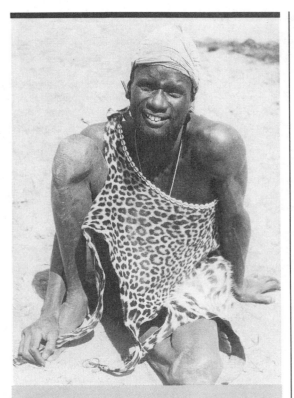

FIGURE 5.7 Leopard Skin Chief
The Nuer, tribal cattle herders, turned to a mediator to settle disputes between segments of the tribe in a blood feud. The leopard skin chief used threats of supernatural retribution to persuade both sides to come to a peaceful solution while providing refuge in his village for the accused until the matter was solved.

Negotiation.   Peaceful resolution of conflict requires communication between the parties involved. Negotiation can be carried out by the disputing parties themselves, but it is often accomplished through **mediation**, which is negotiation carried out by a go-between. It is generally easier than direct negotiation between parties, providing the mediator is neutral. A mediator has no authority to enforce a decision on those involved in a conflict. Instead, as he draws on the desire of the parties involved to avoid a continuation or escalation of their dispute, he also relies on his own prestige and his ability to mobilize community pressure to influence the parties to settle.

Among the Nuer, the person holding the prestigious status known as leopard skin chief had no official authority over others but had ritual responsibilities and served as a mediator between families that were in dispute. The position of leopard skin

chief was held only by a much-respected male whose home could be a sanctuary to which a murderer might flee for safety while a conflict was being resolved. He performed a ritual purification of the murderer and then approached the family of the murderer to determine the number of cattle they were willing to pay to the family of the deceased. Then he visited the aggrieved family to see if they would accept the offer. If the immediate relatives pressed for retaliation, the leopard skin chief might seek the support of more distant relatives to encourage them to accept a settlement. Usually a settlement of about 40 cattle was accepted. Since an unrecompensed death could lead to a feud between the families, the role of mediator was an important one in maintaining social order.

Community action.   Community action is another approach to conflict resolution. The entire community would be mobilized to respond to and resolve the conflict in societies that lack complex kinship organizations and that are small enough to have a vested interest in resolving the conflict among all members of the local group.

——

mediation negotiation between conflicting parties carried out by a neutral third party

Inuit Song Duels

Native Greenlanders had various ways of resolving personal conflicts, including head butting, wrestling, and boxing contests. Perhaps the most interesting method was the song duel described by Rasmussen (1922), quoted in Hoebel (1954). When an individual lacked the physical strength to challenge an opponent to a test of strength, the song duel was an alternate way of seeking justice. It was carried out in front of other members of the community. Following traditional rules for composing the songs, the parties to the conflict would alternately sing insults against their opponent. The songs would outline the grievance or defense and deride the other person. The audience participated by their laughter and applause. As the duel wore on, the audience's laughter sided more and more against one party until the public ridicule was too great for the loser to endure and he would withdraw.

Hoebel recounted a case of a divorced man whose wife married another. The first decided he wanted his wife back and sought to get her by publicly shaming his rival in a song duel that he began with words that accused his rival of wife stealing:

> Now shall I split off words—little, sharp words
> Like the wooden splinters which I hack off with my ax.
> A song from ancient times—a breath of the ancestors
> A song of longing—for my wife.
> An impudent, black-skinned oaf has stolen her,
> Has tried to belittle her.
> A miserable wretch who loves human flesh—
> A cannibal from famine days.

The rival then responded:

> Insolence that takes the breath away
> Such laughable arrogance and effrontery.

Inuit

The Inuit who inhabited Greenland had several interesting methods of resolving conflicts. The most unusual, perhaps, was the song duel. The combatants composed songs deriding their opponent, and performed them in front of an audience who ultimately decided the winner by applause and laughter.

FIGURE 5.8 Inuit Band Authority

Inuit bands had no centralized authority figure who made decisions for the group. Instead, the community as a whole, or the best qualified member in a given situation, took the lead in such matters as organizing a whale hunt, distributing the meat, and arranging an equitable solution to a dispute.

> *What a satirical song! Supposed to*
> *place blame on me.*
> *You would drive fear into my heart!*
> *I who care not about death.*
> *Hi! You sing about my woman who was*
> *your wench.*
> *You weren't so loving then—she was*
> *much alone.*
> *You forgot to prize her in song, in stout*
> *contest songs.*
> *Now she is mine.*

> *And never shall she visit singing, false*
> *lovers.*
> *Betrayer of women in strange*
> *households.*

> Such singing continued back and forth, each contestant hoping to win over the audience and thereby defeat his rival. Songs might be prepared and rehearsed in advance, and in some areas the relatives of each contestant provided a backup chorus in support of their own family member.

Courts. A **court** is a formalized institution that asserts authority over parties in a dispute and over persons accused of violating the law. A court has power to decide cases and impose sanctions. Courts are part of political systems in which governing authorities have the right to exercise control over persons outside their own kinship group, so true courts are found only in chiefdoms and states, societies with centralized political officials.

Religious institutions. According to Black, when governmental agencies of law enforcement are weak, then other means of social control are likely to be more important. As he put it, "Law varies inversely with other social control" (1976, p. 6). Religion is one of the more prominent social institutions that plays a role in social control. The most well-known examples of religious mechanisms for conflict resolution in a legal setting are oaths and ordeals. **Oaths** are ritual acts of swearing innocence on pain of punishment by deities. Where religious belief is strongly held by people, oaths can be a powerful force in determining guilt, since the guilty may fear supernatural retaliation too strongly to take a false oath. **Ordeals** are tests of guilt or innocence in which parties in a conflict are challenged to undertake a dangerous or painful act with the understanding that supernatural influences will grant them success only if they are innocent. Again, the guilty are likely to refuse such tests or fail them, because their religious convictions undermine their confidence. For instance, the Philippine Ifugao people tested the innocence of persons accused of criminal acts by requiring them to reach quickly into a pot of boiling water and remove pebbles from the bottom. The arm of the person who underwent the ordeal was smeared with grease so that if he acted quickly enough, his arm would not be burned. Those who acted out of a confidence born of innocence probably were more likely to pass this than were those whose guilt made them hesitate. Similar tests have been reported in medieval Europe and for the Tanala of Madagascar where the arms of the accused were unprotected from the boiling water by grease. However, a period of several days was allowed to pass before the arms were examined; this lapse of time presumably favored the innocent who acted with less hesitation than the guilty, since those with less severe scalds were more likely to have healed by then.

Violent Conflict Resolution

Conflicts cannot always be ended peacefully. There are a variety of forceful ways in which people attempt to regulate their relationships with one another, including retribution, feuds, raids, and warfare.

Retribution. In many simple societies that have no centralized governmental authority for the enforcement of law, the responsibility for the punishment of wrongs is a legitimate authority of the person

---

court formalized institution that asserts authority over parties in a dispute and over persons accused of violating the law

oaths ritual acts of swearing innocence on pain of punishment by deities

ordeals tests of guilt or innocence by enduring dangerous or painful acts whose rights have been violated. In such cases, law enforcement is synonymous with **retribution**, the personal use of force to redress wrongs. Retribution as a legal principle is not the same as anarchy, since it is legitimate in societies that condone it only when other members of the community recognize that the aggrieved party has a valid complaint that deserves redressing. Crime, anarchy, and other uses of power that are not condoned by the larger community will be seen as illegitimate and punishable.

Feuds. Armed conflicts between two kinship groups that are initiated by one of the groups to avenge a wrong are called **feuds**. The most common cause of feuds is the murder of a member of one of the groups. Feuds may occur between kinship groups that reside in the same community as well as between neighboring groups from different communities. They are most common in societies in which bodies of related males, called **fraternal groups**, work together and feel obliged to protect one another's common interests.

Raids. Organized violence by one group against another to achieve an economic benefit is called a **raid**. Raiding is generally a more recurrent and ongoing process than is feuding, since the latter is stimulated by a specific grievance and may eventually be settled. The economic advantage gained in raiding is likely to be a continuing motivation for this organized violence. Its goal is not to eliminate or even subjugate the enemy permanently, but rather to accomplish a limited objective such as the acquisition of food, cattle, or other valued goods. Where raiding is common, the enemy is likely to be treated as a resource that must be left available for future exploitation.

War. The most extensive form of organized violence is **war**, armed combat between political communities. The nature of war differs according to the complexity of the societies involved. Otterbein (1970) examined cross-cultural data of 50 societies and found that those with more centrally organized political institutions had more complex military organizations, more effective weapons and tactics, and greater mortality in their engagements than did societies with little or no political centralization. In general, warfare was less complex among bands and tribes than among chiefdoms and states. For instance, professional soldiers were lacking in the former

societies, while they were typical in the latter. The tactic of surprise was more characteristic of simpler societies, while warfare was generally more formally arranged and conducted in complex societies.

Otterbein found that the purposes of warfare also differed for the two groups. In bands and tribes, wars were fought by those who were individually motivated to participate because of personal grudges. So battles tended to consist of many simultaneous fights between individuals with little group strategy. Defense of one's own village and the benefits of plunder were the motives for war in bands and tribal societies. Of course, more complex societies also fought wars for these reasons but were additionally guided by motives that were less characteristic of warfare in bands and tribes. Enhancing one's prestige and that of one's family was an especially common motivation in chiefdoms, societies in which competition for prestige was a prominent characteristic. On the other hand, prestige was a less common motive in states where social ranking was more stable and based on a person's membership in a particular social class. While warfare carried out to achieve economic and political control over other communities was a motive found in some of the more complex chiefdoms, it was especially characteristic of states.

War and gender. Otterbein also distinguished between **internal warfare** in which the combat is between neighboring political communities that share the same culture, and **external warfare** in which the conflict is between political communities with different cultures. Internal warfare is especially common among foraging bands and horticultural tribes, while external warfare is more commonly practiced

---

retribution personal use of force to redress wrongs, usually in simple societies with no centralized governmental authority

feuds armed conflicts between kinship groups initiated to avenge a wrong

fraternal groups groups of related males who work together and feel obliged to protect one another's common interests

raids organized violence by one group against another to achieve economic benefit

war organized, armed conflict between political communities

internal warfare fighting between peoples who share the same language and culture

external warfare warfare which is fought for prolonged periods in locations distant from the warriors' home with enemies who speak a foreign language and follow an alien way of life by more complex chiefdoms and state societies. According to Divale and Harris (1976), internal warfare is particularly associated with the systematic subordination of women. Harris (1974) has summarized the impact of this form of warfare on male and female roles:

> Male supremacy is a case of "positive feedback," or what has been called "deviation amplification"—the kind of process that leads to the head-splitting squeaks of public-address systems that pick up and then reamplify their own signals. The fiercer the males, the greater the amount of warfare, the more such males are needed. Also, the fiercer the males, the more sexually aggressive they become, the more exploited are the females, and the higher the incidence of polygyny—control over several wives by one man. Polygyny in turn intensifies the shortage of women, raises the level of frustration among the junior males, and increases the motivation for going to war. The amplification builds to an excruciating climax; females are held in contempt and killed in infancy, making it necessary for men to go to war to capture wives in order to rear additional numbers of aggressive males. (p. 87)

Since female children are often unwanted in these societies because they lack social power but still need to be fed, **female infanticide** has been the major means of population control in most societies throughout human history. Divale (1972) studied foraging and horticultural societies that practiced warfare and found that the ratio of boys to girls aged 14 and under was 128 to 100. Since throughout the world about 105 boys are born for every 100 girls, the extra 23 boys per 100 girls in Divale's sample indicates a higher death rate among girls in these societies.

The female subordination that occurs with internal warfare does not accompany external warfare, in which men are absent from home for prolonged periods while fighting with distant enemies. Women in these societies are likely to be ranked high, since it is they who make the day-to-day economic and internal political decisions of the village while the men are away. In such societies, the gardens and houses are often the property of women, female infanticide and polygyny are likely to be uncommon, and inheritance is usually through the line of female ancestry. The power of men over their wives is minimized by their lack of ownership over their wives' home and gardens as well as their lack of authority over their wives' children, who are members of their mothers' families, not their fathers'. The

male head of the household is not a woman's husband but her brother, who belongs to her own family. In these societies women often had great influence on the political decisions that led to war and that influenced its conduct. Their economic roles were also an important source of power. For instance, Iroquois women were able to control men's wartime activities by withholding the food used to provision long wartime expeditions.

Causes of war. There are diverse theories about the cause of warfare. Ember (1982) examined cross-cultural data and found that scarcity of resources such as food and fuel was one predictor of the frequency of warfare. Vayda (1976) has pointed out that slash-and-burn horticulture is a factor that stimulates internal warfare in many societies, because taking land that has already been worked by neighboring groups may be easier than clearing new land and preparing it for cultivation. Warfare allows horticulturalists to expand geographically when population growth overtaxes local abilities to produce enough food. Divale and Harris (1976) believe that internal warfare is part of a system that helps to limit population growth, because warfare fosters male dominance, subjugation of women, a preference for male offspring, and therefore high rates of female infanticide, which has a major impact on population growth.

Naroll (1966) examined possible causes of the frequency of warfare. He determined that a high degree of military sophistication did not act as a deterrent to war. In fact, societies with a sophisticated military force were not only more aggressive than were militarily less organized societies, but they were more likely to be attacked as well.

································

The Resolution of Internal Conflict

Mediation, feuds, and warfare are typical means of resolving the conflicts that may occur between societies such as tribes, chiefdoms, or states.

----

female infanticide the killing of female infants as a major means of population control in societies that primarily engage in internal warfare

Within the boundaries of societies with similar political or cultural views, however, conflicts may arise that necessitate a different pattern or means of resolution. Internal conflicts include crimes such as theft and murder, acts that all societies regard as disruptive. Internal conflicts may also overturn a government. Revolution and rebellion are dramatic forms of conflict that seek to redress the wrongs a society perceives are being perpetrated by its government.

Crime

No society is free of **crime**, the harming of a person or of personal property by another. But societies do differ in the frequency and likelihood of various kinds of crime and in how they deal with it. People who live in small groups have little opportunity to harm another member of the group while remaining anonymous and profiting by the act. In large societies crime is more feasible because the perpetrator can remain anonymous. The motivation, however, to violate others' rights for personal gain is certainly not accepted by everyone in such societies, so population growth alone cannot be thought of as the cause of the greater rates of crime in such societies. Rather, it appears that crime in large societies is most likely to be resorted to by those who are unable to fulfill the values that a society's culture encourages. Two related factors that differentiate people in this respect are social class and income.

A study carried out by the United States National Commission on the Causes and Prevention of Violence (USNCCPV, 1969) found that violent crimes were 11 times more common in cities of over 50,000 people than in rural areas, and most crimes were committed by young, low-income males who lived in urban slums. Poverty, unemployment, poor education, and inadequate housing seemed to be major factors that created motives for criminal behavior. People in such conditions were unlikely to achieve success by legitimate means, and were therefore more likely than other members of society to undertake illegitimate actions to improve their condition.

Crime varies in frequency from extremely low levels in societies such as the !Kung San foragers of southern Africa (Lee, 1979, 1984) and the Semai horticulturalists of the Malay peninsula (Dentan, 1968), where crime has been described as almost nonexistent, to societies such as the Yąnomamö (Chagnon, 1968), in which about 23 percent of the men of each generation die violently. Nevertheless,

people in all societies have some concept of crime and consider some harmful acts to be legitimately punishable. Theft, assault against members of one's own community, and murder are probably regarded as crimes everywhere.

Although theft is probably regarded as wrong in every society, the definition of theft differs from culture to culture. In many societies, personal property may be freely borrowed without asking unless the owner expressly indicates that an item is not to be taken. This is particularly likely in societies in which generous sharing of resources is common. For instance, Goldman (1972) described property rights among the Cubeo, a horticultural tribe of the Colombian Amazon Basin: "The attitude of the Cubeo toward personal possessions is best described as casual. They are not indifferent to objects but they regard strong proprietary feelings as improper. Among kin [persons who share common ancestors] objects circulate freely; the closer the tie between people the more active the exchanges. Sisters exchange ornaments and trinkets and men borrow freely from one another with or without permission. They seem to be most free with objects of economic utility, such as a canoe, weapons, implements, and somewhat more possessive with objects of personal adornment" (pp. 75–76). In this context of rather nonchalant attitudes about property rights and borrowing, Goldman recounted an interesting story about borrowing among the Cubeo: "On one occasion a visitor from an upriver sib [kinship group] rose to leave, after having spent most of the day in amiable talk, and in a most casual voice said, 'I will take my spear with me.' A young man then went to his quarters and fetched the spear, which the visitor took as he departed. The young man explained that he had been at this man's house during a drinking party. He saw the spear and admired it and took it home without saying anything about it. Theft to the Cubeo is not a matter of purloining an object. It is entirely a matter of attitude. They ask, in a manner of speaking: Is the taking of an object an act of friendship or of hostility?" (p. 76).

Societies also differ in the likelihood of theft. For instance, in foraging bands of 50 or 60 people, it would be difficult if not impossible to steal the personal property of another and remain undetected. Furthermore, it is generally advantageous to let

---

crime the harming of a person or personal property by another others borrow one's tools rather freely, since the fruits of everyone's labor will benefit the entire group. Thus, the very motive for theft can be undermined by cultural practices such as the custom in many hunting and gathering societies of leaving implements outside the hut when it is okay for others to use them.

Homicide is universally regarded as a criminal act, but cultures vary in what they define as homicide. There is probably no society in which the taking of some human life by someone is considered under all circumstances to be murder. Killing is an accepted part of warfare wherever war is found, and avenging a murder by killing the murderer is typically accepted in most societies. Nevertheless, the intentional taking of another life without justification, however justification happens to be defined, is considered murder practically everywhere. An interesting exception to this general rule was reported by Jenness (1922), who asserted that among Copper Eskimo men, the likelihood of their killing at least one person was so high that only repeated offenses were considered to be murder. This was an important distinction, since murder was a capital offense and taking the life of everyone who had killed just once would have been impossible.

Legal response to crime.   In simply organized societies, the enforcement of legal rights is largely left in the hands of individuals and their families. Where the magnitude of the crime threatens to disrupt the community permanently, corporal punishment, confiscation of property, ostracism, or even death are possible sanctions. Bands and tribes are likely to act in ways that are designed to return the group to the balance it had before a law was broken, a concept known as **restitution**.

The exacting of legal punishment has followed the principle of retribution in many societies. For instance, Beattie (1964) reported that the Berbers of North Africa expected exact equivalence in revenge for a death: "So if a man in one group kills a woman in another, the object of the injured group will be not to kill the murderer, but to kill a woman on their opponent's side" (p. 175). This is the same principle of an eye for an eye that was set forth in Hammurabi's famous code: "When a patrician has destroyed the eye of a member of the aristocracy, they shall destroy his eye. If he has broken another patrician's bone, they shall break his bone. . . . If a patrician has knocked out a tooth of a seignior of his own rank, they shall knock out his tooth. . . . If a

FIGURE 5.9   Retribution
Sanctions are formal and informal controls designed to regulate social behavior. When a crime of great magnitude is committed, some societies demand retribution such as these armed dancers in Papua New Guinea, who participate in regulated combat in order to avenge a murder.

patrician struck another patrician's daughter and has caused her to have a miscarriage, he shall pay ten shekels of silver for her fetus. If that woman has died, they shall put his daughter to death."

Law enforcement in complex societies tends toward an emphasis on punishment of the criminal. This is probably because crime in societies with fulltime law enforcement officials tends to be viewed as a threat to the legitimacy of the government's authority. The reaction of the enforcement system in such societies is to eliminate, imprison, or otherwise punish the wrongdoer; punishment typically becomes more important than seeing that restitution is made to the victim. In recent times in the United States and other industrialized countries, efforts have been made to pass various victim compensation laws, but the predominant emphasis in industrialized societies remains punishment; it is still regarded as the victim's obligation to seek recompense through civil suits.

restitution behavior intended to restore the group to the balance it had before a law was broken

Rebellion and Revolution

The most dramatic forms of internal conflict are rebellion and revolution. **Rebellion** is an organized and violent opposition to the legitimacy of a society's current governing body. It is most likely to occur when a significant number of those who are subject to the government's authority feel themselves to be disenfranchised or inadequately represented by their leaders. Rebellion seeks to influence the policies of government and how they are carried out, but it does not attempt to change the nature of the governmental system itself. **Revolution** is the organized use of force to alter the very form of government. It is fostered by the same conditions that lead to rebellion, but is likely to occur when those involved view the very system of government as the source of its illegitimate policy and practices. Both rebellion and revolution have much in common with warfare, since all three represent conflicts, often violent ones, between at least two groups, each of which asserts the legitimacy of its own right to use force for its own political ends.

rebellion organized and violent opposition to the legitimacy of a society's current governing body
revolution organized use of force to alter the very form of government

C H A P T E R   S U M M A R Y

1. Politics, the use of social power to implement public goals, takes different forms in human societies.

2. Governing authority may reside in the local community, a typical trait of band societies.

3. Authority may be vested in the kinship group and in specialized associations that draw their members from the entire community, as in the world's tribal societies.

4. Authority may reside with full-time officials who make up a specialized government, which shares legal authority with its society's kinship groups, as in chiefdoms, or which claims a monopoly over all legitimate uses of political power, as in the states.

5. However they are organized, political systems have a variety of mechanisms for maintaining social order and for reestablishing order when rules are broken.

6. These mechanisms include socialization, values and morality, religion, rewards and punishments, informal community pressure, and law.

7. Law, the most formal means for enforcing obedience to the rules of social life includes both peaceful and potentially violent means for resolving conflict.

8. Extreme levels of violence such as warfare and rebellion occur when conflicts exist either between governments or within a single society.

A N N O T A T E D   R E A D I N G S

Fried, M. (1967). *The evolution of political society: An essay in political anthropology*. New York: Random House, Inc. A theoretical examination of societal differences in terms of their political structures.

Hoebel, E. A. (1954). *The law of primitive man: A study in comparative legal dynamics*. Cambridge, MA: Harvard University Press. The first major attempt to carefully formalize the anthropological analysis of legal ideologies and practices.

Malinowski, B. (1926). *Crime and custom in savage society*. London: Routledge & Kegan Paul, Ltd. A short examination of law by the founder of the American functionalist approach to anthropological analysis.

Nader, L. (Ed.) (1965). The ethnography of law. *American Anthropologist*, special supplement to Vol. 67, pp. 3–32. An important synthesis of anthropological viewpoints on the study of law.

Nader, L., & Todd, H. F., Jr. (1978). *The disputing process: Law in ten societies*. New York: Columbia University Press. An important collection of ethnographic descriptions of how disputes are settled in a cross section of the world's societies.

Roberts, S. (1979). *Order and dispute: An introduction to legal anthropology*. New York: St. Martin's Press. A short book devoted to the understanding of how order is maintained within societies traditionally studied by anthropologists.

PART

III Society and Social Life

124

Humans are not isolated creatures but social ones. It is in our nature to interact with others of our species for reasons of companionship and survival. Chapter 6 details how groups are organized by status, rank, and role behavior in society and describes the rituals within the life cycle that mark the passage of individuals through stages in their life. Chapter 7 describes the systems used to identify our relationships to other members of our family. Chapter 8 illustrates the many forms that marriage takes in societies around the world. An intimate social relationship, it is the basis for the creation of the family, the primary group to which we belong and the basic institution of social life throughout human existence. A new chapter 9 defines the difference between sex and gender and details how the perception of gender affects male and female roles in society.

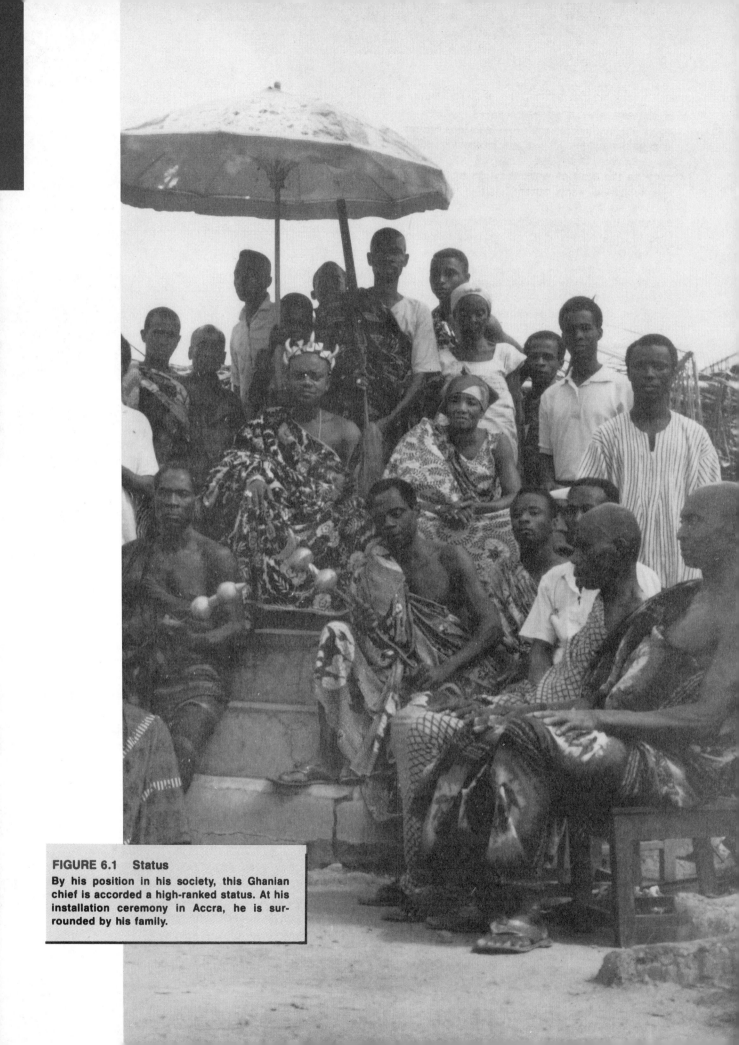

FIGURE 6.1   Status
By his position in his society, this Ghanian
chief is accorded a high-ranked status. At his
installation ceremony in Accra, he is surrounded by his family.

CHAPTER 6

Social Organization and Life Cycle

Nowhere are all people treated equally. In every society, people are organized into groups and levels of honor and social power. Categorizing people on the basis of distinctions such as the kind of work they do or their relationships to each other has the benefit of making social life efficient, orderly, and predictable. But some ways of categorizing people lead to inequalities that are unrelated to people's innate abilities. Such discriminations are made on the basis of historically derived, and therefore culturally diverse, ideas about categories such as race and sex. After examining patterns of social organization and the complexities of racial and sexual statuses, we consider how some of the social statuses we acquire follow one another in a definite sequence from birth to death known as the life cycle.

CHAPTER OBJECTIVES

After reading this chapter, you should be able to:

Define the concept of social organization and its parts.

Discuss the relationships between status, roles, and division of labor.

Explain the relationship of rank to power and prestige.

Compare and contrast the concepts of class and caste.

Discuss the nature and functions of master statuses.

Explain the relationships between biology and statuses.

Analyze the social and psychological functions of rites of passage.

Describe the more common customs in the world concerning pregnancy and childbirth.

Explain the three forms of learning that play a role in socialization.

Describe the more common customs in the world concerning sexuality and puberty.

Describe the more common customs in the world concerning marriage and divorce.

Describe the more common customs in the world concerning old age and death.

Organizational Patterns
Groups
Statuses and Roles
Division of Labor
Rank
Contextual Cues
Master Statuses

Biological Traits and Social Statuses
Statuses Based on Biological Distinctions
Innate Differences vs. Socially Learned Roles

The Life Cycle
Rites of Passage
Pregnancy, Childbirth, and Naming
Enculturation, Childhood, and Adolescence
Courtship and Marriage
Parenthood
Divorce
Old Age
Death

Tinker. Tailor. Soldier. Sailor. Rich man. Poor man. Beggar man. Thief. Imagine yourself digging through old greasy tinfoil and moldy orange peels for your daily dinner. Or imagine yourself in a London Fog trenchcoat on a foggy London morning cautiously peering around a corner to catch a glimpse of the spy carrying an alligator briefcase. Imagine yourself growing up black in the hills of South Africa or white in the Australian outback. Wherever you find yourself in society, your identity is determined both by biology and by culture.

Organizational Patterns

Throughout human history, cultural continuity has been maintained by symbolic communication among members of a particular society. The pattern of that communication is determined by how society is organized. The **social organization** of a society consists of (1) the various groups that form the society, (2) the statuses that individuals may hold, (3) the division of labor, or the way in which the tasks of society are distributed among individuals and groups, and (4) the rank accorded to each group and status.

Groups

Every human society is a **group**, whose members perceive their common identity because of the culture that binds them together. All human societies that have been studied subdivide into smaller groups that coalesce from time to time for specialized activities. Such groups have geographical boundaries,

specifiable members, a common activity engaged in by members, and a division of labor. Basketball fans, for example, when scattered across the country are not a group, but spectators at a specific game are. When a group is formally organized, it may have an explicitly formulated ideology, a goal-oriented "game plan" or set of procedures for carrying out the activity that brings its members together.

The members of social groups generally identify themselves symbolically with a name or some other emblem of their group identity. Commonly, the identifying emblem indicates the activity that draws the members together or represents some other important aspect of the group's characteristics. Thus, the group identity of the United States of America is symbolized by a flag that portrays the political unity of that society's 50 states by a group of 50 stars. The Great Seal of the United States of America contains the image of an eagle clutching an olive branch and arrows, symbols of peace and war, which suggest that the major purpose of the nation as a political entity is to maintain internal order and to defend the group. A smaller, more face-to-face group, such as a basketball team, may identify itself as a unified body by naming itself and by symbolizing its athletic purpose with some symbol of its prowess, such as a charging bull or a flying hawk.

There will also be structured relationships between groups in every society. Interactions by groups are culturally patterned, and may involve hierarchical ranking, with each group having different degrees of honor and social power. Group relationships are sometimes called the **social structure** of a society, to distinguish this aspect of social organization from other aspects such as individual statuses and roles (Service, 1962).

Statuses and Roles

Besides groups, each pattern of social organization also includes several kinds of relationships. All relationships that a person may have with others

---

social organization the relationships between the groups, statuses, and division of labor that structure the interaction of people within society
group two or more individuals engaged in a common activity
social structure the part of social organization made up of groups and their relationships with each other

are called **statuses** and exist in pairs, such as doctor and patient, husband and wife, parent and child, or friend and friend. The **status pairs** of a society are of two types: those in which the holders of the statuses are expected to behave in different but mutually compatible ways, and those in which the holders of the statuses are expected to behave in a similar way toward one another.

Status pairs in which both parties are expected to behave in different but compatible ways are called **complementary statuses**. The status of doctor, for example, requires the existence of the complementary status of patient, that of parent implies that of offspring, and without the status of student there could be no teacher. In each of these cases, the holder of one status of the pair is expected to behave differently from the holder of the second status.

Statuses such as friend, neighbor, enemy, colleague, or ally, on the other hand, imply the existence of two or more holders of the same status who are expected to act toward one another in similar ways. Statuses paired in this way are called **symmetrical statuses**. One cannot be an enemy unless there is someone who will respond in kind as an enemy, too (Watzlawick, Beavin, & Jackson, 1967).

In every society, each person may be involved in many different kinds of relationships and therefore has many different statuses. The same person may be a wife, a mother, a student, an employee, a friend, and a political activist. Some statuses that we have no choice about are known as **ascribed statuses**. These often include characteristics such as gender, family membership, or, in some societies, racial identity. Other statuses must be acquired during our lifetimes and may change as our position in life changes. These statuses, such as team captain, college student, or club member, are known as **achieved statuses**.

The ways in which the holder of a status is expected to behave are called the **roles** of that status. Every status has several different roles, each of which is considered appropriate for certain times and places. For instance, in a classroom students take notes, ask and respond to questions, and occasionally take tests. At home they are expected to read and study assignments and compose term papers. Their written assignments may require that they be able to carry out library research or demonstrate other skills at information gathering. People in these situations behave in the role of student. When these same people go to a party on Saturday night, however, they assume a role other than student and behave differently.

By conforming their behavior to the role expectations of others, holders of a particular status symbolically communicate that they wish to be responded to in a manner appropriate to that specific status rather than to some other status that they might also hold. The team captain is expected to direct action on the field; off the field, the same person may be expected to listen to and respect the opinion of another with whom he or she shares the status of friend. The various status pairs of a society form a pattern of predictable expectations that guide their interactions and simplify social relationships. When team members accept another's status as team captain, they know that during a game their appropriate relationship to the leader is that of followers. Without such role agreements, ball games—and social life—would be somewhat chaotic.

Division of Labor

The day-to-day work that must be done in any society is allocated to people through their statuses. This makes it possible for the members of society to be organized efficiently into a clear-cut, well-known, and effective **division of labor** by which all the tasks of life are accomplished.

Even in those human social systems where few specialists exist, there is some division of labor. In foraging societies, for example, age and gender are the primary bases for assigning the work of life. Even though tasks may overlap and distinctions may not be strictly enforced, males and females in all societies

---

status a culturally defined relationship that one individual may have with one or more other individuals; the position within a group that each member holds

status pair the statuses that two people acquire when they interact, and that together form a relationship

complementary statuses a pair of statuses, each of which has roles that are different from but compatible with the roles of the other

symmetrical statuses a pair of statuses, each of which has the same roles to play with respect to the other

ascribed statuses social positions that one is assumed to occupy by virtue of the group into which one happens to be born—for instance, one's sex or race

achieved statuses social positions that one acquires by demonstrating the necessary role-playing abilities

role the skills, abilities, and ways of acting toward others that belong to each status of a society

division of labor the rules that govern how the day-to-day work of life is divided among the holders of various statuses are generally expected to specialize in somewhat different economic activities, as are the members of different age groups. Typically, in the foraging societies men are assigned the status of hunters, while women specialize as gatherers of wild plants. Children may provide some help around the campsite, fetching water or gathering branches for the fire. Older members of the group may be relied on for their experience in interpersonal and intergroup relations to mediate disputes, negotiate with strangers, or arrange marriages. In societies in which people grow their own food, other forms of specialization develop, and the division of labor may become much more intricate. For instance, individuals or entire villages may specialize in the growing of a particular crop or the manufacture of woven goods or pottery. These are traded to other people or villages in return for their specialties. In industrialized societies, there are so many specialized occupations that a monetary system is needed to organize the exchange of labor.

Rank

Some kinds of work are valued more highly than others. **Rank** is a measure of the relative importance accorded to groups and statuses and the work they do. Holders of highly ranked statuses and members of highly ranked groups generally have more ready access to whatever is valued in their culture than do other members of their society.

Power and honor. Rank has more than one component. According to Kemper (1978), the two characteristics of a status that determine its social rank are the amount of social power and honor[1] associated with it. Power and honor are measures of one's ability to influence others successfully. **Power** is the ability to exercise coercion in obtaining what is sought and to punish the failure of others to comply. **Honor** is the esteem that some statuses confer on those who hold them. The respect that comes to persons such as Supreme Court justices, ministers, or movie stars whose statuses are honored makes it easier for them to accomplish goals and influence others without coercion.

1. Kemper uses the word "status" to refer to what is here called "honor." This reflects the lack of standardization in the terminology of the social sciences. Kemper (1978, p. 378) defines status as "relationship in which there is *voluntary compliance* with the wishes, desires, wants and needs of the other" [italics in original]. To avoid confusion I will continue to use the word "honor" in this discussion wherever Kemper uses "status."

Groups, too, may be ranked in the degree of power and honor that they command. For instance, secret societies and vigilante groups are often characterized by high access to power, but their level of honor may be judged low by others. Service associations such as the Kiwanis or a charity fund-raising group may have little power to obtain social benefits for their members coercively, but they may be highly enough respected to receive voluntary contributions from outsiders.

Like groups, individual statuses may be ranked. In the United States, the occupational statuses of doctor or senator are generally considered more desirable and their holders given more social power and greater incomes than are the occupations of sales clerk, mail carrier, or carpenter.

Societies differ in which statuses are most highly ranked. For instance, in industrialized nations where many of the important relationships in life are based on jobs, occupational status is a major determinant of the rank most people hold. In these societies, the loss of income that comes with retirement is often accompanied by a loss of rank. In societies where kinship relationships determine the most important roles, it is common for rank to increase with age and experience.

Within a status pair, one status may be thought of as the superior of the two and may have access to a greater amount of honor, social power, and/or wealth. Thus, parents are expected to train and control their children rather than the other way around, and it is the teacher who tests and assigns grades to the student.

Class. Ranking of diverse statuses is more common in those societies that have large populations and many differentiated, highly specialized statuses or jobs. These societies are organized into a hierarchical structure that sometimes is subdivided formally into ranked classes. A **class** is a broad stratum that cuts across society and is made up of unrelated families that have more or less equal access

---

rank the relative importance of a status or group as measured by the amount of power and/or honor to which it is entitled

power the ability to exercise coercion in a group in obtaining what is sought

honor the esteem some statuses confer on those who hold them

class a broad, ranked stratum within society made up of unrelated families that have more or less equal power and prestige to income and prestige. Sometimes class membership is determined by birth, and the statuses that individuals may hold during their lifetimes are limited to those of the class into which they are born. In such a case, when people are not permitted to move from one formally demarcated class to another by acquiring a new status, the classes are called **castes**.

caste   a social class determined by birth, so that an individual cannot legitimately change class membership by acquiring a new status

Brahmin   the highest-ranked Hindu caste, members of which are theoretically priests

Kshatriya   the second most important of the Hindu castes, members of which were the traditional warrior-rulers, nobles, and landowners of society

Vaisya   the third-ranked Hindu caste, comprised of commoners

Sudra   the lowest of the Hindu castes, made up of farm artisans, servants, farmers, and laborers

Untouchables   the lowest-status members of Hindu society who belonged to none of the traditional castes and who ritually performed the polluted tasks of life

jati   an occupational subcaste in Hindu society

Caste in India

Caste in India has been described by many anthropologists, including Beals (1974, 1980), Dumont (1970), Kolanda (1978), and Mandelbaum (1972). The system of organizing people socially by grouping them into castes is an ancient practice that is couched in religious concepts and differs somewhat in various parts of India. In simplified terms, there are four major kinds of castes. The first of these, the **Brahmin**, is ranked highest in ritual purity and closeness to God. Members of this caste are priests in theory, although in fact most practice other occupations. Socially, members of the Brahmin caste are accorded greater honor than are those of the lower castes even though they have less power and wealth than many members of other castes. The **Kshatriya** —warrior-rulers, nobles, and landowners— are next in honor. They are thought to be less ritually pure than the Brahmins and are subject to fewer dietary and ritual restrictions than the priestly class. Next come the **Vaisya**, the commoners, and, finally, the **Sudra**, who are the farm artisans, servants, farmers, and laborers. Below all these are the people of no

caste, the so-called **Untouchables** who perform the polluted tasks of life such as removing dead cattle from the village, tanning hides, working leather, and removing human waste.

Although Indian society accords greater honor to the higher castes, it does not link freedom with this honor. Members of the higher castes are hedged about by various restrictions, most notably dietary restrictions. The Brahmins and Vaisya are expected to be strict vegetarians, although the Kshatriya may eat goat, considered a relatively clean animal, and may drink liquor. The Sudra may eat chicken (a less pure animal) as well as goat, and the Untouchables may eat any meat, including beef and pork. In varying degrees the members of higher castes also are expected to avoid physical contact with the members of lower castes.

Within each caste there are many occupational subcastes or **jatis** that are also ranked by ritual purity. Members of each jati have rights over and responsibilities to the members of

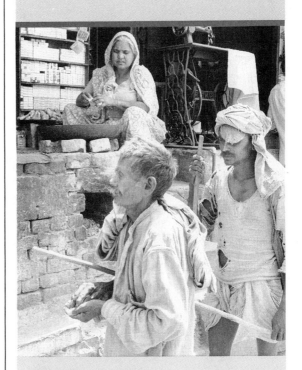

FIGURE 6.2   Caste

The caste system in India is a complex social and religious system of ordering the members of its society. The highest rank is the Brahmin caste and the lowest, the Sudra. Beneath these are the Untouchables, not considered a part of the caste system. These untouchables perform menial tasks such as bricklaying.

other jatis. For instance, potters of the artisan class are expected to make pottery for the farmers, while the farmer is expected to present the potter with a traditional portion of his harvest. The relations between the jatis are most noticeable when a ritual is performed. For instance, Brahmins must officiate using bowls made by the Potter jati and wearing clothes provided by the Weaver jati and washed by the Washer jati. Such rituals portray the interdependence of the various jatis and reassert the rights of each to belong to the community, since all public rituals require the cooperation of all jatis. In everyday economic life, few people in modern India actually make their living on the basis of their jati occupation. Many people may provide services for a fee or follow an occupation different from their traditional jati occupation, since most jatis have more members than are necessary for performing the service. Thus, jati occupations represent more a system of ritual than of real economic ranking.

Hostilities sometimes arise within the system because the different castes each are accorded different amounts of honor, power, and wealth. The Hindu religious ideology helps to minimize these conflicts by asserting that individuals who conform well to the rules that govern their position in life will be rewarded by future rebirth into a higher caste. By accepting the caste system and following its rules, one may eventually attain a sufficient spiritual development to avoid being reborn into the world and its misery. Those who rebel against the rules of caste will be reborn at a lower position, thereby prolonging the cycles of reincarnation and human suffering.

Contextual Cues

No matter how simple or complex a society, each of its members will hold more than one status. Each role of each status has a particular situation in which its manifestation is considered appropriate. In other words, people learn to play each of their numerous roles as they are directed by culturally defined **contextual cues**, which might be the location in which they find themselves, the date and time of day, or the statuses of other persons who are present. Thus, in the United States and Canada, holders of the status of student who find themselves in the context of a classroom during a scheduled class meeting time are expected to play one of their student roles that is appropriate to that set of cues. In another setting, students may relate to a teacher through another of their student-appropriate roles, but one that is more appropriate to the nonclassroom setting. When the teacher leaves, the students' behavior may shift radically as they play the roles of entirely different statuses.

Sometimes conflicting contextual cues occur in the same situation, calling for different roles at the same time. In such circumstances, depending on how different those roles are from one another, the individual may experience an extreme degree of psychological disorientation and confusion technically called **role conflict**. For instance, the first time a newly married couple is visited by their parents in the couple's home, a degree of awkwardness may arise when the young couple attempt to play the role of heads of household in the presence of their parents, who have previously had a monopoly over that superior status.

When people have several statuses that are significantly different in rank, they will tend to adopt the highest status that is appropriate to the situation. The greater the importance that ranking has in a society, the more its members will attempt, wherever possible, to avoid appearing in roles of subordinate statuses. The exception to this rule is that a person who has attained a highly ranked status, such as a senator or a Nobel Prize winner, may play the role of a much lower status as a way of showing respect for his or her subordinates. United States presidents have been photographed in their shirt sleeves on tractors, and Diana, Princess of Wales, has driven a tank while visiting a British military base as ways of "humanizing" themselves in the public eye.

---

contextual cues culturally defined indicators such as setting, date, time of day, or the statuses of other persons present, that determine which roles are appropriate and which are inappropriate to play

role conflict emotional discomfort and confusion experienced in situations in which conflicting contextual cues indicate that an individual should play the roles of more than one of his or her statuses

Master Statuses

The usual pattern in which the setting determines which roles a person may play is altered when he or she holds a master status. A master status is one that is so strongly imbued with importance in the minds of people that it cannot be ignored. For instance, if the chief justice of the United States Supreme Court or a well-known actor were to appear in a college classroom on parents' visiting day, this visitor probably would not be treated as just another parent in the audience. More likely, instead of the situation's defining the status of the visitor, the situation itself would be redefined to fit the visitor's master status. Unlike an ordinary parent, such a visitor would likely be introduced to the class, and the regular lecture might even be preempted by remarks from the guest.

Master statuses may have low rank as well as high. Having a low-ranked master status can overshadow the other statuses a person may hold, even those usually held in high esteem by others. For instance, an alcoholic physician may find it difficult to acquire patients or to obtain referrals from other doctors. Having a low-ranked master status at one time in one's life can bar one from attaining more respected statuses later.

Master statuses of low social rank are sometimes given the special designation of minorities. Minority statuses in United States society include ascribed statuses such as female, African American, Chicano, or Native American, and achieved statuses such as drug addict, prostitute, ex-convict, or mental patient.

Minority status is not necessarily a matter of numbers. In the United States, for instance, females make up slightly more than 50 percent of the population, and blacks constitute large numerical majorities in many cities and counties. Yet birth into either of these statuses may impede acquisition and successful use of highly ranked social statuses. Thus, U.S. women currently hold only about 12 percent of elective offices in a society in which they comprise over half of the total population, and adult black males in the United States suffer from an unemployment rate that is twice that of the adult male work force as a whole.

master status a social status that is so important that it can't be ignored
minorities those with a low-ranked master status, commonly but incorrectly called a "minority group"

An American Master Status

In the United States and Canada, homosexuals have had minority status since they have been identified as a social group. There has been some movement toward acceptance of gays and lesbians since the Gay Liberation Movement of the late 1960s. However, homophobia, fear of and hostility toward homosexuality and homosexuals, is still a common phenomenon: homosexuals are barred from military service; the Boy Scouts of America has denied membership to homosexual boys and excluded gay men as scoutmasters; gay couples lack the legal and economic benefits of marriage, such as inheritance rights and insurance benefits that are available to heterosexuals; in 1986, the U.S. Supreme Court ruled that laws forbidding sexual intimacy between same-sex partners are constitutional. In these and in other ways, lesbians and gays are singled out by public institutions for discrimination that defines them as members of society who are not

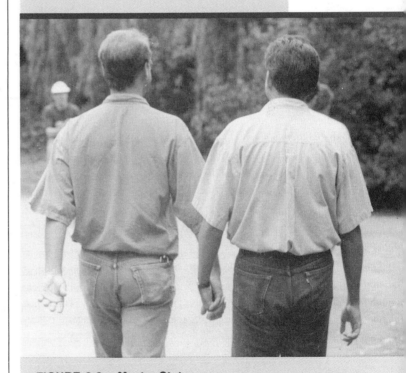

FIGURE 6.3   Master Status
Master status is a position in society a person holds of either high or low rank that cannot be ignored. A low-ranking master status, such as a female, Chicano, or drug addict, is called a minority. In various parts of the world, homosexuals also hold minority status.

entitled to rights and privileges that are taken for granted by heterosexuals.

Homophobia is most likely to occur where the gender roles of men and women are particularly distinct and the roles of women are ranked below those of men. Thus, homophobia and female subordination are related phenomena. George Weinberg (1982), the American psychoanalyst who coined the term *homophobia*, found that the most homophobic individuals were those who associated men's roles with the exercise of power and dominance and women's roles with passivity. Such individuals perceive homosexuals as having abandoned the traditional roles of men or women.

In the view of Adrienne Rich (1980), the subordination of women in a patriarchal society is perpetuated by the assumption that heterosexuality is the normal human state. This assumption, which she calls heterosexism, maintains male dominance by denying the validity of female viewpoints. Charlotte Bunch (1975) has argued that the oppression of homosexuals and of women are linked phenomena, since patriachal institutions control women through heterosexist definitions that assume "that every woman either is or wants to be bonded to a man both economically and emotionally" (1978, p. 180). Heterosexism operates in all institutions, not just in the narrow arena of sex. For instance, Bunch points out (1975, p. 52) that the subordinate roles of women in the workplace—roles such as secretary, waitress, and others—perpetuate economic discrimination because they are built on the assumption that women's proper roles are defined by their relationship to higher status males.

Dennis Werner (1979) found that homophobia was one aspect of a broader opposition to any form of nonprocreative sex. He tested the hypothesis that attitudes toward homosexuality are negative where population growth is desired and permissive where population pressures are severe. He compared a sample of **pronatalist societies**, societies whose customs favor reproduction by forbidding practices such as abortion or infanticide that can limit population growth, with a sample of **antinatalist societies** that permit such practices. In 75 percent of the pronatalist societies, homosexuality was ridiculed, forbidden, or punished, but in 60 percent of antinatalist societies, homosexuality was permitted among at least some members of society. Thus, homophobia and the minority status of homosexuals can be understood as byproducts of values that encourage heterosexual marriage and procreation.

Biological Traits and Social Statuses

In every human society, some of the statuses that people hold are based on observed biological characteristics such as sex, degree of biological maturation, physiological handicap, or skin color. But as we shall see, the analysis of biological observations can be influenced by cultural expectations.

Statuses Based on Biological Distinctions

In all human societies that have been studied by anthropologists, males and females have been expected to adopt lifework and ways of acting thought to be appropriate to their sex. For instance, in foraging societies, the status of hunter is commonly assigned to the males of the group, while the gatherers of wild vegetable foods are usually females. Gender-role distinctions exist everywhere, but they are understood in many different ways. In some groups they are merely convenient ways of dividing up the work, but individuals may frequently do the work usually undertaken by the other gender because it happens to be helpful to do so at the time. In others, crossing gender boundaries is unacceptable and conformity to gender roles has great implications for a person's reputation. In some societies gender roles are accounted for by saying simply that they are traditional. For instance, the Great Basin Shoshoni

pronatalist societies those whose customs favor reproduction and forbid abortion and infanticide
antinatalist societies those whose customs favor low birth rates and thus permit abortion and infanticide

assigned the title of "hunter" to men because they were more likely than women to hunt alone away from camp, yet women and children contributed more physical labor in communal hunting than did the men. In other societies gender-role differences are held to be the result of innate sexual characteristics, although there are important cultural differences in how these physical differences are defined. The Bijagos of Guinea-Bissau, for instance, argue that women are physically stronger than men and cite their ability to go through childbirth as evidence. Yet, heavy labor is assigned to men because they are ranked below women in importance. In European societies it has been common to think of men as physically stronger and therefore better suited to heavy labor, while physically lighter tasks were often given to women. Thus, there is tremendous cultural variation in how gender-role differences are understood and explained.

Similarly, all human societies have used differences in the biological aging process to place individuals into different statuses. Social distinctions involving different behavioral expectations, rights, and responsibilities have been made among infants, children, adults, and the aged.

The blind, deaf, mentally disabled, and other individuals considered to have unusual physiological characteristics are also often set apart in status and may be expected to behave differently.

In many societies today, persons may be categorized and given different roles on the basis of cultural concepts about race. Just as there are cultural differences in how biological sex differences are understood, so there are cultural differences in defining race. The behavioral expectations of individuals based on how they are racially categorized in a particular culture may be highly arbitrary, with no basis in the actual physiological characteristics that differentiate the status holders.

Innate Differences vs.
Socially Learned Roles

Humans may differ from one another in behavioral capacities or generalized tendencies, such as activity level, aggressiveness, or responsiveness to stimuli. Such differences are innate and may result from biologically inherited hormonal and neurological factors. Social roles are not inherited biologically, but rather, as cultural phenomena, are learned. Our inborn predispositions may influence the style with which we play a role, but they do not determine the content of our roles.

Although biology does not control the content of social roles, beliefs about biology may. People who share some biological characteristic may be socialized into playing roles that their culture claims are a natural result of those biological traits. The result is a self-fulfilling prophecy in which playing the learned role seems to prove the culture's association of the behaviors with biology. For instance, an active female child may be subject to intensive social training that leads her to conform to a more passive and nonaggressive role because her society considers these traits attributes of the female status. Similarly, Scott (1969) has described an interesting process by which those with poor vision may acquire the status of blind persons. Having been labeled blind by legal criteria, such persons may begin to interact with various care-giving agencies. In the process of providing their services, these agencies may unwittingly encourage their poorly sighted clients to learn to perceive themselves as helpless. Learning to play the blind role inhibits the use of whatever vision the clients actually possess.

When statuses are assigned to people because of biological characteristics, the roles that they are expected to play are commonly thought of as a natural and inherent result of those biological conditions. In societies where men hold powerful statuses, the culture is apt to contain beliefs that men are somehow naturally more dominant than women. Where one racial group dominates another in the same society, the members who hold the more highly ranked statuses will generally be described as inherent leaders, while those of the subordinate race will be commonly portrayed as naturally lazy, less intelligent, and in need of guidance. This practice of attributing differences in role expectations to the supposed biologically inherited qualities is especially widespread in views commonly held in many parts of the world about racial and sexual differences. The belief that role expectations of members of different racial groups are actually hereditary characteristics is known as **racism**. The belief that role differences between women and men are biologically caused has a parallel name, **sexism**.

---

racism the belief that differences in the expected roles of members of different racial groups are based on the hereditarily controlled behavioral predispositions of those groups

sexism the belief that differences in the sex roles of males and females are biologically determined

Racism.   Though inaccurate and demeaning, racism has evolved because it serves a variety of societal needs such as supporting the political and economic goals of various segments of society. Racism goes a step beyond the mere belief that different races exist. It states that people of different "races" differ in behavioral abilities and that they therefore should play different social roles which, of course, generally reflect the ethnocentric prejudices of the racist, the superior roles being reserved for those who belong to the racist's group.

The racist approach to describing society is predicated on confusing biological heredity with learning culturally assigned roles. In the United States, nearly everyone has heard such racist stereotypes as "White people are natural leaders," "Blacks are natural athletes and can jump higher than whites," and "Jews are born businessmen." The continued existence of such stereotypes that contend that certain ways of acting are inherited through one's biological race readily supports a society's ongoing practice of treating the holders of different racial statuses in different ways.

Such racist ideas tend to inhibit social change by supporting discriminatory policies. Even the so-called minority groups may use racist stereotypes—"Whites are naturally racist"—to gain more power by uniting members of their group in opposition to the status quo. Racism of this type also serves as political leverage when applied against the guilt that many people of the dominant status groups feel about the inequitable past treatment of minority groups.

Whether serving the values of the dominant or subordinate members of a society, racist stereotypes are frequently based on the prejudices of the group that is doing the labeling and may be highly inaccurate. For instance, when Jackie Robinson was attempting to become the first black to enter major league baseball in the United States, newspaper editorials throughout the country contended that to allow blacks to play on major league teams would lower the quality of the game. In that day, blacks were regarded as naturally inferior athletes. Now that it has become commonplace for blacks to be recruited to professional sports, one is more likely to hear the equally racist idea that blacks are inherently superior athletes.

Sexism.   Like racism, sexism treats individuals as if they are by nature constrained by whatever traits are socially imputed to their group, often even after they have demonstrated that the stereotype does not fit them personally. People forget that the role expectations that society may place on a group may be arbitrary and socially learned rather than innate.

Sexist concepts include the ideas that men are instinctively aggressive and females innately passive or nurturing. Only a few years ago in the United States, a father who chose to remain home to care for his children or a mother who sought employment outside the home was sometimes thought of as abnormal. Today, Americans are more accustomed to these new role options for men and women, although women's roles have changed much more than have those of men, and "househusbands" are still far from common. In political elections in the early 1990s, as women's electability has improved, it is not uncommon for male candidates for office who run against women to stress issues such as crime and military defense, which play on public stereotypes about the

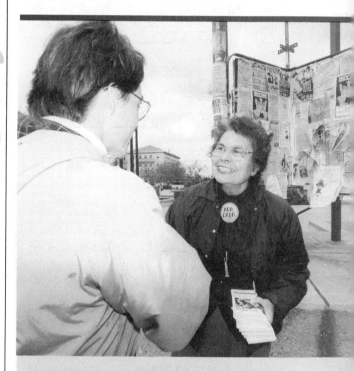

FIGURE 6.4   Female Roles
The expectation that females will follow traditional roles has changed in recent years in the United States. The fact that females have succeeded in such traditionally male roles as politician, physician, or soldier is evidence that gender roles are learned, not biologically inherited. Here, Ada Deer, an American Indian who ran for Congress in 1992 in Wisconsin, distributes leaflets.

need for "masculine" skills, a tactic that implies that men are the better choice by virtue of their sex.

Although there are biological differences between the sexes, it is important not to confuse such differences with those that are based simply on learned gender roles. The fact that individuals are capable of disregarding the traditional role expectations of their group is evidence that there is, in fact, no instinctive impulse for them to follow those roles. The topics of gender and sexism are covered in greater depth in chapter 9.

The Life Cycle

Arnold Van Gennep (1960) has pointed out that as we move from one status to another within the **life cycle**, the life events and status changes that are typically experienced by individuals are commonly proclaimed to other members of society by formal rituals known as life crisis rites or rites of passage.

Rites of Passage

Ceremonies such as christenings, puberty rituals, marriages, and funerals, which we hold whenever a member of society undergoes an important change in status within the life cycle of the group, are considered **rites of passage**. They symbolically dramatize how important status changes are in the eyes of society and help to maintain stability and order while society adjusts to culturally significant changes in people's lives. The acquisition of a new status calls for the successful adoption of a new set of roles by the person who is moving into the new phase of life. The formal dramatization of these changes in a ritual of status change may be psychologically beneficial to those who are beginning roles that they have not practiced before, and to other members of society who must also adopt new ways of relating to them. Four public symbolic rituals are commonly celebrated throughout the world: naming ceremonies, which confer human status on the new member of society and proclaim the parenthood of its caretakers; puberty celebrations, which confer adult status; marriages, which legitimize new sexual, economic, and childrearing obligations; and funerals, which proclaim the loss of human status by the deceased and restructure the ongoing social order.

FIGURE 6.5   Rites of Passage
Rites of passage symbolically dramatize significant changes in people's lives. They not only help the person adjust to his or her new role, but also help other members of the family or of society understand new ways of relating to the person. In Roman Catholic countries such as Mexico, an important ritual in a person's spiritual growth is the taking of the sacrament of Holy Communion. These girls prepare for the ritual with candles, prayer books, and rosary beads.

Pregnancy, Childbirth, and Naming

The first life-cycle change is associated with birth. Yet even before that obviously major event, our parents are experiencing the status changes of pregnancy. The biological facts of conception, pregnancy, and the birth process are interpreted differently

life cycle   the status changes from birth to death that are typical of a particular society
rite of passage (life crisis rite)   a ritual that formalizes a major change in social status

among various cultures. After birth, each society also has its specific ways of raising us.

Pregnancy. People in most societies believe that pregnancy is a result of sexual intercourse, but conception itself is explained in a variety of ways. Often the child is thought of as developing from semen, menstrual blood, or both. In many societies, both the mother and the father are believed to contribute during intercourse to the conception and sometimes to the growth of the child. Sometimes, however, the role of one parent is more important in explaining the origin of the child. For instance, in ancient Greece, the father was thought to plant the child in the mother as one might plant a seed in the field. The mother merely carried the father's child as it grew. Such a metaphor was not uncommon in horticultural societies in which men were dominant. In other societies, where men and women had equal status, the symbols of procreation might emphasize the role of both father and mother in conception. In a few cases, women were thought to become pregnant without the aid of a husband.

Conception Without Sex in the Trobriand Islanders' Ideology

Very few societies view conception as being caused spiritually rather than sexually. Most notable, though, for such beliefs are the native peoples of Australia and the native inhabitants of the Trobriand Islands. Bronislaw Malinowski (1929), who contributed to the development of anthropological research and analytic methods, lived for years among the Trobriand Islanders during World War I. He reported their beliefs about conception in a book ethnocentrically entitled *The Sexual Life of Savages*, from which the following account is derived.

The Trobrianders' ideas about conception are related to their beliefs in reincarnation. The Trobrianders believe that after death the spirit (*baloma*) of a person goes to Tuma, the Island of the Dead, where it enjoys a happier life than that of mortals. Periodically it rejuvenates itself until it decides to return to the world of mortals. Then it transforms itself into a small spirit-infant. The spirit-infant is brought to a human mother-to-be by an older controlling spirit, who usually appears to the woman in a dream to inform her that she is about to become pregnant. This controlling spirit is most often a maternal relative of the woman, or her father.

After revealing its intentions, the controlling spirit lays the child in the woman's head, causing blood from her body to rush there before descending to the womb with the spirit-child. Although intercourse may open the way for the child, it is not thought to cause conception. Actual entry of the child into the mother's womb is apparently thought to be by way of the vagina, since the Trobrianders insist that a virgin is unable to conceive because of her "tightness." After conception the woman's menstrual flow is said to cease because the mother's blood nourishes the body of the infant and helps to build it.

According to Malinowski, the combination of mystical and physiological features of these pregnancy beliefs provided a complete theory of how human life originates. In addition, Malinowski noted that Trobriand social, economic, and political life was carried out within a matrilineal society in which the members of social groups shared maternal ancestors. Thus, in day-to-day social life maternity was a much more influential fact than paternity. Malinowski concluded that the Trobriand ideology of reproduction "also gives a good theoretical foundation for matriliny; for the whole process of introducing new life into a community lies between the spirit world and the female organism. There is no room for any sort of physical paternity" (1929, p. 179).

Malinowski contrasted the Trobrianders' mother-oriented system of thought with the more male-oriented ideology of the missionaries who sought to convert them to a Christian belief system:

We must realize that in the cardinal dogma of God the Father and God the Son, the sacrifice of the only Son and the filial love of man to his Maker would completely misfire in a matrilineal society, where the relation between a father and son is decreed by tribal laws to be that of two strangers, where all personal unity between them is denied, and where all family obligations are associated with mother-line. We cannot, then, wonder that paternity must be among the principal truths to be inculcated by proselytizing Christians. Otherwise the dogma of the Trinity would have to be translated into matrilineal terms, and we should have to speak of a God-kadala (mother's brother), a God-sister's-son, and a divine baloma spirit. But apart from any doctrinal difficulty, the missionaries are earnestly engaged in propagating sexual morality as we conceive it, in which endeavor the idea of the sexual act as having serious consequences to family life is indispensable. (pp. 186–187)

The Trobrianders vehemently opposed the idea of physiological paternity, a belief that is well-suited to a society with a strong patriarchal ideology but not to their own. They characterized the missionaries' belief that sex is the cause of conception as an absurdity and the missionaries, therefore, as liars. For example, Malinowski quotes one of his informants as saying, "Not at all, the missionaries are mistaken, unmarried girls continually have intercourse, in fact they overflow with seminal fluid, and yet have no children" (p. 188). By native logic, if sex were the cause of pregnancy, the unmarried girls would become pregnant more often than older married women, since they engage in sexual intercourse much more often. Yet it is the older married women who have the most children. Another informant argued, "Copulation alone cannot produce a child. Night after night, for years, girls copulate. No child comes" (p. 189), contending thereby that the empirical evidence did not support the view of a relationship between sex and pregnancy. Malinowski also tells us that, "one of my informants told me that

after over a year's absence he returned to find a newly born child at home. He volunteered this statement as an illustration and final proof of the truth that sexual intercourse had nothing to do with conception. And it must be remembered that no native would ever discuss any subject in which the slightest suspicion of his wife's fidelity would be involved" (p. 193).

According to Annette Weiner, the contemporary Trobrianders, who no longer disagree with Western ideas about procreation, continue to use the concept of "virgin birth" as a way of avoiding public shame over infidelity. Weiner, relying on myths and old people's beliefs, argues that the Trobriand ideas about spirits causing pregnancy may have served this purpose even in Malinowski's day. She believes that the implicit understanding that both sexes are part of the process of reproduction existed in ideas that, although spirits cause the pregnancy, sexual intercourse is necessary for the development of the fetus *after* conception: "A man develops and maintains the growth of the fetus through repeated sexual intercourse with his wife" (Weiner, 1976, p. 123).

The Trobriand Islanders' denial that sex causes conception symbolically supported their emphasis on inheritance of both property and familial authority through the mother's line. The concept of a paternal role in the creation of a child would challenge the kinship system around which their political and economic life was built.

(for reference map see p. 92)

On the surface, some societies appear to be unaware of the link between intercourse and conception. Walter E. Roth claimed that the indigenous people of the Tully River of North Queensland, Australia, were ignorant of the role of sex in pregnancy:

A woman begets children because (a) she has been sitting over the fire on which she has roasted a particular species of black bream, which must have been given to her by the prospective father, (b) she has purposely gone a-hunting and caught a certain kind of bullfrog, (c) some men may have told her to be in an interesting condition, or (d) she may dream of having the child put inside her. (quoted in Leach, 1969, p. 87)

On the other hand, Tully River people were aware that copulation causes pregnancy in animals. It is unlikely, therefore, that they were unaware that sex caused pregnancy in humans in a purely physiological sense. However, in any culture, people's ideas about humans are never straightforward descriptions of observed fact, uninfluenced by their values. Their denial of the role of sex in human pregnancy was not simple ignorance; it was a symbolic affirmation of their ideologically important values. According to Leach, the pregnancy beliefs of the people of Tully River are ways of affirming that "The relationship between the woman's child and the clansmen of the woman's husband stems from public recognition of the bonds of marriage, rather than from the facts of cohabitation" (1969, p. 87). The people of Tully River believe that pregnancy is "caused" by a woman's catching the right kind of bullfrog in the same sense that Christians believe that a wife's fertility is "caused" by the rice thrown at her at the end of her wedding ceremony.

Pregnancy rituals. Pregnancy is a time of potential anxiety, since it's fraught with possible negative outcomes such as miscarriage, physical defects in the baby, or death in childbirth for either the infant or the mother. Such anxieties cause people to turn to symbolic **pregnancy rituals** to protect the child and pregnant woman and to aid in a successful birth. These rituals are frequently expected to apply to the husband as well as the pregnant woman. They generally take the form of taboos against doing things that have some similarity to the feared outcomes. For instance, the Great Basin Shoshoni forbid a pregnant woman or her husband to eat either the mud hen, which they called the "fool's hen," or the trout, which flops about when one catches it, since the former might result in the child's being stupid and the latter in its becoming entangled in the umbilical cord during labor.

Among the Aztecs of Mexico, pregnant women were forbidden to look at an eclipse of the sun, which they called *Tonaltiu qualo*, meaning "The sun is being eaten," since to see this phenomenon might result in a lip defect, such as harelip, in the unborn child. As a prophylactic against the effects of accidentally seeing an eclipse, the Aztec mother-to-be might wear an obsidian blade over her breast to protect the child. Formerly, in many parts of the United States one heard advice against eating strawberries or raspberries during pregnancy, because they might result in birthmarks.

On the other hand, some pregnancy rules require behaviors that are similar to the characteristics of a good birth. The Shoshoni father was encouraged to hunt the otter, since this animal is known for its enjoyment of sliding down slippery riverbanks, much as the child was hoped to pass easily through the birth canal. In some groups in the United States, women are encouraged to engage in artistic pursuits such as listening to classical music to increase the chances of the child's becoming artistically inclined.

Abortion. Abortion has been practiced throughout history and in most societies that have been studied by anthropologists. For instance,

George Devereux examined a sample of 350 nonindustrialized societies and reported that intentionally induced abortions were "an absolutely universal phenomenon" (1967, p. 98). More recently, abortion has been studied by anthropologist Suzanne Frayser (1985). Using a sample of 47 societies for which data on attitudes about abortion was available, she found that most societies publicly disapprove of abortion primarily because they are most commonly performed when the circumstances of pregnancy are socially unacceptable, for instance, when the pregnant woman is unmarried or does not want another child.

Devereux (1955) examined the methods of abortion in 400 societies that lacked modern medical techniques. He listed 16 techniques that women commonly use to terminate their pregnancies. They include doing strenuous activity, squeezing or jolting the belly, inserting foreign objects or noxious fluids into the uterus, or taking drugs to harm the fetus or cause it to be expelled. These traditional techniques are generally ineffective and are as likely to harm or kill the woman as the fetus. In contrast, medical techniques developed in this century and now available in most of the world are safer than pregnancy itself when carried out during the first trimester.

Two sociologists, Steven Nock and Paul Kingston, argue that U.S. abortion politics is really a conflict about women's roles. They assert that antiabortion activists "believe men and women to be intrinsically different in their social roles. Women, such individuals believe, are destined to be mothers first and foremost. Because motherhood is women's natural role, anything that makes it less central or less important makes women less important" (1990, p. 209). In their view, "The abortion debate pits traditional women and men against nontraditional men and women. In a very real sense, the argument is over how we as Americans view women: Are they equal to men?" (p. 210).

The view that abortion politics is motivated by gender-related values is supported by the research of James Prescott, a cross-cultural psychologist. He compared the voting records of legislators in Canada and the United States and found that those with antiabortion records were more likely than those with a "pro-choice" voting record to support capital pun-

---

pregnancy rituals religious rules such as taboos designed to protect the unborn child and the mother during pregnancy and childbirth or admonitions to engage in acts believed to be a positive influence on the developing child ishment, the Vietnam war, and military aid to the Nicaraguan "Contras." They were also more likely to oppose handgun controls, the use of medical heroin for dying patients, and to support the illegality of fornication and adultery and the punishment of prostitution. He concluded that opposition to abortion is related to male dominance, opposition to equality for women, and moral fundamentalism.

Prescott found a similar pattern of social values concerning abortion and gender roles in a cross-cultural survey. He compared cultures that denied a woman the right to abortion with those that permitted abortions and found that anti-abortion cultures were also most likely to have practiced slavery, the torture, killing, and mutilation of prisoners of war, the exploitation of women and children, the punishment and/or rejection of premarital and extramarital sex, and the definition of family membership in terms of fatherhood alone (1990, p. 109). In other words, nonindustrialized abortion-intolerant societies have tended to be warlike ones in which the patriarchal domination of women and other minorities was the basis of social life.

It has also been suggested that cultural values concerning abortion are related to the perceived need for population growth. When it is not considered important, women have great latitude in aborting a pregnancy; when it is considered important to increase family size, women often face strict rules against abortion. For instance, Stephen Mosher (1983) has documented the strong governmental role in limiting family size in the People's Republic of China that has led in some instances to coercive pressure on women who have previously had children to undergo abortions, sometimes as late as in the seventh month of pregnancy. In other countries in which the government has supported a population growth policy, women's access to contraceptive information and abortion has been denied by governmental action. Romania under Nicolae Ceausescu—who was overthrown in December of 1989—is a prime illustration of such a country. Karen Breslau, a *Newsweek* correspondent in Bucharest, reported that in 1966, Ceausescu declared, "The fetus is the property of the entire society" and "Anyone who avoids having children is a deserter who abandons the laws of national continuity" (1990, p. 35). Under his pro-childbirth policy, Romania's birthrate nearly doubled. The law forbade sex education and abortion. Women were required to be given pregnancy tests every three months. Pregnant women who miscarried were called in for questioning on suspicion of having had an illegal abortion, and those who did not have children were charged a "celibacy tax" that could be as much as 10 percent of their monthly salaries.

Birth. In most societies, when the woman enters labor she is attended by one or more women who have already experienced childbirth themselves and who help her through the process. Most commonly, birth occurs with the woman assuming a kneeling or squatting position, a posture that facilitates the birth process more than the reclining position traditionally used in many Western hospitals. These upright birthing positions have a beneficial effect on the angle of the birth canal and take advantage of gravity in aiding the passage of the infant.

FIGURE 6.6   Birth
The most common method of giving birth in non-Western societies is for the woman to assume a squatting position. This !Kung San woman is preparing to give birth, with an older woman in attendance who will assist her.

It is only in recent years that Western medicine has begun to abandon its customary treatment of women in labor as if they were ill patients undergoing a surgical procedure. With pressure from women's groups, the role of the woman in her labor has been redefined as an active partner with others involved in the birthing process, and changes have begun to be made in the woman's posture during childbirth that facilitate her role and not simply that of the medical personnel.

!Kung San

The !Kung (pronounced with a click of the tongue first) are a division of the San people. Today they live in the Kalahari desert of Botswana, Namibia, and Angola, but since their food resources are becoming scarce, they have been forced to work on neighboring farms rather than forage. Medical facilities are as inaccessible today as they were when Nisa gave birth.

Nisa's First Labor

Marjorie Shostak has written a fascinating biography of a !Kung San woman, Nisa. The !Kung are the northern linguistic subdivision of the San people, all of whom were foragers in traditional times. The San as a whole occupied lands in Botswana, Namibia, Angola, and South Africa. The !Kung San live mostly in Botswana and Namibia. Nisa's home was in northwest Botswana. !Kung San women faced childbirth without medical facilities or the help of traditional midwives, although they were often helped to give birth by their own or their husband's female relatives. About one woman died for every 500 births, and infant and child death was common. Nisa's account of her first birth is dramatic:

I lay there and felt the pains as they came, over and over again. Then I felt something wet, the beginning of the childbirth. I thought, "Eh hey, maybe it is the child." I got up, took a blanket and covered Tashay with it; he was still sleeping. Then I took another blanket and my smaller duiker skin covering and I left. Was I not the only one? The only other woman was Tashay's grandmother, and she was asleep in her hut. So, just as I was, I left.

I walked a short distance from the village and sat down beside a tree. I sat there and waited; she wasn't ready to be born. I lay down, but she still didn't come out. I sat up again. I leaned against the tree and began to feel the labor. The pains came over and over, again and again. It felt as though the baby was trying to jump right out! Then the pains stopped. I said, "Why doesn't it hurry up and come out? Why doesn't it come out so I can rest? What does it want inside me that it just

stays in there? Won't God help me to have it come out quickly?"

As I said that, the baby started to be born. I thought, "I won't cry out. I'll just sit here. Look, it's already being born and I'll be fine." But it really hurt! I cried out, but only to myself. I thought, "Oh, I almost cried out in my in-laws' village." Then I thought, "Has my child already been born?" Because I wasn't really sure; I thought I might only have been sick. That's why I hadn't told anyone when I left the village.

After she was born, I sat there; I didn't know what to do. I had no sense. She lay there moving her arms about, trying to suck on her fingers. She started to cry. I just sat there, looking at her. I thought, "Is this my child? Who gave birth to this child?" Then I thought, "A big thing like that? How could it possibly have come out from my genitals?" I sat there and looked at her, looked and looked and looked.

The cold started to grab me. I covered her with my duiker skin that had been covering my stomach and pulled the larger kaross over myself. Soon, the afterbirth came down and I buried it. I started to shiver. I just sat there, trembling with the cold. I still hadn't tied the umbilical cord. I looked at her and thought, "She's no longer crying. I'll leave her here and go to the village to bring back some coals for a fire." (1983, pp. 193-194)

Today, 62,000 San people live in the Kalahari desert of Botswana, Namibia, and Angola. None survive in South Africa. Between 2,000 and 5,000 of the San continue to forage, but their food resources are becoming scarcer as agriculture and cattle ranching expands in the areas that surround them. Most of the San have been forced to adopt work as day laborers on neighboring ranches and farms or have migrated to nearby towns in search of work. Their unemployment rate in the towns is high and the San standard of living is probably lower than it was traditionally. Modern medical facilities at the time of childbirth are as inaccessible today as they were when Nisa gave birth to her first child.

Couvade. A few societies, most commonly gardening societies that occupy tropical forest environments, have a custom known as the **couvade**, in which the husband acts as if he is going through labor while his wife is giving birth to their child. This ritual is often performed with the intent of providing religious protection for the newborn child by misdirecting any potentially harmful supernatural powers away from the actual birth that is in process elsewhere.

Why would such a practice be more likely in tropical forests? The groundwork for answering this question was laid by John Whiting (1964), who showed that in societies with protein scarcity—e.g., many tropical forest crops do not have all the amino acids necessary for protein building—children tend to be nursed for long periods. This protects the child from suffering from protein deficiency in its early developmental period. Prolonged nursing is facilitated by rules against the nursing mother's having sex for several years after the birth of a child, since another pregnancy would require weaning the first child. The sex taboo, however, does not prevent the husband from having other wives and continuing his sex life during this period in their households. One result of this arrangement is that a male child spends his early years with no male role model in residence in his mother's household.

If male solidarity is extremely important—for instance, where warfare is common—male puberty rites may be one way of helping the boy finally break his sexual identification with his mother and prove clearly that he has entered the masculine domain. Munroe, Munroe, and Whiting (1973) have argued that the couvade was a possible alternative to male puberty rites in protein-deficient environments where the boy proved his manhood by enduring pain. Where this was not done, the psychological identification with the female role was never fully lost, and the couvade occurred as a symbolic acting out of the female role at the time of childbirth. Be this as it may, the link between the couvade and protein-deficient environments is clear. For instance, the couvade is not found in certain tropical forests such as those of Southeast Asia where pigs and chickens have been domesticated or where vegetable foods are grown that provide all the amino acids necessary for protein synthesis by the human body.

Although many do not accept Munroe, Munroe, and Whiting's rather Freudian interpretation of the significance of the couvade as a completely satisfactory explanation of its presence in protein-deficient environments, the custom does make sense in a rather pragmatic way: Since the father will be absent from the home in which his child will be raised, the couvade publicly affirms his paternity.

Naming. The next important symbolic act in the life of a newborn baby is its **naming ceremony**. In this ritual the baby is officially received into the community of human beings and symbolically given human status by acquiring a human name. In the birth or naming ritual, the infant is commonly brought into contact with those aspects of life that are of central concern to the members of the society into which it is

---

couvade a custom in which the husband acts as if he gives birth to his child

naming ceremony a rite of passage following birth, at which the infant is declared a member of the human group by being given a name

FIGURE 6.7 Naming Ceremony
In most societies, a newborn is named and initiated into the community with the ritual use of whatever element is most meaningful to the survival of the group. In the Christian tradition, water is used as a symbolic cleansing agent. The baby will typically be sponsored by two people who then become its godparents or coparents and aid in its spiritual and sometimes financial upbringing. This Lutheran minister in Stuttgart, Germany, admires the baby she has just baptized.

being received. Thus, among the Samoans of Polynesia and the Yahgan of southernmost Argentina (Cooper, 1946; Murdock, 1934; Service, 1978), both of whom relied heavily on sea products as their main source of food, the newborn child was bathed in the sea shortly after birth. The Mbuti Pygmy of the Ituri Forest of Africa (Gibbs, 1965) grow no food but obtain all their basic needs from the uncultivated resources of the forest; they therefore speak of the forest as their parent and their provider. They initiate their children into the human group in a ritual in which vines from the forest are tied around the children's ankles, wrists, and waists, thereby bringing them into contact with their future livelihood.

Enculturation, Childhood and Adolescence

From birth through adolescence, we humans are raised in some kind of family setting according to the dictates of our culture. Our upbringing usually includes some restrictions on free expression of our sexuality, including taboos against intercourse with certain family members. In many societies, our attainment of sexual maturity is marked by special puberty rites honoring our passage into adulthood.

Enculturation process. The process by which children learn the culture that guides the life of members of their society is known as **enculturation** or **socialization**. Even before they begin to communicate in the language of their society, those around them have begun to mold their behavior so that it will conform to the rules for living that make up their culture.

Anthropologists have long asserted that enculturation occurs partly by imitation and partly by direct teaching through language. Imitative learning, which Edward Hall (1959) calls **informal learning**, results in a greater tolerance for individual stylistic variation and gradual adaptations of older ways of doing things to new situations. Much of what we have learned informally is done automatically, without awareness or concentration and with little or no feeling. When the informally learned rules for doing things are broken, however, anxiety mounts rapidly in all present until someone acts to deal with the rule violation.

Learning that occurs when language is used to admonish us for violating a custom is called **formal learning**. The teacher expresses disapproval of our behavior and suggests an alternative way as the proper, moral, or good way to act. We are conscious of the rules we are following if we learned them formally, since talking about them was part of the learning. Formal ways of doing things are endowed with deep feelings by the participants, and their violation leads to tremendous insecurity in those who rely on them to order and structure their lives. For this same reason, formally learned customs are slow to change.

It is also possible to teach a custom by talking about it, but without expressing disappointment or disapproval of the learner's rule-breaking behavior.

enculturation (socialization)   the process by which children learn the customs, beliefs, and values of their culture
informal learning   learning by imitation
formal learning   learning that proceeds by admonition and correction of the learner's errors, with emotional emphasis on the importance of behaving acceptably

Instead, the new way of acting is explained by giving the logical reason that lies behind it. This form of learning has been called **technical learning** by Hall. People are most highly conscious of technically learned behaviors, since they include explanations of the reasons and benefits of the behaviors. Little emotion is associated with material learned in this way, and it may be replaced readily by new technical ways of dealing with the same situation.

Childhood sexual socialization. Before we are able to play the role of adults with complete success, we must acquire knowledge of the sexual customs of our society. Most societies deal with this necessity in a fairly matter-of-fact way. According to Clellan Ford and Frank Beach (1951), 34 percent of the 95 societies whose sexual customs they surveyed had little or no restriction on sexual experimentation in childhood. Examples of peoples whose attitudes toward childhood sexuality were **permissive** are the Lepcha, an agricultural society in the Himalayas, and the Trobrianders, who live on one of the Melanesian islands. According to Ford and Beach, the Lepcha believed that sexual activity is necessary in order for girls to grow up. Therefore, most girls were regularly engaging in full sexual intercourse by the age of 11 or 12. Among the Trobrianders, boys of 10 to 12 years of age and girls of 6 to 8 years are given explicit sexual training by older companions.

Fifty-one percent of the societies Ford and Beach studied were **semirestrictive**: Young people were expected to follow certain rules of etiquette in their exploration of their sexuality, although no severe punishments were imposed for violations. Only 15 percent of these societies were truly **restrictive** of childhood sexuality, and were most common where male solidarity was economically or politically important and where class distinctions or differences in wealth were important matters. This is certainly understandable, since adults in such societies are likely to have a greater vested interest in the future marriage plans of their children. The more carefully the sexuality of unmarried persons is controlled, the greater are their parents' options in selecting marriage partners for their children.

Puberty rituals. Near the time individuals reach biological maturity, it is common for a **puberty ritual** or **adulthood ritual** to be held. This ritual signals the transition from childhood to adulthood and impresses on both the child and his or her community that the old roles of childhood are to be

set aside and that she or he should be treated as an adult.

In the dominant North American culture, some of the traditional rites of passage are relatively weak or sometimes lacking. For instance, few people in the United States experience any form of true puberty ritual as they near adulthood. Instead we have several less significant transitions, each of which confers some of the rights of adulthood: obtaining a driver's license during the teenage years, graduating from high school, gaining the right to vote at the age of 18, and becoming old enough to legally drink alcoholic beverages at the age of 21. This lack of a clear puberty ritual often creates confusion about the roles we are expected to play and leaves individuals to wrestle alone with what in the United States culture is commonly called an "identity crisis." The existence of this expression in everyday language is evidence of how extensive role confusion is in this society. It suggests the benefits that rites of passage may provide to a society's members by helping them maintain a greater sense of self-confidence as they undergo the normal changes experienced by members of their group.

Not all societies practice puberty rituals, but they are relatively common. In Yehudi Cohen's examination (1964) of 65 societies, 46 had puberty rituals, while 19 did not. He divided these societies into two groups: those with nuclear families only (minimal families that consist only of parents and their children) and those with complex family organizations such as lineages and clans in which many related individuals participate in family affairs (see Chapter 7). He found that in societies based on the nuclear family, where children would be trained from an early age to be socially independent, the probability of puberty rituals was smaller than in those societies with more complex families, where children

---

technical learning learning that occurs when the logical rationales for specific ways of doing things—rather than emotional pressure to behave in that way—are given to the learner
permissive societies those that are tolerant of childhood sexual experimentation
semirestrictive societies those that accept childhood sexual experimentation so long as those involved follow established rules of etiquette and discretion
restrictive societies societies that do not accept childhood sexual experimentation
puberty (adulthood) ritual a rite of passage that formalizes the change from the status of child to the status of adult

were trained to play an interdependent, cooperative role with many other family members.

Social circumstances that foster interdependent role playing can lock people into their current roles and make change difficult without the aid of a mechanism for transformation from one status to another. The puberty ceremony symbolically redefines the child as an adult in a dramatic, public fashion that is difficult for those involved to ignore. The ritual proclaims the changes in rights and responsibilities that everyone in the group must recognize.

Puberty rites for males. For boys, puberty rituals seem to be most dramatic when the transition from boyhood to manhood is potentially difficult. Under such circumstances, male puberty rituals are often severe and painful ordeals, involving ceremonies such as **circumcision** (the surgical removal of the foreskin), **scarification** of the body (decorating the body with a pattern made of scars), tattooing, and the filing or knocking out of front teeth as indicators of adult status.

Whiting, Kluckhohn, and Anthony (1958) found that circumcision of males as a part of initiation rituals is especially associated with three social customs: a taboo on sex between husband and wife for a year or more after the birth of a child, the sharing of sleeping quarters by mother and child with the father's quarters elsewhere, and the establishment of residence by a married couple near the husband's relatives. The first two of these customs make it more difficult for a male child to identify with the male role, since the most available adult role model is the mother. The third, residence of couples near the husband's relatives, is common where male solidarity is important among adults. The conflict between the need to identify with the male group as an adult and the relatively weak childhood tie between father and son makes the transition from childhood to adulthood a stressful one. Hence the dramatic ritualizing of the status change through which a boy proves to the adult male community that he is capable of adopting the adult male role.

Puberty rites for females. J. Brown (1963) found that about half of a sample of 60 societies practiced puberty rituals for girls. These rituals are more likely to occur in societies where the residences of newly married couples are established near the wife's relatives than in societies where daughters leave home when they marry. The puberty ritual emphasizes the young woman's new role. The more important a woman's labor is to the family food supply, the more likely it is that female puberty rituals will be practiced. As with male initiation rituals, painful ceremonies are most likely in societies where the transition from childhood to adult roles is most difficult. For girls, this is in those societies where mothers and daughters share sleeping quarters while the father sleeps elsewhere.

Many societies in which male dominance over women is an important fact of life mutilate the genitals of female children, a practice called **female circumcision**. Hosken (1980) describes the most common forms, their effects, and the cultural settings in which they occur.

Infibulation—an operation performed mostly in childhood by which the sides of the vulva are closed over the vagina—is particularly common where the virginity of wives is important. Following infibulation, sexual intercourse is not possible until the barrier created by the operation is cut, usually by the husband. Deinfibulation is extremely painful. It can result in severe bleeding and can lead to tetanus and other infections that can damage the fallopian tubes and cause sterility. Deaths from medical complications are not uncommon. **Excision**—removal of the pleasure-sensitive clitoris—is performed to reduce a woman's sexual sensations and, thereby, her interest in sex. This is thought to increase her fidelity in marriage, especially in societies where polygyny (where men are permitted to have more than one wife) is practiced, and legitimate opportunities for heterosexual intercourse are less common for wives than for husbands. Excision is sometimes thought to increase female fertility, so it is also practiced to ensure that a woman will have many children.

Female genital mutilation is most common today in the most populous areas of East, Central, and West Africa, in some Middle Eastern countries

---

circumcision the surgical removal of the foreskin from the penis

scarification decorating the body by cutting designs in it and treating them with ashes or other material to ensure that they will produce raised scars

female circumcision mutilation of female genitals, including infibulation and excision, a symbol of male dominance in some societies

infibulation surgical closing of the female vulva over the vagina

excision surgical removal of all or part of the female clitoris

FIGURE 6.8   Puberty Rite for Females
This 12-year-old girl from the Kuria tribe in Kenya has just been circumcised without anesthesia. She carries an umbrella and shilling notes hang from her headdress. The village people dress in tree branches and clap and sing to her. The circumcision of women, traditionally to guard virginity and discourage sexual intercourse, is common in more than 20 African countries. This painful and sometimes dangerous practice is being opposed by many women and some heads of state, but continues to be practiced.

including Egypt and the southern Arabian Peninsula, and in some parts of Indonesia and Malaysia. Excision is practiced by Christian Copts in Egypt, as well as by Egyptian Moslems and by non-Moslem groups in the 26 African countries where it has been documented. Furthermore, although infibulation was not a traditional Western practice, excision was practiced by European and American surgeons into the twentieth century (Barker-Banfield, 1983) as a supposed cure for masturbation and nymphomania, a negative label for sexual desire in females.

Although the practice of female circumcision is still common, it has developed opposition in recent years by a growing number of African and European women who have become concerned especially about the medical dangers it can pose. Efforts by women acting through the United Nations have led a few heads of state to take a position against female circumcision. For instance, Thomas Sankara of Burkina Faso spoke out against female circumcision before he was deposed in 1991. Abdou Diouf of Senegal and President Daniel arap Moi of Kenya have also publicly opposed the practice. Yet, female circumcision continues to have widespread support, not only because of the weight of tradition but also because, for many, the practice became a form of resistance to colonial interference earlier in this century.

Courtship and Marriage

Following the puberty or adulthood ritual, the next common rite of passage is marriage. Cultures handle courtship and mate selection in many different ways. In many societies, marital partners are selected by parents. In others, especially those in which children will establish their own households that are economically independent of their parents, courtship and choice of spouse is a responsibility of the young adults themselves.

Sex without marriage. Following puberty, the majority of societies are quite tolerant of sexual experimentation before marriage. Frayser (1985) found that 64 percent of her cross-cultural sample of 61 societies had little or no restriction on premarital sexual relations. According to Ford and Beach (1952), the least permissive societies are, as might be expected, those in which parents have the greatest interest in controlling the marital choices of their children, societies in which people are ranked by differences in wealth or class membership, and societies in which male solidarity is economically and politically important.

sleep crawling a Samoan sexual practice in which an uninvited youth would enter a young woman's house after dark with the intent of seduction

Courtship in Samoa

In traditional Samoa before contact with Europeans, children were unshielded from the facts of sex, birth, and death. Growing up sharing a house with no walls with 50 or 60 relatives, they did not develop the kind of shame that is connected with sex in societies where privacy is more common. Chastity in daughters was a mark of prestige for families, but, as in all societies, sexual experimentation occurred discreetly. Mead (1928) believed that both men and women were equally free to choose their partners, and her informants claimed that the European concepts of fidelity and jealousy were unheard of.

Etiquette required that a rendezvous be arranged through a go-between, called a *soa*. An unmarried woman might invite a suitor to spend the night with her in her family's home if she did not wish to meet him elsewhere. In such a case, the young man might remove his clothing and grease his body to make it slippery before entering the house after dark when other family members were already asleep. It was expected that he would be discreetly gone before others arose.

This form of courtship gave rise to a custom known as **sleep crawling**, in which an unpopular youth or jilted lover might sneak into the house of a young woman without invitation, in the hope that she might be expecting another lover and allow him to stay once she had discovered the deception. Freeman (1983) regards this as a form of rape and

Samoans

On the island of Samoa in the South Pacific, courtship was generally discreet and sexual liaisons occurred under cover of darkness. Sleep crawling was a focus of courtship in which a young man would hope to gain favor with a woman by sneaking into her room at night uninvited and so impressing her that he would be invited to stay.

believes that a great deal of competition occurred among young men in this practice, due to the great emphasis that Samoan families placed on competition for status and on the chastity of their daughters as a symbol of their family honor. If the woman was not favorably disposed to the sleep crawler, she had the option of rousing her household to chase, ridicule, and beat the intruder for adopting such tactics. If he were publicly identified, a sleep crawler was disgraced and would not be entertained or considered for marriage by other women.

Informal clandestine love affairs in Samoa would eventually lead to the development of more or less permanent primary sexual liaisons between couples that were, in effect, a form of trial marriage. If the couple desired to formalize their relationship by marriage, a courtship process was required in which a go-between would accompany the lover to the woman's family and plead his case for him. After repeated visits, the actual proposal of marriage would be made by the go-between. If the marriage was acceptable to the family, a ceremony would be arranged in which elaborate gift giving took place between the two families.

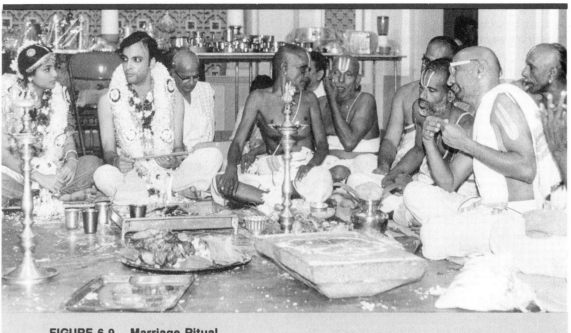

FIGURE 6.9   Marriage Ritual
The marriage ritual differs greatly from culture to culture. This bride and bridegroom sit next to Brahmin priests in a typical high caste wedding in South India.

Marriage ritual.   Once an agreement for marriage partners has been achieved between the families, the actual ritual of marriage may occur. Marriage rituals vary tremendously from society to society. They may involve elaborate symbolism and drama or they may be as simple as a public announcement by a couple that they consider themselves married. Where formal rituals of marriage are customary, the symbolism often emphasizes the union being created between the two families. It may also portray the relations, especially those of a stressful nature, that are expected to exist between the couple and their respective in-laws. For instance, among the Aztecs of Mexico the bride was carried, like a burden, on the back of the old woman who had acted as her matchmaker to the place of the marriage. After lectures by the elders of both families about their new responsibilities as married persons, the capes of the couple were tied together into a knot by which they were joined in marriage.

G. W. Stow (1905) described a South African !Kung San marriage ritual in which the bride is captured by the bridegroom and his family or friends from her defending relatives. During the wedding feast the groom was expected to seize hold of the bride. Then the two families began to fight while the

bride's family focused their attention on beating the groom with their digging sticks. The groom had to succeed in holding onto his bride during this beating for the marriage ritual to be complete. Had he failed, he would have lost his bride.

Parenthood

With marriage may come children, turning the social unit into a family. The relationship between spouses generally changes at the birth of the first child. It creates new obligations for the husband and wife and new demands on their time and energy. Their domestic roles must be adjusted to accommodate their new status as parents. No longer will they have as much exclusive time for each other.

In societies in which the family organization is important economically and politically, entry into parenthood may be formally indicated by a change in the parents' names. Using this custom, called **teknonymy**, a parent might be called Father of Lynn or

---

teknonymy   the custom of referring to a person as the parent of his or her child rather than by birth name

Mother of Kay. Teknonymy is most often practiced by men in societies in which the couple takes up residence with or near the wife's family. Women may practice it as well, but in fewer societies. In either case, it reflects an elevation in the social rank of the individual, since because of the birth of the child he or she is no longer considered an outsider to the family with which the couple resides. The name change calls attention to the greater bond that now exists between the new parent and the in-laws.

Divorce

Not all marriages last until the death of a spouse. In the United States, for instance, between 30 percent and 40 percent of marriages begun in 1989 are likely to end in divorce. Around the world, there are societies with higher and lower rates of divorce. Reasons for divorce vary, but impotence, infertility, infidelity, laziness, and simple incompatibility are common justifications. In probably three-quarters of the nonindustrialized societies that have been studied by anthropologists, women and men have been more or less equal in their right to divorce (Murdock, 1957).

Cross-cultural variations in divorce rates make it possible to discover some of the factors that make divorce less likely. The payment of a marriage gift to the bride's family gives her family a vested interest in the stability of the marriage, since the groom's family is likely to demand return of the payment if the marriage is dissolved. The dowry, a transfer of wealth in the opposite direction, has a similar effect of stabilizing marriage ties. When the couple lives in an extended family, relatives are also likely to have a stabilizing effect on their marriage. Matrilocality, discussed in chapter 8, Marriage and the Family, also is associated with a low divorce rate. Perhaps this is because the control over property this form of residence gives to women is associated with greater than usual social power and honor for women and little familial authority for the husband, who resides with his in-laws. Under these conditions, the frequency of abusive behavior by the husband is also likely to be relatively low.

Old Age

Many of us want to grow older, but we do not want to grow old. The negative feelings we have about aging are partly related to the loss of health and strength that accompany the biological process. So-

cially, aging may also bring a loss of our accustomed rank. What are the factors that contribute to the loss of social power and honor that old age brings in societies such as our own? Cross-cultural research sheds some light on this question.

When postmarital residence rules require a couple to live near one spouse's parents, it is easier for the parents to continue their roles as family heads into their old age. In societies in which the family is a cooperating economic or political group, the status of family head can be a major determinant of an older person's rank in life. According to a study of nonindustrialized societies by Lee and Kezis (1979), nuclear families lack a structure in which parents can maintain their role of family heads into old age. Older people are more likely to have high-ranked statuses in societies in which they live with related married couples and in societies in which descent is traced through only one of the parents (patrilineal or matrilineal societies) rather than through both. However, if an extended family is too large to be easily led by a single family head or couple, decisions may actually be made by smaller groups within the extended family. When the political power or wealth of a family is not consistently related to a particular lineage, parents' rank is not so likely to rise with age as in a system in which it is.

In all societies, the elderly are accorded more respect if they are economically productive. Thus, in industrialized societies where rank is associated closely with wealth and income, the social rank of the elderly tends to decline markedly at retirement.

Death

Simple and obvious criteria such as the absence of breathing, heartbeat, or reaction to pain have been used in societies throughout the world to determine when **biological death** has occurred. With the development of a technology to measure brain functioning directly, in the United States and other industrialized societies, more emphasis seems to be directed toward defining death as the cessation of activity in the cerebral cortex of the brain, the center of intellectual and conscious processes. However, these criteria may not always agree with one another. For instance, the cerebral cortex may no longer be active while the

---

biological death measured by cessation of such organic functions as breathing, heartbeat, reaction to pain, or brain functioning heart and lungs continue to operate, or a person may be comatose and unresponsive to pain, yet later report having been fully aware of the surroundings. Life-support systems used to maintain the vital functions of comatose patients whose heart and lungs have stopped functioning further complicate the process of determining biological death.

Psychological death refers to the process by which people prepare themselves subjectively for their impending biological death. According to Elizabeth Kübler-Ross (1969), who studied dying patients' responses to their circumstances in United States hospitals, the initial reaction of most patients to learning that their illness is terminal is *denial*. Patients refuse to accept the correctness of the diagnosis, insisting that some error has been made or that their records have been confused with those of someone else. Their basic attitude might be summed up as, "There must be some mistake; this cannot be happening to me!" When they finally accept that they are in fact dying, denial is replaced by a period of *anger*, which is characterized by rage, envy, and resentment. In this period, the dominant question is, "Why me, why not someone else?" The anger may be directed at anyone at hand—other patients, doctors, nurses, even family members who come to visit and comfort the person. The third stage is one of *bargaining* for more time. In this stage, patients seek a slight extension of their deadline—to allow doing something "for one last time" or some similar request, in return for which they vow to live a better life. In the fourth stage, *depression* predominates, while the dying person mourns because of the approaching loss of people and things that have been meaningful in his or her life. Finally, a stage of *acceptance* may be reached, a stage of quiet expectation. This is not a stage of happiness, but one of rest in which there are almost no strong feelings and in which the patient's interests narrow as he or she gradually withdraws from everyday life in preparation for what is about to happen. This may be a time of great distress for the patient's family, since they may feel rejected by his or her withdrawal and lack of interest in their visits.

Socially, death brings about the final change of status in the human life cycle—the change from a human status to a nonhuman one. **Social death** is the point at which other people begin to relate to a dying person with behaviors and actions that are appropriate toward someone already dead. Like psychological death, social death may occur before biological death. W. H. Rivers (1926) reported that among the Melanesians, the word *mate*, which means "dead

FIGURE 6.10   Death

A major change in a family or society is the death of one of its members. Many societies have elaborate rituals to help the spirit of the deceased in its journey in the afterlife as well as to help those left behind adjust to the loss. This man participates in Ching Ming Day, an early spring tomb festival in Queens, New York. He says prayers and food and flowers are left at the gravesite.

person," was applied not only to the biologically dead but also to individuals who were gravely ill, close to death, and to the very old who were likely to die soon. The Melanesians, of course, distinguished between biological *mate* and social *mate*. The purpose of referring to those who were close to death as *mate* was that they were treated socially as if they were dead. Such persons might be buried alive so

——

psychological death   the process by which one subjectively prepares for impending biological death

social death   the point at which people respond to a person with the behaviors appropriate to one who is biologically dead that they could proceed to a more pleasant afterlife rather than linger among the living under the unpleasant circumstances of extreme age or terminal illness. Among the Inuit of the Arctic, the survival of hunting families would be endangered if they slowed their wanderings through arctic wastes in search of food to allow the aged or infirm to keep up. Eventually, at the urging of the afflicted party, the Inuit might hold a funeral ceremony and say goodbye to the one who had to be left behind to die so that others might live.

Since all societies must restructure their social relations so that the work of the world may be continued after the death of a member, social death is found in each society. The most dramatic aspect of this social custom is manifest in **funeral rituals**. Funeral rituals provide a mechanism for dealing with and disposing of the body of the deceased and, at the same time, provide a setting in which the survivors can be encouraged to adjust themselves to the person's now permanent absence. As a part of this second role of funeral rituals, issues of inheritance of property rights and of passing on the statuses of the deceased to new persons are dealt with in many societies during or immediately following the funeral.

---

funeral ritual   a rite of passage that formalizes the removal of an individual from the status of living member of the social group

---

The Mapuche Death and Burial Ritual

The Mapuche, a native people of southern Chile, believed, according to Louis Faron (1961, 1968), that death is caused by spiritual powers. The forces of evil known as *wekufe* were usually brought into play by a sorcerer-witch called *akalku*. When a person died, the corpse became dangerous to those who had to deal with it. One or two members of the household washed the corpse, clothed it in its finest garments, and laid it out for display on an altar in the house. After four days, the body was transferred to a canoe-shaped coffin that had been carved from a split tree trunk.

The relatives, especially the women of the family, mourned and lamented the loss, tore their garments, and promised revenge for the death, which they believed to have been

Mapuche

The Mapuche, people native to southern Chile, followed several rituals upon the death of a loved one. They focus on evil spirits as the cause of death. The behavior of the relatives during the "Black Gathering," or wake was believed to influence how the deceased spent eternity.

caused by sorcery. Then came the wake or "Black Gathering." First, the house was purified of evil spirits to prevent them from capturing the soul of the deceased. This was done by horsemen who surrounded the house and shouted at the evil spirits who invariably came in search of the souls of the dead. A four-day-and-night vigil by the relatives followed. This was important, since how the deceased spent eternity—either among the ancestors or in the underworld of witches—depended not on how he or she had lived but on how the mourners conducted themselves during the death ritual. It was their behavior that prevented the witches from stealing parts of the corpse for use in creating a new evil spirit.

After the four days of vigil, the corpse was taken to a bier in a field. There the deceased was praised in several speeches. The coffin was then painted black and decorated with cinnamon, apple, and the shrub maqui. A large wooden cross, a symbol borrowed from Catholicism, was placed at the head of the coffin, which faced toward the east.

Only the closest relatives finally accompanied the coffin to the graveyard. As they returned from the cemetery, ashes were scattered along the way to prevent the spirit from returning to bother the living.

C H A P T E R   S U M M A R Y

1. None of us operates totally independently as isolated, self-sufficient individuals. Each of us lives within a society, and all societies organize their members into groups of various sorts and divide labor among their members.

2. Our social life is also characterized by relationships with many people, each of which involves a status.

3. Each status carries various role expectations defined by our society.

4. Statuses are ranked in power and honor by our society, with some—master statuses—considered so significant that their high or low rank outweighs that of all our other statuses. Low-ranked master statuses are the defining feature of minority groups.

5. Statuses are sometimes assigned on the basis of observable biological facts, such as age, sex, and skin color.

6. Those who believe that the social roles played by minority groups reflect biological realities are called racists or sexists. Racist and sexist thinking typically bars minority group members from access to economic and political power with the rationalization that they cannot handle it.

7. The role expectations that accompany minority group status have little or no relationship to our innate characteristics; they are cultural phenomena, socially learned and enforced.

8. We change in many ways through life, but some of our changes are not unique to us. Rather, they are signs that we are passing through predictable stages in the life cycle.

9. The major stages discussed here are birth, socialization during childhood, marriage, family formation, old age, and death.

10. Societies shape these changes in culture-specific ways, with only a few universals or near-universals such as the incest taboo.

11. Life-cycle changes may be marked by customs such as pregnancy taboos, *couvade*, naming ceremonies, puberty rituals, marriage negotiations, marriage rituals, establishment of residence, divorce, and funeral rites, each of which has specific cultural meanings and purposes.

A N N O T A T E D   R E A D I N G S

Dahlberg, F. (Ed.). (1981). *Woman the gatherer.* New Haven, CT: Yale University Press. Six articles on women's roles from cross-cultural and evolutionary perspectives.

Dalby, L. (1985). *Geisha.* New York: Vintage Books, Random House. A beautifully written and copiously illustrated description of geisha life.

Friedl, E. (1975). *Women and men.* New York: Holt, Rinehart & Winston. A brief but information-packed overview of sex roles and their relationships to variations in culture. Must reading for the major in anthropology.

Kenyatta, J. (1968). *Facing Mount Kenya: The tribal life of the Gikuyu.* New York: Random House. An excellent description of Kikuyu life by a Kikuyu anthropologist. Especially good chapters on life-cycle rituals.

Martin, M. K., & Voorhies, B. (1975). *Female of the species.* New York: Columbia University Press. An examination of the status of women in societies of varying social complexity.

Moore, Henrietta. (1988). *Feminism and anthropology.* Ithaca, NY: Cornell University Press. A good general overview of feminist perspectives on gender.

Moran, Mary. (1990). *Civilized women: Gender and prestige in southeastern Liberia.* Ithaca, NY: Cornell University Press. A recent ethnography on the cultural construction of gender in West Africa.

Rosaldo, M. Z., & Lamphere, L. (Eds.). (1974). *Woman, culture, and society.* Stanford, CA: Stanford University Press. Discussions by female anthropologists of their observations of the status of women in a variety of societies.

Shostak, M. (1983). *Nisa: The story of a !Kung woman.* New York: Random House. A fascinating account of the life history of a woman in a foraging society.

Simmons, L. W. (Ed.). (1942). *Sun Chief: The autobiography of a Hopi Indian.* New Haven, CT: Yale University Press. A fascinating autobiographical account of the life of a Hopi chief, Don Talayesva.

Van Gennep, A. (1960, originally published 1908). *The rites of passage* (S. T. Kimball, trans.). Chicago: University of Chicago Press. The classic discussion of the major changes in status that are celebrated in ritual.

FIGURE 7.1   Kinship

We are all descended not only from our parents but also from their parents and their parents before them. Kinship is a cultural system by which we identify all the members of our family both present and past. This child and her grandmother live in Albuquerque, New Mexico.

CHAPTER 7

Kinship and Descent

Human beings all over the world distinguish their kin from other people. In this chapter, we will see how the concept of kinship is based on various ways of thinking about how children are descended from one or both of their parents and how these parent-child descent ties are used to build up a network that defines those people that are related to one another by kinship. You will learn to recognize different descent systems, some based on the concept of descent from only one parent in each generation and others based on the concept of descent from both parents. We will then consider how different kinds of kinship groups can grow out of these different ways of viewing those related to us. Finally, you will be introduced to the most common kinship terminologies, the systems for naming relatives that are related to the ways in which people think about descent.

CHAPTER OBJECTIVES

After reading this chapter, you should be able to:

Explain the relationship of kinship to descent.

Explain the varieties of cognatic (or nonunilineal) descent.

Explain the varieties of unilineal descent.

Outline the characteristics of the various kinds of unilineal descent groups.

Describe the various kinds of ambilineal descent groups.

Explain the functions of moieties.

Describe bilateral (or noncorporate) descent groups (kindreds).

Discuss the evolution of descent groups.

List the six common types of kinship terminologies.

Explain the building blocks of kinship terminologies.

Explain the conditions that foster each of the six common kinship terminology systems.

Analyze the concept of fictive kinship.

Kinship

Descent Rules
Bilateral Descent
Ambilineal Descent
Unilineal Descent

Descent Groups
Lineal Descent Groups
Bilateral Descent Groups
The Evolution of Descent Groups

Kinship Terminology
Hawaiian
Eskimo
Omaha
Crow
Iroquois
Sudanese

Fictive Kinship

Brother, can you spare a dime? I'm my own grandpa. Sister Sledge. Auntie Mame. Uncle Vanya. Is my mother's new husband's ex-wife's daughter my stepsister? When my mother's sister married a man who already had children, did they become my cousins? If I married a widow and my new stepdaughter married my father, would my father's new son be my half brother or my stepgrandson? How we are related to each other depends on which system of kinship our society utilizes.

Kinship

Kinship is a very human concept. It is the way we keep track of our relationships with others who are connected to us by ties we trace through parents and their offspring. You are my kin if we can find a chain of connected parent-child ties that stretches from you to me. My children are linked to me, their common parent, by a chain one link long. Kin are connected to each other by chains of two similar links. My only niece is my mother's eldest daughter's daughter: she is three parent-child links away from me among my kin. In any human community, some people are thought of as "kin" and others as "not kin," and a particular society's way of defining who are kin may not give equal weight to all connections between biological parents and their offspring. As we shall see, for instance, in many societies, children may be thought of as kin to only one of their parents. Thus, more formally, **kinship** is a system for classifying people who are deemed to be related through culturally defined parent-child ties.

Descent Rules

The cultural recognition of children as kin of one or both of their parents is called **descent**. Although the concept of descent is understood in most cultures as a biological relationship between children and parents, it is not identical to the biological concept of a genetic relationship. Rather, in some societies, such as Canada and the United States, descent is reckoned through both parents, while in others it is traced only through fathers or only through mothers.

Bilateral Descent

If parents came in only one sex, it would be a lot simpler to define our kin. Since they come in two varieties that play different roles in the production of children, the story becomes more complex. For instance, a brother and sister relationship can be traced by the links to a common mother or by links to the same father. Either way works, and my own culture, like that of the Siberian Chukchee or the American Great Basin Ute, considers either chain to be equally valid. So it lets me simply say that my sister and I share the same parents and lets it go at that. This system is based on the principle of **bilateral descent**, a rule that asserts that we are equally descended from both parents and lets us count relatives on both our mother's and father's side of the family. The bilateral system is a common approach. In about 36 percent of societies people consider links through both parents to be equally valid ways of reckoning their kin.

Ambilineal Descent

A variation on the bilateral theme is the idea that we may consider ourselves descended through parents of either sex, but we must choose only one parent for each link that connects a group of rela-

---

kinship a system for classifying people who are related to one another by ties of descent or by ties of marriage
descent the cultural recognition of kinship connections between a child and one or both of his or her parent's kin
bilateral descent a system of tracing descent lines equally through both parents

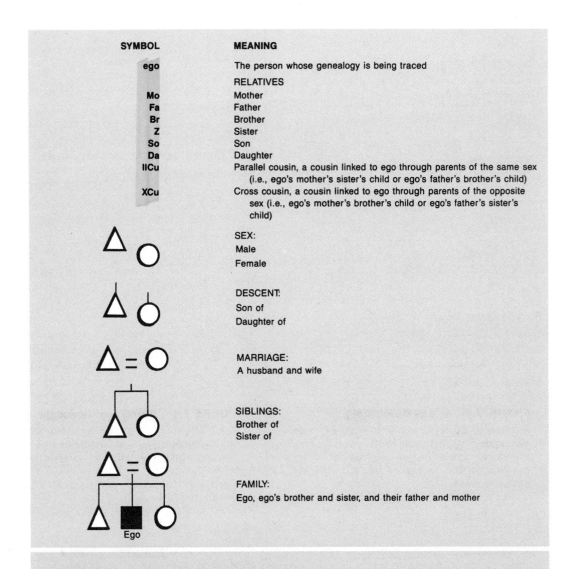

SYMBOL	MEANING
ego	The person whose genealogy is being traced
	RELATIVES
Mo	Mother
Fa	Father
Br	Brother
Z	Sister
So	Son
Da	Daughter
IICu	Parallel cousin, a cousin linked to ego through parents of the same sex (i.e., ego's mother's sister's child or ego's father's brother's child)
XCu	Cross cousin, a cousin linked to ego through parents of the opposite sex (i.e., ego's mother's brother's child or ego's father's sister's child)
	SEX:
	Male
	Female
	DESCENT:
	Son of
	Daughter of
	MARRIAGE:
	A husband and wife
	SIBLINGS:
	Brother of
	Sister of
	FAMILY:
	Ego, ego's brother and sister, and their father and mother

FIGURE 7.2   Interpreting Kinship Diagrams
Kinship diagrams are drawn using a variety of standard symbols. Those shown here are among the most common, and will be used later in this text. The simple family diagram at the bottom could be easily expanded using the same symbols to show ego's uncles, aunts, and cousins. Can you figure out how to do it?

tives. This system, followed in less than 1 percent of societies, is **ambilineal descent**. Using the concept of ambilineal descent, a child might be designated as a relative of either the mother's kin or the father's kin, but not both. A decision had to be made in each generation which parent's group the children would be part of, but the connection might be established through the father in one generation and through the mother in another. The ancient Scottish clans were built up in such a way, so that the relatives who made up a particular clan all could trace themselves back to the founding ancestor of the clan, but not consistently through parents of the same sex.

When grouped by bilateral descent, relatives spread out on both sides of a person's family, creating two groups of equally related kin for each person. In the ambilineal approach, a less predictable group of

ambilineal descent   a system of tracing descent through a parent of either sex, choosing only one parent for each link that connects a group of relatives

158

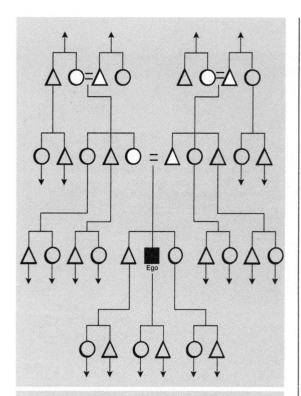

FIGURE 7.3   Bilateral Descent

In bilateral descent, ego is considered to be descended equally from both parents and, therefore, from an increasing number of ancestors on both sides of ego's family, as shown in white.

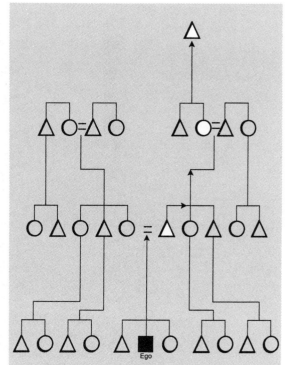

FIGURE 7.4   Ambilineal Descent

Ego's relatives are shown in white. In ambilineal descent, ego's ancestors can be traced through either the father or mother, but not both. Membership in the traditional Scottish clans was based on genealogies that were traced in this way.

relatives is created, one made up of individual families who belong to the entire group in some cases because the father is a member and in other cases because the mother is a member. These two descent systems are sometimes referred to by the general terms **cognatic** or **nonunilineal descent** systems.

Unilineal Descent

Most societies have a narrower way of building up a group of kin that follows a principle called **unilineal descent**, descent through a single sex line, either the father or the mother, rather than through both parents equally. The ancient Greeks, the Lau of Fiji, the Mission Indians of southern California, or the Mossí of the Sudan, and about 44 percent of all societies that anthropologists have studied follow the system of reckoning kin by insisting that kin are only those who are joined by *father*-child ties. This rule for grouping

relatives is called **patrilineal descent**, since it defines children as offspring of their fathers only. Patrilineality is commonly followed in situations that require male solidarity, for instance, in work requiring heavy cooperative labor or in feuding between neighboring groups.

On the other hand, the Navajo of Arizona and New Mexico, the Tuareg of the Sahara Desert, and the Caribbean Goajiro are equally convinced that mother-child links alone should be used. Their ap-

cognatic (nonunilineal) descent   a system of tracing descent bilaterally or ambilineally
nonunilineal descent   cognatic descent
unilineal descent   a system of tracing descent through a single sex line rather than both parents equally
patrilineal descent   a system of descent traced through the father only

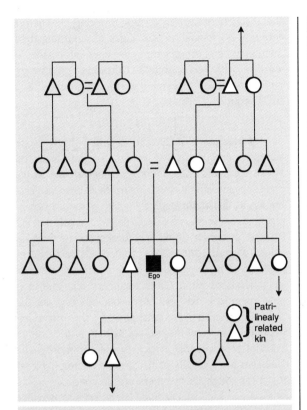

FIGURE 7.5 Patrilineal Descent

In patrilineal descent, a chain of father-child ties links ego to his or her ancestors. Each generation within the descent line consists of siblings who belong to the line of their father and his siblings. Only children of males will continue the line. The children of female members of a patrilineal descent line will belong to their husbands' descent lines. Ego's patrilineal relatives are shown in white.

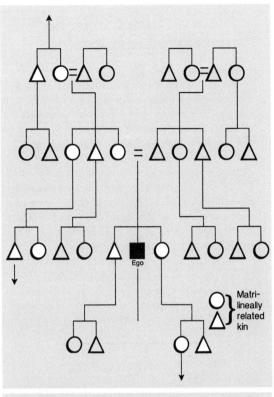

FIGURE 7.6 Matrilineal Descent

In matrilineal descent, a chain of mother-child ties links ego to his or her ancestors. Each generation within the descent line consists of siblings who belong to the line of their mother and her siblings. Only children of females will continue the line. The children of male members of a matrilineal descent line will belong to their wives' descent lines. Ego's matrilineal relatives are shown in white.

proach to counting kin is based upon the principle of **matrilineal descent**. It is shared by about 15 percent of the world's societies. Matrilineality is an effective means of unifying groups of women as decision-making bodies. It is commonly followed as a principle of kinship in societies where men are often absent from the local community.

In about 5 percent of societies, a person may have two separate sets of kin, one designated only through mothers and the other only through fathers. Such a kinship determining rule, called **double descent** or **double unilineal descent**, would be a useful way of keeping track of relatives if, for instance, some property—say, houses and gardens—were inherited from the parent of one sex and other prop-

erty—say, religious rituals and gardening tools—were passed down through the opposite line. Just as patrilineal and matrilineal descent may coexist, ambilineal or bilateral descent may co-occur with matrilineal or patrilineal descent so long as there is some socially useful reason for keeping track of each group.

matrilineal descent a system of descent traced through the mother only
double descent (double unilineal descent) a system of tracing two separate sets of kin, one designated through mothers only and the other through fathers only
double unilineal descent double descent

160

How a Person Can Be His Own Grandfather

I married a widow who had a daughter. My father visited our home frequently, fell in love and married my stepdaughter. Thus my father became my son-in-law, and my stepdaughter my mother, because she was my father's wife. My stepdaughter had also a son; he was of course my brother and at the same time my grandchild, for he was the son of my daughter. My wife was my grandmother, because she was my mother's mother. I was my wife's husband and grandchild at the same time; and as the husband of a person's grandmother is his grandfather, I was my own grandfather.

From an advertisement by Rudolph Oak Hall, 404 Main Street (Dry Goods, Clothing, Gents' Furnishing Goods, Boats, Shoes, Trunks, Valises, Etc., and Millinery), Fayetteville, Arkansas, 1903.

Descent Groups

In all societies, there are social groups whose membership is based on descent. Membership in descent groups may be defined either by the sharing of a common ancestor or by the sharing of a common living relative. Groups whose members share a common ancestor are called **lineal descent groups** or **corporate descent groups**. Descent groups whose members share a living relative are associated with bilateral descent and are called **bilateral descent groups**.

Lineal Descent Groups

There are two kinds of lineal descent groups: unilineal and ambilineal. **Unilineal descent groups** are social groups that are based on either patrilineal or matrilineal descent reckoning. **Ambilineal descent groups** are groups whose members trace their relationship to the common ancestor by using ambilineal descent rules. Both unilineal and ambilineal descent groups share one important characteristic: they are corporate groups, or organizations that continue to exist even though their individual members change over the generations, and they can legally perform

social functions such as owning property, conducting ceremonies, regulating marriages, disciplining their own members, or engaging in legal processes or warfare with other groups. Corporate groups are typically named to symbolize their existence as a social entity.

Lineages. A **lineage** is a kin group which traces its descent from a known common ancestor. When members trace their genealogical ties to the common ancestor through matrilineal descent, it is known as a **matrilineage**; a lineage based on ties of patrilineal descent is a **patrilineage**. Lineages that are formed using an ambilineal descent principle are called **cognatic lineages** or sometimes **ramages** or **septs**. In all three cases, the lineage continues to exist as generations pass. Older members may die, and new members may be born, but so long as the common ancestry is remembered, the surviving members can view themselves as part of a common body of relatives that can carry out common goals. Lineages are typically named for the common ancestor from which its members are descended.

Since each succeeding generation may produce more offspring than made up the previous generation, a lineage may gradually increase in the size of its membership. Thus, lineages may be as small as 30 or 40 people, but may grow to encompass thousands of members. Since growing populations tend to spread out from the location of their ancestral homelands, local segments of a lineage may become involved in activities in which it would be unwieldy and unnecessary to call together all members. So,

---

lineal descent groups those whose members share a common ancestor

bilateral descent groups those whose members share a living relative

unilineal descent group a system of tracing social groups based on a matrilineal or patrilineal descent system

ambilineal descent group a system of tracing social groups based on an ambilineal descent system

lineage a kinship group whose members can trace their lines of descent to the same ancestor

matrilineage a system of tracing descent lines through mothers

patrilineage a system of tracing descent lines through fathers

cognative lineage (ramage, sept) lineage formed using an ambilineal descent system

ramage cognatic lineage

sept cognatic lineage

FIGURE 7.7   Scottish Clan
The tartan, a cross-checkered repeating pattern of stripes or lines woven into a woolen cloth, has come to have great significance in tracing the ancestry of a Scottish clan. The earliest tartan was designed for the Highland 42nd Regiment of Foot, or Black Watch.

growing lineages often fission into smaller sub-lineages over the generations.

Clans.   As generations pass, lineage membership may reach such numbers and such distance from the common ancestry that their exact genealogical ties are no longer remembered, even though surviving members of the total group still regard themselves as relatives. A corporate kinship group of this type is called a **clan** or sometimes a **sib**. Clans may also be differentiated by the rule of descent through which membership is defined. Thus, anthropologists speak of either **matriclans, patriclans**, or **cognatic (or ambilineal) clans**, depending on the descent rule.

The common ancestor of a clan may be so far removed in time that his or her identity may no longer be remembered accurately. As the ancestor's life story is passed down the generations, it may become altered and embroidered with tales that rep-resent the values of clan members more than historical fact. The ancestor may take on heroic proportions and as portrayed by succeeding generations may become more mythological than real. The process by which the folk memories of an important person may become increasingly filled with symbolism that can elevate him or her to a superhuman level is one that operates even in literate societies. In the United States, for instance, children hear mythologized stories of George Washington's inability to tell a lie, and about his having thrown a silver dollar across a river

clan   kinship group whose members believe themselves descended from a common ancestor far enough in the past that they cannot trace their specific genealogical ties to one another
sib   clan
matriclan   clan based on matrilineal descent
patriclan   clan based on patrilineal descent
cognatic clan (ambilineal clan)   clan based on ambilineal descent

162

that is, in some versions, Virginia's smaller Rappahannock and, in others, Washington, D.C.'s nearly mile-wide Potomac. Abraham Lincoln, the Great Emancipator, is remembered as having freed all the slaves in the United States, rather than as just having promised freedom to Southern slaves who joined the Union in fighting the Confederates. When such stories continue to be embellished over many generations, a time may come when it becomes difficult to identify the historically real from the mythological, and the stories about clan ancestors in traditionally nonliterate societies are frequently so filled with superhuman elements that it is impossible to demonstrate that the founder of the clan really existed except in folklore. Indeed, a symbolic ancestor of an existing clan may not even be a human at all. For instance, symbolic clan ancestors are often important animals, plants, or, less often, geographical features in the environment, such as the Bitter-Water or Salt clans of the Navajo.

Clans may have tens or even hundreds of thousands of members. By virtue of their large membership, clans can be very powerful organizations. Like lineages, they are corporate groups that perform a variety of social functions, such as carrying out major ceremonies, owning land or other property, maintaining peaceful relationships between their individual members and the lineages that make them up, handling the legal matters, and regulating the marriage options of their members.

Navajo

The Navajos, most of whom live in Arizona and New Mexico, still rely on traditional matrilineal clan membership as a source of economic and social cohesion as well as for marital regulations. Navajos are forbidden to marry either within their own matriclan or their father's matriclan.

are also considered to be relatives, so a Navajo might describe him- or herself as "born to Bitter-Water [the mother's clan] for Salt [the father's clan]." Clans play an important role in regulating marriage; Navajos are traditionally forbidden to marry either members of their own matriclan or of their father's matriclan. This rule forces marriages to link members of different clans in each generation and is one of the means for maintaining ties of allegiance between members of the various clans in a community.

Considering that there are a large number of Navajos and the clans are spread over a large territory, each Navajo is likely to have many relatives whom he or she has never met. Two Navajo strangers who later discover that they belong to a common clan have the same familial obligations of hospitality and mutual help toward each other as they do to their previously known relatives.

Traditionally, the clan also was responsible collectively for the crimes and debts of its members. This fact, of course, meant that the clan also had authority to control irresponsible behavior in its members. Grazing land, for instance, could not be freely bought or sold by individual persons without permission of other clan members. Clans also controlled inheri-

Navajo Clans

The Navajo who reside in Arizona and New Mexico are a pastoral people who herd sheep and grow corn and other crops in a dry, desert region. They number today over 180,000 people who occupy a reservation territory of more than 25,000 square miles. Though individual families may live miles apart, their unity is aided by a continued reliance on matrilineal clan membership as a source of economic and social cohesion. In the 1940s Kluckhohn and Leighton (1962) found that the Navajo had approximately 60 clans, each bearing the name of a locality. Each clan is likely to have members who live in different communities, and a given local group may be composed of families who belong to 15 or 20 different clans.

A Navajo is born a primary member of the mother's clan, but members of the father's clan tance; goods passed to children from the members of their mother's clan.

Family loyalty still receives support from the traditional clan system of shared economic responsibilities in spite of the fragmenting effects of employment of many Navajos in the industrialized economy of the non-Navajo society that surrounds them. For instance, a Navajo religious ceremony—which might be necessary for the curing of an illness, the reunion of a family member after a period of residence at a nonreservation university, or the celebration of a girl's passage into adulthood—may cost a thousand or more dollars to carry out, an expense that can be too costly for a single household to bear. Such expenses may be supported mutually by nearby members of the person's clan for whom the ritual must be held, a practice that reinforces a tremendous sense of family loyalty, encourages reciprocal responsibilities, and gives cohesion to contemporary Navajo family life.

Phratries. In addition to lineages and clans, there can also be larger unilineal descent groups within a society. A group of clans thought to be related by kinship at a level higher than the clan ancestors is called a **phratry**. It does not necessarily grow from a common ancestral clan. The kinship connection between the clans of a phratry may be merely a social fiction that allows its members to interact as a larger corporate group. That is, a phratry is a group of two or more clans whose members believe and act as if they are somehow related, whether they are really related or not.

Moieties. Sometimes the kinship groups of a society are organized into two major categories or groups, called **moieties**, from a French word meaning "half." Each moiety in this kind of organization is a unilineal kinship group that may consist of a clan or phratry. Moieties usually play a role in the regulation of marriage, by the requirement that the members of each moiety take their spouses from the opposite group. According to Lévi-Strauss (1967), the relationships between moieties may "range from the most intimate cooperation to latent hostility," and in addition to providing spouses for one another's members, "[s]ometimes their role is confined to activities of a religious, political, economic, ceremonial, or merely recreational character" (p. 10). Thus, the two moieties of a society may play other socially reciprocal roles such as providing funerals or hosting feasts for each other. Moieties may also facilitate social specialization by playing complementary roles. For instance, among the Toda of southern India, the clans of one moiety owned all of the sacred herds of dairy cattle and the dairies in which they were kept, but the dairymen of the sacred herds, who were the priests of

Toda society, could be chosen only from the other moiety.

Combinations of lineal descent groups. More than one kind of lineal descent group may operate simultaneously within the same society. For instance, lineages may be the only descent group present in a society; a clan may exist without lineages being differentiated within it; or a clan may be subdivided into identified lineages, each of which carries out activities within the entire clan. Lineages, clans, and phratries may be organized into moieties. As a matter of fact, with one exception, any combination of lineages, clans, phratries, and moieties may occur in a particular society. The exception is merely that when phratries are present, there must also be clans, since phratries are defined as groups of two or more clans.

Bilateral Descent Groups

Descent groups that are not based on descent from a single common ancestor may also exist. Such a group, called a **kindred**, is defined by the kinship relationship all its members have to a living person. A kindred consists of all relatives on both the paternal and maternal sides of the family who are known to a single individual. Brothers and sisters will have

phratry group of clans thought to be related by kinship
moiety one of two basic complementary social subdivisions of a society
kindred a kinship group in a bilateral descent system that consists of the known relatives of an individual

FIGURE 7.8 La Grande Famille

A kindred consists of all relatives on both the paternal and maternal sides of the family who are known to a single individual. This family gathers for a photo at the wedding of their son in Charente Maritime, France.

the same kindred, but other relatives will have kindreds with somewhat different members. For instance, if kindreds included only first and second cousins, then my own second cousin's kindred would include *their* second cousins, who would be too distantly related to me as fourth cousins to be part of *my* kindred.

A person may call upon her or his kindred for aid and support, and kindred can act together as a group on behalf of the individual or siblings to whom they are all related. Unlike unilineal descent groups, kindreds exist only at that time in history when they share a particular living group of siblings. When those brothers and sisters die, their kindred no longer has a uniting focus, so it ceases to exist. Thus, kindreds do not have the quality of being corporate groups that exist beyond the lifespans of the individuals that are born into and die out of them. Neither are they normally responsible for such corporate responsibilities as owning property or conducting religious ceremonies. Rather, their existence is usu-

ally ephemeral. They may be called together for a particular purpose by the individual or sibling group that seeks the support of a body of relatives, but they cease to work together as a group when the purpose is accomplished.

Such kindreds include relatives on both sides of their families; they are the typical descent groups that trace their ancestry bilaterally. They are most common in circumstances in which small family groups are more adaptive than are larger ones and in which individual mobility is high. Thus, they are typical of industrialized societies such as those of North America where children do not normally inherit their homes and occupations from their parents and may even have to leave their home towns to obtain employment. Kindreds are also typical of foraging societies, since small family groups that pursue a migratory life can more readily obtain the wild foods they need to survive in most environments than can larger, permanent family organizations such as lineages or clans.

The Evolution of Descent Groups

The oldest and simplest of human social systems, those founded on foraging economies, do not usually have corporate descent groups. Economic cooperation between intermarried families may create a local extended family of bilaterally related kin in the next generation, but when growth in the local kindred group makes food getting difficult, a breakup of the group is likely to occur. Since their life-style is based on a wandering quest for food, conditions do not foster the easy perpetuation of ongoing kinship ties between neighboring groups over many generations. Nor is there any specific need to do so. Within a generation or two, bilateral kindreds may still be called together for common economic or political action such as family reunions or for the distribution of property upon the death of a family member, but conditions that call for the development of permanent unilineal descent groups do not seem to be present in most such societies.

On the other hand, unilineal descent groups are common in horticultural, pastoral, and agricultural societies. In such societies, when an extended family divides, each smaller group of relatives is likely to establish its new residence within easy access of the other. This pattern of geographical and social dispersal can easily support the formation of lineages or other corporate descent groups as generations pass, if it is economically or politically advantageous to do so. For instance, lineages, clans, and phratries lend themselves readily to the maintenance of cooperating family-based military groups when warfare is an important feature of social life.

Interestingly, larger, socially more complex and specialized societies sometimes shift again toward a bilateral descent system. Where lineages and clans are the basic social building block, these kinship groups typically perform many of the governmental functions that are carried out by specialized non-kinship groups in some of the more complex societies. Thus, for instance, if a society develops a political system that takes over the military role previously played by unilineal descent groups, then bilateral descent reckoning is likely to replace the lineal system that existed before. Similarly, increasing social complexity can fragment matrilineal descent groups because geographical and occupational mobility increases the viability of smaller, economically independent nuclear family groups. Both of these conditions are common in the most industrialized societies of the world today where bilateral descent is the rule.

Kinship terminology is the system people use to identify the distinctions among relatives that are important in their lives. Kin terms may classify relatives in many different ways. For instance, kinship terminologies of different societies commonly may use the potential contrasts between: (1) paternal versus maternal side of the family; (2) generation; (3) relative age; (4) sex; (5) descent ties versus marriage ties; (6) own versus linked descent line; and (7) when descent lines are noted, sex of the linking relative. Thus, actual kinship terminologies are highly varied. Nevertheless, individual systems can be grouped into six common types, called *Hawaiian, Eskimo, Omaha, Crow, Iroquois,* and *Sudanese.* The first two of these are types found in societies with bilateral descent systems, in which relatives on the maternal and paternal sides of the family are equally important in a person's life. The others tend to be associated with societies that use unilineal descent reckoning.

Hawaiian

This is the simplest kinship terminology in the sense that it is the system with the fewest terms. In the **Hawaiian kinship terminology** system, the key distinction is one of generation. Relatives are not distinguished by side of the family (e.g., "aunt" may be either a mother's sister or father's sister). One's affinal (related by marriage) descent line is not distinguished from linked or collateral descent lines, those that parallel one's own line back to a common ancestor. Thus, in Hawaiian kinship terminology, cousins are called by the same kin terms as are one's siblings, commonly translated as "brother" and "sister"; and one's father, father's brother, and mother's brother are all referred to as "father"; and mother, mother's sister, and father's sister are likewise designated by a single term. In its simplest form, Hawaiian kinship terminology may not make any distinction by sex, reducing the system to three basic kin terms: parents, siblings, and children.

The Hawaiian kinship system is especially common where extended families or some other form of corporate descent group, within which the nuclear

Hawaiian kinship terminology simplest kinship designation, using terms parents, siblings, and children

FIGURE 7.9   Hawaiian Kinship Terminology

Hawaiian kinship terminology is most common in societies in which an extended group of relatives joined by bilateral descent live together and share work and child-rearing obligations. Its main emphasis is on distinguishing the members of the family's two adjacent generations—the generation of the parents and the generation of the children. Ego calls his or her parents and their siblings by the same two terms, translatable as "mother" and "father" and calls his or her cousins by terms that can be translated as "brother" and "sister."

FIGURE 7.10   Eskimo Kinship Terminology

Eskimo kinship terminology is most common in societies that trace relationships bilaterally and in which the isolated nuclear family—a husband and wife and their own offspring—is the economically independent work-group of society. This kinship system emphasizes the separateness of ego's nuclear family (ego's parents and siblings) from other relatives by contrasting mother and father with aunts and uncles and by contrasting brother and sister with cousins.

family does not function autonomously, live and work together. It is more common in societies that make use of bilateral or ambilineal rather than unilineal descent systems (Textor, 1967). In other words, Hawaiian terminology emphasizes the cohesion of the extended family or corporate groups, distinguishing only between the generational differences which are important in the etiquette of family interaction in all societies. It should be noticed that the Hawaiian system automatically extends the field of persons who have the same kinds of rights and obligations as members of one's own nuclear family. Thus, on the death of a child's biological father, there are likely to be several other men who will be expected to take responsibility for the childrearing activities that the child's "real" father would have performed. Similarly, the incest taboo is extended to cover a much broader range of relatives, such as cross cousins, than is typical in other systems.

Eskimo

This kinship terminology is the second general type of bilateral kinship system. It is the type with which most North Americans are familiar. In **Eskimo kinship terminology**, the terms for mother, father, brother, and sister are not used for any relatives

outside the nuclear family, and the terms for other relatives such as aunt, uncle, or cousin are the same for the maternal and paternal sides of the family. Cross cousins, children of siblings of the opposite sex, and parallel cousins, children of siblings of the same sex, are not distinguished by different terms, and cousin terms may not even differ by sex.

The simplicity of Eskimo terminology is related to the fact that this system is typically found in societies such as foraging or industrialized societies or in other circumstances in which ego's (the term used to identify the person whose descent line is being determined) most important relatives are her or his closest relatives. Thus, Eskimo terminology is commonly associated with economically independent nuclear families, bilateral descent, and kindreds rather than unilineal or ambilineal descent and lineages, clans, or other corporate descent groups. Data compiled by Murdock (1967) for 71 societies in which Eskimo terminology was used indicated that only 4 had large extended families, and only 13 had unilineal descent groups. In fact, 54 had no corporate descent groups.

Eskimo kinship terminology   bilateral kinship system in which terms for mother, father, brother, and sister are not used for relatives outside the nuclear family

FIGURE 7.11 Omaha Kinship Terminology

Omaha kinship terminology is most often associated with patrilineal descent reckoning. Its terms for relatives contrast those related to ego through patrilineal descent ties (noted in white) to the equivalent relatives of his or her mother's patrilineal group (indicated with a dot). The terminology is more elaborate for ego's own patrilineal relatives than for ego's mother's patrilineal relatives for whom the same terms (Mo and MoBr) are used in both generations.

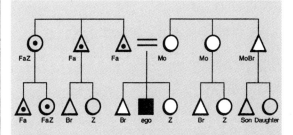

FIGURE 7.12 Crow Kinship Terminology

Crow kinship terminology is most often associated with matrilineal descent reckoning. Its terms for relatives contrast those related to ego through matrilineal descent ties (noted in white) to the equivalent relatives of ego's father's matrilineal group (noted with a dot). The terminology is more elaborate for ego's own matrilineal relatives than for his or her father's matrilineal relatives for whom the same terms (Fa and FaZ) are used in both generations.

The remaining major kinship systems are those associated with unilineal descent systems. They distinguish between maternal and paternal kin, but differ in other ways.

Omaha

This kinship terminology is an example of a **bifurcate merging** system, one that derives its kin terms from two major characteristics: the contrast between paternal and maternal relatives (hence, "bifurcate") and the use of a small number of kin terms to refer to many different kin within each of these two groups (hence, "merging"). The Omaha system is found in societies that have patrilineal descent systems. In the **Omaha kinship terminology** system, members of one's mother's patrilineage are distinguished only by sex regardless of generation. Thus, one term is used for all males of that group (e.g., for mother's brother and mother's brother's son) and another for all females including ego's mother, her sister, and her brother's daughter. In ego's own patrilineage, father is merged with father's brother. Parallel cousins in both lineages are merged with ego's brother and sister, and their children are called by the same term as ego's own children. The bifurcation is a useful way of contrasting the lineage of ego's

mother from that of ego's father, while the merging of terms for parents and their same-sex siblings has the effect of emphasizing lineage cohesiveness. Since the mother's lineage is relatively unimportant in ego's daily life, generational differences in status can be ignored, but in ego's own patrilineage—which is the important corporate group in life—different terms for men of the father's generation and men of ego's own generation are distinguished in recognition of the differences in power and honor that they are likely to have.

Crow

The Crow system is also a bifurcate merging system, but it is the mirror image of the Omaha pattern. Named for a Native North American society, **Crow kinship terminology** is found in many ma-

bifurcate merging kinship terminology derived from contrast between maternal and paternal relatives using a small number of kin terms to refer to many different kin
Omaha kinship terminology patrilineal descent system where mother's patrilineage is distinguished only by sex, regardless of generation
Crow kinship terminology matrilineal descent system where father's matrilineage is distinguished only by sex regardless of generation

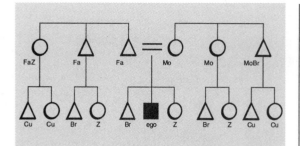

FIGURE 7.13 Iroquois Kinship Terminology

Iroquois kinship terminology tends to be found in societies that use unilineal descent reckoning, especially among those that trace ancestry through matrilineal descent. Societies that follow the Iroquois system instead of the Crow or Omaha systems are believed to place less importance on the solidarity of their unilineal kinship groups and are more willing to permit marriage with cousins on either side of the family. For this reason, paternal and maternal cross cousins are not distinguished from one another, and in some variants of the Iroquois system, parallel cousins are not called "brother" and "sister" as shown in this figure but by another term—thereby indicating their acceptability as potential spouses for ego.

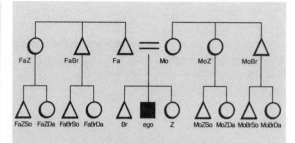

FIGURE 7.14 Sudanese Kinship Terminology

Sudanese, or descriptive, kinship terminology is common in societies that trace descent patrilineally when status distinctions between individual members of both ego's patrilineage and ego's mother's patrilineage are important. Accordingly, the Sudanese system uses a different term for each relative in each patrilineage.

trilineal societies throughout the world. In it the relatives of ego's father's matrilineage are distinguished only by sex, regardless of age or generation, while generational differences are noted within ego's own matrilineage. As with the Omaha system, Crow kinship is highly compatible with a powerful unilineal descent system, in this case emphasizing the importance of the matrilineal kin organization.

Iroquois

Like the Omaha and Crow systems, **Iroquois kinship terminology** is a bifurcate merging system. It, too, assigns different terms for maternal and paternal relatives, while merging father with father's brother and mother with mother's sister. The terms for parallel cousins are similarly merged with the terms for brothers or sisters. The important distinction that separates Iroquois from the Omaha and Crow systems is that in the Iroquois system there is no merging of generations in the lineage that marries into ego's lineage. Instead, ego's cross cousins in

both lineages are merged, minimizing the lineage contrast for members of this one group of kin.

Like Omaha and Crow, Iroquois kinship is most often found in societies with unilineal descent, and it is particularly common in matrilineal societies. Crow, too, is associated with matrilineal social organizations, and Leslie White (1939) suggested that the reason for the presence of one rather than the other may be that the Crow and Omaha patterns are most likely to develop in a society that is firmly unilineal, while the Iroquois system is most likely in either an incipient or weakening unilineal descent system. Goody (1970) has added the idea that the Iroquois pattern is likely to develop when circumstances favor marriage with either maternal or paternal cross cousins rather than with just the cross cousins of one side of the family.

Sudanese

This kinship system has the largest number of kin terms, so it is sometimes also called **descriptive**

Iroquois kinship terminology bifurcate merging system like the Crow and Omaha, but where there is no merging of generations in the lineage that marries into ego's lineage kinship terminology. As do many kinship systems, Sudanese kinship terminology distinguishes parallel cousins from cross cousins. In addition to the nuclear family terms for mother, father, brother, sister, son, and daughter, this system includes cousin, uncle, and aunt terms that distinguish maternal from paternal relatives.

Referring to each relative by a separate term suggests that the distinctions are culturally relevant. In other words, when descriptive terminology is present, a person's behavior is expected to be different toward each relative. For instance, a person would have a different relationship with a maternal cross cousin than with a paternal cross cousin. Relatively few societies have circumstances in which such diversity of kin relations would be necessary, so the descriptive kinship system is a rare one. When it does occur, it is in association with patrilineal descent. Sudanese terminology occurs most often in North Africa.

· ·

Fictive Kinship

Sometimes societies create relationships that are thought of as more or less equivalent to kinship relationships between persons who would otherwise not be considered relatives by either descent or marriage. These so-called **fictive kinship** relationships include adopted relatives who become legal equivalents of those who are relatives by birth. They also include persons thought of as ceremonial or quasi-relatives, whose relationships are secondary to those based on descent or marriage. Such ceremonial kinship relationships are established to fulfill special purposes such as establishing a stable economic bond between two persons or providing foster parents upon the death of the biological parents. Thus, in addition to fully adopted relatives, fictive kin include various kinds of "blood brotherhood" and coparenthood or "godparenthood." Among the Rwala Bedouin, for instance, men sometimes established a brotherhood of *akh* relationship with persons such as traders who were not a part of their own residential groups. This relationship created an obligation to protect the outsider's property. If a raid by one group against the other resulted in the loss of camels by someone who has an *akh* in the raiding group, the *akh* was bound by honor to recover and return those animals from his own kin. This fictive kin relation-

FIGURE 7.15   Fictive Kinship
In many societies, people establish relationships with others that are not based on descent or marriage. These provide a support system in difficult times in addition to kin. Thus, godparenthood, blood brotherhood and sisterhood, and adoption all give the people involved a sense of belonging and security.

ship made it easier for traders to travel safely from group to group to conduct trade, an activity that was beneficial to both the traders and the Bedouin.

▬

descriptive kinship terminology   Sudanese kinship terminology
Sudanese kinship (descriptive kinship) terminology   occurring mostly in North Africa, this system distinguishes maternal and paternal relatives by separate terms
fictive kinship   kinship relationships created by societies toward those who are not otherwise considered relatives either by descent or marriage

─────────────

Godparenthood Among the Chan Kom Maya

The village of Chan Kom in the state of Yucatán, Mexico, was studied in the 1930s by R. Redfield and Villa Rojas (1934). Its 250 people were Maya Indians whose customs had been influenced by 300 years of Spanish colonial domination. One European custom adopted by the people of Chan Kom was the *padrinazgo,* the choosing of godparents for

Chan Kom Maya

The Mayan Indians who lived in the village of Chan Kom in Yucatan, Mexico, adopted the European custom of choosing godparents for their child. Godparents aided the parents in both the physical and spiritual care of the child.

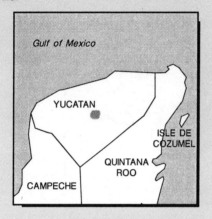

their children at important ceremonial transitions during the life cycle.

The most important godparents were selected at the time of a child's baptism. The godfather, or *padrino*, and godmother, or *madrina*, took on the obligation to act as parents to the child and to aid it in growing up. In return they were treated with particular respect by the child's parents.

Godparents who had less responsibility were chosen for later changes in the life cycle of the child. The second such event was at the time of the *hetzmek*, the native Maya celebration of the change from infancy to childhood, which occurred when the child was old enough to be carried on its mother's hip instead of in her arms. Godparents were also chosen in preparation for marriage. The same-sex godparent instructed the bride or bridegroom in the marriage ritual and gave advice about the responsibilities that came with marriage. Marriage godparents might also admonish their godchildren at later times for not living up to their marriage responsibilities.

Godparents provided support for community values throughout the lives of their godchildren and so helped them to follow the customs of Chan Kom. Parents and godparents also entered into a kind of fictive kinship relationship called the *compadrazgo*, or co-parenthood. This relationship involved formality and the expression of mutual respect and concern for one another's welfare. By extending the sense of intimate kinship obligations to the field of nonrelatives, coparenthood helped to further integrate the community throughout the village.

CHAPTER SUMMARY

1. The ways in which people think about kinship depend upon how they conceive of descent.

2. Children may be thought of as offspring of their mother, their father, or both. Thus, systems of kinship may be based on matrilineal, patrilineal, ambilineal, or bilateral descent.

3. Groups of people thought of as relatives may be organized into corporate groups such as lineages, clans, phratries, or moieties, or into noncorporate kindreds.

4. The various kinds of kinship groups are related to the economic and social conditions in which they are found.

5. Kinship terminology, of which there are six common types, tends to reflect the kinds of conditions with which people must cope as they work together as relatives.

6. The six patterns of kinship terminology are related, though not perfectly, to the kinds of descent systems that are found in each society.

ANNOTATED READINGS

Collier, J. F., & Yanagisako, J. (1987). *Gender and kinship: Essays toward a unified analysis*. Stanford, CA: Stanford University Press. A collection of articles that illustrates recent approaches to kinship that view women and men as equal partners in kinship and marriage.

Keesing, R. M. (1975). *Kin groups and social structure*. New York: Holt, Rinehart & Winston. A study of kinship theory for advanced students.

Graburn, N. (1971). *Readings in kinship and social structure*. New York: Harper & Row. Articles on a wide range of topics and perspectives concerning kinship and society.

Pasternak, B. (1976). *Introduction to kinship and social organization*. New York: Macmillan. Includes an evaluation of theories of kinship and residence.

Schneider, D. M. (1980). *American kinship: A cultural account*. (2nd Ed.). Chicago: University of Chicago Press. A symbolic interpretation of U.S. kinship.

Schneider, D. M., & Gough, K. (Eds.). (1961). *Matrilineal kinship*. Berkeley: University of California Press. Discussions of kinship in a number of matrilineal societies.

Schusky, E. L. (1971). *Manual for kinship analysis*. (2nd Ed.). New York: Holt, Rinehart & Winston. A short course on the basic tools of the trade for recording and analyzing kinship systems. A good starting point for the student who wants an overview of the basics.

Schusky, E. L. (1975). *Variation in kinship*. New York: Holt, Rinehart & Winston. Another good introduction to kinship, descent, and residence.

FIGURE 8.1   Moscow Wedding
Marriage as a social, economic, and sexual union between two or more people is common in most cultures of the world. However, the rules and customs that govern marriage differ from culture to culture. This wedding party is leaving the Tomb of the Unknown Soldier in Moscow, which they visited following their wedding ceremony.

CHAPTER 8

Marriage is defined as a social, economic, and sexual union that takes many forms. In this chapter you will be introduced to the most common marriage forms such as monogamy, polygyny, polyandry, and group marriage, as well as to less common forms such as symbolic, nonsexual, fictive, and homosexual marriage. You will learn about the common rules that govern and restrict the choices of potential marriage partners, and the ways in which marriages are negotiated in traditional societies. Finally, the contrast between nuclear and extended families will be introduced, and you will learn how three or more generations of kin can be united into a single family by different patterns of postmarital residence customs.

Marriage and the Family

CHAPTER OBJECTIVES

After reading this chapter, you should be able to:

Analyze the defining characteristics of marriage.

Explain the basic functions of marriage.

Define the four basic types of marriage.

Explain the adaptive characteristics of each marriage type.

Define the five types of atypical marriage.

Discuss the various forms of homosexual marriage.

Explain the types of rules that influence choice of marriage partner.

Discuss the economic factors in marriage negotiations.

Define the forms of the family and the household.

Define the five basic postmarital residence rules.

Explain the adaptive significance of each of the postmarital residence rules.

Marriage
Functions of Marriage
Types of Marriage
Atypical Marriages

Marriage Choice
Incest Taboo
Exogamy Rules
Endogamy Rules

Negotiating Marriage
Bridewealth
Bride Service
Dowry
Gift Exchange

Postmarital Residence
Virilocality
Uxorilocality
Bilocality
Neolocality
Avunculocality

Family

Something borrowed, something blue. Till death do us part. For time and all eternity. *Tali*-tying. Ghost marriage. Co-marriage. All societies form marriages, but each does it with different styles, rules, and customs.

Marriage

Sex and reproduction are cultural as well as biological phenomena. In all societies, there are customs governing how and under what circumstances they should occur. Marriage plays a central role in these customs. Typically, people marry to legitimize sexual unions and to facilitate childrearing. Nevertheless, the reasons for marrying are diverse, and the families created by marriage differ in many ways from society to society. Ethnographers have reported marriages that are contracted by parents before the birth of a child, marriages that have no public ceremony, marriages that establish no common residence, and marriages between more than two persons, to name but four examples. What then are the minimum defining characteristics of marriage? While the rituals and customs surrounding marriage may differ around the world, the concept of **marriage** may be universally defined as a socially accepted sexual and economic union involving a lasting commitment between two or more people who have parental rights and obligations to any children of the union.

Functions of Marriage

The apparent universality of marriage as an institution suggests that it fulfills a variety of functions in the maintenance and perpetuation of human social life. These functions include chaneling sexual behavior into stable relationships, fulfilling the economic needs of marriage partners, perpetuating a society's kinship groups, and providing an institution for the care of children until they become self-sufficient.

Committed sexual unions. Marriage is more than just a sexual union, since sexual relationships can exist without either a commitment to fidelity or a long-term involvement. Legitimate sexual relationships are recognized in many societies outside the bonds of marriage. For instance, data from the Cultural Diversity Data Base (White, 1987, p. 30) indicate that only 27 percent of 186 societies surveyed have customs that imply the importance of female virginity at the time of marriage. Societies also may approve of sexual relationships outside of marriage between persons who are already married to others. The same Cultural Diversity Data Base (p. 31) indicates that only 44 percent of a sample of 109 societies forbid extramarital sex to both husbands and wives. Another 44 percent accept such behavior by husbands, and only 12 percent by wives.

The Toda of southern India recognized the legitimacy of formalized sexual liaisons between a married woman and certain other men, such as priests, to whom she was not married, so long as the woman's husband gave his approval. For the husband to refuse such requests was considered bad form. The Kalinga of the Philippines institutionalized the taking of mistresses by married men. Children born to the mistresses normally inherited smaller portions of the family property than did the children of the wife. This practice was not followed by all families, but if a wife were barren, taking a mistress was the only legitimate means of perpetuating the man's family without divorce and remarriage—so the wife would often help her husband in the selection of a sexual partner. Gregerson reminds us that sacred prostitution—often performed as part of the rites of a god in a sacred setting such as a temple—was accepted in much of the ancient Near East, India, and Greece and that, according to Herodotus, "every Babylonian woman must have sexual intercourse with a stranger in the temple of Mylitta [a variant of Ishtar or Astarte, a goddess Herodotus equates with Aphrodite] once in her life" (1983, pp. 163–4). Though

marriage   a rite of passage that unites two or more individuals as spouses

FIGURE 8.2 Families of Marriage Partners

Marriage generally creates two sets of in-laws, the families of the partners who assume obligations to the couple as well as to each other. They may provide an economic and emotional support for the couple. In this receiving line at a Christian wedding in Tokyo, Japan, the married couple and their families greet the guests.

sexual unions such as these may be socially approved, they cannot be considered examples of marriage because they lack the public commitment to a lasting relationship and to sexual fidelity that is a defining feature of marriage.

To say that marriages are normally expected to be long-lasting—even lifelong—unions is to recognize that marriage involves a commitment of the partners to one another and to their socially acknowledged partnership. For this reason, marriage usually includes an expectation of fidelity. Cross-cultural data reported by Ford and Beach indicates that in a sample of 139 societies, 61 percent required women to be sexually faithful in marriage, and 53 percent had the same requirement for husbands (1951, pp. 115–116). Reiss (1987) argues that even in cultures that may have formally lenient rules regarding marital fidelity, jealousy may still be caused by infidelity.

One effect of an expectation of fidelity within marriage is to minimize the potentially disruptive

effects of sexual competition. When people marry, the role change typically defines them as inappropriate sexual partners for members of the unmarried group within which courtship is a common pursuit. Being part of a stable relationship thereby permits each partner to devote time, previously taken up by the courtship process, to other pursuits.

Sex and Reproduction Among the Nayar of India

Although marriage is commonly said to be a cultural universal, there is at least one major group within a larger society, the Nayar of Kerala State in southern India, that has no marriages as they have been defined in this chapter.

Nayar

Marriage among the Nayar of southern India consisted first of a *tali*-tying ceremony, which then allowed the young men from the nearby *taravad* and the young girl to have sexual relations. Subsequent *sambandham* marriages also allowed for sexual relations and established paternity. Neither marriage allowed for a common residence.

According to Gough (1959, 1961), the nineteenth-century Nayar were a landowning caste whose men by tradition pursued the occupation of soldiers who hired themselves to the rulers of several neighboring kingdoms. This meant that men were often away from home for extended periods of time. Among the Nayar, children were members of their mother's family and household. Land was owned by a group of relatives who were related through the female line and who lived together as a household. This group, called the *taravad*, was headed by the eldest male of the household.

Each Nayar taravad had a special partnership with several others in the community. At intervals of every 10 or 12 years, the girls of each taravad would go through what was called the *tali*-tying ceremony with a man selected from the linked taravads, who tied a *tali*, a gold ornament, around the neck of the girl. Although it was considered a marriage ceremony, it also marked the transition of the girl into adulthood. Sexual relations were permitted if the girl was old enough; however, the "husband" had no further obligations to his "bride," and her only responsibility to him thereafter was to perform a ceremony at his funeral. Thus, this marriage was essentially a symbolic one.

Having gone through the tali-tying ceremony, the woman was now entitled to enter into *sambandham* relationships with other men of the same or of a higher caste than her own. These, too, might be called "marriages," but they also lacked most of the defining features of marriages elsewhere. Preferred partners were men of the higher-ranking Namboodri Brahmin caste who could not, by rules of their own caste, accept the children of the Nayar "wives" as their own heirs.

The first of these sambandham relationships began with a simple ceremony, as did any others that were intended to involve a lasting sexual relationship. Temporary relationships with other sambandham partners involved no ceremony. Sambandham "husbands" were allowed to spend the evening with their "wives" and were expected to bring small gifts with them at each visit, but a common residence was not established. The Nayar woman continued to live with her own taravad, where her brothers took responsibility for the costs of rearing her children. The woman's taravad benefited from her sambandham relationships in several ways: The woman's children became members of her own taravad and constituted the next generation of her family, and she might receive various services from each of her husbands, who were likely to have a variety of occupations.

Children born to a Nayar woman were legitimate only if paternity was acknowledged by one or more of her sambandham husbands. The designated father was usually one of the men who had been sexually involved with her during the appropriate time for the child's conception, but might also be the man who was currently in the role of a "visiting husband." The fatherhood ceremony consisted of the payment of the midwife's fee, but the "father" had no further economic or social responsibilities for rearing the child. The failure of any of the husbands to acknowledge paternity was considered evidence that the woman had fathered the child with a man of a lower caste or a Muslim or Christian, an offense that was punishable by death or banishment of both the mother and child.

Types of Marriage

Marriages take several forms. Four basic types seem to exist: monogamous, polygynous, polyandrous, or group marriages. These four types differ in the number of persons of one or both sexes who form the marriage relationship and in the circumstances under which each tends to be the idealized form of marriage.

Monogamy. In **monogamous marriages** two persons are joined as spouses. Monogamous marriages are the most common form of marital unit in all societies, even where other forms may be idealized as more desirable. Yet Ford and Beach (1951) found that less than 16 percent of their sample of 185 societies formally *restricted* marriage to the monogamous form. The recently developed Cultural Diversity Data Base (p. 22) supports the Ford and Beach finding with a similarly low figure of 14 percent of a sample of 180 societies and indicates that another 19 percent prefer monogamy without forbidding other marriage forms.

Serial monogamy. In societies such as the United States in which monogamy is the accepted form of marriage, a high rate of divorce and remarriage creates a particular pattern sometimes called **serial monogamy.** Serial monogamy has some characteristics of **polygamy,** the form of marriage in which a person is permitted to have more than one spouse at the same time. In serial monogamy, persons are permitted to have more than one spouse during their lifetimes, but only one at a time.

Polygyny. The form of polygamy in which one man is married to more than one woman at a time is described as **polygynous marriage.** This was actually the *preferred* form of marriage in 83.6 percent of 185 societies surveyed by Ford and Beach (1951). The highest frequency of polygynous families is found in societies in frontier areas; in societies where warfare is common; in societies in which the ratio of adult women to men is high (a condition that is common in either of the two preceding circumstances); and in groups where rapid growth of families is beneficial to family survival. Since the ratio of male to female children is about equal in all societies, relatively few men actually are able to practice polygyny even in societies where it is the preferred marital form. It is practiced most commonly by individuals of high social standing, while most men of lower social standing remain monogamous. Since it generally takes some time and effort to achieve the social standing that makes it possible for a man to have more than one wife, polygyny often involves an age difference between spouses, with older men taking much younger wives. White (1988) has demonstrated that polygyny is organized into two basic patterns: sororal polygyny and male-stratified polygyny. In **sororal polygyny** or **male-ranked polygyny with related co-wives,** a man marries two or more

---

monogamous marriage form of marriage where one man and one woman are joined as husband and wife
serial monogamy a marriage pattern in which individuals of either sex may have only one spouse at a given time, but through divorce and remarriage may have several spouses during their lifetime
polygamy form of marriage where a person is permitted to have more than one spouse at the same time
polygynous marriage form of marriage in which a man has more than one wife
sororal polygyny the form of polygyny in which the wives are sisters
male-ranked polygyny with related co-wives a more descriptive term for sororal polygyny

FIGURE 8.3 Polygyny

While marriage takes many forms, it is a universal phenomenon. This Togolese chief, here posing with a number of his wives, practices polygyny.

FIGURE 8.4   A Polyandrous Wedding Ceremony
One variation in the structure of marriage is the polyandrous type in which one woman marries two men. This Nepalese woman, in the veil, is marrying the two brothers on the left.

closely related women, often sisters. In societies that practice this form of polygyny, social ranking is primarily a matter of individual achievement. A small number of men, such as outstanding hunters, warriors, or shamans, demonstrate their success by marrying a second or third wife. Since male labor is the major contribution to the subsistence income of the family and extra wives are a drain on the man's wealth, he exchanges his individually achieved wealth for wives, and his ability to support them demonstrates his high social rank.

Male-stratified polygyny or **wealth-increasing polygyny** is more common in societies in which there are hereditary classes. In this form of polygamy, a small number of men who hold positions of rank and authority, often older men of wealthy families, marry a larger number of wives, perhaps 20 or 30. In these societies, the labor of women is often economically valuable, and each new wife increases the wealth of the family and its social prominence. It also becomes easier for the husband to acquire yet another wife. In contrast to sororal polygyny, where the wives and their husbands often reside together, these wives often have their own residence so that their economic activities can be carried out with a minimum of direct competition between co-wives.

Polyandry.   It is rare for a woman to have several husbands, as in a **polyandrous marriage**. It is the idealized family type in probably less than 0.5 percent of the world's societies. The most common form of polyandrous union is one in which a woman is simultaneously married to several brothers, a form known as **fraternal polyandry**. It is advantageous where resources are extremely limited. Polyandrous unions have been reported among southern Indian and Tibetan peoples where land is at a premium and cannot easily be further subdivided from one generation to the next. It was also practiced by the Shoshoni of the Great Basin, where a man might temporarily share his wife with a younger brother until he was old enough to make his own way as an independent hunter with his own family. Like polygyny, polyan-

---

male-stratified polygyny   form of polygamy in which a small number of men of high rank and authority marry a larger number of wives
wealth-increasing polygyny   male-stratified polygyny
polyandrous marriage   the form of marriage in which one woman has more than one husband
fraternal polyandry   the form of polyandry in which the husbands are brothers

dry is actually practiced by a minority of women in societies where it is the preferred marital form and gives evidence of a woman's high status.

Polyandrous and Group Marriages Among the Toda

The Toda of Southern India, described in detail by Rivers (1906), were one of the few peoples of the world where polyandry and group marriages were the rule. Marriages were arranged by parents when children were as young as two or three years of age. A marriage united the girl not only to the boy for whom she was originally selected but also to any brothers he might have, including those born after the ceremony. Thus, a Toda wife typically had several husbands who were usually brothers, although she might also enter marriage with other men. Since a woman was considered to be the wife of any of the brothers of a man she married, if brothers entered into marriage with more than one woman, the result was a group marriage in which several women might be wives simultaneously to several men.

Both polyandry and group marriage made it infeasible to keep track of biological paternity, so this concept was unimportant to the Toda. However, since Toda families were patrilineal, fatherhood in its social sense was important. Therefore, the Todas employed a ritual of fatherhood, a ritual that designated a particular man to be the social father of any children a woman bore for a period of years thereafter, whether or not he was their natural father.

Since fatherhood was established by a ritual act, the concept of adultery was irrelevant to the Toda view of family relations. Not only was sexual infidelity by a wife not grounds for divorce—since it would not have affected the legitimacy of a child's rights to inherit from the socially defined father—but it was also so unimportant a concept that there was not even a word for adultery in the Toda language.

(see reference map p. 107)

Group marriage. When several males are simultaneously married to several females, their union is called **group marriage**. Group marriage and

polyandry typically occur together, but group marriage and polygyny do not. This is because polyandry and polygyny are not simple mirror images of one another. Women in polyandrous families in some ways have higher status than those in polygynous families. For instance, the sexuality of plural wives in polygynous families is often jealously guarded by their husbands, but not in a polyandrous society in which married women will have plural mates as a matter of course. On the other hand, no such contrast exists for husbands in these two family types. Polyandrous societies typically have no rules against husbands sometimes marrying plural wives, something that wives in polygynous societies are not likely to be permitted to do. When one of a woman's husbands in a polyandrous society marries another woman—often a sister of the original wife—the new bride also becomes the wife of co-husbands in the original marriage as well. Such simultaneously polyandrous and polygynous families are also considered group marriages.

▬

group marriage the form of marriage in which two or more men are married to two or more women at the same time

Co-Marriage Among the Inuit of North Alaska

According to Burch (1970, 1975), the Inuit of North Alaska once engaged in monogamy, polygyny, polyandry, and a nonresidential form of group marriage that he calls *co-marriage*. Co-marriages were typically contracted to create a kind of fictive sibling relationship between the same-sex partners. This quasi-siblinghood continued into succeeding generations, since the children of both couples in a co-marriage were considered siblings, and their children in turn were accepted as cousins. Thus, co-marriages established long-lasting cooperative bonds between people and their descendants who resided in different locations, a very useful practice in a highly mobile society in which autonomous nuclear families might lack a network of relatives to call upon for help wherever they traveled.

A co-marriage was established when, by mutual agreement, the husbands and wives had sexual intercourse with each other's resi-

Inuit

The Inuit of North Alaska practiced co-marriage, where, by mutual agreement, the husbands and wives had sexual intercourse with each other's residential spouse. This established a situation of mutual support and obligation among the families, crucial to survival in the harsh Arctic environment.

dential spouse. This formality established a co-husband relationship between the men and a co-wife relationship between the women, relationships that included a continuing obligation of mutual aid similar to that of siblings. Such relationships were both emotionally and practically important among the Inuit, since siblings had strong moral responsibilities toward one another, and life in the cold, arctic environment they occupied could be a difficult one for small foraging families when other relatives were not available for cooperative activities.

Atypical Marriages

In addition to the four basic patterns of marriage, a number of other patterns also exist. These marriage forms may be rare or quite common, depending on the society in question, but are generally not the preferred type in any society. They lack one or more of the usual defining characteristics of marriage shared by the four basic types. Atypical marriages include symbolic marriages, nonsexual marriages, fixed-term marriages, fictive marriages, and several forms of homosexual marriage.

Symbolic marriages. As we have seen, marriage is normally created in all societies as a vehicle for establishing economic and social ties between kinship groups and for providing a means of perpetuating the group. However, under some circumstances societies may sanction the establishment of marriages in which these functions do not apply. Such **symbolic marriages** may serve other purposes, as when religious specialists consider themselves married to a deity. The Roman Catholic nun who wears a ring symbolic of her status as a bride of Christ, and who is therefore taboo to others as an object of romantic love, is a Western example of a participant in a symbolic sacred marriage. Mormon religious practice provides another striking example of symbolic marriage: It includes a contrast between a "marriage for time" and a "marriage for eternity." A temporal marriage is one performed outside a Mormon temple. Such marriages end at the death of one partner, lasting only "till death do us part." Eternal marriages, on the other hand, are performed only in a Mormon Temple and are believed to be valid "for time and all eternity" in the eyes of God. An outgrowth of this belief is the practice of performing vicarious marriages between deceased persons and their surviving spouses or even between two deceased persons who were married only temporally while alive. This system of symbolic marriage has a polygynous bias in the Mormon subculture, since a woman whose "eternal husband" has predeceased her may remarry "for time" only, while a man may enter into several "eternal marriages" serially, if one or more of his wives dies before him. When a man who has entered several "eternal marriages" dies, Mormons believe that he will be reunited with all his wives after death.

Nonsexual marriages. Marriages sometimes fulfill their usual economic, kinship, and even child-rearing functions in the absence of a sexual union between the partners. Such **nonsexual marriages** can occur for a variety of reasons. For instance, they may occur in societies that have class differences, for the political or economic benefits to the marriage partners or their relatives, as when a

---

symbolic marriages those marriages not establishing economic and social ties between kinship groups
nonsexual marriages marriages that fulfill economic, social, and kinship functions without sexual union between the partners

royal marriage is negotiated to stabilize a political alliance between two societies. Among Mormon pioneers in the United States, an elderly woman sometimes entered into a nonsexual marriage as a plural wife for companionship or economic security in a precarious environment. In such a role, she might participate in the domestic life of the family, help with housework, and share childrearing responsibilities with her co-wives.

Fixed-term marriages.

Temporary marriages, such as the fixed-term marriages of Iran, legitimize a sexual relationship in which the usual marriage characteristics, such as economic obligations or the expectation of childrearing, may be minimized. In fixed-term marriages, the length of time of the marriage is agreed upon before it begins, so that it will come to an end after a specified period of time or whenever the activities that make it convenient for the couple to remain together have run their course. For instance, fixed-term marriages came into existence in Islam in order for soldiers to have legitimate sexual partners while they were fighting in foreign wars for long periods. At the end of the husband's military duty, his temporary marriage was dissolved, and he was free to return home with no further obligation to the divorced wife.

Fictive marriages.

A marriage can exist legally without a family being established in order to allow one or both partners to obtain social benefits that would be unavailable otherwise. Such a marriage is called a **fictive marriage**. For instance, immigration and naturalization quotas in the United States have resulted in the practice of marriages between U.S. citizens and potential immigrants or resident aliens for no purpose other than to facilitate the immigration or acquisition of citizenship by the noncitizen partner. In such a case, the parties to the marriage may not establish a common domicile or sexual relationship; indeed, they need not be acquainted before the marriage nor see each other again afterwards. This particular example of fictive marriage is one that is legally rejected by U.S. immigration authorities, and those who are involved may be punished by law, but analogous fictive marriages do exist in societies where they are openly accepted as valid means to an end. For instance, among the Kwakiutl it is possible for a man to marry the male heir of a chief as a means of inheriting certain privileges from the father-in-law. When there is no heir to marry, a man may marry the chief's arm or

leg as a legally valid way of becoming an inheritor.

Probably the most widespread forms of fictive marriage are the levirate and the sororate. The **levirate**, a custom mentioned in Deuteronomy 25, is the obligation of a dead man's next of kin, usually one of his brothers, to marry the dead man's widow. Commonly, at least the first child of this union is considered to be the offspring of the first husband. This custom is especially important in societies that stress the importance of the line of descent through males, since it provides a way for men who die without heirs to have descendants. It also cements anew the marriage alliance between the two families whose children were originally united in marriage. At the same time, it provides the widow with someone who will continue to perform the duties of a husband. The **sororate** is a similar custom in which a widower, or sometimes the husband of a barren woman, marries his first wife's sister. Again, at least some of the children born to this second marriage are considered children of the first wife, a particular benefit in societies where ancestry is traced primarily through women. Like the levirate, the sorarate ensures that the marriage tie between the two in-law families is not dissolved by the death of one partner and that the survivor will continue to have a mate.

---

fictive marriage   legal marriage established for both partners to acquire social benefits

levirate   a rule that requires kin of a deceased man to provide his widow with another husband, often one of the deceased man's brothers

sororate   a rule that requires the kin of a deceased woman to provide her widower with another wife, often one of the deceased woman's sisters

ghost marriages   fictive marriages where a close male kinsman of a man or boy—married or unmarried—who died before he had any legal heirs, marries a woman in the name of the deceased

---

Ghost Marriage Among the Nuer of the Sudan

Evans-Pritchard (1951) described an interesting form of fictive marriage practiced by the Nuer, a cattle-herding people who live in the savanna region of the Upper Nile in the Sudan. **Ghost marriages** occur when the close male kinsman of a man or boy—married or unmarried—who died before he had any legal

Nuer

The Nuer of the Upper Nile of the Sudan engage in ghost marriages to provide legal heirs for the deceased relative. The woman is the legal bride of the dead man even though the ceremony and practical aspects of the marriage are conducted by the dead man's relative.

heirs, marries a woman in the name of the deceased relative. The living vicarious husband gives the family of the bride a number of cattle, as the deceased man would have done had he married the woman while he was still alive. Legally, the woman will be the ghost's bride, and all of the children she bears will be his. However, the vicarious husband will be treated in all other respects as if he were the woman's real husband, something that is not true in the case of the levirate. As with the levirate, the purpose of a ghost marriage is to bear children who will be heirs to the deceased husband. However, ghost marriage differs from the levirate in several important ways. A leviratic marriage unites a widow with a surrogate for her deceased husband. The wife in a ghost marriage is not the widow of the deceased, but she becomes his wife through a marriage ritual with a living surrogate after the death of the ghost husband, whom she, in most cases, might never have known while he was alive.

Ghost marriages among the Nuer are almost as common as simple marriages between a man and woman, partly because each ghost marriage tends to create anew the circumstance which requires ghost marriages in the first place: a man who enters a ghost marriage as the vicarious husband obtains no descendants through that marriage; he may well die before he is able to found a lineage of his own, and it will be up to one of his brothers or nephews to enter a ghost marriage in his behalf. Thus the Nuer "solution" to the "problem" of men who die without children perpetuates the very situation it is intended to eliminate. Such a situation suggests that some pragmatic benefits may accrue to Nuer families who practice ghost marriage.

How might Nuer ghost marriage benefit the living? An answer to this question is suggested by other customs related to ghost marriage. The Nuer not only assert that a dead man may be the legal father of children born long after his death, but also that a ghost may continue to own property. When a man dies without heirs, any cattle he may have owned do not revert to the larger family herd, but remain *ghok jookni*, "cattle of the ghost." Such cattle are sacred and may not properly be used for any purpose other than as payment to a bride's family for her bearing of children in the name of the ghost. This restriction has further implications: According to Evans-Pritchard (1966:111), "When Nuer raid a herd to seize cattle in compensation for some injury they will not take cattle reserved for the marriage of a ghost." So the idea that uninherited cattle remain the property of the dead benefits the survivors because such property is still under their control and can be used for several things. The cows may be milked while they are held in trust for the deceased owner, they may be used to obtain a wife for one of their living sons so long as he enters a fictive marriage in behalf of the dead owner of the cattle that pays for the marriage, and they cannot be taken from the family in payment of debts as their other cattle can. Thus ghost marriage is, in reality, part of a larger web of cultural concepts that includes some economic benefits similar to those of family trusts in the United States.

Homosexual marriage. Just as legitimate marriages may exist without a sexual component, nonreproductive marriages may still fulfill the other functions of marriage and be socially accepted. Marriages of this type include those by persons past their reproductive years and homosexual marriages, both of which are legitimate in a large number of human societies. **Homosexual marriages** consist of both male-male and female-female relationships.

A same-sex marriage between partners of more or less equal age is called a **homophilic marriage**. Though not recognized by law except in Holland, homophilic marriage is the form of homosexual relationship most commonly found in industrialized nations. Same-sex marriages in the same generation have been socially accepted in many nonindustrialized societies, but, unlike homophilic marriages, they involve a gender-role change in one partner, who undertakes some of the roles usually assigned to members of the other sex, including the practice of transvestism, cross-sex or gender-mixed dressing. Such relationships have been called **pathic marriages** (Gregerson, 1983) or **intragenerational marriages** (Adam, 1986). Transvestism is generally common as a nonpublic behavior among heterosexually married males who seek a covert means for escaping what they perceive as limitations of accepted masculine roles. Homophilic and pathic marriages may be regarded as culturally patterned variants of same-sex intragenerational relationships.

Societies that historically accepted pathic marriages differed from those that did not in a number of ways. Those that accepted pathic relationships were more likely to have a variety of social traits that are associated with flexibility and adaptability to changing economic circumstances (Crapo, 1987). These include bilateral descent, ambilocal residence or the absence of patrilineal kin groups when patrilocal residence is followed, and social rank based on individual achievement rather than birth into a high-status descent group. Male labor is particularly important in the food-getting activities of these societies, but women have relatively high status both politically and domestically. Wealth-depleting polygyny is common and is one indicator that a male is particularly successful as a provider, since the major source of income is male labor. Both homosexual and lesbian pathic marriages were common in societies with these characteristics, although male pathic relationships were somewhat more widespread in the world's nonindustrialized cultures, probably because the gendered division of income-producing labor created greater economic incentives for male pathic marriages than it did for female pathic marriages.

In societies that accepted same-sex marriages, a pathic male commonly entered marriage as the second "wife" of an already heterosexually married man. This increased the status of the family, which by the addition of the pathic wife, became polygynous. A pathic marriage is a relatively easy way for a man to become a polygynous husband, because, in addition to doing women's work, the gender-crossing wife can help produce income that husbands are usually responsible for alone. The pathic wife may actually increase the income of the family and improve the husband's chances of being able to afford a third wife even sooner.

Lesbian pathic marriages have been common under two circumstances. First, they were found in many of the same societies in which homosexual pathic marriages occurred. But they were sometimes found in the absence of male pathic marriages where polygyny was not a usual marriage form. In these societies, a daughter might be raised as a pathic child by a family that had no son, because a son's economic contributions, such as food obtained by hunting, were vital to family survival. As an adult, a pathic daughter who had learned the roles that usually were carried out by males was permitted to marry in the role of a pathic husband in a lesbian marriage.

---

homosexual marriage   marriage between members of the same sex
homophilic marriage   same-sex marriage without transvestism or change in sex role by one of the partners
pathic marriages   same-sex marriages involving gender-role change in one partner
intragenerational marriages   pathic marriages

Nuer Woman Marriage

Evans-Pritchard's (1951) study of the Nuer of the Sudan reported a form of marriage that he called "woman marriage," in which one woman marries another. She does so exactly as a man does, paying a bride price of cattle to her bride's family. The female husband in such a family acquires cattle when her own kinswomen marry, just as her brothers do and may inherit cattle from her father as if she were a son. Children born to her own wife through the services of a man she chooses for that purpose "are called after her, as though she were a man" (p. 109). Her children address her as "father," and she is "treated by her wives and children with the same deference they would show to a male husband and father" (p. 109). When her daughters marry, she receives the cattle that are normally given a father in payment of the bride price.

Woman marriages may also occur when a female relative of a deceased man marries a wife in the name of the dead kinsman. According to Evans-Pritchard (1951, p. 111), "The persons involved in a marriage of this kind are the dead man, his kinswoman who marries a wife in his name, the wife, and the man who is brought in to cohabit with the wife." The children of this union are legally those of the dead man and will inherit from him.

(see reference map p. 182)

One other form of homosexual marriage is found in a variety of the world's cultures, a form that has been labelled **mentorships** (Herdt, 1981) or **intergenerational marriage** (Adam, 1986). Mentorships are same-sex relationships between older and younger partners in which the older person has the role of husband to the younger same-sex wife. Mentorships often come into existence as a way of solidifying an important social bond such as an economic or political patron-client, master-apprentice, or teacher-student relationship by which younger members of society are socialized into specialized adult skills or knowledge. The younger apprentice may, at the same time, aid his mentor in his pursuit of higher status within the male community. Unlike pathic marriages, which may be life-long relationships, mentorship marriages are usually temporary unions that end when the apprentice-wife graduates into adult life and, potentially, enters into the same kind of relationship as mentor to a younger apprentice. It is usual for both male and female husbands in homosexual and lesbian mentorships to be married simultaneously in heterosexual relationships.

Male mentorships are often a part of the military training system in male-dominant, warlike societies, and may be associated with specialized religious training, where younger males are secluded from contact with females. They may also be common in societies in which men play a socially domi-

nant role, and exercise sexual rights over persons of lower rank, such as women, youths, and slaves (Adam, 1981, 1986). The mentorship marriage occurs during a period of sexual segregation of young men from young women. This minimizes competition between younger and older men for wives, making it easier for high-status, older men to marry a large number of younger women.

In societies with male mentorships, the preferred form of heterosexual marriage is polygyny of the wealth-increasing variety, in which the most highly ranked, older men have a large number of wives whose work is a major source of their income (Crapo, 1987). This form of heterosexual polygyny symbolizes the husband's high social standing and perpetuates his power by ensuring that he will have many children. Since wives in societies that practice wealth-increasing polygyny typically have low status, the position of wife within a male mentorship reinforces the younger male's situation as a socially subordinate person in the male status hierarchy. However, it also provides him with an acceptable sexual outlet during his period of segregation from women and makes the temporary taboo on heterosexuality for young men easier to follow.

Unfortunately, very little is known about female mentorships. A few researchers have suggested the presence of ritualized, intergenerational lesbian relationships in Melanesian cultures in which lactating women nurse prepubescent girls to transmit the life force that is symbolized by milk (Harrisson, 1937, p. 410; R. Kelly, 1976; Godelier, 1982, pp. 97–98; Keesing, 1982; Schwimmer, 1984). Anthropologists have reported female mentorships on Carriacou in the Caribbean (Blackwood, 1985) and in Lesotho in southern Africa (Blacking, 1978; Gay, 1985; Mueller, 1977). In both of these areas, husbands are away from home for prolonged periods as wage laborers, while wives remain home and have responsibility for the running of household affairs. Women in these settings sometimes enter a relationship with a younger woman for both affection and help in household work.

mentorships system of marriage between an older, socially established partner and a younger spouse of the same sex

intergenerational marriage male mentorship

Marriage Choice

Each culture includes various rules that influence the choice of marriage partners. Some of these rules restrict the choices that may be made by proscribing certain persons as possible partners. Other rules require marriage within defined social categories. Some define particular kinds of persons as preferred partners. All three kinds of rules help to narrow the range of appropriate mates from which the selection is made.

Incest Taboo

One rule that seems to be found in almost all cultures is the **incest taboo**, which forbids sexual intercourse between parents and their children, between brothers and sisters, and frequently between other kin as well. There are a few cultures in which exceptions to this rule exist. For instance, the Hawaiian royalty, the kings and queens of ancient Egypt, and the Inca emperors were expected to violate the incest taboo in order to perpetuate their lineages by brother-sister marriages. But societies such as these are rare, and all others forbid sexual contact between parents and children and between siblings. Indeed, most nonindustrialized societies have included a much broader range of kin and even fictive kin, such as nursemaids, under the prohibition.

Nevertheless, there are variations in how effectively incest taboos are enforced. Gregory Leavitt has noted that as societies become technologically and socially more complex and as trade institutions develop, the number of relatives included in the incest taboo declines and punishment becomes less severe (1989).

A variety of theories have been proposed for the existence of an incest taboo in societies throughout the world. These have included biological instinct theories; psychological theories; more recent sociological ideas and political and economic theories. Anthropological theories have emphasized the social functions of the incest taboo and, until recently, have given little attention to issues of the "politics" of incest as an abuse of power within the family.

Biological theories. The earliest explanations of the incest taboo simply attributed its universality to "instinct." This idea has generally been

FIGURE 8.5   Incest Taboo
The choice of a marriage partner is limited in most cultures by restrictive rules. Nearly universal, the incest taboo forbids sexual intercourse between parents and their children and between siblings. In some cultures, such as that of the ancient Egyptians, incest was encouraged in order to perpetuate the royal lineage. Cleopatra was a product of eleven generations of step-sibling inbreeding.

discarded on the grounds that if there were an instinctive avoidance of incest, rules against it would not be necessary, and incest would be unlikely to occur. In fact, incest does occur. For instance, it has been estimated that there may be as many as 50,000 cases of incest per year in the United States.

Later biological theories emphasized the possible detrimental genetic effects of incest on human

---

incest taboo   a rule that forbids sexual behaviors between designated kin, including but not limited to intercourse between parents and children and between siblings groups, but they have not generally remained popular for two reasons. First, most societies have limited knowledge about the nature of biological heredity, and second, it is doubtful that the harmful effects of close inbreeding on a species with fertility rates as high as are typical of human societies could cause its extinction. Therefore, most theorists have looked elsewhere to explain the universality of the incest taboo.

Psychological theories. A psychological approach still advocated is based on Westermark's (1889) notion that "familiarity breeds contempt," that children who are reared together are simply not likely to be sexually attracted to one another due to a kind of "boredom factor." Several studies have suggested that young people are more likely to prefer strangers. For instance, unrelated children reared in the communal dormitories of certain Israeli kibbutzim have a demonstrated tendency to marry persons from other communities. Detractors of these studies argue, on the other hand, that by the time these children are old enough for mate selection, they have been dispersed due to the universal military obligation and would thus automatically choose someone outside their community. Studies of quasi-sibling marriages in Taiwan in which the bride-to-be is raised from childhood by the in-law family have shown such marriages to have higher rates of infertility, impotence, and divorce than other Taiwanese marriages (Wolf, 1966). Although there may be some merit to the idea that sexual attraction is greater between strangers than between persons reared together, this approach is more relevant to sibling incest taboos than to parent-child sex prohibitions and also fails to address the fact that incest does occur.

Sociological theories. The sociological approach emphasizes the role of the taboo in preventing the role confusion that incestuous relationships could have within families if they were acceptable (Starcke, 1889; Malinowski, 1939). If, for instance, a daughter were also a co-wife of her own father, conflict could arise about when it would be appropriate to play a subordinate or equal role with respect to either the mother or the father. This approach is generally regarded as overly simplistic in failing to recognize that humans generally manage to juggle a lot of potential role conflict without tremendous difficulty. For instance, newly married children hosting their parents in their home could experience role conflict over who should play the dominant role in the new

setting, the parents in their traditional role or the children as hosts and family heads. We manage to live with such conflicts and usually work out satisfactory accommodations. Therefore, the incest taboo does not seem to demand role conflict to explain its universality.

A recent variant on Malinowki's sociological approach has arisen among feminist anthropologists, who emphasize the role of gender and relative age differences in social power as a cause of incest. In most societies, male roles have greater access to power than do female roles, and older persons have greater power than younger ones. Both parent-child and sibling violations of the incest taboo can be examined as inappropriate uses of social power by one individual to gain sexual access to another that would otherwise be denied. From this perspective, the purpose of the incest taboo is to protect the rights of the less powerful member of the relationship. The period of childhood socialization is the time during which children acquire the foundations of trust that serve as the basis for their continuing successful interpersonal relationships with other people throughout the rest of their lives. Incest impairs the less powerful person's ability to trust others and form bonds of emotional intimacy. It is therefore a form of victimization where the more powerful individuals in an incestuous relationship will find it inherently difficult to distinguish between their own needs and those of their subordinate victims. The incest taboo, therefore, has the effect of insulating less powerful members of the family from the harm that incest represents.

Economic and political theories. Economic and political implications of the incest taboo maintain a lot of popularity among anthropological theorists (e.g., White, 1948; Harris, 1968). The most common argument insists that prohibiting incest is an indirect means of forcing each new generation to marry outside the natal family. If sex is unavailable between parents and children or between siblings, then marriage between these persons is also impossible. Sexual partners must be found outside the family of origin, and these relationships—when legitimized as marriages—become the basis for economic and political alliances between the in-law families, who may be called upon for aid in times of economic need or political strife, such as when feuds erupt between neighboring families. Families that allow incest tend to be isolates that eventually lose out in competition with families that are more powerful through the marriage alliances. In effect, the incest taboo codifies the rule of "Marry out or die out." This approach sees the incest taboo as a cultural rule that has adaptive value, and is supported by recent research that indicates that incest is more common among marginal and socially isolated families.

Exogamy Rules

When marriages are of practical significance to a family, the culture often has formal guidelines about whom a person ought or ought not to marry. Such rules increase the likelihood that the practical well-being of the kin group will be fostered. The most common examples of such marriage guidelines are **exogamy rules** that require marriage outside designated groups such as one's own lineage or clan.

Rules of exogamy are more than mere extensions of the incest taboo. Where incest taboos specifically govern sexual behavior, rules of exogamy do more than this: they govern marriage rights. Therefore they may exclude from consideration for marriage a broad circle of persons with whom sex is not necessarily forbidden. Thus, rules of exogamy may require marriage outside one's own residential unit as well as outside one's own family. In some societies the local unit is divided into two groups, or moieties, which are each exogamous—so that members of one moiety always marry persons from the opposite moiety, each of which has reciprocal rights and obligations to the another. For instance, members of one moiety may host a funeral when a member of the opposite moiety dies.

Endogamy Rules

On the other hand, **endogamy rules** require that both marriage partners be members of a certain kinship, social, or local group. For instance, a rule of endogamy may require marriage into one's own village, church, or social class. In the traditional castes of India, marriage partners were strictly limited to members of one's own caste, and among the traditional Bedouin, there was a preference for endogamous marriage within one's own patrilineal lineage.

Marriage preference rules single out specific kin as ideal marriage partners. Although the exogamy rules of most societies promote marriage beyond the circle of one's cousins, there are many that

FIGURE 8.6   Exogamy Rules
The rules of exogamy ensure that marriage will occur with an individual outside one's own lineage or clan. The rule is traced back to a time when it was advantageous politically and socially to extend relationships outside of one's group. In preparing for a marriage between two Bedouin groups, this sister of the groom, in a symbol of camaraderie, assumes her brother's role and embraces the bride.

in fact prefer marriage between cousins. Most of these cultures have a rule of preferential marriage between **cross cousins**—cousins who are linked by parents of opposite sex, as children of a brother and sister. In both patrilineal and matrilineal systems of reckoning kinship, cross cousins belong to different

exogamy rule   a rule forbidding an individual from marrying a member of the kinship, residential, or other specified group to which he or she belongs
endogamy rule   requiring marriage within specified kinship categories or other specified social or local groups to which one belongs
marriage preference rules   systems that single out certain kin as ideal marriage partners
cross cousins   cousins who are related through parents of the opposite sex who are usually brother and sister

lineages. With such marriages, members of each family gain in-laws outside their own lineage to whom they can turn for aid in times of need. A common form of cross-cousin marriage is one in which a brother and a sister marry cross cousins who are also sister and brother to each other. In societies where the inequality of the sexes is marked, this is often described as two men exchanging sisters. In such cases, marrying one's brother-in-law's sister does create an added social bond between two men that may benefit them both politically and economically. **Sister exchange**, or, more accurately, **bilateral cross-cousin marriage**, links two lineages over many generations. This system is called "bilateral" because a man's wife is both his mother's brother's daughter and his father's sister's daughter.

A less intense pattern of intermarriage between two lineages is one in which a male of one lineage marries a woman from another lineage in one generation, and his daughter marries into that lineage a generation later. This permits his sister to marry into a third lineage, thereby extending the marriage alliances into an even greater circle of people. This system has been called **patrilateral cross-cousin marriage** because, from the male's point of view, the preferred marriage is with one's father's sister's daughter. Patrilateral cross-cousin marriage permits many lineages to be linked into a circle in which marriage partners flow between lineages in alternate directions every other generation.

An even more common pattern is one in which several lineages are linked into a circle in which the women of each lineage always marry in one direction around the circle, while their brothers marry into the lineage next to theirs in the opposite direction. This marriage system is like the patrilateral marriage system, but the direction of marriages is asymmetric and does not alternate each generation. This system also is known as **matrilateral cross-cousin marriage**, since a wife is always a mother's brother's daughter to her husband.

The rarest form of preferential cousin marriage is marriage with a **parallel cousin** (a cousin who is one's mother's sister's child or one's father's brother's child). Parallel-cousin marriage is found among many Arab societies. It is called *bint'amm* or **patrilateral parallel-cousin marriage**, that is, marriage between a man and his father's brother's daughter. This rule is useful in maintaining solidarity within a lineage, since a man and his father's brother's daughter belong to the same lineage (Barth, 1954; Murphy & Kasdan, 1959). It is especially

helpful, for instance, among Arab Bedouins, where members of the same lineage may be dispersed from one another for long periods of time.

....

Negotiating Marriage

Negotiations before marriage between the two families will emphasize pragmatic issues, such as the size of the payment one family may make to the other, the work and domestic skills of the future spouses, and the like. Less rational matters such as the feelings of the prospective bride and groom for one another are not given as much weight as in societies where large kinship groups are not the major economic and political units of society. Neither the couple's sexual gratification nor their emotional compatibility is of great interest to their respective families. Rather, the couple to be married form a link by which those families are joined in their society's larger arena of politics and economics.

Bridewealth

In perhaps three quarters of the world's societies, marriage negotiations involve the determination of how the prospective groom's family shall recompense the family of the bride-to-be for the loss of her productive and reproductive services (Coult & Haberstein, 1965; Murdock, 1957). This compensation may consist of gifts, known alternatively as the **bride**

---

sister exchange   form of cross-cousin marriage in which a brother and sister marry cross cousins who are also sister and brother to each other

bilateral cross-cousin marriage (sister exchange)   cross-cousin marriage in which a brother and sister marry cross cousins who are also brother and sister

patrilateral cross-cousin marriage   marriage between a male and his father's sister's daughter

matrilateral cross-cousin marriage   marriage between a male and his mother's brother's daughter

parallel cousins   cousins whose common parents are either two brothers or two sisters

bint'amm   patrilateral parallel-cousin marriage

patrilateral parallel-cousin marriage (*bint'amm*)   marriage between a male and his father's brother's daughter

bride price (progeny price)   goods transferred from the groom's kin to the bride's to recompense them for her loss price, **bridewealth**, or **progeny price**. The amount of the bridewealth compensation will reflect the importance of the bride's family compared with that of the groom's, since the bride's status as a married woman and the status of her children will be greater if the compensation is a high one. Bridewealth is found in 60 percent of those societies that anthropologists have investigated. It is particularly common among simpler food-producing societies, such as tribal horticulturalists and noncommercial pastoralists, those that raise animals only for their own use.

Bride Service

Alternatively, compensation to the bride's family may take the form of a period of work to be performed by the groom for his wife's family, in which case it is known as the **bride service**. The bride service has been reported in about 24 percent of societies that anthropologists have studied. It is particularly common among foragers who lack the accumulation of wealth necessary for paying bridewealth.

Bride service also typically differs from bridewealth in that bridewealth is paid at one time, or over a short period, at the beginning of the marriage and permanently validates the marriage, while bride service continually recompenses the bride's family for a prolonged period that may last the life of the marriage. In the words of Schlegel and Eloul (1988, p. 294), in bride service, "marriage is in a constant state of economic negotiation." Nevertheless, even when the bride service is performed for a fixed period of time, the spouses usually have sexual access to one another from the beginning of the period of service, and the legitimacy of children is not affected by being born before the end of the service. Under the custom of bridewealth, however, children may not be considered fully legitimate, particularly in respect to inheritance rights, until the entire progeny price has been paid.

Dowry

In the **dowry**, the benefits flow in the opposite direction from those of the bridewealth or bride service. Here, goods belonging to the bride's family accompany her into the marriage. The wealth is most often controlled by the bride within her new family, but it sometimes is held in trust for her by her husband or his relatives, or it may simply become the

FIGURE 8.7   Dowry
This traditional dowry presentation in what was Czechoslovakia illustrates one way a bride brings a certain amount of wealth with her into the marriage. It both ensures that some of her family property will remain in her family and that the bride will be financially cared for in the event of her husband's death or desertion.

property of the husband's family (Goody & Tambiah, 1973, p. 2). In this case, it is apt to be perceived as a compensation for the economic burden of supporting the woman. Thus, the dowry is not a mirror-image of the bridewealth or bride service, even though it flows in the opposite direction. Like bridewealth and bride service, dowry reflects the status of the woman in a marriage. The first two forms are more likely when a woman's status is high; the dowry is more likely

bridewealth   compensation to the family for the loss of their daughter through marriage
progeny price   bridewealth
bride service   service performed by the groom for the family of the bride to recompense them for her loss
dowry   a payment from the family of a bride to the family of her husband to compensate them for their acceptance of the responsibility of her support

FIGURE 8.8   Gift Exchange
At this wedding in Wenjang, China, guests bring gifts in baskets. Gift giving is part of a system of gift exchange that emphasizes the ties of future interaction that will exist between the families and their children. In gift exchange, the families share items of nearly equal value, whether it be yams, cattle, or silver.

when a woman's status is low (Schlegel & Barry, 1986).

The dowry is most common in more complex societies, especially those whose economy is based on complex agriculture or commercial pastoralism, that is, in societies in which commodities are produced for market exchange and in which there are wealth differences between families. The dowry may be viewed as a kind of advance on a woman's inheritance from her own family; it keeps the wealth within the family by ultimately benefiting the grandchildren of the donors.

Indirect dowry.   Goody (1973) has noted a variant of the dowry that he has called the **indirect dowry**, a payment of goods made by the groom or his family to the bride, either directly to her or to her father, who then passes it to her. Sometimes the father may keep some of this payment before passing the rest on to his daughter, to cover the costs of the marriage preparations or to recompense him for having raised the girl. As with the dowry, the goods

that go to the bride in the indirect dowry are intended to provide security for the bride and her children, especially if she becomes widowed. Coming from her husband's family, the payment may symbolize their commitment to the well-being of the daughter-in-law in her new home.

Gift Exchange

Sometimes the flow of goods between the families who are party to a marriage goes in both directions. Called **gift exchange**, this reciprocal sharing of objects of more or less equal value between the two families emphasizes the ties of future interaction and mutual aid that will characterize the relationship between the families.

▬

indirect dowry   payment of goods made by the groom or his family to the bride either directly to her or indirectly through her father

gift exchange   reciprocal exchange of gifts between families who are party to a marriage

Women exchange. Schlegel and Eloul (1988, p. 292) have pointed out that gift exchange is not perfectly balanced, since one family loses a child, while the other gains a relative by marriage. However, there is one system that overcomes this imbalance. **Women exchange** is a system in which no gifts are passed between the families. Instead, each family gives a female, usually a daughter, as a bride to the other family. Since each family loses a daughter but gains a daughter-in-law, the exchange between the two families is completely balanced.

. . . .

Postmarital Residence

Although marriage joins two kinship groups as allies, the couple joined by the ritual of marriage may be more involved in the daily life of one of their parental kinship groups than the other, depending on where they are most likely to set up their new residence.

Virilocality

According to research by Murdock (1957), in about two-thirds of the world's societies newly married couples are expected to set up residence in or near the husband's family. This form of residence, called **virilocality** or **patrilocality**, is most often found where the solidarity of the male group is very important. Naroll (1973) found that the best single predictor of virilocality was the man's predominance in food production. Its likelihood is increased by other factors that strengthen males' solidarity: e.g., where hunting is a primarily male activity; where food production requires heavy labor; where internal warfare (see Chapter 5) involves fighting between neighboring groups that share a common culture and language; where men have more than one wife; where men wield authority in a political organization that is a source of prestige; or where male accumulation of property is a sign of rank.

Uxorilocality

The second most common residence pattern is **uxorilocality**, formerly known as **matrilocality**. Uxorilocality is found in about 15 percent of societies

and involves the setting up of a residence in or near the residence of the bride's family (Coult & Haberstein, 1965; Murdock, 1934). This is most likely to be practiced where food is provided by simple gardening in environments that do not require heavy labor and in warlike societies where belligerence is most common between distant groups.

Bilocality

A third residential pattern is **bilocality** or **ambilocality**: Residence may be in the home area of either the bride or the groom. This form of residence is practiced in 5 to 10 percent of societies. It permits flexibility of choice in societies in which cooperation within large kinship groups is important but in which it is useful to be flexible about which group a new couple joins, as in agricultural groups where land is limited.

Neolocality

In **neolocality** the couple sets up a residence in some new place apart from either family. This residence pattern provides maximum flexibility in electing a place to live and is most common when the nuclear family of two parents and their children is economically independent and responsible for its

---

women exchange a situation where, rather than exchange gifts between families, they exchange women, so that they lose a daughter but gain a daughter-in-law

virilocality (patrilocality) custom where a newly married couple is expected to set up their residence with or near the groom's family

patrilocality place of residence for newly married couples in or near the husband's family

uxorilocality (matrilocality) the custom in which a newly married couple is expected to set up residence with or near the bride's family

matrilocality the custom in which a newly married couple is expected to set up residence with or near the bride's family

bilocality (ambilocality) the custom in which a newly married couple may elect to set up residence with or near either the bride's or the groom's family

ambilocality the custom in which the residence for a newly married couple may be in the home of either the bride or groom

neolocality the custom in which the newly married couple sets up residence in a new location apart from either of their families own survival. Only about 1 in 20 societies emphasizes neolocal residence. It is most common in industrialized societies.

Avunculocality

In **avunculocality** the couple takes up residence in or near the house of the groom's mother's brother. This form of residence is common in less than 5 percent of societies and occurs only in matrilineal societies where the men of the matrilineage must stay together, as when warfare is common.

. . . .

Family

Marriage legitimizes a sexual union and provides an institutionalized means for producing the next generation. Some group must be charged with the responsibility for rearing the children born from the marriage union. The group in which children are raised is known as the **family**. This group need not be structured solely around the individuals who are united to one another in marriage. When the family does consist of parents and their children, it is called a **nuclear family**. This is the family type that is most familiar to peoples of Western societies in recent times, and it is also typical of foraging societies. However, as the sole basis for households it is a rare family form.

Almost all societies throughout most of human history have had more complex family forms than the nuclear family. These more complex family forms, known collectively as **extended families**, include more individuals than a husband and wife and their children. They are formed when the married couple sets up their residence with one of their families. Extended families usually include three generations: either a pair of grandparents, their sons, the wives of their sons, and all the children of their sons, or a pair of grandparents, all their sons and daughters, and all the children of their daughters. These two basic types of extended family may be further elaborated, depending on the marriage forms involved, since the extended family may include plural spouses in the parental and grandparental generations.

Extended families may live under a common roof or in several closely assembled dwellings. Thus, they may make up a single **household** (residential unit) or several households. In any case, the number of individuals involved in childrearing responsibilities will be much larger in extended families than in nuclear families. Therefore, extended families are likely to have more formally established rules regarding the rights and obligations of various family members to one another than do societies in which nuclear families are the norm.

----

avunculocality the custom in which the newly married couple establishes residence with or near the groom's mother's brother

family the group consisting of married persons, their children, and other relatives who reside with them

nuclear family the form of family that consists only of married persons and their children

extended family the form of family that includes two or more nuclear families and often their parents, who reside together

household a group of people who share a common residence

The Samoan Extended Family and Household

Ella (1895) and Mead (1928) described the traditional Samoan family system, which provides a marked contrast to North American families and households. Among the Samoans, a single household was led by a *matai* or headman, a titled member of the family selected to act as their patriarchal head. The *matai* had life-and-death authority over members of the household and was responsible for carrying out religious rituals for the family. As family head, he also owned the land that was worked by the family members and assigned them their share to work.

Within the extended family group, children were tended by their older siblings. The mothers were thus freed for other activities, and all adult relatives were viewed as having rights over the children of the group. Besides baby-tending, boys under eight or nine years of age and girls who had not yet attained puberty were expected to help adults in many other ways, contributing to the work and welfare of the household. On the other hand, if the demands of the family became too great, children were free to leave home and take up residence with other relatives in another household that they found more congenial.

(see reference map p. 148)

C H A P T E R S U M M A R Y

1. Marriage is a socially accepted sexual and economic union that unites members of previously separate families in a committed relationship that typically involves childrearing expectations.

2. The most commonly recognized marital types are monogamous, polygynous, polyandrous, and group marriages.

3. In many societies there are also symbolic, nonsexual, fictive, fixed-term, and homosexual marriages.

4. Since marriages unite separate families into an in-law relationship with each other, their creation has practical implications for more persons than just the spouses.

5. The choice of marriage partner is restricted in all societies by rules such as endogamy, exogamy, and marriage preference rules.

6. In most societies, the creation of a new marriage traditionally has also involved various practical considerations, such as the payment of goods or service to the family of the bride and the dowry.

7. The size of the family is directly related to customs that govern where a newly married couple is expected to set up their residence.

8. The family established by marriage may vary in size from the nuclear family that is common in Western societies today to the more traditional extended family that has been common in most of the world since the rise of food domestication.

A N N O T A T E D R E A D I N G S

Blackwood, E. (Ed.). (1986). *The many faces of homosexuality: Anthropological approaches to homosexual behavior.* NY: Harrington Park Press. An exceptional collection of essays on the cultural patterns of homosexuality in a variety of different cultural contexts.

Ember, M., & Ember, C. R. (1983). *Marriage, family, and kinship: Comparative studies of social organization.* A collection of cross-cultural studies that test various explanations of human social organization.

Fox, R. (1968). *Kinship and marriage: An anthropological perspective.* Baltimore, MD: Penguin. One of the easiest to follow texts that have been produced on kinship and marriage.

Frayser, S. G. (1985). *Varieties of sexual experience: An anthropological perspective on human sexuality.* New Haven, CT: HRAF Press. One of the most recent attempts to use cross-cultural data to examine the diversity of human sexual customs through time and across cultural boundaries using data from Murdock and White's Standard Cross-Cultural Sample. This book includes important discussions of marriage, family, childrearing, and divorce.

Gregerson. E. (1983). *Sexual practices.* New York: Watts. A well-illustrated and informed discussion of the major topics of the cross-cultural study of human sexuality.

Needham, R. (Ed.). (1972). *Rethinking kinship and marriage.* London: Tavistock. A collection of essays that focus on the cross-cultural study of kinship and marriage customs.

Pasternak, B. (1976). *Introduction to kinship and social organization.* Englewood Cliffs, NJ: Prentice Hall. One of the standard sources on kinship, this book contains information about theories of marriage and the family.

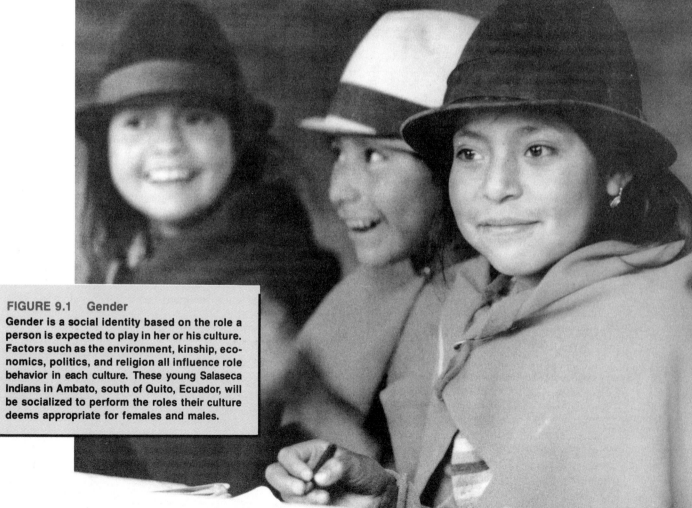

FIGURE 9.1   Gender
Gender is a social identity based on the role a person is expected to play in her or his culture. Factors such as the environment, kinship, economics, politics, and religion all influence role behavior in each culture. These young Salaseca Indians in Ambato, south of Quito, Ecuador, will be socialized to perform the roles their culture deems appropriate for females and males.

Gender

In all societies, ideas about differences between men and women influence the ways in which social roles are assigned. Not all cultures limit gender roles to two categories. In some, the genders of men and women are complemented by an alternative third or even a fourth gender category. A society assigns its genders different degrees of social power and honor. When there are significant differences, the men's roles are typically accorded greater rank. Such differences are influenced by kinship systems, the nature of warfare, and the economic aspects of each society. Religion typically provides support for gender role differences and the gender characteristics of society are typically incorporated into mythology and other religious symbols. The privileged status of men's social roles found in many societies has often caused women's rights to be neglected.

CHAPTER OBJECTIVES

After reading this chapter, you should be able to:

Distinguish between sex and gender.

List some of the common sexual differences in humans.

Define gender.

Discuss cultural differences that have existed in gender roles.

Recognize the effects of gender stereotypes on the roles we learn to play.

Explain the concept of third and fourth genders.

Outline the common patterns of division of labor by gender.

Explain the influences of kinship, economics, religion, and warfare on the relative power and honor accorded the different genders.

Discuss the various aspects of women's rights as human rights.

Discuss the relationships between religion and gender differences.

Man, woman, macho, lady, hunk, broad. We have many different words that have both political and personal significance for the countless ways humans behave in male or female roles. They reveal much about our culture and our attitudes about our social roles. In this chapter, we will explore the ways in which culture molds our beliefs and feelings about sex and gender.

Sex and Gender

The word "sex" is often used as a synonym for "gender" by the public, but anthropologists give different meanings to each word. The term **sex** refers to biological distinctions such as the chromosomal, hormonal, or physical differences between males and females. **Gender** defines the social statuses and roles that people are socialized into based on cultural concepts about the sexes. In this chapter we will look at some of the complexities of both sex and gender.

Sexual Differences

Humans are biological creatures as well as cultural beings. Females and males differ biologically in various ways. Genetically, women have two X chromosomes, and men have an X and a Y. Since only males carry the Y chromosome, the sex of a child is determined by whether it received an X or a Y chromosome from its father.

Males and females differ in both their primary sexual characteristics, such as genitals and reproductive organs, and the secondary sexual characteristics that develop during puberty, such as breast development in females and the development of low-pitched voices and a broad distribution of body hair in males.

Physiologically, males in the human species are slightly larger than females on average, a characteristic known as **sexual dimorphism**. The sexes also generally differ in how strength is manifest. Males typically are able to exert higher levels of energy for short periods, while females tend to have greater endurance and are generally hardier. This distinction can be noticed at all stages of development. For instance, a higher percentage of spontaneous abortions tend to be males, and females seem to have a naturally higher life expectancy, although this is counteracted in many societies by a life-style that increases women's mortality rates.

Some studies also point to basic psychological differences between the sexes. Beatrice Whiting and John Whiting (1975) carried out an in-depth study of children in six different societies where they found a number of psychological characteristics that crosscut cultural boundaries. For instance, boys and girls both showed dependence, but expressed it in different ways: girls tended to seek help and contact, while boys sought attention and approval. They found no differences between boys and girls in seeking and offering friendship to others, and they found that girls behaved as actively as boys. Some differences in the behavior of boys and girls in the six societies, however, were discovered. Boys played more aggressively and in larger groups than girls did, and older boys were more likely to respond to aggression with aggression. Thus, there appear to be some general psychological characteristics that distinguish the sexes even in childhood.

Gender

Gender is a social identity that consists of the roles a person is expected to play because of his or her sex. Whereas we are born with sexual characteristics, our gender is something we must learn. All cultures recognize the existence of at least two genders: females are normally socialized into the roles that lead them into a social identity as women, while males learn men's roles.

---

sex biological distinctions such as the chromosomal, hormonal, or physical differences between males and females

gender social statuses assigned on the basis of cultural concepts about the sexes

sexual dimorphism marked differentiation in size and form of the sexes

Gender stereotypes. It is not surprising that the average differences between males and females figure into **gender stereotypes,** preconceived ideas about how women and men differ in their personality traits, and behavioral skills, and predispositions. However, it is a mistake to believe that biology is the *cause* of gender differences. In the first place, biological differences are average distinctions between males and females as groups, but there is a range of individual differences within both sexes and they overlap more than they differ in most characteristics. Thus, some males may have greater endurance than most females, and some females may be able to exert more strength than most males. If biology *caused* gender differences, then they too would be merely statistical averages between what males and females did socially. But gender differences do not simply arise out of our predispositions to play various roles. Rather, gender stereotypes are *guidelines* that tell us how we are expected to act. It is our culture's gender stereotypes, not biology, that most directly channel us into our different gender roles.

Diversity in Male and Female Roles

Since gender is culturally defined, there are significant differences from culture to culture in the specific roles of men and women. What is thought of as masculine or feminine behavior in one culture may not be thought of in the same way in another culture. Such differences are influenced by many factors such as environmental resources, economics, kinship, politics, and religion. In this section we will explore diversity within gender.

Socialization of Gender Differences

Anthropologists have noted that in every society there are socialization practices that result in differences from the typically expected North American patterns of male and female personalities.

The well-known anthropologist Margaret Mead did fieldwork (1950) among three New Guinea societies in which the ideologies about sex roles were quite different. Her descriptions of the Arapesh,

Mundugumor, and Tschambuli make it clear that how people think about being masculine or feminine is highly variable and determined by culture rather than by any absolute dictates of biology. Although there were gender role differences among the Arapesh, no basic temperamental differences were thought to exist between males and females. Neither men nor women were believed to be driven by spontaneous sexuality, and violence, although tolerated, was not linked with either sex. Men were expected to be gentle, unacquisitive, and cooperative. Women were taught to accept anything out of the ordinary without curiosity. From childhood, they had been actively discouraged from asking questions about anything unusual and from engaging in speculative thought, a pastime that was encouraged in boys.

The people of a not-too-distant tribe, the Mundugumor, were quite different in their attitudes about the sexes. The Mundugumor were headhunters and cannibals, and the life of a male was characterized by fighting and the competitive acquisition of women through warfare. They assumed that there was a natural hostility between members of the same sex. As a result, inheritance of most property crossed sex boundaries with each generation from father to daughter and from mother to son. Compatible with their way of life, both males and females were raised to have violent social personalities and to place no value on sensuality. For instance, breastfeeding of infants was done in a utilitarian way, with no hint of pleasure; nursing was carried out only to give food and never for comfort from fright or pain.

Finally, the Tschambuli, a third nearby group, did distinguish personality differences between men and women, although these expectations differed radically from role expectations of men and women in North America. The Tschambuli preferred marriages in which a man had many wives. Ancestry was traced through the men of the family. Men owned the houses and the land and officially "owned" their wives. But in practice women held the main power in society. It was they who made most of the economic decisions, and they took the initiative in social life. For instance, Tschambuli women were socialized to be sexually aggressive, while the men, who were shy in adolescence, were not.

Mead (1950) summarized her findings:

gender stereotypes preconceived ideas about what behaviors and roles are considered "masculine" or "feminine"

Here, admittedly looking for light on the subject of sex differences, I found three tribes all conveniently within a hundred mile area. In one, both men and women act as we [North Americans] expect women to act—in a mild parental responsive way; in the second, both act as we expect men to act—in a fierce initiating fashion; and in the third, the men act according to our stereotype for women—are catty, wear curls and go shopping, while the women are energetic, managerial, unadorned partners. (p. vi)

These extremely contrasting examples demonstrate that the personalities of men and women in any one society are not unambiguous manifestations of inherent characteristics that are fixed by nature. Rather, they are manifestations of each society's culturally patterned role expectations.

Male and Female Roles in Iran

For an in-depth example of socially patterned status differences between males and females, we can look at Iranian men and women. According to Behnam (1985), the traditional Muslim family traced its ancestry through the father, tended toward marriage between cousins, favored polygyny, and was male dominated. The Iranian family was an autonomous economic unit in production as well as consumption. This lent it great cohesiveness, and the decision making for the domestic group lay in the hands of the male hierarchy within the family. According to Nassehi-Behnam (1985), the economic role of the family made marriage an important union between two family lines, so marital choices were a matter of great importance, with preparations sometimes beginning at birth.

In wealthy Iranian families, the symbolic distinction between the private intimacy of the household and the profane external world of strangers was portrayed by dividing the house into two areas, the private (andaruni) interior of the home, the area of the wife, and the public (biruni) area of the man, the threshold between the home and the outside world. Although the men of the family could enter the private areas of the home, the women were excluded from the public areas.

The responsibility of the woman for domestic work was emphasized by the Islamic religious traditions. The exemplary models of the division of labor within a marriage were Ali, the brother of Muhammad, and Ali's wife, Fatimah. In Islamic hadith or sacred tradition, Fatimah took responsibility for the domestic affairs, such as grinding the flour, baking the bread, and sweeping the house, while Ali took responsibility for all work outside the door of the house, such as bringing the firewood and obtaining food for the family. In the words of Allah as recorded in the Qur'an (4:34), "Men are the protectors and maintainers of women because God has given the one more (strength) than the other, because they support them from their means." Men, in other words, are thought to excel women in natural strength, so it is their responsibility to support their wives. Since a son will bear the economic responsibility of supporting a wife, a daughter need not inherit as much as a son. The Qur'an (4:11) specifies that, "God (thus) directs you as regards your children's (inheritance): to the male, a portion equal to that of two females."

Industrialization has created many strains on the traditional Iranian family structure. Urbanization has drawn many people away from rural areas. Housing problems in the cities make it difficult for extended families to maintain a common residence, further fragmenting the earlier family hierarchies. Industrialization also created increasing opportunities for women to be employed, making divorce easier, since employment permits women to support themselves following divorce. Thus, the divorce rate is three times as high in urban areas as in rural areas (Nassehi-Behnam, 1985).

The revolution of 1979 brought attempts to reestablish the old male/female distinctions, with an increased application of Islamic religious principles in family law and values and repeal of the Family Protection Laws passed in 1972 that granted women the right to divorce, the right to an education and to work without their husbands' consent, and the right to custody of the children as well as restrictions on polygyny. The wearing of the veil by women in public became mandatory, women's employment was restricted, and coeducational schooling was terminated as contrary to Islam.

The efforts of the post-revolutionary government to root out all evidence of Western influence from Iranian life were particularly strong during the 1980s. The Islamic dress code became an important symbol of political loyalty. According to Katayon Ghazi, women who failed to wear the long veil, or chador, and to cover all parts of their bodies except their faces and hands "were harassed and arrested by the revolutionary Komiteh, the Islamic national morality authority, in its crackdown on what were termed obscene trends." Violations of the dress code resulted in imprisonment, flogging, or a heavy fine. For instance, displaying rouge and mascara in public was punishable by 70 lashes. Ghazi reports that Abolhassan Bani-Sadr, the first President after the revolution, asserted "that women must cover every strand of hair because 'research proved female hair had a kind of radiance' that might be tempting to men" (Ghazi, *New York Times,* June 11, 1991, p. A4).

By 1991, civil and revolutionary forces had become integrated. The Komiteh merged with the local police forces. This stabilization of the government reduced some of the zeal with which public morality had been enforced previously. Women's work is still legally restricted, and their testimony remains invalid in court. Women still lack the right to divorce or to leave the country without their husbands' permission. But enforcement of the dress code has been relaxed. Now, according to Ghazi, "most of the violators rounded up on Mohseni Square and herded into buses face far lighter penalties," such as detainment at the Center for Combating Sins for a maximum of 24 hours or even immediate release upon signing a commitment to observe the law (p. A4). Under these relaxed standards, some women have begun to wear more colorful garments and let perhaps an inch of hair show from beneath their scarves.

FIGURE 9.2 Iranian Dress Code

Roles for men and women in Iran follow a long tradition of Muslim heritage, but industrialization and revolution have combined to cause some changes. Women's work is still legally restricted, but the dress code now allows women to wear colorful garments and to show some of their hair beneath their scarves. These shoppers in Teheran illustrate the traditional hair covering (on the right) and the modern.

Common Patterns in Division of Labor

In spite of differences in how gender roles may be structured, there is a pattern to differences in roles that are commonly assigned to women and men. A cross-cultural study by Murdock (1973) revealed that throughout the world, males are almost always responsible for hunting large land and sea animals and game birds and for trapping smaller animals. They are usually expected to fish, to herd large animals, collect wild honey, and to clear the land and prepare it for planting. Women are usually involved in gathering wild plant foods. Other food production activities, such as collecting shellfish, caring for small animals, milking animals, and planting, tending, and harvesting crops, are not consistently assigned to either men or women. As a matter of fact, such tasks

are often roles of either gender. Men usually butcher animals, while women most often cook, prepare vegetable foods, drinks and dairy products, launder, carry water, and collect fuel. Preserving meat or fish for future use may be done by either men or women or by both.

The common division of labor that Murdock reported for food getting and preparation most often associates men with work that requires strength or rapid bursts of energy and women with work in which lower levels of strength are required for longer periods. This pattern seems to apply to other areas of work as well. For instance, men typically do woodworking, including felling trees, preparing wood, and building boats. They also are almost always the ones who mine and quarry stone, smelt ores, and work with bone, horn, and shell. Men usually build houses and make nets and ropes. On the other hand, spinning yarn is almost always done by women. Either or both genders prepare skins and make leather products, baskets, mats, clothing, or pottery. Whyte (1978a) has added to Murdock's list by noting that it is almost always men who are involved in warfare and who hold most positions of political leadership. Weisner and Gallimore (1977) have noted that child care is usually carried out by women.

According to J. K. Brown (1970), two other biological factors in addition to strength and metabolism that have an influence on gender roles are pregnancy and lactation. Since women of childbearing age in most parts of the world spend about half of their time either pregnant or nursing children, it is easy to see why women's roles usually include most of the child care responsibilities as well as other duties that can be carried out while pregnant or tending children. By contrast, men's roles include many activities that take them away from home for long periods, or activities that, although done near the home, must be done without the interruption that child care would involve. In addition, many male activities would be dangerous to children.

The common gender differences in tasks that seem unrelated to either strength or child care may simply be secondary effects of tasks that can be explained in these ways. For instance, men's involvement in making musical instruments is probably influenced by their other work with wood, just as their work at making nets and ropes may arise from the common use of these tools in activities such as fishing, trapping, and smelting. Although men's prominence in warfare may be related to their typically greater size and proportion of muscle to body weight, it is also true that many of men's roles, such as hunting and fishing, take them away from home to locations where strangers are more likely to be encountered. The weapons of war are also typically the same kinds of tools that men are accustomed to using in activities such as hunting. In small-scale societies, the association of men with warfare most certainly increases their likelihood of entering positions of political leadership where decisions are made about matters such as relations with neighboring groups of potential enemies.

Gender Roles and Subsistence

Women in the United States now represent about 40 percent of the paid labor force, and the typical American family has two incomes. Neverthe-

less, women's income has not achieved equality with that of men, and married women's incomes average only about a quarter that of their husbands. This inequality helps to perpetuate women's greater involvement in contemporary American domestic roles. Even when husbands and wives are employed for the same number of hours a week, U.S. women continue to bear the primary responsibility for shopping for groceries and clothing, cooking, doing the family laundry, and caring for the children.

A look at the broad range of human cultures shows clearly that the American division of labor in which men have greater control over family income and women have more responsibilities at home is far from inevitable. Rather, the relative contribution of men and women to subsistence varies considerably, depending on how food is obtained. For instance, women in many foraging societies contribute as much as 80 percent of the calories their families eat (Service, 1962; Lee & DeVore, 1968; Tanaka, 1977). However, on average women's subsistence production in *all* foraging societies represents about 28 percent of the family's food. Women's subsistence contribution tends to be larger than that in societies that practice horticulture or agriculture without irrigation. Peggy Sanday (1973) has reported that women produce from about 33 percent to about 45 percent of the subsistence in such societies (see Figure 9.3). However, more complex forms of food production technology, such as irrigation-based agriculture, are associated with heavy labor. The subsistence contribution of women is low in societies that practice intensive agriculture and is as low as that of foraging women where irrigation is part of the agricultural work. Although industrialized technology reduces the amount of physical labor women must perform well below the levels that are common in agrarian societies, the process of becoming industrialized involves increased poverty and deprivation among women in the lower social classes and rural women.

Third and Fourth Genders

Although all cultures have at least two genders, there are some in which third or fourth genders exist. These typically involve an inversion of the usual association of men's roles with the male sex and of

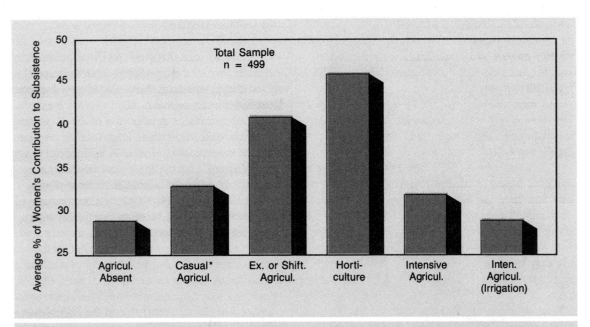

FIGURE 9.3   RELATIONSHIP BETWEEN TYPE AND INTENSITY OF AGRICULTURE AND AVERAGE PERCENTAGE OF WOMEN'S CONTRIBUTION TO SUBSISTENCE

*Less than 5% of total sample.

Source: From Peggy R. Sanday, "Toward a Theory of the Status of Women," *American Anthropologist,* 75 (1973): 1691. Reproduced by permission of the American Anthropological Association.

women's roles with females. Three examples of third and fourth genders are the hijra, the berdache, and the transvestites.

The Hijra

Serena Nanda (1985, 1990) has described the *hijra,* a socially recognized third gender in India. The hijra, most of whom live in cities in north India, are regarded as neither male nor female, but their roles include elements of both. Like the berdaches of the North American Indians, the hijra gender also includes religious roles. As devotees of the Mother Goddess Baluchara Mata, the hijra are expected to undergo a surgical removal of their external genitalia and to live an asexual life. Their sexual abstinence is believed to be a source of sacredness that allows the hijra to give blessings of fertility, prosperity, and health or to cause infertility through their curses. The hijra perform as musicians and dancers at christenings and at weddings. In these roles, the hijra are spiritually identified with the Hindu god Siva, who also plays the roles of singer, dancer, eunuch, and transvestite.

The Berdache

A number of indigenous North American societies had a social status that has come to be known as the **berdache,** a female or male who had adopted a sex role that mixed the gender characteristics of both sexes. The berdache was particularly common among men of Plains Indians tribes where warfare was an almost sacred preoccupation and where the male role placed strong emphasis on demonstrations of pride, bravery, and daring. So the presence of the berdache has long been thought of as a cultural alternative for men who lacked the skill or interest in the aggressive pursuits of the traditional male role (Hoebel, 1949, p. 459). Such a man might instead opt for the life of a berdache by adopting the dress, work, and mannerisms of a woman.

—

berdache   a social status in which males and females adopt the role of the other sex, considered a third gender in some societies

FIGURE 9.4   Berdache

The last of the Crow male berdaches, Finds-Them-And-Kills-Them, illustrates the cross-dressing characteristic of this gender role. Males who assumed some of the work, dress, and behavior of a woman were accepted into their community because the berdache was a legitimate way to express a personality that was not compatible with the traditional Plains Indian man's role.

The berdaches held a sacred status in many Native American societies. Often they played important ceremonial roles, and in some cases all shamans were required to be berdaches. A female who became a berdache actually moved up the status hierarchy and might achieve wealth and social prominence by doing so, since the change allowed her to participate in what were considered the more advantageous male pursuits such as trade. A berdache "man" might marry and even rear children by having another man impregnate his wife, or a berdache "woman" might hire another woman as a surrogate mother.

The Transvestite

We have seen that third and fourth gender roles generally include the expectation of cross-dressing or mixed-gender dressing, behavior known as **transvestism**. The transvestite fulfilled a common expectation of the berdache gender role of the indigenous people of North America and the behavior continues today in contemporary India. In societies in which third or fourth genders are accepted, it serves as a noticeable symbol of a person's special status. In societies in which only two genders are recognized, transvestism tends to be stigmatized and serves a somewhat different function. In these societies, people participate in cross-dressing for brief periods, in rituals, for recreation, or as a form of psychological release from gender-related role stresses. For instance, Richard Doctor, who surveyed research on transvestism, found (1988) that in the United States and Europe, transvestism is most often engaged in by heterosexual males in covert settings.

······································

Gender, Power, and Honor

The approach that analyzes culture and society by examining the relationships among social power, social honor, and gender is called **feminist anthropology**. Studies by feminist anthropologists have revealed some important new insights into the causes of inequality between women and men.

Sanday (1974) has suggested four measures of the social power of women's rank: (1) female control of material things such as land, produce, and crafts outside the domestic unit, (2) demand for women's produce outside the family unit locally or in external markets, (3) women's right to participate in the political process in a way that influences policy affecting those outside their domestic unit, and (4) the presence of female solidarity groups that protect women's political or economic interests. She found that women's rank, evaluated by these measures,

---

transvestism   cross-dressing or mixed-gender dressing, a common part of the berdache gender role
feminist anthropology   the anthropological approach that studies the relationships among social power, social honor, and gender

varied considerably from society to society, and that when women's economic contribution to subsistence was very high or very low compared to men, women's power tended to be low. It was in the middle range, where men and women cooperated in subsistence production and contributed more or less equally to the economy, that women's social power was greatest. This suggests that economic dependency functions to perpetuate low levels of power for women, but that when women become the major economic mainstay of families, men tend to find other spheres for exerting their social power.

Gender Stratification

Gender stratification refers to the differences in social power and honor that may exist between men and women. When there is no significant gender stratification, men and women are more or less equal in the deference and respect they receive and in their abilities to influence political decisionmaking. This can be the case even when women do not normally hold political offices. Where gender stratification is significant, however, women's social power, or honor, or both are low.

In extreme cases of female subordination, women, stigmatized as inferior and spiritually dangerous to men, are in danger of rape, physical and psychological abuse, and murder. Such behaviors that inflict harm on females may even become accepted as valid customs under various circumstances. Carole Sheffield (1987) has called customs that employ violence against females and help maintain male control and domination of females through intimidation **sexual terrorism**.

Rape as social control   In some societies, rape or the threat of rape has been used as a mechanism for controlling women's behavior. For instance, Thomas Gregor (1982) described the Mehinaku of central Brazil, who segregated men and women and had a very strict division of labor by gender. The men's house was a sacred place and a social club from which women were excluded. When women violated rules that forbade them from observing the sacred things of men, the Mehinaku used gang rape as punishment.

Among the Cheyenne Indians of the North American Plains a wife who committed adultery could be punished by gang rape at the husband's request. He would invite the 30 to 40 unmarried men who were members of his military association but not members of his wife's clan to rape her. If she survived the ordeal, she still was stigmatized for the rest of her life.

Chinese footbinding.   Chinese footbinding is a form of physical abuse that became accepted as a custom. Until the 1920s many Chinese families bound the feet of their young daughters very tightly to keep them small into adulthood, a trait that was regarded as beautiful. According to Howard Levy (1966), the custom began within the upper class and demonstrated that a man should support a wife who could not walk well enough to work. Small feet became symbols of aristocracy and beauty, so the practice spread into the middle and even working classes. Normal feet, like those of farm women who had to work, were ridiculed as ugly. The process of binding involved extreme pain and led to permanent deformation of the woman's feet. The custom of footbinding was particularly difficult for poorer women whose feet had been bound but who had to walk in spite of the pain because they had to work. In the late 1920s the Chinese government exerted tremendous pressure against its people to end the custom.

Physical abuse.   The physical abuse of women is a major worldwide problem. For instance, Lori Heise reports that "in Bangkok, Thailand, a reported 50 percent of married women are beaten regularly by their husbands. In the barrios of Quito, Ecuador, 80 percent of women are said to have been physically abused. And in Nicaragua, 44 percent of men admit to beating their wives or girlfriends. Equally shocking statistics can be found in the industrial world" (Heise, 1989a, p. B1). According to Teri Randall (1990), in the United States, abuse by a partner or spouse is the single most common cause of injury to women and their visits to emergency rooms in hospitals. Injuries from abuse by husband or lover are more common than injuries from automobile accidents, muggings, and rapes combined. The annual cost of family violence in the United States includes $44 million direct costs, 175,000 days missed from paid work, 21,000 hospitalizations, 99,800 days of hospitalization, 28,700 emergency room visits, and 39,900 doctor visits.

---

sexual terrorism   customs that employ violence against females in order to maintain male domination

Suttee. Another example of sexual terrorism was the custom of the suttee that was practiced in nineteenth century India. Hindu widows were expected to demonstrate their fidelity and love for their deceased husband by joining him on his funeral pyre. In traditional Hindu communities, the woman's status was defined so intensely in terms of her relationship with a husband that a widow was not permitted to remarry. A widow's sexual behavior would have dishonored her family. Her devotion to her husband, whom she should have loved and honored as a god, was expected to be so great that she would not have wished to survive without him. Mary Daly (1978) reports that since widows had no acceptable means of surviving, those who did not follow the custom of the suttee were sometimes forced into the fire by their relatives.

Purdah. Family honor is extremely important in many Islamic countries, and often deeply depends on the sexual purity of the female members of the family. That purity is ensured by the practice of purdah, or seclusion in which women remain isolated from public view. Common features of purdah are the restriction of women to the inner parts of the home when guests are present and the rule of being veiled when the woman is outside the home. Violations of the rules of purdah are severely punished in some countries that follow the custom. Gideon M. Kressel (1981) analyzed where the murder of sisters or daughters is practiced to restore family honor when the girl or woman has been publicly accused of consorting with a male. The act need not have included sexual intercourse. For instance, Kressel cites the example of a 13-year-old who was drowned after she had been berated by her brother when he caught her holding hands with a boy. The attacker is usually a brother, but is also frequently the father. The victim is most often in her teens, but may be a married woman. The homicide generally occurs after a public attack on the family's honor that the family is unable to address by other means, such as arranging a marriage between the couple. An arranged union may be problematic, however. If the boy were of a lower-ranked lineage, the marriage might not be acceptable to the girl's father, since it would lower the esteem of his lineage. Kressel believes such homicides allow patrilineal kin groups to demonstrate their loyalty to the values of the society in which they are competing for social standing. They enhance the family's prestige and demonstrate the religious commitment of the attacker to societal values.

Gender in Patrilineal Societies

Patrilineal societies, especially those that also practice patrilocal residence, provide a strong structural basis for the subordination of women. Patrilineality defines children by their relationship to their father and his relatives, thereby reinforcing the symbolism of male authority within families. It also can be the basis for uniting brothers in fraternal groups whose solidarity in work and warfare can perpetuate male economic dominance and aggressive roles that carry over into the domestic setting. Patrilocal residence further reinforces male dominance, since it separates married women from their birth families and brings them under the authority of their husbands' relatives. Female subordination in patrilineal, patrilocal societies is not inevitable, however. The structural disadvantages of these societies can be counterbalanced by other economic and political forces, a fact that will be discussed in the section of this chapter on matrifocality.

Male Dominance

A fundamental concept for understanding male dominance is the idea of **patriarchy**, a society in which access to social power and prestige is unequally distributed by gender to men. The culture and customs of a patriarchal society assume that male privilege is normal, and both men and women in such societies may resist challenges to patriarchal institutions. The structure of a patriarchy can make it extremely difficult for members to perceive or acknowledge that some of their customs function in ways that victimize women. As a matter of fact, most of us live in societies in which the privileges of power and prestige are unequally divided in a variety of ways besides gender: race, ethnic origins, religion, and various other social statuses. Gender is but one of the many ways in which inequality can be manifest.

Gender in Matrilineal Societies

Whyte (1978b) examined a cross-cultural sample and found that there was a tendency for women's status to be higher where descent groups were ma-

---

patriarchy a society in which access to social power and prestige is available primarily to men

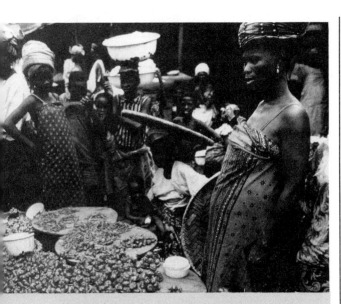

FIGURE 9.5 Matrilineal Societies
Women often own property, hold economic responsibilities, and market produce, thus gaining high status in matrilineal societies. These Nigerian women sell their produce at market.

trilineal and marital residence was matrilocal. In these societies, women often owned property, including houses and food-producing land, held economic responsibilities such as setting prices and marketing produce, and wielded substantial influence in the day-to-day running of community affairs.

Matrifocality

Nancy Tanner (1974) discussed the concept of **matrifocality**, a social system in which high female status is maintained by the absence of men and female control of food production. Matrifocality is common in matrilineal societies, but may also occur in patrilineal societies. For instance, the Igbo of eastern Nigeria is a patrilineal society that follows a patrilocal residence rule at marriage. Igbo men enter polygynous marriages, but since they are involved in long-distance trading that keeps them away much of the time, each wife has her own house and garden and controls the products of her own labor. Marketing of surplus produce occurs locally, where the prices are set by a women's organization. The independence that this matrifocal lifestyle promotes func-

tions to keep women's status high even in this patrilineal, patrilocal society.

Matriarchies.   The idea of *matriarchies*, societies in which men are dominated politically and economically by women, is a common mythological theme in many male-dominated societies. Peggy Sanday (1981a) found that such myths are particularly common in societies where men are the nominal authority figures in families but where women actually have a great deal of autonomy. In these societies, myths of an earlier matriarchy may be indicative of a degree of male anxiety about his authority. It was even suggested by some anthropologists in the last century that there may have been an early period in the evolution of cultures in which matriarchy was the normal social order. However, anthropological fieldwork has never discovered an existing matriarchal society, and the idea that such societies may have existed in the past is rejected by almost all anthropologists today (Joan Bamberger, 1974).

The Causes of Gender Inequality

Various causes have been suggested for gender inequality. Prominent among these have been men's role in warfare and the economic division of labor by gender.

Warfare.   Marvin Harris (1974) points out that the dominance of males in nonindustrialized societies is likely when the male role in warfare is compatible with their day-to-day domination of local community life. Thus, in societies in which warfare is waged primarily between neighboring communities, the type of conflict called internal warfare in chapter 5, the aggressive role of males as warriors is carried over into their daily social roles as leaders of their local communities and families. In such societies, women are expected to play subordinated roles and are often treated as objects of barter between warriors. Divale and Harris (1976) have noted that internal warfare correlates with an unbalanced sex ratio in which there are fewer women than men, which results from the high value placed on sons in

---

matrifocality a society in which high social status is assumed by females primarily because they control food production and because the male is absent much of the time these warlike societies and is partly brought about by the practice of female infanticide. Because the sex ratio imbalance then makes it difficult for young men to find wives, a man's desire to prove his valor in battle and thus obtain a wife can be a powerful psychological motive for participation in warfare.

The role of warfare in the subordination of women does not hold in external warfare when it (or economic activities such as long-distance trade) removes men from their local communities for prolonged periods. The day-to-day economic and political life of local communities is then in the hands of women, and inheritance is typically handed down from mother to child. In such societies, women often have high rank, and men's aggressive warrior roles convey no special privileges on the men when they return home, since property is owned and inherited by women.

Economics. Lisette Josephides (1985) contends that male access to strategic resources is a primary factor in male dominance over women. Friedl (1975) has argued that the crucial issue in the control of economic goods is whether men have exclusive rights to decide how these goods will be used and distributed outside the domestic setting. For instance, the distribution of meat by hunters in foraging bands, the distribution of economic goods by bigmen in horticultural tribes, or the predominance of men in managerial positions that control other employees' salaries can be a source of male dominance when women do not also participate in these roles. In societies where men monopolize these activities, women's contribution to family income might equal or excel that of men, but they are still likely to experience subordination. In effect, male control over the extradomestic use of goods, including resources produced by women, becomes a means for "buying" higher status. Heidi Hartmann (1976) argues that the indirect and impersonal mechanisms of control that emerged with capitalism perpetuated male control over women by enforcing lower wages for women by job segregation, thereby creating pressure for women to marry. This not only advantages men both economically and domestically, but also creates a vicious cycle of subordination for women.

Sanday (1973) has suggested that men's absence from the local community for long-distance trade or for working in distant towns may give women greater local control over important economic resources, but she also has pointed out (1974)

that women's economic productivity is not necessarily reflected in greater social respect. For instance, according to Siegfried Frederick Nadel (1952), among the Nupe of Nigeria, women's economic position is generally much better than their husbands', but Nupe men fear and resent women openly.

The importance of women's control over valued economic resources is illustrated in many western African societies such as the Igbo, where women's roles included the sale of produce in markets controlled by women. In these societies, women had very high social standing. Similarly, among the Plains Indians of the United States, male and female economic roles were very different. Men hunted the bison, an extremely important resource that provided not only food, but also hides, sinew, and bones used to make many tools. However, in spite of men's very aggressive roles when it came to intertribal warfare or the policing of village life, Plains women had very high status that derived, at least in part, from growing the plant foods that were the staples of the Plains diet. The beans and corn they grew met people's nutritional needs for protein even when men brought in no meat from the hunt. Thus, Plains women owned and controlled a critical resource that freed them from economic dependence on men. These examples contrast with the lot of many New Guinea highlands women whose work in the family gardens and in managing the care of the family pig herds was the basic source of food and wealth. Although they produced these goods, the property and produce were considered to be owned by their husbands, so women lacked control over the fruits of their own labor and had rather low social standing.

Mary Nelson (1989) suggests that social change in the roles of women can be a source of antagonism towards them by men. For instance, the Inquisition occurred in Europe during a time when women were entering new forms of employment. Hundreds of thousands of women, particularly those who were not following their traditional gender roles, were accused of witchcraft and put to death—a practice that came to an end soon after men as well as women became potential targets of witchcraft accusations.

In the contemporary secular cultures of the West, many women who move from earlier traditional gender roles to those less traditional are commonly victims of social antagonism. For instance, in the United States, employed women have been accused of causing a supposed decline in family values and an increase in social problems among children. Even psychiatric labeling sometimes has been used to

FIGURE 9.6 Nontraditional Female Roles
Women who move into nontraditional roles may invite social antagonism. In the Middle East, however, women have long been members of the military, as is this soldier in the Iraqi People's Army.

legitimize the victimization of women. In the last century, women who did not conform to mainstream values about gender roles sometimes found themselves defined as mentally ill. More recently, several new gender-related diagnostic categories have been suggested by American mental health practitioners, including one, Self-Defeating Personality Disorder, that portrays battered women as provokers of their own abuse, and another, Paraphilic Coercive Disorder, that potentially could be used by a man as a legal defense against rape.

Gender and Religion

The institution of religion is a powerful force in molding people's attitudes and values. The ideology of religion includes, among other things, creation mythologies using gender symbolism and religious rules that tend to verify men's and women's roles in society. The gendered division of labor within the social structure of religious groups also tends to reflect gender stratification within their societies and is often interpreted as evidence for supernatural support for similar gender stratification in society at large. Thus, religion is often a prominent factor in maintaining gender stratification.

Gender Symbolism

Numerous studies have documented the ways in which a culture's symbolism expresses the social roles of men and women (see Ortner, 1974, and Strathern, 1980). Sanday (1981a) has shown that gender differences often manifest themselves in the descriptions of the world. For instance, in societies in which women are markedly subordinate to men, untamed nature is often regarded as symbolically female in contrast with the "masculine" realm of culture. Patriarchal societies also typically emphasize masculine deities in their mythologies, while egalitarian societies often utilize feminine symbolism. For instance, in egalitarian Iroquois society, the supreme creator was a female deity, the Ancient Bodied One, and it was her daughter who gave birth to humans. On the other hand, the Mosaic deity, Yahweh, was a war god who led the Hebrews in their conquest of Canaan and the building of a kingdom.

Where men's and women's roles are equal in everyday life, female deities are prominent in creation stories, and female symbolism predominates: birth, creativity, and progress that usually originates from *within* something such as water or earth. Female creators work alone or in conjunction with male deities, and bring forth humans from the earth, mold them from clay, transform them from plants or animals, or carve them from wood. The symbolism of female deities is illustrated by the creation story of the Yuchi Indians of North Carolina, reported by Speck (1909, pp. 205–207): Humans originated from the earth that had combined with a drop of menstrual blood that had fallen from the Sun, a female deity.

In contrast, where women's roles are markedly subordinate to those of men, the religious symbolism of creation typically emphasizes male gods who come down from the sky, and themes of warfare, aggression, and sexuality. In these societies, humans are usually created out of the god's body, by acts of sexual intercourse or through self-fertilization by the god. In male-dominant societies, symbolism such as menstruation may be regarded as supernaturally dangerous, especially to men. For instance, according to M. Meggitt, men of the Enga of the western New Guinea highlands obtained their wives from competing neighbors and said, "We marry the people we fight" (1964, p. 218). Enga men believed that women's menstrual blood was a dangerous substance that could destroy men's ability to achieve wealth, pigs, or success in war.

Male-dominant societies also often use cultural symbolism that characterizes females as the originators of various forms of evil, such as sin, illness, and death. For instance, in the Judeo-Christian story of the origin of human beings, it is Eve who succumbs to the temptation of the serpent and commits the first sin, the cause of death and the curse of pain in childbirth. In Greek mythology, illness, greed, and death were released into the world through Pandora's impulsiveness and uncontrolled curiosity.

Gender in the Religious Institution

Where gender equality is present, women's roles are likely to include those of religious practitioners. For instance, among many of the egalitarian Indians of northern California, shamans were always women. Gender stratification, on the other hand, is often associated with practices such as segregating

FIGURE 9.7   Men's House
In many societies, males attempt to retain sole knowledge of myths of human origin and the nature of the supernatural. They exclude women and children from their initiation rites and their separate residences. This is the interior of a men's house in New Guinea.

male and female worshippers, excluding women from religious roles, or restricting them to shamanistic rituals that are subordinate to the ecclesiastical rituals of male priests. Thus, the exclusive ceremonial men's houses of South America and the New Guinea highlands, and comparable ceremonial groups among aboriginal Australians, had political, economic, and religious functions that fostered male dominance. Women were typically forbidden to participate or even observe the religious rituals practiced by men in these settings. In other male-dominant societies, women maintained a separate religious system. For instance, in many Moslem countries where men may hold a number of different positions as ritual practitioners within Islam, the dominant ecclesiastical religion, women may participate in a variety of "women's cults" in which female shamans enter trances and become possessed by spirits to serve as mediums, diviners, and curers for their clients. Similarly, according to I. M. Lewis (1971), Korean shamanism, a religious form that contrasts with the ecclesiastical role of male priests, is primarily a women's activity, providing them with a psychological outlet for the stresses of their subordinated roles in Korean secular life. According to E. Bourguignon and L. Greenberg (1973), in these male-dominant settings, spirit possession symbolism figures prominently in women's religious ritualism.

Women's Rights as Human Rights

A number of countries that have signed international human rights documents that include guarantees of equal treatment of women regularly cite religious values concerning the "sanctity of the family" as grounds for not enforcing these clauses. For instance, Rebecca Cook (1990, p. 22) reports Bangladesh, Egypt, Iraq, Libya, and Tunisia have accepted the UN's 1979 Convention on the Elimination of All Forms of Discrimination against Women, but reserve the right not to follow its obligations when they conflict with Islamic law. Malawi, too, excepts obligations wherever they conflict with its customary law. Iraq, South Korea, and Turkey have maintained the right not to grant women the same rights as men to acquire, change, or retain their nationality. And in Cyprus, Egypt, Iraq, Jamaica, South Korea, Thailand, and Tunisia, where children are deemed to have the nationality of their father, the Convention is not accepted. Leslie Calman has argued that since "women generally have had little influence over political definitions of 'public' morality, the primacy of this value over that of individual rights is detrimental to women" (1987, p. 1).

One major effect of the inequality of women in patriarchal societies is the cultural tendency to equate "human" more readily with men than with women. This is more than a simple matter of semantics. It has tremendous practical significance that adversely impacts women. One effect of this distinction is that the international political concern for "human rights" often focuses on those rights that are of greatest concern to men. For instance, Calman has discussed the fact that political rights violations against women have frequently been treated as a *woman's* issue rather than as a *human* rights issue. This contrast has been exemplified by M. Mejer (1985), who has documented the difficulties of women in obtaining refugee status when they have fled violent and coercive situations. When political issues that concern the violation of women's rights are discussed, they are often treated as a different and less important category.

Margaret Schuler (1986) has summarized some of the major categories of human rights violations that frequently affect women in particular: (1) economic exploitation, including the failure of governments to provide minimum wage laws for occupations filled primarily by women, and the lack of day-care rights, (2) lack of equal treatment of women by family law (such as the failure of governments to grant women the right to obtain a divorce and the imposition of greater punishments for crimes such as adultery, and the lack of inheritance rights), (3) denial of reproductive rights (including the right to contraceptive information, access to safe contraceptive technologies, the right to obtain medically safe abortions, and the right to bear children), and (4) violence and exploitation (including domestic violence, rape, sexual harassment, and coerced prostitution). Calman adds that women's human rights should also be understood to include political rights (such as the right to vote and to hold public office) and the right to an education.

Announcement of Peace Prize

OSLO, Oct. 16 (AP)—Following is the Norwegian Nobel Committee's announcement today that the 1992 Peace Prize had been awarded to Rigoberta Menchú of Guatemala:

The Norwegian Nobel Committee has decided to award the Nobel Peace Prize for 1992 to Rigoberta Menchú from Guatemala, in recognition of her work for social justice and ethno-cultural reconciliation based on respect for the rights of indigenous peoples.

Like many other countries in South and Central America, Guatemala has experienced great tension between the descendants of European immigrants and the native Indian population. In the 1970's and 1980's, that tension came to a head in the large-scale repression of

Quiché Indian

Rigoberta Menchú, a Quiché Indian from Guatemala in Central America, won the Nobel Peace Prize in 1992. She has worked to prevent violence against indigenous people in her native Guatemala and for peace around the world.

FIGURE 9.8   Rigoberta Menchú

Human rights violations around the world have a cultural tendency to be considered more relevant to males than to females. Rigoberta Menchú, a Quiché Indian from Guatemala, has fought to restore rights not only to her own people, but to all people throughout the Americas. She was awarded the Nobel Peace Prize in 1992.

Indian peoples. Menchú has come to play an increasingly prominent part as an advocate of native rights.

Rigoberta Menchú grew up in poverty, in a family that has undergone the most brutal suppression and persecution. In her social and political work, she has always borne in mind that the long-term objective of the struggle is peace.

Today, Rigoberta Menchú stands out as a vivid symbol of peace and reconciliation across ethnic, cultural and social dividing lines, in her own country, on the American continent and in the world. (Golden, *New York Times*, Oct 17, 1992, p. 1)

Economic Exploitation

However poverty is measured, women comprise a major and growing proportion of the world's poor today. This trend is known as the **feminization of poverty**. Poverty is especially a problem of older women and younger women with children. Worldwide, a third of all households are headed by women. Since women receive less income than men in all countries, and since they are so much more likely than men to have to bear the expense of childrearing

alone when a family is headed by one parent, it is not surprising that women are generally poorer than men.

In the United States, the trend toward the poor being primarily women and children began after World War II. According to information from the U.S. Census Bureau, as of 1990, about two-thirds of all people living in poverty in the United States are female. The problem of poverty in single-parent families is particularly acute, since child-care responsibilities often mean making a choice between day-care expenses that make employment unprofitable or accepting low-paid, part-time work that is more compatible with less expensive ways of organizing child care such as pooling work and babysitting with friends or relatives. For many women neither of these options proves successful, and the circumstances of single-parent life force them into dependence on the welfare system. Currently, about half of women in poverty are more or less permanently

feminization of poverty   a growing trend in which women comprise a large proportion of the world's poor reliant on public welfare or on the support of friends or relatives.

Equality in Family Law

The family is considered a separate entity in legal matters. For instance, the enforcement of laws pertaining to families is the authority of kinship groups in chiefdoms. In societies with state governments that monopolize the right to use force, the law often treats the family as a special institution. Laws that do not support the traditional customs of family life may exempt the family from the usual rules of law. Even when family life is not exempted from the principles of law that might impinge on it, enforcement of those laws may not be rigorous. Thus, the legal rights of men and women may differ significantly in matters that members of society perceive as related to the family.

The insularity of the family makes it an institution in which gender inequality can lead to abuses that are not publicly addressed. Thus, in many societies a husband can avoid the charge of murder by asserting that the killing was done in defense of "family honor." For instance, until 1989 Brazilian courts accepted the defense of family honor in cases where it judged that the killing was in response to a wife's adultery.

The right to choose one's own spouse and the right to divorce are not equally available to men and women in many societies. For instance, Gail Cairns (1984) reports that in nine Latin American countries, the grounds for divorce are not the same for men and women. In five countries adultery by a husband is grounds for divorce only if it involves a public scandal, while adultery by a wife is sufficient grounds for a husband to be granted a divorce. In El Salvador, a woman is not permitted to remarry for 300 days after the final divorce decree. In Israel a husband's consent is required for a divorce, and in Middle Eastern countries that follow Islamic law, a similar rule applies unless an exemption is granted by a cleric.

What's in a Name?

In the United States it has been a tradition until recently for a woman to adopt her husband's surname when she marries. The custom is still so common that the government routinely co-operates in name changes with a minimum of formality. It is a rather easy matter for a woman to obtain a new driver's license with a new surname by merely showing a marriage certificate. In Utah, however, two women recently discovered that it is not as easy for that change to be reversed following a divorce.

In 1988 Wendy Jean Alldridge Jorgenson attempted to have her driver's license reissued under her birth name, Alldridge. She presented the motor vehicles department with her divorce decree and her birth certificate. Although the state still had a record of the earlier license under her birth name, she was informed that the department's unwritten policy was to make such a change only if a woman obtained a judicial order to that effect. Ms. Alldridge challenged the legality of the policy in court. In October 1989 U.S. District Judge J. Thomas Greene ruled against her. He informed Ms. Alldridge that she had two alternatives. The first was to have her divorce decree amended to include the name change, which would require her to seek her ex-husband's permission. Otherwise, it would be necessary for her to go through the costly process of requesting a legal name change in court. Ms. Alldridge tried to have the judge's decision overturned, but the 10th U.S. Circuit Court of Appeals upheld the lower court's decision in April of 1991.

Utah is not unique in the United States in assuming that a woman's identity and her name depend on her relationship to a man. In 1990, Lucille Anne Riccitelli of Providence, Rhode Island, decided to resume her birth name to honor her father after he died without any sons. She was successful in having the name on her driver's license and social security card changed, but when she tried to change her name on a joint bank account that she and her mother had at Fleet National Bank, they insisted on a court document to validate the name change. Probate Judge Anthony B. Sciarretta told Ms. Riccitelli that she would have to get her husband's permission before he would grant her request for the name change. Although Ms. Riccitelli's husband, Edward Martin, supported his wife's wish to use her father's surname, she and her husband agreed that requiring his consent was inappropriate, since the requirement treated Ms. Riccitelli as if she were a minor without independent legal rights. Nevertheless, Judge Sciarretta denied her petition because she refused to obtain her husband's permission.

Reproductive Rights

The right to control one's own reproductive life is limited in various ways in most of the countries of the world today. For instance, Mosher (1983) has documented the strong governmental role in limiting family size in the People's Republic of China. Under a legal policy that limits each family to having only one child, women who become pregnant a second time have been put under strong pressure to terminate their pregnancies. In some instances women have been coerced into undergoing unwanted abortions as late as in the seventh month of pregnancy. Diana Russell and Nicole Van de Ven (1976) reported that during the 1960s Puerto Rico's government policy of controlling population growth had resulted in 35 percent of women of childbearing age being sterilized, in most cases without the use of the sterilization consent form required by law. Research indicated that 19.5 percent of these women reported health complications, and 10 percent reported that their relationships suffered as a result of their sterilization.

While some countries have imposed limitations on women's reproductive rights, others, by government action, have limited or denied women's access to contraceptive information and abortion. Karen Breslau (1990) described the extremes that such policy took in Romania under the regime of Nicolae Ceausescu, where governmental concern for the nation's low birth rate practically mandated pregnancy. Romanian law forbade sex education, contraception, and abortion. Women were required to take pregnancy tests every three months at their workplaces. Women who failed to conceive were fined a "celibacy tax" of up to 10 percent of their salaries, and pregnant women who miscarried were suspected of having had an abortion and were summoned for questioning. These policies ended in December of 1989 when Ceausescu was overthrown. Although the Romanian policies represent an extreme, government efforts to increase population are still pursued in many countries through policies that restrict or deny women family planning services.

Violence

While physical abuse by partners is the most common form of violence against women worldwide, there are many other sources of physical harm that commonly impact women more than men. For example, Mitra Das (1989) has documented the rise in frequency of dowry-related wife burnings in parts of India. These developed because of the economic changes that resulted from industrialization, which has particularly affected lower caste families, for whom large dowries have become increasingly important. Decades ago, dowries in India were gifts that a woman received from her parents when she married. Now, the dowry gifts are paid to her in-laws, who many times perceive them to be inadequate, instead of to the bride. Dowry deaths, often caused by setting fire to a kerosene-doused woman, were described as "kitchen accidents." Such a death allowed the family to acquire another dowry when the husband remarried. The problem has become so common that the Ahmedabad Women's Action Group has estimated that as many as 1,000 women may have been burned alive in Gujarat, India, in 1987.

Political Rights

In many countries today, women are denied political rights in a variety of ways. For instance, in Kuwait and Bhutan, men, but not women, have the

FIGURE 9.9   Reproductive Rights
Some governments, such as that of the People's Republic of China, take a strong role in limiting each family to one child. This one-child family in Hohhot, Inner Mongolia, stops to observe something. Behind them are posters providing information about the census that keeps track of population growth.

right to vote. In other cases, human rights violations occur against both men and women, but the violations of women's rights are systematically different from the political abuses that are experienced by men. For instance, both women and men are involved in cases of arrest and detention without trial in a variety of countries and may experience torture as political prisoners. However, politically motivated violence against women frequently involves rape as an aspect of political torture (Adams, 1989; Ashworth, 1986; Anon, 1987, 1989; Heise, 1989b; Tambiah, 1986). Sexual slavery is another human rights violation that particularly affects women. Women in various parts of the world are held forcibly in slavery today, but because this practice is associated with forced prostitution, it has not been addressed as a "human rights" issue in such institutions as the United Nations. Member nations are not required to submit statistics on the practice. Women forced into prostitution under such conditions have not been recognized as deserving of refugee status and receive no special protections, but have, in some countries, been arrested and imprisoned even though their participation in prostitution had been involuntary.

CHAPTER SUMMARY

1. Gender is a social and cultural identity that consists of the roles a person is expected to play because of his or her sex.

2. There is great cross-cultural variety in how the genders are perceived.

3. Some societies have more than two gender categories.

4. In many societies men's gender roles have greater privilege with respect to power and honor.

5. The presence or absence of male dominance is influenced by a society's kinship system, the nature of its warfare, and its economic customs.

6. Religion provides supernatural support for society's gender role traditions and portrays gender differences in the symbolism of its creation stories.

7. Women's human rights have often been ignored in areas such as economics, family law, reproductive rights, protection from violence, and political rights.

ANNOTATED READINGS

Blackwood, E. (Ed.). (1986). *The many faces of homosexuality: Anthropological approaches to homosexual behavior.* NY: Harrington Park Press. A collection of important anthropological articles that examine homosexual roles in a variety of cultural and theoretical contexts.

di Leonardo, M. (Ed.). (1991). *Gender at the crossroads of knowledge: Feminist anthropology in a postmodern era.* Berkeley, CA: University of California Press. A collection of specialized essays on feminist anthropological studies of gender and society.

Ginsburg, F., & Tsing, A. (Eds.). (1990). *Uncertain terms: Negotiating gender in American culture.* Boston: Beacon Press. A collection of essays on gender in America.

Moore, H. (1988). *Feminism and anthropology.* Minneapolis: University of Minnesota Press. Provides a good general overview of feminist perspectives in anthropology.

Morgan, S. (Ed.). (1989). *Gender and anthropology: Critical reviews for research and teaching.* Washington, DC: American Anthropological Association. A review of gender studies that covers both gender roles in the major world regions and a variety of general issues pertaining to gender.

Nanda, S. (1990). *Neither man nor woman: The Hijras of India.* Belmont, CA: Wadsworth Publishing Company. An excellent account of a third gender in India.

Roscoe, W. (1991). *The Zuni man-woman.* Albuquerque: University of New Mexico Press. The life history of We'wha, the most well-known Zuni berdache.

Sanday, P. R. (1981). *Female power and male dominance: On the origins of sexual inequality.* New York: Cambridge University Press. A cross-cultural examination of sex role inequality and the ways in which sex role differences are symbolized.

Sanday, P. R., & Gallagher, R. (Eds.). (1990). *Beyond the second sex: New directions in the anthropology of gender.* Philadelphia: University of Pennsylvania Press. A collection of challenging essays that incorporates new approaches to analyzing gender and culture, including insights into the diversity of ways that culture and gender can be perceived.

214

Humans have built a superstructure of culture using their ability to communicate, to explain their place in the universe, to understand the concept of their own mind and its relationship to others in a society, and to create and enjoy beauty. Chapter 10 looks at patterns of language and learning, the system of symbolizing and communicating meaningful ideas to others. Chapter 11 discusses the most abstract of symbolic systems, the varieties of religious ideologies and rituals that societies develop to give meaning to their place in the universe. Chapter 12 focuses on the individual's relationship to culture, illustrating how it shapes personality, influences states of consciousness, and identifies psychological disorders. Chapter 13 describes the ways that various cultures define beauty and discusses how art forms function in society.

FIGURE 10.1 Communication
Cultural patterns of life are communicated to others by a complex system of signs and symbols. This young boy in front of a mosque in Cairo, Egypt, is not only being given water, but is learning the traditions of his culture through written language on the wall and through the gestures and attitudes of the elder helping him.

CHAPTER 10

Human ways of life are far more varied and complex than those of other animals. This complexity is facilitated by our distinctive ability to communicate the intricacies of these lifeways to other members of our group. Unlike other animals, we tend to portray our concepts by highly arbitrary but mutually accepted symbols, including languages. In this chapter, we will examine these two capacities, learning and symbolizing, which are so fundamental to the origin and perpetuation of the human pattern of life.

Language and Culture

CHAPTER OBJECTIVES

After reading this chapter, you should be able to:

Discuss the contrasts between symbolic communication and sign communication.

Contrast human with nonhuman communication.

Explain the characteristics of nonverbal communication.

Define language.

Explain the biological basis of language.

Outline the structural components of language.

Explain the concept of linguistic relativity.

Discuss the process of language change.

Explain the concept of language families.

Discuss contemporary language diversity.

Dude. Boombox. Beetlejuice. Jive. Lift. Bonnet. All words of the English language. Would you understand what they meant if you were 18 years old? or 80? Lived in California? London? In all parts of the world, and at all ages, humans learn to communicate with each other using a complicated system of vocal sounds that symbolize complex concepts. Language is the primary ability that distinguishes us from other primates.

Human Communication

Analyzing one's experiences, whether internally in thought or externally in communication, involves the manipulation of concepts. **Communication** is the transfer of information embodied in concepts or ideas from one person to another by using observable objects or events such as gestures or spoken words to represent those concepts.

Signs and Symbols

Human communication is a process by which we express meaning simultaneously with signs and with symbols. **Signs** are events such as tears, smiles, clenched fists, or agitated gestures that are spontaneous expressions of our feelings, needs, or concepts that require little conscious effort or learning to master. Thus, when human beings smile spontaneously as a sign of happiness, they use the same facial muscles in all societies around the world. The use of natural signs that express our inner feelings or needs is a form of communication that we share with other animals. Since signs are spontaneous outward expressions of our inner states, we often learn rather easily to recognize the meanings of signs used by other species. For instance, when a dog crouches and tenses its muscles, growls, and bares its teeth, these signs of potential aggression are readily understood not only by dogs and other animals but also by humans.

Symbolic communication is the most distinctive of all human behavioral attributes. It is the use of symbols in communicating that sets us apart from other animals and that serves as the foundation for the extremely complex ways of life found in all human groups. **Symbols** are objects or events such as national flags or spoken words that have no inherent significance, but whose meanings exist only because their users have agreed that they will represent certain other objects or events (White, 1971). Thus, symbols have no innate meaning, and their use and interpretation must always be learned.

The relationship between a symbol and what it represents is not determined by the inherited biological tendencies of the communicator to relate the two to one another. Furthermore, a symbol need not share any physical similarities or physical proximity with its referent. There is, for instance, no reason dictated by human biology or the physical properties of the wavelengths of light that red had to be used to mean "stop" or green to mean "go" in traffic signals, nor is there any compelling reason in human biology or in geometric properties for a stop sign to be octagonal rather than triangular in shape. There may be causal factors in one's history or environment that influence the form of a symbol, but its meaning is essentially arbitrary. Any symbol therefore, may be used to designate any referent. Since the meanings of symbols are a matter of social convention or consensus rather than nature, they can change quite readily even within the lifetimes of their users. Because people can freely assign new meanings to objects or actions, they can communicate extremely complex and subtle messages to one another.

---

communication the transfer of information from one person to another using objects and events as signs or symbols

sign an object or event whose meaning is biologically disposed or based on a similarity or a tendency for two things to occur together in nature

symbol an object or event that represents another object or event because of the agreement among people that it will

Human vs. Nonhuman Communication

Homo sapiens is not the only species of animal that communicates. Many nonhuman animals make use of both biologically innate and learned signs in communicative acts. However, the creation and use of symbols is characteristic of humans alone, and the human use of symbols is central to our most conscious efforts to communicate. Acts such as smiling or crying have rather natural meanings as signs, but they can be consciously manipulated and used in ways that alter their natural meanings and transform them into symbols, as when we smile sarcastically or feign tears or a sad expression to communicate a feeling we are not really experiencing.

In human beings, only the simplest of meaningful signs—those that communicate simple feelings in unconscious or unintentional ways—are biologically preprogrammed. For instance, we express heightened interest in whatever we are observing by an increase in the dilation of the pupil of the eye, a change controlled on an unconscious level by the autonomic nervous system (the part of the nervous system that controls the functioning of involuntary actions such as the beating of the heart). This sign, though unintentional, is communicative, and other persons perceive the change and respond to it. Similarly, the increased muscle tension that signals rising anger is often communicative enough to cause an observer to act more carefully.

In some other animals, even complex communications may be governed by biologically controlled behavioral tendencies. For instance, a fighting timber wolf may indicate its submission by freezing its stance and exposing the vulnerable area of its throat to the attacking fangs of its opponent. This act might seem highly inappropriate and dangerous in the heat of battle, yet the timber wolf has a biological predisposition to signify its acceptance of defeat in this way. And the sign is responded to appropriately: Although the victor grasps the throat of its victim with its mouth as if to bite, its muscles tremble as if strained by the effort to control its enraged attack, and it does not bite to kill. If the submitting wolf remains rigid and unmoving, it will not be bitten, and the victor will continue to strain as if it desires but is unable to bite until, finally exhausted, it releases its hold and begins to walk away. Even now, if the submitting wolf starts to move, a renewed attack will begin until the sign of submission is given again. The process may be repeated several times until the loser manages to escape from the repeated attacks of the gradually tiring dominant animal.

Human Communication With and Without Symbols: Helen Keller

The dramatic impact that symbols have on human behavior is well illustrated by the case of Helen Keller, a person in whom the acquisition of symbols and, hence, the ability to communicate symbolically was delayed until she was almost seven years old. Stricken by illness at the age of 19 months, Helen was left both blind and deaf. Helen lacked the senses through which we normally learn the arbitrarily agreed-on meanings of our communicative acts and through which we usually perceive those symbolic acts themselves. Nevertheless, she needed to communicate and did so by her own signs, acts whose meanings were implicit in the quality of the acts themselves. In her own words:

My hands felt every object and observed every motion, and in this way I learned to know many things. Soon I felt the need of some communication with others and began to make crude signs. A shake of the head meant "No" and a nod, "Yes," a pull meant "Come" and a push, "Go." Was it bread that I wanted? Then I would imitate the acts of cutting the slices and buttering them. If I wanted my mother to make ice cream for dinner, I made the sign for working the freezer and shivered, indicating cold. . . .

About three months before Helen's seventh birthday a teacher, Miss Anne Sullivan, arrived to attempt to train her to communicate by finger spelling. Gradually, Helen learned to spell several words, but she simply used these as she had previously used her own self-invented signs. That is, she had not yet recognized the essence of symbols: Since their meaning is arbitrarily assigned by their users, a symbol may be created to refer to anything. In the words of Anne Sullivan:

Helen has learned several nouns this week. "M-u-g" and "m-i-l-k," have given her more trouble than other words. When she spells "m-i-l-k" she points to the mug, and when she spells "m-u-g," she makes the sign for pouring or drinking, which shows that she has confused the words. She has no idea yet that everything has a name. (p. 253)

In a month of intense teaching, Helen learned only 25 nouns and 4 verbs. Here is her own description of this period of her slow learning of the fingerspelling signs:

The morning after my teacher came she led me into her room and gave me a doll. The little blind children at the Perkins Institution had sent it and Laura Bridgman had dressed it; but I did not know this until afterward. When I had played with it a little while, Miss Sullivan slowly spelled into my hand the word "d-o-l-l." I was at once interested in this finger play and tried to imitate it. When I finally succeeded in making letters correctly I was flushed with childish pleasure and pride.

FIGURE 10.2   Helen Keller
Unable to communicate by speaking and unable to hear, Helen Keller (1880–1968) learned the meaning of words through the complicated method of her teacher forming letters in her hand. This photograph, taken in the early fifties, shows the hand of her companion signing letters in Helen's hand. Helen became a tireless and popular lecturer for the rights of the deaf.

Running downstairs to my mother I held up my hand and made the letters for doll. I did not know that I was spelling a word or even that words existed; I was simply making my fingers go in monkey-like imitation. In the days that followed I learned to spell in this uncomprehending way a great many words, among them pin, hat, cup and a few verbs like sit, stand, and walk. But my teacher had been with me several weeks before I understood that everything has a name. (p. 35)

Helen's slow rate of sign learning was superseded by a remarkably accelerated rate of learning that began when her inborn symbolic abilities became activated in a single dramatic incident. This change was recorded by her teacher in the following excerpt of a letter:

April 5, 1887
We went out to the pump-house, and I made Helen hold her mug under the spout while I pumped. As the cold water gushed forth, filling the mug, I spelled "w-a-t-e-r" in Helen's free hand. The word coming so close on the sensation of cold water rushing over her hand seemed to startle her. She dropped the mug and stood as one transfixed. A new light came into her face. She spelled "water" several times. Then she dropped on the ground and asked for its name and pointed to the pump and the trellis, and suddenly turning around she asked for my name. I spelled "Teacher." Just then the nurse brought Helen's little sister into the pump-house, and Helen spelled "baby" and pointed to the nurse. All the way back to the house she was highly excited, and learned the name of every object she touched, so that in a few hours she had added thirty new words to her vocabulary. Here are some of them: Door, open, shut, give, go, come, and a great many more.

P.S.—I didn't finish my letter in time to get it posted last night; so I shall add a line. Helen got up this morning like a radiant fairy. She has flitted from object to object, asking the name of everything and kissing me for very gladness. . . . I thought my heart would burst, so full was it of joy. (Keller, 1954)

Nonverbal Communication

The two most active forms of interpersonal communication are nonverbal communication and language. **Nonverbal communications** are messages we convey to each other without words. Often they are unconscious expressions of our emotions and may not even be intended as communications. They range from grins and hugs to the space we place between ourselves and others in conversation and our handling of time (as in arriving early or late for an appointment).

Nonverbal Signs

The simplest forms of nonverbal communication are physiological signs, not symbols. For instance, blushing, which communicates embarrassment, is a direct reflection of one's emotional state and is controlled by the autonomic nervous system. Smiling, although it can be consciously controlled and assigned other symbolic meanings in special contexts, is also more generally a direct reflection of happy feelings. As such, it can be observed in deaf-blind individuals as well as in others. Slumping posture will signal submission or defeat without conscious effort; prolonged eye contact can indicate aggression or interest in maintaining contact; staring blankly while avoiding eye contact may signal fear or a desire not to interact. Nonverbal signs communicate the same meanings in every culture. Samoan, Navajo, or Chinese, we all express happiness with the same spontaneous smile, confusion with a distinctively human knit brow, and boredom with a yawn.

Culturally Patterned Nonverbal Symbols

In contrast with nonverbal signs, our nonverbal symbols, such as parting gestures, flirtatious uses of the eyes, and hand gestures of contempt, vary from culture to culture. For instance, throughout Europe when people want to point out the location of something they gesture in the appropriate direction with their hand. The finger closest to the thumb, appro-

FIGURE 10.3   Andamanese Greeting and Parting Customs
Andaman Islanders of either sex greet each other after absences of a few weeks by one sitting in the lap of the other and weeping. Since their etiquette demands crying as a means of expressing sentiment, the Andamanese learn to shed tears on demand.

priately called the "pointing finger" in colloquial English, may also be extended. Shoshoni Indians of the North American Great Basin still use their traditional gesture, pointing with their lips. Many North Americans use a "thumbs up" gesture to express their feeling that things are going well. In Japan this gesture would likely be interpreted to mean "boss" or "father." The German who points to the side of his forehead communicates the same idea—"crazy!"—that the North American may convey by tracing a circle next to the head with the index finger. North Americans point at their chests to indicate "self"; Japanese point to their noses with the same significance.

Our most common nonverbal symbolic communications tend to be performed with the highly visible upper extremities of the body—the hands,

nonverbal communication all transfer of information other than with words that includes such things as volume, pitch, tone of voice, and speed when speaking, as well as non-oral things such as gestures, posture, and use of space and time arms, shoulders, head, and parts of the face. They are often used in situations of purposeful communication: (1) where verbal communication is impossible, as when persons are too distant from one another to hear one another well; (2) where verbal communication is inappropriate, as when the actor wishes to send the message to only one member of a group (but knows others would overhear a verbal message), or when the sender feels that a verbal communication would be too direct or strong in impact; and (3) where their use will provide added emphasis while speaking verbal symbols.

Cultural variations in such symbols may inhibit full communication between people of different cultures, even on a nonverbal level. Greeting is not signified everywhere by a handshake: A kiss, an embrace, or a nose rub will do as well. Among the Toda of India, a woman indicates respect in greeting an elder kinsman by kneeling and lifting his foot to her forehead (Murdock, 1969). A wave of the hand that the European would interpret as a farewell might elsewhere be used as a request to approach. Such differences can lead to misunderstandings between well-intentioned persons from different societies who do not realize that their behaviors are only arbitrarily endowed with meaning and that the same behaviors might denote something different to people from another society.

Proxemics

Even the distance we place between ourselves and others conveys subtle nonverbal meanings. Edward Hall (1969) has studied the ways in which people symbolically structure their nonverbal manipulation of spatial relationships between themselves and others. He refers to the study of people's use of the space around them as proxemics. One finding of proxemic research is that the distance people choose to place themselves from others while communicating with them illustrates how they feel about the interaction. According to Hall, there are four main distances to which North Americans adjust themselves in their business and social relations: intimate, personal, social, and public.

Intimate distance, which is reserved for occasions when caressing and touch are appropriate, varies in the United States from direct contact to one and one-half feet, where persons are still close enough to touch one another easily. We experience others in this zone intensely by many of our senses.

They fill our field of vision, their breathing is audible, and we are aware of their presence by the senses of touch and smell as well. This intimate awareness often leads us to experience the other as an extension of our own self rather than as a separate entity. Intimate distance is normally regarded as too close to be used by adults in public. In crowded situations such as elevators or subways, when one is forced to remain within the intimate distance of strangers, individuals communicate that they are not intentionally intruding on the intimate zone of others by staring impersonally at a distant spot.

The second meaningful zone to which North Americans adjust themselves, called **personal distance**, indicates a close friendship. It extends from $1^{1}/_{2}$ feet to 4 feet. A husband and wife generally place themselves within the first half of each other's personal zone in public or conversational situations, while other friends will normally occupy the farther half of this zone. In many other cultures, the distances for this personal zone are somewhat closer than they are in the United States or northern Europe. This can make it difficult for persons of differing cultural backgrounds to communicate their interest in one another. An Anglo-American may feel ill at ease if a stranger from another society adopts a distance that in the stranger's homeland indicates friendship but which to the Anglo-American seems overly intimate or pushy. When the Anglo-American backs away to a distance at which he or she feels comfortable among friends, the other may mistakenly interpret the nonverbal communication as disinterest. Such misunderstandings can be avoided only if one becomes aware that even the most habitual of human behaviors, because they are very specific and symbolic, have no universal meanings but vary from society to society.

Beyond personal distance is **social distance** of 4 to 12 feet, which is used in more impersonal interactions of a cordial type such as in business transac-

---

proxemics the study of how people structure the space around them when interacting with others

intimate distance the distance from their bodies that people reserve for those with whom they are intimate enough to permit casual touching

personal distance the distance to which people adjust themselves when interacting with close friends

social distance the distance to which people adjust themselves when interacting in impersonal situations such as business transactions

FIGURE 10.4   Proxemics - Social Use of Space
Specific social and cultural rituals determine how people use their individual space. The Taiwanese monks greeting each other (A) are careful to observe a formal social distance. In other cultures (B) the greeting may include close physical contact such as a handshake or a kiss.

tions. **Public distance**, which is greater than 12 feet, is the final zone. The usual distance placed between a teacher or public speaker and most audiences is 12 to about 25 feet. Distances greater than this are used to distinguish important public figures.

Hall (1969) has studied several societies and has found that the distances to which people adjust themselves for intimate, personal, social, or public activities are not the same in every society. For instance, among Germans personal space is expanded to include visible areas far beyond the North American's four-foot space. People are expected to greet formally anyone of their acquaintance who comes into sight and is within hailing distance. This difference shows up in the German preference for solid doors that clearly separate each room in homes and work places, a preference that contrasts with the common North American preference for rooms connected by doorways that have no closeable doors. Typically, the traditional German home or apartment has a lockable door on every room, including the kitchen, allowing Germans to indicate their personal space with a definite boundary. The North American walk-through floor plan with kitchen and dining areas open to and clearly visible from the living room would strike the traditional German family as strange, indeed. Arab homes, on the other hand, are much more open than those in North America. Privacy there is obtained not by physical boundaries but by withdrawal from communication, which may simply mean moving outside personal distance. To North Americans who identify their "selves" with their bodies, this intimacy might seem an invasion of their persons. Yet for Arabs, who have had to adjust to higher population densities in which contact with strangers is difficult to avoid, it is adaptive to learn to isolate their sense of personal identity deeper within their bodies than North Americans do.

Kinesics

Nonverbal communication often accompanies speech, providing the context within which speech is interpreted. Signs such as posturing of the body, gestures, and the use of the eyes communicate the level of interest and involvement in others present or in the subject being discussed. The subtlety and complexity of nonverbal communication provides information about emotions such as love, hate, fear, dependency, submission, dominance, interest, disinterest, or boredom. It therefore defines and expresses the nature of the relationship. Without a successful nonverbal relationship between people, verbal communication may become impossible. For instance, if body movements are too unsynchronized with each other, or if they indicate hostility, successful verbal communication may be impossible.

The study of the body movements that complement speech as a means of communication is called **kinesics**. Ray Birdwhistell (1970) has developed a system for recording those movements with precise detail. He has discovered, for instance, that the human face can make a quarter of a million different expressions. For study purposes, however, 26 symbols are enough to record the basic facial positions. Birdwhistell's system for recording the movements of the entire body uses less than 100 symbols. He has demonstrated that the ability of the human brain to process visual data about other people's body movements is astounding. He estimates that people are capable of processing as many as 10,000 bits of information or percepts per second.

Some nonverbal signs can be brought under more or less conscious control and can become overlaid with symbolic significance that will alter their basic significance as signs. Yet such nonverbal signs still tend to reflect the emotional state of the speaker and thus are limited in their use as a productive communication system. The more usual role of nonverbal communication is to define a relationship between two or more persons and a topic of communication by sending simple, often unconscious messages about how those involved feel about themselves, about each other, and about the ideas being expressed in language (Watzlawick, Beavin, & Jackson, 1967).

....

Language

Language is a symbolizing system that does not rely on body signs in order to communicate. Language is therefore said to be an "open" system of communication because its subject matter is unlimited. New messages can be invented to express

---

public distance   the distance reserved for separating people whose interaction is not intended to perpetuate a social relationship

kinesics   the study of the body movements that accompany speech as a component of communication anything that can be thought. Language can be used to communicate about feelings, things, or persons not only visible at the moment, but also invisible because they are displaced in space or time, as well as things that are nonexistent. Language is a **meta-communication system**—one that can be used to communicate about the process of communication itself. In the following sections, we will examine the distinction between speech and language, the biological basis of humans' capacity for language, the origin of language, the structure of language, the interactions between language and culture, the processes by which languages change and diverge from each other, and the politics of language.

Language vs. Speech

Within the human supply of symbolic skills, language is the most singularly outstanding and systematically organized component. **Language** is the shared system of rules that guides the production of **speech**, the audible symbols that people use to communicate. Every language system is made up of three sets of shared rules: (1) rules for forming the particular speech sounds used in the language, (2) rules for putting the sounds of speech together into words that symbolize concepts, and (3) rules for putting the words together into sentences that portray the relationships between concepts. The existence of a system for organizing speech symbols increases the amount of information that can be communicated with those symbols. If speakers could do no more than simply produce an unstructured list of vocal symbols, then a hearer could associate these utterances with a series of mental concepts. Yet the hearer would have no way of deciding which relationship between the communicated ideas the speaker had in mind. Language thus enables the hearer to decipher the complex ideas expressed by the speaker.

When children begin learning language, they not only learn the vocal symbols of the speech which they hear uttered by others around them, but they also discover the meaningful pattern to the arrangement of these speech sounds. The number of sentences that can be spoken in any language is effectively unlimited. But the existence of a system that governs the organization of words into sentences makes it unnecessary for children to actually hear and memorize each separate sentence before they can communicate any idea they wish to express to someone else (Chomsky, 1971). Having a socially shared

pattern for representing concepts by a series of vocal symbols makes it possible (1) to produce new sentences one has never heard before, (2) to communicate about new concepts, and (3) to interpret correctly new utterances that one hears for the first time.

---

meta-communication system a system of communication that includes the capacity to communicate about itself
language a system of rules that govern the production and interpretation of speech
speech the audible symbols that people use to communicate

Vocal Communication in Nonhuman Primates

Is language unique to the human species? We are now attempting to understand the communication patterns and language potential of other animals, including our own closest relatives. Biologically speaking, human beings are members of a group of animals known as *primates* that consist of the apes, the monkeys, and the small tree-dwelling prosimians. As a group, the primates tend to be social and communicative animals. Nevertheless, the uniqueness of human language is apparent when one compares it with the communication systems of the other primates.

According to Altmann (1973), "For the most part . . . the social signals of monkeys and apes are not semantic: the messages do not stand for something else. They are simply social signals to which a response is given. In this they are much more like the cry of a newborn infant than they are like the speech of human adults." Similarly, Marler (1965) observes, "It begins to appear that a repertoire of from about 10 to about 15 basic sound-signals is characteristic of nonhuman primates as a whole. In some it may prove to be smaller or larger, but it is doubtful if the limits will be exceeded by very much. . . . Comparison with other highly vocal groups of vertebrates that have been closely examined reveals an approximately similar repertoire size." Thus, the nonhuman primates do not seem much different from other comparable animals in their vocal communicative abilities. Symbolic language seems to be a distinctively human trait.

In recent years, the limits of nonhuman primate communicative abilities have begun to be explored through attempts to teach various forms of language to chimpanzees (Mounin, 1976), possibly the most similar to human beings in their biological characteristics. These efforts have revealed a striking capacity in chimpanzees to expand their communication skills. One such study was started in 1966 by Allen and Beatrix Gardner with the chimpanzee Washoe (1969, 1985). A major problem in earlier attempts to teach a human language to chimpanzees had been the chimpanzee's difficulty in forming the sounds used in human speech (Kellog, 1968; Hayes & Nissen, 1971).

The Gardners overcame this problem by teaching Washoe a modified version of *American Sign Language (ASL)*, the gestural language of the deaf in North America. Chimpanzees naturally make use of a variety of gestures when communicating in the wild, and the Gardners' use of ASL proved to be a breakthrough. Within four years, Washoe had mastered more than 130 signs of ASL. In addition to using signs appropriately to name objects (e.g., dog, flower, or shoe), attributes (e.g., red, dirty, or funny), and actions (e.g., give, want, or drink), Washoe learned to combine signs into sequences such as "give" + "tickle." The Gardners and Washoe's later trainer, Roger Fouts, claim that Washoe has mastered something equivalent to grammar in human language. In six successful studies they

FIGURE 10.5   Chimpanzee Signing
In several different experiments chimpanzees have been taught to converse with their trainers, using American Sign Language. Here this chimpanzee asks to hug the cat and gets his wish.

believe they have proven that chimpanzees have at least a basic ability to use language in the human sense. Others disagree. Herbert Terrace (1979) has worked with chimpanzees and has also analyzed videotapes of human/chimpanzee sign language interaction. He and his colleagues, Laura, Pettito, R. J. Sanders, and Thomas Bever, (1979) claim that many of the apparent examples of chimpanzees' combining signs into grammatical sequences are not spontaneous but have resulted from the chimpanzees' responding to subtle cues that the trainers gave. Duane Rumbaugh, H. Warner, and Ernst Von Glasersfeld (1977) began training chimpanzees to communicate by pressing keys embossed with geometric signs. They agree with Terrace that chimpanzees can learn to associate signs with objects and actions and to use signs to make simple requests, but that the chimpanzees that have been taught ASL do not demonstrate a grasp of grammar (Savage-Rumbaugh, Rumbaugh, & Boysen, 1980; Savage-Rumbaugh, Pate, Lawson, Smith, & Rosenbaum, 1983). Rather, they merely string together any signs they know that are relevant to the situation in which they are making a request. Savage-Rumbaugh and her colleagues (1980:60) assert that the most important difference between chimpanzee communication and that of human children is that chimpanzees make requests but do not spontaneously begin to describe their environment. They make sequences like "give orange me give eat orange me eat orange give me eat orange give me you," but they do not make comments such as "The orange is cold" or "The orange juice is sticky" while they are eating the orange.

Another primate language training study has been carried out by Francine Patterson with a gorilla named Koko (1978; see also Hill, 1978). Like Washoe, Koko has been taught American Sign Language. Her vocabulary is over 400 words. It includes words for emotions, such as sadness and shame, that Koko uses to communicate about her own feelings. She has spontaneously used descriptive phrases, such as "finger bracelet" for ring, to refer to things for which she had learned no word from her trainer, an ability that also had been demonstrated by the chimpanzee Washoe; she has been caught lying, when she tried to blame a human for something she had broken, and she has mastered sign language well enough to take an intelligence test designed for human beings, scoring in the low-average range!

We have much to learn about nonhuman primate communication skills—what they have in common with and how they differ from human language. Considering the abilities that nonhuman primates have demonstrated, an intriguing question that remains to be answered is why they have not put these skills to use in the wild, where their communication with one another seems limited to a small number of signs that have very natural expressive meanings. One project now underway that may eventually help us answer questions like this one began at the Institute for Primate Studies in Oklahoma. There, a group of chimpanzees—including Washoe—who have learned American Sign Language were placed together on an island to see if they would use ASL with each other, whether they would learn signs from each other, and whether their skills would be passed on to the next generation (Linden, 1974). In 1980 the project was moved to Central Washington University, where the study of communication between chimpanzees has continued. Roger Fouts and his colleagues have reported that by 1984 Washoe's adopted offspring, Loulis, had learned 28 signs from her mother. By November 1992, the number had reached 78 (R. Fouts, D. Fouts, & D. Schoenfeld, 1984, and R. Fouts, personal communication, November 3, 1992).

FIGURE 10.6   Koko Communicating
Koko, the gorilla made famous by her affection for kittens, has also been taught American Sign Language. Here she is making a sign that indicates the mother in the story is "mad."

In evolutionary terms, chimpanzees and gorillas are our closest living relatives. Perhaps they do have the same basic symbolic capacities as human beings, but the controversy about how closely their communication skills parallel our own continues. The communication skills of these nonhuman primates are tremendously impressive, but whether they can use the "languages" symbolically and not just as systems of meaningful signs remains to be seen. So far none of the primates in these studies have demonstrated that they have Helen Keller's distinctively human insight that *everything* can be given a name.

The Biological Basis of Language

The exceptional human linguistic ability—an ability that has allowed the creation and perpetuation of complex cultures—is made possible by a biologically inherited, specialized set of structures in the brain. The human brain is a complex affair, as yet imperfectly understood. It consists of three major subdivisions: (1) the **brain stem**, which regulates involuntary processes such as breathing and heartbeat and controls basic drives such as hunger; (2) the **cerebellum**, which coordinates muscular activity; and (3) the **cerebral cortex**, the largest and most recently evolved part of the brain, which monitors the senses, controls mental activities, and initiates voluntary activities (see Fig. 10.7).

The cerebral cortex is the area of the brain that analyzes sensory experiences and initiates conscious action. Seen from above, it is divided in half into two major components or hemispheres. Each hemisphere is creased by numerous folds. The specialized language mechanisms of the cerebral cortex are located on only one side of the cerebral cortex—on the left hemisphere for almost all individuals.

Below one of the major creases is **Wernicke's area**, the section of the cortex that receives incoming information about speech sounds. Wernicke's area seems to be the seat of comprehension of speech, of interpreting the meanings of words as well as of formulating verbal messages. Here concepts are apparently translated into their corresponding word representations.

From Wernicke's area, the information is passed on to a larger region of the cerebral cortex called the **association cortex**. It coordinates information from various other parts of the cerebral cortex—such as the hearing centers, the visual centers, and the centers of physical sensation—with the vocal message and provides Wernicke's area with the conceptual information that guides its selection of the appropriate word symbols.

From the association cortex, the linguistic message is sent forward to an area in the front half of the cerebral cortex known as **Broca's area**. There, it organizes the message grammatically and controls information about the sequences of movements necessary for the production of speech. Broca's area is directly in front of an important fold in the cerebral cortex known as the **Fissure of Rolando**, which controls the voluntary movements of various parts of the body. The part of the Fissure of Rolando directly next to Broca's area is the **speech motor area**. This area controls the movement of the vocal cords, tongue, jaws, and lips. Thus, Broca's area seems to be directly in charge of causing this area of the brain to

---

American Sign Language (ASL) a system of hand gesture symbols used by hearing-impaired persons for communicating. Although it is not a verbal system of symbols, ASL may be seen as a true nonverbal language, since it has its own grammar and vocabulary and is not simply a gestural copy of spoken language

brain stem the parts of the brain, except the cerebral hemispheres and cerebellum, that regulate involuntary processes such as breathing and heartbeat

cerebellum the part of the brain below and behind the cerebral hemispheres of the brain that functions in the coordination of muscular activity

cerebral cortex the surface layer of the two large hemispheres of the brain that functions in the analysis of sensory experiences and initiates conscious action

Wernicke's area the part of the cerebral cortex involved in processing speech sounds

association cortex the area of the cerebral cortex that coordinates information from various other parts of the brain

Broca's area the part of the cerebral cortex involved in organizing words into grammatical sequences

Fissure of Rolando a vertical fold in the surface of the brain that separates the motor areas, which control conscious muscle movement, from corresponding areas, which receive sensory informaiton from various parts of the body

speech motor area the part of the cerebral cortex that controls the production of speech sounds

FIGURE 10.7   The Speech Centers of the Human Brain
Without the complex structures in the brain, humans wouldn't have the ability to transform sensory experiences into speech. The speech centers are located in the left hemisphere of the cerebral cortex. Wernicke's area receives speech sounds and interprets them as meaningful. The association cortex coordinates information from other sensory stimuli to allow the brain to select a proper verbal response. Broca's area and the speech motor area control the grammatical sequence of words and the physical movements necessary to produce speech.

move the vocal apparatus in the proper sequences to produce the speech sounds of the message.

There are no *direct* connections between the parts of the association areas that deal with vision, those that pertain to hearing, and those that are related to the motor activities of speech. Lancaster (1968) has pointed out that in monkeys and apes the only way of making these connections involves another region of the brain known as the **limbic system**, which consists of some of the deeper and evolutionarily older areas of the cortex that deal with emotional experience. This may be why vocal communication in the nonhuman primates such as the apes and monkeys is limited to the expression of internal motivational states. In human beings, on the other hand, indirect connections that do not involve the limbic system (and emotion) can be made between the areas of the association cortex, which are connected with the other sensory centers, and the association areas connected to the speech centers (DeVore, 1965). This gives humans the unique ability to withhold vocalizations in moments of emotional excitation and to communicate vocally about facts of

no immediate emotional significance to the speaker, abilities of fundamental importance for symbolic communication.

The Origin of Language

Very little is known about how human language abilities evolved. Unfortunately, spoken language leaves no imprint that can be searched for directly, and humans only began to record language in written form a few thousand years ago. So our investigation of the very beginnings of language must look at indirect evidence. Investigating the fossil record of early human forms for evidence of biological characteristics that are necessary for speaking is one method. Another is determining how people who do not speak the same language have sometimes developed new languages, called creoles.

▬
limbic system   areas within the brain that deal with emotional experience

Biological evolution and language. Clearly, our nearest living relatives, chimpanzees and gorillas, do not use spoken symbols as humans do when speaking. Since it is unlikely that completely sophisticated language skills emerged suddenly, it is commonly assumed that the foundations from which modern languages evolved developed sometime after the separation of the human line from that of the apes about four to six million years ago. Communication among early human ancestors such as the australopithecines of two to four million years ago probably had much in common with nonsymbolic communication in the apes, consisting of vocal calls and gestures. The important question is when and under what circumstances the communication of our ancestors might have taken on the symbolic and, therefore, "open-system" qualities that are characteristic of all modern languages. Some researchers believe that studies of the evolution of the brain and vocal tract may help us pinpoint the transition.

The human brain achieved its modern size among Neanderthals at least 100,000 years ago, and Dean Falk (1975) and Philip Tobias (1983) pointed out that Broca's area was well developed in Neanderthals. Several kinds of archaeological evidence strongly suggest that Neanderthals practiced religious rituals. For instance, at several sites they stored cave bear skulls and leg bones with ceremonial care, and their gravesites indicate carefully prepared burials. Such behavior implies abstract thought and a level of communication that other animals do not demonstrate.

What is not clear, however, is whether Neanderthals' communicative abilities were as sophisticated as human languages are today. Philip Lieberman and E. S. Crelin (1971) studied reconstructions of the Neanderthal vocal tract and found that their throats and mouths were not organized in a way that would have permitted them to produce the sounds found in all modern languages. Jeffrey Laitman (1984) and Lieberman (1984) argue that the modern physical form was not achieved until about 40,000 years ago.

Pidgin and creole languages. There are several situations that bring people together who speak no common language. For instance, in colonial days, masters of plantations might need to communicate with laborers who spoke another language, or in the early days of trading, shipboard life often brought together a crew of many different nationalities who needed to work and communicate together. These and similar situations have given rise to the development of **pidgin languages**, which are simplified versions of one language or a combination of several. Pidgins are simpler in grammar and smaller in vocabulary than are the natural languages that children learn in childhood. However, they have sometimes become the second-generation native languages of entire populations, in which case they invariably develop the greater grammatical sophistication and larger vocabularies that are necessary for use in everyday life. Such true languages that have developed out of pidgins or through the efforts of speakers of several different languages are called **creoles**. There are over a hundred creole languages spoken in the world today. They include Haitian Creole, Hawaiian Creole, São Tomense of Equitorial Guinea, and Srinam of Surinam.

Derek Bickerton (1983) has investigated creoles and has found that they all have a number of characteristics in common. Their grammatical qualities may reflect that of early human language. For instance, in almost all creoles adjectives function as verbs, so there is no need for a "to be" verb to join a subject with an adjective. Thus, in Guyanese Creole "He is tired" is simply "i wiiri." Creoles express future and past tenses by the addition of a particle, such as "shall" or "was" between the subject and the verb, and all have adopted the use of double negatives such as in Papia Kristang "non dag na bait non kyat" (literally, "no dog no bite no cat"), which translates into English as "No dog bit any cat." All creoles also make use of intonation to indicate the difference between questions and statements.

The traits that all creoles have developed may tell us something about the origins of language itself. It was suggested some time ago by the linguist Noam Chomsky (1965) that all natural languages share an underlying grammatical system. Chomsky's views were based on his studies of noncreole languages. He found that certain fundamental grammatical patterns of all languages are variations on a relatively simple, universal system of grammar. This led him to suggest that human children are born with an innate capacity to learn language. According to Bickerton, the notable uniformities among creoles support this idea, and the situations in which creoles emerge make it likely that the basic, innate language patterns are likely to be followed more closely than in languages with

pidgin languages simplified versions of one language or a combination of several
creoles true languages that have developed out of pidgins

longer histories. Thus, in his opinion, the shared grammatical qualities of creoles are likely to be the very ones that were present in the earliest forms of human language.

The Structure of Language

Anthropological linguists who are interested in the structure of languages have shown that all languages have definite patterns in the sounds that their speakers use, in how those sounds are combined to form symbols, and in how those symbols are organized into meaningful utterances. These three structured parts of language are called phonology, morphology, and syntax.

Phonology

The study of sounds used in speech and the rules for producing the sequences of sounds that occur in a particular language is called phonology. The human vocal apparatus is capable of forming a large number of different sounds but the range of sounds actually produced in human languages is relatively small. Although there are at least 3,000 languages in the world, it is possible to record any human language using the International Phonetic Alphabet, which consists of fewer than 100 sound symbols.

The description of a specific language begins by using some of the symbols of this alphabet to record the phones, sounds made by speakers of the language. This record is called a phonetic description of the language. A phonetic transcription of a language records more sound detail than would seem necessary to native speakers. A simple phonetic transcription of verse from the well-known English poem, "The Walrus and the Carpenter" by Lewis Carroll, looks like this:

ðə tʰãym hæz kʰʌ̃m
ðə wɔlrʌs sɛd
tʰu tʰɔk əv mẽni θĩŋz
əv šuz ænd šɪps
ænd silĩŋ wæks
əv kʰæbəjəz ænd kʰĩŋz
ænd way ðə si ɪz bɔylĩŋ hat
ænd wɛðər pʰɪgz hæv wĩŋz.

It is difficult to read a phonetic transcription of one's native language without practice, because it records more information than is needed by fluent speakers who are unconscious of many of the predictable sound patterns in their speech. In every language, some of the phonetically recorded sounds are not meaningfully distinct from one another. Instead, they are simply variants, or allophones, of a more general sound called a phoneme of that language. For instance, a native English speaker is likely to say that the letter *t* in the words "top" and "stop" are the same sound. In fact, this is not the case. In the first word the pronunciation of the *t* ends with a definite explosion of air that is not present following the *t* in the second word. This difference can be demonstrated by pronouncing each word while holding the end of a strip of paper against the upper lip. The paper will flutter only when the word "top" is pronounced.

Once it is determined how the phones of a language are grouped into phonemes, it is possible to record the language phonemically, using a smaller alphabet designed especially for that language. A phonemic alphabet is made by using only one symbol for each phoneme of the language. The phonemes of such alphabets are the smallest meaningful units of sound in a language; substituting one phoneme for another can change the meaning of a word. Thus, if the word *stop* is pronounced so that the *t* is followed by the explosion of air found in its allophone in the word *top*, the word will still be heard by listeners as *stop*. However, substituting the phoneme *l* for *t* will create a different word, "slop."

---

phonology the study of the rules that govern the production and the organization of the sounds of a particular language

International Phonetic Alphabet (IPA) a standard alphabet of nearly 100 sound symbols used by linguists throughout the world for writing phonetic transcriptions of languages

phones smallest sound units of a language

phonetic description descriptions pertaining to the smallest units of sound actually produced by speakers of a language. A phonetic transcription attempts to record all of the sounds consistently produced by the speakers of a language

allophones phonetically variant forms of a single phoneme

phonemic alphabet a written record of a speech that uses an alphabet composed of only one symbol for each phoneme of the language

phoneme the smallest psychologically real unit of sound in a language

A phonemic alphabet records the distinctions in sounds that are psychologically relevant to the native speakers of a language, so it spells words the way they seem to sound to native speakers. In a phonemic transcription of spoken English, the word *hiss* would be written as *his,* and the word *his* would be written as *hiz.* Typically, only between 20 and 45 phonemes are necessary for writing a language. English, for instance, has 45 phonemically distinct sounds. Since the 26-letter alphabet used by English speakers for writing their language is not phonemically accurate, English speakers must learn a complex system of spelling to decipher the conventions they use in writing their language.

Grammar

The analysis of the regular and predictable ways that the sounds of a language are combined to form meaningful utterances is called **grammar**. It has two subdivisions, morphology and syntax.

Morphology. The first of these, **morphology**, is the study of how phonemes are combined into the smallest meaningful units, called **morphemes**. *Alligator, love,* and *Arkansas* are **free morphemes** because they can stand alone as words in sentences. English morphemes such as *-s,* meaning "plural," and *pre-,* meaning "before," are called **bound morphemes** because they cannot serve as words in sentences. Bound morphemes only occur as suffixes or prefixes of other morphemes. Sometimes several morphemes carry the same meaning; for instance *-s,* *-z* (written as an *s* in English), *-en,* and *-ren* all mean "plural." Such morphemes are considered variants of one another, since it is predictable which will be chosen by English speakers to pluralize another morpheme. Thus, *child* combines acceptably only with the plural morpheme *-ren.* Morphemes that carry the same meaning in this way are called **allomorphs** of one another.

Syntax. The second subdivision of grammar is **syntax**. It is the study of the rules for combining morphemes into complete and meaningful sentences. All languages do an adequate job of expressing meanings, but each language has its own distinctive rules that control how one goes about expressing those meanings. Although we each find the conventions of our own language quite natural, seeing how differently other languages operate can give us some idea of the fact that what seems natural to us as native speakers is merely one of many possible conventions.

Languages such as English use word order to indicate differences between the actor and the acted-upon. For instance, there is an important difference of meaning between the two English sentences, *The dog bit the child,* and *The child bit the dog.* In many languages, the distinction between subject and object is instead indicated by subject and/or object suffixes. For instance, in the Latin sentence *Canis infant-em momordit* (literally, "Dog child-object bit"), the suffix *-em* indicates the object. Languages that distinguish subjects and objects in this way can become quite free in their word order. Thus, in Latin *Infant-em momordit canis* also could be used to mean "The dog bit the child." Often, in languages that do not rely on order to indicate subject-object relations, differences in order may convey differences in emphasis. In the two Latin sentences just used, the first might be translated as "The *dog* bit the child," while the second would be "The dog bit the *child*." Some languages have special ways of marking an emphasized word. For instance, in the Andean language Quechua the bound morpheme *-qa* indicates the emphasized topic of a sentence: *Alqu wawa-ta-qa k"ani-rqa* (literally, "dog child-object-topic bite-past"), which might be translated as "The dog bit *the child*," but *Alqu-qa wawa-ta k"ani-rqa* would be "*The dog* bit the child."

Quechua greatly elaborates the process of modifying single words with suffixes to express complex meanings. Thus, the two-word Quechua sentence *Mana kasu-wa-na-yki-chiq-ri-chu* (literally, "Not obey-me-for-you-plural-nicely-question") means "Is it not for you to obey me nicely?" Other languages such as Chinese use but one morpheme per word, so that the Chinese equivalent of "The dog bit

---

grammar the analysis of the regular ways that the sounds of a language are combined to form meaningful utterances. Grammar includes morphology and syntax

morphology the study of how phonemes are combined into the smallest meaningful units of a language

morpheme the smallest meaningful sequence of sounds in a language

free morphemes can stand alone as words in sentences

bound morphemes morphemes that can't stand as complete words

allomorphs variants of a single morpheme that have the same meaning but different phonological structure

syntax the study of the rules for combining morphemes into complete and meaningful sentences the boy" would be *Gǒ yǎo le shǎohái* (literally, "Dog child bite completed"), the time of the action being specified by a particular word *le* that indicates that the action of the verb *yǎo* is completed.

The many languages of the world differ tremendously in their phonologies and grammars. Despite the great diversity in how languages organize a small number of sounds into meaningful sentences, all languages seem equally able to express ideas. As natural as your own language may seem to you after years of use, it is no more fundamentally human in its workings than others. Like all symbolic systems, languages convey meanings effectively simply because their users have learned the same conventions for interpreting those meanings.

Linguistic Relativity

Any idea can be symbolically expressed in any language. Nevertheless, the vocabulary and grammatical variations of different languages do have an impact on (1) which things speakers habitually notice, label, and think about, and (2) how speakers will ordinarily organize their expression of the relationships between these things (Sapir, 1949). The idea that language influences thought processes is expressed in the theory of **linguistic relativity**, sometimes called the "Sapir-Whorf hypothesis" after two of its originators. According to linguistic relativity, what a people habitually think about is a reflection of what the current vocabulary of their language encourages them to notice, and at least some aspects of how people think will be affected by the grammatical relationships demanded by their language. Most anthropological linguists today agree that linguistic relativity should not be understood to mean that language structure *determines* how we think, but that language does have some effect on what we think about most readily and on how we think much of the time.

Effects of Morphology

Benjamin Lee Whorf was an originator of the idea that the superficial and arbitrary grammatical patterns that distinguish one language from another influence the ways in which its speakers habitually think about the world. His strongest case is for the effect that the morphology of a language can have on its speakers' tendency to notice some things readily while failing to pay attention to others. For example, Whorf (1971a) pointed out that one place in which industrial fires frequently begin is the room in which so-called "empty" containers are stored. The word *empty* is a symbol that refers to two somewhat different concepts: It is used to mean (1) "containing only residues, gases, vapor, or stray rubbish," and also, in a more basic sense, to mean (2) "vacuous, inert, or containing nothing." Managers who label the room as a storage area for "empty containers" understand the word in its more specialized association with the first concept; workers are likely to behave around these containers of sometimes volatile residues and gases as if they were inert and vacuous. A worker, for example, who would never consider lighting a cigarette near a "full" gasoline drum might casually do so near an "empty" one, never stopping to think that the volatile gasoline fumes that remain in the empty containers are much more likely to ignite explosively than is the liquid gasoline of the full containers. According to Whorf, the use of a single symbol that represents two different concepts is not uncommon in hazardous situations.

Whorf (1971b) argued that people's names for things often influence how they behave around those things even more than the physical traits of the things themselves. He cited the blower as an example. Physically, a fan is a machine that simply causes air to move. Yet when it is used to make air pass through a room—such as a room for drying materials—because it is called a *blower*, workers are likely to install it so that it *blows* air into the room instead of *pulling* air out of it. The former method of installation is no more efficient and is much more hazardous than the latter, since an electrical fire in the machine itself will be blown into the room. Once begun, the fire will be fanned by a blower installed in this way as long as it continues to function.

Sometimes labels are changed in the hope of avoiding undesirable conditioned responses or of calling forth some hoped-for result. Thus, unpopular wars are called "pacification programs," and the American War Department was renamed the "Defense Department." Similarly, tuna did not become a popular food in the United States until one company began to label it "Chicken of the Sea." And those who wished to support what they called more work-

---

linguistic relativity the idea that the characteristics of a language influence the way that its speakers think able "legal controls" over drug use or prostitution soon recognized that it was better to use such labels for their legislative proposals than to refer to them as attempts to "legalize" these activities. Western science provides a further example of the conditioning effects of verbal symbolic labels: European scientists noted that when they "added heat" to an object, its weight did not change. So for years they searched for evidence of other "weightless substances" before they realized that heat, even though it is labeled by a noun, is actually a process rather than a substance.

Effects of Syntax

Syntactical processes may also affect how speakers of a language think about the world and how they behave, although the influence of syntax is probably not so great as the effects of morphology. One finds numerous examples of correlations between a society's customs and values and the grammatical characteristics of its language. For instance, the Navajo language is highly verb-oriented; even inactive verbs have a structure that implies a state achieved by motion. The language describes the universe as kinds of motion to which subjects may attach themselves but for which they are not responsible. This feature parallels perfectly the Navajo world view, in which the universe is seen as being in a state of dynamic flux and humans as subordinate to a more powerful nature. Similarly, in the Navajo language, it is ungrammatical to use a verb meaning "to cause to do" with a human object. The closest Navajo translation of "I made him go home" would run something like "Even though he did not want to go home, when I asked him to, he did." This is in perfect parallel to Navajo social values, in which coercion is strongly rejected.

Rom Harré (1984) cites examples of Inuit grammar that parallel Inuit ideology. If the Inuit respond to the question "Who is preparing dinner?" their answer, *uva-nga*, does not translate as "I am" but as "The being here-mine." The English "I hear him" becomes in Inuit *tusarp-a-ra*, literally, "his making of a sound with reference to me." In general, where English grammar portrays a person as an "entity" who has attributes and intentions and who intiates actions, Inuit designates a person as the "location" at which qualities and relations occur. This characteristic of Inuit grammar mirrors and supports Inuit social life, in which one's position within the group is much more important than one's

characteristics as an individual. Responsiveness to others is the hallmark of Inuit social interaction: When one laughs, all laugh; when one cries, everyone cries. According to Harré, "At least with respect to a large and varied catalogue of public performances, individual feelings, intentions, and reasonings play a very minor role" (p. 88).

Such parallels between syntax and culture are best viewed as systems like that of the chicken and its egg: It is not clear which came first. Syntax may change to reflect the culture in which the language is spoken, but the habits of thought embodied in that syntax may help to maintain conformity to the rules of the culture by making those rules feel very natural to those who speak the language.

Language, then, seems to have an effect on the way people relate to the world. It is a conscious vehicle of habitual thought. The vocabulary of any language selects segments of reality that its speakers must become aware of when they learn to use their language. And the grammar is a built-in logic system that leads its users to relate the parts of the world to one another in the same way that the grammar organizes the relationships between the words that stand for those parts of the world.

Changes in Language

Since languages are symbol systems, they are highly susceptible to change. Language change may occur as the language is passed, by learning, from one generation to the next. A language may also change as its speakers are influenced by their interaction with speakers of other languages. In the following sections, these processes of linguistic change will be described in detail.

Changes Over Time

Since the sounds used to form the verbal symbols of a language have no necessary connection with the meanings of those symbols, it is possible for both the sounds and the meanings attached to them to change as time passes. Likewise, the customary ways of organizing the verbal symbols into meaningful word order to communicate relationships between the concepts may also change as time passes. Thus, with the passage of time, languages may change in their sound system, their semantic or meaning system, and in their grammatical system. Consider for instance, the differences between contemporary versions of the Lord's Prayer and this Old English version written in the ninth century:

Faeder ūre, thū the eart on heofonum, sī thīn nama gehālgod. Tobecum thīn rīce, Gewurthe thīn willa on eorthan swā swā on heofonum. Urne gedaeghwāmlīcan hlāf syle ūs to daeg. And forgyf ūs ūre gyltas, swā swā wē forgyfath urum gyltendum. And ne gelaed thū ūs on costnunge, ac ālys ūs of yfele. Sōthlīce.[1]

Since language change involves the systems that comprise it, changes occur in systematic or patterned ways. For instance, the change of one sound to a new one expresses itself in every word of the language in which that sound occurs. Compare a list of Old English words of about 1,000 years ago with their modern English equivalents:

Old English	Modern English
hus	house
mus	mouse
ut	out
hu	how

In this list, the Old English *u* represents a sound that would be pronounced approximately as *uw*. Consistently, these same words are pronounced today by English speakers as the vowel sequence *ao*, variously written as *ou* or *ow* in contemporary spelling. That is, the Old English sound *uw* became *ao* in Modern English, consistently changing the pronunciation of all English words in which it occurs.

Dialects

Such changes in language occur gradually with the passage of time. Yet, at any given time, the need to communicate effectively within a social group necessitates a certain degree of mutual sharing in the sounds used to form words, in the meanings of words, and in the grammatical patterns for combining them. So a language changes in the same way for all members of the group. However, when a group is subdivided, either geographically or socially, the members of each group tend to communicate more frequently with each other than with others. One

1. From *Old English: An Introduction* (p. 19) by Robert J. Kispert, 1971. New York: Holt, Rinehart & Winston. Copyright 1971.

result of such isolation is that new ways of speaking that arise in one of the groups may not necessarily pass over into the others. Thus, the language originally spoken in all these groups can gradually change until it is made up of separate **dialects**, mutually intelligible variants of the same language that are shared by different social groups. For instance, the English now spoken in Great Britain differs from the varieties of English spoken in the United States and Australia, although all three varieties developed from the same language that was spoken but a few hundred years ago by emigrants from Great Britain.

dialect a geographical or social subdivision of a language that differs systematically from other such subdivisions of the same language in its vocabulary, grammar, and phonology

Black English Vernacular the everyday speech patterns of African Americans studied in urban centers

Standard English the dialect taught in U.S. schools and used by most people in the United States at least on formal occasions

---

Black English Vernacular

William Labov (1972) studied the everyday speech of African Americans in Philadelphia, New York, and other urban centers in the United States, and recorded the patterns of an English dialect technically called Black English Vernacular or BEV. It differs in several ways from Standard English, the dialect taught in U.S. schools, and used by most people in the United States at least on formal occasions.

One notable difference is the common omission in Black English of forms of "to be." This rule allows a statement such as "You are fast" to be expressed more succinctly as "You fast." Although this deletion of "to be" is not used in Standard American English, it is not at all unusual. For instance, subject and predicate complements are not joined by a "to be" verb in Russian, Hungarian, or Arabic. Black English Vernacular also makes use of various forms of the double negative. For instance, Standard English "There wasn't much I could do" becomes "Wasn't much I couldn't do" in BEV, "When it rained, nobody knew it did" becomes "When it rained, nobody don't know it didn't," and "No cop ever beat me" becomes "Ain't no cop never beat me."

According to Labov, Black English Vernacular is a dialect "that is more different from most other English dialects than they are from each other" (1972, p. 36). However, like any other dialect, most of its grammatical rules are those shared by all dialects of English. Its difference from Standard English is one of degree, not kind.

———

Dialects of the same original language can gradually become so different that their speakers are no longer able to understand one another. English and German are two examples that were at one time in history a single language. Called **Proto-Germanic** by modern students of language, it was spoken on the mainland of Europe in what is now northern Germany by people known as the Angles and Saxons. They left the mainland about 1,500 to 2,000 years ago to become a separate social group in the British Isles, where their isolation allowed the language to change in different ways than it did on the mainland. Since the process of change was systematic in both groups, one finds a system of consistent parallels between the two "daughter" languages, German and English. Compare, for instance, the initial sound of the following word lists from German and English, and notice that the German *z* (written as upper case *Z* in the case of nouns), which is pronounced *ts*, is consistently a *t* sound in English:

German	English
zu	to
zwanzig	twenty
zwölf	twelve
zwitschern	twitter
Zinn	tin

Word-Borrowing

Change in language also occurs when words are borrowed by the speakers of one language from other languages with which they come in contact, especially those spoken by their politically and economically more powerful neighbors. For instance, following the Norman invasion of England in 1066, English speakers began to be influenced by the Old French language of the more powerful Normans. Today, about half of the vocabulary of the English language traces its origins to borrowed Old French words. Approximately two and one half centuries

after the invasion, an early historian, Robert of Gloucester (1300), described in his *Chronicle* the effects of the language of the Norman rulers on English:

Thus cōm, lọ, Engelọnd intō Normandïes họnd;
And thē Normans ne cōūthe spẹ̄ke thọ bote hor owe spẹ̄che, And spẹ̄ke French as hii düde at họm, and hor children düde alsọ tẹ̄che,
Sọ that heie men of this lọnd that of hor blōd cōme Họldeth alle thülke spẹ̄che that hii of hom nọme;
Vor bote a man conne Frenss me teleth of him lüte.
Ac lowe men họldeth tō Engliss, and tō hor owe spẹ̄che zhüte. [2]

(Lo, thus England came into Normandy's hand; and the Normans speak nothing but their own speech, and spoke French as they did at home, and did so teach their children,
So that high men of this land that came of their blood Hold the same speech that they received of them; For except a man knows French men speak little of him. But low men hold to English, and to their own speech yet.)

Those English speakers who had the most contact with the Norman rulers began to adopt Old French terms for elements of Norman life. The speech of the English commoners, because they had much less contact with the Norman rulers, was less influenced. For instance, contemporary English has inherited a distinction between the cooked and live forms of several meat animals. *Mutton*, *pork*, and *beef* were adopted into English from Old French (*moton*, *porc*, and *boef*) for use when serving foods to the Norman rulers. When the animals were still alive and in the keeping of the English peasants, they were called by their original English names, *sheep*, *swine*, and *cow*. These latter three terms have their counterparts, not in French, but in the German words *Schaf*, *Swein*, and *Kuh*, a derivation that reflects the recent separation of English and German from a common ancestral language. Similarly, the word *roast* represents a borrowing from Old French—*rostir*, a verb used by cooks when speaking about preparing meat for their Norman rulers. This aristocratic term did not, however, replace the original

2. From *A Middle English Reader* (p. 210) by Oliver Farrar Emerson, 1923. New York: Macmillan. Copyright 1923.

———

Proto-Germanic English and German that were at one time the same original language

English word *bake*, which continued to be used in the peasant households for the same method of preparing meat, but became an alternative term for essentially the same procedure. *Bake* itself stems from the same original word as the German word *backen*, which means "to bake or roast." Notice that in modern English, one still "roasts pork" (both words being of Old French origin) or "bakes ham" (both Germanic words). Although the foods themselves and the cooking procedures may be identical, the two idioms reflect two socially different speech contexts (Leaf, 1971).

Basic Vocabulary

The tenacity of these Germanic words for things that were important in households suggests that domestic terminology may be somewhat more stable and resistant to externally induced language change than are other parts of a vocabulary. The part of a language that best reflects its internal history consists of those words that are learned by individuals early in their lives in their home setting. Such words are used frequently in normal speech situations. The habit of their use is not easily overcome, and foreign terms are not likely to supplant them (Gudschinsky, 1964). The part of a vocabulary that has these qualities is known as the **basic vocabulary** of a language. It includes such words as *father, mother, brother, sister, head, hand, foot, eat, water, drink, fire, house, earth, sky, sun, moon, star,* and others that designate basic elements of people's social, biological, and physical environments.

By comparing the basic vocabularies of two languages, it is possible to determine whether they developed from the same common ancestral language, proof that may not be evident in comparing the entire contemporary vocabularies of the languages. For instance, the fact that over 50 percent of the entire English vocabulary is derived from French does not indicate that both languages arose recently from a common ancestral language. This distinction becomes clear only when one examines the English basic vocabulary. In this more stable part of the vocabulary, English words generally have their closest counterparts not in French but in the Germanic languages spoken in the region from which the Anglo-Saxon immigrants to England originally came. This common origin of English and German is illustrated by the following basic vocabulary lists:

English	German
father	Vater
mother	Mutter
brother	Bruder
sister	Schwester
hand	Hand
house	Haus
mouse	Maus
water	Wasser
sun	Sonne
moon	Mond
fire	Feuer

Language Families

Such lists of basic vocabulary terms make it possible to compare how many of these items the languages share. It is assumed that the more of these stable items two languages have in common, the more recently they began diverging from a single parent language to become separate languages in their own right. Using this assumption, it is possible to reconstruct a family tree of related languages such as the one that compares the languages of northern Europe in Figure 10.8 on page 238. The branches on this language family tree correspond to major historical occurrences in the societies that led to the separation of the speakers of the original language into separate subdivisions. Thus, the point where Old English separates from the other branches that arose from Proto-Germanic reflects the migration of the Anglo-Saxons from the northern German coast to the British Isles about A.D. 500. After this time the islanders were no longer in intense enough communication with their mainland counterparts to maintain a language unity. This family of languages diverged from a single common ancestral language, called **Proto-Indo-European** by linguists today. It was spoken almost 5,000 years ago. The languages of other parts of the world also have been grouped into similar language families.

---

basic vocabulary   the part of a vocabulary that one learns early in life in the home setting

Proto-Indo-European   the ancestral language from which most of the contemporary languages of Europe, Iran, and India have developed

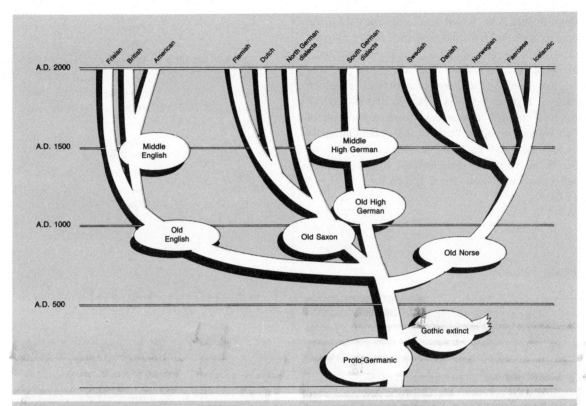

FIGURE 10.8   The Family Tree of Northern European Languages
The root or parent language of Northern European languages is called Proto-Germanic. It in turn is derived from an earlier Proto-Indo-European base, the ancestor of many languages in India as well as Europe.

Glottochronology

A method was developed by Morris Swadesh and Dorothy Lee in the 1950s to estimate the minimum number of years since the divergence of any two related languages. **Glottochronology** makes it possible to assign dates to the various branches in a language family tree. By comparing the basic vocabularies of languages that belong to different language families and have had long written histories, researchers discovered that about 14 percent of a 100-word basic vocabulary was replaced by new words every 1,000 years in all the languages that have been examined in nonisolated societies (Gudschinsky, 1956). Thus, the rate of change in the basic vocabulary, being a constant, can be used to compute the length of time that two languages have been diverging from one another. Since about 14 percent of the basic vocabulary of a parent language will be lost in any daughter language after 1,000 years of change

from that original state, each daughter language will maintain 86 percent of the original vocabulary. Consequently, if one compares lists of 100 basic vocabulary items for two contemporary languages and discovers that they share about 74 basic vocabulary items (86 percent of 86 items), then one may calculate that they were in fact a single language 1,000 years ago. Two languages will share about 55 (74 percent of 74) of the original 100 basic vocabulary items after 2,000 years of separation and about 41 items (74 percent of 55) after 3,000 years of separation (see Figure 10.9).

glottochronology   a technique for calculating the minimal length of time that two related languages have been diverging from a common ancestral language

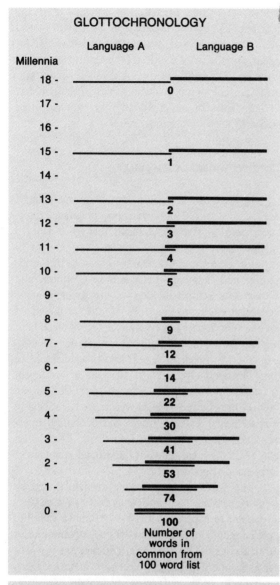

FIGURE 10.9 Glottochronological Change

Human vocabulary shares a common ancestral language or protolanguage. After a period of one thousand years any given language will replace 14 percent of its original vocabulary with new terms. This chart graphically portrays the divergence of languages over a period of time.

Contemporary World Languages

Most estimates indicate that there are at least 3,000 languages spoken in the world today; some estimates indicate there are nearer 5,000. The exact number is difficult to determine because the dialects that make up a language can be very similar to one another, or so distinct that two linguists might not agree on whether they should be called dialects or separate languages. Consider German and Dutch. Although speakers of Bavarian German dialects would be unable to comprehend the dialect spoken in a German village in Schleswig-Holstein near the border of Denmark, the change from one local dialect to the next is too gradual to claim that there is more than one German language in the country. Similarly, the dialects spoken in small towns on either side of the German and Dutch borders may be so similar that the inhabitants of both towns can understand one another. Yet people speak of German and Dutch as if they were separate languages. In fact, some southern German dialects differ more from the nationally preferred way of speaking the modern standard German "language" (which is mostly based on northern German dialects) than some northern dialects in Germany differ from Dutch.

Some languages are spoken by relatively few native speakers. For instance, only a few thousand people speak Shoshoni today. On the other hand, some languages are spoken by many societies with very different cultures. Such languages may cross the borders of modern nation-states and be spoken by millions of people. For instance, English is one of the official languages of India as well as the native tongue of peoples as geographically distant from one another as England, Canada, South Africa, the Falkland Islands, and Jamaica.

The languages spoken by the largest numbers of people today are those that have become the national languages of major nations. The Beijing dialect (formerly called Mandarin) of China is spoken by about 885 million people. English is the next most commonly spoken language of the world, with about 450 million speakers.

In some parts of the world, many different languages are spoken by people who differ relatively little in their culture. Canada maintains two nationally recognized languages, French and English; political speeches and advertising must be carried out in both. In Nigeria about 400 languages are spoken, of which only 3 have been designated as official languages. Such a diversity of spoken languages can create enormous political problems in administering governmental affairs throughout the country. The elevation of one or more languages to official status is intended to alleviate some of these problems. Since government business is largely conducted in an official language, speakers of other languages are expected to learn one of the official languages or find an interpreter when they wish to deal with government administrators. Where national languages exist, they are likely to be the ones used in the school system, with the idea that all citizens should learn to use the national language. Although the selection of one of a society's languages as an official one may simplify some of the problems of governing a linguistically diverse country, the designation of an official language is not without its problems. For instance, speakers of a nonofficial language may find themselves at a political or economic disadvantage compared with others who speak the national language. Such circumstances can lead to political rivalries and conflicts that are difficult to resolve.

Language Politics

Language can reflect political differences or acquire political significance as people from different geographical or cultural areas interact. Two examples of the politics of language are judgments about the acceptability of a dialect or language and the use of language as a symbol of nationalism.

Prestige Dialects

Since different social groups often speak different dialects, inability to speak the dialect of a society's elite may become a means of identifying those who do not belong to the elite, and thus of discrimination. According to Pierre Bourdieu (1982, 1984), speaking the dialect of the politically powerful or of the wealthy class can become a necessary skill for those who wish to participate within these areas of social life. So the dialects of such groups sometimes take on the reputation of being superior to others. Dialects with a reputation of being inherently better than others are called **prestige dialects**.

Prestige dialects are a phenomenon of socially stratified societies such as chiefdoms and states in which social ranking is used to distinguish the power and influence of different groups. Thus, foraging societies such as the Great Basin Shoshoni lacked prestige dialects, but they are common in the world's contemporary nation states. In countries that have one traditionally accepted prestige dialect, it is often one of those spoken in the capital city. In France, it was a dialect of Paris that became the national

standard of "good French." In England it is the dialect spoken by the monarch. In the United States, where the capital was created as a district unconnected with the prior politics of the several states, the nationally preferred dialect taught in the school system is not one of any particular part of the country, but somewhat of an amalgam that is most often spoken by television newscasters.

Language and Nationalism

In contemporary countries that are made up of peoples who speak more than one language, intergroup politics similar to those that give rise to prestige dialects influence language preferences in the political arena. In Canada, for instance, English is the dominant language used for most economic and political transactions in most of the country, while French plays a similar role in the province of Quebec. The country as a whole has recognized both languages as "official" national tongues for the conduct of government business, and products sold in stores throughout the country carry labels that repeat the same information in French and English. In Quebec, the one province in which French-speaking citizens have greater political and economic influence over English-speaking Canadians, French has been given the legal status of the official language of the provincial government.

The political loyalties that are symbolized by preference for one language or another can be powerful enough to express themselves in public hostility between members of different language communities within a country. For instance, competition between native French and English speakers in Canada has erupted into open conflict on more than one occasion, and has been the basis for a secessionist movement within Quebec aimed at founding a separate, French-speaking country in North America. Language as a political rallying point of this kind is not unique to Canada. For instance, the Basque separatist movement in Spain and France has had a long history of armed conflict involving specific language-speaking groups. And in the United States during times of great immigration by non-English-speaking people, there have been two recurring political issues: whether English should be legally declared the country's national language and which language should be used to teach immigrant children in school.

prestige dialects dialects with the reputation of being inherently better than others

CHAPTER SUMMARY

1. The basis for the complexity of human cultures is our ability to form and communicate concepts.

2. Signs are communications that express our feelings directly.

3. Symbols are forms of communication in which one thing is arbitrarily used to represent another, according to socially agreed-on and learned conventions.

4. Human communication is highly symbolic and therefore extremely flexible.

5. While some nonverbal messages such as our gestures, facial expressions, body language, and distances from each other are spontaneous signs of our emotions, even nonverbal communications may be symbolic.

6. Verbal communication—language—is totally symbolic, for speech sounds, written words, and ways of arranging them are uniquely and arbitrarily assigned symbolic meanings within each culture.

7. The capacity for creating and using complex language systems seems to reside within certain areas of the human cerebral cortex.

8. Some nonhuman primates may have similar, though more limited, language capacities as humans, but do not use them unless they are carefully taught to do so.

9. Languages and cultures are so closely linked that the forms and patterns of our speech both affect and reflect how we perceive the world.

10. Languages, like their cultures, change over time with influences from other cultures and their languages.

11. The part of a language that is most resistant to change is its basic vocabulary, which consists of household words taught and used from childhood.

12. Differences and similarities in basic vocabularies allow linguists to trace the historical growth of language families into the many languages and dialects spoken in the world today.

ANNOTATED READINGS

Abu-Lughod, L. (1986). *Veiled sentiments: Honor and poetry in a Bedouin society.* Berkeley: University of California Press. Discusses the uses of Arabic poetry among Egyptian Bedouins.

Appel, R., & Muysken, P. (1987). *Language contact and bilingualism.* London: Edward Arnold. Examines what happens when different languages interact.

Bourdieu, P. (1984). *Distinction: A social critique of the judgment of taste,* trans. R. Nice. Cambridge: Harvard University Press. Discusses the politics of language and the role of language as a source of access to economic and social benefits.

Birdwhistell, R. L. (1970). *Kinesics and context: Essays on body motion communication.* Philadelphia: University of Pennsylvania Press. An exposition of the techniques used for analyzing body movement in nonverbal communication.

Carroll, J. B. (1956). *Language, thought and reality: Selected writings of Benjamin Lee Whorf.* Cambridge, MA: M.I.T. Press. The primary writings of Whorf on the effects of language on thought and action.

Greenberg, J. H. (1968). *Anthropological linguistics: An introduction.* New York: Random House. A good nontechnical introduction to anthropological linguistics.

Hall, E. T. (1959). *The silent language.* Greenwich, CT:

Fawcett Publications. An interesting look at the rules for nonverbal communications in a variety of cultures.

Labov, W. (1972). *Language in the inner city: Studies in the Black English Vernacular.* Philadelphia: University of Pennsylvania Press. The classic investigation of Black Vernacular English that destroyed the myth of the natural superiority of Standard English.

Lakeoff, R. (1975). *Language and women's place.* NY: Harper & Row. A examination of gender differences in language and its social implications.

Lenneberg, E. H. (1967). *The biological foundations of language.* New York: Wiley. The basic text on the biological basis of speech.

Lieberman, P. (1984). *The biology and evolution of language.* Cambridge, MA: Harvard University Press. Examines the fossil evidence for the origin of language.

Mandelbaum, D. G. (1968). *Selected writings of Edward Sapir in language, culture and personality.* Berkeley, CA: University of California Press. A well-chosen collection of the classic writings of the father of American anthropological linguistics.

Trudgill, P. (1983). *Sociolinguistics: An introduction to language and society,* rev. ed. NY: Penguin. A short introduction to the various roles that language plays in social relationships, including gender, class, and ethnicity.

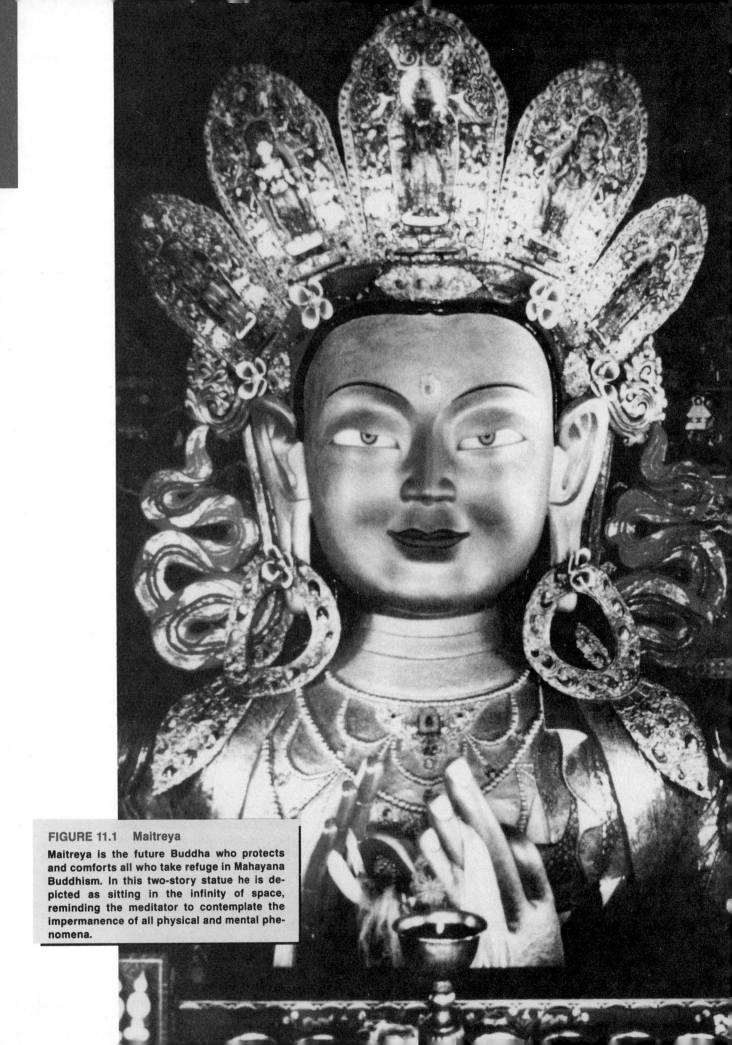

FIGURE 11.1 Maitreya

Maitreya is the future Buddha who protects
and comforts all who take refuge in Mahayana
Buddhism. In this two-story statue he is depicted as sitting in the infinity of space,
reminding the meditator to contemplate the
impermanence of all physical and mental phenomena.

CHAPTER 11

Religion is an organized system of shared supernatural beliefs that gives meaning to perplexing parts of human society and its environment, and a system of rituals by which human beings strive for greater control over themselves and their social and natural environments. Psychologically, the beliefs and rituals of a particular religion symbolically express the kinds of stresses and anxieties that are common among the members of that society. In this chapter we will examine both the psychological and the social aspects of religion.

Religion

CHAPTER OBJECTIVES

After reading this chapter, you should be able to:

Critique the various definitions of religion that have been proposed in the history of anthropology.

Analyze the ways in which people conceive of the supernatural and their relationship to it.

Discuss the relationship between religion and practical aspects of human survival and cultural adaptation.

Define the structure and diversity of religious ideology.

Exemplify relationships between religious ideologies and social organization.

Analyze the nature and functions of ritual in religion.

Explain the different forms of religious social organization.

Discuss the social and psychological functions of religion.

Analyze the cognitive characteristics of religious thought.

Describe the revitalization movement in religion.

Ghosts. Demons. Angels. Witches. Buddha. Shaman. Christ. Do you whistle in the dark as one way of dealing with the unknown silence? Do you sleep with a night-light? Do you avoid stepping on cracks in the sidewalk or walking under ladders? Do you light candles to ward off the demons of darkness in your soul or your world? Every culture has evolved a system of symbolic beliefs and rituals that it uses to define its place in the universe.

The Definition of Religion

Religious beliefs and rituals take so many forms across the world that anthropologists have found it difficult to define religion in a way that encompasses them all. They have agreed, however, that the major characteristics of a global definition of religion include belief in supernatural beings and supernatural power, symbolic expression of feelings, and rituals performed both individually and in groups for the purpose of positively influencing the supernatural powers.

Belief in the Supernatural

Religious beliefs differ from the ordinary day-to-day beliefs that grow out of a mechanistic view of things. Religious beliefs portray the world supernaturally rather than scientifically. They postulate a world of humanlike beings and powers: Gods, angels, demons, ghosts, or forces that respond to rituals and other symbolic acts and that inspire special feelings, such as awe and dread. Anthropologists have attempted to explain the emotionally powerful supernatural beliefs and symbolic rituals of religion in various ways. Their different approaches to analyzing religion have led to a variety of different but complementary definitions.

Belief in supernatural beings. Sir Edward Burnett Tylor (1871), a nineteenth-century Victorian scholar, provided one of the first anthropological definitions of religion: a belief in supernatural beings such as the soul, ghosts, spirits, and gods. According to Tylor, religion functions to provide human beings with explanations of perplexing phenomena such as unconsciousness, sleep, dreams, and hallucinations. Early humans, Tylor contended, created the idea of the soul to account for such phenomena. Unconsciousness, fainting, sleep, and even death could be explained as the soul's departure from the body; dreams could be memories of the soul's experiences as it travels outside the body during sleep; and visions or hallucinations could be simply apparitions of souls and other spirit beings. The idea of the soul also implied the possibility of other spiritual entities such as ghosts, genies, angels, and gods.

Although Tylor's views were useful in pointing out the role that religion plays in providing people with ways of understanding the experiences for which they have no pragmatic explanations, his perspective was narrow. For Tylor, religion was a product of the human intellect; its relationship to emotional life was unimportant.

Belief in supernatural power. An even greater limitation of Tylor's definition was its ethnocentric narrowness in excluding from the realm of religion the belief in formless supernatural powers. Robert Marett (1909) raised this criticism of Tylor and introduced the Melanesian word *mana* to refer to the concept of spiritual power. Mana, which might be thought of as a kind of supernatural electricity, may reside in objects such as a rabbit's foot, a four-leaf clover, in powerful natural phenomena such as thunderstorms, or in anything strange, rare, or dangerous. In doses too large, it can cause harm, illness, or even death, but properly channeled it can be used by human beings to accomplish ends that are unattainable by other means. Mana can increase one's luck, skill, and ability to gain knowledge of hidden things. It is the force behind magic; it is the holiness

religion belief in supernatural power, symbolic expression of feelings, and rituals performed in order to influence the nonhuman realm

mana supernatural power or force

in the ground around the burning bush; it is the sacredness of the Host in the Eucharist; it is Luke Skywalker's Force. As the embodiment of spiritual power in its rawest form, mana inspires the sense of awe and reverence that people of every religion experience when they perceive themselves to be in the presence of the Holy. Though mana makes things more powerful than they normally would be, it does not come and go of its own accord. Like its secular equivalent, electricity, it must be manipulated by human beings to benefit from its power. However, unlike electricity, the manipulation of mana is accomplished through rituals.

Marett believed that the concept of mana was one of the simplest and most widespread of religious ideas. He asserted that it was a more ancient religious concept than the belief in spiritual beings, and that it arose not from intellect but from the emotions.

Where mana plays a prominent role in religion, the concept of taboo is also likely to be important. A **taboo** is a rule that forbids contact with sacred or dangerous things, those filled with so much mana that careless contact with them may harm the unwary. The term was derived from a Polynesian word, *tapu* or *tabu*, which means both forbidden and sacred. Polynesian chiefs were sacred, and their bodies contained so much mana that it was taboo for commoners to touch them, since to do so might kill an ordinary person. Since Tylor's definition failed to encompass mana, an important aspect of religious practice and ideology, Marett broadened it by defining religion as the belief in supernatural things in general.

Recently, a number of anthropologists have attempted to clarify some ambiguities of the word **supernatural**, which has almost always been a central element in Western anthropologists' definitions of religion. Traditionally, the supernatural has been understood to be a realm that transcends the natural senses. It consists of things that are believed to be very powerful but that do not seem to conform to the normal laws that govern the behavior of things in the world. Since the dichotomy between a natural and a supernatural realm has long played a central role in the distinction between science and religion in Western culture, few have felt that the term "supernatural" needed further clarification. However, Cohn (1967) has pointed out that the distinction between a natural and a supernatural realm is not made in most of the world's religions. Neither is there a word in most of the world's languages that translates as "religion." How, then, have anthropologists decided to call be-havior religious when they were studying cultures in which there is no word for religion and no explicit concept of a supernatural realm?

Anthropomorphism. Anthropologists have adopted several different ways of defining the concept of the supernatural. One approach has been to find an alternative concept; another has been to broaden the idea of religion by dropping the concept of the supernatural from its definition. An example of the former approach is found in the work of Stewart Guthrie (1980), who undertook a major survey of the studies of religion and showed that the common denominator in all religious thinking is **anthropomorphism**—assigning human qualities to things that are not human in order to create beliefs in those beings and powers that traditionally have been called supernatural. Thus the word *anthropomorphism* can take the place of *supernatural* in a definition of religion: a system of (1) beliefs in which the nonhuman realm is portrayed as having humanlike qualities, including the ability to respond to symbolic communication, (2) feelings related to those beliefs, and (3) ritual practices that elicit and control those feelings and are carried out either to portray the beliefs or to influence the universe by symbolic communication.

Symbolic Expression of Feelings

The second approach to bypassing the problem of the supernatural, that of dropping the concept altogether, usually involved emphasizing the emotional side of religion over its cognitive aspect, an expression of feelings, not beliefs. An early example of such an approach to religion is embodied in the work of the French anthropologist Emile Durkheim (1915), who focused on the sacred feelings that religion creates in a community of people. By **sacred**,

---

taboo   a rule forbidding contact with sacred things, those containing *mana*
supernatural   that which transcends the natural, observable world
anthropomorphism   using human qualities to explain the nonhuman realm; interpreting or acting toward the nonhuman realm as if it were human, especially as if it were able to respond to symbolic communication
sacred   Durkheim's definition that included feelings of respect, awe, and reverence inspired by things set apart and forbidden

Durkheim meant the feelings of awe, respect, or reverence that were inspired by anything that is set apart and forbidden. Durkheim was concerned with the question of what lies at the root of religious ideas and what maintains them through the generations. He suggested that religious ideas are symbolic representations, metaphors of those aspects of society and culture that inspire feelings of respect, fear, and awe. Durkheim believed that by maintaining and manipulating these feelings in symbolic form, religion perpetuated the sentiments that people must have toward their society if it is to survive. Thus, for Durkheim, religion was society's symbolic worship of itself.

A more recent definition of religion that emphasizes its role in expressing feelings to lend stability to society is one still used by many anthropologists and that was formulated by Clifford Geertz: "A religion is (1) a system of symbols which acts to (2) establish powerful, pervasive, and long-lasting moods and motivations in [people] by (3) formulating conceptions of a general order of existence and (4) clothing these conceptions with such an aura of factuality that (5) the moods and motivations seem uniquely realistic" (1966, p. 4). By eliminating the supernatural from his definition, Geertz has broadened the traditional concept of religion to include any ideological system that people turn to as the ultimate source of their most deeply held feelings. Geertz's definition emphasizes similarities in the deep commitment and behavior of followers of theologies such as Islam or Christianity and of adherents of political ideologies such as Marxism.

Geertz's approach, like that of Durkheim, focuses on the role of religion in validating people's allegiance to their society and culture. Religion, in this view, consists of important symbols that affirm a culturally valued worldview by providing people with ritual settings in which they will feel that those valued beliefs are true even though they may be challenged by experiences outside the religious setting. Thus, for instance, religion can rescue people's faith in spite of disasters, tragedies, and personal difficulties that might otherwise challenge their faith. By explaining life's evils as "God's will," punishment for sin, the results of witchcraft, or with similar religious ideas, these religious concepts help people cope with aspects of life that might otherwise undermine their social commitments and motivations. According to Geertz, it is especially by participating in religious rituals that people repress any contradictions between the world as it ought to be and the world as it is.

Ritual Behaviors

Other anthropologists have shifted their interest away from both beliefs and feelings toward the ritual behaviors that are always a part of the practice of religion. **Ritual** differs from other sorts of behavior in three important ways: it is symbolically meaningful, it is often performed in a repetitive, stereotyped, and predictable way, and it has the intent of manipulating nature through the power of symbols rather than by mechanical means. Typical of those who view ritual as the central element of religion is Anthony F. C. Wallace (1966), who contends that ritual is the central element of religion performed to bring about or to prevent changes in human beings or in nature. Religious beliefs give meaning to the rituals by explaining and interpreting them and by directing the energy of the ritual performance.

Ideology in Religion

Religious ideology, the supernatural beliefs and sentiments of different societies, is extremely diverse, more so than any other aspect of culture. Variability in nonreligious beliefs is directly constrained by the immediate practical results of those beliefs. An oar must be an effective tool for moving a small boat through the water, so ideas about how to build and use an oar do not differ greatly from one society to another. Gender roles may vary across cultures and time, but all cultures must incorporate sexual reproduction into their customs or become extinct. Cultures with automobiles must provide drivers with some guidelines such as a preferred side of the street to drive on to minimize the hazards of traffic. Because religious beliefs are more insulated from such practical considerations, they can be tremendously diverse. But despite the intriguing diversity among religions, it is possible to explain and predict much about religion by considering how it helps people adapt to varying environmental, technological, and social circumstances.

---

ritual behaviors, often performed in repetitive and stereotyped ways, that express people's anxieties by acting them out. May be an attempt to influence the supernatural realm to achieve greater control over the natural world

Diversity of Beliefs

Consider first some examples of religious diversity. Chastity, sexual fidelity, and even celibacy are venerated in some religious traditions. But in southern India until a generation ago, sexual intercourse was a religiously acceptable means of attaining the highest state of spiritual ecstasy, and temple dancers called *devadaasii* shared themselves sexually with priests and other devotees as a sacred act.

Not all witches fly on broomsticks. The Nyakyusa, a farming and herding people of Tanganyika, believe that there are witches living as pythons in the bellies of their human victims, whose insides they gnaw away to satisfy their cravings for flesh (Wilson, 1951). Cannibalism was a sacred act among several peoples in the not too distant past, notably among the Kwakiutl of the British Columbia coast, where the Cannibal Society was the highest ranked religious association. Among the Aztec of Middle America, cannibalism may have played a role in the system of human sacrifice by which the Aztec gods were placated. Estimates of how many people—mostly enemy soldiers—the Aztec sacrificed to the gods and then devoured every year range from about 15,000 to 250,000 people.

Souls come in many sizes and shapes. Among the Shoshoni of the American Great Basin, the soul was thought to be shaped like a small ball of feathers that resided in the forehead. The Jívaro, who were native to the forests of Ecuador, believed that a person might have three kinds of souls: the *nëkás*, the *arutam*, and the *muisak*. The nëkás was an ordinary soul that resided in the bloodstream and perpetuated the individual's personality after death. The arutam was a power-conveying soul that had to be acquired by prayer and fasting. It protected the possessor from death unless it was first lured away by magic. The muisak was an avenging soul that came into being only at the death of a powerful warrior who had a special kind of power-conveying soul. Once it was formed, it sought to kill the murderer.

Many people have worshiped both female and male deities. Others have venerated various types of animals or worshiped deformed children or other humans as deities. The adherents of some North American religions believe themselves immune to poisons, the bites of venomous snakes, or the weapons of enemies as long as they exercise sufficient faith, practice the rituals of their religion assiduously, or wear the proper charms. The possibilities of religious belief have been limited only by human

FIGURE 11.2   Aztec Human Sacrifice
Cannibalism may be one way for a society to impose order on chaos, to regenerate itself, or to communicate with the supernatural. Aztecs sacrificed humans to placate their gods and engaged in ritual cannibalism. This drawing from the Codex Florentino (ca. 1577) shows the sacrifice of a captive warrior impersonating Tezcatliopoca.

imagination. From the unicorns of medieval European folklore to the cannibalistic stone giants of contemporary Shoshoni stories, if something can be imagined, it has probably been a part of the religious ideology of some people somewhere.

The Adaptive Basis of Religious Beliefs

Religious ideology that conflicts too greatly with the nonreligious beliefs and values of a culture, including its survival strategies, will not be readily adopted by the people. For this reason there is a predictable degree of harmony between a people's religion and the rest of their culture. Thus, many differences in religious ideologies may be accounted for as adaptations of culture to differing environmental, technological, and social circumstances.

FIGURE 11.3 Female Deity
**The artifacts and murals at Knossos on the
island of Crete indicate that in the seventeenth
century B.C. one sacred being was a female
deity with women acting as her clergy. She is
depicted holding snakes or with snakes encir-
cling her body, as shown in this ivory and gold
carving. The serpent was a symbol of wisdom
and prophetic counsel.**

Environment. Religious symbolism draws
heavily on features of the natural environment that
are important to the survival of groups. Thus, in
aboriginal Australian religions, one important concept was that every human was born with a special
spiritual relationship with a particular food animal.
For Ituri Forest Pygmies, the forest, as the source of
all necessary resources, was religiously personified
as the spiritual parent of humans, and religious rituals
such as the christening ceremony emphasized the tie
between humans and the forest. And throughout
India, where cattle pull the plow and provide dung to
fertilize the fields and fuel the cooking fires, the cow
is religiously venerated.

The connection between environment and religion runs deeper than the mere borrowing of symbolism from the environment. Cultural ecologists and
cultural materialists have explored ways in which
religious beliefs and practices help societies adapt to
different environmental circumstances. For instance,
Omar Khayyam Moore (1965) has argued that when
hunting peoples such as the Montagnais-Naskapi of
the barren plateau of the Labradorian Peninsula use
divination to decide where to hunt, their technique
randomizes their choices. Although the religious
practice may not improve their chances of hunting
success in the short term, it reduces the likelihood of
overhunting their already scarce food resources for a
long-term benefit.

Technology. One famous proponent of a deterministic view, Leslie White (1971), contended that
the degree to which people view the world around
them in religious terms is inversely related to the
complexity of their technology. The more complex it
is, the more they relate to the world in mechanistic
rather than spiritual ways. In other words, as people
develop direct, pragmatic control over their environment, they may become less likely to seek help from
supernatural powers.

Growth in technological complexity also tends
to accompany growth in population and increasing
social complexity and specialization. These factors
make it increasingly likely that people will feel lost in
a sea of strangers, lacking the power they would like
to have in day-to-day social life. When such people
are alienated from society, they are less likely to
believe in the supernatural. Since religious rituals
reaffirm people's commitment to the fundamental
goals and values of their society, stresses experienced
by the socially alienated tend to be channeled into
coping mechanisms other than traditional religion, an
adaptation referred to as secularization.

Secularization is the process by which nonreligious beliefs expand within an ideology at the
expense of religious ways of thinking. It is a natural

secularization the process by which nonreligious beliefs
expand within an ideology at the expense of religious
thought

result of the more complex technologies and of the greater level of social specialization that results from the increased population densities. The users of those technologies learn to think of the parts of the world that they are manipulating with tools in a more pragmatic and matter-of-fact way than do peoples who control less of their environment technologically. For instance, crop rotation, the plow, fertilization of the soil, and efficient irrigation systems make it much less likely that their users will think of the growth of crops as being dependent upon mysterious spiritual forces than do peoples who rely on rainfall for their food supply.

Complex technologies produce population growth and greater social specialization, which can also foster secularization by undermining the importance of religious ideology. As the number of specialists grows, people are apt to become increasingly aware that many of their survival needs are fulfilled through the services of other human specialists, a perception that can also breed a secular view of life.

Secularization can occur within the religious organization itself. Where technologies produce an economic base that can support a variety of religious specialists such as full-time theologians, religious belief tends to place more stress on organized rational doctrine, and characteristics such as religious ecstasy and altered states of consciousness are likely to be less valued. Thus, when there are full-time religious practitioners who specialize in the performance of rituals, the congregation moves toward less active participation. There may be a rather passive audience fitting themselves into the ritual pattern, not spontaneously but in a highly predictable way. Participation in these rituals also may be motivated largely by a more or less secular desire to be accepted as a conforming member of society rather than by an immediate spiritual need for the rituals.

Social organization. Social organization also affects religious ideology. Guy Swanson has tested the notion that religious beliefs are symbolic representations of what he calls the "sovereign groups" of society, the groups that have "original and independent jurisdiction over some sphere of life" (1960, p. 20) and, thereby, the power to inspire respect and compliance in their members. Using a sample of 50 societies from around the world, he found that strong statistical relationships existed between several common religious doctrines and social traits that could logically be expected to be symbolized by those doctrines.

Swanson found that **monotheism**, the belief in a high god, a supreme being who either created and ordered the universe or at least maintains order within it now, is most likely to be found in societies in which the sovereign, decision-making groups are organized hierarchically so that one of them is superior in rank to at least two levels of groups below it. In such societies, one sovereign group, like a supreme god, can create and maintain order among subordinates.

The belief in superior (but not supreme) gods who control major parts of the universe, such as the weather, the oceans, or agriculture is called **polytheism**. According to Swanson, polytheism reflects specialized purposes in human affairs. A society with many unranked occupational specialties is more likely to have a polytheistic religion than is a society with few such specialties. Similarly, societies with distinct social classes are more likely to have polytheistic religions than are egalitarian societies, since the purposes of these social classes differ one from another. Traditional Indian society with its hereditary social castes and numerous jati occupations had equally diverse, specialized polytheistic deities.

According to Swanson's research, **ancestral spirits** are believed to remain active in human affairs when the kinship organizations that perpetuate the purposes and goals of their deceased members are more complex than the transitory nuclear family. Belief in **reincarnation** is most common in societies in which continuity from one generation to the next is maintained by small, isolated groups whose members are economically interdependent and occupy a common settlement smaller than a village.

Belief in some form of **human soul**, the embodiment of an individual's personality and personal

---

monotheism the belief in a high god, a supreme being who either created the physical universe and other spiritual beings and rules over them or who at least maintains the order of the universe today
polytheism the belief in superior (but not supreme) gods, each of whom controls or rules over some major aspect of the universe
ancestral spirits souls of ancestors who remain interested and involved in affairs of their descendants
reincarnation the belief that the soul of a human being may be repeatedly reborn into the human group to which it previously belonged or as an animal that may be symbolically associated with that group
human soul the supernatural part of the human being that is believed to animate the human body during life or perpetuate the individual's memories or life-goals after death

memories, is almost universal. But Swanson distinguishes between societies in which the soul is believed to be lodged in the individual's body and those in which the soul transcends the body. People are more likely to believe in souls that are intimately tied to the individual's body if they live in societies that have: (1) many different sovereign groups to which everyone must belong, (2) situations in which individuals with conflicting objectives that cannot be reconciled by such means as courts must work together as a group, (3) situations in which groups of individuals whose relationship is not based on their common consent must function as a group to achieve the members' common goals, (4) large-sized settlements, (5) debts, or (6) no sovereign kinship group. All these social traits increase the degree to which individuals are set apart and are socially distinct from each other. Where these traits are absent, the soul is more likely to be conceived in less personal terms as a vitalizing essence, part of a transcendent spirit that animates everyone.

Although all societies have moral and ethical rules that govern the conduct of individuals toward each other, not all societies use the threat of supernatural punishments for the violation of their moral rules. **Supernatural sanctions for violations of moral rules** are most common where interpersonal differences in wealth are prominent, that is, where different groups within society benefit unequally from those rules.

According to Swanson, **sorcery**—the use of rituals to harm another person supernaturally—is most common in societies in which individuals must interact with each other but in which socially approved means for one individual to control another do not exist. In an earlier study of sorcery, Beatrice Whiting (1950) showed that sorcery was most likely

---

supernatural sanctions for violations of moral rules   punishments for immoral acts by spiritual agencies as opposed to human agencies. In most societies, the enforcement of morality is a strictly human responsibility, rather than a religious preoccupation
sorcery   the learned use of rituals to magically control the supernatural realm to achieve human goals

---

India's Sacred Cow

Religious beliefs often serve practical purposes, though these purposes may not be obvious. Such is the case with the sacred cows of India.

Since the British colonial occupation of India, the English phrase "sacred cow" has stood for any custom that is maintained in spite of all rational reasons for its change. The zebu cow, held sacred by Hindus of India, symbolizes gentleness, life, and India itself. The cow is so greatly revered that its protection was written into the constitution. The cow may be neither killed nor molested as it wanders the streets. To the British, for whom cattle were an important food resource, it seemed the height of folly for a society in which hunger and even starvation were significant social problems to support cow reverence instead of cow eating. In spite of the thinly veiled ethnocentrism in this opinion, there is some intuitive merit to the idea that protection of the cow is irrational when its use as food might alleviate a major social problem.

Marvin Harris (1974), who believes that the material conditions of life have a greater impact on an ideology than an ideology does on those conditions, has argued that the custom of cow reverence is integrated with other facts of Indian life in such a way that using cows for food would create more problems than it would solve. Those whose only contact with cattle is the meat section of their local supermarket may be unaware of the great expenditure of resources that goes into the raising of cattle as food. In the United States, for instance, beef cattle are fed from farm-grown foods. Three fourths of the agricultural land in the United States is devoted to growing food for cattle. Since American farmers still are able to produce sufficient food for domestic consumption and export, this cost is well within their means. In India, though, the establishing of this kind of beef industry would remove acreage from the production of food for human beings. The result would be the displacing of millions of farmers and an increase in food costs and hunger.

Indian farmers pen their cows at night but allow them to wander the streets during the day, scavenging their own food. Eating the weeds and plants they find along the way, the cows consume things that are not edible to humans for about four-fifths of their diet. The custom of permitting cows to range freely greatly reduces the amount of labor and feed that farmers must devote to the upkeep of their animals. Allowing cows to wander the streets and fostering cow love benefits the poorest farmers who otherwise could not afford to own a cow or keep it during times of hardship.

Although the cow is not food for its owner, it is an important part of that farmer's means of food production. Teams of oxen are harnessed to pull plows. Cows are milked to provide a small amount of milk for their owners and a few milk peddlers. Cattle also produce dung, which is valuable as fertilizer and fuel in India, a country with little oil, coal, or wood. Cattle dung takes the place of expensive petrochemical fertilizers. It also is burned within the home. Finally, when cattle die from natural causes, the meat is not wasted, for most of it is eaten by members of the lowest castes. The custom of cow worship ensures that the meat reaches the tables of those who could least afford to buy it if it were a market item sought by all.

Perhaps someday beef will be routinely eaten in India, but under current circumstances beef-eating would not be cost-effective, whereas cow reverence is. Far from being a case of the irrationality of religious symbols, the sacredness of the zebu cow in India reflects the real importance of the cow as a resource and means of livelihood in India under the current economic conditions.

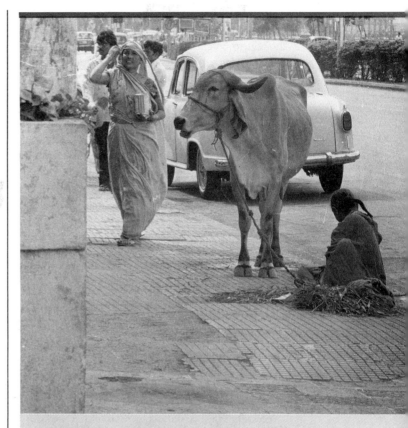

FIGURE 11.4   Sacred Cow of India
The zebu cow is sacred to Hindus of India primarily because it is economically and ecologically more sound to preserve it than to slaughter it. These cows share the road with automobiles and the sidewalk with people.

to be practiced in societies that lack "individuals or groups of individuals with delegated authority to settle disputes" (p. 90) and in which retaliation by peers is the main tool of social control. In addition, beliefs in sorcery and **witchcraft**—a related phenomenon in which the evildoer has an innate ability to harm others without using rituals—are most common in societies that engender severe anxiety about the expression of aggression or sexuality in children during their socialization (Whiting and Child, 1953).

Religious Feelings

Supernatural things are believed to be a source of great power that can be influenced for human ends. Whether perceived as gods, spirits, or mana,

they have the quality of being both nonhuman yet humanlike in their response to symbols. Because they are both powerful and mysterious, they are capable of inspiring strong feelings in humans who approach them. Rudolf Otto (1923) described these intense feelings as the uncanny or eerie sense of awe and dread that people sometimes experience when they are confronted by mysterious things. Such feelings are easily interpreted as a perception of a transcendent, supernatural presence that can fascinate even while it may be feared.

witchcraft the innate ability to influence supernatural forces to operate, usually in ways that are harmful to others without the necessity of using rituals

The "religious thrill" of the ecstatic experience is often associated with trance and is typically thought to be caused by the overpowering presence of supernatural beings or power. Religious ecstasy is accompanied by unusual behaviors such as convulsions and **glossolalia**, a behavior that can vary from groaning to uttering unintelligible sequences of sounds that are commonly called "speaking in tongues" by followers of some North American religions, such as the Holiness churches. Similar ecstatic states have been described in non-Western cultures. For instance, Ruth Benedict described the dance of an initiate into the Cannibal Society, the most sacred society of the Kwakiutl Indians of British Columbia: "He danced wildly, not able to control himself, but quivering in all his muscles in the peculiar tremor which the Kwakiutl associate with frenzy" (1934, p. 180). Similar behavior is found in the spirit possession trances of many cultures around the world, such as the Shoshoni and Koreans (see discussion later in this chapter).

glossolalia   behavior in religious ecstasy that may include groaning and uttering unintelligible sounds

The Holiness Church

"And these signs shall follow them that believe; In my name shall they cast out devils; they shall speak with new tongues; they shall take up serpents; and if they drink any deadly thing, it shall not hurt them; they shall lay hands on the sick, and they shall recover" (Mark: 16-18). Some fundamentalist Christian churches in Appalachia, a coal-mining region in the eastern United States, take these verses to heart and contrast themselves with others who "do not accept the *whole* Word of God." The religious services of the Holiness churches are characterized by much more active participation of the congregation in emotionally charged rituals than is common in the more staid middle-class churches.

In the Holiness way, the emotional experience of the presence of God as the Holy Ghost is a crucial test of the validity of religion. It can be experienced in a variety of ways: loud music and hymn singing are accompanied by dancing, speaking in tongues, spontaneous preaching by any individual who feels inspired to do so, drinking strychnine, and handling poisonous snakes such as timber rattlers and copperheads.

For members of the Holiness churches, the snake is not a symbol of evil, but of God's power over life and death. Handling snakes is a test of faith and a proof of God's love for the faithful. Mary Lee Daugherty, who studied the Holiness churches of West Virginia, interpreted snake handling as their central sacrament. In her view the ecstatic experience of handling serpents counterbalanced the dreariness of a life of poverty and provided a

Holiness Church

Trusting that Jesus will protect them, some members of the Holiness Church handle poisonous rattlesnakes during the singing and dancing that characterize their service. Fundamentalists in the strictest sense, members are centered in the poor Appalachian towns of the southeastern United States.

means for experiencing the power of God's protection in a dangerous environment:

> *The land is rugged and uncompromisingly grim. It produces little except for coal dug from the earth. Unemployment and welfare have been constant companions. The dark holes of the deep mines into which men went to work every day have maimed and killed them for years. The copperhead*

and rattlesnake are the most commonly found serpents in the rocky terrain. . . . Mountain people have suffered terrible pain and many have died from snakebite. Small wonder that it is considered the ultimate act of faith to reach out and take up the serpent when one is filled with the Holy Ghost. (1976, p. 232)

Generally, members of the snake-handling churches are drawn from the poorer, working-class members of Appalachia. They experience a high unemployment rate. According to Daugherty, "The handling of serpents is their way of confronting and coping with their very real fears about life and the harshness of reality . . . in years gone by and, for many, even today" (p. 235). Handling serpents and drinking poison safely also demonstrates that they are valued by God, even if they are not held in high esteem by society.

Serpent handlers know that God sometimes lets even the faithful die from snakebites as a demonstration of the very real danger that they face when they demonstrate their faith in His power over death. Contrary to what outsiders might expect, however, relatively few serpent handlers have died from snakebite. Many have survived numerous bites, and those who have been bitten frequently are praised for their faith and courage.

FIGURE 11.5   Serpent Handlers
Members of the Church of Lord Jesus in Jolo, West Virginia, handle dangerous rattlesnakes and drink strychnine as a part of their worship service. The act for them is not only a test of faith but also a way of affirming the words of the Bible: "They shall take up serpents; and if they drink any deadly thing, it shall not hurt them."

Ritual in Religion

Of the many cultural arenas in which ritual behavior is common, such as play and art, religion is the most publicly encouraged system for the ritual expression of people's concerns and anxieties.

This section will examine the three main roles of ritual in religion: (1) to unite a community emotionally, (2) to portray or act out important aspects of a religion's myths and cosmology, and (3) to influence the spiritual world and thereby the natural world for human beings or, conversely, to help human beings adjust to the conditions of the natural and spiritual realms. These roles of ritual as symbolic communication may be present simultaneously in a single ritual and are not always clearly distinguished in the minds of the participants themselves.

Ritual as Communitas

Victor Turner has emphasized the role of ritual in helping people achieve a sense of unity with each other, a kind of social relationship that he calls **communitas**. During the state of communitas, the normal structure and hierarchy of society is forgotten, and members of the group experience themselves as a community of equals whose individuality may even be submerged into a general sense of fellowship. According to Turner, every society needs the experience of communitas as a source of deeply felt bonding and allegiance—a kind of "mystery of

communitas   Turner's definition of the role of ritual in helping people achieve a sense of unity with each other intimacy"—between the members of the group (1969, p. 139). However, communitas is also potentially dangerous and disruptive to society, since it challenges the basic system of social hierarchy, rank, and power differences as they are usually experienced in day-to-day interaction. The dangers that communitas might otherwise pose to society's power structure are restrained by the fact that this state is typically achieved only during the ritual process.

Rituals, Turner noted, are often described as having three phases. In the first phase, sometimes described as a period of "separation," the participants in the ritual literally may be removed from their normal place of work to a place set apart for the purpose of disentangling themselves from the web of symbols that define the ordinary reality of their culture. The second phase of a ritual is often described as a period of pilgrimage within a spiritual landscape. Turner calls the transition stage between the beginning and end of a ritual the **liminal period.** It is during the liminal phase of a ritual that communitas is characteristic of the participants' feelings toward each other. Finally, participants in rituals are returned to an awareness of the mundane world of normal social life during the phase of reintegration. This tripartite pattern of ritual is particularly common in the rites of transition that societies commonly use to mark the status changes that occur during the life cycle. However, liminality, the state of being "betwixt and between," is also found in social settings where people experience themselves as marginal or inferior in the eyes of others. Thus, people with low-ranked or marginal social statuses—such as slaves, prostitutes, or street people—may experience a strong sense of camaraderie such as is experienced by mainstream members of society only during the communitas of the ritual process.

Ritual as Portrayal

Rituals often involve symbolic portrayals of myths. The Christian ritual that is sometimes called the Sacrament of the Lord's Supper, in which wine and broken bread are shared by members of a congregation, may remind people of the final meal that Jesus and the disciples had together before Jesus' arrest and crucifixion. At the same time, the broken bread and the wine may symbolize or become the body and the blood of Jesus, who Christians believe died as a vicarious sacrifice on behalf of humankind. In addition, the ritual may represent purification and

renewal of the spiritual bonds that unite members of the congregation with their religion as they receive and eat the sacramental meal. Similarly, the baptism by immersion that is practiced in some Christian churches may represent simultaneously a washing away of sin; a portrayal of the death, burial, and resurrection from the dead that most Christians believe Jesus experienced; the spiritual death and renewal by which the individual enters the Christian religion; or the individual's own future death, burial, and hoped-for reawakening to a life beyond the grave. Part of the beauty of a ritual for its participants lies in the multiplicity of meanings it may have for them, a characteristic that may give them the feeling that the ritual embodies meanings transcending those of ordinary symbols.

Ritual as Influence

In their attempt to influence the spiritual or natural worlds for the sake of human beings, some rituals are believed to be coercive in their effect. Others are thought to be more like requests for aid. Usually, they are more coercive when people feel an urgent need for more control over events than they have by nonreligious means. The most coercive rituals are known as **magic.** They are often performed with mechanical precision and careful attention to details, especially when the successful outcome of the magical act is crucial to the performers.

Law of similarity. Sir James Frazer (1922) noted long ago that magic the world over seems invariably to make use of the same two principles: imitation and contagion. **Imitative magic** acts out or portrays what it is intended to accomplish. It uses a principle that Frazer called the **Law of Similarity.** This principle seems to be based on the idea that activities performed that are similar to the desired

---

liminal period   transition stage between the beginning and end of a ritual
magic   the use of rituals that are believed to compel—as opposed to simply making requests of—the supernatural when performed correctly
imitative magic   attempted ritual coercion of the supernatural realm by use of the Law of Similarity
Law of Similarity   the principle that things that are similar to one another are spiritually identical, and can be used in rituals to influence a desired outcome

outcome increase the probability of its occurrence. Thus, magical rituals that follow this principle imitate the thing that they are designed to bring about. Christians who immerse a convert in water to "wash away sin" and Pueblo Indians who whip yucca juice into frothy suds to "bring rain" are both making use of the Law of Similarity. So is the American child who takes care to step over the cracks in the sidewalk, following the admonition in the childhood rhyme, "Step on a crack, and you break your mother's back"—in which there is a similarity in the sound of the words "back" and "crack" and in the appearance of the line of sidewalk blocks and the line of vertebrae in the spinal column.

Law of contagion. The idea that once two things have been in contact with each other they remain in contact on a spiritual level, so that the magical manipulation of one will also affect the other, is called the **Law of Contagion**. **Contagious magic** follows this law. It may be performed on anything that has had contact with the person to be influenced: A lock of the person's hair or a piece of his or her clothing are ideal; fingernail or toenail clippings, dirt from under the nails, or excrement will do just fine; even dirt from the bottom of a footprint will help. In magic designed to harm, the magical poison can simply be poured into the victim's footprint itself. The Law of Contagion is one reason why many people all over the world have two names, one for public use by others and a true, private name known only to themselves and perhaps a few close relatives. Since the name is an extension of the self, so the logic goes, to know someone's true name is to be able to use it as a form of contact in speaking a magical spell. This is why in some parts of the world people customarily change their names as a part of the cure of an illness that is thought to have been magically induced, thus denying the sorcerer a chance for continued mischief by magical contact through the victim's name.

Often, magic employs elements of both the Law of Similarity and the Law of Contagion at the same time. My grandmother in Arkansas, for example, practiced the custom of protecting her children from tetanus by carefully washing the farmyard nail that had been stepped on, covering it with lard, and placing it on the kitchen windowsill. This magical ritual made use of the object that had inflicted the wound—the Law of Contagion—and treated it in a way that she believed would prevent germs from reaching it—the Law of Similarity.

Divination. An important use of rituals to obtain supernatural aid or knowledge is **divination**. Methods of divination can be very creative. Examining the entrails of animals for unusual signs, considering the flight direction of birds or the shapes formed by molten lead poured into water, or checking the lines on people's hands or the date of their birth have all been used as means to answer such questions as, Where is my lost watch? Who committed a particular crime? What kind of person should I marry? Methods of divination fall into two main categories: those in which the results can be easily influenced by the diviner and those in which they cannot. The former include practices such as reading tea leaves or interpreting an astrological sign, casting of the *I Ching*, spreading of *tarot* cards, and randomly selecting a Bible verse, since there is much latitude for subjective interpretation by the diviner. These methods permit the diviner's knowledge of the client's circumstances to play a role in providing answers that are psychologically satisfying to the customer.

Methods that give responses that the diviner is unable to control include such techniques as casting lots or checking whether an object floats on water to answer a question. Like flipping a coin, these tend to randomize the answers. This approach to divination is especially useful when conflicting secular information causes confusion or when divergent opinions must be resolved.

———

Law of Contagion   the principle that things that have been in contact remain supernaturally in contact or that contact between things can be used to transfer *mana* from one to the other
contagious magic   ritual coercion of the supernatural realm by the use of the Law of Contagion
divination   the use of ritual to obtain answers to questions from supernatural sources

The Azande Poison Oracle

Evans-Pritchard described an interesting system of divination that uses poison. The Azande, who live in the Republic of the Sudan, Zaire, and the Central African Republic, consult the poison oracle on all important matters in order to diagnose the cause of an illness, to decide how to conduct vengeance by magic most safely, or to determine who has used

Azande

The Azande, who live in the Republic of the Sudan, Zaire, and the Central African Republic, consult an oracle on important matters of politics or health. The diviner brushes poison into the beak of a chicken as he seeks an answer to his question. For a definitive response, one chicken must die, and another must live.

magic against them. The poison oracle also is consulted to find out if a journey may be undertaken safely or to prepare for any dangerous or socially important activity.

Consulting the poison oracle usually occurs in the bush far from the homestead to maintain secrecy and to avoid people who have not observed the taboos necessary for the oracle to work. Participants must not have sexual intercourse, smoke hemp, or eat elephant's flesh and a number of other foods for several days before consulting the oracle.

The diviner, who with only rare exceptions is a male, scrapes a hole in the ground and places into it a large leaf to hold the *benge*, or oracle poison. He fashions a brush of grass to administer the poison to chickens, several of which are brought by each questioner. When everyone is seated, it is decided how each question will be framed to provide the most information. The diviner then pours water into the leaf bowl and adds the powdered poison. After mixing the paste with his brush, the diviner squeezes the liquid from the brush into the beak of one of the chickens. While several doses are given, the questioner asks the first question repeatedly, ending each time with a request for the poison to kill or to spare the fowl if the answer is affirmative. For instance, a question about whether adultery has occurred might be ended by the questioner's saying:

> *Poison oracle, poison oracle, you are in the throat of the fowl. That man his navel joined her navel; they pressed together; he knew her as woman and she knew him as man. She has drawn badiabe [a leaf used as a towel] and water to his side [for ablutions after intercourse]; poison oracle hear it, kill the fowl. (1937, p. 138)*

The poison used is a red powder prepared from a jungle creeper. The alkaloid that it contains has effects similar to strychnine. Some chickens seem unaffected by it. Others die immediately or soon after it is administered.

In poison oracle divination, there are always two tests of each question, one framed positively and the other negatively. One chicken must die and another must survive to confirm an answer to a question. If both live or if both die, the oracle must be consulted at another time to obtain an answer to the question.

Affecting health. Influential magic also may be used to cause ill health. Illness is a problem with which people must cope in all parts of the world. Although health-related magic is most common in societies that lack complex secular medical technologies, one finds religious rituals for the curing and causing of illness in all the world's societies.

According to Forest Clements (1932), there are six major theories of disease in the world's societies: natural causes, magic, the intrusion of disease objects into the victim's body, soul loss, spirit possession, and taboo violations. Each of these is associated with an appropriate approach to curing the illness.

Those diseases or infirmities that are thought to be the result of natural causes are treated by pragmatic techniques such as setting broken bones and using herbs.

When magic is used to bring about illness or death in a victim, favored materials include things that have been in intimate contact with the victim such as hair clippings, nail parings, excreta, or pieces of the victim's clothing, since they invoke the Law of Contagion and direct the magic more surely to its intended victim than the Law of Similarity alone might. Magic-caused illnesses must be cured by countermagic.

Sending a foreign object, called a **disease object**, into the body of a victim by magic is another favored technique of sorcerers and witches for bringing about illness or death. When a foreign object such as a barbed stick or a stone is believed to have been supernaturally projected into the victim's body, thereby causing pain and illness, the object is removed by massage and sucking.

The fourth cause of illness is **soul loss**, a common malady where independence and self-reliance are important social values. When a soul has left a person's body—whether dislodged from the body by a sudden fright, simply lost during its nightly wanderings, or stolen by another's magic—the body is left without the vitality it needs to survive. If this is believed to be the cause of the victim's ill health, a healer must coax the wayward soul back into the patient's body or recapture it and bring it back.

Spirit possession, the control of a person's behavior by a spirit that has entered his or her body, is common in societies where people are expected to be dutiful and compliant rather than independent and assertive. It requires a ritual of exorcism to remove the offending spirit.

Taboo violation is the only one of the six causes of illness in which magic may not play a role. In many cultures, especially those in which people are expected to learn many rules, it is believed that illness may come not as punishment but simply as a natural consequence of breaking a supernatural rule. Thus taboo violation includes willful breaking of the taboos, but may also include rule breaking that was accidental or even done without the actor's awareness. So the rule breaker is not necessarily held morally responsible for the act, as in the Western concept of **sin**, but may still suffer the consequences. For instance, Apache Indians of the southwestern United States believe that illness may result from using wood for firewood that has been urinated on by a deer even though one is unlikely to know that this is the case. Furthermore, in some societies the illness that follows a taboo violation may strike someone other than the rule breaker—a relative or a neighbor, for instance. When taboo violation is thought to be the cause of illness, confession will play a role in the cure.

What determines whether people will believe that the malicious acts of others, such as sorcerers or witches, are the cause of illness, or will attribute illnesses to other causes? As has been noted, Beatrice Whiting (1950) and Guy Swanson (1960) cited the presence of societal conflicts and the absence of effective social means of resolving them as major causes of the belief in sorcery to work harm. Specific conflicts surrounding sexual jealousy also have been suggested as a basis for witchcraft and sorcery. On the other hand, belief that illness may be caused by nonhuman spiritual beings (spirit possession) seems to symbolize anxiety about the kind of social role one is expected to play. Bourguignon and Greenberg (1973) found that spirit possession is most common in societies in which people are expected to be submissive and compliant, and that spirit loss is most common in societies in which people are socialized to be independent and self-assertive. Illness as a result of taboo violation is found in societies in which conformity to rules is important. For instance, taboo violation is an important cause of illness among the arctic Inuit, whose environment can be quite deadly if one is lax or careless in following the established rules of life.

Death by magic. In some cases, victims of sorcery actually die. Anthropologists have tried for decades to understand the phenomenon of death by magic.

Cannon analyzed cases of so-called **voodoo death** and suggested that the actual cause of death in such cases may be prolonged shock induced by extreme fear. Cannon quotes Herbert Basedow (1907), who graphically described the terrifying ef-

---

disease object an object such as a barbed stick or stone that is magically cast into the body of a victim to cause illness

soul loss in primitive societies, the belief that the departure of the soul from the body, usually caused by a sudden fright, causes the body to weaken and die

spirit possession a trance in which individuals feel as if their behavior is under the control of one or more spirits that have entered their bodies

taboo violation the breaking of a supernatural rule, whether intentional or not. Taboo violations are often believed to be a cause of illness

sin a form of taboo violation in which the rule breaker is thought of as morally responsible for the act

voodoo death death that occurs following a magical ritual performed to kill

FIGURE 11.6 Bone Pointing
A man in the Northern Territory, Australia, shows how the magic bone is pointed at a victim while he is being "sung." It is said that when a victim learns of the ritual even though it is done in secret, he or she may actually die.

fect of sorcery by **bone-pointing** (see Fig. 11.6) in Australia:

> A man who discovers that he is being boned by an enemy is, indeed, a pitiable sight. He stands aghast, with his eyes staring at the treacherous pointer, and with his hands lifted as though to ward off the lethal medium, which he imagines is pouring into his body. . . . His cheeks blanch and his eyes become glossy, and the expression of his face becomes horribly distorted, like that of one stricken with palsy. He attempts to shriek but usually the sound chokes in his throat, and all that one might see is froth at his mouth. His body begins to tremble and the muscles twist involuntarily. He sways backwards and falls to the ground, and after a short time appears to be in a swoon but soon after he begins to writhe as if in mortal agony, and, covering his face with his hands, begins to moan. After a while he becomes more composed and crawls to his wurley [hut]. From this time onwards he sickens and frets, refusing to eat, and keeping aloof from the daily affairs of the tribe. Unless help is forthcoming in the shape of a counter charm administered by the hands of the

"*Nangarri*" or medicine-man, his death is only a matter of a comparatively short time. If the coming of the medicine-man is opportune, he might be saved. (1942, p. 181)

Normally, both fear and anger stimulate the sympathetic nervous system, which regulates the inner organs and the circulatory system. This stimulation prepares the body for prolonged muscular exertion by discharging adrenalin and accelerating the heart rate, by constricting blood vessels during the exertion, and by dilating the bronchioles within the lungs so that more oxygen may be available to the muscles and more carbon dioxide may be expelled. All of these changes prepare the body for the muscular action that may be necessary for the escape from danger. However, when the energy thus made available cannot be used for a prolonged period, the physiological stress of remaining in this state of preparedness for intense action will eventually result in exhaustion and damage to the bodily organs, which may result in death. As Hans Selye (1976) pointed out in his description of the stress response, which he termed the **General Adaptation Syndrome**, these are nonspecific changes that occur in the body as a result of any stress, and even adaptation to a stress-producing event eventually ends in a state of exhaustion. Adaptation to unusual levels of stress cannot go on indefinitely.

In fear-induced shock, the prolonged constriction of the small blood vessels occurs especially in the extremities and the abdominal viscera. The lack of an adequate supply of oxygen in the visceral capillaries causes their thin walls to become more permeable, and blood plasma escapes into the spaces surrounding these small blood vessels in the abdomen. This reduces the volume of blood available in the circulatory system until adequate circulation is no longer possible. The result is a lowering of the blood pressure, which in turn leads to a deterioration of the heart and other organs that normally ensure an adequate circulation of blood to the body. If the cycle is not broken, death is inevitable. The process by which it happens is often speeded by the fact that the

bone-pointing a magical ritual for killing, in which a sharp bone or stick is pointed at or ritually cast into the body of the intended victim

General Adaptation Syndrome the nonspecific changes that occur in the body as a result of stress, as it mobilizes itself to act against the cause of the stress victim may cease to eat and drink, thereby adding even greater stresses to the body. H. D. Eastwell (1982) has argued that dehydration may be the actual cause of death. Since stress that is brought on by fear of sorcery cannot be eliminated by any practical action, death may indeed result unless the fear can be eliminated by a ritual cure.

Death by Sorcery in Dobu

Reo Fortune (1932) gave a graphic account of the use of sorcery to kill among the Dobuans, inhabitants of the Melanesian Islands near New Guinea. The sorcerer and one or more assistants approached the area of the victim's garden in the forest. They rubbed their bodies with magically powerful herbs to make themselves invisible and then crept to the edge of the clearing where the victim was working in the garden. Suddenly, with a characteristic scream, the sorcerer jumped into the clearing. The victim, taken by surprise, would recognize what was happening from the cry and actions of the sorcerer. He or she would be overcome by fear and fall immediately into a faint. The sorcerer was then free to prance about and dramatically act out, in symbolic form, the surgical opening of the victim's abdomen and the magical removal of the entrails and vital organs. After closing the magical wound, the sorcerer would ask the victim, "What is my name?" The victim could not respond, ensuring that the sorcerer would not be identified.

After the sorcerer departed, the victim gradually recovered enough to stagger home and crawl up the ladder to his or her house. Relatives, recognizing the expression of shock and fear on the victim's face, knew what had transpired and began to make arrangements for the funeral. The victim lost all appetite and could die from shock within the next few days.

(see reference map p. 52)

Spiritual healing. Just as ritual is believed to play a prominent role in the causing of illness or even death, religious power is called on in many societies to cure illness. Curing illness is the primary concern of shamans, or inspired religious healers. In societies in which shamans are able to congregate in sufficient numbers, they may form organizations in which they discuss their practices, cooperate with one another in curing patients, and initiate apprentices into the shared secrets of the trade. For instance, among the Iroquois, a native American people who lived in northern New York and were described extensively by Morgan (1851), various illnesses were treated by the members of specialized medicine societies. Among these were the False Face Society, the Bear Society, the Pygmy Society, the Otter Society, the Chanters for the Dead, and the Eagle Society. Each specialized in the treatment or prevention of particular ills and had its own songs and rituals. Those who asked a particular society for a cure became members of that society if the cure was successful, as did persons who dreamed that they must join a society. Thus, following a cure, individuals acquired a new social status and were expected to play a role in the curing of others who became afflicted by the same disease.

The Iroquois False Face Society

The False Face Society is a powerful religious curing society among the Iroquois of the northeastern United States. Their cures are

False Face Society

To cure sick people in their community, the Iroquois False Face Society wear ceremonial masks while they sprinkle the patient with ashes and shake a turtle carapace rattle to dispel the illness. The masks represent spirit forces that heal.

accomplished with the use of wooden masks representing various spirits worn by the members of the society during its ceremonies. The masks characteristically have distorted features created by carving the face into the trunk of a live tree (see Fig. 11.7). During the carving, prayers are made to the spirit force that it represents. After tobacco is burned before the mask, it is cut free, painted, and decorated with hair made from cornsilk or horsehair.

Curing ceremonies take place at the request of the patient's family in the longhouse where they live. The members of the False Face Society don their masks and travel in a group to the patient's house. As they come, they mimic the spirits represented by the masks. Upon entering the patient's house, they sprinkle the afflicted person with ashes and shake their turtle carapace rattles over him or her to drive away the illness. In return for their work, members of the False Face Society are paid with gifts and food.

FIGURE 11.7 False Face Society
The members of the Iroquois False Face Society perform rituals to cure the sick. They wear masks that have been carved from the trunk of a tree and shake their turtle carapace rattles over the patient as they dance in order to drive out the evil spirits causing illness.

The Social Organization of Religion

A hallmark of religion is ritual involvement with others. By participating in the religious rituals of their society, people express a sense of togetherness, unity, and belonging. This group aspect of religious practice fosters deeper loyalty to one's society. To be sure, all religions include rituals that individuals may perform for their own benefit: private prayer to petition the spirits and gods for aid, magic to achieve the same ends more coercively, taboos that are followed to avoid misfortune, and positive acts that foster luck, skill, and safety. However, no religious system is built solely from these individualistic ritual activities. All religions have at least part-time religious specialists who perform rituals for others, and some are organized into more complex communal or ecclesiastical religious groups (Wallace, 1966).

Ritual Specialists

Ritual may be performed by any adherent of a religion, but all religions also have some individuals who specialize in the use of spiritual power to influence others. These include shamans, sorcerers, priests, and witches.

Shamans. The most common kind of ritual specialist in human societies is the inspired, charismatic medical-religious curer called a **shaman**. The term "shaman" was originally borrowed from a seminomadic Siberian people called the Chuckchee, among whom shamanism was a male occupation. According to Waldemar Borgoras (1907), the Chuckchee shaman was a man who was socially withdrawn, listless, and prone to falling into trances before entering the shamanic career. Chuckchee shamans were expected to adopt the dress of women as a symbol of their sacred status. In fact, those

shamans part-time religious practitioners who are believed to have access to supernatural power that may be used for the benefit of specific clients, as in healing or divining shamans who, besides adopting the clothing of women, took on the behavior of a woman and entered into sexual relationships or marriages with men, were thought to be the most powerful.

M. Eliade (1964) has shown that the central feature of shamanistic practice is the ecstatic experience achieved in trance. In the trance state, shamans may send their spirits on errands in service to their clients, or they may invite powerful spirits to enter their bodies and give them power. In spirit travel and possession trances, shamans experience the ecstasy of visions of a world not seen by ordinary eyes. Noll (1985) has argued that the training that sets the shaman apart from other people in the skill of entering trances and experiencing visions is facilitated by visual imaging. With practice the shaman's visions become more vivid and lively, and the shaman learns to control when the visions begin and end and what their content will be. L. P. Peters and D. R. Price-Williams (1980) describe the trance as similar to a waking dream and guided imagery. Further, Price-Williams believes that the true shamanistic trance involves passing over from simple visual imaging into an altered state of consciousness in which the shaman experiences personal "participation and immersion in the imagery content" (1985, p. 656).

Becoming a Shaman Among the Avam Samoyed

Where shamans are formally initiated by others of their kind, the initiation ceremony often enacts a kind of symbolic death, journey through the spirit world where the novice is trained and given the powers of a shaman, and rebirth into the human world. This formula is well illustrated in a story told by Popov (1936) about the vision of a Siberian Avam Samoyed man who received the power to cure. While lying near death from smallpox, his Sickness spoke to him on behalf of the Lords of Water and gave him the new name, Diver. After climbing a mountain, Diver met a naked woman, the Lady of Water, who took him as her child and suckled him at her breast. Her husband, Lord of the Underworld, gave him two guides who led him to the Underworld. There he learned of the diseases, both physical and mental, from which people suffer. Then he

Avam Samoyed

Becoming a shaman involves a formal initiation in most societies. Among the Avam Samoyed of Siberia, the ritual includes a symbolic death, a journey through the spirit world where the initiate is trained, and a rebirth into the human world.

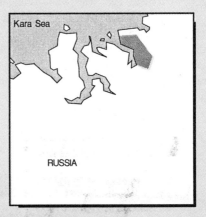

visited the Land of Shamanesses where voice is strengthened, since song is used in cures. On an island in one of the Nine Seas, he found the Tree of the Lord of the Earth. There he was given the wood for making three of the drums that shamans use in their ceremonies. After he received instruction in the medicinal use of seven herbs and in other techniques for curing, he was told that he must marry three women.

Then the initiate was led to another high mountain where he met two women clothed in the hair of reindeer. Each gave him a hair to be used when he used his power to influence reindeer. He crossed a great desert to another mountain. There he was dismembered, and his body parts were boiled in a great cauldron by a naked man who forged his head on an anvil that was used to forge the heads of great shamans. This man taught him to divine whether a cure would be successful, reassembled his body, gave him new eyes capable of seeing into the spirit world, and pierced his ears so they could hear the speech of plants. After all these things, he awoke and found that during the three days of his coma, he had been so close to death that he had almost been buried.

Sorcerers. The antisocial equivalent of a shaman is the sorcerer, a person who uses supernatural power to harm human beings, cause misfortune, illness, and even death. As dangerous as a sorcerer may be, acknowledged practitioners of the art may be tolerated by their neighbors, since their noxious powers may occasionally be sought by others. A sorcerer might, for instance, be hired by persons who believe themselves to have been wronged by others and who seek vengeance by sorcery. Since persons who discover that they have been cursed by a sorcerer may seek the removal of that curse by making amends for the wrong of which they have been accused, the sorcerer's role in society is sometimes similar to that of the law enforcers in societies that have centralized governments.

Navajo Skinwalkers

Among the Navajo of the southwestern United States, it is said that a curer may be seduced by the dark side of power. No human being is all good or all evil. In the Navajo view, we each have both qualities or, more accurately, the capacity to do both good and evil. According to Witherspoon (1977), the goal of Navajo life is to bring one's impulses under control so that one grows and develops through a complete life in a condition of *hózhó*—the state of beauty, harmony, good, and happiness—and then dies naturally of old age and becomes one with the universal beauty, harmony, and happiness that make up the ideal positive environment.

A person's *ch'indi*, or potential for evil, can be controlled by rituals that restore one to a state of *hózhó*. Although the state of inward beauty achieved through living in outward harmony with the ideal environment can be disrupted by contact with dangerous (*báhádzid*) things or by the sorcery of others, perhaps leading to illness or to death, such states can be countered by a traditional ritual chant, or "Sing," of which there are over 60. These channel positive supernatural power by reenacting the Navajo creation myths.

Navajo singers, the curing shamans of the Navajo, also can learn to use the power of ritual to harm other people. Initiation into the world of sorcery carries a high price: The initiate must consent to the death of a close relative. In using rituals to upset the ideal balance of life in others, the sorcerer's *ch'indi* grows stronger and may overwhelm him. Sor-

cerers live a life that inverts the ideals of the Navajo: They gather at night in places avoided by others to do their rituals; they dig up corpses to grind their bones into poisons; they don the skins of wolves and transform themselves into animals. Skinwalkers, as they are called, can travel great distances faster than ordinary humans can imagine. They cast their poisons into the smoke holes of their victims' hogans or magically shoot harmful substances into their bodies.

(see reference map p. 162)

Witches. Shamans and sorcerers share the world of supernatural power with witches, men or women who, like sorcerers, are believed to do evil to human beings. But unlike sorcerers, who must learn the rituals with which they work their harm, witches are thought to be born with the power to harm. Thus, the evil of a witch may do its damage to others even without the witch's conscious intent. They are often viewed as the epitome of evil and may be described in terms that invert the normal qualities of human beings: Witches love the night; they commit incest and kill their own relatives; they may travel on their heads instead of their feet, and may fly as fireballs through the sky. Since witches are different from ordinary humans, the very presence of persons believed to be witches may not be tolerated, and those convicted of being witches are likely to be killed.

Priests. Religious practitioners who have been trained to perform rituals for entire congregations are called priests to distinguish them from their more charismatic counterparts, the shamans. Whereas shamans serve individual clients when called upon to do so, priests perform rituals for a congregation on a full-time or at least regular basis. Priests may be organized into a professional priesthood, a bureaucracy that both organizes the activities of its members and regulates the ritual calendar of the congregations. Unlike shamans, who often are highly charismatic individuals who follow the inspiration of the moment in modifying their ritual performance to fit the needs of their clients, priests maintain the traditional forms of the rituals they have learned.

sorcerers practitioners of magical rituals that are done to harm others

witches persons believed to have the innate supernatural ability to harm others without the use of ritual

Shamanic Religions

Of all forms of religious organization, shamanic religions are the socially simplest and perhaps the oldest. They are based on rituals performed both by nonspecialists and the shamans. Shamans may perform rituals to divine the future or to gain answers to their clients' questions. As spirit mediums, they may be called on to increase the success of a hunt, the fertility of the game, or the growth of crops. The charms they make protect their clients from harm or increase their luck and skill. However, shamans are best known for their skill at manipulating the supernatural to cure illness. Their spiritual powers do not differ in nature from those that nonspecialists may use in their own behalf, but their special status grows out of their reputation for greater skill at manipulating these powers. In addition to their spiritual powers, shamans often possess an impressive body of knowledge about the natural medical effects of a broad range of native plants and other curative materials and techniques. Shamans also draw upon the awe and reverence of their patients for religious power, thereby increasing the patients' confidence in the likelihood of recovery.

On the reservation in Nevada where I did my fieldwork, a Shoshoni *puhakanten*, literally a "possessor of power," still cured the sick. The shaman's spiritual power was brought to him by a spirit partner, a *newe puha-pea*, the Eagle, who first appeared to him in a vision and gave him the power to cure.

When a prospective patient approaches this shaman, the first task is to determine whether he will be able to perform the cure. At the direction of his spirit partner, certain cases—such as those he diagnoses as cancer—must be referred to a medical doctor. To facilitate the diagnosis, the individual who has consulted him may be given an "eagle wing," a fan made of eagle feathers to place above his or her bed that night. That evening, the shaman consults his spirit partner for a diagnosis. On the next day, he will either accept or reject the petitioner as a patient, depending on the diagnosis.

A cure usually begins at sunset in the shaman's home. It is sometimes attended by other interested members of the community. Attendance at a curing ceremony is believed to foster good health in general among those who participate. The patient, who has bathed that morning at sunrise in a local hot spring, provides tobacco that is smoked by the shaman as part of the ceremony. After smoking, the shaman

FIGURE 11.8   Kalahari San Shaman

Shamans are specialists primarily in healing. Extensive training gives them both physical and spiritual knowledge in eliminating the causes of illness. The rituals shamans use may vary from culture to culture but involve chanting, smoking, massaging the body of the patient, and entering a trance state. This Kalahari San shaman, while in a trance, lays his hands on the patient in order to cure him.

begins a chant that he was taught by his spirit partner in his first vision. This chant is a call to the Eagle to come down from his mountain abode and enter the shaman to give him power to cure his patient's illness. He alternately smokes, chants, and massages the patient's body to remove the illness. Following the ceremony, the patient may be given some tasks to perform to complete the cure. For instance, a patient who is suffering from nosebleeds may be required to collect the blood and dispose of it on a red anthill.

shamanic religions   religions in which the only ritual specialist is the shaman, and which contain only individual and shamanic ritual practices

Patients are required to abstain from alcohol to ensure the efficacy of the cure.

Korean religious tradition also includes an important role for shamanic rituals that are performed by a class of female shamans called *mansin*. They obtain their power by becoming possessed by powerful spirits and deities, during which time they carry out rituals that benefit both individuals and groups. They divine the causes of both psychological and physical illnesses, undertake the cures, communicate with the spirits of the dead, placate angry gods, and purify villages that are plagued by evil spirits.

Brian Wilson has described a *kut*, or spirit possession ritual, conducted by a *mansin* to cleanse a village of angry spirits that had caused a series of tragic deaths, a murder and several suicides. The shaman, whom Wilson calls Mansinim, had diagnosed the cause of the problems to be the village's tutelary spirit, who was angry because some members of the community had cut down some trees. According to Wilson:

Mansinim began the *kut* with the *pujong*, or ritual cleansing of the [village] shrine and surrounding area of all polluting elements. While the *paksu* (male shaman) who was working with her this day beat a rapid beat on the drum and gong and chanted the invocational *tokkyung*, Mansinim walked around the concrete *sŏnang* shrine with salt water and ashes and sprinkled the surrounding area using her *Changgun* sword to sprinkle the water. Then she took a bowl of salt and walked around the shrine and sprinkled the salt to drive away any harmful spirits that might have been lurking about. She took two cymbals (*para*) attached to each other by a strip of white cloth and began beating them in a slow, almost funereal rhythm. She walked out in the field, clanging the cymbals, and when I later asked why she said it was to notify the gods and spirits that she was here and that the *kut* was about the begin. The field was marked off with straw rope from which were fluttering red, blue, and green bits of cloth. She marched toward an old tree beside which were the two guardian posts inscribed with the customary *ch'onha tae changgun* [male general of heaven] and *chisang yo changgun* [female general of earth]. She circled the tree three times and bowed, then walked to the base of the mountain overlooking the village and bowed to *San Sin* [the Mountain God]. Walking back to the *sŏnang*, still clanging the cymbals, she bowed before every tree along the side of the path.

She entered the *sŏnang* shrine and bowed. Then she put on the red vest and blue sash of [the god]

Sinjang, the Arrester, and her hands, pressed together in a prayer-like position, began shaking. This is the outward sign that the god has possessed her. She took the sword and trident and began jumping in front of the *sŏnang* shrine. Inside the little house-like shrine was the offering of a pig tied to an upright stone. The stone is the *sŏnang* spirit which guards the village. The villagers say it was miraculously washed up during a flood and deposited in the village.

The *paksu* changed the beat to a dance rhythm and Mansinim took the divinatory flags and danced with them, circling the shrine. Then she danced with a fan and bells. She danced over to the chairman of the Elders' Association and pulled him into the shrine, where he bowed and placed a money offering at the foot of the stone. Mansinim fanned him with both fans. The gods were pleased.

She took the *sin tae* (spirit stick used in divination) and danced with it. A bow signaled the end of that *kori* [one segment of the ceremony].

After lunch the *kut* resumed. Mansinim put on the blue vest and black hat and the *Taegam* [Greedy Provincial Official] danced. Then she put on the *Changgun* ["General's"] costume, took two swords and danced with them inside the shrine compound. Her motions became very mannish and brusque. She stopped dancing and her body shook. *Changgun* had descended. She took her sword and tried to balance it on the flat end of the handle but the wind kept blowing it over. She went out and got the trident while the *paksu* picked up the beat with drum and gong. This time the trident stood, a sign of the favorable presence of *Changgun*. Her body shook again and she began dancing, becoming more animated as she danced and then she began jumping. Finally she faced the assembled villagers and the General spoke to them through her:

You are ungrateful! (*kwaessim hada*)
Do you know which General has come down?
Tosol Changgun ["Heavenly General"] has come down in order to help the people who live in this mountain valley.
I come to this village letting three *mansins* go ahead,
In order to make a success of human wishes.
Because three mansins fervently pray,
Because all the spirits cooperate to make a success of human wishes,
Because villagers ask the *Son Hwang* [the tutelary spirit of the *sŏnang* shrine] spirit for their wishes,
Because villagers offer a whole *ssiru* [steamed rice],

Because villagers offer a whole pig and pray fervently,

Don't worry, I will solve your problem,

I will also open the door to a bright future.

Later in the afternoon, at the end of the *kut*, Mansinim drove the offending *subi* [goblins], *magwi* [demons], *kwisin* [ghosts] and other evil spirits into a dead branch to which had been tied pieces of red and green cloth. With the chairman of the Elders' Association trailing behind she ran across the field and then across another field to the foot of a hill where she untied and burned the colored cloth and 'planted' the tree in the hillside. (1980, pp. 8–10)

Lewis pointed out that spirit possession is a religious practice in which socially powerless members of society are able to assert themselves in ways that society ordinarily forbids and "press their claim for attention and respect" (1971, p. 32). This view of the psychological role of spirit possession seems valid when applied to the *kut* because in Korea, the social roles of women provide few opportunities for achieving high public status. In a discussion of the role of the *mansin* in Korea, Wilson (1980) has painted a poignant portrait of how Mansinim sought the fulfillment that was denied her because of her gender.

Mansinim had had a difficult life: Her father had died when she was three years old, and she worked as a housemaid as a teenager. She entered into an arranged marriage with a man she had never met, and had to live alone in a bomb shelter when her husband went into the army during the Korean War. After the death of two of her children, she suffered from dizzy spells and fits of crying, and was frequently ill. After a violent quarrel with her husband about an affair he had been having, she found her calling as a shaman when she became possessed by the spirit of her mother-in-law during a *kut* ceremony. Wilson has noted that similar hardships seem characteristic of many of the female shamans whose lives he studied.

Yet according to Wilson, Mansinim's role as a shaman was not simply the manifestation of psychological stresses. As a shaman, Mansinim came to be possessed by a variety of powerful spirits and deities such as Tosol Changgun, whose name means "Heavenly General." During her states of possession on ceremonial occasions, Mansinim was able to abandon her prescribed role as a submissive woman, and speak with a religiously legitimated power and authority usually reserved for men in Korean society. In Wilson's opinion, her dominant behavior when pos-

sessed fit her natural predispositions in a healthier way than did any other role available to her.

Possessed of a god, Mansinim was able to express a part of her personality that was otherwise forbidden by her culture. Thus, Mansinim's shamanistic religion offered her a healthy outlet for parts of herself that, otherwise being denied, might have been a source of psychic distress.

Communal Religions

A more complex form of religious organization tends to be found in societies that have slightly larger local groups than those in which shamanic religions predominate. In societies with larger social groups, **communal religions** serve to celebrate the cohesiveness of the group or ease the transition of individuals from one status to another by publicly proclaiming that change in a rite of passage. Like shamanic religions, they are found in many societies where people survive by foraging wild foods. Communal religions also are found in societies where horticulture and pastoralism are practiced.

The group rituals permit broader social participation in the shared concerns of the community or of groups of specialists than do individual or shamanic rituals. The rituals that are most often celebrated in communal religions include rituals to increase the fertility of game or ensure success in hunting; annual rituals to influence the weather, the fertility of crops, and the harvest; social rituals to celebrate changes in status or reinforce the importance of social divisions by sex or age; and ceremonies to reenact the mythology of the group or commemorate cultural heroes, ancestral spirits, or particular deities.

---

communal religions religions that include the performance of rituals by groups of lay practitioners, shamans, or individuals

---

The Rainbringing Ritual of the Jigalong People

According to Tonkinson (1974), the most important yearly ritual of the Jigalong people of the western Australian desert is the rainbringing ritual, called *Ngaawajil*. This ritual reenacts the story of Winba, an old snake-man ancestral being, and other rainmaking beings,

Jigalong People

The Jigalong people of the western Australian desert depend heavily on rain for their subsistence. Thus, they perform a yearly ritual reenacting the story of Winba, a snake man, and other rainmaking spirits in order to ensure that the rains will come.

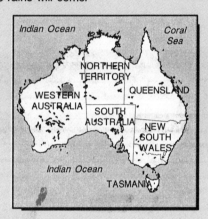

controllers of rain, clouds, thunder, lighting, hail, and other elements of the weather. If the people perform, the annual return of the rains is ensured, as is the increase in the kangaroo and other game animals that depend on the rains for water in the desert environment where the Jigalong people live and hunt.

Since the ritual lasts for many days and consists of a number of ceremonies performed simultaneously in different locations, it requires the cooperation of five male and four female groups, each with its own name, insignia, and ritual responsibilities. Throughout the ritual there is a division of the participants into the two-generation-level moieties of Jigalong life, groupings that unite members of alternate generations (grandparents and grandchildren) and separate members of contiguous generations (parents and children). Thus, the ritual reinforces a major aspect of Jigalong social life by incorporating the moiety division into the structure of the ritual.

The ritual activities occur at two locations, the camp—where men, women, and children participate together in the ritual—and the "men's country" away from the camp—where only initiated males are involved in the ceremonies. At the camp, men and women of appropriate status prepare food for the participants, and members of each moiety engage in chanting and throwing water at members of the other moiety. Away from the camp, the ritual requires two groups or stacks of sacred objects such as rainbow stones to encourage the rainmaking ancestors to bring the rains. These objects are sprinkled with blood symbolic of rain, covered with down feathers symbolic of clouds, and "fed" with ceremonial food and water. The desire for rain is communicated to the rainmaking ancestors by rainmaking snakes believed to live in the piles of sacred objects.

Ecclesiastical Religions

The **ecclesiastical religions** make use of individual, shamanic, and communal rituals, but they add to them a series of rituals performed by **priests**. In ecclesiastical religions priests may perform some shamanistic roles, such as confessor, counselor, and faith healer. However, the priestly hierarchy may not be tolerant of some shamanistic activities, such as seances, faith healing, prophecy, and psychic readings by separate specialists. The hierarchy of priests often frowns on similar behavior in the lay congregation as well, and may forbid practices such as spirit possession trances and the ecstatic speaking in tongues by members of the congregation. Ecclesiastical religions tend to be found in agriculturally based societies, particularly in those with large enough populations to support a variety of full-time specialists.

Polytheism and monotheism. Ideologically, the earliest recorded ecclesiastical religions had poly-

---

ecclesiastical religions religions that include not only individual, shamanic, and communal ritual practices but also a coordinating body of priests who perform rituals on behalf of congregations

priests religious practitioners who perform rituals for the benefit of groups. Often, priests are full-time religious practitioners whose emphasis is on preserving the established ritual forms, rather than on inspiration and innovation in the application of their rituals

Hindu tradition are said to be merely various manifestations of a single, all-encompassing deity.

Olympian religions polytheistic ecclesiastical religions in which the gods or supernatural beings may be loosely ranked but in which no one of the supernatural beings is truly supreme over the others

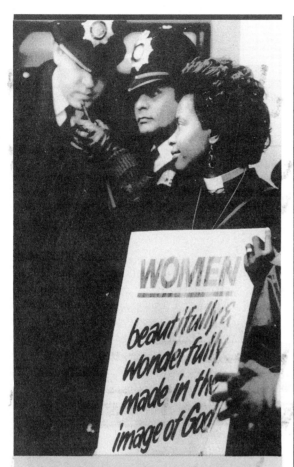

FIGURE 11.9   Ecclesiastical Priests

In 1992 some Western ecclesiastical religions began to admit women to the priesthood, but not without great controversy. Here the Reverend Rose Hudson-Wilkes, a deacon in Wolverhampton, England, demonstrates her support for women priests outside Church House, in London. Priests function as ritual specialists for their congregations in ecclesiastical religions.

theistic beliefs in which a variety of high gods each required the service of special religious practitioners. Wallace (1966) has called these early ecclesiastical religions the **Olympian religions**, to distinguish them from the later monotheistic religions in which the supernatural pantheon of ranked gods is superseded by one in which the highest deity is regarded as a truly Supreme Being, if not the only god in the pantheon. The ancient Greeks, Egyptians, Babylonians, and Romans followed the Olympian pattern, while monotheistic religions are represented today in Judaism, Christianity, Islam, and in modern philosophical Hinduism, in which all of the gods of earlier

Mormon Priesthood and Pantheon

Mormonism was founded in 1824 in the eastern United States by a charismatic leader, Joseph Smith, following a series of visionary experiences, including a visitation by God the Father and Jesus. Today, this religion claims about nine million members worldwide.

Mormonism is an ecclesiastical religion. Its priesthood, which is held only by male members of the church, is organized into a complex hierarchy, presided over by a president. The president of the church is also referred to as the *Prophet, Seer, and Revelator* of the church. As the presiding official of the church, the Prophet is believed to receive direct guidance from God whenever this is necessary for the work of directing the church. Below the Prophet is the Quorum of Twelve Apostles, which is presided over by its own president and two counselors. Below this level are intermediary officers down to the local congregations, called *wards*. The presiding official of the ward is the *bishop*. The bishop is a nonpaid minister, as are all local members of the priesthood. His responsibilities are not to deliver weekly sermons, but to organize and preside over each Sunday's worship services and all other business of the ward. In this work he is aided by his own counselors and a series of priesthood quorums within the ward.

The local priesthood quorums are themselves organized into an age-graded system which is divided into two major components, the lower, or Aaronic Priesthood and the higher, or Melchizedek Priesthood. Boys are typically inducted into the Aaronic Priesthood at the age of 12 as Deacons. Their assignments include passing the Sacrament to members of the ward during the Sacrament meeting each Sunday. At 14 years of age, boys are ordained Teachers and are permitted to prepare the sacramental bread and water used in the service. Sixteen-year-olds become Priests, at which time they receive the authority to bless the Sacrament and to baptize. Eighteen-year-olds receive the full authority of the Melchizedek Priesthood as Elders, including the authority to confirm a baptized person as a member of the church and, by the laying on of hands, to give that person the right to receive direct and personal guidance through the Holy Ghost. At this time, it is expected that worthy males will spend a two-year period as unpaid, full-time missionaries for the church. For most, the next major change occurs at age 45, when men are inducted into a High Priest's quorum.

The women's organization is an auxiliary program, since all policy-making and governing authority is vested in the priesthood. The men's and women's organizations are structurally equivalent, but they differ in authority and responsibility, with the women specializing in supportive service roles. Mormon ecclesiastical values reflect the secular differentiation of male and female roles. According to Shepherd and Shepherd (1984), Mormons are taught to idealize a family pattern in which the husband, as the family's sole source of income, plays a presiding role and in which the wife, as counselor to her husband, specializes in domestic responsibilities.

In addition to a Father in Heaven, Mormon theology includes a divine Mother in Heaven (Heeren, Lindsey, & Mason, 1984). However, Her role in Mormon theology is an auxiliary one, like that of the women's organization within the church or of the wife within the idealized Mormon family. She is never explicitly mentioned in Mormon scriptures, She has no governing authority within the Godhead, and She is not approached in worship in any rituals of the church.

The recurring pattern of presidents and two counselors within the church structure mirrors Mormon theology, which includes a divine pantheon of many gods presided over by God the Father, Jesus Christ, and the Holy Ghost. Jesus, the firstborn spirit child of God, and the Holy Ghost, another spirit son of God, are believed to be fully separate individuals from the Father. Their role in the Godhead is much like that of the counselors to the earthly Prophet of the church. Thus, church organizational structure reproduces forms that Mormons think of as divine in origin and that reinforce the value of a presiding role for males.

Religious Change

Religion tends to be a conservative institution that normally functions as a stabilizing influence within society. It typically emphasizes the importance of tradition and stability, and the perpetuation of beliefs and rituals that have been handed down from the past. Yet, religion does change. Usually, it is a slow and piecemeal process in which religious beliefs and practices usually lag behind social change, and then make small adjustments when the discrepancies grow too large.

Revitalization Movements

Revolutionary change can also occur in religions through a process that Anthony Wallace called a **revitalization movement**, which he described as a "conscious, organized effort by members of society to construct a more satisfying culture" in response to unusual social and cultural stresses (1966, p. 30). According to Wallace, revitalization movements are frequently the bases of new religions, often millenarian in outlook, that promise a return to a more stable and harmonious society.

Revitalization movements typically involve four stages that Wallace termed the steady state, the period of increased individual stress, the period of cultural distortion, and the period of revitalization. The steady state is the normal moving equilibrium of any culture during which change is relatively slow and incremental. A culture can be pushed out of its usual steady state by forces such as "climatic and biotic change, epidemic disease, war and conquest, social subordination, or acculturation" (p. 159). Such forces cause a growing number of individuals to experience individual stress because they interfere with society's ability to meet people's needs. During the period of increased individual stress, crime and illness increase, individual deviance increases, and society appears increasingly disorganized.

A period of cultural distortion can arise if some members of society respond to the increasing stresses

revitalization movement a change in religion described as a conscious effort to construct a more satisfying culture

FIGURE 11.10 Sioux Ghost Dance

The Ghost Dance ritual originated among the Plains Indians in the 19th century as a response to the encroachment of the non-Indian on Indian lands. In each version of the dance the idea was to destroy the non-Indians and bring back to life the spirit of the dead Indians. The Sioux warriors wore Ghost Dance shirts in the belief that they would be protection against bullets. This 1890 drawing by Frederick Remington portrays a Ghost Dance performed by the Ogallala Sioux at the Pine Ridge Agency, South Dakota.

by organizing special interest groups that no longer support the established social order. Instead, the special interest groups struggle to obtain the old benefits of life for their members through previously unacceptable behavior. This is a period of widespread "[a]lcoholism, venality in public officials, the 'black market,' breaches of sexual and kinship mores, hoarding, gambling for gain, 'scapegoating' by attacking other groups or a central bureaucracy, and similar alienated behaviors which, in the preceding period, were still defined as individual deviances" (p. 159). At such times, the old religious rituals, beliefs, and values may be less than satisfying to many, since they are too rooted in earlier, less stressful times to help people cope with new, current problems.

The period of revitalization begins when an "individual or group of individuals constructs a new, utopian image of sociocultural organization" (p. 160). This often occurs when a man or woman who was personally distressed by the lack of order in society undergoes a hallucinatory experience perceived by the distressed person as a religious revelation from a supernatural source. It seems to account for society's turmoil and provides a series of new religious rituals that are intended to help people cope with the new problems that the old religions appear to have failed to address.

When the prophet of the new religion preaches the message to others, those who have been trying unsuccessfully to cope with the same widespread social ills may accept it as a divinely revealed answer to their problems. In fact, converts may be attracted so quickly that the revitalization prophet cannot personally coordinate the activities of the growing organization. At this point, a group of full-time disciples may be appointed to do that. The rapid growth of the new religion is often perceived as a threat by those members of society who still have a vested interest in the old, established institutions, such as government and the previous religious organization. Sometimes the conflict that develops out of this perceived threat ends in the destruction of the new movement by its opponents, but sometimes the revitalization movement achieves dominance and establishes a new steady state.

Revitalization movements were common in many parts of the world among indigenous peoples after they were contacted by the technologically and militarily more powerful European societies. They include the so-called Cargo Cults of Melanesia and Australia, and several nativistic religious movements among American Indians, such as the Handsome Lake religion of the Iroquois, the Ghost Dance religion of the United States' Great Basin region, and the Native American Church that has spread to many parts of the United States. Similar millenarian Christian movements such as Mormonism, Seventh-Day Adventism, the Reverend Sun Myung Moon's Unification Church, Bhagwan Shree Rajneesh's utopian movement in Rajneeshpuram, Oregon, and the Reverend Jim Jones's People's Temple settlement in Guyana, have histories that follow the pattern of revitalization movements.

Why Are People Religious?

Although cultures differ considerably in their religious beliefs, practices, and organizations, there is no known human culture in which religion is absent. There is archaeological evidence that religion has been practiced by our ancestors since at least the time of the Neanderthals, 100,000 years ago. In trying to explain the universal existence of religion in our species, anthropologists usually have considered the role that religion plays in making our social life more successful and the psychological benefits that religion gives us as individuals. The question of whether people also are responding to a true super-

natural realm is, itself, not accessible to anthropological study.

The Maintenance of Social Order

Religion teaches people that they have a place in the universe and a relationship to it. Through the ideology of a religion and through its rituals, people gain a sense of identity and a feeling that life is meaningful. The practice of a religion creates greater solidarity among its participants, enabling them to work more effectively together and accomplish more.

Religion provides guidelines about how human life should be properly conducted and what values should be held. In so doing, it motivates people to follow the customs of their society even in the absence of practical insights about how their actions may benefit it. For instance, farmers suffering the effects of a prolonged drought may be too discouraged to dig yet another well after several failures until a "water witch" assures them of the presence of water at some location. Without such religious sources of motivation, the short-term costs of trying one more time in the face of the previous failures might seem to outweigh the potential long-term benefits.

Social rules that are necessary to the maintenance of order may be supported by the threat of supernatural punishments for their violation or supernatural rewards for their acceptance. This can be especially beneficial to a society that lacks secular means of ensuring obedience to the rules. Viking men were promised the reward of Valhalla for valor in warfare, and Aztec warriors were assured that death in battle led to an eternity in the most glorious of the Aztec heavens, that of their war god, Huitzilopochtli. Among the Rwala Bedouin of northern Saudi Arabia, the pains of Hell awaited those who lied, and for the ancient Egyptians a similar fate was reserved for the stingy.

In situations in which disagreement might be divisive, religion may provide the means to achieve consensus without hard feelings. For instance, divination can be used to find the answer to a question about which the group is hopelessly divided. That solution then can be accepted by all without loss of face.

Finally, the rituals of religion provide emotional release from stresses that might otherwise lead to socially disruptive behavior. When Zuñi farmers blame their crop failures or illness on the malevolent

FIGURE 11.11 Purpose of Religion
Religion gives people answers to important questions about their existence, provides guidelines about how human life should be conducted, and gives people encouragement in times of distress. This priest and his wife give offerings to the Gods during an *odalan,* an Indonesian temple ceremony that takes place every 210 days, at a village near Ubud.

activities of sorcerers in another town and take action to protect themselves through rituals, they may be sparing themselves the strife that might otherwise disrupt their own village if they took out their frustrations on neighbors or relatives.

The Reduction of Anxiety

In addition to benefits to society at large, there are psychological benefits for the individual in the practice of religion. People do not always have as much control over their lives or circumstances as they need to feel secure. When this is the case, the performance of rituals for control through supernatural means can alleviate debilitating anxiety. This is especially true when the anxiety stems from prob-

lems for which no secular remedies are known. More than one anthropologist has noted parallels between shamanistic curing rituals and Western psychotherapeutic practices.

In frightening situations, religion can be a source of strength to stand up to one's fears and overcome them. The prayer uttered privately or the blessing given by another before a dangerous act is undertaken may provide just enough confidence to ensure success. Guilt can be overcome by acts of penance and sacrifice, and shame may be counteracted by demonstrations of piety that restore one's reputation. People who are unable to remove unjust obstacles in their lives can release their anger by acting it out with rituals that direct the power of magic against the source of their frustrations. At times of loss, religion may console the grieving. In

272

these and other ways, religion helps people cope with troubling emotions.

The Cognitive Role of Religion

Religion's role in shaping beliefs is to give people answers to important questions for which they have no scientific or definitive answers: Why do I exist? What will become of me after I die? What are the sun, moon, and stars, and how did the Earth itself come into existence? Who were the first humans, and how did they originate? To such questions, religious ideology usually provides satisfying answers based on supernatural authority.

Some existential questions that deal with meaning and purpose are those with which science is not equipped to deal but for which religion may provide answers. However, the rise of scientific specialists in Western societies led to new answers to many questions that had been handled previously by religious leaders. This sometimes resulted in social conflict between advocates of science and advocates of religion, which, as society became more secular and dependent on rational explanations for natural phenomena, gradually resulted in a major loss of social and political influence by religious professionals. Education, for instance, increasingly came under the control of secular educators. A natural byproduct of the conflict between science and religion was the evolution in Western culture of the idea that scientific and religious ideologies are fundamentally different, perhaps even irreconcilable. This idea is dramatically illustrated in the ongoing attacks on scientific knowledge about the age of the Earth or about human evolution by Christian fundamentalist religious leaders in the United States who reject the notion that scientific insights should be allowed to influence their interpretation of Scripture.

It is true that science and religion differ in the methods and assumptions that they employ to create new ideas. However, it is an error to assume that the cognitive processes involved in religious thinking differ radically from those applied in science. Guthrie has shown that "people hold religious beliefs because they are *plausible* models of the world, apparently grounded in daily experience" (1980, p. 181, emphasis added). Guthrie believes that anthropomorphism (using human qualities to explain the nonhuman realm) is fundamental to religion and that it is anthropomorphism that all religions have in common. He observes that our understanding of our experiences is initially ambiguous, but that we reduce this ambiguity by interpreting experiences in human terms. Whether we do so religiously or scientifically does not matter. We understand new things by finding similarities between them and things we already understand. By thinking of nonhuman phenomena in human terms, the hallmark of religious thinking, we create plausible explanations for the unknown. According to Guthrie, such anthropomorphic explanations are plausible for three reasons: (1) Humans are complex and multifaceted, so similarities can be found between many phenomena and some parts of the human condition; (2) human beings are likely to be found wherever the human observer may be; (3) humans are the most important factor in the human environment. Therefore, anthropomorphic models are readily used by human beings to interpret their experiences, and it is these models and interpretations of the universe as created and governed by unseen humanlike beings that we call religion. Guthrie's view that there is nothing psychologically implausible about religious ways of interpreting experiences implies that when we ask why people are religious, we may be asking the wrong question. Perhaps we should be asking why people sometimes think in nonreligious ways.

C H A P T E R S U M M A R Y

1. Religion is found in all cultures but is subject to greater diversity than any other aspect of culture.

2. Universal aspects that define religion in all societies are the belief in supernatural beings, the belief in supernatural power, the symbolic expression of feelings, and ritual behavior.

3. The great diversity in belief systems may be related to variation in people's social, environmental, and technological contexts and may be seen as helping them adapt to those particular circumstances.

4. Ritual behaviors may serve any of three general functions: uniting a community emotionally, portraying human needs or sacred beliefs, or influencing the supernatural. Rituals may be the province of solo practitioners—shamans, sorcerers, or witches—in small-scale societies.

5. In somewhat larger societies, religion is often a communal matter, with group ceremonies.

6. In large, socially stratified societies, religious specialists are commonly full-time practitioners, organized into the hierarchical systems that characterize ecclesiastical religions.

7. Religion seems to help maintain social order, reduce individual anxiety, and help people make sense of the often puzzling world around them.

8. New religions often arise during times of social stress as revitalization movements that offer solutions to society's problems.

A N N O T A T E D R E A D I N G S

Evans-Pritchard, E. E. (1956). *Nuer religion.* Oxford: Clarendon Press. Based on years of intensive study by one of the greats in British anthropology, this is a classic study of religion in an African society.

Furst, P. T. (Ed.). (1972). *Flesh of the gods: The ritual use of hallucinations.* New York: Praeger. A collection of articles on the use of hallucinogens to achieve altered states of consciousness in religious settings.

Kluckhohn, C. (1944). *Navaho witchcraft. (Papers of the Peabody Museum of American Archeology and Ethnology, Harvard University, 22[2]).* Cambridge, MA: Harvard University Press. An interesting look at a fascinating part of Navajo religious beliefs.

Lehmann, A. C., & Myers, J. E. (1985). *Magic, witchcraft, and religion: An anthropological study of the supernatural.* Palo Alto, CA: Mayfield. A thorough and up-to-date collection of articles on religion.

Lessa, W. A., & Vogt, E. Z. (Eds.). (1979). *Reader in comparative religion* (4th ed.). New York: Harper & Row. The classic comprehensive reader for the anthropology of religion. Must reading for the anthropology major.

Radin, P. (1937). *Primitive religion.* New York: Dover. A classic and insightful view of religion by an excellent writer.

Sharon, D. (1978). *Wizard of the four winds: A shaman's story.* New York: Macmillan. An insightful biography of a Peruvian shaman.

Swanson, G. E. (1960). *The birth of the gods: The origin of primitive beliefs.* Ann Arbor, MI: University of Michigan Press. An often overlooked, but important exploration of the Durkheim view of religious belief as a reflection of the organization of society.

Wallace, A. F. C. (1966). *Religion: An anthropological view.* New York: Random House. An influential look at religion that argued for the centrality of ritual in understanding religion.

Worsley, P. (1957). *The trumpet shall sound: A study of "cargo" cults in Melanesia.* London: MacGibbon & Kee. The classic comparative study of religious revitalization movements in Melanesia.

FIGURE 12.1   Culture and Personality
Personality is formed as much by one's family
as it is by one's culture. In 1992, Russian cos-
monaut Sergei Krikalev spent 313 days in space
during which time his country ceased to exist.
Gorbachev resigned as president, and the cos-
monaut's hometown of Leningrad was renamed
St. Petersburg. Weakened by the time in space
because no agency would accept the responsibility for the space mission, Krikalev's personality will certainly be affected by the changes in
his country.

We like to think of ourselves as unique individuals, yet we tend to be somewhat similar to other people in our society. Our personalities are not merely our own. They are shaped to a great extent by our culture. In this chapter, we will look at how culture provides the limits within which we can express our unique qualities. Culture also provides various ways for interpreting deviant behavior. Such behavior may be valued as creative or it may be stigmatized. Deviant behavior grows out of attempts to relieve the stresses peculiar to life in each society. If these attempts do not fit within the bounds of what others consider normal behavior appropriate for our roles, we may be labeled mentally ill.

Culture, Personality, and Psychological Process

CHAPTER OBJECTIVES

After reading this chapter, you should be able to:

Explain the relationships among personality, socialization, and social roles.

Discuss the relationships among childrearing practices, personality, and a society's secondary institutions.

Explain the role of socialization in culturally patterned gender differences.

Analyze the concept of face-work.

Analyze the relationship between role playing and emotional distress.

Explain the nature and causes of trance.

Discuss the cultural functions of trance states.

Explain the roles of ritual in expressing and alleviating stress.

Explain the nature and causes of deviance.

Discuss how culture influences people's conception of mental disorders.

Discuss the various culture-specific mental disorders.

Stressed out. Cool. Yuppie. Druggie. All-American. Are you self-confident? Shy? Bright? Frightened? Do you listen to AC/DC? Or Mozart? Do you play the violin? Or enjoy basketball? Do you drink Coke? Or Pepsi? Who we are and who we become depend on numerous influences both in our family and our culture.

···

Culture and Personality

In the 1920s, a number of anthropologists began to study the relationship between culture and human psychology. Their school of thought came to be known as **culture and personality** for its emphasis on the close parallels between each society's culture and the common personality characteristics of its people. This early period in the study of culture and its impact on individuals had two thrusts: configurationalism and national character studies.

Configurationalism

The leader in culture and personality studies was Ruth Benedict, a student of Franz Boas. She suggested that each culture molded personalities in distinctive ways. Because of the harmony between a culture and the basic personality type it engendered, culture could be seen as a "personality writ large." Culture, then, is to a society what the personality is to an individual. According to Benedict, each culture is a unique, integrated whole with a distinctive configuration of values and customs that are analogous to "individual psychology thrown large upon a screen, given gigantic proportions and a long time span" (1932, p. 24), a view of culture that is known as

configurationalism. As an example, Benedict characterized the Pueblo societies of the southwestern part of the United States as having a culture that stressed the values of emotional balance, moderation, and cooperation, a configuration she named Apollonian, after Apollo the Greek god of sunlight, music, and poetry (1928, 1934). The socialization of Pueblo individuals based on these values almost guaranteed that their personalities would all be similar. Benedict contrasted the Pueblos with the culture of the Plains Indians, in which emotional extremes were valued. Their customs included the pursuit of valor in warfare as a way of achieving high status and religious practices such as self-torture, vision quests, and the use of drugs to achieve ecstatic experiences, a configuration that she called Dionysian, after the Greek god of wine. These cultural traits resulted in the socialization of individuals into much more aggressive and emotive personalities than were found among the Pueblos.

As another example, Margaret Mead, a student of Ruth Benedict, looked specifically at the adolescent development of young women in Samoa (1928). She found that Samoan adolescence was not characterized by the same turmoil and rebellion that was common among adolescents in the United States. She concluded that the emotionally smoother transition between childhood and adulthood in Samoa was a result of values that stressed harmony and cooperation and customs that permitted their children to learn about and explore their sexuality in a more casual way than was possible in the United States.

Socialization and personality. Our culture is incorporated into our personality through the process of **socialization**, which also guarantees that a culture will be passed from one generation to the next. Much of this socialization occurs during our childhood. Every society has its own customs by which children are raised toward adulthood. For instance, Margaret Mead (1950) pointed out that the warlike, aggressive Iatmul of New Guinea encouraged aggression in their children by allowing them to

---

culture and personality anthropological study of relationship between culture and human psychology
configurationalism Benedict's view of culture as a configuration of values and customs that influence individual psychology
socialization the process of learning a culture and the role-playing skills necessary for social life

cry for long periods before feeding them and then frustrating their attempts to take food. The nearby Arapesh, on the other hand, having a peaceful way of life, indulged their children.

The importance of childrearing customs in influencing the development of personality traits has been illustrated by Cora DuBois (1944). She reported that Alorese children in Indonesia received very inconsistent care from infancy. Mothers had to return to work in the fields within two weeks after the birth of a child, and infants received little attention until they were nursed when their mothers returned late in the afternoon. Once an Alorese child learned to walk, it received even less attention during the day. Weaning occurred before the birth of another child and was promoted by teasing, punishment, or even by sending the child to stay with relatives. As one might expect, Alorese children grew up to be suspicious and pessimistic, with shallow friendships. Alorese religion and art reflected their upbringing. Like parents, Alorese gods were not to be relied on. They had to be placated to avoid their anger. But this was done grudgingly, and religious art was only carelessly crafted, without devotion. Frustration and resentment were central themes of Alorese folk tales and stories.

The anthropologists who pursued personality and culture studies were greatly influenced by Freudian psychology. Abram Kardiner, an influential psychoanalyst, popularized the concept of the **basic personality structure**, which he defined as the "adaptive tools of the individual which are common to every individual in society" (1939, p. 237). Other anthropologists, especially those in the 1950s and later, who dealt with statistical data about the prevalence of personality traits in various societies, took a position that allowed for more variation in the personalities of members of any society by substituting the concept of **modal personality type** for basic personality structure. It referred to the most frequent personality traits that are found in a society. But all followers of the culture and personality approach were searching for some way of relating cultural traits with some kind of predominant personality characteristics that distinguished the members of one society from those of another.

Primary institutions. Kardiner's model of the interaction of culture and personality held that children's personalities are most directly influenced by a society's **primary institutions**, those involved in childrearing. During childhood, our personality is

FIGURE 12.2   Socialization
Socialization is a process by which the customs of a society are passed down from one generation to the next, particularly during childhood. These Yąnomamö boys have learned how to cook lizards, a common food in their culture.

shaped by factors such as how we are fed and cared for, the degree to which we are touched and comforted, how long we are nursed, how we are weaned and toilet trained, and how and what we are taught about human sexuality. Just what are the primary institutions? According to John Whiting and Irvin Child, "The economic, political and social organs of a society—the basic customs surrounding the nourishment, sheltering and protection of its members—seem a likely source of influence on child training practices (1953, p. 310)."

Secondary institutions.   Kardiner further argued that people's personalities shape the **secondary**

basic personality structure Kardiner's term for the adaptive tools used by all individuals in a particular society
modal personality type the most common or typical pattern of personality traits in a particular society
primary institutions the primary care groups related to childrearing, including feeding, weaning, sexual training, and subsistence patterns

institutions of society, those most central to the ideology of a culture, such as religious beliefs and rituals, myths, folktales, humor, recreation, and art styles.

Robert LeVine (1973) has elaborated upon the relationships between primary and secondary institutions by adding an intermediate level that he calls a society's **maintenance system**, the economic and social structure that results from a society's adaptation to a particular environment. It is this system, according to LeVine, that determines the society's childrearing practices, which—mediated by the biological needs, drives, and capacities of these children—result in the development of their personalities. As children grow into adulthood, the basic patterns of their personalities influence how they work and play and are the source of cultural products such as fantasies, forms of recreation, and perceptions of the world as benevolent or dangerous.

Subsistence patterns.   The impact of subsistence patterns on personality development has been investigated by Herbert Barry, Irvin Child, and Margaret Bacon, who compared agricultural societies with those in which people survive by hunting and gathering (1959). They found that the cultures of agricultural societies are more likely to stress compliance in children, while hunting and gathering people are more likely to teach their children to assert themselves as individuals. Whereas self-reliance is an important survival trait among hunters, following an established routine seems more important in the daily lives of agriculturalists. Children who play with and scatter the stored food reserves of agricultural peoples or who get underfoot in their more crowded settlements are not likely to be well tolerated.

National Character

While the culture and personality school of anthropology was developing its model of how socialization influenced personality and how personality, in turn, influenced other aspects of a culture, some members of this field produced a series of studies that came to be known as national character studies. Like the configurationalist descriptions of nonindustrialized societies, **national character studies** were an attempt to identify the psychological characteristics of entire societies, but the focus was on entire nations. A common theme in national character studies was the view that childrearing customs had a major impact on adult personality traits. For

instance, the supposedly strict and early toilet training experienced by Japanese children was claimed to be the foundation for the extreme wartime aggressiveness of Japanese soldiers. The Russian swaddling, the tight wrapping of infants that constrained their arm and leg movements, was said to be the reason why adult Russians had little self control and were given to long periods of brooding followed by outbursts of rage.

National character studies were a product of World War II and of efforts of some American anthropologists to help their government better understand the Japanese (Geoffrey Gorer, 1943; Weston LaBarre, 1945; Benedict, 1946). Since direct fieldwork was impossible, these anthropologists carried out their study of Japanese culture indirectly, by examining Japanese Americans, Japanese films, and previously published documents about Japan. These studies portrayed the Japanese culture as one that instilled obsessive-compulsive traits in its people, characteristics that were manifest in great concern for ritual, order, and cleanliness. Other national character studies were carried out on countries such as the United States (Mead, 1942; Gorer, 1948), Russia (Gorer and Rickman, 1949), and England (Gorer, 1955).

Criticisms of the Culture and Personality School

The early culture and personality studies have been subject to criticism because both the configurationalist studies and the national character studies tended to gloss over individual differences within any society and to over-generalize consistencies of personality. Thus, Benedict's portrayal of the Zuñi was flawed by its failure to acknowledge the existence of conflict, alcoholism, or suicide, all of which did occur among the Zuñi in spite of cultural ideals to the contrary. Mead did discuss several examples of young women whose adolescence was not as conflict-

---

secondary institutions   the institutions in social life that satisfy the needs and tensions not met by the primary institutions, including taboo systems, religion, rituals, folk tales, and techniques of thinking

maintenance system   the parts of the economic and social structure of a society that determine its childrearing practices

national character studies   an attempt to identify the psychological characteristics of entire societies free as she had portrayed Samoan women's lives, but Harris has pointed out that Mead portrayed these women as deviants, not as examples of personality differences (1968, p. 410).

Culture and personality studies have been criticized also for their lack of methodological rigor. The absence of fieldwork in the wartime national character studies introduced errors. For instance, later studies demonstrated that Japanese families were typically less concerned with toilet training than were Americans. The portrayals of cultural characteristics in this early period were also highly impressionistic, a problem that resulted from cultures being described as if every member of society shared exactly the same understandings of their way of life. Thus, culture and personality studies such as Benedict's portrayals of the Zuñi and Kwakiutl have been criticized for failing to recognize the widespread cultural diversity and personality differences that exist in all societies. Furthermore, culture and personality studies were not based on random samples of members of the societies that were being studied, but relied heavily on the intuitions of the investigators when they described the "typical" personality characteristics of a society. For instance, Mead's study of Samoan women was based on interviews of only 50 individuals from neighboring villages, and half of the young women were not yet past puberty. The validity of supposed causal links between childrearing customs and adult personalities was not tested by examining cross-cultural data on other societies with the same childrearing practices. Methodological weaknesses were especially problematic in national character studies, where the peoples being studied were political enemies, and ethnocentric judgments would be a particularly easy source of error. Thus, discussions of rituals in Japanese life were defined with terminology, such as compulsiveness, that was developed within Freudian psychology to characterize a psychological disorder.

Psychological Anthropology

Efforts to overcome the methodological and conceptual weaknesses of the earlier culture and personality researchers led to new approaches to the study of the relationships between culture and the individual, beginning in the 1950s. These more mod-

ern approaches make up today's diverse field of **psychological anthropology**, which has abandoned global characterizations of cultures and intuitive generalizations about personality and has adopted a more empirical approach to data collection that emphasizes statistically testable links between specific aspects of culture and particular psychological processes. Psychological anthropology has taken two major forms. In the first, studies use cross-cultural fieldwork to make comparisons of specific psychological characteristics between different groups within the same culture or between members of different cultures. In the second, cross-cultural survey research emphasizes tests of particular hypotheses about customs and psychology that rely on statistical comparisons of similar data from a large number of societies. Whereas the first approach relies on fieldwork studies, often by teams of researchers, the second approach makes heavy use of the Human Relations Area Files (HRAF) data derived from traditional ethnographies of the world's cultures.

Cross-Cultural Fieldwork

An excellent example of cross-cultural fieldwork by a team of researchers is a project that was headed by Walter Goldschmidt (1965). It investigated the influence of subsistence activities on personality in four East African societies, the Hehe, Kamba, Pokot, and Sebei. The Hehe and Kamba had some historic connection and shared a common language, Bantu. Similarly, the Pokot and Sebei, though distinct, also spoke a common language, Kalenjin, and had some historic continuities. Each of these societies had communities based on pastoralism and communities based on horticulture. Based on data collected by asking questions and by recording responses to inkblots and color slides, the team demonstrated that each of these societies had distinct cultural characteristics. For instance, the Hehe data showed them to be aggressive, formal, mistrusting, and secretive. The Kamba showed psychological traits of extreme male dominance, fear of poverty, and restrained emotions. The Pokot were particularly concerned with cattle, beauty, and sex. And the Sebe were concerned with health and showed more jealousy and hostility than the other groups.

psychological anthropology empirical approach to data collection that emphasizes statistical correlations between culture and psychological processes

By comparing the pastoral and horticultural communities in each of the four East African societies, one of Goldschmidt's team members, Robert Edgerton, was able to demonstrate certain similarities that distinguished pastoralists from cultivators regardless of which society or cultural tradition they belonged to or which language they spoke. He found that the pastoralists were direct and open in their communication, realistic in their outlook, and constricted and controlled in their emotions, while the horticulturalists in all groups tended to be indirect, abstract in their views, more anxious and less able to deal with their emotions as well as less able to control their impulses (1965). Fieldwork studies such as this one have been valuable sources of data about the cultural variables that influence personality differences between groups, since they examine the mechanisms of personality formation in specific, real-life contexts.

Cross-Cultural Surveys

John Whiting and a number of his colleagues have made extensive use of the Human Relations Area Files developed by George Murdock to test a variety of hypotheses regarding relationships between specific customs and personality traits. These studies have generally followed a model derived from Kardiner (see p. 277).

John Whiting and Irvin Child (1953) were the first to use the HRAF in an important study of personality. They found a relationship between childhood experiences and beliefs and religious practices related to illness in societies that lacked complex medical technologies. The frustration of a child's aggression and oral, sexual, and dependence needs was directly correlated with beliefs about the causes of illness and with curing practices. For instance, Whiting and Child found that early punishment of aggression is cross-culturally correlated with a strong belief in sorcery and witchcraft as causes of illness. Similarly, George Wright (1954) has found that in societies where children are severely punished for aggression, the theme of aggression is particularly common in their folk tales. In a similar way, proverbs, riddles, and jokes seem to reflect the psychological preoccupations of a people.

Today, psychological anthropology is a highly varied field within anthropology. Psychological anthropologists specialize in the study of such diverse topics as the relationships between culture and emotions, the development of cognitive skills, the influence of language on perception and on cultural differences in how people classify and understand themselves and their environment, psychological universals in symbolic aspects of culture, and cultural similarities and differences in psychiatric disorders.

....

Personality

In psychological terms, **personality** may be defined as our consistent pattern of behaviors, resulting from internal mechanisms. Although we generally think of our personality as something located within ourselves, anthropologists are more interested in examining it in relation to a complex external cultural system and social pressures. From an anthropological perspective, personality is seen as an individual's pattern of behavior that results from the various social roles that he or she has learned to play. Whereas psychologists tend to be interested in the consistent ways of behaving regardless of the role being played, anthropologists are more likely to be interested in how differences in the individual's style of behaving vary from role to role, depending on the time, place, or social context of the role playing. In this chapter, we will examine the various approaches anthropologists have taken to analyzing the relationships between personality, social roles, and culture.

Personality and Social Roles

Culture defines the nature of a society, the kinds of roles the participants may adopt, and, hence, the ways that people can interact. For instance, among the Cheyenne of the North American plains, the **Contrary Warrior** was expected to interact with others in a different way from other Cheyenne (Grinnell, 1961; Llewellyn & Hoebel, 1941). When Contraries wished to affirm something, they were required to say "No"; to deny, they said "Yes"; when they were asked to go away, it was anticipated that they would approach. Contraries were chosen from the bravest of warriors. They were thought to

▬

personality   consistent pattern of behavior related both to inner forces and to external, cultural, and social pressures
Contrary Warrior   a Cheyenne status that required the reversal of all normal behaviors, reserved for the bravest warriors

be possessed of visionary power and inspired other warriors to fight their hardest. To set the status of the Contrary apart from others, Contraries were expected to do all things backwards, displaying buffoonery even during otherwise solemn occasions.

Status-appropriate roles. Patterns for behavior are laid down in the culture's ideology as rules outlining the status-appropriate roles that people may play when interacting with one another. Personality therefore can be seen as a cultural phenomenon as well as an internal, psychological one—that is, as a culturally controlled pattern in an individual's role playing. Whenever people interact in settings where one of their statuses is appropriate, they normally manifest those parts of their personality that embody the roles of that status.

Each human group is made up of several statuses that the group defines as mutually compatible. When a person attempts to enter a new group, members interact with the newcomer to determine her or his potential to hold a status that the group recognizes as appropriate. This process determines which roles of the group's various statuses the newcomer is capable of playing. In initiating the process, newcomers "present face," that is, communicate to the others the possible social value they claim for themselves. Once admitted to the group, individuals are expected to play a role that supports that face, or social standing. They will be evaluated by the others based on how well they continue to live up to that initial self-portrayal.

---

status-appropriate roles the ways of behaving that are expected of an individual who holds a particular social status in a specific culture

face positive social value a person can contribute to a group; social standing

---

Sorority Rush: An Example of Establishing Face

Whether we are being interviewed for a job, discussing the news of the day with a group of potential new friends, or joining a sorority, our first interactions with others are an attempt to demonstrate that we can be of value to them. If we convince the group that we can fill a role that would benefit it, and if the group convinces us that we have something to gain from playing that role, then we will be taken into the group. Depending on how formally the group is organized, the process may be more or less highly structured, but it is essentially the same in content wherever it occurs.

Consider the case of sorority rush, a more formal example of face-work. On the Utah

FIGURE 12.3 Establishing Face
Face-work is a process by which we attempt to convince others that we would be capable of playing a role in their group. The college sorority or fraternity is a compatible group that represents a particular attitude or ideal. New students seek to be admitted through a series of activities and interviews. Once admitted, they must participate in initiation rites as these young women are doing. in order to save face.

State University campus, Greek Rush Week begins on Monday, when the three sororities set up a registration table in the Student Center. Young women who wish to join a sorority pay a $5 registration fee to demonstrate the seriousness of their intent. They fill out an application giving their names, hometowns, grade-point averages, and interests, as well as identifying immediate relatives who have been sorority sisters. On Tuesday, applicants attend a movie that explains the Greek system: the philanthropies engaged in by each House, the intramural sports played between the Houses, the parties and social events that each hosts, and the activities of Greek Rush Week. The applicants are then divided into groups of 30 or 40 for House Tours through the three sorority Houses near the campus.

During the next three days of Greek Rush Week, the applicants and sorority sisters become more familiar with each other. The sisters must study all applicants' information, learning their names and as much as possible about them. On Wednesday they host half-hour "Halloween Parties" for each group of applicants. The activities include singing and dancing. The applicants and House sisters meet personally at this time. On the next day each House invites a smaller group to return to a "Beach Party." This group includes only those applicants in which each House is most interested. At this party, the sorority sisters talk with the applicants, trying to become better acquainted personally. After the party, the sisters meet to hold an open discussion and vote on each applicant.

On Friday an even smaller group of the most preferred applicants are invited to return to the "Preference Party." The selectiveness of the process works both ways, for even if the applicants are invited by all three Houses, they may attend only two events. Preference Day is the most intimate and emotional of the three days. The goal of the House at this party is to show the value of the sorority to its members, to communicate the closeness of the sisters and how they feel about each other. There is singing, and the senior sisters give talks about what the sorority means to them.

After the Preference Parties, the applicants must indicate their first and second choices of a House on a signed document. Once it is signed, their choices cannot be changed. The sisters of each house write the names of their top choices, and all applicants are ranked based on the total votes they receive. The Greek Council meets and compares the lists from each House with the preferences of the applicants, and each applicant is assigned a House.

On Saturday the applicants pick up the "bids," which inform them which house they have been assigned. They go immediately to the sorority House, where the sisters are waiting outside for them. They are greeted with songs and a welcoming party. At a formal ceremony, applicants now become Pledges, a status they will hold for about eight weeks. At the end of that period, if the Pledge wishes to finalize her entry into the House, she will be initiated into the status of a full member.

Face-work. Much of our day-to-day social interaction is aimed at promoting and protecting our own face and the face of other members of our group. In general, the more highly ranked our social status, the more effort others will expend to protect our face. Erving Goffman (1955) has described as **face-work** the process by which we are maintained in the roles we have been assigned to play. Often, when one first behaves in a way that contradicts the face one has initially espoused, such violations are ignored, and no damage to face occurs. It is then possible for a person to return to the usual role, and social interaction continues according to the normal game plan. If, however, a violation of the norms is brought to public attention—that is, if it becomes publicly labeled as a violation of one's expected "normal behavior"—some work must be done to repair one's damaged face if one is to be accepted again as a fully participating member of the group.

This repair process generally follows a definite sequence, which Goffman has characterized as (1) the challenge, (2) the offering, (3) the acceptance, and

face-work   interaction in which effort is directed to maintaining or returning behavior to roles considered appropriate for members of a group; efforts to maintain or reestablish face

(4) the thanks. In the challenge, the person who has injured or threatened another's face is confronted with the warning that the threatened face will be defended. In the offering, the offender (or, occasionally, another person) is permitted to make amends, perhaps by indicating that the apparent threat was meaningless or unintentional, that it was only a joke, or that it had been unavoidable. The offering may also take the form of excusing the actor from responsibility, as when one attributes an otherwise serious violation of rules to intoxication, fatigue, or illness. At the same time, compensation may be offered to the offended party, and the offender may take on a self-imposed punishment. The recipient of the offering may now indicate acceptance of its sufficiency for reestablishing the original symbolic balance of the group. If this is done, the offender expresses thanks for the forgiveness.

As individuals manifest their personal qualities in social interaction, their behavior is constrained by culturally defined rules for maintaining social order. The personality traits that are considered normal are those that can be integrated successfully into the interactions. Behaviors that consistently disrupt social exchanges are likely to be seen as abnormal or deviant. Each society exists in a unique environment and has particular techniques for obtaining what its people need to survive there. Thus, the cultural ideals of "normal" interaction will be defined differently from society to society.

Individuality and Deviance

Although a culture's ideals and rules for behavior work to create conformity, none of us is identical to anyone else, and each of us brings to the group our own unique predispositions, including how we each respond to socialization. Thus, the actual behavior of individuals varies somewhat from the expectations embodied in their culture about how people should act in various situations. The ways in which individuals may successfully deviate from their culture's rules and the degree of deviation that is tolerated by others differs from culture to culture.

Deviance. To most people, the word *deviance* has a rather negative connotation. In a more technical context, however, it is not limited to negative behavior. **Deviance** is merely behavior that differs enough from what is expected, that it is noticed (Becker, 1963, pp. 8–9; Erikson, 1962, p. 308;

FIGURE 12.4 Cultural Deviance
Ezra Pound (1885–1972) was an American poet most known for his extensive collection of Cantos. In his concern about the causes of World War II, he condemned American participation in broadcasts from Italy. Returning to the United States he was arrested, tried for treason, and finally found insane and mentally unfit for trial. He spent 12 years in St. Elizabeth's Hospital for the criminally insane in Washington, D.C., where he continued to write.

Scheff, 1966). Deviance may be welcomed and praised or rejected and punished. Thus, **creativity** may be considered a kind of deviance from cultural expectations, but it generally results in a valuable new contribution to society and may be rewarded. It is also true that deviation from cultural norms may bring public censure and **stigma**, the loss of rank that accompanies the social rejection of persons who have violated accepted role behavior. For instance, poets or actors sometimes have been imprisoned or confined in mental hospitals by governments who perceived their political commentaries as "traitorous," "pornographic," or "insane."

---

deviance behavior that differs enough from what society expects that others notice and react to it
creativity deviance that results in valuable new contributions to society
stigma loss of rank that accompanies the social rejection of persons who have violated accepted role behavior

TABLE 12.1   Emotional Responses to Inadequate Role Playing

Problem (Context of Stress)	Individual's Interpretation of the Role Playing Difficulty	Individual's Physiological and Behavioral Responses to Tension State**	Individual's Subjective Feeling
UNKNOWN DANGER, NON-SPECIFIC AROUSAL	"I need to act but I don't know what to do. I cannot cope with this."	generalized visceral tension, hyperventilation, breathlessness, tightness of chest, stomach spasms, diarrhea or constipation, rapid heartbeat, respiratory distress, fainting, nausea, sweating, tremor and agitation	ANXIETY (includes frenzy, helplessness, inner conflict, worrying, feelings of loss of self-control)
KNOWN DANGER	"I have too little power."	*facial pallor, coldness of hands and feet, rapid and shallow breathing, rapid heartbeat, immobilization or retreat	FEAR (includes terror, apprehension)
HARM TO ANOTHER	"I have used too much power."	head lowered (lower than in shame), gaze averted with only quick glances at other people, avoidance of eye contact, wringing of hands, face takes on "heavy" look with tightness around eyes, dryness of mouth, tightness of sphincter muscles, preoccupation with concepts of fault and wrongdoing	GUILT (includes self-reproach, remorse)
REJECTION, LOSS, ISOLATION	"I have too little esteem; I am worthless."	*sadness with or without tears, headaches, nasal congestion, swelling of eyes, feelings of hopelessness	GRIEF (includes loneliness, sadness, sorrow, pensiveness)
LOSS OF FACE	"I have claimed too much esteem, and others know of it."	*blushing, lowering or covering of face, gaze averted down and to one side, confusion, body curved inward on itself, curled up, makes self look smaller, eyes closed	SHAME (includes embarrassment, shyness, contriteness, sheepishness, mortification)
FRUSTRATION	"Someone/something stands in my way."	*violence of movement or speech, repetitiveness	ANGER (includes hate, rage, annoyance)

In a given situation, when we fail to respond in a manner appropriate to our status or role, we experience emotional distress.

*From "The Distancing of Emotion in Ritual," by T. J. Scheff, 1977, *Current Anthropology, 18* (3), 483–506.
**Alternatively, any of these may be realized as emotionless and/or distraction.

Note. Ideas about power and esteem adapted from *A Social Interactional Theory of Emotions* by T. D. Kemper, 1978, NY: John Wiley and Sons.

Inadequate Role Playing

Failure to play our roles as we are expected to may bring us personal distress as well as stigma. Every status has a culturally defined rank. To maintain face, the holder of each status is expected to use a particular amount of power and to receive a certain amount of honor. Failure to play one's roles in a way that uses the appropriate level of power or demands the appropriate amount of honor results in emotional distress for the role player.

The most basic form of this subjective distress is anxiety, a general sense of powerlessness and foreboding. Depending on the context in which the stress occurs and on how the individual interprets the situation, anxiety may alternate with more focused distressful feelings (see Table 12.1). Anxiety will take the form of the more concrete emotion fear if the sufferer feels that he or she is playing a role with insufficient power to remain safe from the negative effects of some specific problem. Anxiety alternates with guilt when stress arises from an awareness that one is exercising more power than is personally acceptable. Grief or sadness may be present when the stress-causing situation is understood by the sufferer

as the inability to obtain voluntary esteem from others. Alternatively, anxiety may take the form of shame or embarrassment when there is a possibility that the present esteem of others may be withdrawn, that is, when the stress stems from discovering that one is receiving more honor than one's skills deserve. Any of these four negative, concrete emotions—fear, guilt, grief, and shame—may be avoided if the sufferer has learned to respond to others with anger instead. We feel anger when we hold another person responsible for causing our own distress.

---

anxiety a distressful subjective awareness of stress; a general sense of powerlessness and foreboding without awareness of a specific danger

fear a distressful emotion characterized by concerns about inadequate power to protect oneself from specific danger

guilt a distressful emotion characterized by remorse for having used too much power and having harmed another

grief a distressful emotion characterized by a sense of loss, sadness, and failure to obtain esteem from others

shame (embarrassment) a distressful emotion characterized by a sense of personal ineptness resulting in damage to one's reputation and loss of esteem

anger an emotional state during which another person is held responsible for one's own distress. Anger can substitute for anxiety, fear, guilt, grief, or shame in situations in which those emotions might otherwise be felt

---

Anger and Violence Among the Semai of Malaysia

The Semai horticulturalists of central West Malaysia were described by Dentan as a society whose people were so unaggressive in their customs that they had no need for police, judges, or jails. The very idea of physical violence was so horrifying to them that their word for 'hit' would be translated as 'kill" (Dentan, 1968, p. 58).

In the Semai culture, people learned that anger made them prone to accidents. So instead of getting angry, victimized persons preferred to seek redress for their grievances in ways that did not show anger, such as approaching the offender and asking for compensation. The other person was under some pressure to acknowledge his fault and make amends to avoid further responsibility for ac-

cidents that might befall the already injured person. Even when social problems were not adequately resolved, violence rarely resulted. The injured party might spread gossip and otherwise insult the wrongdoer. These acts were enough pressure for some to resolve the problem finally, but even if they failed, escalation of the hostility did not occur among the Semai.

Dentan supported his description of a society without violence with the fact that the Semai could not remember an instance of homicide, and he could find no instance of murder, attempted murder, or maiming among the Semai from 1956 through 1968. In Dentan's opinion, violence actually seemed to terrify the Semai. They reacted to force with passivity or flight and learned to keep a tight rein over aggressive impulses.

The Semai had no authority figures, even

Semai

Living in central West Malaysia, the Semai are a nonviolent people. In solving social problems, they simply ask for, and expect, compensation for whatever fault was committed against them. They react to force with passivity or flight, and learn to control their own aggressive impulses.

in their families. Parents never coerced their children into specific kinds of behavior, but let them follow their own inclinations. They believed that to pressure children would make them unhappy and, therefore, accident-prone. To teach their children to avoid unacceptable behavior, the Semai used fear in the form of threats of physical punishment. But the threatened blow was never realized; it would be frozen inches away from the child or transformed, at worst, to a slight tap.

That it was situational forces and not just personality that molded people to crime or conformity was illustrated by a further fact about Semai behavior. During the 1950s, the Malaysian government was involved in military conflict with Communist guerrilla forces. When Semai men joined the British military forces and participated in combat, some individuals became noted for the extremes of their fervor in battle. But when the circumstances of warfare led them to kill other human beings, their acts of violence caused them such psychological distress and disorientation that, in order to deal with it, they entered a trance-like state they termed *buul bhiib*, or "blood drunkenness." During the mental dissociation that accompanied this state, they sometimes participated in extremely violent fighting. In Dentan's words: "A typical veteran's story runs like this. 'We killed, killed, killed. The Malays would stop and go through people's pockets and take their watches and money. We did not think of watches or money. We thought only of killing. Wah, truly we were drunk with blood.' One man even told how he had drunk the blood of a man he had killed" (pp. 58–59).

Robarchek and Dentan (1987) have pointed out that many of the Semai who behaved violently were men who had experienced the murder of a number of influential Semai by Communist terrorists. In Robarchek and Dentan's opinion, the Semai soldiers were simply "people with little or no prior experience in either committing or dealing with violence, transplanted from an egalitarian, peaceful society into one that taught and rewarded killing, where they were trained in military behavior, including how to kill" (1987, p. 361). In the "heat, fear, and excitement of a sudden firefight" they did what they had been trained to do against enemies they believed had harmed and killed their own neighbors and friends. Most importantly, the state of "blood drunkenness" that these men experienced was an expression of their horror at their own behavior. Contrary to the implications of its English translation, "blood drunkenness" was a state of mind that was characterized not by a frenzy of blood lust or desire to kill, but "an acute state of nausea, fear, disorientation, and disgust which the sight of human blood evokes among the Semai" (1987, p. 361).

Violence and its accompanying "blood drunkenness" were not typical of Semai soldiers. As a matter of fact, the original Semai unit of over 300 soldiers killed only an average of one person a year over a twenty-year period. It is true that some Semai were certainly capable of extremes of violence when they were removed from their normal cultural environment. But even these Semai veterans were disgusted by their own extreme behavior and were at a loss to explain it. Their traditional nonviolent self-image remained intact when they returned to civilian life, and they reverted to their former gentle and timid style of life.

Stress

Stress is the body's attempt to prepare itself to take action against any problem, whether organic (e.g., a change in brain chemistry), psychological (e.g., learned habits that make it difficult to interact successfully with others), or external (e.g., a major life crisis, such as a divorce). Normally, we prefer to channel the energy mobilized by stress into direct attempts to eliminate the problem. When such pragmatic action is not possible, either because (1) we have not correctly identified the problem, (2) we have not learned a means of dealing with it adequately, (3) we lack the skill to take action successfully, or (4) we have no opportunity to take action, we begin to experience anxiety, conscious awareness, and preoccupation with the stress we feel. Depending on how we interpret the situation, anxiety may be a general, nagging sense of foreboding, or it may take on the more concrete form of one of the distressful emotions: fear, guilt, grief, shame, or anger. Some persons so control the expression of anxiety that they experience **affectlessness**, a kind of emotional lethargy.

The Trance State

One common result of intense or prolonged anxiety is the experience of **trances**, which are sometimes also called **altered states of consciousness**. These are subjective states of mind in which experiences are interpreted not in terms of the normal symbolic categories of one's culture, but in various ways common to all human beings. Trances may be rather mild and undramatic experiences, such as the state of daydreaming or fantasy that we all engage in occasionally when we are tired or bored with our current environment. They also may be rather vivid and dramatic occurrences, such as hypnotic trances or dreams.

Psychologist Arnold Ludwig (1972) reports that the major characteristics of altered states of consciousness are:

1. alterations in thinking
2. disturbance of the sense of time
3. change in emotional expression
4. change in body image
5. distortions in perception

FIGURE 12.5   The Trance State
The trance state, or altered state of consciousness, results in changes in perception of time, space, or mobility. It may be induced by drugs, stress, sensory deprivation, or sensory overload. This San shaman, in a trance state as part of a curing ritual, is being helped to walk.

6. change in the perceived meaning or significance of things
7. a sense that the experiences cannot be described
8. hypersuggestibility, and sometimes
9. a sense of loss of control, and/or
10. feelings of rejuvenation

stress   a physiological response to any demand, characterized by the body's preparing itself for action
affectlessness   the complete control of emotion resulting in lethargy
trance (altered state of consciousness)   subjective state of mind where experiences are not interpreted in terms of normal symbolic categories of one's culture
altered state of consciousness   subjective state of mind where experiences are not interpreted in terms of normal symbolic categories of one's culture

Most of these changes may be results of stress, which may inhibit the usual role of the left hemisphere of the cerebral cortex in initiating action and controlling a person's behavior.

Biological explanations of trances. To understand altered states of consciousness, we must first look at the effects of stress on the brain. In the discussion of a biological basis of language (see Chapter 10), we noted that the human cerebral cortex is divided into two major halves or hemispheres, and that the left hemisphere is more specialized than the right. The left hemisphere has specialized centers that make possible the symbolic skills embodied in language. Since normal human interaction is predominantly a series of symbolic interchanges, the left cerebral hemisphere tends to be dominant in initiating and controlling most human activities. Stress, however, interferes with the symbolic capacity of the human organism. This leaves the right hemisphere, the side of the cerebral cortex that takes the lead in nonsymbolic behavior, to play the dominant role during the expressive acts that are common in rituals. This is a role to which it is well suited, since the right hemisphere's predominant way of operating involves communication by direct representation by signs.

The changes in thinking that are common in altered mental states include increased difficulties in concentration, attention, and memory, all of which are results of stress. There is also a shift away from thinking in terms of cause and effect—a left hemispheric way of organizing thought—toward a mode of thought in which opposites may coexist. The coexistence of opposite meanings is a hallmark of communication by signs: A smile may indicate friendship or sarcasm, tears may signal sorrow or joy, and laughter may express either relief from stress or mounting embarrassment.

It has been noted repeatedly in studies of differences between the left and right hemispheres that the ordering of information in a sequence, such as a chronological listing of events, is a left hemispheric trait. However, the experience of time as a passage of events one after another at a constant, measurable pace is alien to the way in which the right hemisphere orders its memory of events. Therefore, the disturbed time sense common in altered mental states may be a result of a shift away from the predominant influence of the left hemisphere's symbolic conceptualization of time.

Perceptual distortions take their most dramatic form as **hallucinations**, which are like vivid dreams in a waking state. According to Buchsbaum (1979), studies of how the left and right hemispheres communicate suggest that hallucinations may result from the failure of the left hemisphere to suppress incoming fears of the right hemisphere. Normally, this suppression is a result of an inhibitory chemical, **serotonin**, produced in the brain during waking hours (Goleman, 1978; Jacobs, 1978). Both dreams and daydreams are normally produced by brain stem stimulation of various brain centers on a 90-minute cycle (Krupke & Lavie, 1975; McCarley, 1978), and daydreams may be the waking state manifestation of dreams in a washed-out form. Under stressful circumstances, the levels of serotonin in the brain may decline, allowing daydreams to be experienced in the vivid form of hallucinations.

The change in the perceived meaning or significance of things experienced during altered states is called the **eureka experience**, a sudden sense of deep insight into things "as they really are." It occurs because the right hemisphere analyzes experiences not by breaking them up conceptually into parts that are then related to one another by abstract logic, but by weighing the experience in its totality and finding answers in sudden flashes of insight. The left hemisphere solves problems and discovers meaning by the symbolic process of analysis.

Producing trance states. Ludwig (1972) reports five main ways of producing altered states of consciousness: (1) a prolonged reduction of sensory input and/or motor activity; or (2) the opposite condition, namely, sensory and/or motor overload; (3) prolonged increased alertness or mental involvement; or (4) the opposite condition, a prolonged decrease in mental alertness or involvement; and (5) changes in body chemistry. The first of these may be exemplified by trances induced by solitary confinement, so-called "highway hypnosis," (the detached state sometimes experienced by motorists on long, boring stretches of road), or the sensory deprivation

hallucination   a realistic-seeming experience—much like a vivid waking dream—that may include vision, hearing, the sense of touch, smell, and/or taste in the absence of external cause

serotonin   a chemical produced in the brain during waking hours that inhibits the production of dreams or hallucinations

eureka experience   a sense of intensified meaningfulness of experiences that sometimes occurs during an altered state of consciousness associated with *kayak angst* (see p. 297). Examples of the second process are brainwashing, the trances of whirling dervishes, and the frightening encounter or tickling that leads to *latah* (see p. 294). Increased alertness as a path to altered mental states may be seen in the effects of fervent prayer or sentry duty. Decreased alertness is used in some forms of meditation to achieve a mystical mental state. Changes in body chemistry include all the drug-induced altered states of consciousness. All of these conditions interfere with the normal functioning of the central nervous system and produce stress, the source of signalized ritual behavior accompanied by altered states of consciousness.

Trance and ideology. Interestingly, altered states of consciousness may play a part in the development of the ideology of a culture. Whenever people attempt to describe or account for the experiences they have had during an altered mental state, they must use the medium of language, a left hemispheric system of communication. Whatever the particular beliefs by which people make sense of altered state experiences, these beliefs invariably involve some degree of what Leslie White (1971) has called a confusion between self and not-self. This confusion may take one of two forms: either (1) that which lies outside the individual is considered an extension of the individual, as when lightning is thought to be nature's response to a sinful thought; or (2) that which actually occurs within an individual, such as a dream or a hallucination, is spoken of as a truly external event. These responses function to relieve the personal effect of stress, not by eliminating the objective cause of the stress, but by relieving the resulting inner feeling of distress.

Cultural Shaping of Altered States of Consciousness

To the extent that altered states of consciousness are responses to stress, they may be culturally shaped in two dimensions. One dimension is the cultural nature of the stress itself; the other is the way in which altered states of consciousness are culturally defined. One example of how cultural definitions of

trance influence its role in society is the use of dreams to control the supernatural.

Dream-control of the supernatural. D'Andrade (1961) compared societies in which people attempt to contact and control the supernatural through dreams with those societies in which dreams play no such role. He found that societies in which young men move far from their parents when they marry are more likely to make such use of dreams. He suggests that this may be a response to the loss of a parent as a source to turn to in times of need. And societies that have the capacity to store food are less likely to use dreams for supernatural purposes than those that are less able to preserve quantities of food. Since the latter is also likely to emphasize independence and self-reliance as a natural consequence of its low accumulation of foodstuffs, Bourguignon (1974) regards the use of dreams to control supernatural power as a response to stresses generated by the lack of human support that the expectation of self-reliance implies.

Socialization and Trance States

Bourguignon and Greenbaum (1973) have noted that different cultural patterns lie behind two different forms of trance, **spirit travel trance** and **spirit possession trance**. The first is characterized by passivity or even unconsciousness during the altered mental state, which is interpreted as a "trip" in which the spirit leaves the body and communes with supernatural entities. Possession trances, on the other hand, involve a great deal of bodily activity, thought to be under the control of a spirit visitor. These trances are often entered with the aid of repetitive chants and dancing. Unlike participants in spirit travel trances, people who engage in possession trances often experience amnesia about what they said and did while possessed. In spirit travel trances, hallucinations may be vividly recalled and drugs are more likely to be used as an aid to entering the trance.

spirit travel trance a trance in which individuals experience themselves as leaving their bodies
spirit possession trance a trance in which individuals feel as if their behavior is under the control of one or more spirits that have entered their bodies

The spirit travel trances are most likely to be found in societies that place the heaviest stress on independence and assertion. Spirit possession trances, on the other hand, are most common in societies where compliance is expected. Thus, Bourguignon and Greenbaum believe that the type of trance that is more common in a culture is the kind that will most effectively reduce the kind of stress common in that culture. For example, in cultures in which people normally are expected to behave in an independent way, spirit travel trances permit them to be taken care of physically by others while they are on a spiritual trip. The spirits they visit offer help and assistance in a way that is not generally available in normal social settings, thereby fulfilling dependency needs that go unsatisfied in the participants' day-to-day social life. In contrast, in cultures where people usually play a more compliant and dependent role, some may satisfy their normally unfulfilled desires for power and autonomy during a spirit possession trance in which they take on the personalities of the powerful, dominant spirits that animate their bodies. During these possession states they can behave in ways their normal roles do not permit, speaking boldly and acting powerfully. Later, they are not held responsible for behaving aggressively, since they did so in the role of a passive vehicle for the spirit that controlled them and may even claim no recollection of their own trance behavior.

According to Whiting and Child (1953), spirit travel trances were especially common in North America, where they were found in 94 percent of the native societies examined. In contrast, only 25 percent had spirit possession trances. In sub-Saharan Africa, on the other hand, only 36 percent had spirit travel trances, and spirit possession trances were about as common as in North America—26 percent. This may reflect a greater emphasis on self-reliance in traditional North American cultures and a corresponding greater role for fulfilling one's responsibilities to the community in many African cultures.

Emotional Distress and Ritual

Prolonged or intense anxiety may also result in changes in behavior. The behavioral changes that often accompany spontaneous trances begin with a breakdown of old patterns leading to residual rule breaking, behavior that violates the unspoken, taken-for-granted rules of our culture. Sometimes this behavior may result in a creative new solution to the

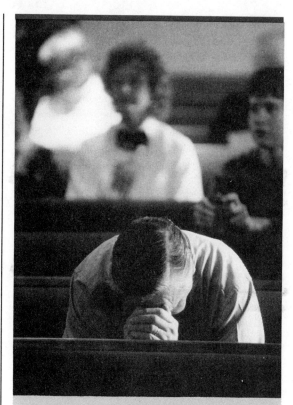

FIGURE 12.6   Religious Ritual

Rituals are specific patterns of behavior that help relieve stress. In times of crisis, religious rituals not only focus our attention elsewhere, but provide some comfort since they are supported by an ideology that people believe can help solve their problems.

original problem. More often it does not. In such cases, our residual rule breaking settles down into highly expressive actions such as a grimace or clenched fists that portray how we feel about the unresolved problem. Whenever it recurs, we are likely to respond with the same expressive acts. Thus, stress-induced residual rule breaking coalesces into ritual, stereotyped repetitive behavior that expresses problems by acting them out. Although ritual acts have no pragmatic effect on the original problem, they do have the psychological effect of reducing our anxiety.

ritual behaviors, often performed in repetitive and stereotyped ways, that express people's anxieties by acting them out. May be an attempt to influence the supernatural realm to achieve greater control over the natural world

Ritual and the control of anxiety. We all spontaneously use rituals when we experience stress that we have not learned to handle in any practical way. Many of our rituals are organized into culturally established patterns that are shared by many people and thought of as *religious* acts. In times of crisis, these religious rituals are available as a source of comfort. Rituals give us something to do when we feel that we must act but do not know what to do. They permit us to channel some of the excess energy of stress into physical action and thereby relieve some of the physiological problems of stress. An even more important role of rituals is to distract us from the stress sensation by focusing our attention elsewhere.

Religious rituals are especially effective in this, since they are supported by an ideology that people believe is a source of supernatural power that can help solve their problems. Following major disasters, such as the 1985 earthquake in Mexico or the 1992 hurricane in Florida, individuals often seek comfort from grief and fear through prayer, both privately and in groups. More idiosyncratic rituals also appear, spontaneously created and carried out with the same emotional benefit of relief from anxiety. For example, people sweeping the steps of a now-demolished house reassure themselves that order can be maintained in the midst of chaos. Others gain solace after the death of loved ones by temporarily denying the loss in word and deed—by preparing food for them as usual at mealtime or even by talking to them as if they were still there. We reassure ourselves in much the same way when we bring flowers or gifts to the bed of someone in a coma, keeping alive the hope of recovery by ritual communication. Rituals give us real benefits in emotionally trying situations, in that while they may not solve the problems that cause us stress, they do help us continue to function in spite of it.

Sometimes, however, our rituals fail to sufficiently allay our worries. When this happens, we may elaborate upon them in a vain attempt to gain control over the anxieties they have not succeeded in eliminating. Then our rituals can interfere with other parts of our lives and become part of a vicious cycle in which we function less and less effectively. It is these rituals that others are most likely to see as evidence of insanity. John Nemiah has reported the case of a young man whose rituals began over his anxiety about not performing well on the job but eventually interfered with his performance:

> A man of 32 who worked on the assembly line of an electronic concern developed the following compelling ritual: before he could solder one piece to another, he had to tap on the workbench 3 times with his left hand and 3 times with his right, followed by stamping 3 times on the floor first with his left foot, then with his right. For a time this merely slowed down his work performance, and he was able to continue his job.
>
> Gradually, however, an element of doubt crept into his mind. After completing a sequence of tapping and stamping, doubting thoughts would flash into his consciousness: "Did I really do it right? Am I sure I tapped 3 times? Did I stamp with my left foot first?" In response to these questions, he had to repeat the ritual to make sure it was perfectly done; but, the more he performed it, the greater his doubt. Before long, almost his entire working day was taken up by his rituals, and he was forced to leave his job. (1975, p. 1246)

Social Stress and Deviant Personality

People who suffer the stigma and emotional distress that can accompany inadequate role playing may occasionally experience spontaneous altered states of consciousness and find themselves engaging in ritual behavior that expresses their distressful feelings. Sometimes, however, individuals become habituated to ritualized behavior and trance states, and this interferes even more with their ability to play acceptable social roles. Such individuals may find themselves reassigned to deviant master statuses, such as "immoral," "possessed," or "insane."

Deviant statuses. A deviant is a person who has been given this label by others for his or her role-playing errors. The specific deviant status assigned will depend on the way in which a person misuses socially assigned power and prestige. The user of an excess of power will be seen as *hostile* and will be described as being prone to anger. The person who consistently uses less power than expected will be seen as *timid* or *fearful*. One who claims the right to an unrealistically high level of esteem will be viewed as *conceited* or *megalomaniacal*. The overly self-denigrating individual will be labeled as *depressive* or *insecure*. Each culture elaborates these four basic categories with labels for subtypes that occur with

---

deviant a person who has been labeled a rule violator by others for his or her role-playing errors high frequency. For instance, in American culture the special term for the person who manifests the hostile use of power by insulting the value of another person is *catty*. One who uses an excess of power to prevent another from terminating a conversation, while remaining overtly oblivious to his or her own violation, will be called a *bore*.

Categories of cultural rules. Rule violations in the use of culturally appropriate levels of power and prestige are common enough in all societies so that every culture is likely to specifically label and define realms within which violations of rules can be grouped. For instance, in the United States, rule violations will be seen as violations of *law* if they result in harm to persons or property. Violations of rules of prestige, which differentiate members of one class from another, are violations of *etiquette*. *Aesthetic* standards are current values about beauty. They include judgments about what things may be compatibly organized together. For instance, North American aesthetic standards preclude the use of Greek columns on a ranch style house, although I suspect that if one grew up with such a style it would not seem strange. As do all symbolic categories, aesthetic standards change. For instance, before the film *Flashdance*, wearing a torn sweatshirt in public was considered unaesthetic in most of America. Law, etiquette, and aesthetics are but three of a much longer list of formally labeled American rule categories.

The precise list of rule categories varies, of course, from culture to culture, and categories that are important in one society may be absent in another. In most societies, for instance, there is no formal category of rules labeled *religious* rules, since the concept of religion as a separate aspect of human life is rare (Cohn, 1967). The one universal fact in categories of rules is that, regardless of how long the list may be, there will always be rules left over that belong to none of the categories. These may be said to make up the *miscellaneous* or **residual rules** of that culture. Although they comprise a leftover category, residual rules are important, since they play a central role in concepts about the most deviant statuses in a society.

Violations of residual rules. Even if a residual rule category is not formally named, the violation of any of these rules elicits a similar reaction from members of society. Scheff (1966) has pointed out that it is the violation of residual norms that results in the labeling of a person as *insane* by other members of society. The violation of legal rules may be abhorred. But such violations are punished at least in part because most members of society can conceive of situations in which they themselves might be tempted to violate the rights of others. Likewise, violation of etiquette is undesirable, but this "poor taste" is understood as evidence of a failure to achieve a desirable level of social ranking, something that not everyone is expected to be able to accomplish. The residual rules, on the other hand, are the rules that are taken for granted, conformity to which is assumed to come naturally to all normal individuals.

Residual rules are the prohibitions that need not be taught; it literally "goes without saying" that they are not to be done. Indeed, the prohibitions embodied in these miscellaneous rules could never be fully codified and formally taught, since the list is, for any culture, an open-ended one that could be added to *ad infinitum*. For example, it is doubtful that any Americans have ever been taught not to remove their shoes and juggle them while carrying on a conversation with a minister. Yet most if not all Americans would immediately recognize such behavior as a rule violation were they to witness it, especially if the actor, on being queried, failed to provide an acceptable rationale for her or his behavior. He or she would be likely to be judged insane.

Stress and residual rule breaking. In the opinion of Scheff (1966), the causes of residual rule breaking are diverse. They include: (1) organic sources such as genetic, biochemical, and physiological problems; (2) psychological sources, such as problems in upbringing and training or maladaptive habit patterns that interfere with one's own success; (3) external stress such as drug ingestion, danger, lack of food and sleep, or sensory overload; and (4) volitional acts of innovation or defiance. The common denominator of all these causes is that residual rule breaking is likely to occur when the individual is experiencing stress, regardless of its sources. Stress is a physiological state that has been studied for years by Selye (1976), who defines it as the nonspecific response of the body to any demand. In the beginning

---

residual rules miscellaneous, normally unspoken rules that people are expected to follow to avoid violating the pattern or style of behavior that is expected in the culture stages of the stress state, the human body is mobilizing itself for action. This state of readiness involves such general bodily changes as increased movement, heightened blood pressure, excess perspiration, and accelerated heartbeat.

When one's culture has provided no normal response to a stressful situation, residual rule breaking does have the potential of being adaptive. By doing things that are not in the normal behavioral repertoire of the culture, the stressed person may discover a creative practical solution to the original stress-inducing problem. In such cases, residual rule breaking may be a source of cultural innovation and change. However, such innovations will be adopted by society at large only if enough others are trying to cope with the same kind of problem and therefore recognize the benefit of the innovation (Wallace, 1961). When this is not the case, they are likely to regard the residual rule breaking as a startling and undesirable form of deviance from the usual behaviors that they expect from one another. This is one reason why people labeled insane are sometimes feared as potentially dangerous.

Mental Disorders and Culture

The concept of insanity is found in cultures throughout the world and may be viewed as a cultural process as well as a psychological one. An analysis of the cultural process involved in defining insanity casts light on the conditions in which a person is given the master status of being insane.

Insanity

As a cultural process, there are two criteria, both of which must be present, for a person to be regarded as insane. The first is the characteristic of residual rule breaking, which Edgerton has described as a state in which "a person's thought, emotions, or behavior appear to others in his society to be unreasonable or irrational, or when his ability to cope with the ordinary demands of life are impaired (1976, p. 63)." As a case in point, Edgerton reports the example of "an elder Sebei man of Uganda who for some years spent most of his waking hours hanging

upside down from the limb of a tree or a rafter in his house. His only comments were: 'I have a chicken in my head' or 'I have countless wives.' Most Sebei easily agreed on labeling him psychotic" (p. 64). This example illustrates the condition of a residual rule-breaker who cannot control his deviant behavior. The second criterion is the judgment that a person lacks control over his or her deviant behavior (Miller, 1974; Murphy, 1976). Thus, **insanity** may be defined as role playing in which a person engages in residual rule breaking that others believe he or she cannot control.

Typically, the insane status that such people acquire is one of the most highly stigmatized in all societies. People who hold this master status are considered the antithesis of whatever their societies regard as normal. Thus, for instance, languages as diverse as Shoshoni and English express the idea of insanity with a word that means "not sane." The Chippewa of northern Wisconsin and northeastern Minnesota, the Cree of northern Manitoba, and the Montagnais-Naskapi of northern Quebec referred to any severe form of insanity as the generic term *windigo* or *wiitiko,* terms that were also names for a mythological giant cannibal with a heart of ice.

Insanity in Western History

Some concept of insanity exists in every culture, but its causes are understood in many different ways. A widespread way of thinking about insanity is the belief that it is related to the supernatural: The insane may be possessed or controlled by malevolent spirits; they may be suffering the effects of sorcery; or they may be witches or sorcerers themselves. Harris pointed out that such views were common in Europe during the fifteenth through seventeenth centuries, a time when the political influence of the clergy was being challenged by a series of grass-roots religious revitalization movements that prophesied the end of the traditional church-state connection (1974, pp. 207–24). During this period, when religious revivalism threatened the established coalition of clergy and the political elite, social deviants, including the insane, were often stigmatized as possessed or in league with the Devil. Treatment for their condition included the execution of witches and painful exorcism rituals that

---

insanity process by which a person acquires and maintains deviant master status of residual rule breaker were designed to make the bodies of possessed persons too uncomfortable for evil spirits to remain.

According to Andrew Scull (1979, pp. 13–49), as the power of the European monarchs grew and that of the clergy waned, the religious model for deviance declined, and socially troublesome people, including vagrants, minor criminals, the physically handicapped, and the insane, were increasingly confined in institutions at the expense of the state. Then, during the period between the mid-eighteenth and the mid-nineteenth centuries, a major change occurred in which the insane came to be distinguished from other deviants and viewed as mentally ill. This was a period of population growth, commercialization of agriculture, and the proliferation of workhouses and other similar institutions for housing the growing number of unemployed who had been dispossessed from the rural areas by the economic changes of industrialization.

In the growing urban centers of Europe, the numbers of unemployed persons were a significant and disruptive social problem. The solution was sought in various forms of confinement: prisons for incarcerating and punishing the criminal poor and vagrants who "refused to work," almshouses and workhouses for helping and training the indigent who were willing but unable to work, and madhouses for the troublesome insane whose bizarre behavior marked them as "incapable" of surviving in the new wage-based economy or abiding by the rules of the almshouses and workhouses. The madhouses were run by medical practitioners whose background and training in the handling of the medically incapacitated was thought to be appropriate for handling the new class of incapacitated mentally ill.

Culture-Specific Forms of Hysteria

In hysteria, an overwhelming anxiety, fear, or sense of powerlessness may be avoided by dissociating oneself from awareness of some aspects of the personality. For instance, in amnesia distressful memories are blocked out of conscious memory. This process occurs without the direct awareness of the afflicted individual. Hysteria may also take the form of conversion of anxiety into what appears to be an organic problem. Some part of the body ceases to function normally, even though there is no medical evidence of real organic impairment. For instance, in hysterical paralysis certain muscles can be used for some activities but not for others that are associated

with emotionally stressful aspects of the individual's life. Tics, tremors, or an inability to speak are other examples of hysterical conversion reactions. As in amnesia, the failure of an organic function seems to occur without the person's conscious recognition or intent.

Although the basic psychological mechanisms by which hysteria is produced may be common to all peoples throughout the world, the specific ways in which hysteria is experienced and communicated are influenced by cultural interpretations of human behavior. Anthropological fieldworkers have reported a variety of culturally specific forms of hysteria in traditional non-Westernized societies.

Amok, which is a hysterical reaction of the dissociation type, is found in New Guinea (Langness, 1965; Newman, 1964). Only young men ages 25 through 35 seem to be afflicted. After an initial depression, the victim enters a phase of anxiety and depression in which experiences take on an unreal quality, and the victim broods over offenses by others. Finally, in a burst of energy, the victim "runs amok," screaming and attacking people and their property. During this stage, the sufferer seems delirious and sometimes unable to hear what others shout at him. After exhausting himself, the victim returns to consciousness but has no memories of what he has done. Among the Gururumba of New Guinea, the individual who was affected by amok was not expected to recompense the victims for the losses he inflicted on them, for his behavior was believed to have been beyond his control, caused by the bite of an aggressive ghost or some similar factor. Additionally, his susceptibility to the disorder was seen as evidence of a weakness in his ability to deal with the normal stresses of Gururumba social and economic life. Therefore, payment of his previous economic debts was no longer vigorously sought by others. Disorders similar to amok were also reported in Malaya, Indonesia, Polynesia, and the Sahara.

Latah, a hysterical dissociation brought on by a sudden startling encounter with dangerous things or by being tickled, was found in Southeast Asia and Mongolia (Aberle, 1961; Van Loon, 1926). After an

hysteria a form of neurosis in which there is ritualistic avoidance of anxiety or ritualistic manipulation of others as a means of avoiding failure
amok a culture-specific hysterical disorder in which young men attack other people and destroy property
latah a culture-specific hysterical disorder that is characterized by uncontrollable imitation of the actions and speech of others

FIGURE 12.7   Culture-Specific Forms of Hysteria

Hysteria is an extreme reaction to fear or anxiety in which some part of the body ceases to function normally. Culture may play a role in the manifestation of hysteria. In some Inuit areas where the environment causes stress and sunlight is decreased, the hysteria may take the form of *pibloktoq* where the victim becomes highly agitated, violent, and runs naked into the icy cold snow.

initial fright reaction, such as tremor and collapse, the victim engaged in compulsive imitation of the actions and speech of others. In Southeast Asia and Indonesia, latah was most common among women, but in Mongolia it was more likely to afflict men.

Imu, which is perhaps simply a variety of *latah*, was found among the aboriginal inhabitants of northern Japan, the Ainu (Winiarz & Wielawski, 1936). Like latah in Southeast Asia, imu mainly afflicted women. Brought on by a sudden frightening experience, such as hearing a loud sound or being bitten by a snake, it begins with an aggressive or fearful startle reaction, followed by automatic obedience to suggestions given by others or its opposite, negativism, and the compulsive imitation of sounds and gestures until the victim is exhausted.

A similar disorder, **arctic hysteria** or *amurakh*, was found among the Yakut and Tungus of northeastern Siberia, where it also was most common among women (Czaplicka, 1914). Like its counterparts elsewhere, it involves compulsive imitation of sounds and gestures. At least in the form experienced by spiritual healers, or shamans, the original attack is brought on by a sudden fright.

Another hysterical disorder with dissociation characteristics was found among the northern native Greenlanders (Foulks, 1972; Gussow, 1960; Wallace,

1972). This affliction is known as *pibloktoq*. After a period of irritability and withdrawal, the victim becomes highly agitated, violent, and talkative. Some victims may tear off their clothing and run naked into the snowfields. Finally, after collapsing from exhaustion and falling into unconsciousness, the victim may recover from the attack with no memory of it. It was found somewhat more commonly in women than in men.

Since pibloktoq was most common in the winter, increased life stresses caused by coping with the rigorous arctic winter in small communities might be a triggering factor in this disorder. However, Wallace

---

imu   a hysterical disorder found among the Ainu of northern Japan characterized by automatic obedience or negativism and uncontrollable imitation of sounds and gestures

arctic hysteria (*amurakh*)   a culture-specific hysterical disorder that is characterized by compulsive imitation of sounds and gestures

amurakh   a culture-specific hysterical disorder that is characterized by compulsive imitation of sounds and gestures

pibloktoq   a culture-specific hysterical disorder characterized by agitated attempts to flee the presence of other people

(1972) has argued that the basic cause of pibloktoq was the Greenlanders' calcium-deficient diet. Since vitamin D—produced by the body when it is exposed to sunlight—is necessary for the body to absorb calcium from food, the seasonal increase in pibloktoq could be explained by the decreased sunlight in winter. Calcium deficiency would impair the functioning of the central nervous system, producing the pibloktoq symptoms of nervous excitability and distortions in thought processes. Other researchers (Foulks, 1972) failed to find significant differences in the serum calcium levels of pibloktoq-prone and normal Greenlanders, so Wallace's calcium deficiency hypothesis remains controversial.

Hsieh-ping is a hysteria found in traditional Chinese societies (Wittkower & Fried, 1957). Sufferers, most commonly women, are believed to be possessed by spirits of dead relatives or friends to whom they have failed to offer the proper respect. It includes symptoms of tremor and disorientation, with clouding of consciousness, delirium, speaking in tongues, and hallucinations.

Saka is an hysterical disorder found among Wataita women in Kenya (Harris, 1957). Sometimes preceded by restlessness and anxiety, an attack begins with convulsive movements in which the upper body trembles and the head shakes from side to side. Occasionally, the victim may repeat actions or sounds thought to be in a foreign tongue. A trance or loss of consciousness and rigidity of the body may follow. Attacks may be precipitated by the sight, sounds, and smells of men or foreigners or even by things associated with them, such as the train whistle or the smell of a cigarette.

Social roots of hysterias. Each of these hysterical disorders is ideologically patterned in such a way that the people among whom it is found understand the symptoms according to their culture's unique system of meanings. Yet, all these disorders share several important characteristics with each other and with the varieties of hysteria described in the Western psychiatric tradition. For instance, in most of these cases, the affliction is more likely to strike women than men, a finding that may reflect women's traditional lack of socially granted power. In those cases where men are prominent victims, they often fail in the goal-oriented masculine roles of their culture, where power is expected to be exercised successfully. Attacks are often set off by a sudden frightening shock or by other stimuli that may call the victims' attention to how little power they have

compared with others. Attacks are followed by great agitation and even violent behavior that is powerful in form, if not in fact. Alternatively, instead of violent agitation, one may find its opposite: behavior that dramatizes the powerlessness of the victim, such as automatic obedience or robot-like imitation of others' sounds and gestures. In either case, the hysterical behavior is generally performed in a mentally clouded, disoriented state of mind. Finally, after termination of this intense and ritualized drama of powerlessness, the victim, who may fall exhausted into a state of unconsciousness or sleep, is likely to experience amnesia concerning the attack itself.

Hysteria and culture. Seymour Parker (1962) has summarized the traits common to cultures in which hysteria is prevalent: (1) early socialization is not severe and there is a high level of need gratification; (2) there is a corresponding emphasis on communalistic values and expectations of mutual aid; (3) the female role is ranked markedly below that of the male; and (4) the religious system often provides models of hysteria-like behavior in spirit-possession rituals. In other words, childrearing practices foster high expectations that others may be relied on to fulfill one's dependency needs; therefore, self-reliance does not reach a high level. Community values support these traits by providing a substantial level of support from others, while at the same time emphasizing conformity to community values.

The dependence on others rather than on oneself for fulfillment of one's needs implies that a person's self-esteem is contingent on the interpretation of his or her value in the eyes of others. Many times, this support for self-esteem is consistently available: children are not dealt with harshly, their wants are quickly fulfilled, and mutual aid among adults communicates their value. But in several areas of life, this system may break down. Women, for instance, are repeatedly reminded that their status is inferior to that of men in both esteem and power. By and large, women in these societies therefore trans-

---

hsieh-ping a culture-specific hysterical disorder that is characterized by tremor, disorientation, clouding of consciousness, delirium, speaking in tongues, and hallucinations

saka a culture-specific hysterical disorder that is characterized by repetition of actions or sounds believed to be a foreign language, and loss of consciousness with body rigidity form their day-to-day stress into negative self-worth. They also, then, are more likely than men to react to sudden dangers with fright that may lead to hysterical breaks with reality. Similarly, symbolic reminders of their inferior status may lead stressed women to fall into hysterical trances.

Social outcasts of either sex are not supported in their self-esteem by these societies. Rather, the communities use subtle and not-so-subtle sanctions to withdraw their support from deviant individuals. For the individual whose self-esteem is dependent on the support of others, this can be disastrous. For example, in traditional Chinese societies, the woman who fails, either out of laxity or poverty, to make the expected offerings to the dead could find herself losing the needed support of her community. This might lead quickly to great anxiety in a person not socialized to self-reliance. Since a married woman leaves her own family to reside with her husband and his kin, she lacks support from her own kin at times of emotional stress. The hysterical reaction that results is believed by those around her to be a manifestation of spirit possession. In performing a cure, the community would reintroduce her into its good graces and the hysteria would subside.

Men who are less active than others or who fail in the pursuit of the male goals in these societies also may develop anxiety about their inadequate personal power. This is likely in situations where they do not have others to whom they may turn for aid without denying the masculinity that they are expected to demonstrate by their independence. When arctic hysteria struck men, it usually struck those whom Edward Foulks described as " 'nervous' young men aspiring to become shamans," that is, young men who were somewhat marginal in secular male pursuits and wished therefore to become spiritual healers (1972, p. 11).

Other Culture-Specific Disorders

Besides the hysterias, other disorders have been described that are uniquely shaped by specific cultures. Among these are kayak angst, susto, koro, and frigophobia.

Kayak angst. *Kayak angst* has been found among the indigenous people of western Greenland (Freuchen, 1935; Gussow, 1963; Honigmann & Honigmann, 1965). It strikes males while they are alone and the sea is calm. The stress results from physical immobility and environmental monotony in a potentially dangerous situation. The reaction begins with confusion, dizziness, and blurring of vision and depth perception. The victim becomes immobilized by fear of capsizing the kayak, a fear that is increased by a sudden chilling of his lower body, which he believes to be caused by water entering the kayak. These attacks may recur and be so incapacitating that the man may refuse to leave shore again, in spite of the economic importance of doing so.

Kayak angst has characteristics that are common in the phobic disorders of Western cultures. In *phobias*, conscious awareness of the true source of anxiety is avoided by displacing fear onto some object that is symbolic of whatever produces the anxiety. The overtly feared object is often something regarded as completely harmless by nonphobic individuals. Phobics may fear kittens, dirt, open fields, closed-in spaces, or almost anything.

Susto. *Susto*, sometimes called *espanto* or *pasmo*, is most common in Latin America (Rubel, 1960). It illustrates what Western psychiatry calls an *anxiety disorder*, which may involve a chronic state of tension and mild apprehension, or temporary but acute and terrifying paniclike reactions that are not associated with any real danger. Susto typically begins following an experience of shame from failure to meet an important social obligation. The victim, whose soul is believed to have been lost because of a sudden fright or some other spiritual cause, becomes withdrawn, listless, and irritable. In addition, the victim loses appetite and experiences rapid heartbeat, nausea and vomiting, diarrhea, and restless sleep troubled by nightmares. Susto seems to combine some elements of depression with its primary symptoms as an anxiety reaction.

---

kayak angst a culture-specific phobic disorder that is characterized by an inordinate fear of being at sea in a kayak

susto (espanto, pasmo) a culture-specific anxiety disorder with depressive features, interpreted by the victim as caused by soul loss

espanto a culture-specific anxiety disorder with depressive features, interpreted by the victim as caused by soul loss

pasmo a culture-specific anxiety disorder with depressive features, interpreted by the victim as caused by soul loss

Koro. *Koro* exemplifies the Western disorder of *hypochondriasis*, a condition characterized by intense preoccupation with physical health, magnifying the sensations of normal bodily fatigue, aches, pains, and a recurring but unfounded fear that the sufferer's complaints are evidence of some dire disease. Koro has been associated most commonly with China and other parts of east and southeast Asia (Hsien, 1963, 1965; Yap, 1963, 1965). Koro attacks often follow a sudden fright. Male victims report that their penis feels cold, numb, and no longer a part of themselves. They fear that it is shrinking and being absorbed into their abdomen, leading to death. Among women, the fears center on the belief that their breasts are being similarly absorbed and that they will die. The cultural parallel of this anxiety about masculinity or femininity is clear: The traditional ideology of Chinese culture classified all things as masculine and feminine on the basis of the *yin* and *yang* or "female" and "male" essences they contain. In China, koro is believed to be caused by an imbalance of yin and yang in the victim. For instance, it is believed that koro can be brought on in men by the loss of semen through masturbation or frequent sexual intercourse, since semen is held to be a source of yang, which represents masculine vitality and strength. Like susto, koro is an anxiety reaction.

Frigophobia. *Frigophobia* or *pa-ling* is a Chinese *obsessive-compulsive disorder* in which anxiety is manifest through repetitive thoughts and acts that are symbolic of the underlying anxiety. Frigophobia involves an obsessive-compulsive need to change clothing repeatedly and to wear it in several layers to avoid heat loss from the cold and from winds (Kiev, 1972; Yap, 1951). The attendant fear of the cold and wind is rationalized by the victim of pa-ling by the belief that either of these may upset the balance of yin and yang necessary to health, and that the resulting loss of vital essence may lead to death. In contrast to the normal use of layered clothing in China, sufferers of frigophobia may spend so much time changing clothes that they are unable to function in their normal responsibilities.

---

koro a culture-specific anxiety disorder characterized by fear of death through loss of sexual essence
frigophobia (*pa-ling*) a culture-specific obsessive-compulsive disorder characterized by fear of loss of body heat

Anorexia Nervosa: A Culture-Specific Disorder in the U.S.

The unique social stresses of the modern United States also lead to culture-specific disorders, including one syndrome in which some young women literally starve themselves to death. Contemporary American culture emphasizes slenderness as a mark of beauty in women. Fashion models, for example, are much more slender than the average Ameri-

FIGURE 12.8   Anorexia Nervosa
In American society, the emphasis on physical slenderness as the standard of beauty has caused the culture-specific disorder of anorexia nervosa. It affects primarily young girls who starve themselves almost to death in order to achieve a slender body.

can woman. The stars of our motion pictures are rarely of average build, and the overweight actress is most often found in a comic role. Diet foods fill an entire section of our supermarkets.

In a society in which youth and slenderness are highly valued, anxiety about weight gain and growing older is also common. As many as 1 in 250 American females between the ages of 12 and 18 years may suffer from a disorder called **anorexia nervosa**. The central characteristics of this disorder are an intense fear of becoming obese, an inaccurate body image, a significant loss of weight, and a refusal to maintain even a minimal normal body weight. The patient refuses to eat and may lose 25 to 30 percent of her body weight. Although the most common pattern is a single episode followed by full recovery, some 5 to 18 percent of cases end in death by starvation.

This condition also may express a fear of the transition from childhood to womanhood. Victims of anorexia nervosa are almost always female. They are frequently described as perfectionistic "model children" who commonly feel inadequate in their social roles and incompetent in their work or school performance.

It is clear from these examples that the culture-specific disorders have much in common with one another. Indeed, the underlying psychological process seems to be the same. Individuals who are faced with stresses that they are unable to relieve by pragmatic action experience emotional distress and begin to manifest that stress by breaking the residual rules of their cultures. These various culture-specific disorders differ from one another mainly in their overt manifestations: The responses to stress are symbolic behaviors that are appropriate to the particular culture.

Causes of Mental Disorders

Some people use altered states of consciousness as coping mechanisms for dealing with stress and then return to their normal behaviors; others get lost in altered states. What prevents some individuals from maintaining an acceptable social role while suffering from stress? The failure may be due in part to individual characteristics that make some people unusually susceptible to the effects of stress. It may also be due in part to the nature and level of the stresses involved. Finally, it also may be partly because the social reactions of others do not give each individual the same opportunity to escape from the anxieties that stress creates.

Individual Susceptibility

Those who prefer to examine insanity from a psychological or biological perspective argue that insanity is at least partially a result of objective abnormalities within the sufferer, rendering him or her incapable of dealing with stresses that most people can handle. This viewpoint is not strictly a Western one. Jane Murphy (1976) points out that one element of insanity in cultures around the world is the belief that those who are truly mentally ill are unable to control the spontaneous rituals that plague them and the onset of their altered states of consciousness. This approach often portrays genetically inherited differences as predisposing factors that are insufficient by themselves to cause insanity. That is to say, genetic inheritance may play a role in setting an individual's level of tolerance for stress, but social stresses—which differ in form from culture to culture—are believed to be the critical triggering forces that precipitate episodes of insanity.

The Social Context

Those who prefer to apply a cultural perspective to the analysis of insanity reject the notion that it

anorexia nervosa a culture-specific obsessive-compulsive disorder characterized by an unrealistic appraisal of one's own body as overweight and by self-starvation

300

is an illness (Szasz, 1970). They assert, in other words, that it is not a problem that arises primarily due to some inherited inadequacy of the individual. The proponents of this approach believe that it is more enlightening to see insanity as a social process in which problematic situations force some members of society to play the role of sick or inadequate individuals. Those who maintain this position argue that the inability to control ritualized behavior and altered states of consciousness—used in many cultures as a criterion for judging a person to be insane—need not always be the result of a real biological incapacity of the individual who plays the sick role.

Another social aspect of insanity is that the same rule violation may be ignored when engaged in by one person, excused when done by another, and seen as evidence of "mental illness" in a third. What accounts for such differences in people's reactions to norm violations?

Research in complex societies has made it clear that the higher one's rank, the easier it is to behave in unusual ways without being labeled as insane. For instance, Hollingshead and Redlich (1953) examined data about schizophrenia from New Haven and surrounding Connecticut towns. Schizophrenia is a striking disorder that is characterized by unusual thought processes and bizarre forms of self-expression. It is sometimes accompanied by hallucinations. Although genetic factors may play a strong role in predisposing individuals to schizophrenic disorders, their social manifestations can be viewed as problems in the process of communication, especially in role acquisition and the presentation of face. Hollingshead and Redlich (1953) found that there was an inverse relationship between social class and schizophrenia. The higher the class, the lower was the percentage of people being treated for schizophrenia. The lowest of five classes made up 17.8 percent of the community's total population, but 36.8 percent of the psychiatric population. It appears, then, that one's social rank may be a factor in determining whether one enters into the socially labelled role of a schizophrenic.

The situation in which a person deviates from the norms of the group may also influence whether or not the behavior is judged insane. For instance, the individual who engages in acts of autistic reverie will not be thought insane if this silent musing is confined to times when he or she listens to music. The person who carries on half of a dialogue with what seems to be an unseen partner will not be thought to be mentally ill if there are cues such as age or setting that suggest an alternative explanation—for instance, a child may talk to an "invisible playmate," and an actor or university professor may rehearse lines for a play or public address. Even the person who claims to hear voices that others do not hear or who "speaks in tongues" and makes unintelligible sounds need not be thought of as strange, if he or she does so only during the services of an appropriate religious organization. On the other hand, these same activities performed in other contexts may lead to the practitioner's being labeled insane.

Since the status of the insane is a master status with low access to both power and prestige, once people have been labeled insane they are likely to continue to be thought of as insane, irrespective of their future behavior. One American researcher, David Rosenhahn (1973), had himself and several other researchers admitted to a number of American mental hospitals as patients. He and his co-researchers discovered that once they had been admitted, even though they behaved normally, the hospital staff, including psychiatrists, psychologists, and psychiatric nurses, failed to recognize that they were actually sane.

The implication is that the researchers' predicament mirrored what happens in social life outside institutions. Once people are branded with a deviant status associated with an altered state of consciousness, others will assume that all their actions spring from that altered state and therefore withhold power and prestige from them, severely restricting the roles they are allowed to play.

---

schizophrenia   a mental disorder characterized by residual rule breaking caused by difficulty in communicating an acceptable social identity. Schizophrenia may include hallucinations and ideas about reality that are greatly at odds with mainstream ideas

C H A P T E R   S U M M A R Y

1. From an anthropological perspective, personality is an individual's patterns of behavior that express the various social roles he or she has learned to play.

2. As children, we are socialized to fit into the patterns of our society. As we take on roles, we learn the behaviors that are considered appropriate for them.

3. These behaviors are what others perceive as our personalities.

4. The socialization customs of each society engender different anxieties in children, and these are expressed in various ways.

5. The socialization that is the source of our personality differences results in the patterns of male and female personality characteristics that are found in societies throughout the world.

6. The social roles which define our personalities are also not the same in every culture.

7. Each society includes different statuses, each with its own culturally defined roles. Normal day-to-day behavior in any society is a matter of trying to play those roles appropriately.

8. In every society, people deviate from their expected roles in ways that may be approved as creative or stigmatized as unacceptably deviant.

9. The stigma of inadequate role playing is often accompanied by emotional distress and sometimes by trances, altered states of consciousness that are interpreted in most societies as evidence of the influence of supernatural forces. Ritual behavior is another common result of anxiety.

10. Those who have such experiences too frequently may be reassigned to a master status such as that of insane person, a status that implies an inability to control one's own behavior.

11. The insane status is found in every culture, but cultures differ in how it is understood.

A N N O T A T E D   R E A D I N G S

Barnouw, V. (1985). *Culture and personality*. (4th ed.). Homewood, IL: Dorsey. An introductory-level text on psychological anthropology.

Bateson, G. (1936). *Naven: A survey of the problems suggested by a composite picture of the culture of a New Guinea tribe drawn from three points of view*. Cambridge, MA: Cambridge University Press. The analysis of a Iatmul ritual that led to Bateson's revolutionary theory of schizophrenia.

Chernin, K. (1981). *The obsession: Reflections on the tyranny of slenderness*. New York: Harper & Row. An examination of the emphasis on slenderness as beauty in American culture.

Hsu, F. L. K. (Ed.). (1972). *Psychological anthropology: Approaches to culture and personality*. Morristown, NJ: Schenkman Press. A basic survey of the field of psychological anthropology for the advanced student.

LeVine, R. A. (Ed.). (1974). *Culture and personality: Contemporary readings*. Chicago: Aldine. A useful collection of papers on cultural and psychological aspects of the human condition, including cultural interpretations of the abnormal personality.

Marsella, A. J., DeVos, G., & Hsu, F. L. K. (Eds.). (1985). *Culture and self: Asian and Western perspectives*. New York: Tavistock Publications. A current examination of the experience of self from a cross-cultural perspective.

Price, W. F., & Crapo, R. H. (1992). *Cross-cultural perspectives in introductory psychology*. Minneapolis/St. Paul: West Publishing. Twenty-five vignettes about cross-cultural research that illustrate various aspects of human psychology.

Price-Williams, D. R. (1975). *Explorations in cross-cultural psychology*. San Francisco, CA: Chandler & Sharp. A short but somewhat technical examination of cross-cultural psychology, with emphasis on cultural relativism in the interpretation of human psychology.

Simons, R. C., & Hughes, C. C. (1985). *The culture-bound syndromes: Folk illnesses of psychiatric and anthropological interest*. Boston: D. Reidel Pub. Co. The most comprehensive survey of the culture-specific mental disorders available. Each disorder is described and then analyzed in terms of contemporary Western psychiatric classification.

FIGURE 13.1 Peruvian Kero
In most cultures, art is integral to the functional object rather than being considered a separate activity, as it is so often in Western culture. This painted wooden beaker, or kero, from the Inca Indians of Peru represents an ocelot head.

CHAPTER 13

Aesthetics and Culture

The human condition includes the ability to experience pleasure in various ways. The expression of these experiences is the basis for play, recreation, ritual, and art, the most distinctive characteristics of a culture. Art is a particularly intriguing and many-faceted aspect of expressive culture, in which people find beauty in the skilled production of meaningful forms as diverse as painting, sculpture, music, dance, and aesthetic forms of speaking. This chapter defines the various categories of expressive culture and analyzes the functions of art in human life.

CHAPTER OBJECTIVES

After reading this chapter, you should be able to:

Discuss the cultural relativity of aesthetics.

Define and illustrate the concepts of aesthetic experience and expressive culture.

Define the nature of play and explain its psychological functions.

Explain the relationships of art to play.

Explain the roles of form, feelings, and meaning in art.

Outline the various forms of art.

Analyze the social functions of art.

Beauty. Pleasure. Disgust. Appreciation. Connoisseurship. Gourmet. Gourmand. Artist. Critic. Dada. "Primitive." Kitsch. Pornography. Sensuality. Jazz. Baroque. Rap. However beauty is defined, humans everywhere react to some things as beautiful and to others as ugly. In this chapter, we will explore the nature of the aesthetic experience and the ways it is culturally patterned.

The Relativity of Aesthetics

The parts of an ideology that comprise the rules by which beauty is to be evaluated are called the **aesthetics** of a culture. Not all cultures have a formally articulated aesthetic, but when members of any society express aesthetic judgments, it is possible to infer the rules to which their evaluations about beauty conform.

Cultural Differences in Aesthetics

Most of the languages of nonliterate societies lack a word for art. This is because in many societies what we call art does not belong to a circumscribed sphere of life, a domain of specialists, but is integrated into the day-to-day activities of the ordinary member of society. Thus, the lack in many cultures of a conceptual category of art, either as an activity or as a class of objects, is not due to a lack of aesthetic appreciation in those cultures, but rather to the fact that art is part of daily living. People everywhere sing, dance and decorate themselves and the objects that they use, placing value only on the beauty they

see in such acts. What they lack is not a sense of artistry but a concept of "art for art's sake." Phrased in this way, the difference between cultures that have such a category and those that do not can be readily understood in *social* terms: A vocabulary that includes the word "art" is the product of a society that has professional artists, persons who make their living by the production of objects that are valued primarily for their aesthetic qualities rather than for their common or utilitarian ones.

Aesthetic locus. Maquet has noted that societies may devote aesthetic effort to different areas of life, and each culture has certain areas in which aesthetic experience is more important than others. He calls such an area an **aesthetic locus** of a culture, which he defines as "the categories of objects in which aesthetic expectations and performances are concentrated" (1986, p. 69). As examples of aesthetic loci he cites the tea ceremony of Japan, the Christian ritual of thirteenth-century Western Europe, and ancestral effigies and masks of many societies in West and Central Africa. Charles Keil (1979) describes dance as the central aesthetic locus of Tiv culture, a horticultural society in West Africa. Men's dances are displays of strength, speed, and agility. They often convey a message that mockingly portrays the effects of disease, sequences of skilled dance being interspersed with segments in which the dancers break step, stagger, and grimace as if from the effects of various dire illnesses. Their dance styles change rapidly; new steps invented by creative individuals are adopted by others and then just as quickly replaced by other fads as new styles are invented. Tiv dance troups tour the country, earning money and fame.

Diversity in aesthetic standards. Standards of aesthetic judgment also vary from culture to culture. For instance, Tipilit Ole Saitoti, a Maasai visitor to Germany, described his reaction to German chamber music:

> One Sunday I was wandering along Ludwig Strasse when I struck up a conversation with a young

---

aesthetics the rules by which beauty is to be evaluated in a culture
aesthetic locus the area of a culture to which a society devotes its aesthetic effort

German woman. She took me to an old church. Two men were before an audience. They held two musical instruments between their knees and shoulders and rubbed them with sticks. They produced strange melodies that rose and fell like waves.

This was the first time I had heard such music, and I was not at all impressed. At the end of each performance the audience stood up and clapped, and the men on the stage bowed their heads in appreciation. The whole thing went on and on, and I was getting bored. My companion loved the show and was very disappointed when I told her that I did not like it. She insisted, *"Das ist gut, das ist gut."* I was used to African rhythms you could dance to, such as Congolese drumbeats. The young woman and I never saw each other again. (1986, p. 108)

A formal set of rules for evaluating the beauty or effectiveness of a work of art is most likely to exist only if a society treats the realm of art as a realm for specialists. For instance, Charles Keil (1979) reports that the Tiv have no word for art and no accepted principles for distinguishing such things as good carvings from bad ones. Nevertheless, they do make individual judgments about which carvings are well done and which are not. Thus, even in societies that have no such specialists, informal aesthetic standards exist implicitly in the consensus of public opinion.

In contrast with the Tiv, the Yoruba, an agricultural people of Nigeria, have a well-developed set of standards for judging beauty in art. Robert Thompson (1968, 1973) had Yoruba critics rank works of sculpture and explain the basis of their judgments. By comparing the opinions of many individuals, he found over a dozen general principles that guided Yoruba aesthetic evaluations. Some of these rules are clearly distinctive to Yoruba aesthetics. For instance, the Yoruba felt that the major parts of a sculpture should be clearly visible, as should any designs with which they were decorated. They also valued sculptures that depicted people in their prime over carvings that portrayed older people, and open-mouthed figures were considered particularly unattractive.

Not only do societies differ in the rules that govern aesthetic standards, but works of art are also not necessarily thought of as creative productions of individual artists. For instance, Paul Bohannan reports his difficulty in adjusting to the "communal" approach of the Tiv to creating and decorating objects. At one point during his fieldwork, he bought tools and tried his hand at making stools and chairs.

But I was not allowed to do it myself. The moment I rested, some bystander would take up the adze and get the work a little farther forward. I, in Western tradition, had a feeling of complete frustration because my "creativity" and my ability were being challenged. For a few days I tried to insist that I wanted to do the work myself, but soon had to give it up because everyone thought it silly and because no one could remember my foible. Eventually, several of our chairs and stools "didn't turn out too badly." I had a hand in all of them, but they are not my handiwork—the whole compound and half the countryside had worked on them. (1961, p. 90)

This communal approach to art was not unique to making furniture. For instance, Bohannan observed the same group involvement in the decorating of personal items such as staffs. He reports that:

The most astounding feature, to me, was that comparatively few of the designs were made by a single individual. As I sat watching a young man of about thirty carve a stick one day, he was called away. He laid aside his stick and the double-edged knives with which he was cutting the design. A guest came in a few moments later, picked up the stick, and added a few designs. A little later, he handed it on to someone else. Four men put designs on that stick before the owner returned and finished it. When he had done so, he held it out for me to copy and said, "It turned out pretty well, didn't it?" (1961, p. 90)

Any society may have formally defined standards of aesthetic judgment and attribute the beauty of individual artworks to the skill of their creators. Yet, a formal aesthetic is most common in complex societies where the economy supports aesthetic specialists such as professional artists and art critics.

Hindu Aesthetics

According to Richard Anderson, Hindu philosophy of art was founded on the concept of *rasa*, "the sensuous pleasure that the aesthetically attuned individual may experience as a result of art—the thrill of excitement or, at the least, the soothing of grief, that can come about when a person is immersed in an art" (1990, p. 166). *Rasa* implies an experience of oneness between the audience and a work of art, a state in which the work of art evokes one of nine basic human emotions—happiness, pride, zest (or laughter), sorrow, anger, disgust, fear, wonder, or tranquility. According to Anderson, "the capacity to feel delight is the basis of erotic art, laughter is elevated by art to become comedy, sorrow is transmuted into pathos, and anger is the basis of furious art" (p. 168). In the state of aesthetic oneness between the beholder and the work of art, a basic human emotion is transformed into a higher feeling, one in which the audience can experience itself at one with Brahma, the highest manifestation of God as Absolute Being, who transcends the limitations of the senses.

So in Hindu philosophy, the essential quality of the aesthetic experience is its ability to help people transcend the idiosyncratic qualities of personal experience and the limitations of mundane senses in order to achieve oneness with that transcendent reality. In this tradition, art does not merely serve religion in the sense of providing moral instruction or of instilling emotions appropriate to a religious setting, as might the murals in a religious building. Art can be coequal with meditation or ritual as an independent way of experiencing the Divine. Indeed, according to the oldest Indian aesthetic tradition, recorded in a third century A.D. document called the *Nātyaśāstra*, Brahma himself created art for the pleasure and betterment of the lesser gods and of mortals.

The Aesthetic Experience and Expressive Culture

Although beauty may be defined differently from culture to culture, the **aesthetic experience**, the pleasure we feel when we recognize something as beautiful, is universal. There are many phenomena that can involve us in an aesthetic experience. Some, like a beautiful sunset, a magnificent vista, the dancing flames in a fireplace, or an awesome thunderstorm, are natural. Others, like an attractively woven basket, an ornamental rug, or an unforgettable mel-

ody, are cultural. The ability to appreciate beauty in things is a biologically based capacity that we all share—the capacity to take pleasure in the senses.

The aesthetic experience is similar to the positive emotional states, but is experienced outside the goal-oriented settings with which the emotions are normally associated. It is a more generalized expression of our ability to experience positive feelings in settings that are not related to specific pragmatic goals, or when negative feelings are evoked in a safe setting. Thus, for instance, we experience aesthetic feelings when a work of art reminds us of one we might love, of a cause we might take pride in, or of successes worthy of striving for.

The various ways in which aesthetic pleasure is given cultural form constitute a society's **expressive culture**. Expressive culture includes aspects of life as diverse as play, games, festivals, sports, and the arts.

Play

Common among mammals, including humans, play has never been defined in a way that everyone accepts. It seems to be intrinsically pleasurable behavior. The activities of play seem to be done because they are fun, rather than to accomplish some utilitarian purpose, even though they do provide practical benefits—the practice of skills that will be used in goal-oriented ways outside the setting of play. Play also has an important symbolic component in which we act out feelings and preoccupations, and often it seems to be done in a trance-like state of mind in which fantasy and imagination overshadow the real world. So one way of defining **play** is as a stress-relieving ritualistic practice of potentially utilitarian behaviors, accompanied by altered states of consciousness in which the perception of external things is altered by the participant's own fantasy. In play, a broom may become a horse to ride, or a chair may become a castle.

Although we sometimes play as adults, spontaneous play is more typical of childhood. It seems to have a number of characteristics that are particularly

---

aesthetic experience   the pleasure we feel when we recognize something as beautiful
expressive culture   expressions of culture such as play, ritual, or the arts
play   stress-relieving ritualistic practice of potentially utilitarian behaviors

beneficial to children. Since children lack the experience and skills necessary for adult functioning, they are likely to experience repeated stress because of their inability to perform many tasks that they attempt. The fantasy of play provides the opportunity to practice various tasks without experiencing anxiety about lack of skill. The pleasurable quality of play provides the motivation for repetition and practice which, in turn, helps children become proficient in motor activities, including complex sequences of acts. The mental component of play allows them to externalize their fantasies. Children can thus project into the outside world those things that are of current concern to them. How this process can help to alleviate stress is most clearly seen in the case of fears. When a child pretends that a pillow is a shark or a crumpled sheet a ghost, the signs of real fear may be evoked when the object is approached or brought closer. These fear signs usually alternate with laughter and a cathartic release from the tension of fear as the child suddenly retreats from the fear-evoking object. This cycle may be repeated many times, as the child alternately seeks to increase the level of fear and then to discharge it. The experience itself may involve real physiological fear. But, as long as the child is able to remember that the situation is only one of "make-believe," he or she is learning that fears are controllable. As the experience of controlled fear is generalized to the thing represented by the play object, the fear of that thing is gradually diminished. It becomes more difficult, in other words, for a child to continue to fear a thing that she or he has learned to *pretend* to fear.

A. C. Cain observed this process in a group of children who were mental patients:

> A considerable component of the erratic behavior of these children has a conscious element—that is, they are "playing crazy." Much, though by no means all, of this activity centers around their past experiences of and continual concerns about "being crazy." While playing crazy may be very quiet and subtle or blatant and obvious, identified as "pretend" by the child or exhaustively "defended" as crazy, it takes varied forms: "looking odd," staring off into space, or acting utterly confused; wild, primitive disorganized ragelike states, odd verbalizations; incoherencies; mutterings; alleged hallucinations and delusions; the child's insistence that he is an animal, goblin, or other creature; or various grossly bizarre behaviors. Most of the children show many of these forms of playing crazy and make clear—though by no means reliable—announcements that they have played crazy or intend to do so, or speak of "just pretending."
>
> At times, the child is quite consciously, deliberately, almost zestfully, playing crazy—he is under no significant internal pressure, is completely in control, and at the end is most reassured. For if one can openly *pretend* to be crazy, how can one really be crazy? (1964, pp. 281-282)

FIGURE 13.2 Play

This child's kite in Alexandra, near Johannesburg, South Africa, may represent for him, the possibility of flight, of freedom, of escape, or it may simply be an object of delight. The activity may help him coordinate eye-hand movements, or gain skill at running. Play is an activity that can relieve stress, provide an opportunity to fantasize, and, especially for children, to practice skills without fear of failure.

Play, of course, may be stimulated by stresses other than those derived from lack of skill, but reduction of the effects of stress—from whatever source—is a consistent factor in play. Indirect release from the subjective aspects of stress accounts for another central quality of play: the pleasure that participants derive from it. People sometimes report that they engage in play for the pure fun of it. But notice that this can be understood as being equivalent to saying that when one plays, subjective distress—the opposite of pleasure—is decreased.

Games

Games are more formally structured than spontaneous play. According to Kendall Blanchard and Alyce Cheska, a **game** is "a competitive activity that involves physical skills, strategy, and chance, or any combination of these elements" (1985, p. 60). J. Roberts, M. J. Arth, and R. R. Bush (1959) view games as models of the conflict-producing situations in society that create anxiety. Games provide an outlet for the expression of anxieties by permitting reenactment of conflicts in a nonthreatening setting, as well as a safe chance to practice the skills needed in conflict situations. Societies with a simple social organization are unlikely to use games of strategy; societies with a complex social organization are. In simpler societies, children are encouraged to be assertive, so strategy is a less important social skill than in more complex societies.

Roberts and Sutton-Smith (1962) found that games of strategy are most popular where obedience is stressed in childrearing. Such games may well reflect anxiety about powerlessness among children who lack the determination to achieve many of their goals directly. Games of chance, on the other hand, are more popular in societies in which duty and responsibility are stressed during socialization. Such games may represent a form of defiance, a psychological release from anxiety about having to be responsible. These researchers also found that games of physical skill tend to be preferred when independence is emphasized during childhood socialization. Such skills help children to succeed at tasks they undertake at their own initiative.

Festivals

Public, secular celebrations, such as festivals carried out for pleasure, are probably the most widely practiced form of adult play. Festivals occur at predictable times of year. They sometimes have religious or political overtones, but they often function as a cathartic outlet from the routine stresses of life. In contemporary nation-states, hundreds of thousands of people may gather for parades, dancing, and other forms of enjoyment at holiday celebrations such as Mardi Gras in São Paulo, Fasching in Hamburg, or New Year's Eve in Times Square and other major cities of America and Europe. Children sometimes have special festivals, such as Halloween, reserved for their own entertainment.

Sports

According to Blanchard and Cheska, **sport** is "a physically exertive activity that is aggressively competitive within constraints imposed by definitions and rules" (1985, p. 60). Sports are more ritually patterned than games. The cultural element of sports can be seen by examining the changes that occur when a sport is borrowed from one culture by another. For instance, when cricket was taken over from the English by the Trobrianders, they transformed it to fit their own traditions of intergroup competition between villages by embellishing it with traditional warfare symbolism.

Art

Art is more than the experience of pleasure or the manifestation of skill. It is a human product that involves skill in its production, evokes feelings, and as Jacques Maquet succinctly put it, "is a part of a socially constructed reality" (1986, p. 8). **Art** is, in other words, a phenomenon of culture, a symbolic expression that is meaningful within a particular cultural tradition and that evokes an aesthetic experience. Alexander Alland has suggested that art is a kind of "play with form" whose products are aesthetically successful and culturally meaningful (1977, p. 39). Unlike ordinary play, it is performed with conscious attention to the meaningfulness of the acts of play or its products.

Although all art involves our senses in ways that demonstrate technical skill in its production, arouse feelings, and convey a message, these three components of art may not be equally prominent in a particular artistic product. In any given artistic work, one of these may be particularly noteworthy. This is true whether the work is in the visual arts such as painting or sculpture, the auditory arts such as music, or the kinesthetic arts such as dance. So artistic products of all types can be classified by their relative emphasis on feelings they arouse, the skill with which

---

game a competitive activity involving physical skills, strategy, and chance in a model of a conflict-producing real-life situation
sport aggressively competitive activity played according to strict rules
art a cultural expression of feeling and meaning in a form that evokes an aesthetic experience in the participant or observer

they were produced, and the meanings that they embody.

Skilled production of form. Although art has much in common with play, it is more than just play. The artist gives conscious attention to how the artistic activity is carried out in a way that is not present in the spontaneity of play. Therefore skill in the production of form has been held by many to be a fundamental quality of art. As long ago as 1916, Franz Boas observed that "All art implies technical skill" (1940, p. 535). Nevertheless, as a disciplined variety of play, artistic acts are creative and innovative within the constraints of the rules that define each form and its various culturally recognized styles. The artist explores the current conventions of an established artistic style, creates new variations on the themes those rules imply, and sometimes alters those rules in creative, new ways. An appreciation for the skill of its producer is also an important aspect of the aesthetic experience of the observer of art.

Artistic skill includes the artist's mastery of execution and judgment about the qualities of form the artistic product must contain to achieve an aesthetic effect. Skill in organizing the composition is crucial to the aesthetic experience in all forms of art. It can be found in the arrangement and choice of instrumentation in a musical score, in the choice of colors and the balance of different forms within a painting, or in the choreography of dance. As with the dexterity that is evidenced by skilled execution, effective choice in the makeup of an artistic product is also a skill that lends pleasure to the aesthetic experience.

FIGURE 13.3   Skill in Art
While most non-Western cultures don't have a concept of "art for art's sake," they do recognize the fact that some artists have greater skill than others. Skill in art involves arranging the materials in an aesthetically pleasing manner, arranging instrumentation in a musical score, or choreographing the steps to a dance. This Inuit is preparing his sculpture in his studio.

Shoshoni Art

Once, while I was doing fieldwork in Nevada, a Shoshoni friend of mine, Dannie Millet, and I were talking about Shoshoni music. He described the music which he used to sing at Fandangos, where people gathered from miles around to enjoy themselves. Songs, he said, were often accompanied by a percussion background of drums or rasps. On impulse, he decided to make a musical rasp and demonstrate it for me. It only took a minute for him to find a cottonwood branch under one of the nearby trees. Then he set about whittling a series of notches down one of its sides. Using a pot from my kitchen as a sounding board, he played and sang some traditional songs so I could hear what Shoshoni music sounded like. In his younger days, he said, he had known enough songs to sing from sunset to sunrise. He graciously let me keep the rasp.

The next morning Dannie called on me unexpectedly. Although it had worked perfectly well as a musical instrument, Dannie had been dissatisfied with the instrument he had made on such short notice. The branch he had found the day before was curved and somewhat asymmetrical. It looked like a branch with notches cut on it, not like an instrument. So that night when he went home, he had spent some time searching out a more suitable branch from which to carve a rasp that was more pleasing to the eye. He had selected a straight branch, about a foot long, and had carefully cut away its surface bark. Then he notched it evenly from one end, but left a suitable hand-hold area at the other. The finished product gave evidence of his skill as a craftsman. It didn't play any better as a percussion instrument—not, at least, to my untrained ear. But it was a better instrument, because Dannie had endowed it with a beauty his first rushed job had lacked, a visual form that demonstrated his technical skill as its maker and that was more pleasing to the eye. Here was art in its most fundamental sense, art as an expression of the artist's desire for a beauty of form that went beyond mere functionality.

(see reference map p. 84)

The expression of feelings in art. Artistic acts and play are both self-rewarding activities that express feelings. Both may be pleasurable and provide cathartic release from the stresses of daily life and work. Also like play, the artistic frame of mind has been described repeatedly in terms suggesting an altered state of consciousness. Artists sometimes describe their creative ideas as if they come to them from somewhere outside themselves, like revelations. In general, all creative acts are intimately related to altered states of consciousness, which in turn are responses to and statements about the stresses of life (Koestler, 1964). Like play, the acts of art are expressive of the hopes, fears, and desires of the actor, but in art, the expressive signs of the tension that exists between reality and desire are consciously refined.

All art expresses feelings as well as craftsmanship and meaning, but there are, historically, styles of art in which emotion is particularly prominent. In European history, for example, music of the Romantic period that followed the more formal Baroque era of music, the "Sturm und Drang" literature of German writers such as Lessing and Schiller, and contemporary horror movies in the United States are all highly emotional.

Meaning in art. In addition to the characteristics it shares with play, art has meaning and makes an intentional statement. Because it is intended as communication, art implies an audience, real or potential, even if the audience is the artist

FIGURE 13.4 Mayan Garment Design
The artist communicates meaning by transforming natural phenomena into designs that are particularly symbolic of her or his culture. The traditional Mayan huipil, a rectangular hand-woven shawl, is decorated with diamond patterns that represent the cosmos, the vulture, a symbol of the weaver's community, and the toad, representing rain and fertility. The ancient weavers of these designs symbolically placed themselves at the center of the world, close to the ancestors who interceded for them with requests to the gods who control order, rain, and life on earth.

alone. The artist transforms raw, natural signs, such as smiles and tears that have universal meanings and that are used intuitively by others, into the symbolic conventions of his or her own culture. Yet, a skilled work of art may be appreciated beyond its original cultural setting. Because symbols of art are derived from natural signs, commentators sometimes speak of art as using a universal language or as making a statement that transcends the narrow confines of its society or time. Nevertheless, since the artistic transformation involves the elaboration of natural signs into a symbolic statement that is particularly meaningful within the cultural tradition of the artist, no work of art is truly universally meaningful.

Intellectual art in which the meaningful component is highly emphasized can be exemplified by Escher prints in which the visual forms have paradoxical relationships with one another, and iconoclastic art such as the works of Andy Warhol and the students of Dadaism. Intellectual artistry is often an important component of the verbal arts, but all forms of art make a meaningful statement. For instance, in the Western musical tradition, Bach, one of the last Baroque composers, is known for the "intellectual" nature of his music. Though his music may be admired for its beauty and the interplay of melodies, he is nevertheless particularly remembered for the remarkable ways in which his music incorporated meanings for those who could discover them. For instance, in his final work, his own name is spelled out in the musical notes employed in its melody—a fact that a German listener is more likely to discover than is a British or American, since the German musical scale includes an H as well as an A, B, and C.

FIGURE 13.5   Decorative Pottery
In some cultures, objects are created simply to decorate the environment of the home or the workplace. The concept of "art for art's sake" may apply to functional objects as well. This jar with four bird figures was purchased in Casas Grandes, Mexico, by the National Museum of the American Indian in New York.

Art Forms

Anthropological research has looked most intensely at the products of artists, since their works are more accessible to objective description and analysis than are their subjective mental states. The major categories of works of art with which anthropologists generally have dealt are visual arts, music, dance, and verbal arts.

The Visual Arts

Probably all languages have a word that stands for visual beauty. In English we say that some things are "good looking." In Shoshoni they are *caan na-pui-tyn*, literally "good itself-look-ing." The Navajo speak of scenery or a location as hó-zhó-ní (literally, "location-beauty-is"). So it is not surprising that there are a large variety of ways of expressing visual beauty, including decorating the human body, designing physical objects that people use, such as baskets, and expressing feelings in paintings and sculpture.

Body decoration. People throughout the world decorate their bodies in various ways to make themselves beautiful. Common forms of body deco-

ration include clothing and jewelery, makeup, tattoos, and scarification. The beauty conferred by decorating the body can have a variety of purposes. For instance, personal adornment may be used to make individuals more attractive, uniforms and decorative insignia may communicate their rank or occupations, and costumes may facilitate play and recreation, sometimes by hiding people's identities and status or even by making them less attractive.

Decorative arts. Sometimes objects are made for purely aesthetic reasons. Paintings, murals, mosaics, and sculptures may be done solely to decorate the environment of a home or workplace. In societies with professional artists, objects of this type may also be treated as "art for art's sake," and stored in museums or privately owned. Similar objects can be found in less complex societies as well. These tend to be of a more personal nature: aesthetic objects of religious significance such as medicine bundles (rab-

FIGURE 13.6   Art and Social Complexity

In this segment (A) of the Dresden Codex, the Opossum God carries the image of the Maize God to a shrine at the entrance of the town. This complicated design that fills its available space is an example of art produced in a stratified society. Illustration (B), by contrast, is produced in an egalitarian society. Its design is simple, repetitive, and surrounded by space.

bit's feet, four-leaf clovers, or other personal religious objects); fetishes (objects containing spirits); mandalas (objects to look at while meditating); ceremonial masks; or paintings used in religious ceremonies.

John Fischer (1961) compared the pictorial art of complex, socially stratified societies with the art of egalitarian societies (those that are usually organized into small, self-sufficient communities, with little differentiation of activities, statuses, or rank). He found that, regardless of the specific symbols used, art in egalitarian societies tends to use symmetrical designs and repetition of simple features. Much of the available space is left empty, and figures are not enclosed by a formal boundary. In stratified societies, by contrast, pictures tend to be asymmetrical and composed of dissimilar elements that are integrated into the full design. The tendency is for little empty space to be left within the field of works

of pictorial art, and figures are often enclosed by well-defined boundaries.

Fischer speculated that symmetry may reflect the basic similarity of the generalized statuses within the egalitarian communities; repetition of simple elements may reflect the similarity of individuals. He suggested that the asymmetrical design of the art of stratified societies may reflect the specialized differences and ranking of statuses; the integration of diverse elements into the design may mirror the high degree of specialization and integration of diverse statuses in complex societies. Fischer also suggested that the greater use of empty space in the art of simple egalitarian societies may represent their relative isolation and self-sufficiency. By contrast, the filling of empty space in the art of complex societies may stem from the lack of isolation of individuals, who learn to find security through establishing a place for themselves in the network of statuses that makes up the community. Similarly, the enclosing boundaries may represent the imposition of controls on the behavior of individuals—since many rules imposed from above is a social trait most characteristic of the socially stratified societies.

Music

The study of **music**, rhythmically organized, scaled tones that produce melodic sound, and its relationship to culture is the subject matter of a specialized subfield of anthropology called **ethnomusicology**.

Scales. A **scale** is a sequence of tones that ends with a return to a tone that has a frequency twice that of the starting tone. The European tone scale that Americans are familiar with is an octave of eight tones (CDEFGABC) in which one of two different pitch intervals may occur between each succeeding tone pair. In any sequence of eight tones of increasing pitch, the eighth will have a frequency of twice that of the first tone, which has the psychological effect of making it sound like a higher pitched version of the first. The pitch intervals between succeeding tone pairs (C-D, D-E, F-G, G-A, and A-B), called "whole steps," are twice the interval between the two remaining tone pairs (B-C and E-F), which are called " half steps." The interpersion of whole and half steps depending on the particular scale. Since the Middle Ages, European music has also employed five other tones within the octave (C#, D#, F#, G#, and A#), each of which is a half step above or below its adjacent tones.

Ethnomusicologists have discovered that very different musical scales are found in many other societies. These include scales of as few as 2 or 3 tones or more than 12. Scales of 5, 6, or 7 tones are the most common. For instance, the Japanese use a scale whose octaves are of 5 equidistant notes, the Javanese use scales of 5 and scales of 7 notes, and Arabic music uses octaves of 17 and 24 tones. Most musical scales are rooted in a single tone to which melodies frequently return and on which they end.

Barbara Ayres has found cross-cultural support for connections between child-rearing practices and tonality. Noting that laboratory animals that were stressed before weaning engaged in more exploratory behavior as adults, she suggested that a similar relationship might be found in humans between early

stress, such as scarification, nose piercing, or circumcision before two years of age, and extensive tonal ranges in adult music (1968). Alan Lomax found another intriguing cultural difference in tonal ranges: the pitch interval in song was greater in foraging societies where the group had to cover larger territories in the quest for food (1962).

Rhythm. The timing and stressing of tones within a melody is called **rhythm**. It is highly varied from society to society. For instance, rhythm may be characterized by patterns of stressed tones arranged in regular groupings, or meters. Western music traditionally relies on meters of two, three, four, or six beats, with variations in the patterns of which beats are stressed and which are unstressed. Asymmetric meters are also possible and are quite common in Asian music. Much African drum music is characterized by great rhythmic complexity in which accents, meters, or even beats change in different segments of the music.

Ayres also examined the rhythms infants are exposed to when carried, to see if these influenced the rhythm of a society's music. She found that when children are regularly carried in slings, pouches, or shawls, so that they experience the movement of walking by the person who carries them, musical rhythms tend to have regular beats (1973). In contrast, where children are strapped to a cradle board or spend time in cradles, the rhythms of adult music tend to have irregular beats or free rhythm.

Lyrics. Musical melodies can be hummed or chanted, using nonsense syllables to sing the tones. In all parts of the world, music is sometimes conveyed with **lyrics**, words that convey a message. Music was studied in great detail by Alan Lomax (1968), who found the songs of complex societies to be wordier than those of simple societies. He pointed out that precision in enunciation also tends to increase with social complexity. Lomax noted that choral singing and counterpoint, the addition of independent melo-

---

music rhythmically organized scaled tones that produce melodic sound
ethnomusicology the study of music and its relationship to culture
scale a sequence of tones that ends with a return to a tone that has a frequency twice that of the starting tone
rhythm the timing and stressing of tones within a melody
lyrics words in a musical piece that convey a message

dies above or below the main one, are most common where cooperative labor is the hallmark of work. Polyphony, the singing of two or more melodies simultaneously, is most common in societies where women contribute at least half of the food.

Dance

Rhythmically patterned human movement performed for aesthetic pleasure is called **dance**. It is typically accompanied by music or song, and often has a place in religious ritual as well as in secular life. Lomax studied dance as a cultural art form, and found that "movement style in dance is a crystallization of the most frequent and crucial patterns of everyday activity" (1968, p. 237). For instance, the postures adopted in work frequently are found in the dance style of a society. Dance styles also vary between societies with simple subsistence technologies and those with complex food production techniques. For instance, foraging bands and gardening tribes make more use of simple up-and-down movements such as hopping and side-to-side steps such as shuffling, while the dance styles of agricultural chief-

FIGURE 13.7   New Guinea Dancers
Dance styles reflect social complexity just as does art and music. In less complex societies, it is common for people to do similar hopping steps or side-to-side shuffling steps in groups, as these New Guinea dancers are doing. In complex societies, movement may involve many parts of the body, and may include a hierarchy of performers, such as in dance performances.

doms and states are more likely to include movements in many parts of the body, such as the hands, arms, and torso (Lomax and Arensberg, 1977).

The Verbal Arts

The **verbal arts**, sometimes called **oral literature**, include myths, legends, rhetoric, folk tales, proverbs, riddles, jokes, and other forms of art that are based on language and that enrich the human experience.

Myths.   Stories that recount the origin of such things as the gods, the universe, human beings, animals, and plants are considered **myths**. They may explain how human ways of life began, the nature of death, and the afterlife. Usually myths are placed in the distant past and involve supernatural beings. For example, the Shoshoni of the Great Basin desert tell of a time when the sun was so close to the earth that people were dying, and the plants of the earth were burned up so there was no food to be found. Cottontail, one of the creatures of the earth, determined to kill the sun and set things right. He took some rocks as weapons and traveled toward where the sun rises until it got too hot for him. Then he began to burrow until he got to his destination. He made a hunting blind and waited until the sun came up. When the sun arose, Cottontail threw a rock at the sun and killed him. It was so hot that Cottontail was scorched, which left him brown, as he is to this day. After a while, the sun revived, but Cottontail removed the sun's gallbladder and told the sun that he must go up higher in the sky so that all people might have light to gather food, but not be burned. Out of the sun's gallbladder, Cottontail fashioned the moon, which also went up to the sky.

According to Clyde Kluckhohn (1965), five themes seem to be found in the myths of every society: great natural catastrophes (most often by flood, but sometimes by earthquake, hurricane, or

---

dance rhythmically patterned human movement performed for aesthetic pleasure
verbal arts (oral literature) various forms of speaking for aesthetic pleasure, including orating, reciting myths, and telling folktales
oral literature various forms of speaking for aesthetic pleasure, including orating, reciting myths, and telling folktales
myths stories that recount the origin of such things as gods, the universe, animals, and plants

fire), monster-slaying, incest (usually by brother and sister), sibling rivalry, and castration (in real or, more often, symbolic form). The list clearly deals with anxiety-related matters that must be dealt with by peoples the world around.

Legends. **Legends** are very similar to myths, but usually deal with a more recent period of time than myths, and their central characters are heroes and heroines of great stature who are usually responsible for the origin of a particular society or culture. Although they are usually regarded as real persons, they are often thought to possess superhuman qualities and to embody the central values of their society. The legendary figures of American culture are noted for their individualism, self-reliance, strength, and cleverness. They stand up for their ideals against great odds, triumphing over adversity. George Washington is one American legendary figure who actually existed, yet time has endowed him with stature somewhat above that of a real person. He is remembered in American folklore as being unable to tell a lie even as a child. At one time, it was said that he was strong enough to have thrown a silver dollar across the Rappahannock River. In many parts of the country, the river in this story has become the much wider Potomac. Other American legends are based on purely fictional characters, like Johnny Appleseed, whose exploits included the planting of apple trees throughout the New World.

Legends are not limited to stories that claim to have been passed down from an earlier era. New legends can arise in each generation and be an active part of people's sense of their current place in the broader scheme of things. For instance, legends of a hitchhiker who admonishes people about their obligations and then vanishes mysteriously have been common for generations in the U.S. Intermountain West. In early October 1992, I heard a contemporary version of this legend by a woman who told me that an acquaintance of hers had been driving near Ogden, Utah, when she picked up an elderly hitchhiker with white hair and a white beard. He asked her if she had enough food in storage to see her through difficult times. When she responded that she did not, he told her that she should have a good food supply laid aside by January. When she next looked in the rearview mirror, he was no longer in the back seat of the car. Shocked, she pulled to the side of the freeway to ponder the remarkable incident. Shortly thereafter,

a highway patrol officer stopped to see if she needed any assistance. When she recounted her experience, the officer told her that she was the sixth person who had told him the same story that day. The vanishing hitchhiker legend has a very active life. A week after I heard this particular version, the Salt Lake City newspapers reported that many people were telling variations of the same tale, and the highway patrol office had received numerous calls of inquiry. Such stories function to support an Intermountain tradition of self-sufficiency, an important social value in this American subculture.

Rhetoric. Formal speech that follows the traditional rules of a particular culture is called **rhetoric**. Most societies acknowledge a distinction between ordinary, everyday speech and elegant speech used for special occasions. It is particularly common in societies with class differences to provide formal education, at least to the elite members of society, in styles of public speaking that are judged to be refined and aesthetically pleasing. For instance, among the Aztecs, members of the nobility received special training in public speaking, including the use of metaphors, poetry, proverbs, and other ways of embellishing their speaking. Effective speech was so highly valued by the Aztecs that they had many euphemisms for describing people's manner of talking: An argumentative person who insisted on the last word was "wooden-mouthed," when one was too easily offended and responded by scolding others it was said that "words are his food," a chatterer was "swallow-mouthed," and the Aztec ruler was called the *tlatoani*, "the one who speaks," because his authority derived from his oratorical skills.

Folktales. **Folktales** are fictional stories told primarily for entertainment, but that also teach a moral principle or a practical lesson. Aesop's fables capture the essence of folktales told both for pleasure and to teach a lesson, as do many of Grimm's fairy tales. Folktales are commonly placed in a timeless setting and vague location. They portray the basic

---

legends stories that describe heroes and heroines who are usually responsible for the origin of a culture or society
rhetoric formal speech that follows the traditional rules of a particular culture
folktales stories told for entertainment that teach a moral principle or a practical lesson

dilemmas with which people must grapple as they strive to attain the goals of their culture. For instance, many European folktales are built around the theme of a poor but beautiful young girl who is often mistreated by her evil stepmother or sisters but who, by some type of magic or supernatural intervention, is rescued from her life of drudgery and raised to high status as the wife of a handsome prince. Against the backdrop of European social systems in which the female role traditionally included domestic chores and economic dependence on an income controlled by fathers and husbands, such folktales can be seen as stress reduction through wish fulfillment. They also contain the moral: dutiful little girls will be rewarded. In the United States, a popular series of folktales are those about the fictional character Paul Bunyan, whose exploits included the creation of Puget Sound. The telling of Paul Bunyan stories reinforces historic U.S. values of expansiveness and pride in heroic individualism.

Folktales include many forms of story telling and humor that communicate messages of folk wisdom, giving people a sense of their common heritage and cultural identity. This can be illustrated by the common Sufi stories about the wise fool, Mulla Nasrudin, who, through his foolish simplicity, teaches important moral principles. For instance, in one story, Nasrudin began a sermon to a crowd by announcing that he had a message of the greatest importance and asking them if they knew what he was about to tell them. When the people responded that they did not, he walked away muttering that if they were so unenlightened, it would be a waste of time trying to explain it to them. When he returned the next day and posed the same question, the audience, thinking they had better answer differently than they had the day before, called out "We do! We do!" To this, Nasrudin responded, "Well, then I don't need to explain it to you!" and left. On the third day, the villagers, hoping to maneuver Nasrudin into revealing his secret, had prepared themselves by agreeing that half the crowd would say yes, but that the other half would say no. But upon receiving this mixed response to his query, Nasrudin simply said, "Then let those who know explain it to those who do not," and left. To Sufis, this tale, told with much humor at Nasrudin's failure to reveal an important message because of his own foolishly concrete interpretation of what others said to him, does contain an important message. It reiterates a Sufi belief in the foolishness of seeking truth in an intellectual treatise instead of by listening to God through one's own heart.

Appalachian Storyteller

In a ramshackle home on a mountainside in the Appalachian hills, Ray Hicks, 69, has become a legend in the art of storytelling. He is known primarily for his mastery of 18 "Jack Tales," which tell the story of a clever, poor boy, Jack, who overcomes adversity with skill, cleverness, and good work.

Jack Tales, or similar stories, were once told all across Europe and were collected by the Grimm brothers in Germany around 1812. The stories were passed down in the oral tradition to Hicks's ancestor, Council Harmon, who died in this country in 1896 at the age of 93, and to Hicks, in an unbroken line of eight generations. They have become a metaphor for growing up poor in Appalachia. "The Jack Tales is how it feels to be a poor person," says Mr. Hicks (De Parle, *New York Times*, p. B7).

All the Jack Tales contain the elements of poverty, anger, wisdom, cunning, and heroics

FIGURE 13.8   Appalachian Folktales
On a mountain top in the Appalachian hills of North Carolina, Ray Hicks, 69, has become famous for telling the tales of Jack, a poor boy who conquers his adversaries in a dangerous world with kindness and cunning and emerges a hero. In an era of folktelling festivals, where the stories and techniques are largely imitative, Hicks is an original, telling his stories in a rambling fashion with a thick Southern accent.

Ray Hicks

In Beech Mountain, North Carolina, on the Tennessee border, Ray Hicks, 69, is famous for telling his "Jack Tales." Based on stories first collected in 1812 by the German brothers Jakob and Wilhelm Grimm, Hicks inherited them from his ancestors who traveled to America in colonial times.

on the part of the young boy, Jack. In "Soldier Jack," for example, Jack ties up Death in a magical sack. In "Jack and the Bean Tree," he steals a sleeping giant's quilt, and escapes by hiding the giant's boots. In a story of courtship, Jack outwits a farmer who challenged anyone wanting to court his daughter to make a rabbit stay within the boundaries of a circle 10 feet wide. The danger was real, since the farmer would chop off the suitor's head if the rabbit escaped. If the rabbit stayed, the farmer would lose his head. Through generously sharing his lunch, Jack obtained a stick which, when placed in the circle, magically kept the rabbit within the boundaries. Thus, through generosity, courage, and a little magic, Jack became a hero, and married the farmer's daughter.

Proverbs.   Like myths and legends, **proverbs** embody the basic values of a culture, but in a form that can readily express issues that concern people in a particular society. Their brevity makes it possible for proverbs to be inserted into conversations, where they can be used to cast light on the topics being discussed, comment on the propriety of a state of affairs, call others to take action, or even mildly rebuke another person without direct confrontation. In accordance with the work ethic, Americans remind each other that "the early bird gets the worm." The Aztec leader who was informed about disputes among the commoners might have responded, "My task is to guard turkeys. Shall I peck at those who peck at one another?" He meant that it was no more his fault that the commoners contended among themselves than it was the fault of the turkey guardian that turkeys pecked one another. Proverbs are often highly idiomatic, using symbolism that is drawn from the life experience of a particular society. For this reason, they may be difficult for members of other societies to decipher correctly.

Riddles.   **Riddles** are mental puzzles told for entertainment. By describing common things in novel ways, they challenge hearers to exercise their ability to see similarities between common things that are not usually associated with one another. They are a source of information about the things that a people consider noteworthy in their environment, how they classify things, and what aspects of things they judge to be relevant. For instance, Aztec riddles about spindles are often related to pregnancy. Perhaps the most obvious analogy is that the spindle grows in size as it is filled, just as a woman does in pregnancy. However, a more subtle message carried by these Aztec riddles is one of classification: They reiterate the idea that the spindle is symbolically associated with the woman's role.

Jokes.   **Jokes** and other forms of humor have long been recognized for their role in helping people relieve the tensions of their way of life. Since the major anxieties differ from society to society, so does the type of humor. Consider the Inuit of northern Alaska and Canada. They live in a harsh environment that challenges the limits of their skill. The ability to endure pain and to cope skillfully with potentially disastrous situations is necessary for survival in the far north. The people's reaction to many near-disas-

---

proverbs   short statements that illustrate the basic values of a culture
riddles   mental puzzles told for entertainment
jokes   humor that is intended to help relieve the stress of everyday life

ters is one of mirth. For instance, they might laugh uproariously at the tale of a party of travelers who are spilled into the wet snow, lose their dogs when their sled tips over, or lose their sled when it slides from the trail onto rotten sea ice and breaks through. Despite the inconveniences, the possible disaster of the party's being thrown into the freezing seawater has been escaped. Even those who were involved in the situation might react with immediate laughter at their relief, before settling down to the unpleasant task of retrieving their dogs and damaged goods.

The Olfactory and Gustatory Arts

Smell and taste are the chemical senses. Their evolutionary importance has often been linked to their role in the recognition of what is edible and what is not. Just as vision and hearing are important to many forms of artistic expression, the senses of smell and taste also have been sources of aesthetic experience. For instance, perfumes and scents have been used since early times to make people more attractive. The ancient Egyptians mixed perfumes into cones of butter that they placed on their heads during parties so that the melting butter would release a pleasant scent. Today, perfume production is a multibillion dollar a year industry worldwide. Various kinds of incense are burned to produce an attractive scent in the rituals of diverse religions. For instance, the Aztec and Maya of Middle America used a resin called copal as well as pine pitch as an offering to the gods, and Christians, Hindus, and Buddhists throughout the world burn incense as a symbol of purification, prayer, and piety.

The enjoyment of food involves both taste and smell. In all societies, individuals express preferences for one food over another, and sometimes make judgments about how well a food has been prepared. In some cultures, the ability to make such judgments is the basis for an aesthetic of foods and eating. For instance, the French distinguish between the *gourmand* and the *gourmet*; English speakers contrast the glutton with the epicurean. But even in societies that may lack terms to distinguish one who takes aesthetic pleasure in food and eating from one who merely eats without aesthetic reflection, eating is sometimes an event of special importance that is expected to bring particular pleasure.

Special attention to food preparation can have important significance in religious settings, at important family functions, and as an aspect of political

ceremonies. In the United States, most families have formal practices that relate to meals on at least certain holidays, such as Passover, Christmas, or Thanksgiving Day. In tribal societies, food preparation and feasting is a common part of the celebrations hosted by big men and big women, and sharing food can be an important act in finalizing political arrangements between allies or former enemies.

In chiefdoms, the high rank of political leaders is often acknowledged by sumptuary laws that permit certain foods to be eaten only by the chiefs. For instance, Trobriand Island chiefs were ceremonially presented the finest yams as gifts from members of their wives' clans, and only chiefs were permitted to have the best gardens. In societies that have class distinctions, rules of etiquette that distinguish upper class members of society from others always include rules about socially preferred ways of preparing, presenting, and eating foods, and sumptuary rules may also distinguish the aristocracy from commoners in the kind of foods that each may eat.

Tea Ceremony in Japan

One of the most famous artistic functions of food is the role of tea in the Japanese tea ceremony called *chanoyu*, "boiling water for tea." The tea ceremony has its origins in Kyoto during the fifteenth century. The custom of drinking *matcha*, powdered green tea whipped into boiling water, had been brought to Japan from China by Japanese Zen Buddist monks trained in China during the thirteenth century. Tea was used in temples as an aid to meditation. During the turmoil of the fifteenth century, the ceremonial drinking was introduced into the aristocratic courts by scholars and aesthetic advisers from the Zen monasteries.

The tea ceremony symbolically bridged the gap between the aristocracy and the peasants. The small, separate "grass hut" tearoom, in which the host or tea master guided a small group of friends in the meditative sharing of tea, imitated the construction of peasant thatched houses. The utensils, carefully chosen for their aesthetic harmony, were arranged on shelves or in an alcove after the manner of a Buddhist altar. The aesthetic emphasis in each tea ceremony was the concept of *wabi*, or elegant simplicity, that highlighted the transience of human life and the importance of experiencing each gathering in the seclusion of the tearoom as a unique and valuable moment. The importance of the tea ceremony was emphasized by recording it in a tea ceremony diary.

The tea ceremony remains an important focus of Japanese aesthetics today. The basic pattern of a ceremony begins with the cleaning of the tearoom hut and the surrounding garden. The host lays a fire in a sunken hearth or brazier and begins to boil the water, then places a scroll and flower arrangement in the utensil alcove. The guests rinse their hands and mouths at an outdoor water basin and enter the tearoom quietly. The host greets the guests, then brings the utensils and water from the pantry and puts each in its proper place. To prepare the tea, the host must wipe the tea scoop and ladle with a silk cloth, remove the lid from the boiling kettle, and place it on a special stand. The host then washes the bamboo whisk and wipes the tea bowl with a cotton cloth. Two scoopfuls of tea are put into the bowl, and a ladleful of hot water is poured into it. The mixture is whisked into frothy tea that is served to the first guest as the host bows. Each guest is served in the same way, and as each finishes drinking, the host cleans each tea bowl. The host then removes the implements to their alcove and bows to the guests from the pantry.

The austerity of the tea ceremony and its symbolism of humility and simplicity are captured in a poem by Fujiwara Teika (1162-1241):

> As far as the eye can see,
> No cherry blossom,
> No crimson leaf,
> A thatched hut by an inlet,
> This autumn evening.

Like foods, tobacco and snuff have been used for the pleasure they afford the senses of smell and taste. Tobacco was originally used by American Indians in religious rituals, but non-Indian peoples adopted it and spread it throughout the rest of the world, primarily as a recreational substance. Although the European use of tobacco was secular rather than religious, and although the acceptability of smoking waxed and waned, early smoking customs developed an aesthetic that had a definite aura of ritual and propriety. Men gathered in "smoking clubs" that rented pipes and sold tobacco. Elaborate rules governed the behavior of these gentlemen.

The Functions of Art

Art has an effect on the individual and on a particular culture in a society. Psychologically, art enhances life by adding beauty to our surroundings. It is a source of pleasure and relaxation from the stresses of life. Socially, art plays a number of different roles by virtue of its capacity to embody symbolic significance to its audience.

Art and Social Organization

Art fulfills a number of important social functions. It is used to communicate the various statuses people hold. It can play a role in regulating economic activities. And it is almost always a means for expressing important political and religious ideas and for teaching principles that are valued in society. These and other social uses of art function to preserve the established social organization of each society.

Status Indicators

One of the social functions of art is the communication of status differences between individuals. For instance, gender differences in body decorations and dress are typical of cultures throughout the world. Age differences may be similarly indicated. Puberty rituals often include tattooing, scarification of the body in decorative designs, or even filing of the teeth to distinguish between children and adults. Social class differences in complex societies also involve aesthetic markers such as the clothing people wear and the kinds of artworks they use as decorations of their homes. According to Sahlins (1976), social and economic class, age, and gender differences are noticeable even in the kinds of fabrics people's clothing is made from. For instance, silks in most societies are predominantly worn by women, especially those who are part of the upper classes and those who are middle-aged.

Economic Functions

Economic life, by virtue of its practical importance to our survival and to our standard of living, can sometimes be a source of conflict between groups that must carry out exchange with one another. Sometimes art, perhaps because it is valued for its nonutilitarian qualities, can play a role of maintaining harmony in such settings. This was one of the functions of the Kula Ring exchange of ceremonial necklaces and armbands among islanders such as the Trobrianders and Dobuans (see p. 89).

Religious Functions

Much of the dramatic and emotional impact of religion derives from its use of art. Religious rituals everywhere include song and dance performances, and the visual arts function to heighten the emotional component of religious experience in all parts of the world, by portraying important scenes and symbols from religious history and mythology. In some cultures, art and religious ritual are inseparable. For instance, among the Abelam of Papua New Guinea, all art is produced for use in rituals.

FIGURE 13.9 Navajo Sand Painting
Art can be used for practical rather than aesthetic purposes. Religious rituals, for example, are often accompanied by appropriate music, practitioners may wear garments richly decorated, and may use implements that are beautifully created or designed for the purpose. This Navajo sand painting is used in a ceremony intended to cure an illness.

Didactic Functions

Art is often employed as a means for teaching important cultural ideas and values. For instance, hymns in Western religions express theological concepts and encourage the support of specific religious values. Daniel Biebuyck has analyzed the use of art to embody moral and ethical principles by the Lega people of Central Africa. Lega ethical ideals are codified in figurines of humans and animals made of ivory, pottery, bone, wood, and wickerwork. The figurines are used in the initiation and training of men into prominent positions within Lega society. Each of these statues is associated with one or more aphorisms, a concise statement that alludes to a general ethical concept. For instance, one figure is a carved stick

> whose top is slit so as to suggest an open mouth. . . . The object illustrates the saying, "He who does not put off his quarrelsomeness will quarrel with something that has the mouth widely distended." (In other rites this idea may be rendered by a crocodile figurine with widely distended jaws.) The aphorism alludes to the disastrous effects of quarrelsomeness and meddlesomeness. (1973, p. 217)

Thus, Lega figurines were not only works of art, they were also devices for teaching important moral principles to each new generation. At the same time, their ownership by older men who had achieved initiation into the highest levels of society functioned to perpetuate respect for the moral wisdom of the leaders in the established social hierarchy.

Political Functions

Art often functions to legitimize the authority of government. Mount Rushmore, in South Dakota, memorializes four American presidents who were selected for their symbolic association with messages about values of individualism and democracy. The statue Mother Russia commemorates the enduring will to survive of the Russian people. The British Crown Jewels, by virtue of their artistry and the symbolism of precious stones that originated throughout the Commonwealth, celebrate the value of the institution of the monarchy. And the ornately carved Golden Stool of the Ashante of southern Ghana, with the distinctive myth of its supernatural origins, reinforces the legitimacy of the Ashante king and the unity and stability of Ashante society. Douglas

Fraser's account of the myth of the Golden Stool illustrates the interconnectedness of art and the social order. In this story, the chief priest of the first king of the new Ashanti Confederacy

> promised the king and the nation that he would call down from the skies a supernatural stool of solid gold which would enshrine and protect the soul of the nation. As a precondition to fulfilling his promise, however, he demanded that the ancestral (blackened) stools, state shields, state swords, and other regalia of all the member states be surrendered to him. This was done, and he buried them in the bed of the Bantama River in Kumasi. The purpose of this action was twofold: to ensure that no item of regalia in the new kingdom could have a longer history than the Golden Stool and hence take precedence over it, and, by depriving the formerly independent states of the relics of their respective pasts, to pave the way toward a new and broader union. (1972, pp. 139–140)

As a statement about the legitimacy of governmental authority, art is a conservative force in society. In this role, it is intended to elicit loyalty and to stabilize society and its political system. Governments also sometimes deliberately employ this aspect of art as propaganda urging public action that supports official policy. Thus, propagandistic art embodies both didactic and political functions.

CHAPTER SUMMARY

1. Art is a culturally relative phenomenon, both in the degree to which explicit aesthetic rules exist for judging artistic beauty and in the nature of those rules.

2. In all societies, human beings take pleasure in the experience of beautiful things.

3. The aesthetic experience is culturally organized into activities such as play, recreation, ritual, and art.

4. Play is the spontaneous stress-relieving behavior in which the practice of potentially utilitarian skills is facilitated by fantasy.

5. Recreations such as games, sports, and festivals are socially organized forms of play.

6. Art is a disciplined form of play that utilizes the skilled production of forms that are both expressive of feelings and culturally meaningful.

7. The artforms of any society may be classified by the senses they predominantly utilize.

8. Art fulfills a variety of social functions, including communicating status, facilitating economic processes, instilling rituals with meaningful feelings, supporting the political system, and teaching social values.

ANNOTATED READINGS

Alland, Alexander. (1977). *The artistic animal.* NY: Doubleday Anchor Books. A simple introduction to the biological basis of and the cultural influences on art.

Anderson, Richard L. (1990). *Calliope's sisters: A comparative study of philosophies of art.* Englewood Cliffs, NJ: Prentice Hall. A comparative study of the aesthetics of 10 societies, ranging from foragers to industrialized agriculturalists.

Dundes, Alan. (1980). *Interpreting folklore.* Bloomington: Indiana University Press. A collection of articles on the study of folklore.

Hannah, Judith L. (1979). *To dance is human.* Austin: University of Texas Press. A cross-cultural study of dance that examines the functions of dance in various kinds of social organizations.

Lomax, Alan. (1968). *Folksong style and culture.* American Association for the Advancement of Science, Publication no. 88. Washington, D.C.: American Association for the Advancement of Science. The groundbreaking study of folksong styles throughout the world.

Maquet, Jacques. (1986). *The aesthetic experience: An anthropologist looks at the visual arts.* New Haven: Yale University Press. An anthropological approach to the visual arts that integrates the study of Western and non-Western traditions into a single model.

Cultural Change and Diversity

The dynamics of change are predicated on the readiness of a culture to accept and adapt to it. Innovations and change may take the form of invention, discovery, borrowing, or diffusion. As specific adjustments to the natural environment or as responses to neighboring societies and their cultures, cultural change has dramatically altered life in many nations. Simple nonstate societies are few in number today due to the rapid expansion of state societies into their territories. Although industrialization has brought great power to some nations, the majority of the world's peoples still live as peasant food-producers in politically and economically subordinated segments of nation-states.

This unique examination of American culture reveals a complex society full of contradictions in the way it handles its life cycle changes, determines its role expectations, and balances its basic value systems. Traditional concepts of competitiveness, conformity, and the work ethic are contrasted with a love for fun, individualism, and a nostalgia for the simpler past.

Human cultural systems are dynamic. The pace of change is rapidly accelerating today as societies communicate more easily with one another and learn to adapt more readily to a complex, technological way of life. Chapter 14 details this process of cultural evolution, focusing on the interrelationships among technology, social organization, and ideology and illustrates how this process affects contemporary world societies. Chapter 15 takes a unique anthropological view of contemporary American culture.

FIGURE 14.1 Dial "S" for Soothsayer
Combining African tradition and Western marketing techniques, Liza Khumalo of Johannesburg, South Africa, is a star among the new breed of telephone diviners. She wears the traditional sangoma of the soothsayer, a woolen wig, arranges her tools, including shells and bones, and sits by the phone waiting for customers who pay about $2 a minute to get answers to their questions.

Cultural Evolution and the Contemporary World

Human cultural systems do not remain forever stable. In adjusting to the world around them, to the effects of population growth, and to the influence of other groups, human beings adopt new and different ways of manipulating their environment, of organizing themselves, and of thinking and communicating. Over the millennia, societies have evolved from simple hunting and gathering ways of life to extremely complex ones based upon industrialized technologies. In this chapter we will explore the process of cultural change and the forces that have influenced the rise of societies that have greater technological and social complexity. We will consider whether technological progress is synonymous with progress in the quality of life. We will also examine the diverse contemporary world, in which hunting and gathering cultures that have changed little over thousands of years coexist with rapidly modernizing industrial cultures whose trappings range from superhighways, heart transplants, and cable television to polluted air and water. Between these two extremes, the mass of humanity are peasants, living from the land by hand labor, with little income for luxury goods.

CHAPTER OBJECTIVES

After reading this chapter, you should be able to:

Discuss the ways in which cultural change occurs.

Analyze the interrelationships among the three cultural subsystems: technology, social organization, and ideology.

Contrast specific and general evolution.

Explain the principles of cultural evolution.

Discuss the nature and causes of alienation.

Discuss the processes of acculturation, ethnocide, and genocide.

Analyze the process of industrialization.

Compare and contrast developed and underdeveloped societies.

Recount the history of feudal and colonial peasantries.

Describe the nature and likely future of contemporary peasantries.

Explain the work of applied anthropology.

Explain the role of population control in developing nations.

Tai Chi. Cannes. PC compatible. Yeltsin. Clinton. Bosnia Herzegovina. Are we becoming a global culture? Is there any area of the world that has not seen the golden arches? Or not felt the influence of a microchip? What has made us what we are, and how do we maintain individual and cultural autonomy in a world that is becoming culturally unified?

....

The Process of Change

Cultural traits are subject to many change-promoting influences, both internal and external. As one trait changes, others also shift, ultimately altering the nature of the entire cultural system.

Cultural Dynamics

No culture is completely static. Cultural changes may arise within a society, or they may result from the cultural influence of one society on another. The primary forms of change are innovation, diffusion, and acculturation.

Innovation. The development of any new characteristic within a culture that occurs as a result of discovery or invention can be called an **innovation**. **Discovery** involves noticing something that has not been noticed before, while **inventions** involve putting previous cultural elements together in some new way. Discoveries and inventions do not occur randomly, since the current cultural pattern of thinking in any society prepares people to notice or accept some new things more readily than others, and cultural values

will favor some forms of change over others. If innovations depart too radically from the current way of thinking, they may not be valued or may even seem bizarre to most members of society and, thus, will not be accepted. In a culture with a high degree of role specialization, it is possible for some members of society to have experiences that are so uncommon in society at large that the insights they produce will be regarded as insignificant, foolish, or of no practical use. For instance, Gregor Mendel, a nineteenth-century Austrian monk, spent years cultivating plants, and in the process developed revolutionary new ideas about genetics that were shelved for years. It was only much later that growing interest in evolutionary theory among biologists provided a place where Mendel's discoveries proved to be very useful and enlightening to the scientific community.

Diffusion. Cultural changes that occur as a result of the influence of one society on another are referred to as **diffusion**. Anthropologists generally distinguish between two forms of diffusion: **direct borrowing** of traits and **stimulus diffusion**, in which the idea of the trait rather than the trait itself passes from one people to another. In both cases, the trait is likely to be modified in form, use, and meaning, to fit into the way of life of the recipient society. But the greatest changes occur in stimulus diffusion when the trait is created anew by the borrowing society to meet its own needs.

Tobacco provides an example of what changes occur in a directly borrowed trait. It was originally used in religious rituals in Native American cultures. In the process of being assimilated by other cultures, both the crop and methods of its preparation have been greatly modified. It is now used in many parts of the world as a recreational substance, rather than

---

innovation   changes in a culture as a result of discovery or invention

discovery   the development of new insights and ideas

invention   the act of combining preexisting cultural traits in new ways

diffusion   the passage of a cultural trait such as customs, artifacts, and ideas from one society to another

direct borrowing   the adopting of a cultural trait by one society from another with relatively little change in form, as exemplified by traits acquired through trade or imitation

stimulus diffusion   the borrowing of the idea for a cultural trait by one society from another, with the implementation of that idea being more or less determined within the borrowing culture for religious purposes (Linton, 1936). The transmission of writing from Mesopotamia to Egypt illustrates how the form of a trait may be changed when it is borrowed through stimulus diffusion. It is believed by many that the idea of writing was borrowed by the Egyptians, but instead of using Mesopotamian written symbols, the Egyptians created entirely new pictorial forms to write their own language.

Acculturation. When two or more cultures interact intensely so that they change in the process of adjusting to each other, anthropologists term the adjustments **acculturation**. The process of cultural change may begin before members of the two societies actually meet, as technological traits from one society are traded through intermediary societies until they reach far distant groups. But acculturation occurs most dramatically when two societies are interacting directly. As each adopts the other's technological, social, and ideological traits, it becomes more like the other. When one of the societies is politically, economically, and technologically less powerful than the other, it will change the most. When this process is carried to an extreme, the subordinate culture can change so much that it is hardly distinguishable from the dominant one. As a more powerful society extends its boundaries and politically subordinates a less powerful people within its own native territory, the indigenous people generally come to have very little influence on the political decision making of the society that governs them.

The process of acculturation can take place forcibly, for instance, through military domination. It also can occur more peaceably through mechanisms such as trade. As members of the less powerful society seek to acquire useful materials from their more powerful trade partners, their own way of life changes in the process. Acculturation eventually can lead to the extinction of an entire culture even though its people survive (see also p. 000).

The general long-term effects of the interaction of societies of unequal power have been formulated by David Kaplan (1960) as the **Law of Cultural Dominance:** "That cultural system which more effectively exploits the energy resources of a given environment will tend to spread in the environment at the expense of less effective systems." Any interacting cultures have some effect on each other. But, since more traits flow from the dominant to the subordinate culture, the latter is the one more likely to be radically altered—if it survives the effects of contact with the more powerful society at all.

FIGURE 14.2   Acculturation

The Ainu, an indigenous people who live on Hokkaido, Japan's northernmost island, are fighting to maintain their own autonomous culture rather than be completely assimilated by the Japanese. The battle is being led by Masanori Toyooka, on the right. He hopes to obtain four islands as a home for the Ainu from the Russians, who seized them in World War II. Fusae Doi, on the left, works with him to preserve Ainu handicrafts.

The Law of Cultural Dominance is not an invariable process. Cultures differ in their receptivity to acculturation on the basis of their degree of evolutionary adaptation. Some technologically simple societies have been remarkably resistant to the effects of cultural change at the hands of more powerful societies. Ruth Benedict (1934) pointed out long ago that the Pueblo Indians have had a long history of rather successful resistance to the effects of cultural traits of neighboring peoples. Nevertheless, in the general evolutionary scheme, societies with greater technological control over energy resources have fairly consistently expanded while technologically simple societies are becoming fewer each year.

acculturation   the process in which one culture adapts to the influence of another culture by borrowing many of its traits
Law of Cultural Dominance   the cultural system that effectively exploits the energy resources of a given environment has the tendency to spread into that environment at the expense of less effective systems

Interrelationships Among Technology, Social Organization, and Ideology

Change may begin within any aspect of culture, but is likely to then affect other aspects of culture as well. The major goals of culture-guided behaviors are manipulation of the external environment with a technology, social interaction within a social organization, and symbolic expression of experiences that are made meaningful by a shared ideology. These three major subsystems of culture—technology, social organization, and ideology—are related, and change within any one will affect the others (see Fig. 14.3).

Evolution through technological change.

Technology—the means by which energy is drawn from the environment and used within a society—is considered by some anthropologists to be the area most likely to be the leading edge of cultural change. Leslie White formalized this idea as the **Basic Law of Cultural Evolution**: "Other factors remaining constant, culture evolves as the amount of energy harnessed per capita per year is increased, or as the efficiency of the technological means of putting the energy to work is increased" (1971, pp. 368–369). Due to the extreme reliance of humans on tools to maintain life, changes in the tool kit of a society have profound effects on the nature of the society itself and on a people's understanding of the world.

The economy has the most immediate technological effect on the social organization, because its structure determines the division of labor in the production and distribution of subsistence goods. Population size is affected too: The more effective a subsistence technology becomes at providing energy beyond the minimum necessary for survival, the larger the population will grow. As the population expands, there will be a corresponding increase in the complexity of the social organization and other parts of the technology. With increasing numbers of statuses and specialization—and interdependence of statuses—new and more complex means of political control will develop. New specialized political statuses take over roles previously fulfilled by kinship. Societies with the most complex technologies also tend to be those that are most highly stratified with ranked statuses, some of which have access to great amounts of power, prestige, and control over the material wealth of the society.

Technological changes will be reflected in ideological adjustments, first as new informal patterns of ideas and feelings arise and later as the formal, conscious ideology finally accommodates to the new circumstances. The ideology may reflect technological or social innovation by actually adding new beliefs.

A classic example of the effects of technological change on social organization and ideology is the case described by Sharp (1952) of the introduction of steel hatchets to the Yir Yiront, an Australian hunting and gathering society that previously had known only the stone axe. Among the Yir Yiront, stone axes were manufactured only by adult men and were exclusively their property. They were, however, commonly used by women, by men who owned no axe of their own, and by children, all of whom had to borrow one from an adult male kinsman. The process reinforced the authority of the kinship system that structured the society, and the axes themselves served as symbols of masculinity and male dominance in the social and economic system. Enter the European missionaries, who attempted to help the Yir Yiront "improve their conditions of life" by distributing or trading to everyone steel axes which, being technologically more efficient tools, were to help the natives "progress." What the missionaries did not understand was that this change undermined the authority of the adult males of the society and eventually had a disruptive effect on the economic system of the Yir Yiront as well, since their trade with neighboring peoples was motivated by the need to acquire stone to manufacture the axes. The festive annual gatherings at which trade previously had occurred began to lose their social importance and excitement as trading partnerships weakened. A man might find it easier to obtain a steel axe from white men by selling his wife's favors than by traditional means, an outcome hardly foreseen by the European missionaries!

Evolution through social change.

Cultural change may begin not only within the technological subsystem but also within the social organization. As a population grows, the number of social relationships increases, and new ways of coordinating society are needed. New statuses and institutions arise in response to these pressures. In very simple societies, the family is the fundamental institution of social control. It educates the young, produces food and

---

Basic Law of Cultural Evolution concept that increases in energy harnessed or in efficiency of its use through technological change are the primary cause of cultural evolution

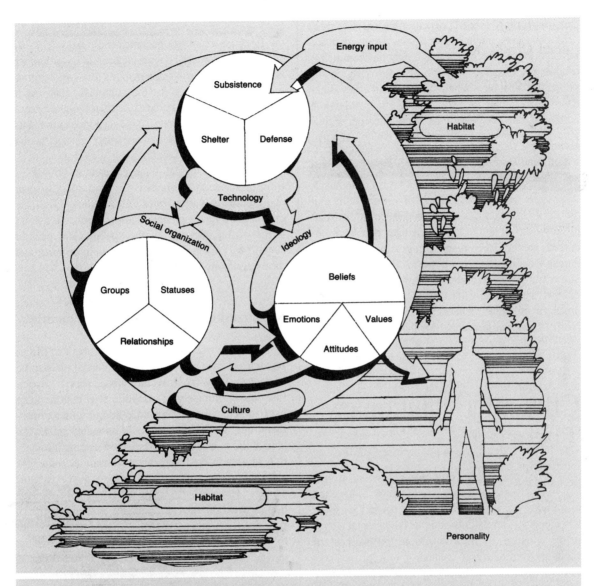

FIGURE 14.3   Cultural Subsystems
This chart shows the relationship of the cultural subsystems of technology, social organization, and ideology. Change in any one will affect the others.

other economic goods, carries out judicial activities when members violate important rules, and performs other "governmental" functions. As societies increase in population and density, new institutions arise to help coordinate human interaction. One important new institution is the special-interest nonkinship association—groups such as the local militia composed of all young men of the group, the voluntary fire brigade, or the harvest cooperative group. Larger-scale societies begin to develop full-time specialists and other new statuses and groups such as full-time governmental specialists, draft laborers, religious leaders, and standing armies.

As the social organization becomes more complex, cultural changes are reflected in the society's technology and ideology. For instance, when producers begin to specialize in the manufacture of a given item, it tends to become more standardized in form. Ideologically, as governmental specialization develops, members of the society increasingly value order and stability, even at the expense of individual autonomy.

Evolution based on ideological change.
Adjustments in the cultural subsystems that are initiated in the ideological realm may be exemplified by processes such as the birth of a new religious or political philosophy. When successful, the new doctrine is proclaimed by a social body organized by the author of the new teachings. New ideologies thus give rise to new social structures, which, in turn, influence the functioning of the culture's technology. An ideology may, on the other hand, slow the process of change. The Old Order Amish of Pennsylvania are a well-known example of a social body that for ideological reasons has remained highly resistant to the complex technological changes that have occurred among their neighboring Americans. The Amish have maintained a horse-and-buggy transportation system, a horse-drawn plow subsistence technology, and a home life largely unaffected by the presence of radios, televisions, and other common North American household appliances.

Cultural Evolutionary Theory

The observable differences among tribes, bands, chiefdoms, and states (see Chapter 5) have led a number of anthropologists to speculate about whether these levels constitute developmental stages in the advance toward civilization, the progress of societies from one stage to another, or improvements in the quality of life. In asking such questions, they have tried to formulate general laws that can be applied to the process of cultural evolution in all societies.

Specific and General Evolution

The existence of extensive parallels in the development of early civilizations suggests that the evolution of ways of life is as orderly as biological evolution. Marshall Sahlins and Elman R. Service (1960) and Service (1971) have clarified the regularity of cultural evolution by pointing out that cultures change in two fundamentally different ways: (1) through a process of **specific evolution**, or change in the direction of increasing adaptive specialization; and (2) through a process of **general evolution**, or change in the direction of increasing complexity. In the first, a way of life becomes more adjusted to its specific environmental circumstances—in a word, more specialized. In the second, new parts of a total environment are drawn upon by the cultural system. As a culture becomes more complex, it relates to its environment in radically new ways, harnessing greater amounts of energy for new uses. Qualitative change is the hallmark of general evolution.

While biological changes cannot be passed from one species to another, the traits that arise in one culture may pass over into another. Thus, the evolutionary development of cultures must be seen in terms of the interplay of the specific and general evolutionary changes that occur within cultures and the interactions between cultures.

Stabilization vs. Evolutionary Potential

It is the interaction between cultures that makes possible an interplay between the forces of specific and general evolution. Acting alone, specific evolution leads ultimately to stability. If a culture were ever to achieve a perfect adaptation to its environment, any further change would be maladaptive. If a way of life is relatively inefficient in helping a society to deal with its environment, it is a simple matter for a people to improve their adjustment to the circumstances. However, the more efficient a way of life becomes in making use of the resources available to a people, the more expensive and difficult it becomes to implement each new increase in efficiency, so that change in the direction of greater adaptation gradually slows and a way of life becomes more stable. This fact has been referred to by Thomas Harding (1960) as the **Principle of Stabilization**. On the basis of this principle, Sahlins and Service (1960) have formulated what they call the **Law of Evolutionary Potential**, which states that a culture's capacity to

---

specific evolution change in the direction of increasing adaptive specialization

general evolution change in the direction of increasing complexity

Principle of Stabilization the concept that the more efficient a culture becomes at harnessing energy for society, the more expensive and difficult it becomes to implement new means of increasing efficiency

Law of Evolutionary Potential the concept that a culture's capacity to move from one general evolutionary stage to another varies inversely with the degree of its specific evolutionary adaptation to its environment move from one general evolutionary stage to another varies inversely with its degree of specific evolutionary adaptation.

If it were not for general evolution, interacting cultures would continue increasing their adaptations to their environments and to each other until a final stability would be achieved among them. But, as we have seen, under certain circumstances cultures may adapt to their environment in ways that cause a qualitative change in social complexity and power. General evolutionary change inevitably disrupts the previous balance of power between neighboring societies. As each new general evolutionary stage is achieved, societies at the new level expand at the expense of simpler, less powerful cultures. Some of these simpler societies may be absorbed. Others may be driven out of their territory or annihilated as the more complex society expands in population and acquires new territory. Still others may adopt the new technology themselves and thus enter the new level of general evolution. The latter will eventually need to improve the efficiency of their use of the technology that made the transition to the new stage possible. As this process occurs, the earlier dominant societies of this stage are likely to achieve a high degree of social stability sooner than latecomers do.

Leapfrogging

When considered in light of the Law of Evolutionary Potential, the first culture to make the transition from one general evolutionary level to the next becomes specialized in a technology, making it difficult to move to an even more complex stage. Rather, it is the backwater cultures, those that are less specifically adapted to their current situation, that have the greatest chance to leap ahead in power and complexity by adopting and implementing radically new technologies. This fact has been formulated into another general law of cultural evolution, called the Law of Local Discontinuity of Progress. This law states that successive stages of general evolutionary change are not likely to be achieved in the same locality. General evolutionary change tends to occur in a kind of leapfrogging way, with the dominant centers of world power shifting from one area to another over the centuries.

Elman R. Service (1971) believes that this leapfrogging process is likely to continue into the future. It is his contention that, should no unpredictable factor such as a war intervene, the most likely course of future events is one in which Western civilization will be eclipsed by some of the currently underdeveloped nations. Service writes, "Those nations that are now the most advanced in the present coal and oil complex have less potential for the full and efficient use of the industry of the future than certain hitherto 'underdeveloped' regions which could build a new civilization well-adapted to such a base" (p. 42).

The forces of industrialization, of course, still are spreading gradually throughout the world. In Western Europe and North America, the process was a gradual one that began with quite small-scale industries and expanded to the large and complex international industrial corporations of today over a period of centuries. The social, political, and ideological life of these regions was gradually transformed to fit the needs of the developing industrial complex. Those areas of the world that are just now beginning the process of industrialization are naturally seeking to do so quickly. In Service's words, "They will begin with the latest and most advanced of the known technologies and attempt to create the complete industrial complex at once, skipping whole epochs of our development" (1971, pp. 44–45).

In the process of worldwide industrialization, Service expected that at least some of the developing nations would surpass the status of the United States and the Soviet Union as the world's dominant powers, both politically and economically. However, other factors besides a culture's ability to change readily must be considered in assessing trends in cultural development. Part of the adjustment of a culture to its specific environment is its relationship to other cultures with which it must interact. In the contemporary world, the global nature of economic forces and the political and economic influences of the world's dominant nations are major factors in how the rest of the world's cultures are changing. It is quite possible that these influences will inhibit the traditional leapfrogging pattern of cultural change.

Progress?

Does technological progress also produce progress in quality of life? The major changes that occur

---

Law of Local Discontinuity of Progress the idea that the successive stages of general evolutionary change are not likely to occur in the same locality in societies when technologies harness more energy are increases in population, the number of statuses and groups, and the specialization of roles. Inherent in these changes is an increased interdependence of everyone in society. Individuals have less autonomy and less ability to fulfill their own needs and must rely upon others to perform necessary tasks for which they themselves lack the skills. In general, family continues to play a role as an economic group in consumption, but tends to lose its role as a production and distribution group. The role of kinship as an economic and political force also declines. In the realm of ideology, more and more facets of life need to be understood in mechanistic rather than spiritual terms, for the role of religion declines as a culture becomes more generally evolved. All of these trends tend to make the lives of individuals less and less secure and stable, which has an important psychological impact on modal personality types.

Alienation. The major psychological effect of individuals' decreasing autonomy and control over their own lives is referred to as alienation. The concept of alienation is most strongly associated with Karl Marx (1961), who argued in 1844 that alienation develops when the work of individuals ceases to satisfy human needs directly and becomes instead merely a means of satisfying those needs indirectly. In the simplest societies, individual roles are highly generalized, and each individual possesses most of the skills necessary for survival. For instance, if a woman is hungry, she takes up a basket and a digging stick (often of her own making) and goes in search of food. This direct relationship between work and personal needs leads to a sense of fulfillment in work. As societies become more complex, however, persons work not to satisfy their immediate physical needs but merely to obtain some object such as money that can later be used to satisfy those needs. The labor is a step removed from the purpose for which it is ultimately performed. A telephone operator may spend the day pushing buttons in service of others, an activity that has no obvious connection with obtaining food or shelter or any other personal need. He or she may receive payment for this work only once a month and is not likely to feel the same personal satisfaction in that daily work as does the hunter in manufacturing the salmon spear or rabbit snare that will be used to obtain the day's meal. The effects of alienation are multiplied when individuals must work for others in order to survive. Under such conditions, even the direct products of a

worker's labor do not belong to him or her, and this lack of control reduces the sense of satisfaction for having created some useful or aesthetic object.

High specialization of labor also leads to competition among interdependent specialists. Each attempts to obtain the most possible from his or her goods or services at the expense of others. Such competition also increases the sense of alienation from society as a source of human security and meaningfulness.

The first anthropologist to emphasize the concept of alienation in the study of human cultures was Edward Sapir. He went so far as to suggest that cultures could be rated in terms of how "inherently harmonious, balanced, self-satisfactory" they are, a view that has received little attention from other anthropologists (1924, p. 410). Although he did not suggest that there is a direct relationship between the complexity of a society and the degree to which its culture is "a spiritual hybrid of contradictory patches, of water-tight compartments of consciousness that avoid participation in a harmonious synthesis," there is an obvious parallel between his views and Marx's concept of alienation (p. 410).

....

The Vanishing of Nonstate Societies

As the cultures of the world evolved, societies at each new general evolutionary level were technologically and socially more powerful than those of the preceding levels. Throughout the history of cultural evolution, societies with less dense populations have been displaced by those with technologies that have allowed their populations to grow increasingly powerful. Tribes have displaced bands, and chiefdoms have expanded at the expense of both band and tribal peoples. The process continues today as the state-level societies take control of territories that once belonged to nonstate peoples. As this happens, more and more of the nonstate societies of the world are becoming extinct.

▬

alienation dissociation of workers from ownership of things they produce, accompanied by feelings of powerlessness and boredom

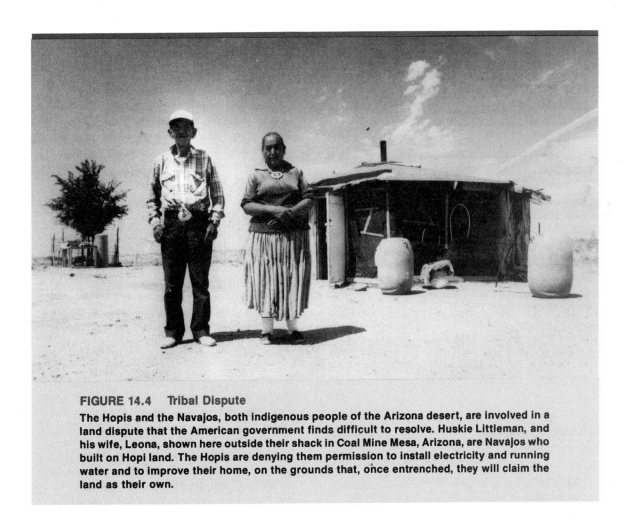

FIGURE 14.4 Tribal Dispute

The Hopis and the Navajos, both indigenous people of the Arizona desert, are involved in a land dispute that the American government finds difficult to resolve. Huskie Littleman, and his wife, Leona, shown here outside their shack in Coal Mine Mesa, Arizona, are Navajos who built on Hopi land. The Hopis are denying them permission to install electricity and running water and to improve their home, on the grounds that, once entrenched, they will claim the land as their own.

Indigenous Peoples

Today, relatively few bands, tribes, and chief-doms still exist, and the number is declining each year. The expansion of state societies into territories once occupied by nonstate societies has given rise to groups called **indigenous people,** who are the native people of an area now controlled by a state political system within which they have little or no influence. Today, about 200 million people, or 4 percent of the world's population, have this status. As we shall see, however, most indigenous people do not continue to live their ancestral way of life. Those who do are an even smaller minority.

According to Burger (1987, p. 11), indigenous peoples live on all five continents. They are found in about half of the 161 member states of the United Nations. In North America there are about 2.5 million Native Americans. There are between 25 and 30 million indigenous Indian people in Central and South America and about 60,000 Sami (formerly known as Lapps) in Scandinavia. Maoris make up about 240,000 of New Zealand's population. There are about 250,000 Aboriginal Australians. The re-maining 136 million indigenous peoples are found in Asia: about 6.5 million in the Philippines, 11 million in Burma, 500,000 in Thailand, 51 million in India, and 67 million in China.

Once, the ancestors of today's indigenous peo-ples occupied most of the world. Conquest and colonization changed that. Many have been dispos-essed of their traditional lands and have resettled.

---

indigenous people a group of people whose occupation of an area precedes the state political system that now controls that area, and who have little or no influence within that political system

Those whose lands were of little use to the national economies of the conquering states remain in their native territories, although even these people have typically been forced into restricted areas such as the Indian reservations of the United States. The territories of today's indigenous peoples, such as deserts, tundras, forests, mountains, and islands, can be termed **frontier areas**, lands that are unproductive for industrialized agriculture. But the insulation that frontier areas have provided in the past is weakening. Their natural resources are gradually attracting more and more outsiders, both individuals and corporations, which are seeking to exploit them for the benefit of the more urbanized economies of the states that claim sovereignty over them. In many places around the world, indigenous peoples are disappearing because of these outside influences.

frontier areas unproductive lands for industrialized agriculture opened to settlement by national governments that do not recognize the claims of the indigenous population

Western Shoshoni Land Rights in the United States

Denying indigenous peoples the right to control their own lives is not just a thing of the past. It continues to occur wherever indigenous peoples are found. The ongoing political contest between the Western Shoshoni of the North American Great Basin region and the American government is just one powerful example of how once sovereign societies lose their autonomy to powerful nations.

In 1863 the United States government signed the Treaty of Ruby Valley with the Western Shoshoni who occupied a 43,000 square-mile territory that included parts of southern California, the eastern half of Nevada, and parts of Idaho. This treaty was unusual in the history of relationships between the United States and American Indian societies because it ceded no land to the United States, which was still involved in a civil war and was concerned with ensuring the continued flow of gold from California. The Shoshoni did agree to end warfare against the United States and to allow the construction of roads, railways, and telegraph lines through mining settlements within their territory. Over the next 125 years, the United States govern-

ment obtained billions of dollars worth of resources from Western Shoshoni lands under this arrangement.

During the 1920s conflicts over land use increased between the Shoshoni and non-Indian settlers. In 1934 the United States government installed a tribal council form of government among the Shoshoni, a system that was fundamentally different from their traditional way of governing. In 1946 Congress created the Indian Claims Commission, which would be authorized to adjudicate Native American land claims against the United States. The legislation authorized lawyers who represented Indians in such cases to be paid 10 percent of any awards the commission made to Indians. In the same year, the Bureau of Indian Affairs persuaded one group of Shoshoni, the Temoak Bank, to file a claim for compensation for the loss of Shoshoni lands. The Temoak understood the purpose of this claim to be the recovery of their control over their traditional lands.

The law firm appointed by the Bureau of Indian Affairs to represent the Shoshoni was the same one that had drafted the legislation creating the claims commission. Other Western Shoshoni bands protested that their land had never been ceded to the United States, and that to accept compensation would amount to selling their lands. In 1951 the law firm petitioned the claims commission to recognize that its actions in behalf of the Temoak Shoshoni actually represented the interests of the entire Western Shoshoni people. A group of Temoak Shoshoni were selected by the law firm as the "exclusive representatives" of the Western Shoshoni. Those who disagreed with its plans were dismissed from the group. Despite objections by the majority of the Shoshoni involved, the petition was granted by the commission. The Temoak and other Shoshoni soon learned that the law firm was not attempting to secure a ruling that would recognize their ownership of their traditional land; instead it was seeking a monetary award.

In 1962, the Indian Claims Commission noted that it had been "unable to discover any formal extinguishment" of Western Shoshoni lands in Nevada. However, on February 11, 1966, the law firm that ostensibly represented the Shoshoni's interests *against* U.S encroachment on Shoshoni lands, *stipulated* that the Shoshoni had ceded 24 million acres of land to the United States (including 16 million acres that were occupied by no one but Shoshoni

Indians), and arbitrarily fixed the date of that stipulated loss as July 1, 1872, the middle day of the year, but otherwise a date of no known historical significance. The law firm requested that these lost lands be paid for and that land values in mid-1872 be used to compute the amount of the compensation. In 1972 the Indian Claims Commission concluded that the lands of the Western Shoshoni had been "taken" in the nineteenth century by "gradual encroachment of whites, settlers and others."

Since the Temoak were now convinced that their lawyers were serving the interests of the United States government, instead of Indian interests, the Temoak fired the law firm as their agents. However, the Bureau of Indian Affairs refused to recognize the right of the Temoak to do so and continued to renew the firm's contract "in the Indians' behalf." In effect, the lawyers were now being employed by the government to act as representatives of the Indians against their clients' own wishes and to pursue a course of argument favored by the government.

The Western Shoshoni hired their own lawyer and appealed the Commission's ruling in the U.S. Court of Claims. The Court refused to rule on the issue of who held title to the traditional Shoshoni lands, but awarded the Shoshoni $26,154,600 for the loss of 24 million acres, land that by 1979 values would have been worth more than $40 billion. The law firm that had been contracted by the Bureau of Indian Affairs was paid $2.5 million "for services rendered."

To pay the Shoshoni for the lands they had now lost, the U.S. Department of Interior transferred $26,145,189.89 (the amount of the award less $9,410.11 as an offset against goods it claimed the government had delivered to the Shoshoni in the 1870s) into a trust account held by the U.S. Treasury Department in behalf of the Shoshoni. Accumulating interest since 1979, this money now amounts to 70 million dollars. The Western Shoshoni have refused to accept receipt of this money since that date. Their purpose had never been to sell their territory, but to gain recognition of their ownership of it. As of November, 1992, the Western Shoshoni have unsuccessfully continued their efforts to reassert their sovereignty over their traditional lands.

(see reference map p. 84)

Extinction

Although there are still 20 million indigenous people in the world, many indigenous cultures have become extinct. There are three general ways in which indigenous cultures disappear: acculturation, ethnocide, and genocide.

Acculturation. When two previously distinct cultures come in contact, they both change. This process, called acculturation, was discussed in detail on p. 327. We should note here, however, that while acculturation generally causes both cultures to change, it can change a culture so much that it soon loses most of its own traditional characteristics and in effect, becomes extinct.

Ethnocide. Sometimes the destruction of a traditional way of life is carried out by deliberate, systematic policies of the dominant culture. Such a process is called **ethnocide**. The effect of ethnocide is that a group is denied the right to enjoy, develop, and disseminate its own traditional culture and language. Politically dominant societies may legally require that indigenous peoples send their children to schools that train them in the dominant culture and language. In some cases these are boarding schools, where the children must live for long periods of time, far from their own families. Often the use of their native language is not only discouraged but also forbidden and punished. Removed from the normal process of socialization in their own native culture, they return home ill-equipped to carry on their parents' way of life. Missionary efforts also have contributed to the destruction of indigenous ways of life by attacking traditional religious beliefs and working for the abolition of all forms of marriage other than monogamy (Ribiero, 1971; Walker, 1972).

Genocide. Related to ethnocide, the destruction of a culture, is the practice of **genocide**, the systematic destruction of a people. Many of the indigenous people of the world have been and are

---

acculturation the process in which one culture adapts to the influence of another culture by borrowing many of its traits

ethnocide the systematic destruction of a traditional way of life

genocide the systematic extermination of a people

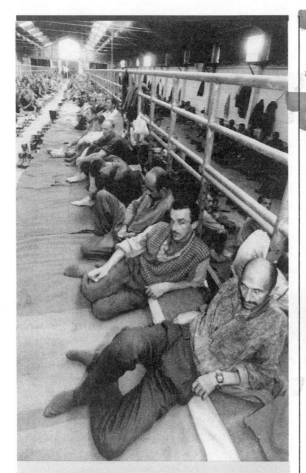

FIGURE 14.5   Genocide

The systematic destruction of a people has taken place around the world, most recently in Bosnia-Herzegovina. These Muslims and Croatians were being kept as prisoners of war by the Serbs in a detention camp in Manjaca, northwest of Sarajevo, in 1992 as the Serbs bombarded and destroyed the former capital of Yugoslavia.

being systematically exterminated. Military campaigns against native peoples have been only one way in which the extinction of whole societies has occurred. Biological warfare also has been used. In the earlier days of United States history, clothing and blankets infected with smallpox and other diseases were distributed to some Native Americans, ostensibly as gifts. Colonial people also had given gifts of poisoned foods to indigenous people and had sometimes hunted them for sport (Bonwick, 1870; Calder, 1874; Horwood, 1969). In the past decade in many parts of Latin America, Indians have been killed by settlers moving onto their traditional lands. This

private warfare is carried out with guns, bombs, dynamite, and even rapid-fire weapons from helicopters by private individuals, while national governments have turned a blind eye to the killing. In some cases, despite the presence of indigenous people, government agencies have declared traditional native lands to be "empty" and therefore legitimately available for settling by nonindigenous farmers, miners, and land speculators. For instance, in 1978, in the Department of Alta Verpaz, Guatemala, non-Indian landowners tried to evict Kekchi Indians from lands they had lived on for generations. When the Indians protested to the mayor in the nearby town of Panzos, 100 were killed and 300 wounded. Within four years the federal government had defined all Indians as "subversives," and a military campaign against them had begun. In 1982, government forces massacred 302 Chuj Indians in the village of Finca San Francisco in the Department of Huehuetenango. The only survivors were 20 men who were away from the village at the time. Over a six-month period, between 2,000 and 10,000 Indians were killed by government forces. As of 1992, over a million people have been displaced from their homelands by these conflicts, and about 200,000 have left the country to find refuge in other parts of Central America.

Thomas Gregor has reported the impact of the immigration of nonindigenous people into one Latin American country:

> In 1500 explorer Pedro Cabral landed on the coast of Brazil and claimed its lands and native peoples for the Portuguese empire. Since that time Brazilian Indians have been killed by European diseases and bounty hunters, forced off their land by squatters and speculators, and enslaved by ranchers and mine owners. Today the Indians, numbering less than one-tenth of the precontact population, inhabit the most remote regions of the country. (1983, p. 1)

The effects of such violence have penetrated even into indigenous groups that have had little direct contact with outsiders. Gregor has described the Mehinaku, a single village tribe that lives in a vast protected reservation in the Mato Grosso of Brazil. Despite their official protection and relative isolation, contact with Brazilians has been sufficient to undermine the security of their lives. Gregor quotes one Mehinaku villager: "Last night my dream was very bad. I dreamed of a white man" (p. 1). According to the Mehinaku, such dreams portend illness. The symbolism is apt since, in the words of Gregor,

FIGURE 14.6   Global Forum

Representatives of the Chilean Mapuche-Pehuenche Indians arrive at the '92 Global Forum in Rio de Janeiro to attend a forum of the Indio '92 Conference. Indigenous people around the world met to discuss living conditions in their respective countries and to formulate policies that will help them maintain their autonomous cultures in a rapidly homogenizing world.

"In the early 1960s, almost 20 percent of the tribe died in a measles epidemic, and the villagers continue to suffer from imported diseases for which they have neither natural nor acquired immunity" (p. 2).

The Effects of Industrialization

One fundamental factor sealing the doom of many nonstate societies and altering the nature of all the world's cultures has been **industrialization**. Beginning with the Industrial Revolution in Great Britain in the latter half of the eighteenth century, many cultures have joined the movement away from home production of goods to large-scale, mechanized fac-

tory production requiring great inputs of capital. This shift has brought profound alterations in all aspects of life, including changes in economic systems, growth of populations, and concentration of people around cities. Even those societies that have not industrialized are now defined and affected by their lack of industry.

Indigenous Peoples Today

In response to the influx of outside forces such as the logging and mining industries, indigenous peoples throughout the world are forming organiza-

---

industrialization   the process of change from an economy based on home production of goods to one based on large-scale, mechanized factory production

338

tions to influence both national and international policies that affect their autonomy. According to Julian Burger, one of the major causes of this coalescence of indigenous organizations has been the "massive explosion of demand for natural resources on the world market . . . [that] has stimulated vigorous exploration and exploitation" of the territories of indigenous peoples (1987, p. 44). For instance, in 1974 the International Indian Treaty Council was formed in the United States to bring Native American concerns before international bodies such as the United Nations. It obtained status as a nongovernmental consultative organization at the UN in 1977. In 1978 Native Americans also formed the Indian Law Resource Center to support Indian legal rights in the U.S. court system and through international groups such as the United Nations Commission on Human Rights. Many such organizations now exist throughout most of the world. A similar international organization, the World Council of Indigenous Peoples, was organized in 1975. Its members are made up of delegates who now represent over 35 million of the world's indigenous peoples. In 1982 in response to the demands of indigenous peoples' organizations, the United Nations Commission on Human Rights "established an annual Working Group on Indigenous Populations to gather information about the situation of indigenous peoples world-wide and make recommendations about future international laws to protect their rights" (Burger, 1987, p. 61).

The Yąnomamö Today

Frontier lands occupied by indigenous people often attract citizens of the larger nation states, who then claim sovereignty over them. The Yąnomamö of Brazil and Venezuela have experienced a large influx of Venezuelan and Brazilian farmers, loggers, and miners who are radically changing their ancestral environments in the hopes of quick profits. Like other indigenous peoples who are not well represented in the governments that control them, the Yąnomamö and their traditional way of life have received little protection from either the Venezuelan or Brazilian governments. For instance, in 1975, about 4,500 of Brazil's 10,000 Yąnomamö Indians lived in an area of northern Amazonia that the government had ostensibly set aside as a reserve to protect them from outside incursion. But this land, now

called the Yąnomamï Park, has continued to attract mining companies and illegal settlers. By June of 1991, some 45,000 gold and tin miners had entered Yąnomamö lands, and opposition to the establishment of a Yąnomamö reserve was strong. For instance, in response to protests about the incursion of others into the Yąnomamï Park, the Governor of Roraima, Brazil, said "An area as rich as this, with gold, diamonds and uranium, cannot afford the luxury of preserving half a dozen Indian tribes which are holding up development" (Wright, 1982, p. 29).

The cavalier attitude of government leaders to the plight of the Yąnomamö is particularly interesting when actual government practice is contrasted with what one might expect if the legal rights of the Yąnomamö were actually enforced. For instance, Brazilian law guarantees the rights of Indian peoples to their land. The Indian Statute of 19 December 1973 gives "the Indians and native communities in the terms of the constitution, permanent possession of the land they inhabit, recognizing their right to exclusive usufruct of the natural wealth and all the utilities existing on that land" (Act No. 6001, Art 2, Par IX). The act also required the government to formally define the exact boundaries of the lands of each Indian group within five years. Nevertheless, by 1978, only a third of the native Indian territories had been formally defined, and the National Indian Foundation (FUNAI), the government agency charged with the protection of Indian rights, had been taking no action against the non-Indian colonizers who had entered these areas.

In addition to losing their lands to the more powerful immigrants who have laid claim to the resources they contain, the Yąnomamö have suffered tremendously from the diseases that have come with the immigrants. The Venezuelan Yąnomamö have experienced epidemics of measles and whooping cough that have killed as many as 30 percent of some communities, and they are currently threatened with extinction by diseases such as tuberculosis and malaria. In their isolated, frontier setting, the Yąnomamö lack the immunity and the medical facilities to protect them from these diseases.

Efforts to acculturate the Yąnomamö have included the use of enforced recruitment of Yąnomamö children into a boarding school far from their homes. Jacques Lizot has described how Yąnomamö children were enticed away from their homes with candy, soft drinks, or invitations to ride on motor boats, and then taken to the boarding school with no explanation to their parents. There, every effort was made to eliminate all vestiges of their Yąnomamö identities: their hair was cut, their names were changed, and they were required to survive on foods to which they were unaccustomed, while the adults proceeded to "educate" them about their own inferiority and the necessity of learning a new language and new customs.

The Yąnomamö, like other indigenous peoples, have escalated their efforts to control their own destinies. One Yąnomamö leader, Davi Kopenawa Yanomami, has described the current plight of his people:

My Yanomami people know, they see what is happening to our community, and they see what is happening to our relatives in other communities. They are terrified of the miners, of the [polluted] rivers.

The miners invaded our reserve and came to our communities feigning friendship; they lied to us, they tricked us Indians, and we were taken in. Then their numbers grew; many more arrived, and they began bringing in machinery that polluted the river. The pollution killed the fish and the shrimp, everything that lived in our rivers. (Albert, 1991, p. 52)

The outcome of the Yąnomamö efforts to obtain self-determination within a protected reserve is still in question, and their efforts to affect public opinion and national policy continue. However, they recently experienced one important breakthrough in their efforts toward their cultural survival. On November 15, 1992, the then-Brazilian president Fernando Collor de Mello established the long-promised reserve for the Yąnomamö Indians. The Brazilian reserve is situated next to a similar Venezuelan Yąnomamö reserve, and the two reserves contain 68,331 square miles of land.

(see reference map p. 36)

Developed and Underdeveloped Societies

Societies may be categorized in a number of ways. One simple distinction commonly is made on the basis of industrialization. **Developed countries** are the industrialized nations of the world: the countries of North America, Europe, Japan, Taiwan, and Russia. **Underdeveloped countries** are the remaining, largely nonindustrialized world societies, including all of Africa, Asia (excluding Japan, Taiwan, and Russia), and Latin America. The distinction between developed and underdeveloped countries is widely used, but the dichotomy is simpler than the reality it represents. The world's underdeveloped countries vary from extremely poverty-stricken societies in which hunger and starvation are daily problems to others that have incorporated a great deal of industrialized technology into their economy and will soon be viewed as having become developed countries. Those underdeveloped countries that are making major gains in industrialization are sometimes referred to as **developing countries** in recognition of the changes they are undergoing.

As of mid-1985, three-fourths of the human population lived in underdeveloped nations (Kent & Haub, 1985). Living standards are very low in these areas, and their current economies often will not support industrial development. Most underdeveloped countries suffer from severe shortages of land, capital, or labor. Land is often largely owned by a small, elite minority, with the remainder severely fragmented into plots too small to do more than meet the minimal needs of the families who farm them. The results of the absence of capital include roads that are impassable when it rains, schools that lack enough books, and per capita incomes that are extremely low. The average per capita gross national product of the underdeveloped nations is 640 U.S. dollars, compared with 10,700 U.S. dollars for the developed world (Haub & Kent, 1988). The population of the underdeveloped world is a more rural one than that of developed countries: While 73 percent of the people in developed societies live in urban areas, only 37 percent of the people in underdeveloped countries do so. As developing countries are drawn into the world-

---

developed country   a nation in which industrialization has become the primary basis of the economy
underdeveloped country   nation with a largely nonindustrialized economy
developing country   underdeveloped nation undergoing industrialization

wide network of industrialized economies, they change in a variety of ways that are discussed in the following sections of this chapter.

Economic Change

Industrialization has greatly influenced the economic and social life of societies in which it has occurred. Preindustrial economies are fundamentally systems of family-based production, with the food and other goods produced used primarily by the families themselves. Farming peoples who produce for their own consumption are more likely to diversify into as many as 20 to 30 different kinds of crops and animals. This diversity minimizes their risks and maximizes their autonomy. Trade exists mostly to distribute the surpluses from the family and community stock rather than to specialize in the production of food or other goods for the purpose of trade. Market-oriented farmers tend to invest in a smaller number of more specialized crops.

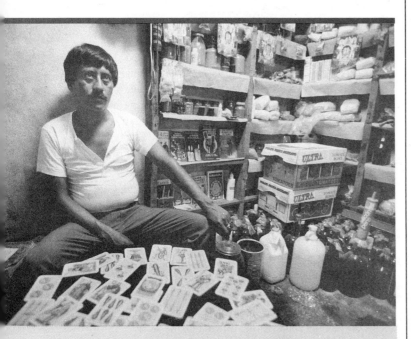

FIGURE 14.7   Catemaco Shaman

In Catemaco, a Mexican town with a tradition of witchcraft, Jorge Jáuregui, otherwise known as the Infernal Goat, worries that the North American Free Trade Agreement of 1992 will adversely affect his ability to cure people in the traditional way with dried tree bark, dead snakes, and magic potions.

With industrialization comes a major increase in the number of specialized occupations. It has created a great demand for wage laborers at centralized locations who do not produce their own food, thus creating a situation where the economy is no longer a family-oriented subsistence activity but a market-oriented enterprise.

Industry also fosters the production of nonessential food crops, such as cocoa and coffee, and nonfood products, such as wool for textiles or sisal for twine and cordage manufacture. So industrialization fosters a move of a large percentage of farmers away from staple food production. In an industrialized economy, the food-producing sector of farming becomes increasingly competitive, mechanized, expensive, and competitive, so that small-scale farms become less and less viable.

Urbanization

Agriculture created towns and cities long before industrialization began, but industrialization greatly fostered the growth of cities. Since the large-scale manufacture of marketable goods and trade go hand in hand as industrialization proceeds, industrialized centers of manufacture tend to be located in urban centers along the routes of trade. As industry produces a growing demand for labor, workers are drawn out of rural areas into the cities to find employment, and urban areas grow in population.

In 1900 only 13.6 percent of the world's population lived in cities. By 1988 the portion of the world's population living in urban areas had risen to 45 percent (Haub & Kent, 1988), and it is expected to climb to 60 percent by the year 2020 (Murphy, 1985). Part of the process of urbanization has been an increase in the size of cities. In 1950 there were only 2 cities with more than 10 million inhabitants: the New York/New Jersey urban complex and London. In 1990 there were more than 10 such cities, the largest of which was Tokyo/Yokohama with 27 million people (see Table 14.1).

World Population Growth

In addition to becoming more concentrated in cities, the world's population has grown in general as industrialization has increased our life expectancy, through factors described in the next section, "Indus-

TABLE 14.1   World's Ten Largest Cities

1950	Population (in millions)	1990	Population (in millions)	2000 (proj.)	Population (in millions)
1. New York-N.E. New Jersey	12.3	1. Tokyo-Yokohama	27.0	1. Mexico City	27.0
2. London	10.4	2. Mexico City	20.2	2. Tokyo-Yokohama	27.0
3. Rhine-Ruhr	6.9	3. São Paulo	18.1	3. São Paulo	25.4
4. Tokyo-Yokohama	6.7	4. Seoul	16.3	4. Seoul	22.0
5. Shanghai, Mainland	5.8	5. New York-N.E. New Jersey	14.6	5. Bombay	15.4
6. Paris	5.5	6. Osaka-Kobe-Kyoto	13.8	6. New York-N.E. New Jersey	14.6
7. Buenos Aires	5.3	7. Bombay	11.8	7. Osaka-Kobe-Kyoto	14.3
8. Chicago-N.W. Indiana	4.9	8. Calcutta	11.7	8. Teheran	14.3
9. Moscow	4.8	9. Buenos Aires	11.5	9. Rio de Janeiro	14.2
10. Calcutta	4.6	10. Rio de Janeiro	11.4	10. Calcutta	14.1

Sources: 1950 information from United Nations, Department of International Economic and Social Affairs, 1985. 1990 and 2000 information from the 1992 *Information Please Almanac*, 1991. New York: Houghton Mifflin, pp. 134–135.

trialization and the Quality of Life." The history of human population can be described as a long period of slow growth followed by a relatively recent explosion that reached its fastest rate of expansion in 1965, when world population was increasing at about 2 percent per year. The period of slow growth ended with the development of agriculture about 10,000 years ago; the continuing rapid explosion started with the Industrial Revolution.

A third of a million years ago, in the time of *Homo erectus*, the human population of the entire world was less than 1 million people. When food domestication began, about 10,000 years ago, there were still fewer than 10 million people in the world. By A.D. 1 the figure was about 300 million. It reached half a billion in A.D. 1650, and the first billion was achieved about A.D. 1800. By July of 1986 the figure had reached 5 billion. Using the same beginning

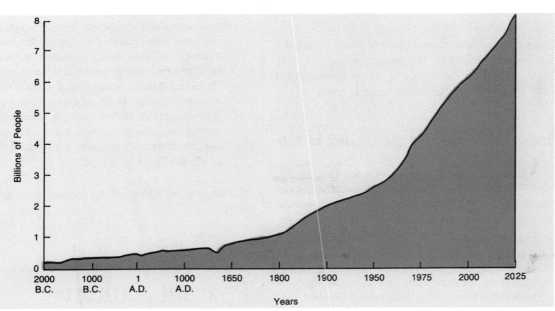

FIGURE 14.8   World Population Growth Through History

The growth of the population of the world has historically been a long, slow process until the Industrial Revolution, which initiated a rapid growth period.

FIGURE 14.9   Hand Looms Fall Silent
Mohandas K. Gandhi early in this century preached the simple virtue of wearing khadi, an unrefined cotton cloth hand-woven on India's looms. It became a symbol of self-reliance and loyalty to the state of India. With the introduction of industrialization, the end of government subsidies for the hand looms, and changing attitudes, more than 5,000 looms in Delhi itself are idle.

point, a population of one billion required a third of a million years to reach. The second billion took only about 130 years, the third just 30 years, the fourth only 15 years, and the fifth a mere 11 years!

Industrialization and the Quality of Life

Industrialization does provide benefits. Its productivity is much greater than that of hand labor, which frees many members of society to pursue the specialized occupations that do not exist in preindustrial societies. Thus, industrialization brings to society new goods and new services, raising the standard of living and extending life expectancy, which are the result of many factors: better nutrition and security from famine; improved housing and sanitation; decline in the rate of disease and lower mortality rates in all age categories because of medical specialists and other health care providers.

But industrialization also has its costs. Growth in industry is paralleled by growth in air and water pollution. As population grows, increased demand for goods can lead to the depletion of nonrenewable resources such as minerals and fossil fuels and to the overuse of potentially renewable ones. The urban growth that an expanding population fosters brings crowding and its attendant problems of unemployment, poverty, poor health and nutrition, and crime. It is ironic that industrialization can create both many new jobs and high unemployment, wealth and poverty, abundant foods and poor nutrition. Many of these problems grow out of the fact that although industrialization creates wealth, that wealth is not necessarily equitably distributed. Without exception, the process of industrialization has been accompanied by increasing disparities in the wealth, power, and honor of the social classes that are part of all state-level societies. At times, these inequities can be the source of major social problems.

Another effect of the spread of industrialization is the increasing economic interdependence of the entire world. Over a decade ago, Eric Wolf wrote:

> On one level it has become a commonplace to say that we all inhabit 'one world.' There are ecological connections: New York suffers from the Hong Kong flu; the grapevines of Europe are destroyed by American plant lice. There are demographic connections: Jamaicans migrate to London; Chinese migrate to Singapore. There are economic connections: a shutdown of oil wells on the Persian Gulf halts generating plants in Ohio; a balance of payments unfavorable to the United States drains American dollars into bank accounts in Frankfurt or Yokohama; Italians produce Fiat automobiles in the Soviet Union; Japanese build a hydro-electric system in Ceylon. There are political connections: wars begun in Europe unleash reverberations around the globe; American troops intervene on the rim of Asia; Finns guard the border between Israel and Egypt. (1982, p. 3)

The interconnectedness of the world is even greater today.

Peasant Cultures

Since the beginning of urbanization, the contrast between urban centers of power and wealth and less influential rural food-producing areas has been a fact of human life. As societies have grown in social complexity, the discrepancy between the political power and prestige of the urban elite and other members of society changed from a strictly urban-rural distinction to one of social elites versus peasants. **Peasants** are food producers whose economic life centers on using family-based labor, and who consume most of what they grow. Since peasants must produce their own food, they do not specialize in cash crops. They may produce some crops for sale, or hire out their own labor to supplement their incomes, but their cash incomes are too low to change their material condition and, consequently, their socially subordinate status. Typically, peasants use nonindustrialized, hand-labor techniques that yield only a minimal subsistence for their own families, yet in a seeming contradiction, need large families to ensure that they have enough labor to produce the food they need. They are largely rural peoples, but some peasants live in urban areas where they can supplement their incomes from small-scale gardening with income from paid labor. Peasants are economically and politically dominated by a governing class of which they are not a part. They rarely control their own political destinies. Their food production is generally part of the larger society's economy, but they have little influence on its operation. In most societies, peasants do not own the land that they work.

Feudal Peasantries

In preindustrial times, peasants were part of political systems in which local aristocratic leaders, who claimed ownership of the land, granted the **feudal peasants** the privilege to use the land to grow their own food in return for rent or service. According to G. Dalton (1969), the relationship between peasant and lord in feudal times involved responsibilities and obligations on the part of the land owner as well as the peasant. For instance, the feudal lord provided military and police protection for the peasants, settled disputes, and fed them in times of hardship. Peasants' lack of land ownership probably always has been a source of dissatisfaction in most feudal societies (Wolf, 1969), but the conditions of peasant life probably worsened following industrialization, when contracted wage labor replaced the earlier paternalistic feudal system, and the peasant was forced to provide for all his own needs. In the industrialized economic system, the obligations of the propertied classes ended with the payment of the wage.

Colonial Peasantries

Following the development of industrialized food production and transportation technologies, the subordination of peasantries intensified. Industrialization opened the door for colonial empires to spread into distant parts of the world, where inexpensive peasant labor made possible the cheap extraction of natural resources for the benefit of the colonial administrations and their homelands. **Colonial peasants** were encouraged, sometimes economically and sometimes by the pressure of military might, to move from the production of food to the production of nonfood export crops and to engage in labor for pay. As Frances Lappé and Joseph Collins have said:

> Colonialism destroyed the cultural patterns of production and exchange by which traditional societies in "underdeveloped" countries previously had met the needs of the people. Many precolonial social structures, while dominated by exploitative elites, had evolved a system of mutual obligations among the classes that helped to ensure at least a minimal diet for all. A friend of mine once said: "Precolonial village existence in subsistence agriculture was a limited life indeed, but it's certainly not Calcutta." The misery of starvation in the streets of Calcutta can only be understood as the end-point of a long historical process—one that has destroyed a traditional social system. (1977, p. 76)

The colonial subordination of peasantries can be seen as a process in which some societies have been underdeveloped to the benefit of others (Rodney, 1972). Colonial administrations encouraged the production of cash crops such as cotton, cocoa, coffee, sugar, and tobacco for export at the expense of the staple foods that had been produced previously.

---

peasants people who use nonindustrialized, labor-intensive techniques for producing food and who are politically and economically subordinate to a governing class of which they are not a part and with whom they have little influence

feudal peasants food producers in preindustrialized societies who pay rent or perform service for the privilege of farming lands owned by local aristocratic officials, who have obligations to provide police and military protection, judicial services, and care for the peasants in times of hardship

colonial peasants members of peasant societies that were politically and economically dependent on a foreign state that perpetuated its economic exploitation of the peasant area by military domination

FIGURE 14.10   Somali Peasant

Warring factions in Somalia have prevented many crops from being harvested in the mid-1990s. With the fall of the dictator Mohammed Siad Barre, farmers have been assisted in planting crops again in some areas. Sharif Abdul Nur plants sorghum seeds in the town of Habarre, north of Baidoa, and hopes to purchase a herd of camels, the mainstay of Somali economy. In fleeing the war, Sharif's 33 camels were stolen by the guerrillas.

These export crops were selected for their high-priced value in the home market relative to their shipping costs and not for their value as foods. The methods used to bring about this shift to cash crop production included physical force and taxation. In some cases, foreign governments or private individuals claimed ownership of native lands and forced the native people to work the fields as slaves, wage laborers, or dispossessed tenant farmers. The profits remained in the hands of the foreign interests. Thus, through various means, previously self-sufficient farmers could no longer grow enough food to meet their own needs. Ironically, even though peasant peoples throughout the world are basically farmers, the peasant societies have had to become major food importers to feed themselves. This has locked them firmly into the world economy which today is dominated by the industrialized nations.

Contemporary Peasantries

Today, most of the people in the world can be classified as peasants, members of a social class of traditional, family-based food producers who are subordinate to an urban-based administrative class in each of their societies. The economies of these societies are, themselves, highly influenced by worldwide economic forces that are beyond their control. Because of the small volume of their specialized cash crops, the peasants lack the cash flow to pay for the equipment and services that would be necessary to industrialize their farming techniques. Neither is their economic base sufficient for state taxation to sustain the bureaucratic social benefits available in urban centers. Traditional credit and rental arrangements in peasant communities often are based on commodities rather than money, and exchange is centered on small marketplaces in which individual peasants act as "penny capitalists," selling their few surplus products or selling their labor on a piecemeal basis. Since in many peasant societies much of the most productive land is owned by a wealthy elite—who long ago converted it to the production of cash crops—peasants find it difficult to produce sufficient foods on their "postage stamp" farms to meet their own nutritional needs. Much of their cash income is devoted to the purchase of food, and typically the cash incomes that they obtain prove insufficient to meet the expenses of life in an industrializing society.

Peasant societies are not all identical. They are found in various environments and use many different types of subsistence technologies. Jon Moris (1981) has outlined nine basic subsistence styles of most of today's peasants:

1. Pastoralists and ranchers with low-density populations that are spread over large territories.

2. Tenant farmers who grow one or two market crops such as coffee or hemp on irrigated farmland.

3. Laborers who live and work on foreign-owned large farms or estates and who grow export crops such as rubber or tea.

4. Farmers who rely on natural rainfall in isolated pockets of semiarid lands and hilly areas with steep slopes that are suited only for hand-growing techniques and who market only what they don't need.

5. Peasants who live by labor-intensive farming in impoverished conditions in crowded smallholdings.

6. Landless peasant workers or dispossessed tenant farmers in government-organized settlements and frontier areas.

7. Aged, sick, and uneducated peasants in impoverished rural communities, who depend on remittance income from younger members of the community who work in other areas.

8. Refugees and former tenant farmers who have become landless and dispossessed.

9. Peri-urban squatters who live in densely settled, often illegal, communities near urban areas and support their families by gardening "postage stamp" farms and working in the neighboring cities.

Migrant Labor and Women's Status in Lesotho

The case of Lesotho is a particularly interesting example of the domination of peasant economic and social life by forces that lie beyond the control of the people involved. Lesotho is a small, mountainous kingdom that is entirely surrounded by the Republic of South Africa. Its major internal subsistence resources are agriculture and cattle herding, but most of its best agricultural lands were lost to South Africa in a series of wars that ended in 1868. So Lesotho has become a labor-reserve area for South Africa and relies heavily on the remittances from migrant workers there.

Since the loss of Lesotho's best agricultural lands, tremendous population growth forced the expansion of cultivation into many areas that had previously been used for cattle grazing. As formerly seasonal pasturage in the highlands came to be used throughout the year, their productivity was undermined by overgrazing and erosion. Lesotho agriculturalists in this century found it became unprofitable to export grain because of import tariffs imposed by neighboring governments; grain must now be imported from South Africa to feed Lesotho's growing population. Indeed, about 40 percent of food consumed in Lesotho is imported. Cash income is also important to Lesotho men, because the traditional bride price required for marriage is now usually made in cash payments. Today, the majority of cash income for the people of Lesotho comes from wages earned by migrant laborers who work primarily in the mines of the Republic of South Africa.

According to Safilios-Rothschild (1985), nearly half (47.7 percent) of Lesotho men are absent from home, working as migrant laborers starting at about the age of 20 years. Males who take employment in South Africa may stay away for 1 to 2 years at a time, after which South African law requires that they return home for several months before resuming work. Typically, migrants are away from home for a total of 15 to 20 years, between the ages of about 20 and 50 years.

Lesotho women have been forbidden since 1963 by South African law to enter South Africa as migrant laborers, and women are not permitted to reside with their husbands at the mines. Thus, between 40 and 60 percent of Lesotho's married women are left behind to

Lesotho

The women of Lesotho in South Africa have very little status even with the introduction of cooperative agricultural associations and industrialized tools and techniques. Women do not have the training to join the associations and often have to hire men to irrigate the crops, thus increasing their expenses.

manage on their own (Gordon, 1981, p. 59; Palmer, 1985, p. 18), and between 60 and 70 percent of rural households are headed by women. They can rely on little male help, even from their own kin, in their agricultural work, since the half of the male population who are engaged as migrant laborers are those in their most productive working years. Working husbands may have a portion of their wages remitted to their families in Lesotho, although Mueller (1977) indicates that most migrants prefer to send only small amounts and bring most of their savings home when they return during their leaves. Safilios-Rochschild indicates that 90 percent of migrant miners do not send regular remittances, and only 30 to 35 percent of rural female-headed households receive any at all (1985, p. 304).

The absence of migrant husbands takes a high toll in the lives of Lesotho women. Gordon (1981) found that the longer migrant husbands had been absent from home, the greater were the levels of stress reported by their wives. This was partly because husbands' commitment to their wives declined the longer they were away from home, resulting in decreases in remittances and increases in di-

vorces or separations. Widowhood is also common among wives of migrant laborers, due in part to the much greater age of husbands in Lesotho marriages and in part to the high death rate in mining.

The economic consequences of separation and divorce are not limited to the loss of a woman's remittance income. Since land is owned only by men, legal divorce results in the loss of access to the former husband's lands. Furthermore, a divorced woman is not viewed as an acceptable spouse by other men if her ex-husband had not paid a full bride price before the divorce.

Widowhood also brings economic hardships. Traditionally, a third of a widow's lands were repossessed by her husband's family, and although this custom is no longer legal, it is often still followed in the more rural areas. Widows also face the prospect of lifelong responsibility for agricultural work that would otherwise be taken over by their husbands at the end of their work in the mines. Nevertheless, few widows remarry, because doing so would require them to give up all rights to their deceased husbands' fields, house, property, and children—all of which would revert to his relatives (Bardill & Cobbe, 1985).

One response to the poverty related to traditional hand-labor-based agricultural production has been the formation of cooperative agricultural associations in which members can pool their resources for their mutual benefit. The government has encouraged such efforts by offering agricultural credit to cooperatives that become legally registered.

Ironically, the poorer, female-headed households in rural areas have difficulty meeting the requirements for registration, since they must have formal training in managerial, cooperative, bookkeeping, and marketing skills. Such training is offered by the government in town centers rather than in rural areas, where the poorest households are found. Thus, less-needy households in and near the towns are closer to the training centers than are rural households in general. Female heads of households in the rural areas also find it more difficult to arrange to do their agricultural work and tend their children while attending such training than do male heads of households. These barriers to women's ability to obtain agricultural assistance are difficult to challenge, since there is a widespread assumption that female-headed households have access to migrant husbands' remittances and are, therefore, less in need of financial assistance than are male-headed households.

A second important response to the economic difficulties of life in Lesotho has been the government's attempt to increase agricultural production through the introduction of industrialized tools and techniques. According to Riley (1989), these efforts have focused on making loans available to farmers for the purchase of irrigation equipment, such as pumps, pipe, and sprinklers, and cultivation equipment such as rototillers, push cultivators, and—in very few cases—tractors. This has increased productivity, but it has also increased labor and expenses among women heads of household. For instance, irrigation has increased the necessity of weeding and transplanting and harvesting, all of which are traditionally women's work in Lesotho.

Irrigating, on the other hand, is viewed in Lesotho as men's work, so women heads of household are faced with the additional expense of hiring men to do such work as moving irrigation pipe and sprinklers.

Thus, along with the increased productivity that industrialized technology is bringing to Lesotho has come a dramatic increase in costs to women. They continue to be responsible for almost all domestic tasks and have larger expenses, more agricultural work, and devote more time to money-producing activities than before development projects started. In spite of these changes, few agriculturists have achieved self-sufficiency in food production, so foreign employment continues to keep a majority of men away from home and unable to break the cycle of increasing work for women as agricultural development proceeds.

Change in peasant societies. The economic limitations of peasant life are not easily overcome. Robert Chambers has stressed the fact that rural poverty often goes unnoticed or misunderstood by outsiders (1983). Most peasants live in conditions that are geographically or socially too far removed from the lives of urban elite policy-makers for governments to understand their real needs. Thus, government efforts to improve the conditions of peasant life are often based on faulty assessments of what needs to be done. They too often fail to appreciate the necessity of incorporating peasants' own insights about their needs into the policy and process of development.

Some observers also feel that a major obstacle to change lies in the peasants' own attitudes. According to Foster (1967), life in peasant societies often leads to a rather fatalistic, dreary outlook in which the drudgery of life is not believed to bring much reward, since the achievement of one person can only be accomplished at the expense of another. Foster has called this outlook the **image of limited good**. Because of this view of life, peasants are commonly jealous of success, and peasant life contains many social pressures not to excel over one's peers. Lewis (1966) saw this life-style as fostering attitudes that cause peasants and other poverty-stricken people to think only of today, to spend and consume what they have right now since saving for tomorrow seems futile. Lewis called this approach to life the **culture of poverty**.

Although this outlook certainly is not the underlying cause of the impoverished conditions of peasants in most parts of the world, it can make it difficult for peasants to take part effectively in opportunities for social change.

Wolf (1966) believes there are more substantial reasons why change is difficult in peasant circumstances. Peasants are slow to join forces to overcome exploitation, because they are individually bound into vertical political ties or "patron-client" relationships with more wealthy and powerful individuals on whose aid they depend in times of need. To work with other peasants for the common good is to sever these personally advantageous ties, so peasant communities are caught in a cycle of competition among individuals and factions.

Scott (1976) points out that the status quo does provide the peasant with a buffer from adversity. Peasant community expectations have a leveling ef-

image of limited good a fatalistic outlook common in situations of peasant poverty, in which the drudgery of life is not believed to bring much reward, since the achievement of one person can only be accomplished at the expense of another

culture of poverty an approach to life often found in situations of poverty in which actions are directed only to satisfying the needs of the present, by spending and consuming all income, because saving for the future seems futile

FIGURE 14.11   Canadian Indian Rights
Ovide Mercredi, a woodlands Cree, is chief of the Assembly of First Nations, representing 633 Indian communities. His goal is to incorporate Indian rights into Canada's evolving constitution, thus giving indigenous people the right to self-government with political powers equal to that of the federal or provincial governments. A lawyer, who takes as his role model the Rev. Dr. Martin Luther King, Jr., Mercredi here meets with a member of the audience after speaking to a youth conference in Ottawa.

fect that limits the poverty into which any one member of the society can sink. The maintenance of "commons"—lands available to all, for instance as pasturage—is an example of the buffers against adversity that are built into the peasant community. Commercialization, according to Scott, is actually a threat to peasant security, since it undermines the mechanisms that provide that security in impoverished circumstances.

Nelson and Water (1984) argue that prices in peasant markets are quite unstable and seasonally variable, since peasants market only the surplus that their families do not need for food. They tend to rely on relatives for credit and assistance, and lack sufficient cash incomes to support markets that sell factory-produced goods. Nelson and Water believe this situation is self-perpetuating, because reliance on family for labor and economic support leads to large family size, and increased population growth leads to reduced savings and investment. This, in turn, neces-

sitates greater reliance on family labor and traditional means of production.

Although there are many features of life in peasant societies that make change difficult, it would be a mistake to assume that change is impossible. Peasants have been ready to revolt against the system that maintains their landlessness and poverty when opportunities for successful uprisings have presented themselves. Many social scientists believe that peaceful improvement of peasant conditions is also possible. Popkin (1979) portrays the peasant life-style as a rational response to the tight constraints that limit their production and to the high degree of risk they face in making a living. He contends that when markets and opportunities exist, peasants respond by increasing output.

Applied Anthropology and Cultural Change

As anthropologists have studied the problems of nonindustrial populations, many have felt a growing obligation to apply their insights to achieve constructive change in areas such as overcoming the cycle of poverty in peasant societies. Because of these concerns, the subfield of anthropology called **applied anthropology** was created. It uses anthropological knowledge to improve social policy decisions aimed at resolving social problems. Applied anthropologists working in developing countries have pointed out that their problems are not merely technological in nature. Technological change is intimately connected to the social and ideological aspects of a culture, and can sometimes create unforeseen problems. Yet the social and ideological aspects of development often have been overlooked by the governmental administrators and technicians who have been given responsibility for improving conditions among peasant populations.

Fisher (1972) describes a number of reasons why government-sponsored development projects often fail. The list demonstrates that project failures are more typically social and ideological than technological in nature.

applied anthropology   the attempt to use anthropological skills and insights to aid in the process of cultural development in nonindustrialized parts of the world or to aid in private and public policy making

1. Projects intended to improve the lot of the peasant poor often are designed by persons who are unfamiliar with life in the peasant community, and these projects are imposed from the outside.

2. The governments involved sometimes fail to commit resources that are necessary for the projects to succeed.

3. Goals and resource allocations may be revised in the middle of a project without regard to the effects on work in the community setting.

4. Often, the resources may be spread too thinly to be effective in any one area.

5. Erroneous assumptions are commonly made about the effectiveness or capabilities of the institutions involved in the project, or the human element in the real work of project implementation may not be fully taken into account.

6. The various governmental ministries involved in the work may not coordinate their efforts.

7. Finally, demand for the new product created by the peasants is often insufficient for the work to become self-sustaining, and the yield or output projections may be inconsistent with the level of management available.

. . . .

The Future of the Peasant World

In spite of the difficulties in planned cultural change, the life of peasant villagers, who make up the majority of the world's inhabitants, is changing due primarily to the green revolution and new techniques for contraception.

The Green Revolution

The spread of scientific farming techniques is the result of what has been called the **green revolution**, the use of modern plant breeding to produce hybrid crop varieties that are much more productive than many traditional crops. The production of high-yield, fertilizer-intensive, fast-maturing crops is spreading quickly into the world's villages, along with year-round irrigation and multiple cropping. The green revolution has been particularly successful in improving the income base of peasant farmers in parts of Asia and India. Hayami and Kikuchi (1981) report that by the early 1980s the introduction of irrigation systems, modern varieties of increased-yield food plants, and fertilizer technology had begun to counteract the previous inability of peasants to produce enough food to meet the demands created by population growth. In the view of Hayami and Kikuchi, the critical problem in peasant village development is achieving peasant labor productivity sufficient to counteract the strong population pressure on limited land resources. The green revolution has been one important factor in solving this problem. The successes have been great enough that a number of underdeveloped countries are becoming increasingly competitive in the world marketplace. On the other hand, many poor peasant farmers cannot afford to adopt the costly new technologies.

Population Control in Developing Nations

A second major force that has had a tremendous impact on the lives of peasant peoples in the past half-century has been the introduction of new, affordable contraception throughout much of the Third World. Scientific contraceptive technologies have proven to be an effective way of countering the problem of population pressure. For instance, Critchfield noted in 1981 that "in places as scattered as China, India's Kerala and Karnataka states, Sri Lanka, and Java and Bali in Indonesia, annual population growth rates have plummeted from $2^{1}/_{2}$–3 percent in the early sixties to 1–$1^{1}/_{2}$ percent now— mostly in the five years 1975 to 1980. Elsewhere, though less spectacularly, fertility [the number of children born per woman] has been declining for the first time in the modern era" (p. 322). These trends have continued in parts of the Third World where governments have advocated the widespread use of contraception to keep population growth from overburdening the ability of the agricultural base to provide food. Some developing countries such as the

---

green revolution use of modern plant breeding to produce high-yield, fertilizer-intensive, fast-maturing crops

People's Republic of China and Singapore have adopted even stronger measures.

Nearly one-fourth of the human population, over one billion people, live in the People's Republic of China, and over half of those people are under 33 years of age (Tien, 1983). Both the absolute size of the Chinese population and the large percentage of the population represented by people of reproductive age make population control a major concern in China. A high fertility rate might well overcome China's ability to feed its population in the future, much less to achieve the status of a developed nation. For these reasons, the Chinese government has taken more extreme measures than have many developing countries, and they appear to have been quite successful at reducing the fertility rate. One means of lowering the fertility rate is to delay the average age of marriage. The current legal age for marriage in China is 20 for women and 22 for men. However, the main efforts to reduce fertility involve direct intervention in family planning. As Article 53 of the revised 1978 constitution of China states, "The state advocates and encourages birth planning." Using newspapers, radio, and television, the government actively publicizes and encourages the goal of limiting births to one child per family. Bonuses, larger pensions, free health care for the child, priority in housing, and the promise of education and employment priorities for the child are all used as inducements for voluntary commitment to having only one child. County birth planning offices supply contraceptives and subsidize local health centers for IUD insertions, sterilizations, and abortions.

Peer pressure also is used to achieve the goal of one child per family in China. At the local level, the government has organized a system of fertility committees throughout the country that meet with individuals and create social pressure for conformity to government goals in family planning. Families are encouraged to publicly commit themselves to having only one child, although in deference to the strong value that Chinese peasants still place on sons, a second child is considered acceptable if the first is a daughter. The weight of public opinion is brought to bear on individuals who refuse to support the national goal of reduced population growth. A liberal policy on abortion and social pressure to terminate pregnancies after the second birth have reduced China's total fertility rate to only 2.74 children per family, a rate about half of what it was in 1970 and equivalent to that of developed countries.

Singapore, where 2.6 million people occupy a mere 200 square miles, is one of the three most densely populated countries of the world. By 1969 the government began providing free family planning services, including abortion and sterilization. Government policy was to encourage small families. Women received maternity leave only for their first two children. The medical fees for the delivery of babies were greater for each successive child. Income tax exemptions applied only to the first two children. Subsidized housing was denied to large families. In 1983 the government began offering a cash payment equal to the average yearly income of a family in Singapore to any woman who was sterilized after her second child. Singapore's strict policies were so successful that by 1985 fertility had dropped from its earlier rate of 4.5 to only 1.4 children per family and efforts to slow population growth were ended.

In developed countries where the costs of population growth have not been felt so strongly, it is difficult for many people to accept the degree to which the governments of China and Singapore are intervening in the reproductive lives of their citizens. These measures are more readily comprehended in light of the terrible costs that high fertility rates have had in slowing the process of economic development in much of the world. Remaining underdeveloped takes its toll, not only as an absence of the material luxuries associated with industrialization, but also as hunger and high mortality rates. Life expectancy at birth in the underdeveloped countries is now 58 years, compared with 72 years in developed nations. In light of the advantages of successful development, similar governmental measures to control fertility rates may become common in other parts of the developing world.

CHAPTER SUMMARY

1. Cultures change—often in the direction of increasing complexity—through local discoveries and inventions, and borrowed innovations.

2. As changes occur in technology, social organization, or ideology, they affect the whole culture, which then adjusts.

3. The interrelated signs of increasing complexity are: harnessing of more energy per capita, increased specialization of labor, greater population density, greater status-ranking, decreasing emphasis on kinship, decreasing individual independence, more centralized political control, and more secular ideology.

4. The changes through which societies pass may be categorized as specific evolution (adaptation and specialization) or general evolution (qualitative change toward greater complexity).

5. Specific evolution tends to stabilize a society (the Principle of Stabilization).

6. General evolution moves a society toward increasing complexity, unless such change is inhibited by the effects of the society's previous adaptation.

7. Indigenous cultures are becoming more and more scarce, either through adaptations to the dominant cultures that surround them or through forced takeovers of their ancestral lands, ethnocide, and genocide.

8. Industrialization has brought profound economic changes, population growth, concentration of population around cities, and both positive and negative effects on the quality of life.

9. The majority of the world's people are affected by these trends but still live as peasants, practicing small-scale food production for their own needs.

10. Some anthropologists apply their knowledge of societies around the world to help solve social problems.

ANNOTATED READINGS

Bernard, H. R., & Pelto, P. J. (Eds.). (1972). *Technology and social change.* New York: Macmillan. An important collection of case studies of the effects of the introduction of Western technology on a variety of cultures.

Bodley, J. H. (1975). *Victims of progress.* Menlo Park, CA: Cummings. A discussion of the destructive effects of contact with industrialized societies on traditional societies.

Chambers, R. (1983). *Rural development: Putting the last first.* Essex, England: Longman Scientific and Technical. A standard text on development.

Geertz, C. (1963). *Agricultural involution: The processes of ecological change in Indonesia.* Berkeley, CA: University of California Press. An already classic study of cultural change and the interactions of technology and the agricultural habitat.

Sahlins, M., & Service, E. R. (Eds.). (1960). *Evolution and culture.* Ann Arbor, MI: University of Michigan Press. A thoughtful examination of various views on cultural evolution.

Service, E. R. (1978). *Profiles in ethnology.* New York: Harper & Row. A well-written series of ethnographic descriptions of a variety of the world's traditional cultures. Must reading for the anthropology major.

Service, E. R. (1962). *Primitive social organization.* New York: Random House. A very useful reference work on the social organization of traditional societies, written from an evolutionary perspective.

Steward, J. H. (1955). *Theory of culture change.* Urbana, IL: University of Illinois Press. A collection of the basic papers on cultural evolution by one of the most influential twentieth-century cultural evolutionists.

FIGURE 15.1   American Culture
Because of its diversity, a truly American culture is difficult to define. Apple pie and ice cream. Hot dogs and ball games. For every stereotype, one can think of aspects of American culture that defy it. Sushi and Chardonnay. Warlocks and Warhol.

Historically, anthropologists have taken as their objects of study the cultures of the world's small-scale, technologically simple societies. Few have attempted to analyze the cultures of large-scale societies such as America.[1] By and large, anthropologists have tended to give priority to the study of simple societies because they represented a rapidly disappearing source of information about the human condition. Sociologists have studied social patterns in industrialized societies, but their interests generally have not centered on cultural questions, and far too little empirical fieldwork exists on American lifeways to develop an adequate model of American culture as a whole. Yet anthropology's relevance to American culture lies in making it meaningful within the context of other cultures in the world.

Contemporary American Culture

C H A P T E R   O B J E C T I V E S

After reading this chapter, you should be able to:

Discuss the economic differences among the American social classes.

Analyze the minority statuses of race and gender in the United States.

Analyze politics, law, and crime in the United States.

Discuss the characteristics of the American family.

Describe the customs associated with pregnancy, childbirth, infancy, and childhood in the United States.

Discuss American adolescence, courtship, and marriage customs.

Discuss illness and old age in the United States.

Explain the role of religion in American life.

Discuss the basic American drives and values.

Explain the influence of population growth on American life.

1. For convenience, *America* will be used in this chapter to refer to the United States only, rather than to all the countries of North, Central, and South America.

American Social Organization
The Economic Base
Social Class
Gender Relations in the United States
American Politics
Law and Violence
Family

The Life Cycle in America
Pregnancy and Childbirth
Infancy and Childhood
Adolescence and Courtship
Marriage
Illness
Old Age and Death

American Ideology
Religion in America
American Drives and Values
The Changing Context of American
    Values and Drives

The Mets. The Jets. Pizza. Pepsi. Tacos. Sushi. Chop Suey. Madonna. Pavarotti. Jordan. Bird. How would you identify a typical North American culture if you were an anthropologist studying it? Would it depend on where you first set your sights? Los Angeles. New Orleans. Baltimore. Minneapolis. Has the great melting pot of American society grown too complicated to be defined? Or is that diversity still its strength and its hope?

American Social Organization

American society is composed of about 258 million people who live in cities of up to several million. Such a large population can only be sustained with a rather complex social organization that has many highly specialized statuses, social classes, and a hierarchy of political and economic power. We will examine the social organization of American society by considering the basic economic differences in U.S. statuses, the role of race and gender in the United States, the American political organization, the life cycle, and American ideology.

The Economic Base

The American people are supported by an industrialized technology based primarily on fossil fuel burning and water-powered generators. About 46 percent of the population make up the employed civilian labor force of about 120 million. Another 19 million are government workers. The American economy is productive enough that only about 30 percent of the labor force is involved in the production of goods, while the rest are service providers. Food is produced for the entire society by only 1.7 percent of the labor force, a decline from 38 percent in 1900. America's high productivity has led to a relatively low demand for labor throughout most of its history. As a result, the United States rarely has had an unemployment rate less than about 6 percent of the labor force except in time of war, and the unemployment rate often has risen well above 10 percent.

Social Class

Ideologically, Americans have not traditionally viewed their society as one made up of separate classes. Yet, as in other industrialized societies, the people of America do not all have equal access to the goods or services produced by its labor force. For instance, in 1989 the median income of American families was $21,921. At the same time, 21.5 percent had incomes of less than $10,000, while 4.2 percent received $75,000 or more. American society, in other words, is socially stratified into classes that differ in their share of the country's wealth (see Table 15.1). The American class system is somewhat ill-defined, in that the American ideology itself has traditionally denied its very existence as a formal structure. Polls have indicated that some 80 percent of Americans claim membership in the middle class. Interestingly, this figure includes both some persons who by technical standards would be considered members of the lower class and others who are technically of upper-class background. The failure of Americans to formally recognize that there are classes within their social system has been made easier by a traditionally high level of mobility within the American class system.

Occupation. An important measure of one's position within the American class system is one's occupation. The American economy is based primarily on market exchange. Rather than producing goods for direct exchange, most Americans are employed by someone else. In return, they are compensated with an income that they then exchange for the services and goods that they require. The size of their personal income depends largely, though not entirely, on the prestige ranking of their income-producing status.

TABLE 15.1 Percent Distribution of Income of U.S. Families, 1990

Families	Percent
Poorest fifth	4.6
Second fifth	10.8
Third fifth	16.6
Fourth fifth	23.8
Wealthiest fifth	44.3
Top 5 percent	17.4

Source: The World Almanac and Book of Facts 1993. New York: Pharos Books, p. 395.

The least prestigious and least well paid of the economic statuses are **unskilled laborers.** They usually are paid by the hour or by the quantity of goods that their work produces. Unskilled laborers often are hired for part-time or seasonal work such as food bagging at supermarkets, waiting on tables at restaurants, and harvesting crops on farms. Many of these jobs are held by young people who are not yet economically self-sufficient, by a disproportionate percentage of ethnic minorities, and by migrant workers.

Pink collar occupations are jobs traditionally held by women: waitress, sales clerk, secretary, telephone operator, and public school teacher (see Table 15.2). There is some variation in the prestige and incomes associated with these jobs, but in the main they fall below average in both measures. This category of low-level human service and informa-

TABLE 15.2 Percent Representation of Women in Occupations, 1989

Occupations	Percent
All occupations	45.2
Managerial/professional	45.2
Executive, administrative, managerial	39.8
Teachers, college and university	38.7
Teachers, except college and university	73.3
Professional workers	50.4
Technical/sales/administrative support	64.9
Sales workers, retail and personal service	49.3
Administrative support, including clerical	80.0
Information clerks	97.2
Service workers	60.4
Personal service	15.6
Precision production, craft, repair	8.6
Operators, fabricators, laborers	26.0
Farming, forestry, fishing	16.5

Source: Statistical Abstract of the United States: 1991 (111th ed.), [Table No. 652, p. 395], by U.S. Bureau of the Census, 1990, Washington, DC: U.S. Government Printing Office.

tion-processing jobs has been the fastest growing of the occupational categories since about 1950. Since World War II, tens of millions of jobs were opened up in this category. Since they were low-paid new jobs, rather than ones previously held by men, they were readily obtained by women without their being seen as competing with men for jobs (Harris, 1981). In the past decade the percentage of women employed in the better-paid, higher-status occupations has been gradually increasing but still remains low.

---

unskilled laborers low-paid workers, including part-time or seasonal workers, who usually are paid by the hour or for the quantity of goods they produce

pink collar occupations service occupations that largely are held by women

Comparative Worth in the United States

The concept of pay equity or comparative worth in the United States is one illustration of the role of cultural values in determining economic worth. Traditionally, United States employers have emphasized that the supply and demand of available employees is one reason they pay different salaries for different jobs. Thus, when many potential employees apply for a position, it can be filled at a low salary. On the other hand, when few apply for a specific position, the employer will have to offer a higher rate of pay. This view that the market itself determines the worth of particular jobs has led many employers to argue that the major reason for the lower average income of women employees compared with male employees has been that women simply prefer to apply for kinds of work that command lower levels of pay!

Others, however, have recognized that discrimination may play a role not only in what positions women are hired for but also what they may be paid. For instance, Toth (1986) has shown that as women in the United States have begun to move into the traditionally high-paying field of public relations, salaries have fallen, as has the social rank of this profession. Despite this attempt of many women to enter a prestigious and well-paid profession, they are typically paid from $6,000 to $30,000 less than their male counterparts who have had a similar education and the same number of years in service. Indeed, the salary gap between men and women over a 10-year career can be over 1 million dollars.

It has been argued that because of discrimination and other nonmarket factors in creating lower than average salaries for women and other minorities, a simple supply and demand concept is inadequate as the sole basis to determine the salary that a position should command. Adherents of the comparative worth position hold that the dollar value of the pay for a job should be determined only in part by the supply and demand factor; the characteristics of the job itself should also be considered. For instance, the length of previous experience and the level of education or training required to perform the work; the level of technical or verbal skill it requires; the amount of responsibility it entails for equipment, operations, or the safety of others; the degree of mental or physical effort the job demands; and the nature of the working conditions, such as noise or hazards, are possible factors to consider when determining the pay scale for a job. A position that is hazardous and requires great skill and previous training might be paid more than a safe job that requires little skill and training. Furthermore,

and this is the crucial point of the comparative worth approach, two very different jobs in the same company that are equivalent in these characteristics should receive equivalent pay. Thus, first-year clerk-typists and construction workers, entry-level secretaries and mechanics, or nurses who must spend two to four years in college and carpenters who must serve up to a four-year apprenticeship, might represent positions in a three-tiered pay system in the same company.

By 1989 all but five state governments in the United States had given some study to the issues of pay equity. According to the National Committtee on Pay Equity, "Twenty states have made pay equity adustments to one or more female-dominated or disproportionately-minority job classification through collective bargaining and/or litigation" in public sector jobs (1989, p. 14). Comparative worth pay plans also have been initiated in a number of larger United States corporations such as AT&T, BankAmerica, Chase Manhattan, IBM, Motorola, and Tektronix already, and they have been considered legislatively in about 30 states. Whether a comparative worth viewpoint will become the predominant United States system for setting pay scales remains to be seen.

Blue collar workers are manual laborers other than farm workers. Although they command little prestige, some of these statuses have access to above-average incomes due to the economic importance of the commodities and services that they control. Examples of blue collar workers are garbage collectors, dockhands, factory workers, taxicab and bus drivers, janitors, and supervisors of manual laborers.

White collar occupations are clerical workers, sales workers, technical workers, managers, and administrators. Their work is primarily the providing of services. Although many of these occupations are fairly prestigious and relatively well paid, over the years many white collar offices have become more and more like factories in the repetitive nature of the routine work.

Professionals are typically self-employed providers of services whose work generally requires a graduate-level university degree. Included in this category are the most prestigious nongovernmental

occupations such as medical doctors, lawyers, scientists, and university faculty. These highly ranked positions, as well as highly ranked governmental positions, generally have been dominated by men (see Table 15.3).

Historically, the simplest means to climb to a higher position within the class system was through the educational system, since higher-ranked occupations generally have required a higher level of education than have lower-ranked ones. Indeed, it is common for many employers in the United States to

blue collar workers nonfarm manual laborers

white collar occupations service-providing occupations such as clerical, sales, managerial, and administrative jobs

professionals self-employed, college-educated service providers

TABLE 15.3 U.S. Occupations Held Predominantly by One Gender, 1991

Occupation	Percent Held
Nine Jobs Where Men Are Scarce:	*by men*
Prekindergarten and kindergarten teachers	2.2
Dental assistants	1.1
Secretaries	0.8
Receptionists	2.8
Licensed practical nurses	3.9
Child-care worker (outside private households)	3.7
Welfare service aides	10.2
Textile sewing machine operators	9.5
Librarians	12.7
Six Jobs Where Women Are Scarce:	*by women*
Automobile mechanics	0.7
Surveyor and mapping scientists	11.0
Aerospace engineers	3.7
Lawyers	12.2
Police and detectives	12.6
College and university teachers	34.7

Source: Statistical Abstract of the United States: 1992 (112th ed.), [Table No. 629, pp. 392–394], by U.S. Bureau of the Census, 1992, Washington, DC: U.S. Government Printing Office.

require an educational background in prospective employees that goes far beyond what is actually needed for the work itself. This system, in which education is strongly rewarded as a means of raising one's rank within the class system, keeps potential workers in school for a longer period of time before they begin full-time work than might otherwise be the case. This has been one means by which the number of people in the labor pool, and therefore the unemployment rate, has been kept lower in the United States than it otherwise would have been.

Although opportunities for upward social mobility have been high in America, so have the chances of moving down in the occupational ranks. For instance, a decline in the demand for a product or service can make it impossible for a person who is qualified for a high-ranked occupation to obtain employment, and persons already employed may lose their positions. Thus, engineers who are educationally too specialized in their skills to move readily from one high-ranked position to another may find themselves bagging groceries, and recent university graduates may be forced to accept employment driving cabs. A great deal of personal anguish may accompany such downward shifts in social rank.

American Factories in Mexico

Today the international economy of all nations is affected by the economic life of all others. This interdependence of national economies is well illustrated by the role of U.S. corporations in Mexico.

In 1964 the U.S. Congress drastically curtailed the movement of migrant labor from Mexico into the United States. This resulted in an unemployment crisis in Mexico. In response to this problem, the Mexican Border Industrialization Program was established a year later. It encouraged foreign corporations to open assembly plants in Mexico to help alleviate the unemployment crisis. Today in Mexico there are over 1,600 U.S. and Canadian companies, including American Hospital Supply, Chrysler, Coleman Products, Fischer-Price, Foster Grant Corp., General Electric, ITT, Levi-Strauss, Mattel, National Semiconductor, Samsonite Corporation, Sears, Union Carbide, Velcro USA Inc., and Xerox, in a 1,950-mile-long (3,218 kilometers) free trade zone along the Mexican–U.S. border.

Multinational companies now employ over 426,000 Mexican workers in assembly plants called *maquiladoras*. Unassembled parts are stored by American companies in warehouses on the U.S. side of the border and shipped daily into nearby Mexican towns for assembly. For instance, in El Paso, Texas, over 700 trucks ferry parts across the border each day to maquiladoras, where they are processed by Mexican maquiladora workers, who are paid wages that typically range from $3.85 to $5.00 per day.

U.S. multinational companies save thousands of salary dollars for each worker they employ in a foreign assembly plant, but the savings do not end there. The Mexican Free Trade Zone was established with the understanding that corporations that moved there would not be taxed by the Mexican government, and when the assembled goods are returned to the U.S., the value-added tax that is paid to the U.S. government is based only on the low cost of the Mexican labor. Since the goods are then sold at U.S. retail market prices, determined as if they had been manufactured in the United States, the maquiladora system results in tremendous profits for corporations that participate.

In addition to tax benefits, corporations also save in health and safety expenses. Mexican workers can be employed in conditions that would violate U.S. health and safety regulations. For instance, maquiladora electronics employees work with toluene, PCBs, and solvents that can cause chloracne, skin cancer, and leukemia. Company doctors routinely dismiss such problems as unrelated to working conditions. Although Mexican law requires companies to grant female employees liberal childbirth leave benefits, companies routinely require women job applicants to submit to pregnancy tests before they are hired. There is a very high turnover rate among employees—women typically work only about seven months for a given company. Thus in practice, companies rarely have to grant the maternity leave that is guaranteed by law.

Nogales, Mexico, is an interesting example of a border town that has been greatly influenced by the maquiladora system. In 1975 there were 50,000 inhabitants there. In 1989 the population had swelled to 150,000 with jobless people who had migrated from other parts of Mexico to find work either in maquiladoras or as day-laborers in American Nogales, just across the border. Many of the immigrants live in squatter settlements in crude, self-built shacks. Technically illegal, these settlements have no electricity, sewage facilities, or permanent water supplies. The 65 maquiladoras employ 20,000 of Nogales' new residents for about $3.74 a day. Although this might be a good wage in much of Mexico, prices in border towns such as Nogales approximate those of neighboring U.S. towns. Thus, maquiladora workers must pay $2.61 for a gallon of milk. Ground beef costs $1.42 a pound, and cheese costs $2.47 a pound.

Many of the maquiladora workers in Nogales are single parents, but there are only two day-care centers, each with a capacity of about 45 children, for factory workers' children. So tremendous problems exist related to the large number of "latch-key" children, many of whom have no alternative but to remain at home in the squatter settlements during the day. Since wages are so low in the assembly plants, and since a woman may have to spend more than half her income to pay someone to watch her children, many children 14 years of age and older go to work in the plants.

The Mexican government has had little effect in trying to improve working conditions in the maquiladoras. Typically the assembly plants are nothing more than cinder block buildings that can literally be vacated by the company overnight. Companies have little invested in the properties themselves and can easily move their operations to other Third World countries if the profitability of their Mexican plants declines. Thus the Mexican government hesitates to press too strongly for higher salaries or for better health and safety.

In addition, the U.S. dollars that enter the Mexican economy have become increasingly important to Mexico, especially since the devaluation of the peso in 1976 cut workers' real wages by 50 percent. So the government has had to make some concessions to keep foreign industries that threatened to leave. Maquiladoras were exempted from various worker-protection requirements, given the right to dismiss workers without severance pay, and allowed to keep workers on "temporary" status for as much as three months. In the attempt to further attract American companies, Mexican Nogales passed local laws that forbade the formation of unions and made it illegal for foreign companies to pay their workers more than the legal minimum wage. The North American Congress on Latin America (1979) estimated that Motorola was able to save four million dollars a year by moving from Phoenix to Nogales, and that General Electric saved between $10,000 and $12,000 per worker by operating its assembly plant in Juarez instead of in the United States. Under these circumstances, it seems unlikely that the lot of maquiladora workers is likely to change in the near future.

Minorities

Minority statuses in the United States include many groups defined by similar characteristics such as ethnic and religious similarities, race, and gender. **Ethnic group** identity is based on shared customs, such as those of immigrants from various European countries, especially of southern and eastern Europe. Religious minorities as well, such as Moslems, Buddhists, Rajneesh, Amish, Hutterites, and Mormons exemplify groups that have not re-

ethnic group   minority group whose identity is based on shared customs, especially of immigrants

FIGURE 15.2   Minority Status
**Minority status in the United States is based
not only on ethnic and religious affiliations,
but on race, gender, and sexuality as well.
Keith Meinhold was discharged by the Navy
after admitting he engaged in homosexual behavior. In a legal battle that followed, a federal
judge ordered the Navy to reinstate Meinhold.
Here he returns to duty at Moffett Naval Air
Station, Mountain View, California, in November 1992.**

ceived total acceptance as members of the American mainstream. Sexuality and gender are also important in American culture as determinants of minority status. Thus, homosexual Americans continue to experience social, economic, and even legal discrimination as minorities, and many aspects of women's roles in America are most fruitfully understood in the context of women's minority status.

Race. Historically, racial statuses have had an important influence on social relations in the United States. For instance, at one time over three-quarters of the states in the United States eventually passed laws prohibiting interracial marriages. That is, those of nonwhite racial statuses were forbidden to marry whites, although nonwhite races were not consistently forbidden to intermarry with one another. Nineteen states still had such laws in 1968, when they were struck down by the Supreme Court of the United States as unconstitutional. Despite legislation that has attempted to eliminate racial discrimination, the class system in the United States continues to reflect the historical discrimination against members of minorities. Holders of minority racial and ethnic statuses in the United States have had unequal opportunities to achieve highly valued social positions and high-income occupations. As a result, races and ethnic groups are socially and economically stratified in the United States. According to the United States Bureau of the Census, whites possess a disproportionate share of the higher socioeconomic statuses, and nonwhites are disproportionately relegated to low socioeconomic positions (see Fig. 15.3).

Maintenance of different ways of treating socially designated races is not without its cost. Consider this example based on information from the *Statistical Abstract of the United States 1969* and on the *Statistical Abstract of the United States 1989* (U.S. Department of Commerce, 1969 and 1990): In 1900 the life expectancy of whites in the United States was nearly 150 percent that of blacks. The difference can be attributed to a higher infant mortality rate among African Americans, a differential access to adequate medical treatment and hospital facilities, and the debilitating effects of the lower-class jobs available to black men. By 1960, the gap had closed somewhat with a general rise in the standard of living, but the white population could still look forward to an average of 7 more years of life than was available to the black population. By 1995, the white life expectancy is expected to reach 76.8 years, 4.4 years more than that of African Americans. Thus, currently, in every generation of 76.8 years, 4.4 years of life are denied to 33 million African Americans, an equivalent of 145,200,000 years of human life wasted needlessly. This loss of life is due to social and economic inequalities that have existed since the founding of the country, and would currently be equivalent to the deaths of 30,283 18-year-olds each year.

It is in effects such as the lowered life expectancies and living standards among those who hold minority racial statuses that racism makes itself felt in its most harmful way. To those who feel its effects,

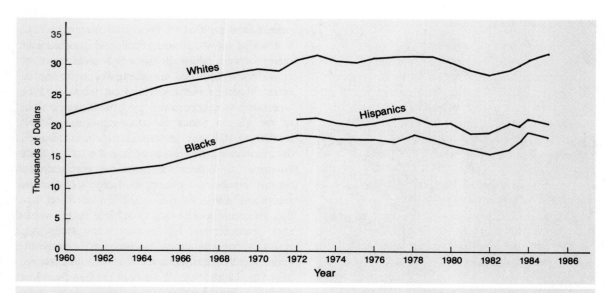

FIGURE 15.3   U.S. Median Family Income by Race in Constant (1990) Dollars
According to the United States Bureau of the Census, whites have a greater share of income than any other race, and the gap seems to be widening rather than narrowing. Thus, despite overt legislation to the contrary, attitudes toward minorities and few opportunities for advancement have combined to keep American society stratified.

Source: Statistical Abstract of the United States: 1992 (112th ed.) [Table 696, p. 445], by U.S. Bureau of the Census, 1991, Washington, DC: U.S. Government Printing Office.

even more abhorrent than ethnocentrism or racial prejudice is the fact that these attitudes may become the basis of social policies, supported by the weight of law or custom, that perpetuate arbitrary and harmful inequalities between peoples. Great harm may be done even without any outward show of prejudice or violence.

Native Americans.   One of the most distinctive illustrations of the minority status in American society is the example of Native Americans. In mid-1989 there were about 1,737,000 million persons in the United States who were legally defined as Native Americans. The impact of minority status on the indigenous Americans is clear: Indians have the lowest life expectancy, at 63 years, and the highest unemployment rates, about 50 percent, of any group in the United States. They also fall below the nation as a whole in average income, housing, and education.

Originally, Native Americans were the only inhabitants of the lands now under control of the United States government. Now, they find themselves in the unusual position of being both citizens of

the United States and of tribal groups that the Supreme Court has called "domestic dependent nations" of the United States (*Cherokee Nation v. Georgia,* 5 Pet. 10 [1831]). This ambiguous legal state of affairs stems from the political history of relations between the U.S. government and the original Native American societies that it conquered as it expanded its borders.

From the viewpoint of Native Americans, the founders of what was to become the United States entered North America as immigrants. Although the incoming population was originally small, its numbers grew rapidly from continued immigration, and its economic and political power increased based on the development of industry and technology. Initially, the U.S. government formally recognized the sovereignty of Indian tribes. The Northwest Ordinance of 1787, ratified by the First Congress in 1789, declared, "The utmost good faith shall always be observed towards Indians; their lands and property shall never be taken from them without their consent."

Nevertheless, as the immigrant population expanded across much of the North American continent, its citizens entered lands occupied by Native

Americans, who found themselves overwhelmed by U.S. military power. When Native American societies did attempt to regulate their relations with the U.S. government and minimize the loss of their own lands and cultural identities by the negotiation of treaties, they were at first treated as foreign nations. Thus Indian tribes typically ceded some of their lands to the United States while reserving other lands to themselves, and the United States acknowledged Indian sovereignty over their own lands, while sometimes promising economic aid and educational rights to the tribal groups in return for the ceded lands.

Indian–U.S. relations never remained as clear-cut as the contents of these treaties suggest, however. The expansion of the U.S. domain eventually engulfed the various Indian territories, and left Native American societies in a more powerless position than that of other peoples who had entered into treaties with the United States. In 1823, the Supreme Court declared that the U.S. government had the right to govern Indians, saying that "the discovery and conquest gives the conquerors sovereignty over and ownership of the lands obtained" (*Johnson v. McIntosh*, 21 U.S. 542). Thus, lands Indian peoples thought they had reserved to themselves through treaties became officially administered as parts of the United States itself. Indian tribes were no longer to be treated as sovereign nations within their own territories, but as dependent peoples of the United States government. This process was formalized when the U.S. Congress unilaterally passed legislation that declared all Indians born within the territorial limits of the United States were U.S. citizens.

Following the extension of U.S. citizenship to Native Americans, it was easy to forget that "reservations" were U.S. lands that had been held in trust for Indians who had not yet adjusted to mainstream American life. U.S. treaty obligations to residents of Indian lands came to be seen by many non-Indians as "special treatment" by the federal government. There followed a period during which tribes were encouraged to disincorporate as tribal entities in return for settlement of claims that they had unsuccessfully pursued for lands they had lost to states and to the federal government. Some tribes ceased to exist under this policy. Others remained. Today, there are still 287 Indian reservations in the United States, governed in part by the tribes, in part by federal bureaus, and in part by the states in or next to which they are located.

The uneasy mix of governing powers that controls the destinies of reservation residents is a continuing source of conflict, both among Native Americans and between reservation governments and non-Indian political bodies. For instance, Cree Indians and other tribes whose traditional lands straddled the U.S.–Canadian border were guaranteed the right to pass unimpeded from one country to the other by an early treaty between the U.S. and Canada. This right is still in force, although U.S. border officials occasionally express annoyance at its use by Indians whose vehicles are immune to the searches that may legally be made of other vehicles that cross the border.

Many times the legal conflicts over Indian rights become major court cases because of the economic interests that are at stake. For instance, treaties with Lumhi Indians and several other tribes in the state of Washington have guaranteed them free and unregulated fishing rights. These rights have been challenged by representatives of the commercial fishing industry and by government agencies concerned with recreational fishing, both of which have economic interests in the maintenance of fishing quotas that those treaties prevent them from imposing on members of the tribes. In Utah, important legal cases have been fought in the 1980s over whether the state government has the right to tax oil companies for oil produced by wells on the Ute Indian reservation, and over the right of the tribe to exercise police authority over predominantly non-Indian towns that exist within the Ute reservation. In 1989, the Ute government declared that the federal government and the state of Utah had abrogated their contractual obligation to build irrigation projects on the reservation in return for rights to irrigated water that flows from the reservation—opening the way for the tribe to withhold that water in the future. In Idaho, a conflict continues that threatens a major source of revenue for the Shoshoni and Bannocks Indians of the Fort Hall Reservation. For years, sales of goods such as cigarettes at untaxed prices have been an important attraction for tourist dollars on the reservation. The Idaho state government is now asserting that this practice is illegal, and that the tribe must collect state taxes on all such sales. The tribal government, on the other hand, asserts that the state of Idaho has no authority over tribal business practices, since reservation lands are not legally part of the state. A similar conflict is occurring between the state of New York and two Indian tribes, the Mohawks and the Seneca.

Sometimes the conflicting views of Indian authority to govern their own lands have reached the point of forceful and even violent confrontations. For instance, in 1986 when the city of Scottsdale, Arizona, refused to renegotiate the rights for non-Indian use of Pima highway, an important commuter road on reservation land, the tribe finally closed the highway to further use by non-Indians. Bonfires and barricades stopped the flow of traffic until the city government capitulated. Most recently, in July of 1989 the New York state police sealed off the St. Regis Indian Reservation because Mohawk Indians had continued to open gambling casinos to tourists from New York, a state that does not allow gambling. After several raids of the reservation casinos by state police, a Mohawk group called the Sovereignty Security Force blocked the main highway in protest against state and federal agencies that they believed were intervening illegitimately in the internal affairs of the tribe by attempting to prohibit gambling, a source of millions of dollars of revenue that the tribal government had authorized. New York state troopers responded with checkpoints of their own on roads into the reservation. As of November 1992, New York state troopers were still posted on the reservation, and the conflict was still unresolved.

The unusual legal situation of America's indigenous peoples is a complicated tangle of conflicting views about who has sovereignty over reservation lands. Tribal, state, city, and federal governments are all involved. Sometimes the tribes themselves are factionalized over who best represents their interests, and within the federal government conflicts sometimes arise about which government body is responsible for determining policy towards reservations. For instance, usually the Bureau of Indian Affairs is the dominant federal party, but in some cases, policies that influence Indian lands adjacent to national forests or parks are set by the National Forest Service or National Park Service. Since vast sums of money are often at stake in these conflicts, they are likely to continue.

Legal Gambling on Indian Reservations

In the United States, about 150 gambling casinos and bingo parlors represent a billion-dollar-a-year source of income on Indian reservations, where about 50 percent of the population is unemployed. Although all but two states permit some form of legal gambling, the flow of revenues from states into the reserva-

tions has been politically controversial. In 1988 the U.S. Congress passed the Indian Gaming Regulatory Act, which made gambling on Indian reservations dependent on the status of gambling in the states in which the reservations are located. Under this law, if states have legal gambling, then they must negotiate "in good faith" with tribal governments about allowing gambling on the reservations as well. The issues often turn on what constitutes "good faith" negotiating by the states, and on identifying the forms of gambling that fall into the same class as those allowed under state law. Several tribes have filed lawsuits against states to attempt to force them to negotiate compacts with the tribes. In one such case, the U.S. District Court decided against the Ponca tribe, ruling that the state of Oklahoma could not be forced to conclude a gambling compact with the tribe. Under this interpretation of the law, states would be able to prevent gambling on Indian reservations simply by refusing to sign a compact with the tribes.

On April 4, 1992, U.S. Interior Secretary Manuel Lujan sent a memo to then-President Bush's chief of staff to indicate that he had reversed his earlier position in support of legalized gambling on Indian reservations. He argued that the policy might be interpreted as being contrary to the Bush administration's position on family values, especially in states that opposed gambling.

Eight days after Secretary Lujan's memo was reported in the news media, FBI agents began a series of raids on Indian reservations in Arizona to enforce the new rules on reservation gambling. Gaming is legal in Arizona, but the state has refused to accept gambling machines on reservations, where gambling generates $45 million a year for Indians. Casinos, a major source of family income for some tribes, were closed on the Fort McDowell–Yavapai reservation near Phoenix, the Tohono O'odham and Pascua Yaqui reservations near Tucson, the Tonto Apache reservation in Payson, and the Yavapai reservation near Prescott. On the Fort McDowell Reservation, FBI agents entered casinos and loaded $3 million worth of video gambling machines into eight moving vans. Yavapai Indians on that reservation responded by blocking exits from the parking lot with cars, trucks, and road-grading equipment. After Arizona Governor Fife Symington negotiated a truce, 30 federal agents were allowed to leave the casino in which they had taken refuge. Indians kept the parking lot under a 24-hour watch, while they continued to negotiate their right to gaming on the reservation.

On May 12, 1992, Governor Symington told representatives of seven Indian tribes that he would favor letting tribes reinstitute the same type of gambling that they had had before the raids. Negotiations regarding gambling resumed after Indians agreed to allow the FBI to warehouse the video slot machines until a formal agreement was reached with the state. After three months of negotiations, the FBI returned the 349 machines to the Fort McDowell reservation, under an agreement that they would not be used for gambling until the negotiations with the state were concluded. The tribe placed the gaming machines in a warehouse just outside a casino. Along with the machines, the FBI also presented the tribe with a bill for $104,102 for storage of the machines during the three months that the federal agency had held them.

Gender Relations in the United States

With industrialization, the means of subsistence for most families has become labor for income rather than food production. In many societies, including European countries during the rise of industrialization and, more recently, in other parts of the developing world, men were drawn more fully into the industrialized sector of the economy than were women. This process increased the economic dependence of women on men historically, and is having a similar effect in many other industrializing nations today.

In the United States, women are holders of minority status, a low-ranked master status that tends to overshadow the other statuses they may hold. Like racism, this sexism creates inequalities of opportunity. Thus, women in the United States today make up almost three-quarters of the poor.

Occupational discrimination. Several limitations have been formally placed on women in the United States on the basis of the idea that societal norms should reflect the biological differences of the two sexes. Among the strongest of these limitations has been the so-called **"protective" legislation** that was overtly designed to protect the female, thought

FIGURE 15.4   Maya Angelou
Perhaps as a symbol of President Bill Clinton's attitude toward providing more opportunities for women and minorities in government, he asked the poet, playwright, and historian Maya Angelou to write a poem and read it at his inauguration. Ms. Angelou, born in a segregated Arkansas in 1928, hoped that her presence at the inauguration would provide the impetus for a nation to unite and develop a truly egalitarian society.

of as the "weaker sex," from exploitation in the labor market. In many states, for instance, laws have forbidden employment of women in positions that require them to lift more than a nominal amount of weight. On the basis of such laws, many individual women who were perfectly capable of meeting the demands of a particular job have been denied employment "for their own protection," not because of

"protective" legislation laws that are ostensibly intended to prevent the exploitation of women, but which in practice create social barriers against the full participation of women in social life outside the domestic sphere; for instance, many states in the U.S. have laws that prohibit the hiring of women into occupations that require the employee to lift more than 35 pounds

TABLE 15.4   Percentage of Women Holding Political Positions in the United States, 1992

	Number	Percent of Women
Supreme Court	1	11.1
Senate	6	6.0
House	47	11.0
Governors	3	6.0

Source: Taylor's Encyclopedia of Government Officials: Federal and State 1991–1992, John Clements, Ed. Vol. 13, 1992. Dallas, Texas: Political Research Inc., pp. 59–275. Updated by *USA Today,* Nov. 5, 1992, p. 7A.

evidence that they lacked the necessary skills, but because they were female.

In the decades beginning with the 1960s, the status of women in the United States has improved as their percentage in the labor force has increased. Nevertheless, although traditionally male occupations are becoming increasingly available to women, the roles of women are still particularly limited in areas, such as politics in which social power is wielded (see Table 15.4).

American Politics

The American political system has been dominated historically by two major political parties, and one commonly hears political issues discussed as if Americans fall simply into one of two fundamentally contrasting camps, liberals and conservatives. However, the actual political makeup of Americans is more complex than this suggests. A 1987 *Times Mirror* survey of American political attitudes found that there were three important personal orientations and six values from which the major American voting blocks were really formed. The personal orientations included differences in (1) religious faith, (2) alienation, a sense of powerlessness and distrust of government, and (3) financial pressure. For instance, politically active Americans tended to be more religious than average, and both Democrats and Republicans had important religious constituencies among their party members. The political value differences that divided groups of American voters were (1) the degree of their tolerance for people with different life-styles and the expression of non-mainstream ideas, (2) the importance they placed on

social justice for minorities and the needy, (3) the level of their anticommunism, (4) the stress they placed on faith in their country's ability to solve its problems, (5) their attitudes about the size and effectiveness of government, and (6) their feelings about the power and influence of business corporations.

The *Times Mirror* survey found that a full 11 percent of Americans were totally uninvolved in public affairs and politics. These people never voted. They tended to be young and poorly educated. Their greatest concerns were unemployment, poverty, and the threat of nuclear war.

The Republican party.   The Republican party is most staunchly supported by two main groups: *enterprise Republicans*, and *moral Republicans*. Enterprise Republicans are affluent, educated, almost exclusively white Americans who are particularly probusiness and antigovernment in their values. Moral Republicans represent 11 percent of the adult population and about 14 percent of voters. As a group, they are middle-aged Americans with middle incomes who hold strong and very conservative political views on social and foreign policy issues. They are strongly "anticommunist" and antiabortion and favor prayer in the public schools and the death penalty. They also favor social spending by government except when it is specifically targeted for minorities. Moral Republicans are regular churchgoers, and many are born-again Christians. Like enterprise Republicans, they are largely white.

The Democratic party.   The backbone of the Democratic party is a coalition of five different groups: *New Deal Democrats, Sixties Democrats,* the *partisan poor,* the *passive poor,* and *seculars.* New Deal Democrats are older Americans who have moderate incomes and little financial stress. Many are of blue-collar and union background. Almost a third of this group are Catholic. They favor restrictions on abortion and support school prayer and social spending except for minorities. The Sixties Democrats are a well-educated group that includes a large number of females and blacks. They favor government spending on social programs, including programs specifically for minorities, and they tend to be somewhat less anticommunist than other groups. The partisan poor is a very low-income group that is strongly concerned with issues of social justice. They favor social spending but oppose tax increases. They also favor the death penalty and school prayer, but are divided on the abortion issue. The passive poor feel less economic pressure than the partisan poor and are less critical of their society. They favor social spending, oppose cuts in defense spending, and are moderately antiabortion. The seculars are well-educated, mostly white, and generally middle-aged. They are the only nonreligious group in the political spectrum. They strongly support personal freedom, favor cuts in military spending, and oppose school prayer, antiabortion legislation, and increased aid to minorities.

There are three remaining voting groups. These are the *upbeats*, the *disaffecteds*, and the *followers*. Upbeats are young, optimistic persons who have great faith in their country. They too are largely white. Their main political concerns are the budget deficit and other economic issues, and they lean toward Republican candidates in their voting. Disaffecteds also lean toward the Republican party. They are alienated, pessimistic, and skeptical of both big business and big government, but they are promilitary, support capital punishment, and oppose gun control. Followers usually lean toward Democratic candidates but sometimes support Republicans. They have little faith in their society, but tend also to be uncritical of either government or business.

The political rhetoric of the two-party system emphasizes the differences between the ideologies of the parties, as if there were no middle ground. Yet the American electorate is extremely diverse, and both parties unite people with important value differences. The election of a candidate from either party requires the support of a coalition of these different groups, and the wooing of the upbeats, disaffecteds, and followers is particularly important to both parties.

The 1992 presidential election illustrates the diversity of the American electorate. Dissatisfaction with the country's economic performance and job cutbacks led to strong voter turnout, especially among the traditional Democratic party supporters. Governor Bill Clinton received about 82 percent of the African American vote in this election and got some support from enterprise Republicans. Among the crucial swing voters, the upbeats and followers, also influenced by economic issues, voted for Clinton, after having supported Reagan and Bush in the previous elections. Many of the disaffecteds, on the other hand, moved toward third-party candidates, the most well-known being H. Ross Perot, a prominent businessman. Another important variable in this election was gender. Women, especially those who were single parents and influenced by concerns about

FIGURE 15.5   Presidential Debate

During the second presidential debate, October 1992, independent candidate H. Ross Perot (left center) speaks as U.S. president George Bush (foreground) and Democratic presidential candidate Governor Bill Clinton respond. The presence and popularity of the third party candidate proved that the American system of government is diverse and that the electorate is engaged in making its voice heard.

economic needs, education, and reproductive choice, voted in record numbers for the Democratic candidate.

So it can be argued that the political rhetoric of liberal versus conservative is an oversimplification of a more complex state of affairs. The centrist tendencies of both political parties may be seen best in the actual day-to-day practice of American legislative politicians after their election, when mutual respect, compromise, bipartisan cooperation, and diplomatic statesmanship are commonly emphasized.

Law and Violence

Americans view themselves as a peace-loving people who fight only when forced to. Nevertheless, the actual level of violence within the society is quite high. For instance, the homicide rate in the United States is among the highest in the world's industrialized nations. According to the annual *Uniform Crime Reports* of the FBI, the rate of murder and negligent homicide in the United States for 1991 was 98 per million people. This is about three times the rate among their culturally related Canadian neighbors to the north. In 1991, there were 24,700 murders and nonnegligent manslaughter cases in the United States. Other violent crimes also are frequent. It is estimated that there were 106,590 forcible rapes in the United States in 1991 and 687,730 cases of robbery. Although Americans frequently complain that their judicial system is overly lenient with criminals, American courts convict a higher percentage of accused persons than do the courts of most other industrialized nations. Once convicted, American criminals are given and actually serve longer sentences than do their European counterparts. In 1991, there were an estimated 789,261 persons in American jails and prisons, an increase of almost 7 percent from 1990.

Family

Americans often refer to the family as the basis of their society. In a culture in which individuals must compete with one another for success, the family is one of the few relatively safe havens of close emotional ties and cooperation. However, the actual role of family in American society is minimal in contrast to most other societies, and single parent families are very common.

The limited role of the family. The American family has lost most social functions beyond the basic socialization of children and the consumption of goods. Unlike families in peasant cultures, American families typically are not production units, but rather consumption units. In a sense, the American family could be defined as the group that eats together, but, since the rise of television, even this definition of the family might be invalid.

Even with industrialization, earlier American families often were held together by the presence of a mother whose work was home-centered. Before the development of effective contraceptive techniques, it was simply easier for the wife to rear her children at home until about the age of 40, and for the husband to seek employment outside the home. With increasingly effective birth control technology, the period of childbearing has declined from about 18 years in 1900 to about 6 years in 1980, and the average number of children born to a couple is now less than 2. As the economic importance of domestic production declined, and the American housewife was left in a dependent economic role, she began to seek employment outside the home. Today, over 60 percent of American women are employed outside the home.

Since labor in America is extremely specialized, children are likely to enter occupations different from those of their parents. The family therefore has ceased to play any important educational role beyond the early socialization of children. After they learn the basic skills of language and acquire their society's basic values, ideas, and customs from their family, children receive most of their formal education in adult life skills through state and private educational organizations. However, although children often enter occupations requiring different skills from those of their parents, their occupations are not likely to differ greatly in rank. The occupational choices of children, therefore, are influenced by their parents' occupations, income, and social status, mediated by such other factors as their place of residence and the quality of the schools available.

The American family is not an autonomous spiritual center for its members; religious ritualism within the family, where it occurs, is practiced as an extension of the rituals of a larger religious body that unites members of many family groups on the basis of a common religious ideology. The family is not a center of authority, either. A complex state-level government monopolizes the right to exercise all legal force, so the American family is lacking in all governmental authority outside the governing of the family itself.

Fragmentation of families. Historically, the American family has been built around a norm of monogamous marriage—an exclusive, lifelong bond between one man and one woman. This ideal once fit into an extended family form, but industrialization has shrunk the family unit to the nuclear family, which is more readily adaptable to the demands of a highly mobile society. Different family members are not likely to find employment in the same place, and job changing is frequent. Even the ideal of monogamous marriage has been influenced by the demands for social mobility. The increasing self-sufficiency of women has been paralleled by a rising divorce rate; the current average length of marriage is less than five years. Since 70 to 80 percent of divorced persons remarry, the American marriage system sometimes has been called **serial monogamy**, a form somewhere between strict monogamy and true polygamy (see Chapter 8).

The Life Cycle in America

In every society, we pass through the same age-related stages: birth, childhood, adolescence, perhaps marriage, old age, and death. But how we experience each one is strongly molded by our culture. Even in the United States, where rites of passage are minimal and socialization diffuse, we tend to experience the life cycle in ways that are unique to our culture.

Pregnancy and Childbirth

Like those of many other societies, American culture includes several traditional pregnancy taboos and admonitions. One of these is the idea of **marking**. According to this belief, children may be influenced by things that are done by or that happen to their mothers during pregnancy. For instance, birthmarks might be attributed to the mother's having eaten too many strawberries, raspberries, or other red foods. The most common expression of the concept of marking in the United States today is in admonitions to do things believed to influence the child in positive ways. For instance, a pregnant woman may hear that by spending time listening to classical music, reading good literature, and immersing herself in art she may predispose her child to similar pursuits. The concept of the marking of an unborn child by its mother parallels the idea that, after birth, mothers have the principal psychological influence on the development of the child and therefore usually receive greater credit or blame for what the child becomes.

Most Americans regard it as desirable for a woman to seek the services of a physician—most of whom are male in the United States—about two months into her pregnancy. This doctor will evaluate the health of the woman, check the progress of the pregnancy, and deliver the baby. However, this ideal is not always possible for those with low incomes, due to the high costs of medical treatment and hospital care. For most Americans the preferred place for the delivery still is a hospital in the presence of the physician and one or more nurses.

There is, however, an increasing return to the less expensive system of delivery at home with the aid of a nurse-midwife who, at the same time, offers more personalized care than does the hospital system. Many hospitals, in turn, are beginning to shift from the use of specialized labor and delivery rooms to the use of birthing rooms, which can save as much as half the hospital costs for a normal delivery.

Parents begin selecting a name for the child months before the birth. Most American families have no formal customary rules for selecting the name, such as a requirement to name the child after a particular relative. Since the selection of the name is largely an aesthetic issue, the popularity of different names rises and falls over the generations much as do fashions in dress. Names like Blanche, Gertrude, Mildred, Helen, Edith, or Ada for girls and Edgar, Orville, Leonard, Albert, or Herbert for boys, which were common among people born 80 years ago, are uncommon in 1992, when such names as Kirsten, Jason, and Jonathan are used frequently. Names are officially given without ceremony immediately after birth when the attending physician fills out a birth certificate to be filed in the county records. A religious naming ceremony may be conducted for the child a few weeks later.

About 1.6 million legal abortions occur in the United States each year. Between 90.5 and 93 percent of these are performed during the first 12 weeks of pregnancy. A total of 99.2 percent are performed before 20 weeks, and only about 100 (less than 0.01 percent) are performed after 24 weeks. It is estimated that about 46 percent of U.S. women will have

---

serial monogamy a marriage pattern in which individuals of either sex may have only one spouse at a given time, but through divorce and remarriage may have several spouses during their lifetime

marking the idea that the behaviors of a woman during pregnancy may influence the physical or psychological characteristics of the unborn child

368

an abortion. Although the frequency of abortions has not increased significantly since *Roe v. Wade* and is no greater than it was in the 1860s, abortion has become a major political issue in the United States (Doerr & Prescott, 1990, p. xv).

Infancy and Childhood

After a period when breast-feeding was not common, it appears to be increasing once again. Today 83 percent of mothers nurse their infants for at least six months, but not usually for much longer. Most American mothers stop nursing their children far short of the several years that is common in many of the world's nonindustrialized cultures.

Americans socialize their children differently, depending on the sex of the child. Symbolically, the color pink is associated with girls and blue with boys as appropriate for clothing and decorations of the baby's crib. It has been noted that mothers speak more to girl babies than to boys, and fathers tend to play in a rougher, more jostling fashion with their male children. Before six months of age, male babies are touched more frequently by their mothers than are girls, but after six months of age the opposite is true. Boys are given less emotional support throughout the rest of their lives and learn rapidly that "big boys don't cry." Instead of emotional support from others, they are encouraged to obtain pleasure from success in competition and in demonstrating skill and physical coordination. Girls are encouraged to take care in making themselves pretty, and their clothing is often designed more for eye appeal than for practicality in play. By and large, differences in the socialization of children reflect a stereotype of gender differences that views males as strong, active, unemotional, logical, dominant, independent, aggressive, and competitive and females as weak, passive, emotional, intuitive, supportive, dependent, sociable, status-conscious, shy, patient, and vain. In the past 20 years, stereotypes such as these have changed tremendously among university students, but there is little evidence that this is the case for American society at large.

Adolescence and Courtship

At 5 years of age, most American children are enrolled in school. Schooling is typically required by most states until the age of 16, which also is a common age for driving privileges to be obtained. There is no widespread practice of puberty rituals, and other adult rights and responsibilities, such as military service, voting rights, and the right to purchase alcoholic beverages, are acquired at different ages up to the age of 21. The absence of a clear-cut transition from childhood to adulthood results in a great deal of uncertainty and turmoil about appropriate role behavior during adolescence.

During the teenage period, American adolescents explore their identities as social beings as they practice the skills necessary to achieve an independent adult status. Acceptance by their peers becomes extremely important, and adolescents begin to create a sense of independent functioning by adopting new values that are in harmony with their peer group and with the social milieu outside their family. In this period of dating, adolescents begin to learn the skills of courtship and lay the foundations for their adult sexual identities. Although American ideals historically have required that both sex and pregnancy be delayed until after the marriage ceremony, the majority of both unmarried males and females experience sex by age 19. Tanfer and Horn (1985) found that in 1983, 82 percent of unmarried women aged 20 through 29 had experienced sexual intercourse. In 1989 there were 880,000 pregnancies among adolescent women aged 15 through 19. About 391,000 of these pregnancies were aborted, and about 312,500 babies were born out of wedlock. This represented 63.9 percent of all births to women of this age in that year (*Statistical Abstract of the United States,* 110th ed.).

Marriage

Americans are marrying later today than they were a generation ago. The median age of males marrying for the first time is nearly 26 years, and for females it is slightly over 23 years. The ideal of romantic love as a basis for marriage is perhaps nowhere else in the world so strongly supported as it is in the United States.

Why is romantic love such an important ideal in the American courtship and marriage system? One factor, certainly, is the economic unimportance of the nuclear family as a unit of production in American society. As industrialization undermined the economic role of the extended family, the marital choices of children grew increasingly independent of parental authority. As parental decision making in the choice

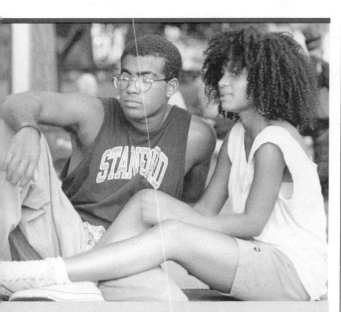

FIGURE 15.6 Romantic Love
Romantic love as a basis for marriage is a highly regarded value in the United States, even though its ideal still generally perpetuates the economic dependence of women on men.

marry a partner who lives within a few miles of them. Ineichen (1979) found that almost 65 percent of a sample of 232 married couples lived in the same city before they married, most of them coming from the same area or adjacent areas of the city.

Initial attraction is likely to be based on superficial, easily observable characteristics such as physical attractiveness, dress, and evidence of social power and prestige. After meeting one another, couples' compatibility of values and attitudes is especially important. Agreement on religious, sexual, familial, and political values is a good predictor of the development of a stable relationship (Kerkhoff, 1962). Burgess and Wallin (1953) found that engaged couples were remarkably similar in their physical attractiveness, physical health, mental health, social popularity, race, religion, parents' educational levels, parents' incomes, and the quality of their parents' marriages. Thus, similarity seems to be an important element in the attraction that leads to relationships.

The love ideal continues to shape relationships after marriage. S. S. Bean examined television soap operas for their portrayal of relationships within the family. Each weekday over 18 million Americans watch these dramatizations of human relationships, even though the basic story lines are repeated over and over. According to Bean, "The triangle involving ties of love and marriage with various complications is the most frequently occurring plot" (1981, p. 61). The American family is depicted in soap operas as composed of two sets of relationships: husband-wife and parent-child. Both are ideally composed of two and only two interacting persons. That is, problems arise in either relationship if the interactions involve three persons, as when either husband or wife becomes involved with another person, or when parents fail to relate as a unit to the child. Bean claims that according to the ideals held forth in soap operas, "The love between husband and wife is romantic love, the source of which is mysterious so that it may begin and may end suddenly. It just happens to people (one falls, not jumps)" (p. 70).

Illness

Americans predominantly espouse a secular, medical model of illness rather than a spiritual model. This feature corresponds to the existence of an extensive system of health care that is based on a scientific view of illness. Secular medicine has been successful enough in combating disease to make the

of mates declined, emotional attraction grew increasingly central to the process of mate selection. Another factor in the maintenance of the ideal of romantic love appears to be the dependent economic status of women. The romantic ideal stresses the role of women as objects of love, valued for their emotional, aesthetic, nurturing, and moral contributions to society rather than for their economic productivity and practical contributions outside the domestic sphere. Thus, the ideal of romantic love seems to play a role in perpetuating the economic dependence of women on men. This romanticism of women as love objects also explains why, contrary to the popular American stereotype, it seems to be men who are the more romantic sex among Americans. Zick Rubin (1973) studied attitudes of dating couples at the University of Michigan, and found that women were more likely than men to focus on practical issues in spouse selection rather than romantic considerations.

Just how does mate selection actually proceed? Several researchers suggest a model that involves a sequence of stages. First, proximity is an important factor. People are most likely to get together with those whom they are likely to encounter. Thus, in spite of their mobility, most Americans actually status of physician one of the most prestigious and well-paid in the American social system. In 1988, the average net income (take-home pay after expenses such as taxes and malpractice insurance) of an American medical doctor was $117,800. As of 1989, there were 548,000 medical doctors practicing in the United States. This means that there was one physician for about every 460 Americans in that year. In the same year, there were approximately 1,595,000 active registered nurses and 631,000 practical nurses in the United States, and over 3,000,000 auxiliary health workers such as nurse's aides, orderlies, attendants, and nonnursing health aides. As these figures suggest, health care is a major component of the American social and economic system. Without counting administrative personnel in hospitals, laboratory technicians, or paraprofessionals, nearly 1 in every 37 Americans is involved in the medical health care profession.

In 1992 there were about 7,000 hospitals and nearly 26,000 nursing homes in the United States and approximately one and one-third million hospital beds for patients. Given the large number of patients who must be dealt with in the hospital setting, it is understandable that hospital rules, regulations, and procedures generally are designed for the benefit of the hospital personnel—to make their work easier and more efficient. Although the standardization of hospital routines may have an overall effect of improved efficiency in patient care, one by-product of such standardization is a depersonalization of the patient as an individual. A person entering treatment in a hospital setting undergoes a status change, a loss of the usual prestige and access to decision-making power accorded normal members of society (Goffman, 1961). Patients are expected to give up their normal autonomy and to passively accept hospital routines and treatment procedures, despite the existence of a Patient's Bill of Rights since 1972. This document, formulated by the American Hospital Association and generally given to each patient as he or she is admitted, states, among others, the following major rights:

1. The patient has the right to considerate and respectful care.

2. The patient has the right to information concerning his diagnosis, treatment, and prognosis.

3. The patient has the right to enough information so that he or she can give informed consent to the procedure contemplated.

4. The patient has the right to refuse treatment to the extent permitted by law.

5. The patient has a right to every consideration of his or her privacy concerning his or her medical care. (adapted from *The World Almanac and Book of Facts, 1993,* p. 231)

Old Age and Death

In the United States, old age generally is thought of as beginning around the age of retirement from employment and the age of eligibility for old-age Social Security benefits. With retirement comes a loss of many of the usual activities and social contacts that make life meaningful for the active person, as well as a loss of the prestige and income associated with productive occupations. This stage of the life cycle is the one most likely to be described as a time of loneliness and boredom. The low level of prestige and power associated with old age qualifies the aged in America for a minority status.

Death in America has been largely removed from the familial context by other social institutions that have taken over the management of the dying and the dead. Hospitals and nursing homes care for the terminally ill and insulate the surviving family members from much of the dying process. Americans are likely to die in either a hospital or a nursing home, often in isolation from their family members. Traditionally, doctors and nurses have tended to avoid telling terminal patients that they were dying. A specialized funeral industry exists to take care of the practical necessities preparatory to burial, and to usher the survivors through the funeral and mourning process.

American Ideology

Despite its social diversity, the United States has not only a rather standardized approach to the life cycle but also a recognizable pattern of beliefs. Those explored here are religious ideology and the framework of American values and drives.

Religion in America

Americans tend to view the universe in mechanistic terms, and, historically, a scientific world view has been held central to their approach to everyday problems. The government recognizes no official religion, for the Bill of Rights of the United States Constitution guarantees a separation between church and state. Nevertheless, the American government traditionally has fostered religion in general, granting tax-exempt status to churches and their properties, while Americans as a people tend to view membership in a church, synagogue, or equivalent religious organization to be evidence of full allegiance to one's community. The church was once the center of local community life, and Americans still tend to participate in religious activities more frequently than do most Europeans.

Currently 65 percent of Americans hold formal membership in a religion, and about 40 percent attend religious services in a typical week (*The Statistical Abstract of the United States,* 110th ed., Table 76). Most belong to Christian churches, Protestant denominations being the most common. Judaism is America's most visible non-Christian religion, but one also finds Buddhists and Muslims in most American communities, as well as adherents of several other religions, especially indigenous varieties of Christianity. Native American religion and organized witchcraft are found throughout the country, but these have entered the mainstream consciousness less well than have the other organized religions. About 5 percent of Americans espouse no religious belief, and another 5 percent who do assert a belief in God or a Universal Spirit express no preference for a particular religion (the Gallup Report, 1985, pp. 13, 50). Interestingly, the American tendency to emphasize membership and participation in religious organizations over religious belief is also found among nonbelievers: for instance, the American Atheists have formed their own quasi-religious organization.

Bellah (1967), a Harvard sociologist who has specialized in the study of religion, has formulated a concept that the basic religious dimension of American life is a **civil religion** that coexists with the formally organized religions. The American civil religion is integrated into American social and political life and draws predominantly from Christianity and Judaism for its symbolism. Its God is the author of order, law, and morality and is actively involved in history, especially in American history, much like the God of ancient Israel. According to Bellah, the symbolism of American civil religion portrays America as the modern equivalent of the biblical Israel and the American Founding Fathers as the inspired prophets of American history. The Declaration of Independence, the Constitution, and Abraham Lincoln's Gettysburg Address are the three sacred documents of American civil religion. The first two grew out of the American Exodus from Europe, the symbolic Egypt from which God led people to the American Promised Land, which God set up as a light to all the world. Whereas Washington was the American Moses, Lincoln was the counterpart of Jesus, the wise and compassionate hero who counseled love of neighbor and whose life was taken by his enemies. Lincoln's Gettysburg Address, the New Testament of American sacred literature, is built around themes of death and rebirth such as "these honored dead," "conceived in liberty," and "a new birth of freedom." Bellah describes the calendar of the American civil religion as consisting of Memorial Day, on which American communities honor their martyred dead, Thanksgiving Day, which integrates the family into the civil religion in a ceremonial feast of thanks to God for the bounties of American life, and the less overtly religious holidays of the Fourth of July, Veterans Day, and the birthdays of Washington and Lincoln. The recent addition of Martin Luther King Jr.'s birthday to U.S. holidays, to symbolize and encourage interracial respect, may be viewed as an extension of the American sacred calendar since Bellah originally proposed it.

American Drives and Values

As we saw in looking at the components of culture in general (Chapter 2), every society has certain ideas about how people should relate to each other and to the universe. But human behavior is characteristically symbolic and therefore subject to diverse interpretations. Scholars have commonly asserted that these value systems and the behavior they guide may coalesce into distinctive patterns (Kroeber, 1944). And in a society with as large a population as that of the United States, the broad generalizations that are necessary for the formulation

---

civil religion   a system of religious beliefs and values that is integrated into the broader, nonreligious aspects of society and is shared by its members regardless of their affiliation with formally organized religious organizations; in America, a system of largely Judeo-Christian religious symbolism within which the American political system is portrayed as divinely sanctioned and American society is viewed as God's modern chosen people of abstract values do not apply uniformly to all American subcultures, either past or present.

Nevertheless, there does seem to be a fair consensus in the writings of anthropologists and sociologists about the most important values that typify the dominant American way of life. These include emphasis on personal goal-directed effort, individualism, progress, freedom, equality, democracy, and an external conformity that is personally motivated by love of country, cooperation for the common welfare, a sense of personal morality and fair play, or the desire for social acceptance.

Although a great deal of agreement exists about the specific values that find their place in the American ideology, social scientists differ with one another in their efforts to find a pattern in American values. One attempt to reduce the complexity in the diverse list of values that have been ascribed to American culture is that of Jules Henry (1963). Henry has suggested a distinction between what he calls drives and values. **Drives** are motives that people actually pursue, sometimes at great cost, rather than those to which they merely give lip service. Since it is in pursuit of their culture's drives that people invest their time and energy, drives represent the things that people value most strongly in the practical sense. They also are the source of stresses in life. What Henry calls **values** represent ideals that people long for but do not necessarily pursue. They are often opposites of drives, since they might give release from the stresses created by the pursuit of drives. Henry describes the roles of drives and values:

> Drives are what urge us blindly into getting bigger, into going further into outer space and into destructive competition; values are the sentiments that work in the opposite direction. Drives belong to the occupational world; values to the world of family and friendly intimacy. Drives animate the hurly-burly of business, the armed forces and all those parts of our culture where getting ahead, rising in social scale, outstripping others, and merely surviving in the struggle are the absorbing functions of life. When values appear in these areas, they act largely as brakes, on drivenness. (p. 14)

At the time of his writing early in the 1960s, Henry saw America as a culture driven by the needs for achievement, competition, profit, mobility, security, a higher standard of living, and expansiveness. American values—in effect, the things Americans long for as a result of being caught up by these drives—include such sentiments as love, kindness, quietness, contentment, fun, honesty, decency, relaxation, and simplicity.

Henry's drives may be understood as ideological reflections of the technologically and economically dictated means for achieving the necessities of life (see Table 15.5). Industrialization has created three prominent drives in American society: conformity, the work ethic, and competitiveness. These, colored by their counterbalancing values—self-reliance, fun, and personableness—can be seen as the basis of the distinctive pattern of American culture.

Conformity. All cultures impose a degree of **conformity** to socially determined norms, but not all peoples value conformity to the same degree or become driven by their efforts to conform. The drive to conform is typical of large-scale industrialized societies, because individuals in these societies make their living by selling their labor as a commodity. Income is partly contingent on conformity to the organizational and sometimes personal ideals by which supervisory personnel and management evaluate employees. Organizational efficiency is fostered by harmonious cooperation and "pulling together." Being "out of step," "rocking the boat," or "quota busting" are likely to be seen as forms of troublemaking precisely because they involve disruption of the routine of the group. One's economic security, personal prestige, and even status-linked rank are easily endangered by too much nonconformity.

The drive for conformity motivated by the need for greater security is manifest in several ways: allegiance to the nation, to one's occupation, religion, ethnic group, and race; cooperation for the common welfare; and support for equality. The Americans' allegiance to others seems largely motivated by the wish to avoid public criticism. It includes the positive sentiments of patriotism, loyalty, and love of country, but it is here that one also finds

---

drives the ideals that people actively pursue, sometimes at great cost, rather than those to which they merely give lip service

values subjective reactions to experiences expressed in terms of good or bad, moral or immoral; the ideals that people long for but do not necessarily pursue. Values are often opposites of drives

conformity a central drive in American culture, motivated by the obligation to defer to the authority of others in many areas of life

TABLE 15.5   The Relationship Between Drives and Values in American Culture

Social Traits Resulting from Industrialization and Role Specialization	Resulting Drives	Subtypes and Examples of Drives	Counter-Balancing Values	Examples of Values
Dependent status in employment ("self-alienation")	Conformity	*Allegiance* in-group sentiments; ethnocentrism; xenophobia; patriotism *Cooperation* obedience to authority; respect for law and office; opposition to boat-rocking and trouble-making *Equality* equality of opportunity; good citizenship; denial of class distinctions; mass education; democracy	Self-reliance	Freedom, autonomy, independence; the Marlborough Man; hero worship; preference for charismatic leaders; opposition to authority figures (politicians, etc.); desire for popularity; self-discovery; self-fulfilled meditation; favoring the underdog
Nonownership of products of own labor ("object alienation")	Work ethic (i.e., work is good in its own right, instead of in terms of its products)	*Optimism* future-orientation; desire for progress, improvement, getting ahead *Energy/Effort* effort-optimism; personal effort, vigor, and initiative; opposition to laziness and sensuality of youth *Purposefulness* purposeful recreation; pragmatic ingenuity; diligence; applied knowledge	Hedonism/ Pleasure/ Aesthetics	Spontaneity and "nowism"; pleasure, relaxation, existentialism; veneration of wisdom and maturity; Santa Claus; nostalgia for carefree days of youth; desire for loss of control, "letting one's hair down," "getting crazy," and being taken care of; reckless abandon
Insecure status ("social alienation")	Competitiveness	*Competition* competition in recreation, scorekeeping; oneupmanship; status climbing and desire for upward mobility; free enterprise system; multiple party system in government *Materialism* material acquisitiveness; profit motive; quest for luxuries; high standard of living; conspicuous consumption; "keeping up with the Joneses" *Mobility* physical mobility; expansiveness; desirability for change and novelty; American restlessness; wanderlust	Personableness	Generosity, charity, kindness; relaxation of interpersonal relationships; love; openness; honesty; resentment of quota-busting over-achievement and those in high office; desire for physical security; desire for simplicity; idyllic pastoral existence; myth of the Noble Savage; American familialism; nostalgia for "good old days," roots; desire for security, stability

FIGURE 15.7   Conformity
Conformity is typical of large-scale industrialized societies, because income is largely determined by the ability of individuals to cooperate within the structure of the group. Allegiances to one's occupation, religion, race, or team is instilled at a young age. These All-American cheerleaders of the National Cheerleading Association huddle on the steps of the American Museum of Natural History in the rain awaiting the start of Macy's Thanksgiving Day Parade in New York City.

the darker side of American drives: ethnocentrism, antipathies toward outsiders or foreigners, racism, and sexism.

Conformity in America, Germany, and Japan

Although America shares a drive for conformity with other cultures, especially with other industrialized nations, the specific influence that this drive has is tempered by various other factors, such as how formally or informally it is taught, and how other drives and values modify the manifestations of conformity. German and Japanese cultures also emphasize conformity. Both differ from American culture in teaching this drive more explicitly and formally.

The traditional German emphasis on the importance of order in social life, orderliness in private life, and respect for authority and obedience are all summed up in the common expression, *Ordnung muss sein!* ("There must be order!"). The typical heroes of traditional German literature were individuals who because of a personal flaw of character were unable to conform to the dictates of the social order and who were tragically doomed because of this flaw. All this explicit emphasis on the subordination of individual needs to the society's need for order is likely to strike the American as too intolerant of individual differences and too restrictive of individual freedom to be palatable. Americans, too, conform, but they learn this drive more informally and are less conscious of conforming to society's rules for living. The American drive for conformity is ironically overshadowed by strong support for the value of self-reliance. American conformity is more a result of a search for friendship, respect, social power, and income, or of avoiding rejection, than it is a formal recognition of the importance of social order for its own sake. Americans are much more likely than are Germans to describe their conformity as a simple by-product of their personal and inner-regulated morality or their desire to be good neighbors, rather than as evidence of respect for the authority of society as a whole over their lives as individuals.

The Japanese, whom Germans have called "the Germans of the East," have a similarly formal emphasis on the importance of conformity to the rules of social life, but they place greater emphasis on the necessity of orders being imposed from those of higher authority. At the same time, they express more ambivalence about this state of affairs. Like Americans, the Japanese stress the importance of competition and success, but their emphasis is on competition between groups rather than individuals. Loyalty to the team counts more heavily than the individual's ability to excel. Whiting (1979) has compared the Japanese and American approaches to baseball and reports a consistent Japanese willingness to sacrifice outstanding individual team members when their lack of cooperative team spirit threatens the sense of *wa*, or group harmony. Whiting summarizes the different feelings about individualism and cooperation in the two cultures:

> The U.S. is a land where the stubborn individualist is honored and where "doing your own thing" is a motto of contemporary society. In Japan, kojinshugi, the term for individualism, is almost a dirty word. In place of "doing your own thing," the Japanese have a proverb: "The nail that sticks up shall be hammered down." It is practically a national slogan. (p. 60)

Self-reliance. The drives of conformity are counterbalanced by idealized values of **self-reliance**, expressed in praise of freedom, liberty, grass-roots government, and independence. The value placed on autonomy is manifest in the glorification of such heroes as Daniel Boone, John Wayne, James Bond, Luke Skywalker, and Indiana Jones who embody the traits of rugged individualism, self-motivation, and self-reliance. The well-known American distaste for politics and the commonly held view that "all politicians are crooks" are expressions of antipathy for "the Establishment," the system of authority that requires conformity. Americans prefer to follow the political leaders who show charisma in handling themselves, thereby "rising above the office." The desire for popularity is a more personal expression of this same value, as is rooting for the underdog and the covert admiration that Americans tend to feel for the individual who stands up against great odds or successfully "bucks the system." (This can be illustrated by the real-life popularity of Ross Perot in the 1992 elections, and by the success of such films as *Indiana Jones and the Temple of Doom, Star Wars,* and *Death Wish.*) The overcoming of impossibly powerful adversaries by a hero with great personal skill is perhaps the most common theme in American literature, and the great popularity of the James Bond movies in the 1960s and the Rocky and Rambo movies in the 1980s illustrates how long-lived this value has been during a quarter-century of great change.

Traditionally, the value of self-reliance has been especially emphasized for men, but women have become increasingly more self-reliant and powerful in American society. This change is also being expressed in the more frequent portrayal of self-reliant women in American films such as *Alien, Thelma and Louise,* and *Norma Rae.*

Francis Hsu believes that self-reliance in America is the central preoccupation from which all our other values arise. Hsu's self-reliance has as its primary psychological manifestation the fear of dependence. He contrasts Chinese and American society in respect to the ideal of self-reliance:

> A man in traditional China where self-reliance was not an ideal may have been unsuccessful in his life. But suppose in his old age his sons were able to provide for him generously. Such a person not only was happy and content about it; he was likely also to beat the drums before all and sundry to let the world know that he had good children who were supporting him in a style to which he had never been accustomed. On the other hand, an American parent who has not been successful in life may derive some benefit from the prosperity of his children, but he certainly will not want anybody to know about it. In fact, he will resent any reference to it. At the first opportunity when it is possible for him to become independent of his children, he will do so.
>
> Therefore, even though we may find many individuals in traditional China and elsewhere who were in fact self-sufficient, and even though we may find individuals in America who are in fact dependent upon others, the important thing is that where self-reliance is not an ideal, it is neither promoted nor a matter of pride, but where it is an ideal, it is both. In American society the fear of dependence is so great that an individual who is not self-reliant is a misfit. "Dependent character" is a highly derogatory term, and a person so described is thought to be in need of psychiatric help. (1961, p. 250)

Hsu argues that self-reliance is actually an impossible goal to achieve. Human society is based on mutual dependence on our fellow human beings, and no one can meet his or her technological, social, intellectual, or emotional needs in isolation. Therefore, Hsu believes that the American ideal of self-reliance creates contradictions that lead to insecurity in the lives of individuals: Self-reliance means imperma-

---

self-reliance a value central to Americans that emphasizes the importance of independence, autonomy of the individual, and the primacy of the individual over the group

376

nence in relationships and competition for status, which in turn requires conformity to organizations or peer groups. "In other words," Hsu explains, "to live up to their core value orientation of self-reliance, Americans as a whole have to do much of its opposite. Expressed in the jargon of science, there is a direct relationship between self-reliance and individual freedom on the one hand and submission to organizations and conformity on the other" (p. 250).

The work ethic. An industrial technology leads to a high degree of labor specialization, in which many individuals must work competitively to produce goods that they themselves do not own and that will be consumed by others. Under such circumstances, it is the labor itself that is rewarded, and work becomes a drive in its own right rather than simply the necessary means to create something of significant value to the worker. This **work ethic** may develop under other circumstances in societies with a nonindustrialized technology, but it would seem to be an inevitable drive wherever industrialization is prominent.

In normal day-to-day terms, it is work of a practical nature rather than work for work's sake that is likely to receive the greatest reward. Therefore, the work ethic is best understood as a drive that is more or less synonymous with a positive attitude toward pragmatic effort or accomplishment. The person who is well socialized for living in accordance with a work ethic will be optimistic, energetic, and purposeful. The specific evidences of a work ethic are manifestations of one of these three aspects.

Optimism is a positive expectation that the future is potentially better than the present state of affairs. In America one finds a traditional emphasis on progress, improvement, diligence, getting ahead, the expectation that children should grow up to be better and more successful than their parents, and the idea that, no matter how badly things are going, "Tomorrow is another day."

The emphasis placed on **energy** includes positive reactions to such traits as vigor, activity, personal effort, and initiative, as well as negative responses to "laziness," passivity, and sensuality. In the opinion of Cora DuBois (1955), these traits form the underlying basis of the "cult of youthfulness" for which Americans are still famous.

Where a work ethic is prominent, effort of any kind will be admired. But effort directed purposefully toward the achievement of specific ends will be more applauded than effort for which no clear

purpose is evident. **Purposefulness** as an aspect of the work ethic is manifest in the national emphasis on pragmatism, ingenuity, inventiveness, and applied science, and in the attitude that recreation, vacations, and other pleasurable activities should be undertaken because they are beneficial rather than for the sake of the pleasure itself. For instance, when I was a child, my father emphasized that meals should not be eaten for the pleasure of eating, but because food is neces-

work ethic a central drive of American culture in which work is felt to be good in and of itself—a feeling fostered by an economic system in which individuals must work competitively to produce goods that they themselves do not own and that will be consumed by others

optimism a positive American expectation—fostered by the work ethic—that the future is potentially better than the present

energy a positive American reaction—fostered by the work ethic—to such traits as vigor, activity, personal effort, initiative, and youthfulness

purposefulness a manifestation of the American work ethic that asserts the importance of goal-directed effort

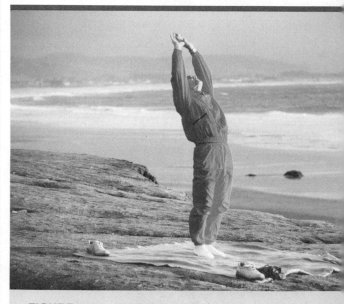

FIGURE 15.8 Relaxation

As a counterpoint to the overriding drive of purposefulness, one component of the work ethic, Americans find many ways to relax. While some choose to be spectators at concerts or sports events, or rent movies for their VCR, others choose to relax by running, working out in the gym, or meditating.

FIGURE 15.9   Thrill Seeking
In a society that is statistically aging, youthfulness is still the ideal. This is manifest not only in dress styles and the promotion of slender bodies through advertising, but also through the popularity of such thrill-seeking activities as white water rafting, parasailing, and bungee jumping. Despite the authorities' concern for its danger, many people still choose to throw themselves over a cliff attached to it by nothing but an elastic cord around their ankle.

sary so that one can work. He also insisted that the only good music is music with lyrics that convey a message. The value of purposefulness also was manifest in the attitude common among Americans of several generations ago that sex should be for procreation and not merely for pleasure. Of the three components of the work ethic, purposefulness seems to have remained the most prominent into the 1990s, while optimism in particular has become much less common as the gap has widened between the haves and the have-nots.

The idealized values that serve as brakes on these work ethic drives of future-oriented optimism, energetic effort, and purposefulness are nostalgia for the "good old days" (the presumably carefree, less hectic days of the past), relaxation, and fun. The latter is the value placed on spontaneity and the "Be

here now" existential philosophy, the desire for enjoyment and pleasurable recreation, and the covert admiration for disaster-courting thrill-seekers.

Competitiveness. Along with conformity and the work ethic, **competitiveness** is the third major American drive. Like the others, its existence is inherent in an industrialized society. In such social systems, the products of labor usually are owned by someone other than the worker who produces them, and the working person generally is dependent on someone else for his or her livelihood. Since these conditions prevail in America, Americans must sell their labor as if it were a commodity. Economic statuses are insecure and dependent because they are organized around authority relationships, and because holding them successfully is predicated on "selling oneself" effectively. It is the insecurity of American life that is the basis for the emphasis on the "spirit of competition."

Within the economic sphere, this drive manifests itself in the recurrent praise of the profit motive and the ideal of a free enterprise system, one in which economic competition is unhindered by noneconomic forces. Socially, the concept of enlightened self-interest is an attempt to reconcile the potential conflicts between drives of competition and drives of conformity, as noted by the French nobleman Alexis de Tocqueville over 100 years ago:

> In the United States there is hardly any talk of the beauty of virtue. But they maintain that virtue is useful and prove it every day. American moralists do not pretend that one must sacrifice himself for his fellows because it is a fine thing to do so. But they boldly assert that such sacrifice is as necessary for the man who makes it as for the beneficiaries. (republished, 1969, p. 525)

Status climbing and upward social mobility are American drives derived from competitive circumstances. The extreme emphasis on competition as a social good even carries over into the realm of relaxation and recreation. Even though Americans assert the idealized value that "it's not who wins the game that counts, but how you play the game," this statement is probably best understood as a wistful but

competitiveness a central drive in American culture—fostered by the need to sell one's labor as a commodity—that emphasizes excelling over others

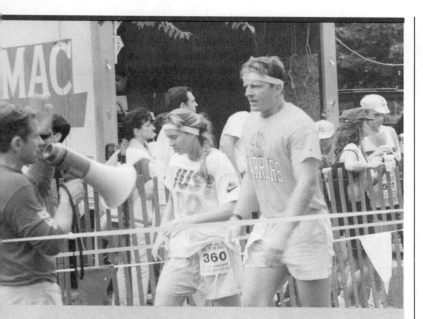

FIGURE 15.10   Competition
Competitiveness is a major drive in the American psyche manifesting itself in economic situations, social situations, and in sports.

The Changing Context of American Values and Drives

The difference between American values and drives and those emphasized in other industrialized societies may reflect the evolutionary adaptation of American society to its unique social and physical environments. Historically, America was one of the first societies in which the benefits of industrialization could be obtained by building a society to fit the growing technological apparatus, rather than by trying to fit an industrialized economy into a pre-existing social order. In America, factories could be built to house the new tools instead of trying to fit equipment into the buildings of a previous generation, as was done in Europe. Cities grew up in a frontier society, and their form could be guided by technological and economic needs as they arose. In Europe, centuries-old cities that had grown up reflecting the needs of a preindustrial age were a factor with which the new technology had to cope. America's backwater frontier status was therefore an advantage that made it possible to obtain the greatest social benefits from its developing way of life.

Population patterns.   The population of the United States has been growing at an accelerating rate throughout most of its history (see Fig. 15.11). One important implication of this growth was what appeared to be an ever-expanding consumer market. This social condition encouraged technological growth and economic expansion. In the early phase of industrialization, the amazing material output of this new mode of production encouraged rapid population growth, since consumers were needed to use the goods that were manufactured. Much of this growth was accomplished through a rapid influx of immigrant consumer/workers. Yet, there are limits on the number of people who can be supported by any mode of production. The more closely the limit is approached, the more that members of the growing population must compete with one another to obtain both jobs and access to products. The growing competition results in increasing costs to obtain the necessities of life, which eventually must counterbalance the forces that induced the initial rapid population growth.

Thus, at some point, the rate of growth begins to decelerate. In the United States, it took almost two centuries for this deceleration to begin. It was not until the early 1960s that the rate of American

unrealistic protestation against the practicalities of a way of life in which "nice guys finish last." Americans continue to teach their children to keep score when playing games, a practice that the traditional Zuñi of the American Southwest would have eschewed as abhorrent.

American material acquisitiveness also must be seen as a manifestation of competitiveness. In a society in which, by Old World standards, the majority has never suffered from a lack of physical security or even luxury, materialism is best understood not as physical need but as a manifestation of the competitive desire to "keep up with the Joneses," that is, as evidence of one's competitive success. Social movement often is accompanied by physical mobility—the expansiveness of American society and the "don't fence me in" restlessness.

The idealized values that counter the implicit conflict and potential hostility in competition include relaxed interpersonal relations, friendliness, frankness, love, kindness, decency, openness, and good sportsmanship. Charity and generosity also are valued as contrasts to the drive to make a profit. Simplicity, idealization of the idyllic pastoral life, and the myth of the noble savage are values that counterbalance the drives of material acquisitiveness.

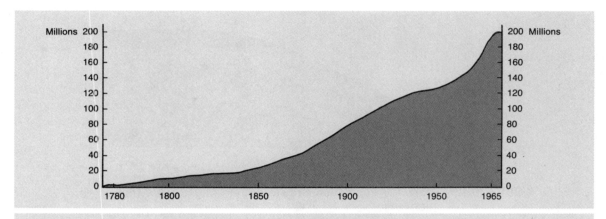

FIGURE 15.11   Population Growth in the United States from 1780–1965
In the early period of industrialization, population growth is encouraged by an expanding consumer market and an expanding industry to accommodate the growing need for jobs, which in turn creates new goods for the expanding market. This period of growth is obvious through 1965 in the United States.

Source: Statistical Abstract of the United States: 1986 (106th ed.) [Table No. 1, p. 5], by U.S. Bureau of the Census, 1985, Washington, DC: U.S. Government Printing Office.

population growth stopped increasing. Since then, although it still is growing, it has been doing so at an ever-slowing rate. If this trend continues, it is estimated that the population of the United States will reach 310.8 million in 2080 (see Fig. 15.12). Most of the growth will occur by 2030, when the population will be about 304.8 million. After 2030 the growth rate will be relatively slow. If the growth rate were not to decelerate, the competition for the goods produced would be so great that it would result in a decline in the standard of living of the population as a whole. Thus, it is likely that the total population will finally level off. Given these past population changes, current patterns, and projected changes, it is possible to consider the implications of population growth rates on American ideology during three phases of population growth: the initial period of accelerating growth, the current period of decelerating growth, and the projected period of nongrowth in the population.

The period of growth.   During the initial period of industrialization in the United States, the population was growing at a faster rate each decade. The internal consumer market seemed to offer unlimited potential for the expansion of sales. The same population growth represented a growing number of people in need of jobs, a further reason for expansion

of industry. Under such circumstances it is no surprise that growth would be equated with progress and bigger with better, while material acquisitiveness would be seen by many as a basic aspect of human nature. The traditional American value system and drives have their roots in the social conditions of this period.

The surplus output of the new industrial system made it possible to drain off some of the capital to expand the industrial mechanism itself, while still leaving enough to support the workers. Major public works projects such as highways, hydroelectric dams, airports, and mass public educational facilities could be financed by creating debts that would have to be paid back by future citizens. Since the population was growing at an accelerating rate, this meant that the costs of growth would be spread out more and more thinly with each year.

The period of transition.   In the 1960s, however, important changes in American values developed. The cost of living grew rapidly, affecting childrearing expenses. As the fertility rate fell, population growth decelerated. Middle-class families found it increasingly difficult to maintain their standard of living unless both spouses were employed. The divorce rate continued to grow tremendously during this period. During the 1960s the United

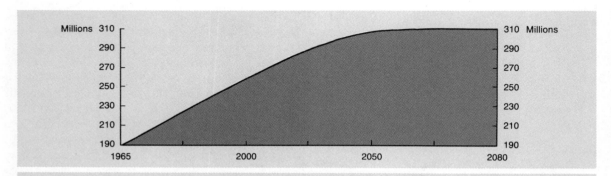

FIGURE 15.12   Projected Population Growth in the United States from 1965–2080

When a growing population begins to compete for the available goods and services, the standard of living begins to stabilize and population growth decelerates. This period began in the 1960s in the United States. It is projected that population growth will level off by the year 2030.

Source: Statistical Abstract of the United States: 1986 (106th ed.) [Table No. 1, p. 5], by U.S. Bureau of the Census, 1985, Washington, DC: U.S. Government Printing Office. Also from "Projections of the Population of the United States by Age, Sex and Race: 1983–2080" in *Current Population Reports: Population Estimates and Projections* (Series P-25, No. 952) [Table 2, p. 30], by U.S. Bureau of the Census, 1984, Washington, DC: U.S. Government Printing Office.

States also was becoming more and more heavily involved in an unpopular foreign war.

The initial ideological response to these changing social circumstances took form during the political and social turmoil of the student and minority protests of the 1960s. During this period, many people noted the discrepancy between traditional drives and values and the current social circumstances. They formulated a new ideology—called the **counterculture**—with its own system of values and drives as a part of their opposition to the established social order.

Born in a period of intense political activism, the central counterculture drive was one that is necessary when people attempt to establish any new political movement: conformity to the ideas and practices of the new movement. Members of the counterculture were expected to be politically active in anti-war and "anti-Establishment" programs. These included a variety of symbolic shock tactics such as the adopting of radically new modes of dress, grooming, and language, and the espousal, at least verbally, of new and more permissive sexual customs. These behaviors had two important functions: (1) They were forms of political expression aimed at directly challenging customary, taken-for-granted symbols of conformity to the traditional social sys-tem; and (2) they simultaneously served as new symbols of group membership and cohesiveness. In the counterculture movement, failure to conform to the new group standards and failure to adopt an activist posture brought loss of esteem and personal distress.

As an offsetting value, the counterculture maintained the traditional American emphasis on self-reliance. But this established American value was spoken of in ways that contrasted with the usual ways of glorifying self-reliance. Counterculture self-reliance was described as noncompetitive individualism that rejected the traditional emphasis on acquisition of luxuries, rank within the established social order, and conformity to traditional morality.

Although the counterculture valued conformity and self-reliance, as did the mainstream culture, counterculture values did fundamentally diverge from those of the established value system in certain

counterculture   a movement of the 1960s that, in response to the increasing cost of living and the perceived unresponsiveness of the established political environment to people's changing needs and goals, attempted to reformulate the American value system by inverting many traditional values areas: (1) the rejection of materialism, monetary success, traditional education, pragmatic scientific rationality, efficiency, and cost-effectiveness as rationales for decisions, (2) an emphasis on sensory experiences and introspection as a source of knowledge in preference to abstract conceptual logic and objectivity, and (3) a quest for a return to harmony with nature as opposed to mastery over nature.

The period of stabilization. The counterculture was the initial awakening to the fact that traditional American values no longer fit the new social conditions. Nevertheless, its ideology was largely a reaction against the contemporary political and economic conditions of its day and not a true adjustment to the social conditions that have prevailed since the rate of population growth began to decline. As such, it was doomed to fall by the wayside as the mainstream American system of values and drives gradually were adjusted to the problems that arise when a society approaches the upper limits of its social and economic growth.

Following the 1960s, these new values and drives began to impress themselves on the public consciousness. The changes that reflect these new values and drives have been described commonly, if not completely accurately, as a return to political conservatism, a reawakening of religious fundamentalism, a decline in optimism, and a reassertion of a practical interest in job security. Perhaps the major change within the American system of drives and values has been a shift within the work ethic away from the optimism drives—such as the traditional emphasis on progress, getting ahead, and the future—toward a greater drive for achieving security in the present. Before the 1970s the word *progress* was equated with change of almost any kind. America was one of the few places where, instead of being encouraged to grow up to be just like their parents, children were expected to learn more and achieve a higher standard of living than their parents had. This is no longer so. Now the goal of young adults is the much less expansive one of achieving economic security or of simply "making ends meet."

Probably the two most fundamental changes in American ideology that have resulted from the economic pressures of the sixties through the eighties have been changes in ideas about the roles of men and women and changes in attitudes toward sex. The pre-sixties idea that a married woman should be economically dependent on a working husband has ceased to be feasible. It is not surprising, then, that not only has it become acceptable for women to seek employment, but Americans also increasingly view an economically productive life as essential to a woman's self-fulfillment as a person.

Childrearing is now extremely costly. Today it costs well over $250,000 to raise a child through four years of college. It is certainly not surprising, then, that the average couple now has fewer than two children. The turn-of-the-century attitude that procreation was the only acceptable reason for sex is no longer tenable as the primary way in which Americans view their sexual lives. Increasingly, Americans are understanding sex primarily in the context of pleasure rather than reproduction.

The desire for economic security has shown itself in enrollment trends in American universities. Enrollments have shifted in the past decade away from the humanities, arts, and social sciences toward applied fields that offer a more secure promise of employment. On the job, the traditional American value of expansiveness has declined, and workers are changing jobs less frequently than they used to, even within companies. The desire for a greater sense of security also may be seen in trends toward more conservative political views, the rise of the yuppie attitude, and in a reawakening of religious interests. The percentage of Americans today who are members of a church is greater than it was a generation ago. The 1970s and 1980s also saw a resurgence of religious fundamentalism and political conservatism among members of society who have felt particularly disenfranchised by the continuing trend of secularization within society at large.

The second major change in American drives has been in the acquisition of material goods. Although this drive is still with us, the role of **conspicuous consumption**—the acquisition and use of a surplus of goods as a way of competitively demonstrating one's success and prestige—is becoming less feasible for Americans. Instead, there is a growing emphasis on finding ways to conserve and extend the life of material goods. This trend is seen in such examples as the increasing popularity of smaller automobiles with greater gasoline mileage, the frequent discussion by the news media of ways in which conservation of energy and natural resources can be supported

———

conspicuous consumption   the acquisition and use of a surplus of goods as a way of competitively demonstrating one's success and prestige

382

by citizens, the extension of tax credits for home insulation, the establishment of recycling centers, and the passage of laws that require environmental impact studies before major building projects are undertaken.

If American population growth patterns continue as has been predicted, stability rather than change will be the order of the day. Upward social mobility may be expected to become increasingly difficult as that stabilization is approached. The role of universities as a traditional means for upward mobility is likely to decline as the costs of a university education continue to grow beyond the means of more of the population. This process alone may ensure that the most prestigious occupations in the American economy will become more or less self-perpetuating across generations: Those who can afford to support their children through a university education will be those whose income is great enough to do so by virtue of their own university degrees. For reasons of political tradition, Americans may remain resistant to any official recognition of classes. Nevertheless, it is unlikely that we will remain as successful during the coming half century as we have been in the past at denying that there are differences in income, power, and prestige within our society.

It may be argued that many of our problems as a society have been intimately linked to the rapid pace of change in American life throughout most of our history, and that with stability may come a lessening of many of these problems. At the same time, however, a greater awareness of the effects of social, cultural, and subcultural differences on our way of life—a major concern of the field of anthropology—is likely to be crucial if a harmonious stability is to be achieved. Certainly, a more widespread recognition of the existence of social differences will make it more difficult to perpetuate the extremes of inequality that have long characterized U.S. society.

I will remind those of you who are not consoled by such thoughts that the very best of us these days are poor prophets, and the scenario of stability that I have sketched may not come to pass. The potentials embodied in new technologies such as computer communications and atomic or solar power—if they can be harnessed successfully for mass consumption—could bring about vast and beneficent changes in the lives of most Americans if they are ever developed to their full extent. Even more dramatic means for raising our standard of living as a society may yet be discovered. These as well as more tragic unpredictables, such as nuclear war, may circumvent the scenario that I have suggested as our most likely future. Yet, until those unpredictables become facts instead of mere possibilities, a course toward greater social stability appears to be most likely in the next century.

External relations are another matter. As the effects of industrialization continue to spread around the world at the expense of technologically less complex ways of life, the cultures of the world are becoming more and more economically and politically interdependent. In this broader context, our future depends on what happens abroad as well as at home. Our relations with developing nations are likely to remain in a continuing state of flux as industrialization spreads and new power blocs and coalitions develop with the goal of ensuring the political and economic self-interest of developing nations. How we shall fare in this process will depend largely on a recognition that our own national self-interest is not likely to be furthered in the long run by a narrowly ethnocentric view of the other cultures with which we share the world.

CHAPTER SUMMARY

1. In contrast to the American ideal of a classless society with equality of opportunity, the reality is an unequal distribution of wealth and status that may stabilize or become more distinct in the near future.

2. In contrast to the ideal of a peace-loving people, the United States has a high rate of crime.

3. Families, assumed to be the core of society, have little power and often are broken by divorce.

4. Birth is being treated more personally than in the past, but socialization of children perpetuates outdated stereotypes.

5. Adolescents turn to their peer groups for socialization and sex, with a high rate of teenage pregnancies. Marriages are occurring later and breaking up sooner.

6. Illness is treated according to a medical model, with the elderly placed in institutions to die.

7. In terms of ideology, the majority of Americans belong to some religious group or perhaps subscribe to the patriotic "civil religion."

8. Driven by an emphasis on conformity, the work ethic, and competitiveness, Americans tend to balance these drives with contrasting values, such as love of fun, charity, and nostalgia for simpler times.

9. As the limits to growth are approached, the mainstream seems to be turning toward an emphasis on security and on conservative use of resources.

ANNOTATED READINGS

de Toqueville, A. (1945). *Democracy in America*. New York: A. A. Knopf. Originally published in 1835, this classic description of American life was so insightful that it still rings true today.

Ginsberg, F. (1989). *Contested lives: The abortion debate in an American community*. Berkeley, CA: University of California Press. An ethnographic study of the grass roots abortion politics in an American community.

Gorer, G. (1964). *The American people: A study in national character*. New York: W. W. Norton & Company. Revision of a classic description of the United States.

Harris, M. (1981). *America now: The anthropology of a changing culture*. New York: Simon & Schuster. A provocative look at the effects of technological and economic change in American culture since World War II.

Hsu, F. L. K. (1983). *Rugged individualism reconsidered: Essays in psychological anthropology*. Knoxville, TN: University of Tennessee Press. Comparisons of traditional Chinese and American cultures by an anthropologist who was born in China.

Jorgensen, J. G., & Truzzi, M. (1974). *Anthropology and American life*. Englewood Cliffs, NJ: Prentice Hall. A useful collection of articles by anthropologists on American culture.

Moffatt, M. (1989). *Coming of age in New Jersey: College and American culture*. New Brunswick, NJ: Rutgers University Press. A fascinating anthropological study of the sexual and academic adventures of adolescents at a major American university in the 1980s.

Schneider, D. M. (1968). *American kinship: A cultural account*. Englewood Cliffs, NJ: Prentice Hall. An examination of the role of kinship in the U.S.

Warner, W. L. (1953). *American life: Dream and reality*. Chicago: University of Chicago Press. An early study by an anthropologist of life in a U.S. city.

West, J. (1945). *Plainville, U.S.A.* New York: Columbia University Press. One of the first descriptions by an anthropologist of life in a small U.S. town.

GLOSSARY

Page references indicate where term is defined.

acculturation the process in which one culture adapts to the influence of another culture by borrowing many of its traits 327, 335

achieved statuses social positions that one acquires by demonstrating the necessary role-playing abilities 129

adaptation adjustment of an organism to a particular environment 60

aesthetic experience the pleasure we feel when we recognize something as beautiful 306

aesthetic locus the area of a culture to which a society devotes its aesthetic effort 304

aesthetics the rules by which beauty is to be evaluated in a culture 304

affectlessness the complete control of emotion resulting in lethargy 287

agriculture the intensive working of land for food production through the use of tools and techniques such as the plow, irrigation, soil fertilization, and animal traction 74

alienation dissociation of workers from ownership of things they produce, accompanied by feelings of powerlessness and boredom 332

allomorphs variants of a single morpheme that have the same meaning but different phonological structure 232

allophones phonetically variant forms of a single phoneme 231

altered state of consciousness subjective state of mind where experiences are not interpreted in terms of normal symbolic categories of one's culture 287

ambilineal descent a system of tracing descent through a parent of either sex, choosing only one parent for each link that connects a group of relatives 157

ambilineal descent group a system of tracing social groups based on an ambilineal descent system 160

ambilocality the custom in which the residence for a newly married couple may be in the home of either the bride or groom 191

American Anthropological Association major professional organization for anthropologists in the United States 20

American Sign Language (ASL) a system of hand gesture symbols used by hearing-impaired persons for communicating. Although it is not a verbal system of symbols, ASL may be seen as a true nonverbal language, since it has its own grammar and vocabulary and is not simply a gestural copy of spoken language 228

amok a culture-specific hysterical disorder in which young men attack other people and destroy property 294

amurakh a culture-specific hysterical disorder that is characterized by compulsive imitation of sounds and gestures 295

ancestral spirits souls of ancestors who remain interested and involved in affairs of their descendants 249

anger an emotional state during which another person is held responsible for one's own distress. Anger can substitute for anxiety, fear, guilt, grief, or shame in situations in which those emotions might otherwise be felt 285

animal-focused foraging fish and animal life provide basic food supply where plants are scarce 66

anorexia nervosa a culture-specific obsessive-compulsive disorder characterized by an unrealistic appraisal of one's own body as overweight and by self-starvation 299

anthropological linguists cultural anthropologists who specialize in the study of communication, human languages, and their role in human social life 8

anthropomorphism using human qualities to explain the nonhuman realm; interpreting or acting toward the nonhuman realm as if it were human, especially as if it were able to respond to symbolic communication 245

antinatalist societies those whose customs favor low birth rates and thus permit abortion and infanticide 134

anxiety a distressful subjective awareness of stress; a general sense of powerlessness and foreboding without awareness of a specific danger 285

applied anthropology the attempt to use anthropological skills and insights to aid in the process of cultural development in nonindustrialized parts of the world or to aid in private and public policy making 348

archaeologists cultural anthropologists who study the material remains of earlier societies in order to reconstruct their cultures 6

arctic hysteria (amurakh) a culture-specific hysterical disorder that is characterized by compulsive imitation of sounds and gestures 295

arid lands areas of low annual rainfall and sparse cover with low-growing desert shrubs 59

art a cultural expression of feeling and meaning in a form that evokes an aesthetic experience in the participant or observer 308

ascribed statuses social positions that one is assumed to occupy by virtue of the group into which one happens to be born—for instance, one's sex or race 129

association cortex the area of the cerebral cortex that coordinates information from various other parts of the brain 228

attitude a subjective reaction to an experience expressed in positive or negative terms 30

authority the legitimate right, delegated to a person, to use power or force 102

avunculocality the custom in which the newly married couple establishes residence with or near the groom's mother's brother 192

balanced reciprocity gift given with expectation of a return gift shortly 87

band a seminomadic, kinship-based society with no full-time government, economically based on a foraging subsistence technology 63, 102

barter form of exchange of goods by trading 94

Basic Law of Cultural Evolution concept that increases in energy harnessed or in efficiency of its use through technological change are the primary cause of cultural evolution 328

basic personality structure Kardiner's term for the adaptive tools used by all individuals in a particular society 277

basic vocabulary the part of a vocabulary that one learns early in life in the home setting 237

behavioral superstructure those behaviors most closely linked to a culture's ideology, including art, ritual, recreation, philosophy, science 51

beliefs ideas people hold about what is factual or real 26

berdache a social status in which males and females adopt the role of the other sex, considered a third gender in some societies 201

bifurcate merging kinship terminology derived from contrast between maternal and paternal relatives using a small number of kin

terms to refer to many different kin 167

bigmanship economic entrepreneurship by persons in horticulture societies who encourage economic production and gift giving in their communities to achieve public recognition and respect 91

bilateral cross-cousin marriage (sister exchange) cross-cousin marriage in which a brother and sister marry cross cousins who are also brother and sister 188

bilateral descent a system of tracing descent lines equally through both parents 156

bilateral descent groups those whose members share a living relative 160

bilocality (ambilocality) the custom in which a newly married couple may elect to set up residence with or near either the bride's or the groom's family 191

bint'amm patrilateral parallel-cousin marriage 188

biological and psychological needs the needs for nutrition, reproduction, bodily comforts, safety, relaxation, movement, and growth 46

biological anthropologist physical anthropologist 8

biological death measured by cessation of such organic functions as breathing, heartbeat, reaction to pain, or brain functioning 150

Black English Vernacular the everyday speech patterns of African Americans studied in urban centers 235

blue collar workers nonfarm manual laborers 356

bone-pointing a magical ritual for killing, in which a sharp bone or stick is pointed at or ritually cast into the body of the intended victim 258

boreal forests heavily wooded regions dominated by coniferous trees 60

bound morphemes morphemes that can't stand as complete words 232

Brahmin the highest-ranked Hindu caste, members of which are theoretically priests 131

brain stem the parts of the brain, except the cerebral hemispheres and cerebellum, that regulate involuntary processes such as breathing and heartbeat 228

bride price goods transferred from the groom's kin to the bride's to recompense them for her loss 188

bride service service performed by the groom for the family of the bride to recompense them for her loss 189

bridewealth compensation to the family for the loss of their daughter through marriage 189

Broca's area the part of the cerebral cortex involved in organizing words into grammatical sequences 228

carrying capacity a particular environment's ability to support a species on the available resources 60

caste a social class determined by birth, so that an individual cannot legitimately change class membership by acquiring a new status 131

cerebellum the part of the brain below and behind the cerebral hemispheres of the brain that functions in the coordination of muscular activity 228

cerebral cortex the surface layer of the two large hemispheres of the brain that functions in the analysis of sensory experiences and initiates conscious action 228

chief presiding redistributive and political official of a chiefdom society or of a subdivision of a chiefdom, whose legal authority extends in at least some areas over members of families other than his or her own 93

chiefdom a society, often of many villages, that has a government capable of coordinating social action within and between villages but in which governmental authority is balanced by the legal autonomy of families in many areas 107

circumcision the surgical removal of the foreskin from the penis 146

civil religion a system of religious beliefs and values that is integrated into the broader, nonreligious aspects of society and is shared by its members regardless of their affiliation with formally organized religious organizations; in America, a system of largely Judeo-Christian religious symbolism within which the American political system is portrayed as divinely sanctioned and American society is viewed as God's modern chosen people 371

clan (sib) kinship group whose members believe themselves descended from a common ancestor far enough in the past that they cannot trace their specific genealogical ties to one another 161

class a broad, ranked stratum within society made up of unrelated families that have more or less equal power and prestige 130

cognatic (nonunilineal) descent a system of tracing descent bilaterally or ambilineally 158

cognatic clan (ambilineal clan) clan based on ambilineal descent 161

cognative lineage (ramage, sept) lineage formed using an ambilineal descent system 160

colonial peasants members of peasant societies that were politically and economically dependent on a foreign state that perpetuated its economic exploitation of the peasant area by military domination 343

commodities goods, services, and intangible items that are determined to be useful or valuable in a particular culture 80

communal foraging cooperative food gathering where fish and small game are meat resources and plants are easily collected 64

communal religions religions that include the performance of rituals by groups of lay practitioners, shamans, or individuals 265

communication the transfer of information from one person to another using objects and events as signs or symbols 218

communitas Turner's definition of the role of ritual in helping people achieve a sense of unity with each other 253

competitiveness a central drive in American culture—fostered by the need to sell one's labor as a commodity—that emphasizes excelling over others 377

complementary statuses a pair of statuses, each of which has roles that are different from but compatible with the roles of the other 129

configurationalism Benedict's view of culture as a configuration of values and customs that influence individual psychology 276

conformity a central drive in American culture, motivated by the obligation to defer to the authority of others in many areas of life 372

conspicuous consumption the acquisition and use of a surplus of goods as a way of competitively demonstrating one's success and prestige 97, 381

consumer market where basic needs of consumers are met by the system of production, and competition for sales may focus on nonessentials 99

consumption final use by a society of goods and services 96

contagious magic ritual coercion of the supernatural realm by the use of the Law of Contagion 255

contextual cues culturally defined indicators such as setting, date, time of day, or the statuses of other persons present, that determine which roles are appropriate and which are inappropriate to play 132

Contrary Warrior a Cheyenne status that required the reversal of all normal behaviors, reserved for the bravest warriors 280

corporation association of employers and employees that is legally entitled to act as a single person to produce goods or provide services 98

counterculture a movement of the 1960s that, in response to the increasing cost of living and the perceived unresponsiveness of the established political environment to people's changing needs and goals, attempted to reformulate the American value system by inverting many traditional values 380

court formalized institution that asserts authority over parties in a dispute and over persons accused of violating the law 118

couvade a custom in which the husband acts as if he gives birth to his child 143

creativity deviance that results in valuable new contributions to society 283

creoles true languages that have developed out of pidgins 230

crime the harming of a person or personal property by another 121

cross cousins cousins who are related through parents of the opposite sex who are usually brother and sister 187

cross-cultural comparison basing general conclusions about the nature of culture and its influence on society on the comparison of a diverse sample of cultures from many parts of the world, so that those conclusions will be generally valid for the human condition as a whole 14

cross-cultural research research that bases its conclusions on data drawn from many diverse ways of life rather than just one 5

Crow kinship terminology matrilineal descent system where father's matrilineage is distinguished only by sex regardless of generation 167

cultural anthropologists anthropologists who specialize in the study of culture in general, or of specific cultures 5

cultural ecology the study of the ways in which cultures adapt to their specific habitats 49

cultural evolutionism the nineteenth-century emphasis on analyzing cultures in terms of their development through a series of stages from savagery to civilization 16

cultural materialism analyzes technological and social variables in explaining ideological facts of culture 50

cultural relativism principle that cultural traits are best understood in the context of the cultural system of which they are a part; the attempt to avoid the narrow bias of judging a custom or entire culture on the basis of one's own cultural values; the view that meanings of behaviors are best understood when interpreted in terms of the culture of the actors 17, 38

culture a learned system of beliefs, feelings, and rules for living around which a group of people organize their lives; a way of life of a particular society 5, 24

culture and personality the field of anthropology that studies how culture affects psychological traits and personality characteristics 19, 276

culture areas geographical areas in which different societies share a complex of cultural traits due to similar adaptations to their environmental zone and to the effects of diffusion of cultural traits through those societies 18

culture of poverty an approach to life often found in situations of poverty in which actions are directed only to satisfying the needs of the present, by spending and consuming all income, because saving for the future seems futile 347

culture shock the loneliness and depression that are often experienced when one is in a foreign cultural setting 35

dance rhythmically patterned human movement performed for aesthetic pleasure 314

descent the cultural recognition of kinship connections between a child and one or both of his or her parent's kin 156

descriptive kinship terminology Sudanese kinship terminology 169

developed country a nation in which industrialization has become the primary basis of the economy 339

developing country underdeveloped nation undergoing industrialization 339

deviance behavior that differs enough from what society expects that others notice and react to it 283

deviant a person who has been labeled a rule violator by others for his or her role-playing errors 291

dialect a geographical or social subdivision of a language that differs systematically from other such subdivisions of the same language in its vocabulary, grammar, and phonology 235

dialogic model an approach to ethnographic narrative that engages the anthropologist and natives of a culture in a give-and-take exploration of cultural meanings 45

diffusion the passage of a cultural trait such as customs, artifacts, and ideas from one society to another 18, 326

diffusionism the early twentieth-century approach to analyzing cultures that emphasized the historical reconstruction of the influences of one culture on another in contrast to the more general evolutionary perspective of earlier anthropologists 18

direct borrowing the adopting of a cultural trait by one society from another with relatively little change in form, as exemplified by traits acquired through trade or imitation 326

discovery the development of new insights and ideas 326

disease object an object such as a barbed stick or stone that is magically cast into the body of a victim to cause illness 257

distribution movement of resources or goods from where they are found or produced to where they will ultimately be used 86

divination the use of ritual to obtain answers to questions from supernatural sources 255

division of labor the rules that govern how the day-to-day work of life is divided among the holders of various statuses 129

domestic economy the reproductive, economic, and social behaviors that characterize life within the family or household 51

double descent (double unilineal descent) a system of tracing two separate sets of kin, one designated through mothers only and the other through fathers only 159

double unilineal descent double descent 159

dowry a payment from the family of a bride to the family of her husband to compensate them for their acceptance of the responsibility of her support 189

drives the ideals that people actively pursue, sometimes at great cost, rather than those to which they merely give lip service 372

dry-land gardening planting in arid environments using several forms of irrigation 70

ecclesiastical religions religions that include not only individual, shamanic, and communal ritual practices but also a coordinating body of priests who perform rituals on behalf of congregations 266

economics system by which people obtain or produce, distribute, and consume material goods and services 80

emic analysis description of a culture as it would have meaning for an insider 41

emotion a pleasant or unpleasant subjective reaction to an experience, characterized by varying degrees of muscle tension and changes in respiration and heart rate 28

empiricism the viewpoint that conclusions should be based on careful observation and description, rather than on abstract theorizing 17

enculturation (socialization) the process by which children learn the customs, beliefs, and values of their culture 144

endogamy rule requiring marriage within specified kinship categories or other specified social or local groups to which one belongs 187

energy a positive American reaction—fostered by the work ethic— to such traits as vigor, activity, personal effort, initiative, and youthfulness 376

environmental values attitudes that define our relationship to the environment 113

Eskimo kinship terminology bilateral kinship system in which terms for mother, father, brother, and sister are not used for relatives outside the nuclear family 166

espanto (susto, pasmo) a culture-specific anxiety disorder with depressive features, interpreted by the victim as caused by soul loss 297

ethnic group minority group whose identity is based on shared customs, especially of immigrants 358

ethnocentrism the attitude that one's own culture is the only good one and that other cultures are more inferior to one's own the more they differ from it 35

ethnocide the systematic destruction of a traditional way of life 335

ethnographers cultural anthropologists who spend prolonged periods living with and describing the cultures of specific peoples 5

ethnographies descriptions of customs, beliefs, and values of individual societies 5

ethnologists cultural anthropologists who formulate general laws of culture based on the study of the ethnographies of many diverse societies 5

ethnomusicology the study of music and its relationship to culture 313

ethnoscience (cognitive anthropology) systematically describes a culture by analyzing the linguistic categories used by informants to discuss their society 45

etic analysis description of a culture in categories based on universal principles 41

eureka experience a sense of intensified meaningfulness of experiences that sometimes occurs during an altered state of consciousness 288

excision surgical removal of all or part of the female clitoris 146

exogamy rule a rule forbidding an individual from marrying a member of the kinship, residential, or other specified group to which he or she belongs 187

expressive culture expressions of culture such as play, ritual, or the arts 306

extended family the form of family that includes two or more nuclear

families and often their parents, who reside together 192

external warfare warfare which is fought for prolonged periods in locations distant from the warriors' home with enemies who speak a foreign language and follow an alien way of life 119

face positive social value a person can contribute to a group; social standing 281

face-work interaction in which effort is directed to maintaining or returning behavior to roles considered appropriate for members of a group; efforts to maintain or reestablish face 282

family the group consisting of married persons, their children, and other relatives who reside with them 192

fear a distressful emotion characterized by concerns about inadequate power to protect oneself from specific danger 285

feelings subjective reactions to experiences as pleasant or unpleasant, good or bad. Feelings include emotions, attitudes, and values 26

female circumcision mutilation of female genitals, including infibulation and excision, a symbol of male dominance in some societies 146

female infanticide the killing of female infants as a major means of population control in societies that primarily engage in internal warfare 120

feminist anthropology the anthropological approach that studies the relationships among social power, social honor, and gender 48, 202

feminization of poverty a growing trend in which women comprise a large proportion of the world's poor 210

feudal peasants food producers in preindustrialized societies who pay rent or perform service for the privilege of farming lands owned by local aristocratic officials, who have obligations to provide police and military protection, judicial services, and care for the peasants in times of hardship 343

feuds armed conflicts between kinship groups initiated to avenge a wrong 119

fictive kinship kinship relationships created by societies toward those who are not otherwise considered relatives either by descent or marriage 169

fictive marriage legal marriage established for both partners to acquire social benefits 181

fieldwork the basic tool of anthropological research in which information is gathered from the context in which it naturally occurs 9

Fissure of Rolando a vertical fold in the surface of the brain that separates the motor areas, which control conscious muscle movement, from corresponding areas, which receive sensory information from various parts of the body 228

folktales stories told for entertainment that teach a moral principle or a practical lesson 315

foraging a subsistence technology based on gathering wild plant foods, hunting, and fishing 62

formal learning learning that proceeds by admonition and correction of the learner's errors, with emotional emphasis on the importance of behaving acceptably 144

fraternal groups groups of related males who work together and feel obliged to protect one another's common interests 119

fraternal polyandry the form of polyandry in which the husbands are brothers 178

free morphemes can stand alone as words in sentences 232

frigophobia (*pa-ling*) a culture-specific obsessive-compulsive disorder characterized by fear of loss of body heat 298

frontier areas unproductive lands for industrialized agriculture opened to settlement by national governments that do not recognize the claims of the indigenous population 334

function the contribution that any one cultural trait makes to perpetuating the unity, equilibrium, and adaptation of a way of life within its environment 18

functionalism the approach to analyzing cultures by examining the mechanics of society while it is in equilibrium, as opposed to the more historical emphasis of diffusionism or the developmental emphasis of evolutionism 18

funeral ritual a rite of passage that formalizes the removal of an individual from the status of living member of the social group 152

game a competitive activity involving physical skills, strategy, and chance in a model of a conflict-producing real-life situation 308

gender social statuses assigned on the basis of cultural concepts about the sexes 196

gender stereotypes preconceived ideas about what behaviors and roles are considered "masculine" or "feminine" 197

General Adaptation Syndrome the nonspecific changes that occur in the body as a result of stress, as it mobilizes itself to act against the cause of the stress 258

general evolution change in the direction of increasing complexity 330

generalized reciprocity gift given with no expectation of immediate exchange 87

general-purpose money universal medium of exchange used to buy and sell any item 95

genocide the systematic extermination of a people 335

ghost marriages fictive marriages where a close male kinsman of a man or boy—married or unmarried—who died before he had any legal heirs, marries a woman in the name of the deceased 181

gift exchange reciprocal exchange of gifts between families who are party to a marriage 190

glossolalia behavior in religious ecstasy that may include groaning and uttering unintelligible sounds 252

glottochronology a technique for calculating the minimal length of time that two related languages have been diverging from a common ancestral language 238

grammar the analysis of the regular ways that the sounds of a language are combined to form meaningful utterances. Grammar includes morphology and syntax 232

grasslands areas that cover 26 percent of the Earth's surface, with grasses of different types 59

green revolution use of modern plant breeding to produce high-yield, fertilizer-intensive, fast-maturing crops 349

grief a distressful emotion characterized by a sense of loss, sadness, and failure to obtain esteem from others 285

group two or more individuals engaged in a common activity 128

group marriage the form of marriage in which two or more men are married to two or more women at the same time 179

guilt a distressful emotion characterized by remorse for having used too much power and having harmed another 285

hallucination a realistic-seeming experience—much like a vivid waking dream—that may include vision, hearing, the sense of touch, smell, and/or taste in the absence of external cause 288

Hawaiian kinship terminology simplest kinship designation, using terms parents, siblings, and children 165

hermeneutic anthropology examines the interaction between fieldworker and native informant 44

holistic emphasizing the full range of relations among parts of a system and the ways the operation of those parts helps to perpetuate the whole system 5

homophilic marriage same-sex marriage without transvestism or change in sex role by one of the partners 183

homosexual marriage marriage between members of the same sex 183

honor the esteem some statuses confer on those who hold them 130

horticulture cultivation of crops using simple hand tools such as the hoe and digging stick and without fertilization of the soil, crop rotation, and often without irrigation 69

household a group of people who share a common residence 192

hsieh-ping a culture-specific hysterical disorder that is characterized by tremor, disorientation, clouding of consciousness, delirium, speaking in tongues, and hallucinations 296

Human Relations Area Files (HRAF) a research data pool containing information on over 335 major societal groups, each coded for the presence or absence of about 700 cultural and environmental traits 14

human soul the supernatural part of the human being that is believed to animate the human body during life or perpetuate the individual's memories or life-goals after death 249

hysteria a form of neurosis in which there is ritualistic avoidance of anxiety or ritualistic manipulation of others as a means of avoiding failure 294

ice-zone regions of permanent snow and ice 60

ideal culture the ways people perceive their own customs and behaviors, often more a reflection of their feelings and ideals about what it should be rather than an accurate assessment of what it is 31

ideological communication communication that reaffirms people's allegiance to their groups and creates a sense of community by asserting its ideology 26

ideology the consciously shared beliefs and feelings that members of a society consider characteristic of themselves 26

image of limited good a fatalistic outlook common in situations of peasant poverty, in which the drudgery of life is not believed to bring much reward, since the achievement of one person can only be accomplished at the expense of another 347

imitative magic attempted ritual coercion of the supernatural realm by use of the Law of Similarity 254

imu a hysterical disorder found among the Ainu of northern Japan characterized by automatic obedience or negativism and uncontrollable imitation of sounds and gestures 295

incest taboo a rule that forbids sexual behaviors between designated kin, including but not limited to intercourse between parents and children and between siblings 185

indigenous people a group of people whose occupation of an area precedes the state political system that now controls that area, and who have little or no influence within that political system 333

indirect dowry payment of goods made by the groom or his family to the bride either directly to her or indirectly through her father 190

individual foraging men and women gather their own plant foods; women provide for the children 64

industrialization the process of change from an economy based on home production of goods to one based on large-scale, mechanized factory production 337

industrialized agriculture the use of an industrialized technology and other techniques such as chemical soil fertilization to obtain high levels of food production per acre 76

infibulation surgical closing of the female vulva over the vagina 146

informal learning learning by imitation 144

innovation changes in a culture as a result of discovery or invention 326

insanity process by which a person acquires and maintains deviant master status of residual rule breaker 293

intergenerational marriage male mentorship 184

internal warfare fighting between peoples who share the same language and culture 119

International Phonetic Alphabet (IPA) a standard alphabet of nearly 100 sound symbols used by linguists throughout the world for writing phonetic transcriptions of languages 231

interpretive anthropology explains how each element of a culture relates meaningfully to its original context 43

intimate distance the distance from their bodies that people reserve for those with whom they are intimate enough to permit casual touching 222

intragenerational marriages pathic marriages 183

invention the act of combining pre-existing cultural traits in new ways 326

Iroquois kinship terminology bifurcate merging system like the Crow and Omaha, but where there is no merging of generations in the lineage that marries into ego's lineage 168

jati an occupational subcaste in Hindu society 131

jokes humor that is intended to help relieve the stress of everyday life 317

kayak angst a culture-specific phobic disorder that is characterized by an inordinate fear of being at sea in a kayak 297

kindred a kinship group in a bilateral descent system that consists of the known relatives of an individual 163

kinesics the study of the body movements that accompany speech as a component of communication 224

kinship a system for classifying people who are related to one another by ties of descent or by ties of marriage 156

koro a culture-specific anxiety disorder characterized by fear of death through loss of sexual essence 298

Kshatriya the second most important of the Hindu castes, members of which were the traditional warrior-rulers, nobles, and landowners of society 131

language a system of rules that govern the production and interpretation of speech 225

latah a culture-specific hysterical disorder that is characterized by uncontrollable imitation of the actions and speech of others 294

law cultural rules that regulate human behavior and maintain order 114

Law of Contagion the principle that things that have been in contact remain supernaturally in contact or that contact between things can be used to transfer *mana* from one to the other 255

Law of Cultural Dominance the cultural system that effectively exploits the energy resources of a given environment has the tendency to spread into that environment at the expense of less effective systems 327

Law of Evolutionary Potential the concept that a culture's capacity to move from one general evolutionary stage to another varies inversely with the degree of its specific evolutionary adaptation to its environment 330

Law of Local Discontinuity of Progress the idea that the successive stages of general evolutionary change are not likely to occur in the same locality 331

Law of Similarity the principle that things that are similar to one another are spiritually identical, and can be used in rituals to influence a desired outcome 254

legal authority legitimate right to compel others to obey the law and to punish those who violate it 114

legal rights and duties rules that define relationships between people by specifying the type of recompense an injured person should receive 114

legends stories that describe heroes and heroines who are usually responsible for the origin of a culture or society 315

levirate a rule that requires kin of a deceased man to provide his widow with another husband, often one of the deceased man's brothers 181

life cycle the status changes from birth to death that are typical of a particular society 137

limbic system areas within the brain that deal with emotional experience 229

liminal period transition stage between the beginning and end of a ritual 254

lineage a kinship group whose members can trace their lines of descent to the same ancestor 160

lineal descent groups those whose members share a common ancestor 160

linguistic relativity the idea that the characteristics of a language influence the way that its speakers think 233

lyrics words in a musical piece that convey a message 313

magic the use of rituals that are believed to compel—as opposed to simply making requests of—the supernatural when performed correctly 254

maintenance system the parts of the economic and social structure of a society that determine its childrearing practices 278

male-ranked polygyny with related co-wives a more descriptive term for sororal polygyny 177

male-stratified polygyny form of polygamy in which a small number of men of high rank and authority marry a larger number of wives 178

mana supernatural power or force 244

market a system of distribution for goods and services based primarily on the use of established locations 93

marking the idea that the behaviors of a woman during pregnancy may influence the physical or psychological characteristics of the unborn child 367

marriage a rite of passage that unites two or more individuals as spouses 174

marriage preference rules systems that single out certain kin as ideal marriage partners 187

Marxist anthropology the study of the effects of class conflict on social and cultural change 48

master status a social status that is so important that it can't be ignored 133

matriclan clan based on matrilineal descent 161

matrifocal societies societies in which the primary solidarity relations involve women 111

matrifocality a society in which high social status is assumed by females primarily because they control food production and because the male is absent much of the time 205

matrilateral cross-cousin marriage marriage between a male and his mother's brother's daughter 188

matrilineage a system of tracing descent lines through mothers 160

matrilineal descent a system of descent traced through the mother only 159

matrilocality the custom in which a newly married couple is expected to set up residence with or near the bride's family 191

mediation negotiation between conflicting parties carried out by a neutral third party 116

mentorships system of marriage between an older, socially established partner and a younger spouse of the same sex 184

meta-communication system a system of communication that includes the capacity to communicate about itself 225

minorities those with a low-ranked master status, commonly but incorrectly called a "minority group" 133

mixed forests temperate climate with conifers and broadleaf trees 58

modal personality type the most common or typical pattern of personality traits in a particular society 277

mode of production the work practices by which people apply their subsistence technology within a particular environment 50

mode of reproduction the technology and practices operating within a particular social environment that influence the size of the society's population 50

moiety one of two basic complementary social subdivisions of a society 163

money standard medium of exchange that has a mutually agreed-upon value 94

monogamous marriage form of marriage where one man and one woman are joined as husband and wife 177

monotheism the belief in a high god, a supreme being who either created the physical universe and other spiritual beings and rules over them or who at least maintains the order of the universe today 249

moral values attitudes or feelings that govern our relationships with our fellow human beings 113

morpheme the smallest meaningful sequence of sounds in a language 232

morphology the study of how phonemes are combined into the smallest meaningful units of a language 232

mountain lands a variety of environments, often within short distances of one another 59

multilinear evolution an approach to cultural evolution that emphasizes the divergent paths that each culture follows as it adapts to its local environment 47

music rhythmically organized scaled tones that produce melodic sound 313

myths stories that recount the origin of such things as gods, the universe, animals, and plants 314

naming ceremony a rite of passage following birth, at which the infant is declared a member of the human group by being given a name 143

national character studies an attempt to identify the psychological characteristics of entire societies 278

natural selection the process whereby those members of a species that are better adapted to their environment contribute more offspring to succeeding generations than do other members 61

negative reciprocity one group or individual in a reciprocal exchange system attempts to get more than it gives 90

neoevolutionism a view of cultural evolution that describes culture as "a mechanism for harnessing energy and of putting it to work" and that measures cultural evolution by the amount of energy that a society's technology harnesses per capita per year 46

neofunctionalism contemporary approach to studying functional processes of cultural systems, with emphasis on the ways in which conflict may be one of the mechanisms by which cultural stability is maintained 48

neolocality the custom in which the newly married couple sets up residence in a new location apart from either of their families 191

nonindustrialized (or traditional) agriculture intensive crop cultivation using simple tools such as hoes, shovels, and animal-drawn plows 74

nonscientific beliefs beliefs that grow out of people's feelings 27

nonsexual marriages marriages that fulfill economic, social, and kinship functions without sexual union between the partners 180

nonunilineal descent cognatic descent 158

nonverbal communication all transfer of information other than with words that includes such things as volume, pitch, tone of voice, and speed when speaking, as well as non-oral things such as gestures, posture, and use of space and time 221

nuclear family the form of family that consists only of married persons and their children 192

oaths ritual acts of swearing innocence on pain of punishment by deities 118

Olympian religions polytheistic ecclesiastical religions in which the gods or supernatural beings may be loosely ranked but in which no one of the supernatural beings is truly supreme over the others 267

Omaha kinship terminology patrilineal descent system where mother's patrilineage is distinguished only by sex, regardless of generation 167

optimal foraging theory asserts that foragers use food resources in direct proportion to the caloric effort required to obtain them 66

optimism a positive American expectation—fostered by the work ethic—that the future is potentially better than the present 376

oral literature various forms of speaking for aesthetic pleasure, including orating, reciting myths, and telling folktales 314

ordeals tests of guilt or innocence by enduring dangerous or painful acts 118

ownership the right to use property and the right to deny use rights to others as long as one owns the property 84

parallel cousins cousins whose common parents are either two brothers or two sisters 188

participant observation the technique of cultural anthropology in which the researcher spends a prolonged period participating with and observing subjects in their natural setting, as opposed to studying them in a laboratory setting 9

pasmo (susto, espanto) a culture-specific anxiety disorder with depressive features, interpreted by

the victim as caused by soul loss 297

pastoralism a subsistence technology based on animal husbandry 72

pathic marriages (intragenerational marriages) same-sex marriages involving gender-role change in one partner 183

patriarchy a society in which access to social power and prestige is available primarily to men 204

patriclan clan based on patrilineal descent 161

patrilateral cross-cousin marriage marriage between a male and his father's sister's daughter 188

patrilateral parallel-cousin marriage (bint'amm) marriage between a male and his father's brother's daughter 188

patrilineage a system of tracing descent lines through fathers 160

patrilineal descent a system of descent traced through the father only 158

patrilocality place of residence for newly married couples in or near the husband's family 191

peasants people who use nonindustrialized, labor-intensive techniques for producing food and who are politically and economically subordinate to a governing class of which they are not a part and with whom they have little influence 343

permissive societies those that are tolerant of childhood sexual experimentation 145

personal distance the distance to which people adjust themselves when interacting with close friends 222

personality consistent pattern of behavior related both to inner forces and to external, cultural, and social pressures 280

phoneme the smallest psychologically real unit of sound in a language 231

phonemic alphabet a written record of a speech that uses an alphabet composed of only one symbol for each phoneme of the language 231

phones smallest sound units of a language 231

phonetic description descriptions pertaining to the smallest units of sound actually produced by speakers of a language. A phonetic transcription attempts to record all of the sounds consistently produced by the speakers of a language 231

phonology the study of the rules that govern the production and the organization of the sounds of a particular language 231

phratry group of clans thought to be related by kinship 163

physical (biological) anthropologists anthropologists who specialize in the study of the evolutionary origins of the human species, the relationships between the human species and other living primates, the physical variations within the human species today, and the relationships between human biology and our species' cultural capacities 8

pibloktoq a culture-specific hysterical disorder characterized by agitated attempts to flee the presence of other people 295

pidgin languages simplified versions of one language or a combination of several 230

piety attitudes that define our relationship to the supernatural and that may manifest themselves in certain behaviors 113

pink collar occupations service occupations that largely are held by women 355

plant-focused foraging plant resources are readily available, allowing hunting expeditions far from campsite 66

play stress-relieving ritualistic practice of potentially utilitarian behaviors 306

polar lands regions of cold climates near North and South poles 60

political economy the reproductive, economic, and social behaviors that are typical of life outside the family or household 51

politics manner in which power is achieved and used to create and implement public goals 102

polyandrous marriage the form of marriage in which one woman has more than one husband 178

polygamy form of marriage where a person is permitted to have more than one spouse at the same time 177

polygynous marriage form of marriage in which a man has more than one wife 177

polyphony diversity of viewpoints within a single culture 45

polytheism the belief in superior (but not supreme) gods, each of whom controls or rules over some major aspect of the universe 249

postmodernist anthropology a humanistic approach to anthropology that rejects the notion of ethnography as a detached, scientifically objective process and proposes the view that culture is composed of a constantly changing, open-ended, and ambiguous system of meanings that are negotiated and renegotiated by members of society as they interact with one another 44

power the ability to exercise coercion in a group in obtaining what is sought 130

prairies areas with tall varieties of grass that tolerate wetter climates 59

pregnancy rituals religious rules such as taboos designed to protect the unborn child and the mother during pregnancy and childbirth or admonitions to engage in acts be-

lieved to be a positive influence on the developing child 140

prestige dialects dialects with the reputation of being inherently better than others 240

priests religious practitioners who perform rituals for the benefit of groups. Often, priests are full-time religious practitioners whose emphasis is on preserving the established ritual forms, rather than on inspiration and innovation in the application of their rituals 266

primary institutions the primary care groups related to childrearing, including feeding, weaning, sexual training, and subsistence patterns 277

Principle of Stabilization the concept that the more efficient a culture becomes at harnessing energy for society, the more expensive and difficult it becomes to implement new means of increasing efficiency 330

professionals self-employed, college-educated service providers 356

progeny price bridewealth 189

pronatalist societies those whose customs favor reproduction and forbid abortion and infanticide 134

"protective" legislation laws that are ostensibly intended to prevent the exploitation of women, but which in practice create social barriers against the full participation of women in social life outside the domestic sphere; for instance, many states in the U.S. have laws that prohibit the hiring of women into occupations that require the employee to lift more than 35 pounds 363

Proto-Germanic English and German that were at one time the same original language 236

Proto-Indo-European the ancestral language from which most of the contemporary languages of Eu-

rope, Iran, and India have developed 237

proverbs short statements that illustrate the basic values of a culture 317

proxemics the study of how people structure the space around them when interacting with others 222

psychological anthropology empirical approach to data collection that emphasizes statistical correlations between culture and psychological processes 279

psychological death the process by which one subjectively prepares for impending biological death 151

puberty (adulthood) ritual a rite of passage that formalizes the change from the status of child to the status of adult 145

public distance the distance reserved for separating people whose interaction is not intended to perpetuate a social relationship 224

purposefulness a manifestation of the American work ethic that asserts the importance of goal-directed effort 376

racism the belief that differences in the expected roles of members of different racial groups are based on the hereditarily controlled behavioral predispositions of those groups 135

raids organized violence by one group against another to achieve economic benefit 119

ramage cognatic lineage 160

rank the relative importance of a status or group as measured by the amount of power and/or honor to which it is entitled 130

rank societies kinship groups in a chiefdom that are ranked in a social rather than occupational hierarchy 108

real culture culture portrayed in terms of the actually observable behaviors of a people 31

rebellion organized and violent opposition to the legitimacy of a society's current governing body 123

reciprocity sharing of surpluses with the understanding that the party receiving the gift will respond in kind in the future 86

redistribution commodities are contributed by all members of a group to a common pool from which they will be distributed to where they will be used 90

reincarnation the belief that the soul of a human being may be repeatedly reborn into the human group to which it previously belonged or as an animal that may be symbolically associated with that group 249

religion belief in supernatural power, symbolic expression of feelings, and rituals performed in order to influence the nonhuman realm 244

residual rules miscellaneous, normally unspoken rules that people are expected to follow to avoid violating the pattern or style of behavior that is expected in the culture 292

restitution behavior intended to restore the group to the balance it had before a law was broken 122

restrictive societies societies that do not accept childhood sexual experimentation 145

retribution personal use of force to redress wrongs, usually in simple societies with no centralized governmental authority 119

revitalization movement a change in religion described as a conscious effort to construct a more satisfying culture 268

revolution organized use of force to alter the very form of government 123

rhetoric formal speech that follows the traditional rules of a particular culture 315

rhythm the timing and stressing of tones within a melody 313

riddles mental puzzles told for entertainment 317

rite of passage (life crisis rite) a ritual that formalizes a major change in social status 137

ritual behaviors, often performed in repetitive and stereotyped ways, that express people's anxieties by acting them out. May be an attempt to influence the supernatural realm to achieve greater control over the natural world 246, 290

role the skills, abilities, and ways of acting toward others that belong to each status of a society 129

role conflict emotional discomfort and confusion experienced in situations in which conflicting contextual cues indicate that an individual should play the roles of more than one of his or her statuses 132

sacred Durkheim's definition that included feelings of respect, awe, and reverence inspired by things set apart and forbidden 245

saka a culture-specific hysterical disorder that is characterized by repetition of actions or sounds believed to be a foreign language, and loss of consciousness with body rigidity 296

sanction action taken by legal authorities responding to violations of law 114

savannas tropical areas of tall grasses and drought-resistant undergrowth 59

scale a sequence of tones that ends with a return to a tone that has a frequency twice that of the starting tone 313

scarification decorating the body by cutting designs in it and treating them with ashes or other material to ensure that they will produce raised scars 146

schizophrenia a mental disorder characterized by residual rule breaking caused by difficulty in communicating an acceptable social identity. Schizophrenia may include hallucinations and ideas about reality that are greatly at odds with mainstream ideas 300

scientific beliefs beliefs that are based on the desire to solve the practical day-to-day problems of living 27

scrub forests regions between coasts and mountains with mild, wet winters and hot, dry summers 59

secondary institutions the institutions in social life that satisfy the needs and tensions not met by the primary institutions, including taboo systems, religion, rituals, folk tales, and techniques of thinking 278

secularization the process by which nonreligious beliefs expand within an ideology at the expense of religious thought 248

sedentarism living in permanent or semipermanent settlements 68

self-reliance a value central to Americans that emphasizes the importance of independence, autonomy of the individual, and the primacy of the individual over the group 375

semirestrictive societies those that accept childhood sexual experimentation so long as those involved follow established rules of etiquette and discretion 145

sept cognatic lineage 160

serial monogamy a marriage pattern in which individuals of either sex may have only one spouse at a given time, but through divorce and remarriage may have several spouses during their lifetime 177, 367

serotonin a chemical produced in the brain during waking hours that inhibits the production of dreams or hallucinations 288

sex biological distinctions such as the chromosomal, hormonal, or physical differences between males and females 196

sexism the belief that differences in the sex roles of males and females are biologically determined 135

sexual dimorphism marked differentiation in size and form of the sexes 196

sexual terrorism customs that employ violence against females in order to maintain male domination 203

shamanic religions religions in which the only ritual specialist is the shaman, and which contain only individual and shamanic ritual practices 263

shamans part-time religious practitioners who are believed to have access to supernatural power that may be used for the benefit of specific clients, as in healing or divining 260

shame (embarrassment) a distressful emotion characterized by a sense of personal ineptness resulting in damage to one's reputation and loss of esteem 285

shifting cultivation slash-and-burn horticulture 69

sib clan 161

sign an object or event whose meaning is biologically disposed or based on a similarity or a tendency for two things to occur together in nature 218

sin a form of taboo violation in which the rule breaker is thought of as morally responsible for the act 257

sister exchange form of cross-cousin marriage in which a brother and sister marry cross cousins who are also sister and brother to each other 188

slash-and-burn cultivation (swidden horticulture) a form of farming in which the land is prepared by cutting and burning the natural growth and in which several plots, in various stages of soil depletion, are worked in a cycle 69

sleep crawling a Samoan sexual practice in which an uninvited youth would enter a young woman's house after dark with the intent of seduction 148

social anthropology Radcliffe-Brown's idea that social interactions are important in determining customs of a culture 45

social death the point at which people respond to a person with the behaviors appropriate to one who is biologically dead 151

social distance the distance to which people adjust themselves when interacting in impersonal situations such as business transactions 222

social organization the relationships between the groups, statuses, and division of labor that structure the interaction of people within society 128

social structure the part of social organization made up of groups and their relationships with each other 45, 128

socialization the process of learning a culture and the role-playing skills necessary for social life 112, 276

sociobiology emphasis on role of natural selection on genetic predispositions for specific behaviors 50

sodality volunteer associations whose members are drawn from several tribal families 105

sorcerers practitioners of magical rituals that are done to harm others 262

sorcery the learned use of rituals to magically control the supernatural realm to achieve human goals 250

sororal polygyny the form of polygyny in which the wives are sisters 177

sororate a rule that requires the kin of a deceased woman to provide her widower with another wife, often one of the deceased woman's sisters 181

soul loss in primitive societies, the belief that the departure of the soul from the body, usually caused by a sudden fright, causes the body to weaken and die 257

special-purpose money medium of exchange restricted to the buying and selling of a single commodity 95

specific evolution change in the direction of increasing adaptive specialization 330

speech the audible symbols that people use to communicate 225

speech motor area the part of the cerebral cortex that controls the production of speech sounds 228

spirit possession a trance in which individuals feel as if their behavior is under the control of one or more spirits that have entered their bodies 257

spirit possession trace a trance in which individuals feel as if their behavior is under the control of one or more spirits that have entered their bodies 289

spirit travel trance a trance in which individuals experience themselves as leaving their bodies 289

spiritual values attitudes that define our relationship to the supernatural and that may manifest themselves in certain behaviors 113

sport aggressively competitive activity played according to strict rules 308

Standard English the dialect taught in U.S. schools and used by most people in the United States at least on formal occasions 235

state a society with a centralized government that monopolizes the legal authority to use force 110

status a culturally defined relationship that one individual may have with one or more other individuals; the position within a group that each member holds 129

status income goods produced over and above subsistence needs 97

status pair the statuses that two people acquire when they interact, and that together form a relationship 129

status-appropriate roles the ways of behaving that are expected of an individual who holds a particular social status in a specific culture 281

steppes areas that cover stretches of southeastern Europe and Asia, with a short, hardy variety of grass 59

stigma loss of rank that accompanies the social rejection of persons who have violated accepted role behavior 283

stimulus diffusion the borrowing of the idea for a cultural trait by one society from another, with the implementation of that idea being more or less determined within the borrowing culture 326

stress a physiological response to any demand, characterized by the body's preparing itself for action 287

structural-functionalism determining customs of a culture by the analytical method of social anthropology 46

structuralism Lévi-Strauss's concept of underlying unity of all cultures to think in dualities 42

subculture variations of a culture shared by different groups within a society 25

subsistence how people obtain the necessities of life, particularly food, from the environment 62

subsistence economy when people consume most of what they produce 96

subsistence income each family produces goods for its own consumption 96

subsistence technology the tools and techniques by which people obtain food 62

Sudanese kinship (descriptive kinship) terminology occurring mostly in North Africa, this system distinguishes maternal and paternal relatives by separate terms 169

Sudra the lowest of the Hindu castes, made up of farm artisans, servants, farmers, and laborers 131

supernatural that which transcends the natural, observable world 245

supernatural sanctions for violations of moral rules punishments for immoral acts by spiritual agencies as opposed to human agencies. In most societies, the enforcement of morality is a strictly human responsibility, rather than a religious preoccupation 250

survivals remnants of earlier social customs and ideas that can be used to reconstruct the evolutionary past of societies 17

susto (espanto, pasmo) a culture-specific anxiety disorder with depressive features, interpreted by the victim as caused by soul loss 297

swidden horticulture slash-and-burn horticulture 69

symbol an object or event that represents another object or event only because of the agreement among people that it will 24, 218

symbolic marriages those marriages not establishing economic and social ties between kinship groups 180

symmetrical statuses a pair of statuses, each of which has the same roles to play with respect to the other 129

syntax the study of the rules for combining morphemes into complete and meaningful sentences 232

Systema Naturae the book in which Carolus Linnaeus classified plants and animals into a hierarchical system based on their degree of similarity to one another 16

taboo a rule forbidding contact with sacred things, those containing *mana* 245

taboo violation the breaking of a supernatural rule, whether intentional or not. Taboo violations are often believed to be a cause of illness 257

taiga swampy coniferous forests of the northern lands south of the tundras 60

technical learning learning that occurs when the logical rationales for specific ways of doing things—rather than emotional pressure to behave in that way—are given to the learner 145

technology tools and techniques through which human beings harness the energy available in their environment 46

teknonymy the custom of referring to a person as the parent of his or her child rather than by birth name 149

trance (altered state of consciousness) subjective state of mind where experiences are not interpreted in terms of normal symbolic categories of one's culture 287

transhumance a form of pastoralism in which only a part of the group moves with the herd; some stay in villages and grow crops year-round 72

transvestism cross-dressing or mixed-gender dressing, a common part of the berdache gender role 202

tribe a semisedentary kinship-based society without a full-time government. Most tribal societies are economically based on a simple food domestication subsistence technology, either horticulture or pastoralism 68, 105

tropical forests regions with warm climates and abundant rainfall, plants, and animal life 59

tundra level treeless plains in the arctic and subarctic regions of North America, Asia, and Scandinavia 60

underdeveloped country nation with a largely nonindustrialized economy 339

unilineal descent a system of tracing descent through a single sex line rather than both parents equally 158

unilineal descent group a system of tracing social groups based on a matrilineal or patrilineal descent system 160

universal application principle that legal authority should apply uniformly in similar situations 114

unskilled laborers low-paid workers, including part-time or seasonal workers, who usually are paid by the hour or for the quantity of goods they produce 355

Untouchables the lowest-status members of Hindu society who belonged to none of the traditional castes and who ritually performed the polluted tasks of life 131

uxorilocality (matrilocality) the custom in which a newly married couple is expected to set up residence with or near the bride's family 191

Vaisya the third-ranked Hindu caste, comprised of commoners 131

values subjective reactions to experiences expressed in terms of good or bad, moral or immoral; the ideals that people long for but do not necessarily pursue. Values are often opposites of drives 30, 112, 372

verbal arts (oral literature) various forms of speaking for aesthetic pleasure, including orating, reciting myths, and telling folktales 314

virilocality (patrilocality) custom where a newly married couple is expected to set up their residence with or near the groom's family 191

voodoo death death that occurs following a magical ritual performed to kill 257

war organized, armed conflict between political communities 119

wealth-increasing polygyny male-stratified polygyny 178

Wernicke's area the part of the cerebral cortex involved in processing speech sounds 228

white collar occupations service-providing occupations such as clerical, sales, managerial, and administrative jobs 356

witchcraft the innate ability to influence supernatural forces to operate, usually in ways that are harmful to others without the necessity of using rituals 251

witches persons believed to have the innate supernatural ability to harm others without the use of ritual 262

women exchange a situation where, rather than exchange gifts between families, they exchange women, so that they lose a daughter but gain a daughter-in-law 191

work ethic a central drive of American culture in which work is felt to be good in and of itself—a feeling fostered by an economic system in which individuals must work competitively to produce goods that they themselves do not own and that will be consumed by others 376

BIBLIOGRAPHY

Aberle, D. F. (1961). 'Arctic hysteria' and latah in Mongolia. In Y. A. Cohen (Ed.), *Social structure and personality: A casebook* (pp. 471–475). New York: Holt, Rinehart & Winston.

Adam, B. D. (1981). *Christianity, social tolerance and homosexuality: A symposium.* Paper presented at the Society for the Study of Social Problems, Ontario, Canada.

Adam, B. D. (1986). Age, structure, and sexuality: Reflections on the anthropological evidence on homosexual relations, *Journal of Homosexuality, 11*(3/4), 19–33.

Agar, M. H. (1980). *The professional stranger: An informal introduction to ethnography.* New York: Academic Press.

Albert, B. (1991). A Yanomami leader speaks: A message from Davi Kopenawa Yanomami. *Anthropology Newsletter, 32*(6), 52.

Alland, A. (1977). *The artistic animal: An inquiry into the biological roots of art.* Garden City, NY; Doubleday.

Altman, S. A. (1973). Primate communication. In G. A. Miller (Ed.), *Communication, language and meaning: Psychological perspectives* (pp. 84–94). New York: Basic Books, Inc.

Amnesty International. (1992). *Women in the front line: Human rights violations against women.* NY: John D. Lucas Printing.

Anderson, L. (1990). *Calliope's sisters: A comparative study of philosophies of art.* Englewood Cliffs, NJ: Prentice Hall.

Angeloni, E. (Ed.). (1987). *Annual Editions: Anthropology.* Guilford, CT: The Dushkin Publishing Group.

Ashworth, G. (1986). Of violence and violation: Women and human rights. *Change Thinkbook* No. II. London: Change.

Ayres, B. C. (1968). In A. Lomax (Ed.), Folk song style and culture. *American Association for the Advancement of Science,* Publication No. 88. Washington, DC.

Ayres, B. C. (1973). Effects of infant carrying practices on rhythm in music. *Ethos, 1,* 387–404.

Bamberger, J. (1974). The myth of matriarchy. In M. Rosaldo & L. Lamphere (Eds.), *Women, culture, and society* (pp. 263–388). Stanford: Stanford University Press.

Barker-Banfield, G. J. (1983). The spermatic economy: A nineteenth century view of sexuality. In Dr. T. Altherr (Ed.), *Procreation or pleasure: Sexual attitudes in American history* (pp. 47–70). Malabar, FL: Robert E. Krieger Publishing.

Barnes, G. H., & Dummond, D. W. (Eds.). (1934). *Letters of Theodore Dwight Weld, Angelina Grimké Weld and Sarah Grimké: 1822–1844* (Vol. 1). New York: Appleton-Century.

Barnouw, V. (1985). *Culture and personality.* (4th ed.). Homewood, IL: Dorsey.

Barry, H., III, Child, I. L., & Bacon, M. K. (1959). Relation of child training to subsistence economy. *American Anthropologist, 61,* 51–63.

Barth, F. (1954). Father's brother's daughter marriage in Kurdistan. *Southwestern Journal of Anthropology, 10*(1), 164–171.

Basedow, H. (1925). *The Australian aboriginal.* Adelaide: F. W. Preece & Sons.

Bates, M. (1967). *Gluttons and libertines: Human problems of being natural.* New York: Vintage Books.

Bateson, G. (1936). *Naven: A survey of the problems suggested by a composite picture of the culture of a New Guinea tribe drawn from three points of view.* Cambridge, MA: Cambridge University Press.

Beals, A. M. (1974). *Village life in south India.* Chicago: Aldine.

Beals, A. M. (1980). *Gopalpur.* New York: Holt, Rinehart & Winston.

Bean, S. S. (1981). Soap operas: Sagas of American kinship. In S. Montague & W. Arens (Eds.), *The American dimension: Cultural myths and social realities* (pp. 61–75). Sherman Oaks, CA: Alfred Publishing Co.

Beattie, J. (1964). *Other cultures: Aims, methods, and achievements in social anthropology.* New York: Free Press.

Becker, H. S. (1963). *Outsiders: Studies in the sociology of deviance.* NY: Free Press.

Behnam, D. (1985). The Tunis conference. *Current Anthropology, 26,* 555–556.

Bellah, R. (1967). Civil religion in America. *Daedelus.* Winter, 1–21.

Benedict, R. (1928). Psychological types in the cultures of the Southwest. *Proceedings of the Twenty-Third International Congress of Americanists,* pp. 572–581.

Benedict, R. (1932). Configurations of culture in North America. *American Anthropologist, 34,* 1–27.

Benedict, R. (1934). *Patterns of culture.* Boston, MA: Houghton Mifflin.

Benedict, R. (1946). *The chrysanthemum and the sword.* Boston: Houghton Mifflin.

Bernard, H. R., & Pelto, P. J. (Eds.). (1972). *Technology and social change.* New York: Macmillan.

Bickerton, D. (1983, July). Creole languages. *Scientific American,* pp. 116–122.

Biebuyck, D. P. (1973). *Lega culture.* Berkeley: University of California Press.

Binford, L. R. (1968). Post-Pleistocene adaptations. In L. R. Binford & S. R. Binford (Eds.), *New perspective in archaeology* (pp. 22–49). Chicago: Aldine.

Bird, C. (1973). *Born female: The high cost of keeping women down.* New York: David McKay.

Birdwhistell, R. L. (1970). *Kinesics and context: Essays on body motion communication.* Philadelphia, PA: University of Pennsylvania Press.

Black, D. (1976). *The behavior of law.* New York: Academic Press.

Blacking, J. (1978). Uses of the kinship idiom in friendships at some Venda and Zulu schools. In J. Argyle & E. Preston-Whyte (Eds.), *Social system and tradition in Southern Africa* (pp. 101–117). Cape Town: Oxford University Press.

Blackwood, E. (1985). Breaking the mirror: The construction of lesbianism and the anthropological discourse on homosexuality. *Journal of Homosexuality, 11*(3/4), 1–17.

Bloomfield, L. (1933). Dialect geography. In H. Hoijer (Ed.), *Language history* (pp. 321–345). New York: Holt, Rinehart & Winston, Inc.

Blount, B. G. (1974). *Language, culture and society: A book of readings.* Cambridge, MA: Winthrop.

Blumenbach, J. (1775). *De Generis Humani Varietate Nativa.* Göttingen. Translated by T. Yshe as *On the natural history of mankind* (1865) in The Anthropological Treatises of Blumenbach and Hunter (p. 145–276). London: Anthropological Society.

Boas, F. (1888). *The central Eskimo.* (Annual Report, 6). Washington, DC: Bureau of American Ethnology.

Boas, F. (1911). Handbook of American Indian languages. Smithsonian Institution, Bureau of American Ethnology, Bulletin 40. Washington, DC: Government Printing Office.

Bodley, J. H. (1975). *Victims of progress.* Menlo Park, CA: Cummings.

Bogoras, W. (1907). *The Chukchee—religion.* (Memoirs of the American Museum of Natural History, No. 11, Part 2). New York: American Museum of Natural History.

Bohannan, P. (1955). Some principles of exchange and investment among the Tiv. *American Anthropologist, 57,* 60–70.

Bohannan, P. (1963). *Social anthropology.* New York: Holt, Rinehart & Winston.

Bohannan, P., & Glazer, M. (Eds.). (1973). *High points in anthropology.* New York: Alfred A. Knopf.

Bohannan, P., & Middleton, J. (Eds.). (1968). *Marriage, family, and residence.* New York: Natural History Press.

Bonwick, J. (1884). *The lost Tasmanian race.* London: S. Low, Marston, Searle, & Rivington.

Boserup, E. (1965). *The condition of agricultural growth: The economics of agrarian change under population pressures.* Chicago: Aldine-Atherton.

Bourdieu, P. (1977). *Outline of theory of practice* (R. Nice, Trans.). Cambridge: Cambridge University Press.

Bourdieu, P. (1982). *Ce que parler veut dire.* Paris: Fayard.

Bourdieu, P. (1984). *Distinction: A social critique of the judgment of taste* (R. Nice, Trans.). Cambridge: Harvard University Press.

Bourguignon, E. (1974). Culture and the varieties of consciousness. *Addison-Wesley Module in Anthropology* (No. 47). Reading, MA: Addison-Wesley Publishing.

Bourguignon, E., & Greenberg, L. (1973). *Homogeneity and diversity in world societies.* New Haven, CT: Human Relations Area Files.

Breslau, K. (1990, January 22). Overplanned parenthood: Ceausescu's cruel law. *Newsweek,* p. 35.

Briggs, J. (1980). Kapluna daughter: Adopted by the Eskimo. In Spradley & D. McCurdy (Eds.), *Conformity and Conflict* (4th ed., pp. 44–62). Boston: Little, Brown & Company.

Briggs, J. (1986). Kapluna daughter. In P. Golde (Ed.), *Women in the field: Anthropological experiences* (pp. 19–44). Berkeley: University of California Press.

Brown, J. (1963). A cross-cultural study of female initiation rites. *American Anthropologist, 656,* 837–853.

Brown, J. K. (1970). A note on the division of labor by sex. *American Anthropologist, 72,* 1073–1078.

Brown, S. J., & Batty, J. C. (1976). Energy allocation in the food system: A microscale view. *Transactions of the American Society of Agricultural Engineers, 19*(4), 758–761.

Buchsbaum, M. S. (1979). Tuning in an hemispheric dialogue. *Psychology Today, 12*(8), 100.

Bunch, C. (1975, Fall). Not for lesbians only. *Quest: A Feminist Quarterly,* (Theories of Revolution) *2*(2) 50–56.

Bunster, X. (1984). The torture of women political prisoners: A case study in female sexual slavery. In K. Barry, C. Bunch, & S. Castley (Eds.), *International feminism: Networking against female sexual slavery* (pp. 94–102). New York: International Women's Tribune Centre, Inc.

Bunzel, R. (1952). *Chichicastenango: A Guatemalan village* (*Monographs of the American Ethnological Society, 22*). New York: J. J. Augustin.

Burch, E. S., Jr. (1970). Marriage and divorce among the north Alaska Eskimos. In P. Bohannan (Ed.), *Divorce and after*. Garden City, New York: Doubleday.

Burch, E. S., Jr. (1975). *Eskimo kinsmen: Changing family relationships in northwest Alaska*. American Ethnological Society Monograph 59. St. Paul: West.

Burger, J. (1987). *Report from the frontier: The state of the world's indigenous peoples*. London: Zed Books Ltd.

Burgess, F. W., & Wallin, P. (1953). Homogamy in social characteristics. *American Journal of Sociology, 49*, 109–124.

Burling, R. (1970). *Man's many voices: Language in the cultural context*. New York: Holt, Rinehart & Winston.

Cain, A. C. (1964). On the memory of 'playing crazy,' in borderline children. *Psychiatry, 27*, 281–282.

Cairns, G. (1984). Law and the status of women in Latin America: A Survey. *Development Law and Policy Program Working Paper No. 13*. New York: Columbia University.

Calder, J. E. (1874). Some accounts of the wars of extermination, and habits of the native tribes of Tasmania. *Journal of the Anthropological Institute of Britain and Ireland, 3*.

Callender, C., & Kochems, L. (1983). The North American berdache. *Current Anthropology, 23*(4), 443–456.

Calman, L. J. (1987, September). Are women's rights human rights? *Women in International Development Working Paper No. 146*. East Lansing, MI: Michigan State University.

Campbell, S. (1983). Kula in Vakuta: The mechanics of *keda*. In J. Leach & E. Leach (Eds.), *The kula: New perspectives on Massim exchange*. Cambridge: Cambridge University Press.

Cannon, W. B. (1942). Voodoo death. *American Anthropologist, 44*, 169–181.

Carneiro, R. (1970). A theory of the origin of the state. *Science, 169*, 733–738.

Carneiro, R. (1978). Political expansion as an expression of a principle of competitive exclusion. In R. Cohen & E. Service (Eds.), *Origins of the state* (pp. 205–233). Philadelphia, PA: ISHI.

Carroll, J. B. (1956). *Language, thought and reality: Selected writings of Benjamin Lee Whorf*. Cambridge, MA: M.I.T. Press.

Casagrande, J. B. (Ed.). (1960). *In the company of man: Twenty portraits by anthropologists*. New York: Harper & Row.

Cassirer, E. (1944). *An essay on man: An introduction to a philosophy of human culture*. New Haven, CT: Yale University Press.

Chagnon, N. A. (1974). *Studying the Yąnomamö*. New York: Holt, Rinehart & Winston.

Chagnon, N.A. (1983). *Yąnomamö: The fierce people* (3rd ed.). New York: Holt, Rinehart & Winston.

Chomsky, N. (1965). *Aspects of the theory of syntax*. Cambridge, MA: The M.I.T. Press.

Chomsky, N. (1971). Language acquisition. In J. P. B. Allen & P. Van Buren (Eds.), *Chomsky: Selected readings* (pp. 127–148). London: Oxford University Press.

Clements, F. E. (1932). *Primitive concepts of disease*. (Publications in American Archaeology and Ethnology, *32*[2]). Berkeley, CA: University of California Press.

Clifford, J. (1983, Spring). On ethnographic authority. *Representations, 1*, 118–146.

Clifford, J., & Marcus, G. (1983). *Writing culture: The process and politics of ethnography*. Berkeley: University of California Press.

Codere, H. (1950). *Fighting with property*. (*Monographs of the American Ethnological Society, 18*). New York: J. J. Augustin.

Codere, H. (Ed.). (1967). *Kwakiutl ethnography*. Chicago: University of Chicago Press.

Coe, R. (1970). *The sociology of medicine*. New York: McGraw-Hill.

Cohen, Y. A. (1964). *The transition from childhood to adolescence: Cross cultural studies in initiation ceremonies, legal systems, and incest taboos*. Chicago: Aldine.

Cohen, Y. A. (Ed.). (1974). *Man in adaptation: The cultural present*. Chicago: Aldine.

Cohn, W. (1967). "Religion" in non-western culture? *American Anthropologist, 69*, 73–76.

Conklin, H. C. (1956). Hanunóo color categories. *Southwestern Journal of Anthropology, 11*, 339–344.

Cook, R. J. (1990, Fall). Taking women's rights seriously. *WID Bulletin, 6*(1) 22–23.

Cooper, J. M. (1946). The Yahgan. In J. H. Steward (Ed.), *Handbook of South American Indians* (Vol. 1, pp. 97–98). Washington, DC: Smithsonian Institution, Bureau of American Ethnology. Bulletin 143.

Coult, A. D., & Habenstein, R. W. (1965). *Cross tabulations of Murdock's world ethnographic sample*. Columbia, MO: University of Missouri Press.

Council of State Governments, The. (1986). State elective officials & the legislature: 1985–86. Lexington, KY: Author.

Cowley, G., with Murr, A., DeLaPena, N., & Quade, V. (1989, June 26). The plunder of the past. *Newsweek*, pp. 58–60.

Crane, J., & Angrosino, M. V. (1974). *Field projects in anthropology: A student handbook*. Morristown, NJ: General Learning Press.

Crapo, Richley H. (1987). Sexuality and kinship: Factors in the cross-cultural patterning of homosexuality. Paper presented at the annual meetings of the American Anthropological Association, Critchfield, R. (1981). *Villages*. Garden City, NY: Doubleday Anchor Press, Chicago.

Culbert, S. S. (Ed.). (1982). *The world almanac and book of facts*. New York: Newspaper Enterprise Association.

Czaplicka, M. A. (1914). *Aboriginal Siberia: A study in social anthropology*. Oxford, CT: Clarendon.

Dahlberg, F. (Ed.). (1981). *Woman the gatherer*. New Haven, CT: Yale University Press.

Dalby, L. (1985). *Geisha*. New York: Random House, Vintage Books.

Dalton, G. (1969). Theoretical issues in economic anthropology. *Current Anthropology, 10*, 63–102.

Daly, M. (1978). *Gyn-ecology: The metaethics of radical feminism*. Boston: Beacon Press.

D'Andrade, R. (1961). The anthropological study of dreams. In F. L. K. Hsu (Ed.), *Psychological anthropology* (pp. 296–332). Homewood, IL: Dorsey.

Darwin, C. (1857). *On the origin of species*. New York: Atheneum.

Darwin, C. (1965). *The expression of emotions in man and animals*. Chicago, IL: The University of Chicago Press. (Facsimile reprint of 1859 edition)

Das, M. (1989). *Dowry violence against women in India*. Unpublished Master's thesis, Colorado State University, Fort Collins, CO.

Dentan, R. K. (1968). *The Semi: A nonviolent people of Malaya*. New York: Holt, Rinehart & Winston.

Dentan, R. K. (1988). Rejoinder to Nanda. *American Anthropologist, 90*(2), 423.

Derrida, J. (1976). *On grammatology*. Baltimore, MD: Johns Hopkins University Press.

Devale, W. T., & Harris, M. (1976). Population, warfare and the male supremacist complex. *American Anthropologist, 78*, 521–538.

Devereux, G. (1967). A typological study of abortion in 350 primitive, ancient, and pre-industrial societies. In H. Rosen (Ed.), *Abortion in America*. Boston: Beacon Press.

DeVore, P. (1965). Language and communication. In P. L. Devore (Ed.), *The origin of man* (pp. 77–77a). New York: The Wenner-Gren Foundation for Anthropological Research.

Dibble, C. E., & Anderson, A. J. O. (Trans.). (1950–1969). *Florentine codex: General History of the things of New Spain* (Vols. 1-12). Salt Lake City, UT: The School for American Research and the University of Utah.

Divale, W. (1972). Systematic population control in the middle and upper Paleolethic: Inferences based on contemporary hunters and gatherers. *World Archaeology, 4*, 222–243.

Divale, W., Chambaris, F., & Gangloff, D. (1976). War, peace and marital residence in pre-industrial societies. *Journal of Conflict Resolution, 20*, 57–78.

Divale, W., & Harris, M. (1976). Population, warfare and the male supremacist complex. *American Anthropologist, 78*, 521–538.

Doctor, R. F. (1988). A review of the literature on transvestism and transsexualism. In R. F. Doctor, *Transvestites and transsexuals: Toward a theory of cross-gender behavior* (pp. 39–71). New York: Plenum Press.

Doerr, E., & Prescott, T. W. (1990). Abortion rights and fetal personhood (2nd ed.). Long Beach, CA: Centerline Press.

Douglas, M. (1966). *Purity and danger: An analysis of conflicts of pollution and taboo*. New York: Praeger and London: Routledge & Kegan Paul.

Douglas, M., & Isherwood, B. (1979). *The world of goods: Toward an anthropology of consumption*. New York: W. W. Norton.

Downie, D. C., & Hally, D. J. (1961). A cross-cultural study of male transvestism and sex-role differentiation. Unpublished manuscript. Dartmouth College.

DuBois, C. (1944). *People of Alor: A social psychological study of an East Indian island* (Vols. 1-2). Minneapolis, MN: University of Minnesota Press.

DuBois, C. (1955). The dominant value profile of American culture. *American Anthropologist, 57*, 1232–1239.

Dumont, J. P. (1978). *The headman and I: Ambiguity and ambivalence in the fieldwork experience*. Austin: University of Texas Press.

Dumont, L. (1970). *Homo heirarchicus*. Chicago: University of Chicago Press.

Durkheim, E. (1915). *The elementary forms of the religious life*. J. W. Swain (Trans.). London: Allen & Unwin. (Original work published 1912)

Eastwell, H. D. (1982). Voodoo death and the mechanism for dispatch of the dying in East Arnhem, Australia. *American Anthropologist, 84*, 5–18.

Edgerton, R. B. (1965). Cultural vs. ecological factors in the expression of values, attitudes, and personality characteristics. *American Anthropologist, 67,* 442–447.

Edgerton, R. B. (1976). *Deviance: A cross-cultural perspective.* Menlo Park, CA: Cummings.

Eichenlaub, J. E. (1963). *The marriage art.* New York: Dial Press.

Eliade, M. (1964). *Shamanism: Archaic techniques of ecstasy.* Princeton, NJ: Princeton University Press.

Ella, S. (1895). The ancient Samoan government. *Australasian Association for the Advancement of Science, 5.* Brisbane, Australia.

Ember, M. (1982). Statistical evidence for an ecological explanation of warfare. *American Anthropologist, 84,* 645–649.

Ember, M., & Ember, C. R. (1983). *Marriage, family, and kinship: Comparative studies of social organization.* New Haven, CT: Human Relations Area Files.

Emerson, O. (1923). *A Middle English reader.* New York: Macmillan.

Erikson, K. T. (1962). Notes on the sociology of deviance, *Social Problems, 9,* 307–314.

Evans-Pritchard, E. E. (1940). *The Nuer: A description of the mode of livelihood and political institutions of a Nilotic people.* London: Oxford University Press.

Evans-Pritchard, E. E. (1951). *Kinship and marriage among the Nuer.* New York: Oxford University Press.

Evans-Pritchard, E. E. (1956). *Nuer religion.* Oxford: Clarendon.

Falk, D. (1975). Comparative anatomy of the larynx in man and the chimpanzee. *American Journal of Physical Anthropology, 43,* 123–132.

Faron, L. C. (1961). *Mapuche social structure: Reintegration in a patrilineal society of central Chile.* Urbana, IL: University of Illinois Press.

Faron, L. C. (1964). *Hawks of the sun: Mapuche mortality and its ritual attributes.* Pittsburgh, PA: University of Pittsburgh Press.

Faron, L. C. (1968). *The Mapuche Indians of Chile.* New York: Holt, Rinehart & Winston.

Fillmore, R. (1989). Ph.D. survey results: 1988 doctor rate update. *Anthropology Newsletter, 30*(3), 30–32.

Fischer, A. (1986). Field work in five cultures. In P. Golde (Ed.), *Women in the field: Anthroplogical experiences* (pp. 267–289). Berkeley: University of California Press.

Fischer, J. (1961). Art styles as cultural cognitive maps. *American Anthropologist, 63,* 80–84.

Fischer, J. (1972). Why do prospects fail to come up to expectations? *CENTO Seminar on Agricultural Planning* (pp. 106–113). Ankara, Turkey: Public Relations Division, Central Treaty Organization.

Fischer, M. M. J. (1987). Beyond otherness, or the spectacularization of anthropology. *Telos, 71,* 161–170.

Flannery, K. V. (1971). The origins and ecological effects of early domestication in Iran and the Near East. In S. Struever (Ed.), *Prehistoric agriculture* (pp. 50–79). Garden City, NY: Natural History Press. (Original work published in P. J. Ucko & G. W. Dimbleby, *The domestication and exploration of plants and animals.* [1969]. Chicago: Aldine)

Ford, C. S., & Beach, F. A. (1951). *Patterns of sexual behavior.* New York: Harper & Row.

Fortune, R. (1932). Incest. *Encyclopedia of the Social Sciences, 7,* 620–622.

Fortune, R. F. (1963). *Sorcerers of Dobu: The social anthropology of the Dobu Islands of the Western Pacific.* New York: E. P. Dutton. (Original work published 1932)

Foster, G. (1965). Peasant society and the image of limited good. *American Anthropologist, 67,* 293–315.

Foucault, M. (1977). *The archeology of knowledge.* London: Tavistock.

Foulks, E. F. (1972). *The arctic hysterias of the north Eskimo* (No. 10). In Maybury-Lewis, (Ed.), *Anthropological Studies.* Washington, DC: American Anthropological Association.

Fouts, R. S., Fouts, D. H., & Schoenfeld, D. (1984, Spring). Cultural transmission of a human language in a chimpanzee mother-infant relation. *Sign Language Studies, 42,* 1–17.

Fox, R. (1967). *Kinship and marriage: An anthropological perspective.* Baltimore, MD: Penguin.

Frake, C. O. (1961). The diagnosis of disease among the Subanum of Mindanao. *American Anthropologist, 63,* 113–132.

Frake, C. O. (1964). A structural description of Subanum religious behavior. In W. Goodenough (Ed.), *Explorations in cultural anthropology* (pp. 111–129). New York: McGraw-Hill.

Fraser, D. (1972). The symbols of Ashanti kingship. In D. Fraser & H. M. Cole (Ed.), *African art and leadership* (pp. 261–293). Madison: University of Wisconsin Press.

Frayser, S. G. (1985). *Varieties of sexual experience: An anthropological perspective on human sexuality.* New Haven, CT: Human Relations Area Files.

Frazer, J. (1910). *Totemism and exogamy* (Vols. 1-4). London: Macmillan.

Frazer, J. (1922). *The golden bough: A study in magic and religion* (Vols. 1-12). New York: Macmillan. (Originally printed in 12 vols., London: Macmillan)

Freeman, D. (1983). *Margaret Mead in Somoa: The making and unmaking of an anthropological myth.* Cambridge, MA: Harvard University Press.

Freuchen, P. (1935). *Arctic adventure.* New York: Farrar & Rinehart.

Fried, M. H. (1967). *The evolution of political society: An essay in political anthropology.* New York: Random House.

Friedl, E. (1975). *Women and men: An anthropologist's view.* New York: Holt, Rinehart & Winston.

Frisch, R. (1975). Critical weights, a critical body composition, menarche and the maintenance of menstrual cycles. In E. Watts, F. Johnston, & G. Lasker (Eds.), *Biosocial interrelations in population adaptation* (pp. 309–318). The Hague: Mouton.

Frisch, R., & McArthur, J. (1974). Menstrual cycles: Fatness as a determinant of minimum weight for height necessary for their maintenance or onset. *Science, 185,* 949–951.

Furst, P. T. (Ed.). (1972). *Flesh of the gods: The ritual use of hallucinations.* New York: Praeger.

Gallup Report, The. (1985, May). *Religion in America, 50 years: 1935–1985.* Reprint No. 236.

Gardner, B. T., & Gardner, R. A. (1969). Teaching sign language to a chimpanzee. *Science, 165,* 664–672.

Gardner, B. T., & Gardner, R. A. (1985). Signs of intelligence in cross-fostered chimpanzees, *Philosophical Transactions of the Royal Society of London,* B308, 150–176.

Gay, J. (1985). Mummies and babies and friends and lovers in Lesotho. *Journal of Homosexuality, 11*(3/4), 97–116.

Geertz, C. (1963). *Agricultural involution: The processes of ecological change in Indonesia.* Berkeley, CA: University of California Press.

Geertz, C. (1966). Religion as a cultural system. In M. Banton (Ed.), *Anthropological approaches to the study of religion.* London: Tavistock.

Geertz, C. (Ed.). (1971). *Myth, symbol, and culture.* New York: W. W. Norton.

Geertz, C. (1972). Deep play: Notes on the Balinese cockfight. *Daedalus, 101,* 1–37.

Geertz, C. (1973). *The interpretation of cultures.* New York: Basic Books.

Ghazi, K. (1991, June 11). Inch by inch, the women let their hair down. *New York Times,* p. A4.

Gibbs, J. L. (Ed.). (1965). *Peoples of Africa.* New York: Holt, Rinehart & Winston.

Ginsburg, F., & Tsing, A. (1990). *Uncertain terms: Negotiating gender in American culture.* Boston: Beacon Press.

Gloucester, R. of. (1905). *Robert of Gloucester's chronicle: How the Normans came to England.* In O. F. Emerson, *A Middle English Reader* (pp. 203–210). New York: Macmillan.

Godelier, M. (1982). *La production des grandes hommes: Pouvoir et domination masculine chez les baruya de nouvelle-guinée.* In A. Verdiglione (Ed.), *Sexualité et pouvoir.* Paris: Fayard.

Goffman, E. (1955). On face-work: An analysis of ritual elements in social interaction. *Psychiatry, 18,* 213–231.

Goffman, E. (1961). *Asylums.* New York: Anchor.

Goffman, E. (1967). *Interaction ritual: Essay on face-to-face behavior.* Garden City, NY: Doubleday.

Goldman, I. (1972). *The Cubeo: Indians of the northwest Amazon.* Urbana, IL: The Illinois University Press.

Goldman, M. F. (1986). The Soviet Union: Striving for the ideal. In M. F. Goldman (Ed.), *Global Studies: The Soviet Union and Eastern Europe.* Guilford, CT: The Dushkin Publishing Group, Inc.

Goldschmidt, W. (1965). Variation and adaptability of culture. *American Anthropologist, 67,* 400–447.

Goleman, D. (1978). Why the brain blocks daytime dreams. *Psychology Today, 9*(10), 69–70.

Gona, D. (Ed.). (1987). *State elective officials and the legislature: 1987–1988.* Lexington, KY: Council for State Governments.

Goode, W. J. (1963). *World revolution and family patterns.* New York: Free Press.

Goodenough, W. H. (1956). Componential analysis and the study of meaning. *Language, 32,* 195–216.

Goody, J. (1970). Cousin terms. *Southwestern Journal of Anthropology, 26,* 125–142.

Goody, J. (1973). Bridewealth and dowry in Africa and Eurasia. In J. Goody & S. J. Tambiah (Eds.), *Bridewealth and Dowry.* Cambridge: University of Cambridge Press.

Gordon, E. (1981). An analysis of the impact of labour migration on the lives of women in Lesotho. *Journal of Development Studies, 17*(3), 59–76.

Gorer, G. (1943). Themes in Japanese culture. *Transactions of the New York Academy of Sciences* (Series II), *5,* 106–124.

Gorer, G. (1955). *Exploring English character.* London: Cresset.

Gorer, G. (1964). *The American people: A study in national character.* New York: W. W. Norton.

Gorer, G. (1966). *The danger of equality*. London: Cresset.

Gorer, G., & Rickman, J. (1949). *The people of great Russia*. London: Cresset.

Gough, K. (1959). The Nayars and the definition of marriage. *Journal of the Royal Anthropological Institute, 89*, 23–34.

Gough, K. (1961). Nayar: Central Kerala. In D. Schneider & K. Gough (Eds.), *Matrilineal Societies*. Berkeley: University of California Press.

Graburn, N. (1971). *Readings in kinship and social structure*. New York: Harper & Row.

Greenberg, J. H. (1968). *Anthropological linguistics: An introduction*. New York: Random House.

Gregerson. E. (1983). *Sexual practices: The story of human sexuality*. New York: Watts.

Gregor, T. (1982, December). No girls allowed. *Science82 Magazine, 3*(10), 26–31.

Gregor, T. (1983). Dark dreams about the white man. *Natural History, 92*(1), pp. 8–14.

Grinnell, G. B. (1961). *The Cheyenne Indians: Their history and ways of life* (Vol. 2). New York: Cooper Square Publishers.

Gross, L., Aurand, S. K., and Adessa, R. (1988). *Violence and discrimination against lesbian and gay people in Philadelphia and the Commonwealth of Pennsylvania*. Philadelphia: Philadelphia Lesbian and Gay Task Force.

Gudschinsky, S. C. (1956). The ABC's of lexicostatistics (glotto-chronology). *Word, 12*, 175–210.

Gussow, Z. (1960). Pibloktoq (hysteria) among the polar Eskimo: An ethnopsychiatric study. In W. Muensterberger & S. Axelrad (Eds.), *The psychoanalytic studies of society* (Vol. 1). New York: International University Press.

Gussow, Z. (1963). A preliminary report of kayak-angst among the Eskimo of West Greenland: A study in sensory deprivation. *International Journal of Social Psychiatry, 9*, 18–26.

Guthrie, S. (1980). A cognitive theory of religion. *Current Anthropology, 2*, 181–203.

Habermas, J. (1976). *Legitimation crisis*. T. McCarthy (Trans.). London: Heinemann.

Hahn, E. (1990). Raising eyebrows in Tonga. In P. R. DeVita (Ed.), *The humbled anthropologist: Tales from the Pacific*. Belmont, CA: Wadsworth Publishing Company.

Hall, E. T. (1959). *The silent language*. Greenwich, CT: Fawcett Publications.

Harding, T. G. (1960). Adaptation and stability. In M. D. Sahlens & E. R. Service (Eds.), *Evolution and culture* (pp. 45–68). Ann Arbor, MI: University of Michigan Press.

Harner, M. (1977). The ecological basis of Aztec cannibalism. *American Ethnologist, 4*(1), 117–135.

Harré, R. (1984). *Personal being*. Cambridge, MA: Harvard University Press.

Harris, G. (1957). Possession 'hysteria' in a Kenya tribe. *American Anthropologist, 59*, 1046–1066.

Harris, M. (1968). *The rise of anthropological theory: A history of theories of culture*. New York: Crowell.

Harris, M. (1974). *Cows, pigs, wars and witches: The riddle of culture*. New York: Random House.

Harris, M. (1979). *Cultural materialism: The struggle for a science of culture*. New York: Random House.

Harris, M. (1981). *America now: The anthropology of a changing culture*. New York: Simon & Schuster.

Harris, M. (1986). *Good to eat*. New York: Harper & Row.

Harrison, T. (1937). *Savage civilization*. London: Victor Gollancz.

Hartmann, H. (1975). Capitalism, patriarchy, and job segregation by sex. *Signs: Journal of Women in Culture and Society, 1*(3), 137–169.

Haub, C., & Kent, M. (1988). *1988 world population data sheet*. Washington, DC: Population Reference Bureau.

Hayami, Y., & Kikuchi, M. (1981). *Asian village economy at the crossroads: An economic approach to institutional change*. Tokyo: University of Tokyo Press and Baltimore, MD: The Johns Hopkins University Press.

Hayes, K. J., & Nissen, C. H. (1971). Higher mental functions of a home-raised chimpanzee. In A. M. Schrier & F. Stollnitz (Eds.), *Behavior of nonhuman primates* (Vol. 4, pp. 59–115). New York: Academic Press.

Heeren, J., Lindsay, D. B., & Mason, M. (1984). The Mormon concept of mother in heaven. *Journal for the Scientific Study of Religion, 23*(4), 396–411.

Heise, L. (1989a, March/April). Crimes of gender. *World · Watch, 2*(2), 12–21.

Heise, L. (1989b, April 8). The global war against women. *Washington Post*, pp. B1, B4.

Herdt, G. (1984). *Ritualized homosexuality in Melanesia*. Berkeley: University of California Press. (Originally published in 1982. London: Mitchell Beazley Publishers)

Herek, G. M. (1989). Hate crimes against lesbians and gay men. *American Psychologist, 44*(6), 948–955.

Herskovits, M. J. (1940). *The economic life of primitive peoples*. New York: Knopf.

Hill, J. (1978). Apes and language. *Annual Review of Anthropology, 7,* 89–112.

Hoebel, E. A. (1949). *Man in the primitive world.* New York: McGraw-Hill.

Hoebel, E. A. (1954). *The law of primitive man: A study in comparative legal dynamics.* Cambridge, MA: Harvard University Press.

Hoijer, H. (1964). Cultural implications of some Navaho linguistic categories. In D. Hymes (Ed.), *Language in culture and society: A reader in linguistics and anthropology* (pp. 142–153). New York: Harper & Row.

Hollingshead, A. B., & Redlich, F. C. (1953). Social stratification and psychiatric disorders. *American Sociological Review, 18,* 163–169.

Holmberg, A. R. (1950). *Nomads of the long bow: The Sirionó of eastern Bolivia.* Institute of Social Anthropology Publication No. 10. Washington, DC: Smithsonian Institution.

Honigmann, J. J., & Honigmann, I. (1965). *Eskimo townsmen.* Ottawa: University of Ottawa.

Hosken, F. P. (1980). Women and health: Genital and sexual mutilation of women. *International Journal of Women's Studies, 3*(1–3), 300–316.

Hsien, R. (1963). A consideration on Chinese concepts of illness and case illustrations. *Transcultural Psychiatry Research, 15,* 23–30.

Hsien, R. (1965). A study of the aetiology of koro in respect to the Chinese concept of illness. *International Journal of Social Psychiatry, 11,* 7–13.

Hsu, F. L. K. (1961). *Chinese and Americans: A study of two cultures.* New York: Henry Schuman.

Hsu, F. L. K. (Ed.). (1972). *Psychological anthropology: Approaches to culture and personality.* Morriston, NJ: Schenkman.

Hsu, F. L. K. (1983). *Rugged individualism reconsidered: Essays in psychological anthropology.* Knoxville, TN: University of Tennessee Press.

Human rights violations against women in Turkey. (1989, Spring). *Interact (A Human Rights Bulletin About Women Prisoners of Conscience),* pp. 3–10.

Hymes, D. (1964). *Language in culture and society: A reader in linguistics and anthropology.* New York: Harper & Row.

Hymes, D. (1967). Models of interaction of language and social setting. *Journal of Social Issues, 23*(2), 8–28.

Ineichen, B. (1979). The social geography of marriage. In M. Cook & G. Wilson (Eds.), *Love and attraction.* New York: Pergamon.

Jacobs, B. L. (1978). Serotonin, the crucial substance that turns off dreams. *Psychology Today, 9*(10), 70–71.

James, P. E. (with collaboration by Kline, H. V. B., Jr.). (1959). *A geography of man.* Boston: Ginn.

Jenness, D. (1922). *The Life of the Copper Eskimo,* Report of the Canadian Arctic Expedition, 1913–1918, Vol. 12. Ontario, Canada: The National Museum of Canada.

Johnson, P. (1979). *The civilization of ancient Egypt.* London: Weidenfeld & Nicholson.

Joint Economic Committee, Congress of the United States. (1986). Concentration of wealth in the U.S.: Trends in the distribution of wealth among American families. Washington, DC: U.S. Government Printing Office.

Jorgensen, J. G., & Truzzi, M. (1974). *Anthropology and American life.* Englewood Cliffs, NJ: Prentice Hall.

Josephides, L. (1985). *The production of inequality: Gender and exchange among the Kewa.* NY: Tavistock.

Kaplan, D. (1960). The law of cultural dominance. In M. D. Sahlins & E. R. Service (Eds.), *Evolution and culture* (pp. 69–92). Ann Arbor, MI: University of Michigan Press.

Kaplan, D., & Manners, R. A. (1972). *Culture theory.* Englewood Cliffs, NJ: Prentice Hall.

Kardiner, A. (Ed.). (1939). *The individual and his society.* New York: Columbia University Press.

Keesing, R. M. (1975). *Kin groups and social structure.* New York: Holt, Rinehart & Winston.

Keesing, R. M. (1982). Introduction. In G. Herdt (Ed.), *Rituals of manhood: Male initiation in Papua New Guinea* (pp. 1–43). Berkeley: University of California Press.

Keil, C. (1979). *Tiv song.* Chicago: University of Chicago Press.

Keller, H. (1954). *The story of my life.* Garden City, NY: Doubleday & Company.

Kellog, W. N. (1968). Communication and language in the home-raised chimpanzee. *Science 162,* 423–427.

Kemper, T. D. (1978). *A social interactional theory of emotions.* New York: John Wiley & Sons.

Kent, M. M., & Haub, C. (1985). *World population data sheet.* In E. M. Murphy *World population: Toward the next century.* Washington, DC: Population Reference Bureau.

Kenyatta, J. (1968). *Facing Mount Kenya: The tribal life of the Gikuyu.* New York: Random House.

Kerkhoff, A. C., & Davis, K. E. (1962). Values consensus and need complementary in mate selection. *American Sociological Review, 27,* 295–303.

Kiev, A. (1972). *Transcultural psychology.* New York: Macmillan.

Kispert, R. J. (1971). *Old English: An introduction.* New York: Holt, Rinehart & Winston.

Kluckhohn, C. (1944). *Navaho witchcraft. Papers of the Peabody Museum of American Archeology and Ethnology, Harvard University, 22*(2). Cambridge, MA: Harvard University Press.

Kluckhohn, C. (1965). Recurrent themes in myth and myth-making. In A. Dundes (Ed.), *The study of folklore* (pp. 158–168). Englewood Cliffs, NJ: Prentice Hall.

Kluckhohn, C., & Leighton, D. (1962). *The Navaho.* Garden City, NY: Doubleday. (Originally published 1946 by the President and Fellows of Harvard University)

Koestler, A. (1964). *The act of creation.* New York: Macmillan.

Kolanda, P. (1978). *Castes in contemporary India.* Menlo Park, CA: Cummings.

Kolata, G. B. (1974). !Kung hunter-gatherers: Feminism, diet and birth control. *Science, 185,* 932–934.

Kramer, S. N. (1959). *History begins at Sumer.* Garden City, NY: Doubleday.

Kressel, G. M. (1981, April). Sororicide/filiacide: Homicide for family honour. *Current Anthropology, 22*(2), 141–158.

Krige, E. J., & Krige, J. D. (1943). *The realm of the rain-queen.* London: Oxford University Press.

Kroeber, A. L. (1939). Cultural and natural areas of native North America. *American Archaeology and Ethnology, 38.*

Kroeber, A. L. (1944). *Configurations of culture growth.* Berkeley, CA: University of California Press.

Kroeber, A. L., & Kluckhohn, C. (1952, November 1). *Culture: A critical review of concepts and definitions. Papers of the Peabody Museum of American Archaeology and Ethnology, 47.* (Reprinted by Random House, n.d.)

Krupke, D. F., & Lavie, P. (1975). Ultradian rhythms: The 90-minute clock inside us. *Psychology Today, 8*(11), 54–57.

Kübler-Ross, E. (1969). *On death and dying.* New York: Macmillan.

LaBarre, W. (1945). Some observations of character structure in the Orient: The Japanese. *Psychiatry, 8,* 326–342.

Labov, W. (1972). *Language in the inner city: Studies in the black English vernacular.* Philadelphia: University of Pennsylvania Press.

Lacan, J. (1967). *Ecrits.* Paris: Seuil.

Laitman, J. (1984, August). The anatomy of human speech. *Natural History,* pp. 20–27.

Lancaster, J. B. (1968). Primate communication systems and the emergence of human language. In P. C. Jay (Ed.), *Primates: Studies in adaptation and variability* (pp. 447–454). New York: Holt, Rinehart & Winston.

Langness, L. L. (1965). Hysterical psychosis in the New Guinea highlands: A Bena Bena example. *Psychiatry, 28,* 258–277.

Lappé, F. M., & Collins, J. (1977). *Food first: Beyond the myth of scarcity.* New York: Random House.

Lawless, R., Sutlive, V. H., Jr., & Zamora, M. D. (1983). *Fieldwork: The human experience.* New York: Gordon & Breach.

Lazarus, R. S. (1991). *Emotion and adaptation.* NY: Oxford University Press.

Leach, E. (1969). Virgin birth. In E. Leach, *Genesis as myth and other essays.* London: Jonathan Cape.

Leaf, M. (1971). Baking and roasting: A compact demonstration of a cultural code. *American Anthropologist, 73,* 267–268.

Leavitt, G. C. (1989). The disappearance of the incest taboo: A cross-cultural test of general evolutionary hypotheses. *American Anthropologist, 91,* 116–131.

Lee, G. R., & Kezis, M. (1968). Family structure and the status of the elderly. *Journal of Comparative Family Studies, 10,* 429–443.

Lee, R. B. (1969). !Kung Bushman subsistence: An input-output analysis. In A. P. Vayda (Ed.), *Environment and cultural behavior: Ecological studies in cultural anthropology.* Garden City, NY: The Natural History Press.

Lee, R. B. (1972). *The Dobe !Kung.* New York: Holt, Rinehart & Winston.

Lee, R. B. (1979). *The !Kung San: Men, women and work in a foraging society.* Cambridge: Cambridge University Press.

Lee, R. B. & DeVore, I. (Eds.). (1968a). *Man the hunter.* Chicago: Aldine.

Lee, R. B. & DeVore, I. (1968b). Population growth and the beginnings of sedentary life among the !Kung Bushmen. In B. Spooner (Ed.), *Population growth: Anthropological implications* (pp. 329–342). Cambridge, MA: M.I.T. Press.

Lehmann, A. C., & Myers, J. E. (1985). *Magic, witchcraft, and religion: An anthropological study of the supernatural.* Palo Alto, CA: Mayfield.

Lehmann, H. E. (1975). Schizophrenia: Clinical features. In A. M. Freedman, H. I. Kaplan, & B. J. Sadock (Eds.), *Comprehensive textbook of psychiatry-II* (Vol. 1, pp. 890–923). Baltimore, MD: Williams & Wilkins.

Lehne, K. (1976). Homophobia among men. In D. David & B. Brannon (Eds.), *The forty-nine percent majority* (pp. 66–88). Redding, MA: Addison-Wesley.

Lenneberg, E. H. (1967). *The biological foundations of language*. New York: Wiley.

Lessa, W. A., & Vogt, E. Z. (Eds.). (1979). *Reader in comparative religion*. (4th ed.). New York: Harper & Row.

LeVine, R. A. (1973). *Culture, behavior and personality*. Chicago: Aldine.

LeVine, R. A. (Ed.). (1974). *Culture and personality: Contemporary readings*. Chicago: Aldine.

Levi-Strauss, C. (1950). *Sociologie et anthropologie*. Paris: Presses Universitaires de France.

Lévi-Strauss, C. (1955). The structural study of myth. *Journal of American Folklore, 67*, 428–444.

Lévi-Strauss, C. (1967). *Structural anthropology*. C. Jacobson & B. G. Schoepf (Trans.). New York: Anchor Books by arrangement with Basic Books, Inc.

Levy, H. S. (1966). *Chinese footbinding: The history of a curious erotic custom*. New York: Walton Rawls.

Lewis, I. M. (1971). *Ecstatic religion*. Baltimore: Penguin Books.

Lewis, L. S., & Brissett, D. (1967). Sex as work: A study of avocational counseling. *Social Problems, 15*(1) 8–18.

Lewis, O. (1966). Culture of poverty. *Scientific American, 215*, 19–25.

Li, An-che. (1937). Zuñi: Some observations and queries. *American Anthropologist, 39*, 62–77.

Lieberman, P. (1984). *The biology and evolution of language*. Cambridge, MA: Harvard University Press.

Lieberman, P., & Crelin, E. S. (1971). On the speech of Neanderthal. *Linguistic Inquiry, 2*, 203–222.

Linden, E. (1974). *Apes, men and language*. New York: Penguin.

Linnaeus, C. (1735). *Systema naturae per regna tria naturae secundum classes, ordines, species cum characteribus, differentiis, synonymis, locis*. Stockholm: Laurentii Salvii. (1956 photographic facsimile of the First Volume of the Tenth Edition. London: British Museum [Natural History])

Lizot, J. (1976). *The Yanomami in the face of ethnocide*. The International Work Group for Indigenous Affairs, Document 22.

Llewellyn, K. N., & Hoebel, E. A. (1941). *The Cheyenne way*. Norman, OK: University of Oklahoma Press.

Lomax, A. (1962). Song structure and social structure. *Ethnology, 1*, 425–451.

Lomax, A. (1968). *Folk song style and culture* (Publication No. 88). Washington, DC: American Association for the Advancement of Science.

Lomax, A., & Arensberg, C. M. (1977). A worldwide evolutionary classification of cultures by subsistence systems. *American Anthropologist, 18*, 659–708.

Lowie, R. H. (1937). *The history of ethnological theory*. New York: Holt, Rinehart & Winston.

Ludwig, A. M. (1972). Altered state of consciousness. In C. T. Tart (Ed.), *Altered states of consciousness* (pp. 11–24). Garden City, NY: Doubleday. (Original work published 1966, *Archives of General Psychiatry, 15*, 215–234)

Lustig-Arecco, V. (1975). *Technology: Strategies for Survival*. New York: Holt, Rinehart & Winston.

Maine, H.S. (1879). *Ancient law: Its connection with the early history of ideas, and its relation to modern ideas*. London: J. Murray.

Malinowski, B. (1922). *Argonauts of the western Pacific*. New York: Dutton.

Malinowski, B. (1926). *Crime and custom in savage society*. London: Rutledge & Kegan Paul.

Malinowski, B. (1929). *The sexual life of savages in northwestern Melanesia: An ethnographic account of courtship, marriage and family life among the natives of the Trobriand Islands, British New Guinea*. New York: Harcourt, Brace & World.

Malinowski, B. (1939a). The group and the individual in functional analysis. *American Journal of Sociology, 44*, 938–964.

Malinowski, B. (1939b). *Sex and repression in savage society*. London: Kegan Paul, Trench, Trubner & Co.

Malinowski, B. (1945). *Dynamics of culture change: An inquiry into race relations in Africa*. (P. Kaberry, Ed.). New Haven: Yale University Press.

Mandelbaum, D. G. (1968). *Selected writings of Edward Sapir in language, culture and personality*. Berkeley, CA: University of California Press.

Mandelbaum, D. G. (1972). *Society in India*. Berkeley, CA: University of California Press.

Marcus, G. E. (1986). Afterword: Ethnographic writing and anthropological careers. In J. Clifford & G. E. Marcus (Eds.), *Writing culture* (pp. 262–266). Berkeley: University of California Press.

Marcus, G. E., & Cushman, D. (1982). Ethnographies as texts. *Annual Review of Anthropology, 11*, 25–69.

Marcus, G. E., & Fischer, M. M. J. (1986). *Anthropology as culture critique: An experimental moment in the human sciences*. Chicago: University of Chicago Press.

Marett, R. R. (1909). *The threshold of religion*. London: Methuen.

Marriage: A garment of society. (1984). *Mahjubah*, *3*(3), 16–19.

Marsella, A. J., DeVos, G., & Hsu, F. L. K. (Eds.). (1985). *Culture and self: Asian and western perspectives*. New York: Tavistock Publications.

Martin, M. K., & Voorhies, B. (1975). *Female of the species*. New York: Columbia University Press.

Marx, K. (1961). *Economic and philosophic manuscripts of 1844*. Moscow: Foreign Language Publishing House.

McCarley, R. W. (1978). Where dreams come from: A new theory. *Psychology Today, 12*(7), 15–20.

Mead, M. (1928). *Coming of age in Samoa: A psychological study of primitive youth for western civilization*. New York: Morrow.

Mead, M. (1942). *And keep your powder dry: An anthropologist looks at America*. NY: Morrow.

Mead, M. (1950). *Sex and treatment in three primitive societies*. New York: Mentor.

Meggit, M. (1964). Male-female relationships in the highlands of Australian New Guinea. In J. B. Watson (Ed.), *New Guinea: The central highlands*. American Anthropological Association Special Publication 6 (No. 4, Pt. 2). Washington, DC: American Anthropological Association.

Mejer, M. (1985, May). Oppression of women and refugee status. *International Seminar on Refugee Women* (pp. 30–38). Amsterdam: Dutch Refugee Association.

Miller, S. N. (1974). The playful, the crazy and the nature of pretense. In E. Norbeck (Ed.), *The anthropological study of human play* (Rice University Studies *60*[3]), 31–52. Houston, TX: William Rice University.

Minister of Supply and Services, The. (1988). *Canada yearbook: 1988*. Ottowa: The Minister of Supply and Services.

Minturn, L., & Lambert, W. W. (1964). *Mothers of six cultures: Antecedents of child rearing*. New York: Wiley.

Montagu, A. (1974). *Man's most dangerous myth: The fallacy of race*. Fair Lawn: Oxford University Press.

Montagu, A. (Ed.). (1980). *Sociobiology examined*. New York: Oxford University Press.

Montagu, A. (1986). *Touching: The human significance of the skin* (3rd ed.). NY: Harper & Row.

Morgan, L. H. (1851). *League of the ho-de-no-saunee or Iroquois*. Rochester, NY: Sage & Brothers.

Morgan, L. H. (1877). *Ancient society*. New York: World.

Moris, J. (1981). *Managing induced rural development*. Bloomington, IN: International Development Institute.

Mosher, S. (1983). *Broken earth: The rural Chinese*. NY: Free Press.

Mounin, G. (1976). Language, communication, chimpanzees. *Current Anthropology, 17*, 1–21.

Mueller, M. B. (1977). *Women and men in rural Lesotho: The periphery of the periphery*. Waltham, MA: Brandeis University.

Munroe, R. L., & Munroe, R. H. (1977). Male transvestism and subsistence economy. *The Journal of Social Psychology, 103,* 307–308.

Munroe, R. L., Munroe, R. H., & Whiting, J. (1973). The couvade: A psychological analysis. *Ethos, 1*(1), 30–74.

Munroe, R. L., Whiting, J. W. M., & Hally, D. J. (1969). Institutionalized male transvestism and sex distinctions. *American Anthropologist, 71*(1), 87–91.

Murdock, G. P. (1934). *Our primitive contemporaries*. New York: Macmillan.

Murdock, G. P. (1950). Family stability in non-European cultures. *Annals of the American Academy, 272,* 195–201.

Murdock, G. P. (1957). World ethnographic sample. *American Anthropologist, 59,* 664–487.

Murdock, G. P. (1967). *Ethnographic atlas*. Pittsburgh: The University of Pittsburgh Press.

Murdock, G. P., Ford, C. S., Hudson, A. E., Kennedy, R., Simmons, L. W., & Whiting, J. W. (1981). *Outline of cultural materials* (5th ed.). New Haven, CT: Human Relations Area Files.

Murdock, G. P., & Provost, C. (1973). Factors in the division of labor by sex: A cross-cultural analysis. *Ethnology, 12,* 203–225.

Murphy, J. M. (1976). Psychiatric labeling in cross-cultural perspective. *Science, 191*(4230), 1019–1028.

Murphy, R. F., & Kasdan, L. (1959). The structure of parallel cousin marriage. *American Anthropologist, 61,* 17–29.

Musil, A. (1928). *Manners and customs of the Rwala Bedouins*. New York: The American Geographical Society.

Nadel, S. F. (1952). Witchcraft in four African societies: An essay in comparison. *American Anthropologist, 54,* 18–29.

Nader, L. (Ed.) (1965). The ethnography of law. *American Anthropologist* (Special supplement to Vol. 67, pp. 3–32).

Nader, L., & Todd, H. F., Jr. (1978). *The disputing process: Law in ten societies*. New York: Columbia University Press.

Nanda, S. (1985). The Hijras of India: Cultural and individual dimensions of an institutionalized third gender role. *Journal of Homosexuality, 11*(3/4), 35–54.

Nanda, S. (1988). More dialogue on the 'blood-thirsty' Semai. *American Anthropologist, 90*(2), 422–423.

Nanda, S. (1990). *Neither man nor woman: The Hijras of India.* Belmont, CA: Wadsworth Publishing Company.

Naroll, R. (1966). Does military deterrence deter? *Trans-Action, 3*(2), 14–20.

Naroll, R. (1973). Holocultural theory tests. In R. Naroll & F. Naroll (Eds.), *Main currents in cultural anthropology* (pp. 309–384). New York: Appleton-Century-Crofts.

Nash, M. (1966). *Primitive and peasant economic systems.* San Francisco: Chandler.

Nash, N. C. (1992, August 17). A cup of coca tea, anyone? Bolivia sees a market. *New York Times,* p. 2.

Nassehi-Behnam, V. (1985). Change and the Iranian family. *Current Anthropology, 26,* 557–562.

National Center for Health Statistics, Vital and Health Statistics. (1963). *Divorce statistics analysis United States* (Series 21, No. 13, Table C). Washington, DC: U.S. Government Printing Office.

National Committee on Pay Equity. (1989). Pay equity activity in the public sector: 1979–1989.

Neale, W. C. (1976). *Monies in societies.* San Francisco: Chandler & Sharp.

Needham, R. (Ed.). (1972). *Rethinking kinship and marriage.* London: Tavistock.

Nelson, M. (1989). Why witches were women. In J. Freeman (Ed.), *Women: A feminist perspective* (4th ed.) (pp. 335–350). Mountain View, CA: Mayfield.

Nemiah, J. C. (1975). Phobic neurosis. In A. M. Freedman, H. I. Kaplan, & B. J. Sadock (Eds.), *Comprehensive textbook of psychiatry-II* (Vol. 2, pp. 1247–1255). Baltimore, MD: Williams and Wilkins.

Neusner, J. (1979). *The Talmud as anthropology.* NY: The Jewish Theological Seminary of America.

Newman, P. L. (1964). Wild man behavior in a New Guinea highlands community. *American Anthropologist, 66,* 1–19.

Nock, S. L., & Kingston, P. W. (1990). The political institution: The politics of abortion. In S. Nock & P. W. Kingston (Eds.), *The sociology of public issues* (pp. 194–213). Belmont, CA: Wadsworth Publishing Company.

Noll, R. (1985). Mental imagery cultivation as a cultural phenomenon: The role of visions in shamanism. *Current Anthropology, 26,* 443–461.

O'Kelley, C. G. (1980). *Women and men in society.* New York: Van Nostrand.

Okonjo, K. (1976). The dual-sex political system in operation: Igbo women and community politics in midwestern Nigeria. In N. J. Hafkin & E. G. Bay (Eds.), *Women in Africa.* Stanford: Stanford University Press.

Ortner, S. B. (1974). Is female to male as nature is to culture? In M. Z. Rosaldo & L. Lamphere (Eds.), *Women, culture, and society* (pp. 67–87). Stanford, CA: Stanford University Press.

Ortner, S. B., & Whitehead, H. (Eds.). (1981). *Sexual meanings: The cultural construction of gender and sexuality* (pp. 80–115). London: Cambridge University Press.

Otterbein, K. F. (1970). *The evolution of war.* New Haven: Human Relations Area Files.

Otto, R. (1923). *The idea of the holy: An inquiry into the non-rational factor in the idea of the divine and its relation to the rational.* J. W. Harvey (Trans.). London: Oxford University Press.

Palmer, I. (1985). *The impact of male out-migration on women in farming.* West Hartford, CT: Kumarian Press.

Parker, S. (1962). Eskimo psychopathology in the context of Eskimo personality and culture. *American Anthropologist, 64,* 76–96.

Pasternak, B. (1976). *Introduction to kinship and social organization.* Englewood Cliffs, NJ: Prentice Hall.

Patterson, F. (1978). Conversations with a gorilla. *National Geographic, 154*(4), 438–465.

Paul, R. A. (1978). Instinctive aggression in man: The Semai case. *Journal of Anthropology, 1*(1), 65–79.

Pelto, P. J., & Pelto, G. H. (1978). *Anthropological research: The structure of inquiry* (2nd ed.). New York: Cambridge University Press.

Perham, M. F. (1937). *Native administration in Nigeria.* London: Oxford University Press.

Peters, L. G., & Price-Williams, D. R. (1980). Towards an experiential analysis of shamanism. *American Ethnologist, 7,* 397–418.

Pike, K. (1954). *Language in relation to a unified theory of the structure of human behavior, Vol 1.* Glendale: Summer Institute of Linguistics.

Polyani, K. (1966). *Dahomey and the slave trade.* Seattle: University of Washington Press.

Popkin, S. L. (1979). *The rational peasant: The political economy of rural society in Vietnam.* Berkeley: University of California Press.

Popov, A. A. (1936). *Tavgytsy: Matgerialy po ethnografi avamskikh i vedeyevskikh tavgytzevi.* Moscow and Leningrad: AN, Trudy Instituta Anthropologii i Ethnografii I, 5.

Pospisil, L. (1971). *Anthropology of law: A comparative theory.* New York: Harper & Row.

Pospisil, L. (1972). *The ethnology of law.* (Module 12). Reading, MA: Addison-Wesley Modular Publications.

Poussaint, A. F. (1967, August 20). A Negro psychiatrist explains the Negro psyche. *New York Times,* Section 6, pp. 52–80.

Powell, B., & Jacobs, J. A. (1983). Sex and consensus in occupational prestige ratings. *Sociology and Social Research 67*(4), 392–404.

Prescott, J. W. (1990). Personality profiles of 'pro-choice' and 'anti-choice' individuals and cultures. In J. W. Prescott & E. Doerr (Eds.), *Abortion rights and fetal "personhood"* (pp. 109–110). Long Beach, CA: Centerline Press.

Price-Williams, D. R. (1975). *Explorations in cross-cultural psychology.* San Francisco, CA: Chandler & Sharp.

Price-Williams, D. R. (1985). On mental imagery and shamanism. *Current Anthropology, 26*(5), 656.

Price-Williams, D. R. (n.d.). The waking dream in ethnographic perspective. In B. Tedlock (Ed.), *Dreaming: The anthropology and psychology of the imaginal.* Albuquerque, NM: University of New Mexico Press.

Rabinow, P. (1977). *Reflections on fieldwork in Morocco.* Berkeley: University of California.

Radcliffe-Brown, A. R. (1952). *Structure and function in primitive society.* London: Oxford University Press.

Radcliffe-Brown, A. R. (1958). Taboo. In W. A. Lessa & E. Z. Vogt (Eds.), *Reader in comparative religion: An anthropological approach* (pp. 45–68). Evanston, IL: Row, Peterson.

Radin, P. (1937). *Primitive religion.* New York: Dover.

Randall, T. (1990). Domestic violence intervention calls for more than treating injuries. *Journal of the American Medical Association, 264*(3), 939–940, 943.

Rappaport, R. A. (1967). Ritual regulation of environmental relations among a New Guinea people. *Ethnology, 6,* 17–30.

Rappaport, R. A. (1968). *Pigs for the ancestors: Ritual in the ecology of a Papua New Guinea people.* New Haven, CT: Yale University Press.

Rassmussen, K. (1922). *Grønlandsagen.* Berlin: Gyldendal'scher Verlag.

Rattray, R. S. (1923). *Ashanti.* London: Oxford University Press.

Rattray, R. S. (1929). *Ashanti law and constitution.* London: Clarendon Press.

Redfield, R., & Rojas, A. V. (1934). *Chan Kom, A Maya village.* Carnegie Institution Publication 448. Washington, DC: The Carnegie Institution.

Reiss, I. L. (1986). *Journey into sexuality: An exploratory voyage.* Englewood Cliffs, NJ: Prentice Hall.

Ribiero, D. (1971). *The Americas and civilization.* New York: Dutton.

Rich, A. (1980). Compulsory heterosexuality and lesbian existence. *Signs: Journal of Women in Culture and Society, 5*(4), 631–660.

Riley, P. J. (1989). *The effect of newly introduced technology on women agriculturalists in Lesotho.* Final Report, USAID Lesotho Consultancy.

Rivers, W. H. R. (1901). Introduction and vision. In R. C. Hadden, (Ed.), *Reports of the Cambridge anthropological expedition in the Torres Straits, 2*(1). Cambridge, England: The University Press.

Rivers, W. H. R. (1905). Observations on the senses of the Todas. *British Journal of Psychology, 1,* 321–396.

Robarcheck, C. A. (1987). Blood drunkenness and the bloodthirsty Semai: Unmaking another anthropological myth. *American Anthropologist, 89*(2), 356–365.

Robarcheck, C. A., & Dentan, R. K. (1979). Conflict, emotion, and abreaction: Resolution of conflict among the Semai Senoi. *Ethos, 7,* 104–123.

Roberts, J., Arth, M. J., & Bush, R. R. (1959). Games in culture. *American Anthropologist, 61,* 597–605.

Roberts, J., & Sutton-Smith, B. (1962). Child training and game involvement. *Ethnology, 1,* 166–185.

Roberts, S. (1979). *Order and dispute: An introduction to legal anthropology.* New York: St. Martin's.

Robinson, J. T. (1972). *Early hominid posture and locomotion.* Chicago: University of Chicago Press.

Rodney, W. (1972). *How Europe underdeveloped Africa.* London: Bogle-L'Ouverture Publications.

Rosaldo, M. Z., & Lamphere, L. (Eds.). (1974). *Woman, culture, and society.* Stanford, CA: Stanford University Press.

Roth, W. E. (1903). Superstition, magic and medicine. *North Queensland Ethnographic Bulletin 5.* Brisbane: G. A. Vaughn, Government Printer, Home Secretary's Department.

Rubel, A. J. (1960). Concepts of disease in Mexican-American culture. *American Anthropologist, 62,* 795–814.

Rubin, Z. (1973). *Liking and loving: An invitation to social pyschology.* New York: Holt, Rinehart & Winston.

Ruby, J. (Ed.). (1982). *A crack in the mirror: Reflexive perspectives in anthropology.* Philadelphia: University of Pennsylvania Press.

Rumbaugh, D. M., von Glasersfeld, E. C., Warner, H., et al. (1977). A computer-controlled language training system for investigating the language skills of young apes. *Biological Research Methods and Instruments, 5,* 355–362.

Russell, D. E. H., & Van de Ven, N. (Eds.). (1976). *Crimes against women: Proceedings of the international tribunal.* Millbrae, CA: Les Femmes.

Sachs, J. (1992, March). Building a market economy in Poland. *Scientific American,* pp. 34–40.

Safilios-Rothschild, C. (1985). The persistence of women's invisibility in agriculture: Theoretical and policy lessons from Lesotho and Sierra Leone. *Economic Development and Cultural Change, 33*(1), 299–317.

Sahlins, M. D. (1960). The origins of society. *Scientific American, 203,* 76–89.

Sahlins, M. D. (1962). *Primitive social organization: An evolutionary perspective.* New York: Random House.

Sahlins, M. D. (1968). *Tribesmen.* Englewood Cliffs, NJ: Prentice Hall.

Sahlins, M. D. (1972). *Stone age economics.* New York: Aldine.

Sahlins, M. D. (1976). *Cultural and practical reason.* Chicago: University of Chicago Press.

Sahlins, M. D., & Service, E. R. (1960). *Evolution and culture.* Ann Arbor, MI: University of Michigan Press.

Saitoti, T. O. (1986). *The worlds of a Maasai warrior: An autobiography.* Berkeley: University of California Press.

Sanday, P. R. (1973). Toward a theory of the status of women. *American Anthropologist, 75,* 1682–1700.

Sanday, P. R. (1974). Female status in the public domain. In M. Rosaldo & L. Lamphere (Eds.), *Women, culture, and society* (pp. 189–206). Stanford CA: Stanford University Press.

Sanday, P. R. (1981). *Female power and male dominance: On the origins of sexual inequality.* New York: Cambridge University Press.

Sapir, E. (1924). Culture, genuine and spurious. *American Journal of Sociology, 29,* 401–429.

Sapir, E. (1949). *Language: An introduction to the study of speech.* New York: Harcourt, Brace & World.

Sapir, E. (1970). Language. In D. G. Mandelbaum (Ed.), *Edward Sapir: Culture, language, and personality* (pp. 1–44). Berkeley, CA: University of California Press.

Saussure, F. de. (1959). *Course in modern linguistics.* W. Baskin (Trans.). New York: The Philosophical Library.

Savage-Rumbaugh, E. S., Pate, J. L., Lawson, J., Smith, S. T., & Rosenbaum, S. (1983). Can a chimpanzee make a statement? *Journal of Experimental Psychology: General, 112*(4), 457–492.

Savage-Rumbaugh, E. S., Rumbaugh, D. M., & Boysen, S. L. (1980). *American Scientist, 68,* 49–61.

Scheff, T. (1966). *Being mentally ill: A sociological theory.* Chicago: Aldine.

Scheff, T. (1977). The distancing of emotion in ritual. *Current Anthropology, 18*(3), 483–506.

Schlegel, A., & Barry, H., III. (1986). The cultural consequences of female contribution to subsistence. *American Anthropologist, 88,* 144–150.

Schlegel, A., & Eloul, R. (1988). Marriage transactions: Labor, property, status. *American Anthropologist, 90*(2), 291–309.

Schneider, D. M. (1968). *American kinship: A cultural account.* Englewood Cliffs, NJ: Prentice Hall.

Schneider, D. M. (1980). *American kinship: A cultural account.* (2nd ed.). Chicago: University of Chicago Press.

Schneider, D. M., & Gough, K. (Eds.). (1961). *Matrilineal kinship.* Berkeley: University of California Press.

Schuler, M. (1986). Women and the law. In R. S. Gallin, M. Aronoff, & A. Ferguson (Eds.), *The women and international development annual: Vol. 1* (pp. 155–187). Boulder, CO: Westview Press.

Schusky, E. L. (1971). *Manual for kinship analysis* (2nd ed.). New York: Holt, Rinehart & Winston.

Schusky, E. L. (1975). *Variation in kinship.* New York: Holt, Rinehart & Winston.

Schwimmer, E. (1984). Male couples in New Guinea. In G. Herdt (Ed.), *Rituals of manhood: Male initiation in Papua New Guinea* (pp. 248–291). Berkeley: University of California Press.

Scoditti, G. (1983). Kula on Kitava. In J. Leach & E. Leach (Eds.), *The Kula: New perspectives in Massim exchange.* New York: Cambridge University Press.

Scott, J. C. (1976). *The moral economy of the peasant: Rebellion and subsistence in Southeast Asia.* New Haven, CT: Yale University Press.

Scott, R. (1969). *The making of blind men.* New York: Russell Sage Foundation.

Scull, A. (1979). *Museums of madness: The social organizations of insanity in nineteenth century England.* New York: St. Martin's Press.

Seager, J., & Olson, A. (1986). *Women in the world: An international atlas.* NY: Simon & Schuster.

Selye, H. (1976). *The stress of life.* New York: McGraw-Hill.

Service, E. R. (1962). *Primitive social organization: An evolutionary perspective.* New York: Random House.

Service, E. R. (1971). *Cultural evolutionism: Theory in practice.* New York: Holt, Rinehart & Winston.

Service, E. R. (1975). *The origins of the state and civilization: The process of cultural evolution.* New York: W. W. Norton.

Service, E. R. (1976). *Culture and practical reason.* Chicago: University of Chicago Press.

Service, E. R. (1978). *Profiles in ethnology.* New York: Harper & Row.

Service, E. R. (1979). *The hunters* (2nd ed.). Englewood Cliffs, NJ: Prentice Hall.

Sharon, D. (1978). *Wizard of the four winds: A shaman's story.* New York: Macmillan.

Sharp, L. (1952). Steel axes for stone age Australians. In E. H. Spicer (Ed.), *Human problems in technological change* (pp. 69–90). New York: Russell Sage Foundation.

Sheffield, C. (1987). Sexual terrorism: The social control of women. In B. B. Hess & M. M. Ferree (Eds.), *Analyzing gender: A handbook of social science research.* Newbury Park, CA: Sage.

Shepherd, G., & Shepherd, G. (1984). *A kingdom transformed: Rhetorical patterns with institutionalization of Mormonism.* Salt Lake City, UT: University of Utah Press.

Shostak, M. (1982). *Nisa: The life and words of a !Kung woman.* New York: Random House.

Sihler, A. L. (1973). Baking and roasting. *American Anthropologist, 75,* 1721–1725.

Simmons, L. W. (Ed.). (1942). *Sun Chief: The autobiography of a Hopi Indian.* New Haven, CT: Yale University Press.

Simons, R. C., & Hughes, C. C. (1985). *The culture-bound syndromes: Folk illnesses of psychiatric and anthropological interest.* Boston: D. Reidel

Speck, F. (1909). Ethnology of the Yuchi Indians. *University of Pennsylvania, Anthropological Publications of the University Museum, 1,*(1). Philadelphia: University of Pennsylvania Press.

Spindler, G. D. (Ed.). (1970). *Being an anthropologist: Fieldwork in eleven cultures.* New York: Holt, Rinehart & Winston.

Spradley, J. F. (1980). *Participant observation.* New York: Holt, Rinehart & Winston.

Stephens, W. N. (1963). *The family in cross-cultural perspective.* New York: Holt, Rinehart & Winston.

Steward, J. H. (1938). Great-Basin sociopolitical groups. *Bureau of American Ethnology Bulletin 120.* Washington, DC: U.S. Government Printing Office.

Steward, J. H. (1955). *The theory of cultural change: The methodology of multilinear evolution.* Urbana, IL: University of Illinois press.

Stockwell, E. G., & Laidlaw, K. A. (1981a). *Third world development.* Chicago: Nelson-Hall.

Stockwell, E. G., & Laidlaw, K. A. (1981b). *Third world: Problems and prospects.* Chicago: Nelson-Hall.

Stow, G. W. (1905). *The native races of South Africa: A history of the intrusion of the Hottentots and Bantu into the hunting grounds of the Bushmen, the aborigines of the country.* London: S. Sonnenschein.

Strathern, M. (1980). No nature, no culture: The Hagen case. In C. P. MacCormack & M. Strathern (Eds.), *Nature, culture and gender* (pp. 174–222). Cambridge: Cambridge University Press.

Sussman, R. (1972). Child transport, family size and the increase in human population size during the neolithic. *Current Anthropology, 13,* 258–267.

Svenson, F. (1980). Aboriginal peoples of Siberia. In G. Ashworth (Ed.), *World minorities in the eighties.* Sunbury, England: Guttermaine House.

Swanson, G. E. (1960). *The birth of the gods: The origin of primitive beliefs.* Ann Arbor, MI: University of Michigan Press.

Swartz, M. J., Turner, V. W., & Tuden, A. (Eds). (1966). *Political Anthropology.* Chicago: Aldine.

Szasz, T. (1970). *Ideology and insanity: Essays on the dehumanization of man.* Garden City, NY: Doubleday.

Tambiah, Y. (1986). Sri Lanka: Violence and exploitation. In M. Schuler (Ed.), *Empowerment and the law: Strategies of Third World women* (pp. 145–154). Washington, DC: Overseas Education Fund.

Tanaka, J. (1977). Subsistence ecology of the Central Kalahari !Kung. In R. B. Lee & I. Devore (Eds.), *Kalahari hunter gatherers* (pp. 99–119). Cambridge, MA: Harvard University Press.

Tanfer, K., & Horn, M. (1985). Contraceptive use, pregnancy and fertility patterns among single American women in their 20's. *Family Planning Perspective, 17*(1), 10–19.

Tanner, N. (1974). *Marifocality in Indonesia and Africa and among black Americans.* In M. Z. Rosaldo & L. Lamphere (Eds.), *Women, culture, and society.* Stanford, CA: Stanford University Press.

Terrace, H. S. (1979). *Nim.* New York: Knopf.

Terrace, H. S., Pettito, L. A., Sanders, R., & Bever, T. G. (1979). Can an ape create a sentence? *Science, 206*, 891–902.

Terrace, H. S., Pettito, L., Sanders, R., & Bever, T. G. (1980). On the grammatical capacity of apes. In *Children's language* (Vol. 2., pp. 371–495). New York: Garner Press.

Thomas, E. M. (1959). *The harmless people*. New York: Knopf.

Thompson, R. F. (1968). Aesthetics in traditional Africa. *Art News, 66*(9), 44–45, 63–66.

Thompson, R. F. (1973). Yoruba artistic criticism. In W. L. d' Azevedo (Ed.), *The traditional artist in African societies* (pp. 19–61). Bloomington: Indiana.

Tien, H. Y. (1983). China: Demographic billionaire. *Population Bulletin, 38*(2). Washington, DC: Population Reference Bureau.

Times Mirror. (1987). The people, press & politics. Reading, MA: Addison Wesley.

Tobias, P. V. (1983). Recent advances in the evolution of hominids with especial reference to brain and speech. *Pontifical Academy of Sciences Scripta Varia, 50*, 85–140.

Toqueville, A. de. (1969). *Democracy in America*. New York: Knopf. (Originally published as *De la démocratie en Amérique* [1835]. London: Saunders & Otley)

Toelkin, B. (1979). *The dynamics of folklore*. Boston: Houghton Mifflin.

Tonkinson, R. (1974). *The Jigalong mob: Aboriginal victors of the desert crusade*. Menlo Park, CA: Cummings.

Torture and mistreatment of prisoners. (1982, May). A stern, steady crackdown: Legal process and human rights in South Korea. *Asia Watch*, pp. 87–107.

Toth, E. L. (1986). *The velvet ghetto*. Research Report. San Francisco: International Association of Business Consultants Foundation.

Toth, E. L. (1989). *Beyond the velvet ghetto*. Research Report. San Francisco: International Association of Business Consultants Foundation.

Tyler, E. B. (1871). *Primitive culture: Researches into the development of mythology, philosophy, religion, language, art and custom*. London: J. Murray.

Uberoi, J. P. S. (1962). *The politics of the Kula ring: An analysis of the findings of Bronislaw Malinowski*. Manchester: University of Manchester Press.

United Nations. (1989). The prospects of world urbanization as of 1984–1985. New York: United Nations.

U.S. Bureau of the Census. (1984). Projections of the population of the United States by age, sex and race: 1985–2080. In *Current population reports: Population estimates and projections* (Series P-25, No. 952). (Table 2, p. 30). Washington, DC: U.S. Government Printing Office.

U.S. Bureau of the Census. (1985). *Statistical abstract of the United States: 1986* (106th ed.). Washington, DC: U.S. Government Printing Office.

U.S. Bureau of the Census (1989). *Statistical abstract of the United States: 1989* (109th ed.). Washington, DC: U.S. Government Printing Office.

U.S. Department of Labor, Employment and Training Administration. (1977). *Dictionary of occupational titles*. Washington, DC: U.S. Government Printing Office.

U.S. Federal Bureau of Investigation. (1985). *Uniform Crime Reports*. Washington, DC: U.S. Government Printing Office.

U.S. National Commission on the Causes and Prevention of Violence. (1969). *Justice: To establish justice, to ensure domestic tranquility*. Final Report. Washington, DC: U.S. Government Printing Office.

Van Allen, J. (1976). 'Aba riots' or Igbo 'women's war'? Ideology, stratification, and the invisibility of women. In N. J. Hafkin & E. G. Bay (Eds.), *Women in Africa*. Stanford: Stanford University Press.

Van den Berghe, P., & Barash, D. (1977). *Human family systems: An evolutionary view*. New York: Elsevier Science Publishing Co.

Van Gennep, A. (1960). *The rites of passage*. S. T. Kimball (Trans.). Chicago: University of Chicago Press. (Originally published 1908)

Van Loon, F. H. G. (1926). Amok and latah. *Journal of Abnormal and Social Psychology, 21*, 434–444.

Vayda, A. P. (Ed.). (1969). *Environment and cultural behavior: Ecological studies in cultural anthropology*. New York: Natural History Press.

Vayda, A. P. (1976). *War in ecological perspective*. New York: Plenum.

Vayda, A. P., & Rappaport, R. A. (1968). Ecology: Cultural and noncultural. In J. H. Clifton (Ed.), *Introduction to cultural anthropology*. Boston: Houghton Mifflin.

Vetter, B. M., & Babco, E. L. (1986). *Professional women and minorities: A manpower resource data service*. Washington, DC: Commission on Professionals in Science and Technology.

Walker, E. (1972). *The emergent Native Americans*. Boston, MA: Little, Brown.

Wallace, A. F. C. (1961). *Culture and personality*. New York: Random House.

Wallace, A. F. C. (1966). *Religion: An anthropological view*. New York: Random House.

Wallace, A. F. C. (1972). Mental illness, biology, and culture. In F. L. K. Hsu (Ed.), *Psychological anthropology* (pp. 363–402). Cambridge, MA: Schenkman.

Warner, W. L. (1953). *American life: Dream and reality*. Chicago: University of Chicago Press.

Watzlawick, P., Beavin, J. H., & Jackson, D. (1962). *Pragmatics of human communication: A study of interactional patterns, pathologies, and paradoxes*. New York: W. W. Norton.

Weinberg, G. (1982). Homophobia. In O. Pocs (Ed.), *Annual editions: Readings in human sexuality, 85/86* (pp. 8–10). Guilford, CT: The Dushkin Publishing Group.

Weiner, A. B. (1988). *The Trobrianders of Papua New Guinea*. NY: Holt, Rinehart & Winston.

Weisner, T. S., & Gallimore, R. (1977). My brother's keeper: Child and sibling caretaking. *Current anthropology, 18,* 169–180.

Werner, D. (1979). A cross-cultural perspective on theory and research on male homosexuality. *Journal of Homosexuality, 4,* 345–362.

West, J. (1945). *Plainville, U.S.A.* New York: Columbia University Press.

White, D. R. (1987). *Cultural diversity data base*. La Jolla, CA: National Collegiate Software Clearinghouse.

White, D. R. (1988a). Causes of polygyny: Ecology, economy, kinship, and warfare. *American Anthropologist, 90*(4), 871–887.

White D. R. (1988b). Rethinking polygyny: Co-wives, codes, and cultural systems. *Current Anthropology, 29*(4), 529–572.

White, L. A. (1939). A problem in kinship terminology, *American Anthropologist, 41,* 569–570.

White, L. A. (1943). Energy and the evolution of culture. *American Anthropologist, 45,* 335–356.

White, L. A. (1948). The origin and prohibition of incest. *American Anthropologist, 50,* 416–435.

White, L. A. (1949). *The science of culture: A study of man and civilization*. New York: Grove Press.

White, L. A. (1959). *The evolution of culture*. New York: McGraw-Hill.

White, L. A. (1971). *The science of culture: A study of man and culture*. New York: Farrar, Straus & Giroux.

Whitehead, H. (1980). The bow and the burden strap: A new look at institutionalized homosexuality in native North America. In B. B. Whiting & J. W. M. Whiting (Eds.) (in collaboration with Richard Longabaugh), *Children in six cultures: A psycho-cultural analysis*. Cambridge, MA: Harvard University Press.

Whiting, B. (1950). *Paiute sorcery (No. 15)*. New York: Viking Fund Publications in Anthropology.

Whiting, J. W. M. (1959). Cultural and sociological influences on development. In *Growth and development of the child in his setting* (pp. 3–9). Baltimore, MD: Maryland Child Growth and Development Institute.

Whiting, J. W. M. (1964). Effects of climate on certain cultural practices. In W. H. Goodenough (Ed.), *Explorations in cultural anthropology: Essays in honor of George Peter Murdock* (pp. 175–195). New York: McGraw-Hill.

Whiting, J. W. M., & Child, I. L. (1953). *Child training and personality: A cross-cultural study*. New Haven, CT: Yale University Press.

Whiting, J. W. M., Kluckhohn, R., & Anthony, A. S. (1958). The function of male initiation ceremonies at puberty. In E. E. Maccoby, T. M. Newcomb, & E. L. Hartley, *Readings in social psychology* (pp. 359–370). New York: Holt, Rinehart & Winston.

Whiting, R. (1979, September 25). You've gotta have 'Wa.' *Sports Illustrated*, pp. 60–71.

Whorf, B. L. (1971a). Languages and logic. In J. B. Carroll (Ed.), *Language, thought and reality: Selected writings of Benjamin Lee Whorf* (pp. 233–245). Cambridge, MA: The MIT Press.

Whorf, B. L. (1971b). The relation of habitual thought and behavior to language. In J. B. Carroll (Ed.), *Language, thought, and reality: Selected writings of Benjamin Lee Whorf* (pp. 134–159). Cambridge, MA: The MIT Press.

Whyte, M. K. (1978a). Cross-cultural codes dealing with the relative status of women. *Ethnology, 17,* 117.

Whyte, M. K. (1978b). *The status of women in preindustrial societies*. Princeton, NJ: Princeton University Press.

Wilson, B. (1980). Kut: Catharsis, ritual healing or redressive strategy? Paper presented at the Conference on Korean Religion and Society. Mackinac Island, MI.

Wilson, E. O. (1975). *Sociobiology: The new synthesis*. Cambridge, MA: Harvard University Press.

Wilson, E. O. (1978). *Human nature*. Cambridge, MA: Harvard University Press.

Wilson, M. H. (1951). Witch beliefs and social structure. *American Journal of Sociology, 56,* 307–313.

Winiarz, W., & Wielawski, J. (1936). Imu—A psychoneurosis occuring among Ainus. *Psychoanalytic Review, 23,* 181–186.

Witherspoon, G. (1977). *Language and art in the Navajo universe*. Ann Arbor, MI: University of Michigan Press.

Wittfogel, K. (1957). *Oriental despotism: A comparative study of total power*. New Haven, CT: Yale University Press.

Wittkower, E., & Fried, J. (1957). A cross-cultural approach to mental health problems. *American Journal of Psychiatry, 116*, 423–428.

Wolf, A. (1966). Childhood association and sexual attraction: A further test of the Westermarck hypothesis. *American Anthropologist, 72*, 503–515.

Wolf, A. (1969). Adopt a daughter-in-law, marry a sister: A Chinese solution to the problem of incest taboo. *American Anthropologist, 70*, 864–874.

Wolf, E. R. (1964). *Anthropology*. Englewood Cliffs, NJ: Prentice Hall.

Wolf, E. R. (1966). *Peasants*. Englewood Cliffs, NJ: Prentice Hall.

Wolf, E. R. (1969). *Peasant wars of the twentieth century*. New York: Harper & Row.

Wolf, E. R. (1982). *Europe and the people without history*. Berkeley: University of California Press.

Worsley, P. (1957). *The trumpet shall sound: A study of "cargo" cults in Melanesia*. London: MacGibbon & Kee.

Wright, G. D. (1954). Projection and displacement: A cross-cultural study of folk-tale aggression. *Journal of Abnormal and Social Psychology, 49*, 523–528.

Wright, R. (1982, Spring). The Yanomami saga. *Cultural Survival Quarterly, 6*(2).

Yap, P. M. (1951). Mental illness peculiar to certain cultures: A survey of comparative psychiatry. *Journal of Mental Science, 97*, 313–327.

Yap, P. M. (1963). Koro or suk-yeong—An atypical culture-bound psychogenic disorder found in southern Chinese. *Transcultural Psychiatric Research, 1*, 36–38.

Yap, P. M. (1965). Koro: A culture-bound depersonalization syndrome. *British Journal of Psychiatry, 111*, 43–50.

Zelnick, M., & Kantner, J. (1977). Sexual and contraceptive experiences of young unmarried women in the United States, 1976 and 1971. *Family Planning Perspectives, 9*, 55–71.

Zetterberg, P. (Ed.). *Conference on Evolution and Public Education: Resources and References*. St. Paul, MN: University of Minnesota Center for Educational Development.

INDEX

Page references in bold indicate a glossed term.

CREDITS & ACKNOWLEDGMENTS

Photos in the contents in brief and the part openers are from the following sources: AP/Wide World, Israeli Tourist Office, National Museum of the American Indian, M. Marcuss Oslander, Leopold Pospisil, Elizabeth Ross, Brian Spykerman, UNICEF, United Nations

Chapter 1 2 UNICEF; 6 Napoleon Chagnon; 8 ©1985 David Weintraub—Photo Researchers; 16 The Granger Collection; The Bettmann Archive, Inc.; 17 The Bettmann Archive Inc.; 19 The Bettmann Archive, Inc.

Chapter 2 22 Michelle V. Agins—The New York Times; 25 UN photo; 28 ©David Austen—Woodfin Camp; 33 Vickie Jensen; 39 Pamela Carley; 42 Henri Cartier-Bresson—Magnum; 47 UPI/Bettmann; 48 Robert Fox—Impact Visuals; 49 ©Kal Muller—Woodfin Camp

Chapter 3 56 UN photo; 63 Lee—Anthro Photo; 66 Eastcott/Momatiuk—Woodfin Camp & Assoc.; 69 UN photo; 70 ©Marc & Evelyne Bernheim—Woodfin Camp & Assoc.; 72 Roland Michaud—Woodfin Camp & Assoc.; 74 UN photo; 76 USDA

Chapter 4 78 UN photo; 81 Rickey Rogers—The New York Times; 82 Owen Franken—Stock•Boston; 86 Irven DeVore—Anthro Photo; 88 Blair Seitz—Photo Researchers, Inc.; 91 The Oriental Institute, The University of Chicago; 92 Annette Weiner; 93 Annette Weiner; 94 UN photo; 96 UN photo; 98 Blair Seitz—Photo Researchers

Chapter 5 100 AP/Wide World; 103 Reuters/Bettmann; 104 Museum of the American Indian; 108 Agence France-Presse; 113 The Granger Collection; 115 ©1984 Nancy J. Pierce—Photo Researchers; 116 J. F. E. Bloss—Anthro Photo; 117 American Museum of Natural History, Neg. # 2A3766; 122 ©Fred McConnaughey—Photo Researchers, Inc.

Chapter 6 126 UN photo; 131 UPI/Bettmann; 133 ©Emilio A. Mercado—The Picture Cube, Inc.; 136 Morey Gash—The New York Times; 137 ©1987 Miguel Sayago—Photo Researchers, Inc.; 141 Shostak—Anthro Photo; 144 ©Margot Granitsas—Photo Researchers, Inc.; 147 Waigwa Kiboi—The New York Times; 149 UN photo; 151 ©Katrina Thomas—Photo Researchers, Inc.

Chapter 7 154 ©M. B. Duda—Photo Researchers, Inc.; 161 Eastcott/Momatiuk—Woodfin Camp & Assoc.; 164 Mark Antman—The Image Works; 169 ©1992 Jim Pickerell—Stock•Boston

Chapter 8 172 Jim Harrison—Stock•Boston; 175 ©1983 Robert A. Isaacs—Photo Researchers, Inc.; 177 UN photo; 178 Schuler—Anthro Photo; 185 UPI/Bettmann; 187 Abuhugbod—Anthro Photo; 189 Eastcott/Momatiuk—Woodfin Camp & Assoc.; 190 Cary Wolinsky—Stock • Boston

Chapter 9 194 UN photos; 199 Katayon Ghazi—The New York Times; 202 The National Museum of the American Indian/Smithsonian Institution, Neg. # 34256; 205 Owen Franken—Stock•Boston; 207 Christopher Morris—Black Star; 208 American Museum of Natural History, Neg. # 125283; 210 Agence France-Presse; 212 UN photo

Chapter 10 216 UN photo; 220 The Bettmann Archive, Inc.; 221 American Museum of Natural History, Neg. #32102; 223 Rene Burri—Magnum; Keystone Press Agency, Inc.; 226 H. Terrace; 227 The Gorilla Foundation

Chapter 11 242 Brian Spykerman; 247 American Museum of Natural History, Neg. # 292759; 248 Museum of Fine Arts, Boston; 251 Kit Porter; 253 Melissa Springer—The New York Times; 258 Australian News & Information Bureau; 260 American Museum of Natural History, Neg. # 319671; 263 Irven DeVore—Anthro Photo; 267 AP/Wide World; 269 The Granger Collection; 271 UN photo

Chapter 12 274 AP/Wide World; 277 Victor Englebert—Photo Researchers, Inc.; 283 UPI/Bettmann; 287 M. Shostak—Anthro Photo; 290 B. Daemmrich—Stock•Boston; 295 Jim Carter—Photo Researchers, Inc.; 298 ©1982 Susan Rosenberg—Photo Researchers, Inc.

Chapter 13 302 The National Museum of the American Indian/Smithsonian Institution, Neg. # 7944; 307 UN photo; 309 ©Eastcott/Momatiuk—Woodfin Camp & Assoc.; 310 Illustration by Elizabeth Ross from "Living Maya" by Walter F. Morris, Jr., Harry N. Abrams, Inc., 1987; 311 The National Museum of the American Indian/Smithsonian Institution, Artifact # 11/9957; 312 American Philosophical Society, Smithsonian Institution; 314 George Holton—Photo Researchers, Inc.; 316 Kenneth Murray—The New York Times; 320 The National Museum of the American Indian, Smithsonian Institution, Neg. # 4771.

Chapter 14 324 Tim Zielenbach—The New York Times; 327 James Sterngold—The New York Times; 333 Cary Herz—The New York Times; 336 AP/Wide World; 337 Agence France-Presse; 340 Stephen Ferry—The New York Times; 342 Edward A. Gargan—The New York Times; 344 Fiona McDougall—The New York Times; 348 Horacio Paone—The New York Times

Chapter 15 352 UN photos; Pamela Carley; 359 Reuters/Bettmann; 363 Stephen Matteson—The New York Times; 365 Reuters/Bettmann; 369 ©1987 Arvind Garg—Photo Researchers, Inc.; 374 G. Paul Burnett—The New York Times; 376 ©Gerd Ludwig—Woodfin Camp & Assoc.; 377 ©1992 Douglas Mason—Woodfin Camp & Assoc.; 378 M. Marcuss Oslander

STAFF

Editor M. Marcuss Oslander
Production Manager Brenda S. Filley
Art Editor Pamela Carley
Designers Richard Stalzer and Charles Vitelli
Typesetting Supervisor Libra Ann Cusack
Typesetter Juliana Arbo

Graphic Assistants Lara M. Johnson, Meredith Scheld, Julie Armeno
Editorial Assistant Diane Barker
Photo Researcher Wendy Connal
Cover design by Richard Stalzer
Photo, "Faces of India," by Lindsey Hebberd—Woodfin Camp & Assoc.